BERKSHIRE
ENCYCLOPEDIA OF SUSTAINABILITY
VOLUME 6

MEASUREMENTS, INDICATORS, AND RESEARCH METHODS FOR SUSTAINABILITY

Editors Ian Spellerberg, *Lincoln University, New Zealand;*
Daniel S. Fogel, *Wake Forest University;* Sarah E. Fredericks, *University of North Texas;* Lisa M. Butler Harrington, *Kansas State University*

Digital editions

The *Berkshire Encyclopedia of Sustainability* is available through most major e-book and database services (please check with them for pricing). Special print/digital bundle pricing is also available in cooperation with Credo Reference; contact Berkshire Publishing (info@berkshirepublishing.com) for details.

For information, contact:
Berkshire Publishing Group LLC
122 Castle Street
Great Barrington, Massachusetts 01230-1506 USA
info@berkshirepublishing.com
Tel +1 413 528 0206
Fax +1 413 541 0076

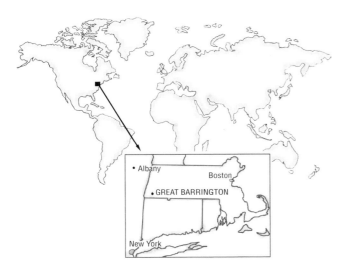

Library of Congress Cataloging-in-Publication Data

Berkshire encyclopedia of sustainability: / measurements, indicators, and research methods for sustainability, edited by Ian Spellerberg, Daniel S. Fogel, Sarah E. Fredericks, and Lisa M. Butler Harrington.
    v. cm.
  Includes bibliographical references and index.
  Contents: vol. 6. Measurements, indicators, and research methods for sustainability—
  ISBN 978-1-933782-40-9 (vol. 6 print : alk. paper)
    1. Environmental quality—Encyclopedias.   2. Environmental protection—Encyclopedias.   3. Sustainable development—Encyclopedias.
  I. Spellerberg, Ian.   II. Fogel, Daniel S.   III. Fredericks, Sarah E.   IV. Harrington, Lisa M. Butler.

Berkshire encyclopedia of sustainability (10 volumes) / edited by Ray Anderson et al.
    10 v. cm.
  Includes bibliographical references and index.
    ISBN 978-1-933782-01-0 (10 volumes : alk. paper) — 978-1-933782-00-3 (10 volumes e-book) — ISBN 978-1-933782-15-7 (vol. 1 print : alk. paper) — ISBN 978-1-933782-57-7 (vol. 1 e-book) — ISBN 978-1-933782-13-3 (vol. 2 print : alk. paper) — ISBN 978-1-933782-55-3 (vol. 2 e-book) — ISBN 978-1-933782-14-0 (vol. 3 print : alk. paper) — ISBN 978-1-933782-56-0 (vol. 3 e-book) — ISBN 978-1-933782-12-6 (vol. 4 print : alk. paper) — ISBN 978-1-933782-54-6 (vol. 4 e-book) — ISBN 978-1-933782-16-4 (vol. 5 print : alk. paper) — ISBN 978-1-933782-09-6 (vol. 5 e-book) — ISBN 978-1-933782-40-9 (vol. 6 print : alk. paper) — ISBN 978-0-9770159-0-0 (vol. 6 e-book) — ISBN 978-1-933782-69-0 (vol. 7 print : alk. paper) — ISBN 978-1-933782-72-0 (vol. 7 e-book) — ISBN 978-1-933782-18-8 (vol. 8 print : alk. paper) — ISBN 978-1-933782-73-7 (vol. 8 e-book) — ISBN 978-1-933782-19-5 (vol. 9 print : alk. paper) — ISBN 978-1-933782-74-4 (vol. 9 e-book) — ISBN 978-1-933782-63-8 (vol. 10 print : alk. paper) — ISBN 978-1-933782-75-1 (vol. 10 e-book)
    1. Environmental quality—Encyclopedias.   2. Environmental protection—Encyclopedias.   3. Sustainable development—Encyclopedias.
  I. Anderson, Ray, et al.
    HC79.E5B4576   2010
    338.9'2703—dc22   2009035114

Contents

List of Entries

Reader's Guide: Articles by Category

Note: most articles appear in more than one category

CONCEPTS AND THEORIES

Challenges to Measuring Sustainability

Citizen Science

Community and Stakeholder Input

Externality Valuation

Intellectual Property Rights

Quantitative vs. Qualitative Studies

Regulatory Compliance

Risk Assessment

Sustainability Science

Systems Thinking

Triple Bottom Line

Weak vs. Strong Sustainability Debate

IMPACT AND IMPLEMENTATION

Agenda 21

Ecological Impact Assessment (EcIA)

Energy Labeling

Environmental Impact Assessment (EIA)

Framework for Strategic Sustainable Development (FSSD)

Global Reporting Initiative (GRI)

Global Strategy for Plant Conservation

Gross Domestic Product, Green

Gross National Happiness

Human Development Index (HDI)

$I = P \times A \times T$ Equation

Intergovernmental Science-Policy Platform on Biodiversity and Ecosystem Services (IPBES)

International Organization for Standardization (ISO)

The Limits to Growth

Millennium Development Goals

National Environmental Accounting

Reducing Emissions from Deforestation and Forest Degradation (REDD)

Risk Assessment

Strategic Environmental Assessment (SEA)

List of Contributors

Abadie, Luis María
Basque Centre for Climate Change (BC3)
Ecolabels (co-author: Ibon Galarraga)

Allison, Elizabeth
California Institute of Integral Studies
Gross National Happiness

Anderson, Mark W.
University of Maine, Orono
New Ecological Paradigm (NEP) Scale

Antal, Áron
Corvinus University of Budapest
*International Organization for
    Standardization (ISO)* (co-authors:
    Gyula Vastag and Gergely Tyukodi)

Asher, Jana
StatAid
Human Development Index (HDI)
    (co-author: Juan Carlos Rosa)

Basile, George
Arizona State University
*Framework for Strategic Sustainable
    Development (FSSD)* (co-authors:
    Karl-Henrik Robèrt and Göran Broman)

Belzile, Jacqueline
University of British Columbia
Focus Groups (co-author: Gunilla Öberg)

Binder, Claudia
University of Munich
Material Flow Analysis (MFA)

Boyd, Doreen S.
University of Nottingham
Remote Sensing

Broman, Göran
Blekinge Institute of Technology
*Framework for Strategic Sustainable
    Development (FSSD)* (co-authors:
    Karl-Henrik Robèrt and George Basile)

Bruce, C. Andrea
University of the West Indies
Systems Thinking
(co-authors: Anthony M. H. Clayton and
    Nicholas Radcliffe)

Campagna, Michele
University of Cagliari
Geographic Information Systems (GIS)

Clarke, Matthew
Deakin University
Genuine Progress Indicator (GPI)

Clayton, Anthony M. H.
University of the West Indies
Fisheries Indicators, Marine (co-author:
    Michael Haley)
Systems Thinking (co-authors: Nicholas
    Radcliffe and C. Andrea Bruce)

Colbeck, Ian
University of Essex
Air Pollution Indicators and Monitoring
    (co-author: Zaheer Ahmad Nasir)

Comtois, Claude
Université de Montréal
Shipping and Freight Indicators

Dornbos, William E.
Yale University
Environmental Performance Index (EPI)
  (co-authors: John W. Emerson, Marc A.
  Levy, and Daniel C. Esty)

Dutfield, Graham
University of Leeds
Intellectual Property Rights

Edens, Bram
Statistics Netherlands
National Environmental Accounting

Eggers, Dee
University of North Carolina at Asheville
Regulatory Compliance

Emerson, John W.
Yale University
Environmental Performance Index (EPI)
  (co-authors: Marc A. Levy, William E.
  Dornbos, and Daniel C. Esty)

Engelman, Robert
Worldwatch Institute
Population Indicators

Ernstson, Henrik
Stockholm University & University of
  Cape Town
Social Network Analysis (SNA)

Esty, Daniel C.
Yale University
Environmental Performance Index (EPI)
  (co-authors: John W. Emerson, Marc A.
  Levy, and William E. Dornbos)

Evely, Anna Clair
University of St. Andrews
Community and Stakeholder Input

Fogel, Daniel S.
Wake Forest University
University Indicators (co-author: Emily
  Yandle Rottmann)

Fredericks, Sarah E.
University of North Texas
Challenges to Measuring Sustainability
Environmental Justice Indicators

Galarraga, Ibon
Basque Centre for Climate Change (BC3)
Ecolabels (co-author: Luis María Abadie)

Gale, Robert
University of New South Wales
Triple Bottom Line

Gerber, Nicolas
University of Bonn
Biological Indicators—Genetic (co-author:
  Jan Henning Sommer)

Gimblett, Randy
University of Arizona
Computer Modeling

Glass, Jacqueline
Loughborough University
Design Quality Indicator (DQI)

Goodall, Melissa
Antioch University New England
Global Environment Outlook (GEO) Reports
(co-author: Maria Ivanova)

Grissino-Mayer, Henri D.
The University of Tennessee
Tree Rings as Environmental Indicators
(co-author: Grant L. Harley)

Grobecker, Anna
European Business School
Global Reporting Initiative (GRI)
(co-author: Julia Wolf)

Grynspan, Rebeca
United Nations Development Programme
Millennium Development Goals (co-author:
Luis F. Lopez-Calva)

Haberl, Helmut
Alpen-Adria Universitaet Klagenfurt,
Wien, Graz, Office Vienna
*Human Appropriation of Net Primary
Production (HANPP)*

Hackett, Steven C.
Humboldt State University
Weak vs. Strong Sustainability Debate

Haley, Michael
EcoReefs Inc.
Fisheries Indicators, Marine (co-author:
Anthony M. H. Clayton)

Hall, C. Michael
University of Canterbury
Advertising

Harley, Grant L.
The University of Tennessee
Tree Rings as Environmental Indicators
(co-author: Henri D. Grissino-Mayer)

Harrington, Lisa M. Butler
Kansas State University
Sustainability Science

Henley, Jane
World Green Building Council
Building Rating Systems, Green (co-author:
Michelle Malanca)

Herring, Horace
The Open University
Energy Efficiency Measurement

Hildén, Mikael
Finnish Environment Institute (SYKE)
Ecosystem Health Indicators (co-author:
David J. Rapport)

Hughes, Robert M.
Amnis Opes Institute & Oregon State
University
Index of Biological Integrity (IBI)

Ivanova, Maria
University of Massachusetts, Boston
Global Environment Outlook (GEO) Reports
(co-author: Melissa Goodall)

Jacoby, Jill B.
University of Wisconsin, Superior
Participatory Action Research

Jones, Kevin Edson
University of Alberta
Citizen Science

Kontogianni, Areti
University of the Aegean
Externality Valuation

Kwak, Thomas J.
United States Geological Survey
Fisheries Indicators, Freshwater

Lang, Daniel J.
Leuphana University of Lüneburg
Transdisciplinary Research (co-author:
   Arnim Wiek)

Levy, Marc A.
Columbia University
Environmental Performance Index (EPI)
   (co-authors: John W. Emerson, William
   E. Dornbos, and Daniel C. Esty)

Lopez-Calva, Luis F.
The World Bank
Millennium Development Goals (co-author:
   Rebeca Grynspan)

MacKenzie, Catherine P.
University of Cambridge
*Reducing Emissions from Deforestation and
   Forest Degradation (REDD)*

Malanca, Michelle
World Green Building Council
Building Rating Systems, Green (co-author:
   Jane Henley)

Malandrino, Ornella
Salerno University
Energy Labeling

Mayer, Audrey L.
Michigan Technological University
Gross Domestic Product, Green

Milne, Janet E.
Vermont Law School
Taxation Indicators, Green

Morse, Stephen
University of Surrey
Development Indicators
Sustainable Livelihood Analysis (SLA)

Nasir, Zaheer Ahmad
University of Essex
Air Pollution Indicators and Monitoring
   (co-author: Ian Colbeck)

Notarnicola, Bruno
University of Bari Aldo Moro, Taranto, Italy
Life Cycle Assessment (LCA) (co-authors:
   Ettore Settanni and Giuseppe Tassielli)
Life Cycle Costing (LCC) (co-authors: Ettore
   Settanni and Giuseppe Tassielli)

Öberg, Gunilla
University of British Columbia
Focus Groups (co-author: Jacqueline Belzile)
Quantitative vs. Qualitative Studies

Pearman, Peter B.
Swiss Federal Research Institute WSL
Biological Indicators—Species (co-author:
   Niklaus E. Zimmermann)

Proto, Maria
University of Salerno
Life Cycle Management (LCM)

Radcliffe, Nicholas
Stochastic Solutions Ltd. & Edinburgh
   University
Systems Thinking (co-authors: Anthony M.
   H. Clayton and C. Andrea Bruce)

Rapport, David J.
EcoHealth Consulting
Ecosystem Health Indicators (co-author: Mikael Hildén)

Robèrt, Karl-Henrik
Blekinge Institute of Technology
Framework for Strategic Sustainable Development (FSSD) (co-authors: Göran Broman and George Basile)

Robertson, G. Philip
Michigan State University
Long-Term Ecological Research (LTER)

Rosa, Juan Carlos
StatAid
Human Development Index (HDI) (co-author: Jana Asher)

Rosenthal, Amy
Natural Capital Project at the World Wildlife Fund
Intergovernmental Science-Policy Platform on Biodiversity and Ecosystem Services (IPBES)

Rottmann, Emily Yandle
McGuireWoods, LLP
University Indicators (co-author: Daniel S. Fogel)

Rowell, Arden
University of Illinois College of Law
Cost-Benefit Analysis
Risk Assessment

Sarzynski, Andrea
University of Delaware
Carbon Footprint

Sawyer, John William David
Department of Conservation, New Zealand
Global Strategy for Plant Conservation

Schaldach, Rüdiger
University of Kassel, Germany
Land-Use and Land-Cover Change

Schmitt, Peter
Nordregio (Nordic Centre for Spatial Development)
Regional Planning

Settanni, Ettore
University of Bari Aldo Moro, Taranto, Italy
Life Cycle Assessment (LCA) (co-authors: Bruno Notarnicola and Giuseppe Tassielli)
Life Cycle Costing (LCC) (co-authors: Bruno Notarnicola and Giuseppe Tassielli)

Smith, M. Alexander
University of Guelph
Species Barcoding

Smith, William K.
Wake Forest University
Biological Indicators—Ecosystems

Sommer, Jan Henning
University of Bonn
Biological Indicators—Genetic (co-author: Nicolas Gerber)

Spangenberg, Joachim
Helmholtz Centre for Environment Research, Halle, Germany
Agenda 21

Spellerberg, Ian
Lincoln University, New Zealand
Volume Introduction

Sroufe, Robert P.
Duquesne University
Supply Chain Analysis

Supino, Stefania
Salerno University
Social Life Cycle Assessment (S-LCA)

Sutton, Adrienne J.
NOAA Pacific Marine Environmental
   Laboratory
Ocean Acidification—Measurement

Tassielli, Giuseppe
University of Bari Aldo Moro, Taranto, Italy
Life Cycle Assessment (LCA) (co-authors:
   Bruno Notarnicola and Ettore Settanni)
Life Cycle Costing (LCC) (co-authors: Ettore
   Settanni and Bruno Notarnicola)

Testa, Mario
University of Salerno
Business Reporting Methods

Therivel, Riki
Levett-Therivel Sustainability Consultants,
   United Kingdom
Strategic Environmental Assessment (SEA)

Treweek, Jo
Treweek Environmental Consultants,
   United Kingdom
Ecological Impact Assessment (EcIA)

Turner, Graham M.
CSIRO Ecosystem Sciences
The Limits to Growth

Tyukodi, Gergely
Corvinus University of Budapest
*International Organization for
   Standardization (ISO)* (co-authors: Gyula
   Vastag and Áron Antal)

Vastag, Gyula
Pannon University & Corvinus University
   of Budapest
*International Organization for
   Standardization (ISO)* (co-authors:
   Gergely Tyukodi and Áron Antal)

Wackernagel, Mathis
Global Footprint Network
Ecological Footprint Accounting

Wiek, Arnim
Arizona State University
Transdisciplinary Research (co-author: Daniel
   J. Lang)

Wolf, Julia
EBS Business School
Global Reporting Initiative (GRI) (co-author:
   Anna Grobecker)
Organic and Consumer Labels

York, Richard
University of Oregon
$I = P \times A \times T$ *Equation*

Zimmermann, Niklaus E.
Swiss Federal Research Institute WSL
Biological Indicators—Species (co-author:
   Peter B. Pearman)

Berkshire Encyclopedia of Sustainability

- Volume 1: *The Spirit of Sustainability*

- Volume 2: *The Business of Sustainability*

- Volume 3: *The Law and Politics of Sustainability*

- Volume 4: *Natural Resources and Sustainability*

- Volume 5: *Ecosystem Management and Sustainability*

- Volume 6: *Measurements, Indicators, and Research Methods for Sustainability*

- Volume 7: *China, India, and East and Southeast Asia: Assessing Sustainability*

- Volume 8: *The Americas and Oceania: Assessing Sustainability*

- Volume 9: *Afro-Eurasia: Assessing Sustainability*

- Volume 10: *The Future of Sustainability*

green press INITIATIVE

Berkshire Publishing is committed to preserving ancient forests and natural resources. We elected to print this title on 30% postconsumer recycled paper, processed chlorine-free. As a result, we have saved:

12 Trees (40' tall and 6-8" diameter)
5 Million BTUs of Total Energy
1,144 Pounds of Greenhouse Gases
5,161 Gallons of Wastewater
327 Pounds of Solid Waste

Berkshire Publishing made this paper choice because our printer, Thomson-Shore, Inc., is a member of Green Press Initiative, a nonprofit program dedicated to supporting authors, publishers, and suppliers in their efforts to reduce their use of fiber obtained from endangered forests.

For more information, visit www.greenpressinitiative.org

Environmental impact estimates were made using the Environmental Defense Paper Calculator. For more information visit: www.edf.org/papercalculator

Introduction to Volume 6: Measurements, Indicators, and Research Methods for Sustainability

Measurements can be made in many ways. Sometimes we use meters to measure things: most people, for instance, are familiar with the meter in a motor vehicle that measures speed (speed*ometer*), and measuring temperatures has been undertaken for many years with the use of thermo*meters*. The information provided by such meters helps us to manage our own safety and our health. There are many kinds of meters, some of which are very relevant to sustainability. The world meter, for example, quite startling to look at and think about (see it at www.worldometers.info/), measures the current world population, as well as other things that increase in number, one by one, faster than the human eye can track. During production of this volume in 2011, the sixth of the *Berkshire Encyclopedia of Sustainability*, the world population passed 7 billion (7,000,000,000).

Measuring and Sustainability

Some of us may ask, "Why measure things—what's the incentive?" The promise of a reward or a prize has sometimes been the incentive to measure what's happening or to measure where we are. For example, the ancient Greek thinker Eratosthenes first calculated (remarkably accurately, considering) the circumference of the Earth and proposed a system of latitude and longitude in order to measure one's location on the planet's surface. Latitude was easy to determine for navigators at sea—those who most depend on this measurement: they simply had to look to the stars to find their relative east or west position on the ocean. It took until the seventeenth century, however, to develop an accurate way of determining longitude at sea, a navigational problem with enormous consequences. Ships loaded with precious cargo from far-off lands were being lost at an alarming rate because ship captains had no way of determining their north–south position. What led to the eventual discovery of a way

to measure longitude? Essentially, several governments offered prizes, and fame and fortune, to the person or people who could solve the problem.

Another incentive to measure what is happening around us is the concern held by many that we are not living within nature's limits. Convincing evidence exists that we are making a continuing, unsustainable, and inequitable use of nature and the environment. Therefore we need information to help us shape policy and to help us manage what we have. As the old adage says, "You cannot manage what you don't measure." Those words are especially relevant to sustainability. For example, measuring the size of fish populations, or the level of acidification in oceans, or what contributes to a carbon footprint are actions whose results can help us monitor the condition of (and changes in) our environment.

Measuring things may seem straightforward, but there are many exciting challenges involved. One is to identify and agree on what best to measure. Keeping in mind the sustainability objective, is it better to measure by single entities (such as the number of trees in a plantation or the amount of waste going to a landfill), or is it better to measure holistically (environmental and social impacts, or gross domestic happiness, or energy efficiency). There is also the challenge of how to measure sustainability as a whole, and to track progress (or lack of progress) toward sustainability. Just as the environment is continually changing, so is the economic world. For example, what happens when Green Company X decides to ship their parts from an entirely different region of the world because their usual supply chain got interrupted by, say, flooding or a tsunami, both of which have happened in the early twenty-first century? How does this choice affect Green Company X's global environmental footprint? Then there are wild cards to watch out for. What if communal Laundromats come into fashion and people stop buying their own washing machines? Bring in the contentious topic of nanomaterials that never need washing (or indeed, washing machines that never need replacing), and the complications increase exponentially. These are just a few examples. They are simplistic but they do demonstrate the interrelated nature of economics and ecology.

A second challenge is to decide how often to measure. One-off measurements may in some instance be appropriate but more often than not there is a need to take measurements at intervals over time. This is called monitoring, and it is used to help detect trends. It is not just a question of deciding the frequency of the measurements but also the duration of the time over which trends may or may not be detected. A danger lies in being selective when it comes to choosing the time period, because one time series can be quite different from another time series. Such selectivity has found its way into the controversies about global temperature trends. Depending on which time periods researchers select, the results will show either decreases or increases in global temperature.

Measuring cause and effect is likely the most difficult challenge because it is not always easy to link a possible cause to an observed effect. This dilemma also has been at the heart of controversy about the causes of climate change. Are such changes and trends random events? Is there really a link between the increasing levels of carbon dioxide in the atmosphere and increasing global temperatures? These questions have concentrated the minds of scientists and scientific organizations around the world. The consensus attributes increasing levels of carbon dioxide in the atmosphere to human activity and industrial activities, and it acknowledges that accumulation of this and other gases is having an effect on global temperatures and climate change.

For the sake of sustainability, never before has there been a need to have the best science and most competent scientists provide information on which to base environmental management and policies. This is not to say that good science alone is sufficient. Policy decisions are often made not by scientists but by laypeople, and very often the decision is not based on science but on ethics. To manage our resources and environmental practices we do need to measure. But due to a lack of data (and to uncertainties and complexities of gathering data), the connection between science and policy is not always direct. There has also been a tendency for measurements and monitoring to take place—just for the sake of measuring and monitoring. Indeed, some would say that the biggest challenge in

the past has been the lack of a mechanism for evaluating measurement as a tool to change or affect policy.

But even more urgent than the need to measure things is the need to make clear that measuring is not enough. Measuring our impact is one of the first steps toward acting on the knowledge that choices we make in our daily lives affect the sustainability of our planet. We will revisit that theme in volume 10, *The Future of Sustainability.* In the meantime, the articles in this volume provide a necessary framework to examine the tools that researchers and scientists may use to do the crucial job of measuring our impact on the Earth.

How do we, in fact, deal with the complexities of measuring nature and the environment? Experience has shown that the diversity of things being measured can become overwhelming. The Earth's ecosystems and the ways to manage them are so unfathomably complicated (a topic covered in depth in volume 5 of this series, *Ecosystem Management and Sustainability*) that we often need to resort to very, very complicated methods to determine what is going on. For example, modeling (which is both an art and a science), has been used widely to help understand the changes taking place around us. Experience has also taught us that because of this complexity it is sometimes easier to use indicators.

Indicators

Strictly speaking, indicators include both indicators and indices. Both terms are widely used in sustainability studies and often used to good effect. An indicator is the presence or absence or condition of something. For example, obesity is an indicator of an unhealthy life style. This simple observation indicates (is an indicator of) an unhealthy life style. The observation neither confirms nor denies that unhealthy eating is the cause. An index is a measurement or calculation. (*Indices* is the plural form of the term preferred by most to distinguish it from *indexes,* the plural used for the alphabetical "back-of-the-book" lists we use to locate information.) For example we use body-mass indices to determine if our height-to-mass ratio is healthy. Another example could be based on waste management. The observation that materials are going to landfill could be said to be an indicator of an unsustainable society. An index of poor waste management could be the amount of waste per capita. Such an index could be used to compare the performance of cities in regard to their waste management. Both indicators and indices have a very important role in helping to achieve sustainability, but both need to be used with an understanding of the context for selecting the indicator or calculating the index. That is why research is so important, be it economic, cultural, social, or environmental.

Research for Sustainability

Research is about seeking the truth. Research is about asking the right question. Research is about methods, methodology, gathering data, analysis, interpretation, application, and presentation of results. Research is about trying to be objective and separating fact from opinion. It can become complicated. Of course the downside of all this complicated research is that all researchers (scientists in particular), tend to get caught up in their work and perhaps lose sight of the importance of what they are measuring in the first place.

Research is about communication. Researchers must consider how they can best get their point across to the average person. Of all the challenges researchers face, effective communication with laypeople can be the most daunting, but it is the most crucial factor when attempting to increase public awareness of sustainability studies.

Long-Term Planning

Another interesting research challenge explored in this volume involves the ways in which the application of research results may have implications in both the short term and in the long term. Although it is difficult to predict what the long-term effects might be, it is important to try and assess what such impacts could be, whether environmental, social, cultural, and/or economic. For example, if a government invests a certain amount of money in solar or wind energy, the following question must be asked: "What are the likely repercussions in ten or twenty years, in terms of job creation, industrial output, and general home consumer behavior?" If a neighborhood votes down a new golf course in favor of a nature preserve, or decides to bring back long-defunct train service, what effect will those decisions have on area real estate prices? Looking back to the mid-twentieth century, who could predict that the liberal use of herbicides and insecticides would have a catastrophic effect on nature? It took a courageous US journalist in the early 1960s (Rachel Carson) to challenge the lack of long-term thinking. Clearly, it's important to figure out both the short-term and long-term

repercussions of policies that governments, international agencies, and even local communities make.

Research and Decisions

Good research is so very important because we need to do our best to obtain the best results so that we can then try to make the best interpretations of the data, whether in terms of the implications of climate change, or the impacts of public versus private transportation, or in terms of the establishment of marine and nature preserves. People need to trust science and scientists. People need to believe the scientists who are telling them that their big cars are contributing to the melting of ice caps in faraway places, or that their electricity is burning up our resources of coal. People often need to learn from scientists *why* these things are so before they are inclined to do something about them. But think of the classic "simple" question, "Why does the sky appear to be blue?" The world is a very complicated place and it is often difficult to describe these things. Communication and trust are extraordinarily important in applying research to the real world.

What You'll Find in This Book

Volume 6 presents a thorough and accessible overview of the ways in which sustainability is charted worldwide. Some articles introduce basic concepts, such as qualitative versus quantitative data or the "weak" versus "strong" sustainability debate. Other articles describe how indicators have been used to address climate change, soil conservation, agriculture, and mining. Research analysts explain the modes and media through which these measurements are broadcast, stressing the importance of developing methods that can be understood by experts and laypeople. The researchers also examine the process of monitoring, itself a highly interesting topic very relevant to national or international policy, law, rules, and regulations. This volume divides the material into six sections; as with most things on this planet, many articles fit into more than one category.

Concepts and Theories

Articles on topics that explore measurement concepts and theories, such as "Intellectual Property Rights," "Systems Thinking," the "I = P × A × T Equation," (which specifies that environmental *Impacts* are the combined product of *Population, Affluence,* and *Technology*), "Quantitative vs. Qualitative Studies," and "Community and Stakeholder Input" help us to examine the ways in which we study and measure things. Are we going about it the right way, generally speaking? What happens when the developed world's standards of living are applied to the (upwardly mobile, and quickly) developing world? What can we learn by studying how others do things, in the classroom, in the lab, or in the workplace? What influence can "regular" people and their communities have on how their environment's resources get allocated? Why is it important that researchers be trained in both quantitative (dealing with "how much") and qualitative (dealing with "how and why") methods of research? In a nutshell, these questions are important so that their research asks the right questions in the first place.

Impact and Implementation

Global programs for measuring sustainability have a tremendous impact on the ways in which sustainability studies may be implemented to effect change. Articles such as "Reducing Emissions from Deforestation and Forest Degradation (REDD)," the "Global Strategy for Plant Conservation," the "Global Reporting Initiative (GRI)," and "Green Building Rating Systems," provide examples of efforts worldwide. These programs are often, although not always, United Nations–sponsored, and are a heartening indication that people around the world can work together to solve problems. Other topics such as "Risk Assessment" explore the ways in which businesses and governments (and even individuals) can anticipate the environmental impacts, either positive or negative, of various plans of action.

Indicators

The presence or the absence of something can reveal a "big picture" of the impacts stemming from different social, economic, and environmental spheres: fisheries (freshwater and marine), air pollution, population, environmental justice, and the relative effects of various green taxation strategies.

It may be hard to believe, but some indicators can be used to monitor past environmental events. Such topics include the study of tree rings (dendrochronology) that allow us to peer into the past and learn something about conditions and changes in the climate hundreds

and thousands of years ago. Indices such as the Index of Biological Integrity (IBI), which scientists base on a number of different biological indicators (such as species abundance and distribution), are used to determine the relative health of aquatic ecosystems. Several articles in this category study facets of the relatively new field of industrial ecology, such as "Life Cycle Assessment, "Material Flow Analysis," and "Supply Chain Analysis."

Methods of Displaying Results

Results from monitoring may be presented in many different ways. The choice of the method is an integral part of communication and depends largely on the audience. It is imperative that we must have good "communication." This category covers topics such as "Advertising," "Ecolabels," "Energy Efficiency Measurement," and "Organic and Consumer Labels." An example of the need to communicate what all the facts and figures mean is the so-called Climategate scandal that began in late 2009, during which several climate scientists at the University of East Anglia in the United Kingdom (who were eventually exonerated for their actions) circulated emails among themselves, wondering how best to make their data (which unequivocally stated that the world's climate was becoming warmer) more readily understood by the public. Word quickly got out that the scientists were exaggerating the dangers of climate change, when in fact they were simply grasping at the best way to make an extremely complicated subject more easily understood by policymakers and the general public. This unfortunate episode has likely set back the general public's trust in climate science by many years, but we can only hope that we have learned from our mistakes.

Research Methods and Measurement Tools

Do we have the best tools to research these important issues? This category explores the fascinating range of research options open to us in such articles as "Geographic Information Systems (GIS)," "Long-Term Ecological Research (LTER)," "Social Network Analysis (SNA)," and "Computer Modeling." Although many of these methods are technology based, other articles, such as "Focus Groups," "Citizen Science," and "Transdisciplinary Research," explore ways in which scientists (and others) can use relatively simple methods—such as getting different peoples' opinions and strengths involved in the research process—to do the job correctly.

Planning for the Future

Measuring the impacts of the world population on nature and the environment must be based on the best science and be undertaken by the most competent scientists. This is the basis for achieving change. There has to be change in all levels of education so as to achieve sustainability. There has to be a change in behavior so that there is no longer inequitable and unsustainable use of nature and the environment. We must embrace the inspiring innovations brought to us from monitoring, indicators, and research so as to learn to live within nature's limits. That's what sustainability is all about.

In the time (roughly twelve or thirteen minutes) that it has taken you to read this introduction, the world population has increased by around 3,000 people. That's a measurement to think about.

The Editors
Ian Spellerberg
Daniel S. Fogel
Sarah E. Fredericks
Lisa M. Butler Harrington

Acknowledgements

Berkshire Publishing would like to thank the following people for their help and advice in various matters. In a project of this scope there are many to acknowledge, of course, but these people deserve our special thanks:

Jim Karr, *University of Washington*.

Mathis Wackernagel, *Global Footprint Network*.

Julie Newman, *Yale University*.

Robert Melchior Figueroa, *University of North Texas*.

Neal Cantin, *The Australian Institute of Marine Science*.

Timo Koivurova, *University of Lapland*.

Emilie Beaudon, *University of the Arctic*.

John Dettmers, *Great Lakes Fishery Commission*.

Weslynne Ashton, *Illinois Institute of Technology*.

A

Advertising

Advertising plays a major role in influencing consumption and therefore in sustainability. It is regarded both as a tool that can be used to encourage sustainable behavior and also as an integral part of a consumer culture that is the antithesis of sustainable consumption. Research on the relationship between advertising and sustainability faces challenges of evaluating product claims as well as understanding the influence of advertising on consumption.

Although the term *advertising* is often used synonymously with *marketing*, it should more accurately be regarded as the promotional dimension of marketing. Advertising is significant for three main aspects of sustainability, each operating at a different scale of consumption and each with its own set of research and measurement issues. At a *microscale level*, advertising is related to the promotion of products and services that support sustainability. Such products and services are often promoted by social marketing campaigns of government and nonprofit organizations in order to encourage more sustainable forms of behavior from all consumers. At a *mesoscale level*, advertising is relevant to the development of environmental or green advertising, which usually refers to advertising that has been specifically developed to appeal to the needs and interests of consumers concerned with sustainability issues, such as the environment or social justice. At the *macroscale level*, advertising is regarded as symbolic of the consumer culture that dominates contemporary capitalism. Such a culture is regarded by some as a barrier to the development of sustainable forms of consumption and has therefore been the subject of anti-advertising or culture-jamming campaigns. The different interpretations of the relationship of advertising to sustainability reflect broader positions regarding whether advertising is a neutral tool or whether it is something inextricably tied to unsustainable mass consumerism.

Each of these different scales of the relationship between advertising and sustainability entails different ways of measuring sustainability along with different research approaches and the use of indicators. A key research area involves finding ways in which studies undertaken at different scales and utilizing different approaches may be integrated or reconciled.

Advertising to Encourage Sustainability

Advertising to encourage sustainability is a promotional aspect of social marketing and socially responsible commercial marketing. From the perspective of sustainability, social marketing uses commercial marketing approaches in order to influence the voluntary behavior of target audiences to improve their own contribution to sustainability and/or that of the society of which they are a part. Such an approach is therefore intermediate between education for sustainability, which emphasizes information and generating awareness, and regulatory approaches (which may have a social marketing dimension). Social marketing differs from socially responsible marketing in that the former focuses on using advertising to make sustainable behavior happen, with the research tending to center on the extent of behavioral change, while the latter promotes tangible or intangible products that are already regarded as sustainable, with research concentrating on the actual sustainability of the products or consumer perceptions of sustainability. The target audiences of such advertising campaigns are also not necessarily consumers who are committed to or interested in sustainable actions or products (Hall 2012).

An example of a social marketing advertising campaign to encourage more sustainable behavior is persuading people to consume less water, which is a significant issue given growing demands for water in the face of drought, population growth, and forecasts of reduced or increased variability in supply as a result of climate change (Jorgensen, Graymore, and O'Toole 2009). Such advertising to a broad audience may focus on price and cost advantages to the consumer rather than emphasizing the environmental benefits. At their simplest, measurements of the success of such campaigns look at changes in the consumption of the resource that authorities are trying to conserve. Research on a 2001 advertising campaign to reduce water consumption in Israel found that 76 percent of responders were willing to save water after being exposed to the campaign, with an average saving of 15 percent in water consumption. Measuring resource use alone in a short time frame will not, however, provide information about the extent of fundamental behavioral change. An indication of the difficulties of advertising in encouraging long-term behavior was that only 38 percent of the respondents thought that they would continue to save water after the advertising campaign finished (Heiman 2002). This suggests that research is required that tracks consumption behavior over time in order to identify the factors that encourage the adoption of new consumptive practices. As such ongoing monitoring may prove expensive, its use may be restricted to only a limited number of agencies or companies. As the next section notes, research may more fruitfully concentrate on specific advertising campaigns rather than long-term behavioral modification.

Green Advertising

Environmental advertising, or green advertising, is often regarded as synonymous with advertising that encourages sustainability. This represents a relatively narrow interpretation of sustainability that tends to ignore issues of equity and social justice, with such concerns often addressed in advertising that promotes fair trade and human rights.

Green advertising developed hand in hand with the growth of green marketing in the 1960s and 1970s and is broadly subject to the same research issues and debates. The US professors of marketing George Zinkhan and Les Carlson defined green advertising as "promotional messages that may appeal to the needs and desires of environmentally concerned consumers" (Zinkhan and Carlson 1995, 1). Research based on such a narrow definition tends to focus more on the relative appeal of different messages rather than the extent to which they actually contribute to sustainability. The marketing

researcher Subhabrata Banerjee and colleagues offered a definition of green advertising as any advertisement that met at least one of the three following criteria (Banerjee, Gulas, and Iyer 1995):

- explicitly or implicitly addresses the relationship between a product/service and the biophysical environment
- promotes a green lifestyle with or without highlighting a product/service
- presents a corporate image of environmental responsibility

This very broad definition raises more substantial issues regarding the relationship between advertising message, behavior, and contribution to sustainability.

Regardless of differences in definition, both approaches seek to utilize advertising research to identify the extent to which consumer behavior—including product purchasing, resource consumption, and product perceptions—changes after exposure to particular advertising messages and media. At its simplest, this is a three-stage process that looks at a consumer before, during, and after experiencing an advertisement. Regardless of whether the research focus is on a product or promotion of a lifestyle, the first stage seeks to gain a broad understanding of consumer behavior and purchasing patterns. If geared toward commercial green advertising, it is likely that research will examine product purchase and perceptions as well as the relationship to company brands. Such background research to the preparation of advertising campaigns is usually conducted by interviews or surveys and by focus groups.

In the second stage, concentration is on the experience of the advertisement and/or the overall campaign. This is usually undertaken by what is known as pretesting or copy testing, involving the analysis of audience levels of attention, linkage of advertisements to specific brands, motivations to purchase, and communication (i.e., likelihood of encouraging positive spread by word-of-mouth). Although research on brand linkage, communication, and motivation is usually done via questionnaire or focus group, the level of consumer attention to an advertisement is increasingly measured by attention tracking (usually with a pointing device such as a computer mouse) or eye tracking (which uses a device for measuring eye positions and movement in relation to visual images). Such pretesting of an advertisement may occur before it is officially released and may therefore result in modifications to maximize consumer attention and emotional involvement.

The third stage, post-testing, usually consists of longer-term tracking studies that examine consumer recall of advertisements and any resultant behavioral change, including stated attitudes and preferences, consumption and purchasing patterns, and brand relationships. Most tracking studies of advertisements get respondents to answer questions related to advertisement recognition and aided and unaided brand or product awareness. Post-testing may be part of a specific research exercise undertaken for a campaign or be incorporated into ongoing panel or population surveys.

A major issue in green advertising has been the extent to which the products and services that have been advertised actually contribute to sustainability and the extent to which advertising has deliberately deceived consumers in order to gain sales or improve product or corporate image. Advertising claims with respect to the environment or to the sustainability of a product can be classified into six categories, each of which has its own specific research context:

- *Product claims* point out the environmentally friendly or sustainable attributes that a product possesses and is usually assessed by quantifiable studies against accepted standards, although these may vary from country to country, as for example with respect to the use of terms such as *organic*.
- *Process claims* deal with an organization's internal technology, production technique, product life cycle analysis, and/or disposal method that generates environmental or sustainable benefits. These claims are usually assessed via quantitative systems analysis.
- *Image orientation* associates an organization with a sustainability or environmentally related cause or activity in order to benefit from consumer or public support. Image orientation is usually studied via methods such as consumer surveys and semiotic analysis, although it may also be subject to content analysis.
- *Environmental fact* involves a statement that is ostensibly factual in nature from an organization about the environment or its condition, in relation to some aspect of its product or service. Depending on the nature of the claim it may be subject to both qualitative and quantitative study.
- *Societal fact* involves a statement that is ostensibly factual in nature from an organization about socioeconomic impact, equity, society, or a community or its condition in relation to some aspect of its product or service. Societal facts are often more difficult to evaluate than environmental claims as they tend to be more complex because of the range of perceptions, interests, and values that may be involved.
- *Combined claims* appear to have multiple facets or dimensions; that is, it reflects some combination of product claim, process claim, image orientation, and environmental or societal fact. Examination of combined claims usually requires an integrated analysis using both qualitative and quantitative research methods.

Product claims have become a central point for criticism of green and sustainable advertising with many jurisdictions having weak or no independent regulation of advertising claims with respect to sustainability. For example, the UK government's Department for Environment, Food and Rural Affairs (DEFRA) only provides guidance on green claims, although they do suggest that such claims should be clear, accurate, relevant, and verifiable. Apart from the issue of the testability of claims that products are eco- or environmentally friendly, uncertainty may even exist over what constitutes the product. In the case of bottled water, for instance, the product could be either the water or the container (Pearce 2010).

Consumer Culture and Culture Jamming

The third main relationship between advertising and sustainability is the role of advertising in consumer culture. From a critical consumer-culture perspective, the driving force behind consumerism is usually held to be multinational firms operating in a capitalist system, who have fabricated a consumer culture (Klein 2005). Advertising messages essentially legitimate consumerism via a mass-media industry that is lacking space for the expression of differing views (Rumbo 2002), including those with respect to sustainability issues such as climate change. From this perspective, corporations and marketers have greater knowledge of and control over communication processes, creating an irreversible communication flow in which the rights and responsibilities of citizens have been reduced to being members of a consuming public.

In response, a counter-institutional movement has emerged that seeks to develop more democratic and sustainable forms of advertising and consumption, one that is often referred to as *culture jamming* (Carducci 2006). Sven Woodside, in a master's degree thesis for the University of Amsterdam, provides a comprehensive definition of culture jamming as "the innovative and alternative ways in which people are offering a form of creative, non-violent resistance against the way we view the world, either for the sake of the interruption or for getting an alternative message across" (Woodside 2001, 9).

Critical research on the relationship between consumer culture and advertising does utilize commercial advertising research methods; however, these are understood within a broader social scientific methodological and theoretical framework that recognizes the political dimensions of research (Binay 2005). From this perspective and given advertising's role in the promotion of unsustainable consumption, advertising research is not a value-neutral tool and instead needs to be understood within a context of interests, power, and values. Therefore, research on the political dimensions of advertising as well as culture jamming will often include public policy analysis and sociologically oriented studies that move beyond the strongly psychological emphasis of traditional commercial advertising research.

Future Contribution

Advertising is integral to contemporary consumer culture and is therefore a major focal point for those who advocate more-sustainable forms of consumption, yet advertising can also be used as a tool to promote more-sustainable products and behaviors. The debate on the extent to which advertising and advertising research is value neutral with respect to its influence on sustainability is likely to continue well into the future. Despite research indicating that voluntary standards for environmental and sustainable advertising are insufficient to ensure the legitimacy of product claims, and therefore their impacts, the power of advertising, corporate, and media interests is such that there is little enthusiasm from policy makers for more regulatory approaches to advertising and green-product claims and branding.

C. Michael HALL
University of Canterbury

See also Challenges to Measuring Sustainability; Citizen Science; Ecolabels; Energy Labeling; Focus Groups; Organic and Consumer Labels; University Indicators

FURTHER READING

Banerjee, Subhabrata; Gulas, Charles S.; & Iyer, Easwar. (1995). Shades of green: A multidimensional analysis of environmental advertising. *Journal of Advertising, 24*(2), 21–31.

Binay, Ayse. (2005). Investigating the anti-consumerism movement in North America: The case of Adbusters. (Doctoral dissertation). Austin: University of Texas at Austin.

Carducci, Vince. (2006). Culture jamming: A sociological perspective. *Journal of Consumer Culture, 6,* 116–138.

Goodrich, Kendall. (2010). What's up? Exploring upper and lower visual field advertising effects. *Journal of Advertising Research, 50*(1), 91–106.

Hall, C. Michael. (2012). *Tourism and social marketing.* London: Routledge.

Heiman, Amir. (2002). The use of advertising to encourage water conservation: Theory and empirical evidence. *Journal of Contemporary Water Research and Education, 121,* 79–86.

Jorgensen, Bradley; Graymore, Michelle; & O'Toole, Kevin. (2009). Household water use behavior: An integrated model. *Journal of Environmental Management, 91*(1), 227–236.

Klein, Naomi. (2005). *No logo: No space, no choice, no jobs.* London: Harper Perennial.

Pearce, Fred. (2010, March 23). Green advertising rules are made to be broken: A UK government checklist of claims for advertisers will fail to stop cynical greenwash without a legally enforceable framework. *The Guardian.* Retrieved November 11, 2011, from http://www.guardian.co.uk/environment/2010/mar/23/green-claims

Pieters, Rik, & Wedel, Michel. (2004). Attention capture and transfer by elements of advertisements. *Journal of Marketing, 68*(2), 36–50.

Rumbo, Joseph D. (2002). Consumer resistance in a world of advertising clutter: The case of Adbusters. *Psychology and Marketing, 19*(2), 127–148.

Woodside, Sven. (2001). Every joke is a tiny revolution: Culture jamming and the role of humour. (Master's thesis). Amsterdam, The Netherlands: University of Amsterdam, Media Studies.

Zinkhan, George M., & Carlson, Les. (1995). Green advertising and the reluctant consumer. *Journal of Advertising, 24*(2), 1–4.

Agenda 21

The United Nations' Agenda 21 plan called for the establishment of indicators for sustainable development. In a broad consultative process, governments, institutions, and organizations developed, tested, and revised these indicators. The latest revision aims at harmonizing the indicators with the Millennium Development Goals, a set of eight sustainability goals. The indicators are used not only in the national sustainable development reports to the United Nations, but they stimulated other indicator programs.

Agenda 21 is a United Nations (UN) plan on sustainable development. The UN Conference on Environment and Development (UNCED), held in 1992 in Rio de Janeiro, Brazil, developed the plan. Agenda 21 is a comprehensive plan regarding human impacts on the environment for UN member organizations, major organizations, and governments. More than 178 governments approved the Rio Declaration on Environment and Development and the Statement of Principles for the Sustainable Management of Forests.

The declaration contains forty chapters. Chapter 40 of Agenda 21 calls for improvement in the informational basis of sustainability issues so governments and organizations can make policy decisions on these issues. This task includes better data (collection, analysis, selection, evaluation, and availability) and the development and application of indicators—that is, measures of progress—that help evaluate the advancement countries and organizations make toward sustainable development. The document says nothing, however, about the kind and quality of the indicators that countries, international bodies, and nongovernmental organizations need to develop.

Origins

In its first session, the Commission for Sustainable Development (CSD) called for the development of indicators providing a basis for countries and organizations to measure progress toward sustainable development. The CSD directed governments to integrate these indicators into the reports they make to the CSD. Responding to this demand, governmental and nongovernmental organizations on all levels began to develop indicators of sustainable development. Many of them could draw on earlier work, resulting in a wealth of indicators and methodology proposals available in a relatively short time. More than thirty UN agencies, Bretton Woods Institutions like the World Bank, other multinational and international institutions like the Organisation for Economic Co-operation and Development (OECD) and the European Union, and representatives of nongovernmental organizations cooperated in these processes. The Scientific Committee on Problems of the Environment (SCOPE) had its own Sustainable Development Indicators (SDI) process. These organizations merged their contributions into a draft problem analysis and a work program. The CSD 3—that is, the third meeting of the Commission for Sustainable Development—accepted the preliminary list of indicators in 1995 and adopted a five-year work program that involved several stages: consensus building on a core list of indicators of sustainable development; development of the related methodology sheets; policy discussions and widespread dissemination of this work; testing; and evaluation and revision of the indicators.

The work program defined the indicators' purpose as tools for guiding political decisions toward sustainable development, improving information and data collection, and enabling country-specific analyses of the states' progress toward sustainable development.

Based on this decision and an implementation plan, the work program developed indicator methodology sheets. The Division for Sustainable Development (DSD) and the Statistics Division, both within the United Nations Department of Economic and Social Affairs, jointly drafted for discussion the first set of indicators of sustainable development. This draft then became the focus of a broad consensus-building process that included a number of organizations within the United Nations system and other international organizations, both intergovernmental and nongovernmental, and relevant research institutes. DSD presented the results to CSD 4 in 1996 and published them in what has become known as the *Blue Book*. With this publication, including indicators and methodology sheets, the DSD achieved a remarkable breakthrough. Other UNCED follow-up indicator processes have been less successful, as the fifteen-year-long failure among the signatories of the Biodiversity Convention to agree upon a set of indicators for the biodiversity convention illustrates.

Quality Criteria

The United Nations formulated quality criteria for SDI in its 1995 Programme of Work on Indicators of Sustainable Development, the objective of which was to provide SDI to national governments so they could use the indicators to make decisions on sustainable development. The program states that SDI in general should be "representative of an international consensus to the extent possible"; that is, the scientific community should widely acknowledge the SDI. SDI should be relevant, covering crucial aspects of sustainable development. They should be "understandable, that is to say clear, simple and unambiguous," and quantifiable. Finally, the indicators should be "limited in number, remaining open ended and adaptable to future developments" (United Nations 1995). The sheer number of 134 indicators and 125 corresponding methodology sheets, however, does not exactly respect the last criterion.

Three additional conditions apply for governments and organizations reporting indicators to the CSD: the indicators must be "primarily national in scale or scope"; "realisable within the capacities of national governments, given logistics, time, technical and other constraints"; and broadly cover Agenda 21 and all aspects of sustainable development to give a comprehensive plan of action (United Nations 1995). These sensible recommendations make sure governments and organizations can produce indicators of sustainability and that the international community will accept them. The CSD's request that indicators should be "dependent on data that are readily available or available at reasonable cost to benefit ratio, are adequately documented, of known quality and updated at regular intervals" is an obstacle to developing up-to-date indicators and monitoring systems that are applicable to the present day (United Nations 1995). The criteria result in a focus on indicators for historic incidences of stresses to the environment. These indicators may have been of political relevance at a particular time in the past and led to data collection to monitor environmental issues. Such a procedure unfortunately is unable to react proactively to potential threats to the future, or at least in due time when first symptoms appear.

All of these recommendations cannot be met at all times, nor are they of equal importance in all circumstances. Good indicator systems, however, should always strike a balance among the recommendations without neglecting a specific element. Because these demands refer to the whole set of indicators, the development of indicator systems requires careful attention not only to the quality of the individual indicators but to the system as such. Combining indicators with different strengths and weaknesses can thus lead to a balanced and meaningful system.

Structure

Environmental, social, and economic dimensions of sustainable development make up the forty chapters in Agenda 21. Agenda 21 structured the 1996 CSD indicators, which followed and reported the agenda chapter by chapter. An institutional factor is inherent, but Agenda 21 does not explicitly define it. Countries cannot govern sustainably without appropriate institutions.

The classification of indicators in each chapter builds upon the concept of pressure–state–response indicators that the OECD promoted. (See figure 1 on page 8.) The OECD system, however, focused on environmental stresses, ignoring socioeconomic causes. In most cases the system missed the links to the driving forces of environmental degradation. This system assumed a causality chain (pressures causing state changes, which provoke responses). In order to be suitable for monitoring progress in the broad sense of Agenda 21, the United Nations modified the concept: the work program and, subsequently, the indicator system went beyond the OECD structure by integrating the economic and the social dimension into the framework, resulting in the need to extend the category of "pressures" to the more general "driving forces." As the United Nations gave up the intention to reflect causal relationships from pressure to

Figure 1. Pressure–State–Response: The Basis for Indicator Building

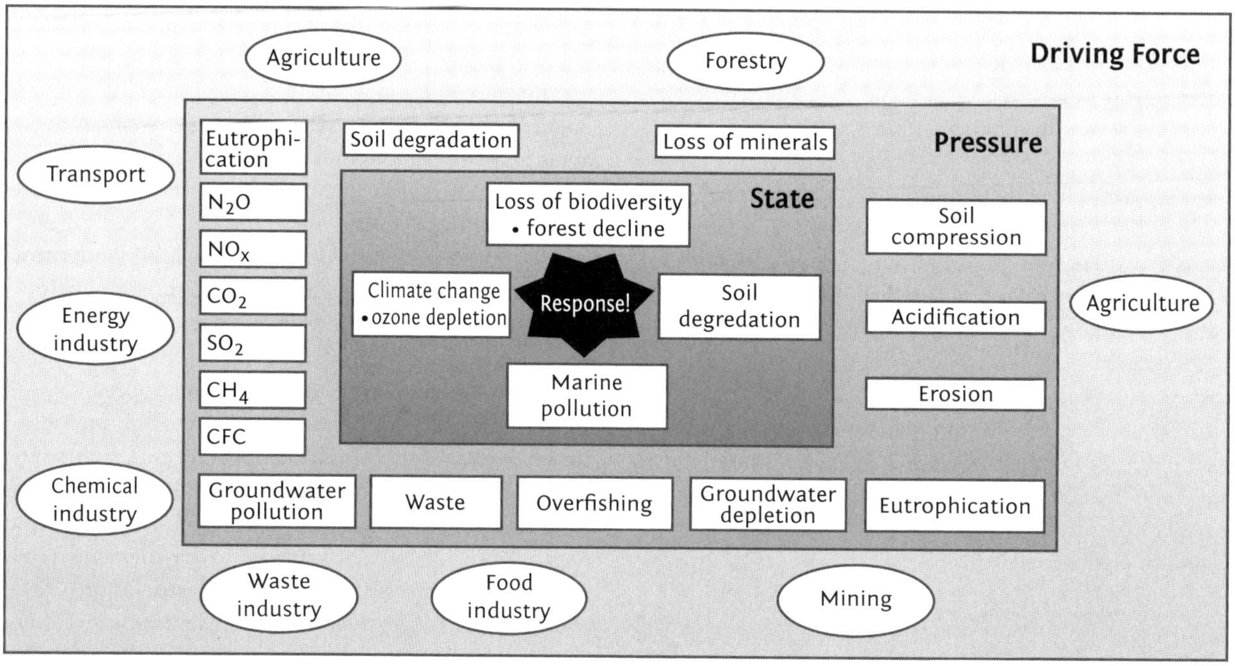

Source: author.

This figure shows the correlation between human activity (driving forces), and the pressures they place on the environment. The resultant effect is indicated by the state of the environment, which in turn elicits a response or action.

response, the indicator set did not address causality; the proposed indicators only incidentally identified the driving forces causing a specific state and the policy responses to this state. The driving force–state–response (DSR) system provided a useful descriptive framework because researchers could describe nearly every problem of sustainability by listing causes, damages or impacts, and possible countermeasures. By its very definition, however, the system lacked analytical and thus policy-steering capabilities.

Revisions

The next crucial step was testing the CSD SDI, an exercise involving twenty-two pilot countries from global North and South, starting in 1997. The CSD published a pilot countries' report at the end of 1999. The report outlined lessons learned regarding possible improvements in the methodology. It highlighted problems such as the lack of causality, a deficit in addressing the interlinkages between the four dimensions (environmental, economic, social, and institutional) existing in reality, and the insufficient level of detail and coherence caused not least by the limitation to three categories D, S, and R—at least driving forces and pressures could be separated to support policy formulation. Critics claimed 134 indicators were insufficient to provide a complete picture of

sustainability, but too high for policy communication; combining a smaller core set of indicators plus an extended number of prospective indicators might help.

The DSD revised the indicator set in 2000, based on these recommendations. They reduced the SDI set to fifty-eight core indicators embedded in a theme/subtheme framework. This set replaced the DSR categorization and the chapter-by-chapter structure, but the DSD still organized it along the four dimensions of sustainable development (social, economic, environmental, and institutional). They took the majority of the indicators from the existing set, modified some, and added others based on internal debates, suggestions from the CSD expert group on sustainability indicators, and the testing results. The DSD presented these indicators to the UN CSD 9 in 2001, which met them with considerable skepticism. The United Nations published the indicators as the second edition of the *Blue Book,* the UN SDI compendium and methodology handbook. Like the World Summit on Sustainable Development in Johannesburg 2001, CSD 11 in 2003 and CSD 13 in 2005 encouraged countries to further work on indicators for sustainable development based on their specific conditions and priorities. CSD 13 invited the international community to support developing countries' efforts.

In 2005 the UN Division for Sustainable Development decided to review the CSD indicators again, for two main reasons. Since the publication of the previous set, knowledge of and experience with sustainable development indicators of countries and organizations had increased significantly, along with an emphasis on measuring progress on achieving sustainable development, including the Millennium Development Goals (MDG), at the national and the international levels. The MDG comprise eight goals, which range from eradicating poverty to ensuring environmental sustainability. The review process synchronized CSD SDI and the MDG indicators, plus some sectoral indicators, like those under development for the biodiversity convention also adopted in Rio in 1992. The UN Department of Economic and Social Affairs felt that a major revision of the indicator set would not be appropriate, given the intensive testing of the previous SDI set. They consequently conducted the review with a relatively small number of resources over an eighteen-month period.

The revised set of CSD indicators maintains the basic structure of the second set, but also contains a number of important changes. The CSD, most importantly, gave up the four dimensions of sustainability as an organizing principle and removed the institutional indicators from the set. The institutional indicators refer to the societal conditions of sustainable development, such as "strengthening the role of major groups," "information for decision-making," or "integrating environment and development in decision making," conditions outlined in the original Agenda 21 document (United Nation Sustainable Development 1992). This unfortunate move reflects the policy debate that treated institutional problems as an issue external to sustainable development—only the "international legal instruments and mechanisms" are still on the agenda and will be dealt with at the UN Conference on Sustainable Development (UNCSD) in Rio de Janeiro in 2012 (Rio+20), twenty years after the UNCED conference 1992.

The new CSD indicators contain a set of fifty core indicators, as part of a larger set of ninety-six indicators of sustainable development. CSD has retained the basic framework but has adapted themes and subthemes; for example, it introduced a new theme on poverty. Updating old and introducing new indicators plus harmonizing methodologies and expanding definitions improved the coherence of the CSD SDI with MDG indicators.

Impacts

Many countries, particularly in the developing world, used the CSD indicators they already produced for their annual country reports to the CSD as starting points when they developed national indicator sets on sustainable development. For countries with weak statistical capabilities, UN statistics provided the support for strengthening the data-gathering and data-processing infrastructure and enabled them to build the capability to provide indicators to the United Nations.

Although no one so far has undertaken a detailed analysis of the impact of the CSD work program on national indicators of sustainable development, a number of general conclusions emerge from assessing the country reports. The historical focus of the CSD on indicators and their national adaptation provided a useful and timely forum for participatory processes developing national-level indicators. Besides its direct effects, the CSD work on indicators thus had an important indirect impact. Most countries have taken up the flexible theme/subtheme framework with adaptations. It is currently the dominant framework for national indicators of sustainable development.

Context

Parallel to the CSD indicator system, other actors undertook SDI work. The Global Reporting Initiative (GRI), founded in 1997, publishes indicator sets for business sustainability that incorporate social responsibility reporting. The current version, called G3 (updated to G3.1 in March 2011; G4 will be published in 2013), defines a set of core information every participant has to provide, plus a series of additional sector-specific indicators that include the public sector. The UN secretary-general advises members of the UN Global Compact, a cooperative structure of the United Nations (6,263 business participants and 2,781 nonbusiness participants that have subscribed to ten core sustainability-related principles and to reporting on the progress they make), to use the GRI indicators for their reports. By July 2011, GRI has expelled more than 2,400 companies for failing to properly inform their stakeholders on progress made, a name-and-shame strategy.

Simultaneous to the work on the CSD indicators, the UN Department of Economic and Social Affairs started a process to develop indicators monitoring changing consumption and production patterns. The process could have complemented the UN SDI set, making it more sensitive to developments in affluent countries than the current sets. Despite international discussions on the issue and endorsements for the development of a sustainable consumption action plan at the 2002 World Summit on Sustainable Development (Rio+10) in Johannesburg and the subsequent Marrakech Process, a ten-year plan for sustainable production and consumption, CSD 19 failed to adopt this action plan in 2011.

Outlook

The future of the UN indicator work, based on Agenda 21, is difficult to predict. It will to a large degree depend on what decisions world leaders make at the Rio+20 UN Conference on Sustainable Development (UNCSD) in June 2012. The more innovative and ambitious the decisions are, the higher the demand for monitoring systems including SDI will be.

Attempts at streamlining international reporting obligations will go on, standardizing indicators covering similar themes in different reporting systems. The structure of the CSD SDI offers enough flexibility for governments, businesses, and organizations to adapt it without weakening its core messages. Several factors could strengthen it. The set could properly reflect the key issue of the Rio+20 summit, the Green Economy. The second UNCSD issue, institutions for sustainable development, could be reintegrated into the CSD SDI. The CSD SDI could more specifically address sustainable consumption. Enhancing the relevance of the indicator set for assessing the sustainability performance of affluent countries by these or other means will be a condition for its permanent relevance on a global scale.

Joachim H. SPANGENBERG
*Helmholtz Centre for Environment Research,
Halle, Germany*

See also Development Indicators; Environmental Performance Index (EPI); Genuine Progress Indicator (GPI); Global Environment Outlook (GEO) Reports; Human Development Index (HDI); Millennium Development Goals; Sustainable Livelihood Analysis (SLA)

FURTHER READING

Bossel, Hartmut. (1999). *Indicators for sustainable development: Theory, method, applications. A report to the Balaton Group.* Winnipeg, Canada: International Institute for Sustainable Development (IISD).

Global Reporting Initiative (GRI). (2006). Reporting framework: G3 online. Retrieved August 9, 2011, from http://www.globalreporting .org/ReportingFramework/G3Online/

Global Reporting Initiative (GRI). (2011). Reporting framework: G3.1 guidelines. Retrieved August 9, 2011, from http://www.globalreporting.org/ReportingFramework/G31Guidelines/

Hák, Tomáš; Moldan, Bedřich; & Dahl, Arthur Lyon. (Eds.). (2007). *Scientific Committee on Problems of the Environment (SCOPE) Series: Vol. 67. Sustainability indicators: A scientific assessment.* Washington, DC: Island Press.

International Institute for Sustainable Development (IISD). (2010). Compendium: A global directory to indicator initiatives. Retrieved August 8, 2011, from http://www.iisd.org/measure/compendium/

Moldan, Bedřich, & Billharz, Suzanne. (Eds.). (1997). *Scientific Committee on Problems of the Environment (SCOPE) Series: Vol. 58. Sustainability indicators: A report on the project on indicators of sustainable development.* Chichester, UK: John Wiley & Sons.

Spangenberg, Joachim H. (2009). Sustainable development indicators: Towards integrated systems as a tool for managing and monitoring a complex transition. *International Journal of Global Environmental Issues, 9*(4), 318–337.

United Nations (UN). (1993). *Agenda 21: Earth summit. The United Nations programme of action from Rio.* New York: United Nations.

United Nations (UN). (1995). Report of the Secretary-General, Commission on Sustainable Development, 3rd session 1995, Item 3(b) of the provisional agenda, Chapter 40: Information for decision-making and Earthwatch, E/CN.17/1995, Work Program on Indicators of Sustainable Development, UN /E/CN.17/1995/18. New York: United Nations.

United Nations Department of Economic and Social Affairs (UNDESA). (1998). *Measuring changes in consumption and production patterns: A set of indicators* (ST/ESA/264). New York: United Nations.

United Nations Department of Economic and Social Affairs (UNDESA). (2007). Indicators of sustainable development: Guidelines and methodologies (3rd ed.). Retrieved January 17, 2012, from http://www.un.org/esa/sustdev/natlinfo/indicators/guidelines.pdf

United Nations Department of Economic and Social Affairs, Division for Sustainable Development (UNDESA-DSD). (1996). Indicators of sustainable development: Framework and methodologies. Retrieved January 17, 2012, from http://www.un.org/esa/sustdev/natlinfo/indicators/indisd/english/english.htm

United Nation Sustainable Development. (1992). United Nations Conference on Environment & Development, Rio de Janeiro, Brazil, 3 to 14 June 1992: Agenda 21. Retrieved January 20, 2012, from http://www.un.org/esa/sustdev/documents/agenda21/english/Agenda21.pdf

Air Pollution Indicators and Monitoring

As air pollution has become widely recognized as an issue affecting human health and the sustainability of the environment, scientists and policy makers have developed indices to measure and report on levels of pollution. Although they are in widespread use, the indices have not been standardized, and different indices measure different components of pollution.

Anthropogenic air pollution (pollution caused by people) has existed since prehistoric humans' first fires. Even the ancient Greeks and Romans were aware of the problem. As early as 1661, the English author John Evelyn wrote about London's air quality in a pamphlet called *Fumifugium*, stating "inhabitants breathe nothing but an impure and thick mist, . . . corrupting the lungs and disordering the entire habit of their bodies." The Industrial Revolution resulted in further widespread air pollution. Since the 1950s, a variety of legislation has been introduced to reduce emissions, but, at the same time, increased use of motor vehicles has introduced new air pollutants. Outdoor air pollution is now estimated to cause 1.3 million deaths worldwide per year (WHO 2011a).

The public is often confused by the information it receives about pollution concentrations and health effects. To help clarify the situation, several agencies have formulated air quality indices to provide a universal platform to compare and assess the impact of the various pollutants. Air quality monitoring, however, requires a network of sophisticated and high-maintenance equipment. The use of bioindicators—organisms that exhibit different responses to different levels of pollution or by accumulation of a pollutant—has been growing. Biomonitoring is used to complement existing air pollution networks.

Background

Air pollution is the presence of any physical, chemical, or biological agent that modifies the natural characteristics of the atmosphere. According to the US Environmental Protection Agency, air pollution is "the presence in the outdoor atmosphere of one or more air contaminants in sufficient quantities and of such characteristics and duration as to be injurious, or tend to be injurious to human health and welfare, plant or animal life, or to property, or which unreasonably interferes with the enjoyment of life and property or the conduct of business" (US Department of Commerce 1978). Air pollution depends upon many factors, including climate, as well as political, economic, and industrial development. It can be considered on many levels, from local to global. For example, on a continental scale, acid rain in Scandinavia is considered to be the result of pollution from the United Kingdom and western Europe, while the release of greenhouse gases is a global problem.

The composition and relative level of pollutants in the atmosphere differs significantly in urban and rural environments, resulting from a variety of natural sources (such as volcanoes, dust storms, forest fires, and pollens) and anthropogenic activities (such as industrial processes, motor vehicle exhaust, heat and power generating facilities, and combustion). All of these produce pollutants that impair the quality of the atmosphere. The use of biofuels in homes in developing countries not only pollutes the outdoor environment but is also responsible for poor indoor air quality and results in around 2 million deaths annually in the developing world (WHO 2011a).

The Industrial Revolution, technological advancements, and the increased use of motor vehicles have contributed greatly to the deterioration of air quality. At the same time, the impact of air pollution on human health and the environment began to be systematically documented during this same period. Scientists have identified a range of ambient air pollutants and their emission sources, but data relating to their concentrations and impact on human health and ecosystems is available for only a limited number of air pollutants.

Air pollutants exist as aerosols (tiny liquid and solid particles), particulates (solid particles that may be larger in size), and gases. They can enter the air directly (primary pollutants, such as oxides of sulfur, nitrogen, and carbon; organic compounds; particulate matter; and metal oxides) or be formed via chemical reactions in the atmosphere (secondary pollutants formed under the influence of light energy: photochemical oxidants). Along with six criteria pollutants (carbon monoxide [CO], nitrogen dioxide [NO_2], ozone [O_3], lead [Pb], particulate matter [PM], and sulfur dioxide [SO_2]), the United States Environmental Protection Agency (EPA) has identified a large number of air pollutants that are known to cause or may reasonably be believed to cause adverse effects on human health or adverse environmental effects. Initially, 187 specific pollutants and chemical groups were identified as hazardous air pollutants (HAPs), and the list has been modified over time. For example methyl ethyl ketone was removed from the list in 2005, ethylene glycol monobutyl ether in 2004, and caprolactam in 1996 (US EPA 2007).

Due to improved emission control technologies and strict legislation, the levels of ambient air pollutant concentrations in developed countries have fallen considerably, but they remain a serious environmental health problem in a large number of low- and middle-income countries, particularly in megacities (those with more than 10 million people). The World Health Organization (WHO) estimates that a quarter of the world's population is exposed to unhealthy concentrations of air pollutants, and outdoor air pollution is responsible for 1.3 million deaths annually around the world (WHO 2011a).

Among air pollutants, fine particulate matter is of greatest concern due to its association with a variety of acute and chronic illnesses, such as lung cancer and cardiopulmonary diseases. (Because particulate matter is so small, it can easily be inhaled.) According to WHO, fine particulate matter is responsible globally for 9 percent of lung cancer deaths, 5 percent of cardiopulmonary deaths, and about 1 percent of respiratory infection deaths (WHO 2011b). National and international ambient air quality regulations and standards have been introduced to protect human health and ecosystems. The threshold concentrations of various pollutants are set after a detailed review of available scientific evidence of their impacts on human health.

To ensure that the established national or international ambient air quality standards are being met, continuous monitoring of the various air pollutants is carried out at fixed monitoring stations in different locations. The public, however, typically is unaware of the links between air pollution and health and does not really understand existing air quality information. Air quality indices have been developed as a tool to inform the public of potential health problems related to air quality or pollutant concentrations.

Air Quality Indices

Air quality indices (AQI) are categorical, generally based on numeric ranges, and are computed by different governments and agencies to report the quality of air with reference to health risks. The higher the AQI, the higher the health risk to the population of that region. To calculate the AQI, ambient air concentrations of various pollutants are continuously monitored at nationwide networks of monitoring stations, and these concentrations are transformed into an index. Numerical values are given in ranges with reference to a health risk or level of air pollution, and each range is typically assigned a color code together with a description. The functions and scales used to convert concentrations of various air pollutants to AQI vary widely among countries (Plaia and Ruggieri 2011).

In 1976, the EPA developed the first air quality index, called the Pollutant Standard Index (PSI), based on carbon monoxide, sulfur dioxide, particulate matter with a diameter of 10 micrometers (PM_{10}), ozone, and nitrogen dioxide. In 1999, the Air Quality Index (US EPA 2009 and 2011) replaced the PSI, and the index was extended to include $PM_{2.5}$ (particulate matter with a diameter of 2.5 micrometers) as well as PM_{10}. Despite some limitations (for example, limited applicability to regions other than the United States and no consideration of the cumulative effect of multiple pollutants), the AQI is widely used. Many countries, however, continue to use PSI because they do not monitor $PM_{2.5}$ (Cheng et al. 2007).

The EPA calculates the AQI for five air pollutants regulated by the US Clean Air Act. Twenty-four-hour concentrations of these pollutants are measured and reported in six reference categories and symbolized by different colors. An AQI value of 100 corresponds to the national air quality standard for the pollutant. A value of 50 represents good air quality with little potential to affect public health, while an AQI value over 300 represents hazardous air quality. (See table 1 on page 13.)

A website developed by a number of US agencies provides the public with easy access to national air quality information (AIRNow n.d.). This site provides daily AQI forecasts as well as real-time AQI conditions for more

TABLE 1. EPA Air Quality Index

Air Quality Index Levels of Health Concern	Numerical Value	Meaning
Good	0 to 50	Air quality is considered satisfactory, and air pollution poses little or no risk
Moderate	51 to 100	Air quality is acceptable; however, for some pollutants there may be a moderate health concern for a very small number of people who are unusually sensitive to air pollution.
Unhealthy for Sensitive Groups	101 to 150	Members of sensitive groups may experience health effects. The general public is not likely to be affected.
Unhealthy	151 to 200	Everyone may begin to experience health effects; members of sensitive groups may experience more serious health effects.
Very Unhealthy	201 to 300	Health warnings of emergency conditions. The entire population is more likely to be affected.
Hazardous	301 to 500	Health alert: everyone may experience more serious health effects.

Source: EPA (2009).

This widely distributed chart generally includes color coding from green for good to maroon for hazardous.

than three hundred cities across the United States. It also provides links to more detailed state and local air quality information.

In Europe, methods and systems used to report air quality vary greatly. A recent European Union (EU) project called CITEAIR gives details for the different countries (van der Elshout and Léger 2007).

The United Kingdom has its own index. In its 2012 revision, carbon monoxide was dropped, $PM_{2.5}$ was added, and index bands for PM_{10}, nitrogen dioxide, and ozone were made more stringent (Department for Environment Food and Rural Affairs 2011). The Daily Air Quality Index, as it is now called, reports the level of air pollution in terms of four air pollution bands (low, moderate, high, or very high) and a ten-point index. The air quality index is based on short-term health effects. (See tables 2 and 3, on pages 14 and 15.)

Air quality indices are now in widespread use. There is no consensus, however, either on the scale or the number of bands. Table 4, on page 15, shows that France, for example, uses a scale of 1 to 10, while Australia uses 0 to 200; both have six bands. All air quality indices have a common aim to reduce adverse health effects from short-term increases in air pollution. Some display a bias toward regulatory issues and others to health effects. As shown in table 3, on page 15, the index is often accompanied with health advice. There is no common approach. In some indices the advice varies by pollutant, whereas in others separate advice may be given for non-risk groups and at-risk groups. Without a consistent approach, a comparison of AQI values is difficult and of limited usefulness.

A number of innovative methods have also been used to inform the public about air pollution. These include

TABLE 2. UK Daily Air Quality Index Bands

Band	Index	Ozone	Nitrogen Dioxide	Sulphur Dioxide	PM2.5 Particles	PM10 Particles
		Running 8 hourly mean	Hourly mean	15 minute mean	24 hour mean	24 hour mean
		μgm^{-3}	μgm^{-3}	μgm^{-3}	μgm^{-3}	μgm^{-3}
LOW						
	1	0–33	0–66	0–88	0–11	0–16
	2	34–65	67–133	89–176	12–23	17–33
	3	66–99	134–199	177–265	24–34	34–49
MODERATE						
	4	100–120	200–267	266–354	35–41	50–58
	5	121–140	268–334	355–442	42–46	59–66
	6	141–159	335–399	443–531	47–52	67–74
HIGH						
	7	160–187	400–467	532–708	53–58	75–83
	8	188–213	468–534	709–886	59–64	84–91
	9	214–239	535–599	887–1063	65–69	92–99
VERY HIGH						
	10	240 or more	600 or more	1064 or more	70 or more	100 or more

Source: COMEAP (2011).

*The concentration of an air pollutant is given in micrograms (one-millionth of a gram) per cubic meter of air, or µgm-3.

Indices in different countries vary widely, but like this UK index, many provide a stepwise decrease in air quality with accompanying health risks.

TABLE 3. Health Advice Relating to the UK Air Quality Index

Air Pollution Banding	Value	Accompanying Health Messages for at-Risk Groups and the General Population	
		At-Risk Individuals	General Population
Low	1–3	Enjoy your usual outdoor activities.	Enjoy your usual outdoor activities.
Moderate	4–6	Adults and children with lung problems (and adults with heart problems) who experience symptoms should consider reducing strenuous physical activity, particularly outdoors.	Enjoy your usual outdoor activities.
High	7–9	Adults and children with lung problems, and adults with heart problems, should reduce strenuous physical exertion, particularly outdoors, and particularly if they experience symptoms. People with asthma may find they need to use their reliever inhaler more often. Older people should also reduce physical exertion.	Anyone experiencing discomfort such as sore eyes, cough, or sore throat should consider reducing activity, particularly outdoors.
Very High	10	Adults and children with lung problems, adults with heart problems, and older people, should avoid strenuous physical activity. People with asthma may find they need to use their reliever inhaler more often.	Reduce physical exertion, particularly outdoors, especially if you experience symptoms such as cough or sore throat.

Source: COMEAP (2011).

TABLE 4. Air Quality Indices in Various Countries and Regions

Country	Index Value	Named Bandings	Pollutants Included
Australia	200	6	$CO, NO_2, O_3, PM_{10}, SO_2$
Belgium	10	10	NO_2, O_3, PM_{10}, SO_2
Canada	100	10	$CO, NO_2, O_3, PM_{10}, SO_2$
European Union (CITEAIR)	100	5	$CO, NO_2, O_3, PM_{10}, SO_2$
France	10	6	NO_2, O_3, PM_{10}, SO_2
Germany	100	6	$CO, NO_2, O_3, PM_{10}, SO_2$
Ireland	100	5	NO_2, O_3, PM_{10}, SO_2
United Kingdom	10	4	$NO_2, O_3, PM_{2.5}, PM_{10}, SO_2$
United States	500	6	$CO, NO_2 , O_3, PM_{2.5}, PM_{10}, SO_2$

Source: Adapted from COMEAP (2011).

balloons (in Paris), photo journals (in Beijing), a digital exhibition (in Madrid), a living light (in Seoul), and lasers (in Helsinki). These will continue to evolve, and, no doubt, in the future individuals will be able to access information on their own personal exposure based on knowledge of their daily routine and lifestyle.

Ian COLBECK and Zaheer Ahmad NASIR
University of Essex

See also Biological Indicators—Species; Carbon Footprint; Environmental Performance Index (EPI); Externality Valuation; Land-Use and Land-Cover Change; Ocean Acidification—Measurement; Reducing Emissions from Deforestation and Forest Degradation (REDD); Regulatory Compliance; Shipping and Freight Indicators; Tree Rings as Environmental Indicators

FURTHER READING

AIRNow. (n.d.). Homepage. Retrieved January 5, 2012, from http://airnow.gov/

Cheng, Wan-Li, et al. (2007) Comparison of the revised air quality index with the PSI and AQI indices. *Science of the Total Environment*, *382*, 191–198.

Committee on the Medical Effects of Air Pollutants (COMEAP). (2011). Review of the UK Air Quality Index. Retrieved January 5, 2012, from http://www.comeap.org.uk/images/stories/Documents/Reports/comeap review of the uk air quality index.pdf

Department for Environment Food and Rural Affairs (Defra). (2011). Notification of changes to the Air Quality Index. Retrieved February 8, 2012, from http://uk-air.defra.gov.uk/news?view=158

Plaia, Antonella, & Ruggieri, Mariantonietta. (2011). Air quality indices: A review. *Reviews in Environmental Science and Biotechnology*, *10*(2), 165–179.

United States Department of Commerce. (1978). Air pollution regulations in state implementation plans: Tennessee (PB-290 291). Retrieved February 8, 2012, from http://www.ntis.gov/search/product.aspx?ABBR=PB290291

United States Environmental Protection Agency (EPA). (2007). Modifications to the 112(b)1 hazardous air pollutants. Retrieved February 8, 2012, from http://www.epa.gov/ttn/atw/pollutants/atwsmod.html

United States Environmental Protection Agency (EPA). (2009). Air Quality Index: A guide to air quality and your health. Retrieved January 5, 2012, from http://www.epa.gov/airnow/aqi_brochure_08-09.pdf

United States Environmental Protection Agency (EPA). (2011). Air Quality Index (AQI): A guide to air quality and your health. Retrieved January 5, 2012, from http://cfpub.epa.gov/airnow/index.cfm?action=aqibasics.aqi

van den Elshout, Sef, & Léger, Karine. (2007, June). Comparing urban air quality across borders. Retrieved January 5, 2012, from http://www.airqualitynow.eu/download/CITEAIR-Comparing_Urban_Air_Quality_across_Borders.pdf

World Health Organization (WHO). (2011a). Air quality and health. Retrieved January 5, 2012, from http://www.who.int/mediacentre/factsheets/fs313/en/index.html

World Health Organization (WHO). (2011b). Global Health Observatory (GHO). Mortality and burden of disease from outdoor air pollution. Retrieved January 5, 2012, from http://www.who.int/gho/phe/outdoor_air_pollution/burden/en/index.html

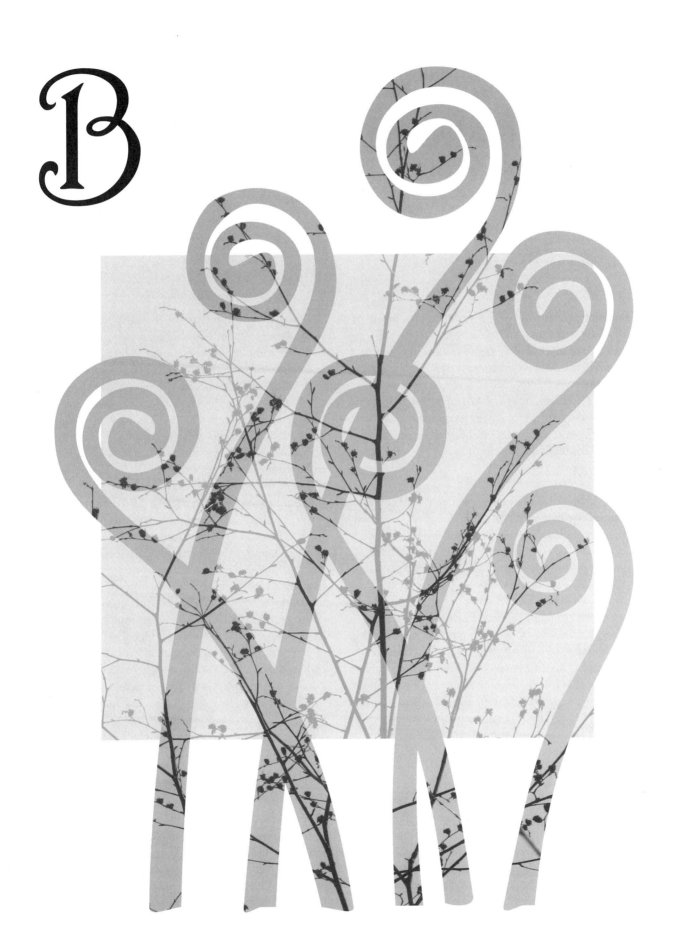

B

Biological Indicators– Ecosystems

In the pursuit of environmental sustainability, researchers look for indicators that give early warning of ecological changes, especially those that could lead to a cascading effect of disrupted ecosystems. Some indicators on the genetic and species levels have been identified. More challenging is the identification of specific fragile ecosystems whose stability can serve as a monitor for effects of environmental stress, including that predicted from global climate change.

Some ecosystems are more sensitive to change than others. Similar to the more common practice of identifying individual species that can provide an early indication of negative impacts (such as exotic species invasions, pollution, or climate change impacts), one can also recognize particularly sensitive ecosystems. Their recognition involves identification not of individual species, or even community-level effects, but of changes in the energy transfer processes and nutrient recycling that define an ecosystem. Ecosystem vulnerability, resilience, and resistance to disturbance are all factors that could be used to identify early indicator ecosystems, ones that will be impacted negatively first among all others. Criteria that could be used to define a potential indicator ecosystem include how sensitive (easily perturbed) is the process of primary production, or the transfer of energy upward into higher trophic levels, or the decomposition processes that return nutrients to the soil. Vulnerability to trophic cascades, in which change in one level of a food chain leads to wider disruption of the chain, is a more specific example of the sometimes rapid destabilization that can lead to major impacts on ecosystem stability and services, including species extinction. Identifying indicator ecosystems is a greater challenge than identifying indicator species and, thus, is a rarer undertaking.

One source of information that may be synonymous with identifying an indicator ecosystem is the recognition that some ecosystems are more fragile (less stable) and vulnerable to anthropogenic disturbance than others (see review by Nilsson and Grelsson 1995). In general, ecosystems that are slow to recover from perturbation are considered not very resilient. Examples of this include high-elevation alpine or high-latitude tundra environments, where short growth seasons do not allow recovery either from natural perturbations, such as fire or landslides, or from a host of anthropogenic impacts ranging from human footprints to mining activities. In these ecosystems, plant growth and decomposition are both severely constrained due to low temperatures. High species and population turnover, plus species abundance and composition, can also reflect ecosystem vulnerability or fragility. These are common characteristics of alpine and tundra ecosystems, as well as others, such as deserts, where precipitation and prolonged drought can severely limit the growth season. On a global ecosystem scale, climate change parameters such as elevated atmospheric carbon dioxide (CO_2) can strongly influence plant productivity and climate warming, which can possibly lead to a host of changes in energy flow and nutrient recycling within the Earth's ecosystem.

An important, if not critical, challenge today is the identification of the most fragile ecosystems, those that, like the canary in the coal mine, will provide an early warning for recognizing ongoing and future ecosystem impacts due to global climate change. Predicted climate change includes atmospheric warming and elevated CO_2 in the atmosphere, leading to such changes as a higher frequency and intensity of droughts, floods, hurricanes, and other forms of extreme, episodic events. Sea level rise is also predicted. Which ecosystems are most vulnerable to these conditions is difficult to assess, and most likely there are many that are equally vulnerable, though in response to different stress factors among those operating simultaneously. Regardless, certain ecosystems might be identified based on their vulnerability to specific stress factors related to climate change and anthropogenic disturbance. This identification must also be tempered by the importance of particular ecosystems to feedback effects that could lead to either negative or positive accelerations, possibly leading to a tipping point in ecosystem stability. For example, the large plant biomass found in a tropical rain-forest ecosystem generates a major sink for CO_2 absorption from the atmosphere. Disruption of this large, critical sink for CO_2 absorption from the atmosphere could lead to even greater increases in atmospheric CO_2 and major impacts on the global carbon balance. In addition, perturbation of this ecosystem, such as over-harvesting or slash-and-burn agricultural practices, could also jeopardize global biodiversity due to the large percent of global species found in these forests. In this sense, tropical rain forests could be considered critical ecosystem indicators of potential alterations in our global ecosystem.

Attempts to list and recognize vulnerable ecosystems include British Columbia's Ministry of the Environment program called Sensitive Ecosystem Inventories (SEI), through which remnants of rare and fragile terrestrial ecosystems are targeted for survival management. The viewpoint of this government agency is that these particularly sensitive ecosystems are important for both habitat and species diversity, elimination of which could have cascading and possibly devastating effects on other ecosystems considered more stable and less vulnerable. Besides attention to terrestrial ecosystems, there have been organized attempts at identifying especially fragile marine ecosystems, ones that could also be used as early indicator ecosystems (Roberts et al. 2010). The observed loss of species numbers or entire ecosystems such as coral reefs is now targeted within SEI, as well as in other projects around the world. The loss of sea ice in the higher latitudes and resultant increased soil respiration from the exposed land could lead to major effects on the global CO_2 balance, atmospheric CO_2, and climate change on a global ecosystem scale. Indeed, spatial scale must be a major consideration in evaluating ecosystems as early indicators of harmful effects.

The major challenges of identifying indicator ecosystems still lie in our estimates of their relative vulnerability, resilience, and resistance to disturbance. Ranking even the most obvious examples of ecosystem vulnerability remains difficult, if not impossible, and attempts at ranking are often based mainly on valuation of the ecosystem services provided to humankind. Researchers face difficulties as they pursue identification of indicator species; such difficulties are amplified when pursuing the successful identification of indicator ecosystems by the astounding complexity of an ecosystem compared to a single species. Regardless, as the list of articles on different websites can verify, the number of sensitive ecosystems continues to grow daily (see e!Science News n.d.).

William K. SMITH
Wake Forest University

See also Biological Indicators—Genetic; Biological Indicators—Species; Ecosystem Health Indicators; Intergovernmental Science-Policy Platform on Biodiversity and Ecosystem Services (IPBES); Long-Term Ecological Research (LTER); New Ecological Paradigm (NEP) Scale

FURTHER READING

e! Science News. (n.d.) Science news articles about "sensitive ecosystems." Retrieved February 6, 2012, from http://esciencenews.com/dictionary/sensitive.ecosystems

Gunderson, Lance H., & Holling, C. S. (2002). *Panarchy: Understanding transformations in human and natural systems.* Washington, DC: Island Press.

Nilsson, Christer, & Grelsson, Gunnel. (1995). The fragility of ecosystems: A review. *Journal of Applied Ecology, 32*(4), 677–692.

Roberts, C.; Smith, C.; Tillin, H.; & Tyler-Walters, H. (2010). Review of existing approaches to evaluate marine habitat vulnerability to commercial fishing activities (Report SC080016/R3). Rotherham, UK: Environmental Agency.

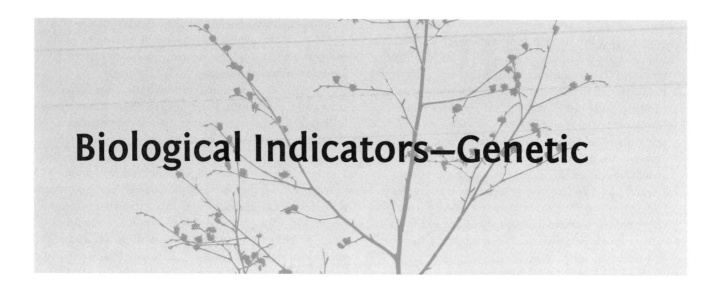

Biological Indicators—Genetic

Genetic diversity is the basis for species and ecosystem diversity and includes the diversity of all genetic characteristics and the degree of their distinctiveness. Diversity is essential to the adaptability of populations, species, and ecosystems to environmental change. International initiatives have helped move forward the application of genetic diversity indicators to conservation and sustainability policies, but more work in this direction is needed.

Biodiversity, the diversity of life on Earth, can be measured and described at different levels of complexity, ranging from genes to species and ecosystems. The concept of biodiversity represents a noncomplementary, hierarchical approach, with the higher levels comprising all information from the lower ones (see Figure 1 on page 21). Genetic diversity, the diversity of all genetic characteristics, builds the basis for diversity at all higher levels. Genetic diversity is crucial to foster evolutionary processes through natural selection. Moreover, genetic diversity directly influences species diversity, as well as ecosystem functions and ecosystem services (Hughes et al. 2008). The US researchers Richard Lankau and Sharon Strauss (2007) have shown that preserving diversity requires preserving the processes that support genetic diversity, and vice versa.

Levels of Biodiversity

The basic unit for measuring genetic diversity is the gene. Genes are sections of the deoxyribonucleic acid (DNA) macromolecule that are separated from other genes by noncoding DNA regions. In higher organisms (animals, plants, and fungi), DNA is stored mainly in the form of chromosomes in the cell nucleus. Most sexually reproducing organisms are diploid, meaning that every individual possesses two sets of chromosomes, one coming from the mother and the other from the father. Both chromosomes are identical in size and shape and in the arrangement of genes. The genes are arranged in a linear sequence on a chromosome, and each gene has a unique location. This location is called the locus (plural: loci), and the specific gene at each of the loci on the two chromosomes is called an allele. A gene usually has two alleles: one from the mother and one from the father. If both alleles of that gene are identical, the gene is homozygous; if they differ, the gene is heterozygous. Genes for which only one allele exists are called monomorphic, as compared to those with several alleles, which are called polymorphic.

The sum of genes of an individual is called a genotype. Each cell of an individual organism contains the exact same genetic information, but there are no different individual organisms that contain the exact same genotype (with the exception of clones resulting from nonsexual reproduction and monozygotic twins).

The different characters of individuals or species (as, e.g., the shape of plant flowers or of the bill of birds) result from different combinations of genes in these individuals. The sum of all morphological characters is called the phenotype. The phenotype traditionally has been the basis for classifying nature and naming morphologically similar entities.

Modern molecular phylogenetic approaches allow the direct analysis of genetic information at the DNA level, and the resulting hypothesis on phylogenetic relationships can be used for classifying the organisms. So far, most of these new classifications affect family and above-family levels, and only in very rare cases is genetic diversity that is revealed by molecular data adequately linked to species names.

Figure 1. The Nested Character of Biodiversity and Its Components

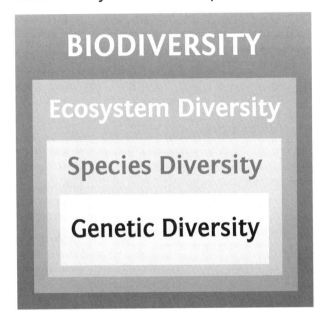

BIODIVERSITY

Ecosystem Diversity

Species Diversity

Genetic Diversity

Source: authors.

Biodiversity can be measured at different levels, ranging from genes to species and ecosystems. Because of the hierarchical character of this system, the higher levels include all information from the lower ones.

Species are the fundamental units of biodiversity. Species diversity is by far the most prominent indicator of biodiversity. It can, for instance, be approximated simply by the number of species occurring within a certain area (species richness), an indicator that can be expanded to incorporate qualitative aspects such as rarity and complementarity, or by indicators of species evenness (i.e., the variability in species abundances). There are, however, several different and partly competing concepts of what constitutes a species. The most commonly used definition states that a species comprises a population of individual organisms that can interbreed to produce fertile offspring. This is known as the biological species concept (Mayr 1942). Yet individuals, populations, breeds, and so on may differ genetically within one species. In contrast, a morphological species concept, which describes species based on morphological similarities or differences, is useful as it helps to classify diversity on Earth more easily. Genetic diversity is often defined as the diversity within species (Magurran 2004); however, genetic information, for instance indicating how distinct the genotype of species *x* is from species *y*, can also be applied to biodiversity indicators at higher (community, landscape, or system) levels.

Ecosystem diversity describes the diversity of different communities of species and their interactions. It is the most abstract level of biodiversity and completely encompasses species diversity as well as genetic diversity.

Genetic Indicators and Biodiversity

The South African conservation biologist Belinda Reyers (2010) recognizes that biological diversity is multifaceted and reviews the categories of biodiversity indicators developed to date. Citing the Millennium Ecosystem Assessment (2005) and a study by Andrew Balmford, professor of conservation biology at the University of Cambridge, and colleagues (2008), Reyers lists the following three components of biodiversity: diversity, quantity, and condition (all measurable at the three levels discussed above). In the diversity category are indicators such as species or gene richness and distinctiveness. Quantity indicators refer to the extent and distribution of species or ecosystems, as well as to measures of abundance and population size. Condition indicators include those that reflect threat status to species and ecosystems, or fragmentation and integrity of populations.

Different components or even levels of diversity do not necessarily exclude each other in their application as diversity indicators. For instance, a genetic diversity metric can complement a species richness index, adding the dimension of genetic distinctiveness between species to their number as a qualitative addendum.

Major Indicators of Genetic Diversity

Scientists talk about the in situ and ex situ storing of genetic information, referring respectively to the genetic information "stored" in species living in their natural environment and in species conserved outside of their natural environment (e.g., seed banks, germplasm banks, natural history collections, botanical and zoological gardens). Similarly, indicators sometimes refer specifically to in situ or ex situ genetic diversity.

Specific genetic indicators of note include allelic richness, which describes the number of alleles (different forms of the same gene) per locus (position of a gene) within a population. Several modifications of this indicator exist that refer either to number, frequency, evenness, or average proportion (heterozygosity) of loci carrying two different alleles. The variation in allelic states can be measured using molecular markers in the laboratory (see Hughes et al. 2008).

Genetic variance, or coefficient of genetic variance, is an indicator that quantitatively describes the continuous variability of a phenotypic trait among individuals within a population that is caused by heredity (see Hughes et al.

2008). It contributes one part to the variance in trait that can either be genetic driven or environment driven. The identification of the genetic-driven variance requires detailed knowledge of the genome as derived by experiments (same genotypes are grown in different environments and vice versa).

The indicator referred to as genetic distance describes the difference in genotypes between two populations. A commonly used fixation index ranges from 0 (identical) to 1 (different species). This indicator compares the diversity of randomly selected alleles of a subpopulation with that of the complete population (see Hughes et al. 2008).

The Biodiversity Indicators Partnership (BIP) of the Convention on Biological Diversity (CBD) has identified a number of potential indicators, all work in progress. Two trends in genetic diversity are explicitly named. The first is trends in ex situ crop collections. An indicator reflecting this trend would provide an assessment of how well we are able to manage (i.e., maintain or even increase) the genetic diversity of crops. BIP partners are currently developing an enrichment index to that effect that should measure how collections around the world (either as seed banks, germ-plasm banks, or fields banks, i.e., live growing plants) reflect the collections enrichment in terms of the number of species they contain, the number of new species entering the collection, and the number of countries represented in the collection. The second trend specified by the BIP is genetic diversity of terrestrial domesticated animals. BIP partners are developing an indicator that should capture the status (such as "at risk") of domesticated animal populations. The indicator will be based on more than thirty species of birds and mammals and covering more than eight thousand breeds, incorporating data on the size and structure of the breed populations. This indicator will serve as an approximation to genetic diversity, as it does not account for the degree of within-breed or between-breed diversity.

The concept of genetic distinctiveness has been used to develop several indicators of genetic diversity and can be found in the literature of different fields, across disciplines ranging from biology to economics. Phylogenetic diversity, for example, describes the relationship of species according to their evolutionary history. During evolution, genetic isolation of different populations may result in speciation events in which species, though genetically identical at the point of isolation, develop independently into new species from that point onward. Hence, the number of common traits shared among species and the number of distinct traits provide information about their phylogenetic distinctiveness. This distinctiveness can be graphically expressed on a phylogenetic tree by the length of its branches. (See figure 2 on page 23.) The earlier a species developed in evolutionary history, the more unique traits it carries and the higher is its contribution to phylogenetic diversity. In other words, the loss of an evolutionary unique species leads to a higher loss of evolutionary history than the loss of an evolutionary young species, whose genetic information is to a large extent shared with many other species (Mace, Gittelman, and Purvis 2003).

Many different biodiversity indices or measures have been developed based on these concepts, some of them dating from the early 1990s (e.g., Faith 1992; Vane-Wright, Humphries, and Williams 1991; Weitzman 1992).

Additional studies have used genetic distinctiveness data obtained through a process of DNA hybridization, examining the DNA of each possible pair of species (or individuals of a same species) within a given group. The differences in the positioning of crucial chemical elements between this hybrid DNA and one of the two original species (called the tracer) gives the measure of genetic difference (Weitzman 1992). Another approach has been to measure the loss of species genetic diversity, based on similar DNA data, to evaluate the amount of genetic diversity that is lost when a species (or more) is taken out of the reference set (Gerber 2011). Graphically, this measure tries to approximate the length of the phylogenetic tree branch that would be cut from the tree if a species were removed from it.

Another technique used in the study of genetic distinctiveness is DNA barcoding—identifying species using a short DNA section of a marker gene. In general, mutations of genes occur at a rather constant rate; thus the more similar the analyzed DNA section between two individuals or species, the closer they are related taxonomically. For DNA barcoding, noncoding sections of the DNA are used because mutations in these sections do not influence the genetic traits (see Moritz and Cicero 2004).

Figure 2. Sample Phylogeny with Four Species

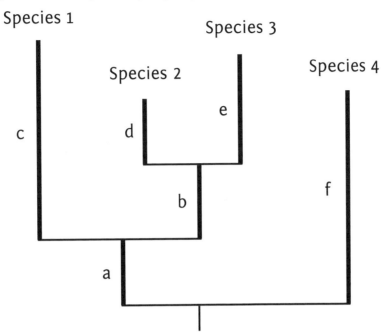

Vertical length (broad segments) represents evolutionary change.

Group A: Species 1, 2, and 3
        ED = evolutionary diversity = a+b+c+d+e

Group B: Species 1, 2, and 4
        ED = evolutionary diversity = a+b+c+d+f

ED (Group A) is smaller than ED (Group B)

Source: authors.

Phylogeny is the history of evolution of a species (or other taxonomic group, e.g. genus or family). The branch lengths in the graph represent the number of derived traits, a measure of genetic distinctiveness between species. The longer the vertical segments, the more evolutionary change is embodied by that species.

Applications for Conservation and Sustainability

Most genetic indicators were developed parallel to the progress in genetics during the twentieth century, especially after the identification of the DNA molecular structure in 1953 by the US scientists James D. Watson and Francis Crick. The application of genetic diversity indicators in the context of the conservation and sustainable use of biodiversity, though still in its infancy, is an extremely important area for continued development. The genetic diversity of populations, species, or ecosystems is crucial to their resilience and adaptive capacity. The more genetically diverse a population is, the more

different options are stored in the genetic code to adapt to changing environments, such as climate change, pathogens, or pests, and the higher is the chance that some individuals will survive and reproduce. If the size of a population falls below a critical level, the remaining genotypes may be not diverse enough to maintain ecological fitness, a situation referred to as a genetic bottleneck. Even if the population's size increases afterward, its genetic diversity is enduringly impoverished. Many species that are threatened with extinction are undergoing this fate (e.g., the cheetah, giant panda, and rhinoceros).

The indicators identified by the BIP group described above are of easy and intuitive use to policy makers; however, as discussed, they are coarse approximations of the actual genetic diversity. Other indicators track more closely evolutions in genetic diversity, but are on the other hand less transparent, which might make them less appealing for policy work.

Challenges

Indicators of genetic diversity to date have had little bearing on sustainability and conservation policy. Reasons for this are probably multiple, ranging from ease of communication and transparency to data availability and applicability to conservation goals.

As of 2011, the indicators developed by the BIP will find applications in policy, but they only capture restricted dimensions of genetic diversity, such as gene richness, and fail to capture the extent of genetic variation (the concept represented by the phylogenetic tree branch lengths). So far, they only relate to gene banks and domesticated species and do not consider unmanaged or "wild" biodiversity and its contribution to ecosystem service provision. One reason for this may be that indicators capturing genetic variation (and having a more direct link to sustainability) are complex and require data and knowledge that is still not available for the majority of species. It is important to develop genetic diversity indicators applicable to policy settings that can best promote conservation and sustainable use of resources. As an example, the coffee beans commercially grown in the world today are genetically very similar. Wild *Coffea arabica* landraces (local varieties that have developed largely by natural processes), which hold more genetic diversity and potential to adapt to future shocks (such as pests or climate change), are concentrated in the Ethiopian Afromontane rain forest, which is quickly disappearing. In order to support the owners of this pool of coffee genetic diversity (i.e., financially reward its conservation), indicators linking genetic diversity to sustainability would help.

Another area needing attention is the political process of handling issues of property rights over the use and sharing of benefits arising from genetic diversity. This is the topic of the protocol adopted in 2010 by the CBD entitled "Access to Genetic Resources and the Fair and Equitable Sharing of Benefits Arising from their Utilization," often referred to as the Nagoya Protocol on Access and Benefit Sharing, or ABS (CBD 2010).

The application of adequate genetic diversity measures and indicators is a prerequisite for the implementation of purposeful policies for the conservation and sustainable use of biodiversity. Neglecting the genetic level in this respect would disclaim the intrinsic value of the evolutionary memory of millions of organisms derived through ages of natural selection processes. Any loss of genetic diversity is irreversible, and a species that goes extinct can never be revitalized. Hence, the utilities of considering the genetic level of biodiversity are manifold. First, it ensures the highest possible adaptive capacity of populations, species, and ecosystems to changing environmental conditions and thereby facilitates the constant supply of ecosystem goods and services. Second, genetic diversity provides important information for breeding and cultivation of crops and livestock, the pharmaceutical industry, and many other potential applications. Altogether, genetic diversity enhances the resilience capacity of ecosystems and thereby provides mankind with invaluable insurance against future challenges as yet unknown.

Current Situation and Outlook

The best-studied indicators of genetic diversity relate to domesticated populations (livestock and crops), while adequate indicators at community or ecosystem levels that are relevant for sustainability issues are as yet largely lacking. Even though the relevance of genetic diversity is generally acknowledged, little effort is evident toward implementing genetic diversity conceptually in conservation action plans and considerations of sustainable use of biodiversity (Laikre et al. 2010). To fulfill the political goals raised by the CBD and other international initiatives, it is imperative that more research capacities be invested in better understanding and in development of methods and tools that will allow genetic diversity at all levels of biodiversity to be appropriately measured, monitored, and conserved.

Nicolas GERBER and Jan Henning SOMMER
University of Bonn

See also Biological Indicators—Ecosystems; Biological Indicators—Species; Ecosystem Health Indicators; Global Strategy for Plant Conservation; Index of Biological Integrity (IBI); Intergovernmental Science-Policy Platform on Biodiversity and Ecosystem Services (IPBES); Long-Term Ecological Research (LTER); Species Barcoding

FURTHER READING

Balmford, Andrew, et al. (2008). The economics of biodiversity and ecosystems: Scoping the science. Cambridge, UK: European Commission.

Barros, Edmundo. (2007). Soil biota, ecosystem services and land productivity. *Ecological Economics, 64*(2), 269–285.

Convention on Biological Diversity (CBD). (n.d.). COP 8, decision VIII/15: Framework for monitoring implementation of the achievement of the 2010 target and integration of targets into the thematic programmes of work. Retrieved August 30, 2011, from http://www.cbd.int/decision/cop/?id511029

Convention on Biological Diversity. (2010). Access to genetic resources and the fair and equitable sharing of benefits arising from their utilization. Retrieved December 17, 2011, from http://www.cbd.int/iyb/doc/prints/factsheets/iyb-cbd-factsheet-abs-en.pdf

Costanza, Robert, et al. (1997). The value of the world's ecosystem services and natural capital. *Nature, 387,* 253–260.

Crozier, Ross H. (1992). Genetic diversity and the agony of choice. *Biological Conservation, 61*(1), 11–15.

Faith, Daniel P. (1992). Conservation evaluation and phylogenetic diversity. *Biological Conservation, 61*(1), 1–10.

Falconer, Douglas S., & Mackay, Trudy F. C. (1996). *Introduction to quantitative genetics* (4th ed.). Essex, UK: Longman Group Ltd.

Forest, Felix, et al. (2007). Preserving the evolutionary potential of floras in biodiversity hotspots. *Nature, 445,* 757–760.

Gaston, Kevin J. (2009). Biodiversity. In William J. Sutherland (Ed.), *Conservation science and action.* Oxford, UK: Blackwell. doi:10.1002/9781444313499.ch1

Gerber, Nicholas. (2011). Biodiversity measures based on species-level dissimilarities: A methodology for assessment. *Ecological Economics, 70*(12), 2275–2281.

Haig, Susan M. (1998). Molecular contributions to conservation. *Ecology, 79,* 413–425.

Hartl, Daniel. L., & Clark, Andrew G. (1997). *Principles of population genetics.* Sunderland, MA: Sinauer.

Hughes, A. Randall; Inouye, Brian D.; Johnson, Mark T. J.; Underwood, Nora; & Vellend, Mark. (2008). Ecological consequences of genetic diversity. *Ecology Letters, 11,* 609–623. doi:10.1111/j.1461-0248.2008.01179.x

Krajewski, Carey. (1994). Phylogenetic measures of biodiversity: A comparison and critique. *Biological Conservation, 69,* 33–39.

Kumar, Pushpam. (Ed.). (2010). *The economics of ecosystems and biodiversity: Ecological and economic foundations.* London: Earthscan.

Laikre, Linda. (2010). Genetic diversity is overlooked in international conservation policy implementation. *Conservation Genetics, 11,* 349–354.

Laikre, Linda, et al. (2010). Neglect of genetic diversity in implementation of the Convention on Biological Diversity. *Conservation Biology, 24*(1), 86–88.

Lankau, Richard A., & Strauss, Sharon Y. (2007). Mutual feedbacks maintain both genetic and species diversity in a plant community. *Science, 317*(5844), 1561–1563.

Linder, H. Peter. (2005). Evolution of diversity: The Cape flora. *Trends in Plant Science, 10*(11), 536–541.

Lynch, Michael, & Walsh, Bruce. (1998). *Genetics and analysis of quantitative traits.* Sunderland, MA: Sinauer Associates.

Mace, Georgina M.; Gittleman, John L.; & Purvis, Andy. (2003). Preserving the tree of life. *Science, 300,* 1707–1709.

Magurran, Anne E. (2004). *Measuring biological diversity.* Hoboken, NJ: Wiley-Blackwell Publishing.

Mayr, Ernst. (1942). *Systematics and the origin of species from the viewpoint of a zoologist.* New York: Columbia University Press.

Millennium Ecosystem Assessment (MA). (2005). *Ecosystems and human well-being: Biodiversity synthesis.* Washington, DC: World Resources Institute.

Moritz, Craig, & Cicero, Carla. (2004). DNA barcoding: Promise and pitfalls. *Public Library of Science Biology, 2*(10), 1529–1531.

Noss, Reed F. (1990). Indicators for monitoring biodiversity: A hierarchical approach. *Conservation Biology, 4*(4), 355–364.

Reyers, Belinda. (2010). Measuring biophysical quantities and the use of indicators. In Pushpam Kumar (Ed.), *The economics of ecosystems and biodiversity: Ecological and economic foundations* (pp. 113–148). London: Earthscan.

Understanding Evolution. (2008, December). Tough conservation choices? Ask evolution. Retrieved October 25, 2011, from http://evolution.berkeley.edu/evolibrary/news/081201_phylogeneticconservation

Vane-Wright, R. I.; Humphries, C. J.; & Williams, P. H. (1991). What to protect? Systematics and the agony of choice. *Biological Conservation, 55*(3), 235–254.

Walpole, Matt, et al. (2009). Tracking progress toward the 2010 biodiversity target and beyond. *Science, 325*(5947), 1503–1504.

Weitzman, Martin. L. (1992). On diversity. *The Quarterly Journal of Economics, 107*(2), 363–406.

Biological Indicators—Species

The assessment of complete levels of species richness is time intensive and expensive, potentially consuming limited resources for conservation action. Biologists have found that some smaller groups of species can be used as indicators of the total number of species, while other groups seem unrelated to the complete list of species in a region. This research has produced effective approaches to identifying, confirming, and using biological indicators of species richness.

The amount of effort that it would take to completely enumerate all species is impressively large, requiring potentially decades of work. A complete survey of the species in even a small area in a highly diverse tropical region could be a mammoth undertaking. Conservationists require information on the spatial distribution of species so that limited conservation resources can be used most effectively, while managers need to evaluate the effects of management action on species as a whole and in target groups of species. For these reasons, biologists have sought to define and evaluate relationships between the presence of members of a group of species at a study site or region—that is, potential indicator species—and the overall number of species at sites. If a potential indicator group is relatively small and easy to evaluate, then focusing on the distribution and number of those species could greatly facilitate biodiversity assessments by decreasing the time requirements and expense of sampling, identifying, and recording species from the areas under consideration.

Development of Indicator Species Research

While the first instances of the use of indicator species in the scientific literature date to the late 1940s, these early uses were entirely in the context of relating species to environmental conditions, such as nutrient availability, the presence of polluting chemicals, or the general quality of air or water (see Ellenberg 2009, first published in 1963). Later, in their critique of the haphazard use of vertebrate species as indicators, the US biologist Peter B. Landres and his coauthors provided a definition of indicator species that has gained general acceptance in the scientific literature: "An indicator species is an organism whose characteristics (e.g., presence or absence, population density, dispersion, reproductive success) are used as an index of attributes too difficult, inconvenient, or expensive to measure for other species or environmental conditions of interest" (Landres, Verner, and Thomas 1988, 317). In the last years of the twentieth century and the early twenty-first century, interest has grown in the use of species indicators for the assessment of biodiversity.

Early studies of the use of indicator species as surrogates for levels of species richness—that is, the number of species in a defined area—began to appear in the early 1990s. These studies successfully identified major research themes that continue to influence research on and application of indicators of species richness as conservation tools. The Arizona State University ecologist David L. Pearson and the Italian entomologist Fabio Cassola conducted one of the first peer-reviewed studies on the use of indicator species to evaluate species richness in other taxa (named groups of related species, e.g., birds, butterflies). They found that the correlation (r, a measure of the degree to which two variables covary, taking values from -1 to 1) between the number of tiger beetle (Coleoptera: Cicindelidae) and bird species, evaluated in squares measuring 275–350 kilometers on a side, varied markedly among North America, Australia, and India ($r = 0.375, 0.531$ and 0.726, respectively; Pearson and Cassola 1992, 386). These positive relationships could be useful in conservation planning, decreasing the amount of effort needed to estimate levels of species richness in other taxa. Pearson and Cassola further suggested that tiger beetles possessed important characteristics that could be used to identify groups of species that might be good candidates for study as potential indicators of richness in other taxa. These characteristics included (1) a stable taxonomy (i.e., names well agreed on by experts), (2) well-understood ecology, (3) ease of observation and handling, (4) broad geographic distribution and range of habitat use by the group, (5) specialization of each species in a narrow range of habitats, (6) patterns of species richness that are highly correlated with those of vertebrate and other invertebrate taxa, and (7) some species of potential economic importance within the group. This set of characteristics is desirable no matter what group of species is proposed as a potential indicator group.

Two additional groundbreaking studies provided key observations that have influenced the further development of indicators of species richness. First, the 1992 study by the US researcher Randall T. Ryti addressed the use of several taxa as a basis for the selection of sites for inclusion in systems of nature reserves. Ryti selected potential reserve sites using lists of the species of birds, mammals, and plants in canyons in San Diego County, California, and lists of species in these taxa, plus reptiles, on islands in the Gulf of California. His simple algorithm for selecting reserve sites stipulated that each species must be represented in at least one site and in this sense the sites were "complementary." Ryti found that the minimum number of sites that were necessary to represent the complete set of species varied among the study taxa. For example, only two canyons, representing 3.2 percent of the total canyon area, were necessary to represent all bird species, but ten canyon reserves and 66 percent of the total canyon area were necessary to represent all the plant species (Ryti 1992, 406). Further, when the reserves were chosen using one group, the proportion of the other species in other taxa that were represented varied substantially among the taxa. For example, on the three Gulf of California islands that were necessary to represent all twenty-nine species of birds, 73.5 percent of plant species were represented, while only 61 percent of reptile species were covered (Ryti 1992, 407). These results demonstrated that the degree to which the protection of species of one taxon acts as a "conservation umbrella" for the species in other taxa could vary when reserves were chosen based on site complementarity for the protection of species in one taxon. The use of groups of potential indicator species to select complementary sites for conservation continues to be a promising topic of active research.

The second seminal study in the development of the literature on species richness indicators concerns the identification of hotspots of species richness (i.e., sites with unusually large numbers of species) to serve as priority sites for conservation. The British population biologist John R. Prendergast and his co-authors, in their 1993 paper in the journal *Nature,* addressed whether sites that are numerically species-rich for one taxon were also species-rich for other taxa. These authors were also interested in whether rare species tended to occur in areas that have high species richness. Birds, butterflies, and dragonflies were chosen to represent well-studied taxa that were often proposed as indicators. Liverworts were chosen as a group that drew little conservation interest. Aquatic flowering plants (angiosperms) were chosen as an indicator of aquatic habitat quality. Species lists were compiled for square cells that were 10 kilometers on a side, in a grid that covered Britain. Hotspots for a taxon comprised the top 5 percent of cells in terms of species richness of the taxon. Prendergast and his colleagues found that hotspot cells for many pairs of taxa were positively associated, but the maximum value of overlap was only 34 percent (for dragonflies and butterflies; Prendergast et al. 1993, table 2). None of the cells was a hotspot for all five taxa, and out of 2,761 cells exactly two cells were hotspots for four taxa. The authors also found that about 17 percent of the rare species (ones present in fifteen cells or fewer) were not found in hotspots. The authors note, however, that if one were to protect all bird hotspots (116), most species in the other four groups would also be protected. Many studies subsequent to this one have addressed the degree to which sites with high species richness for different taxa co-occur in a geographic area. The accumulation of studies regarding biological indicators of species richness has led to the development of closely related concepts that have particular applications in conservation, a diversification of the focus of work on indicator species approaches to conservation assessment, and an overview of the effectiveness of biological indicators of species richness.

In summary, spatial richness patterns for different taxa covary spatially, although the degree of correlation varies among taxa under consideration. Careful selection of focal species groups, based on data from the system at hand, is thus essential to identifying useful indicator relationships. We now examine how the identification of biological indicators of species richness has developed following these key early studies.

Indicator Strategies

Determination of indicators of species richness has been addressed using several different strategies. A first strategy, the development of global biodiversity trend indicators, seeks to describe global trends in species richness using a set of taxa that are chosen because of their inherent interest and the availability of data to support the assessment of trends at the population level. A second strategy of indicator development assesses surrogate relationships between groups of species (the indicators) and different groups of species in the same or, potentially, other taxa (adopting a term from Latin: the *indicandum*). These surrogate approaches include seeking strong correlative patterns among taxa in the distribution of species richness across a set of sites; identifying the correlative relationship between species richness and the distribution of endemic species, that is, ones found only in a relatively restricted area; determining the correlative relationship between the number of "higher" taxa (usually genera or families) and the number of species in those taxa; and defining predictive statistical models that are trained with site-specific data on the presence or abundance of some species and the overall species richness in a larger group. These approaches differ in terms of the data they use and the information they supply.

Global Indicators and Trends

One approach to the quantification of species richness focuses on making a global assessment of the temporal trend in characteristics of populations of many species. The choice of taxa is made based on the interest that conservationists have for the taxa and on the availability of data. One of these indices, the Living Planet Index, started out as a World Wide Fund for Nature (WWF) project with the objective of communicating population trends to a wide audience. This index summarizes population trends in over 4,218 populations of 1,411 species (Collen et al. 2008, 320). A time series of these data shows that most groups of vertebrates have experienced decreasing population abundance.

The Red List of Threatened Species, or Red List Index (RLI), is another global index that uses data from the International Union for Conservation of Nature (IUCN) on levels of the endangerment of species. The primary strength of this index, according to the UK conservation biologist Stuart Butchart and his co-authors, is that it is globally comprehensive, which is accomplished by evaluation of the endangerment of nearly all known species in the focal taxa (Butchart et al. 2006). Finally, the Global Wild Bird Index (WBI, a project of the Biodiversity Indicators Partnership) compiles population data on avian species. These population data can be broken down in a number of ways and analyzed to understand trends in bird populations that are specific to particular regions, habitats, and ecological characteristics of birds. For example, the UK biologist Richard Gregory and his co-authors analyzed population trends in woodland birds in Europe, finding them to be negative: −13 percent for

common forest birds and −18 percent for forest specialist species (Gregory et al. 2007, 86). Overall, these global indicators provide important summary information on trends in the status of species for conservation and policy makers.

Congruence and Complementarity Methods

There are two primary methods by which indicator relationships are developed using lists of the species that are known from a set of sites and the values of species richness that can be derived from these lists. The first approach, called the *congruence method*, identifies the correlation between values of species richness in a proposed group of indicator species and species richness values in one or more other groups of species at the same sites. For example, the Swiss biologists Peter Pearman and Darius Weber examined data on the species composition of birds, butterflies, and vascular plants from 134 cells, each 1 square kilometer, of the Swiss Biodiversity Monitoring program (BDM). The species richness values of butterflies and plants reciprocally explained approximately 32 percent of the variability in species richness. The congruence between butterflies and plant species richness was statistically meaningful, but not particularly strong, while the associations between the richness of birds and richness in the other two taxa were much weaker (Pearman and Weber 2007, 115). In a negative example, the Swedish biologist Karolina Vessby and her coauthors examined species richness in groups of beetles, bees, plants, and birds at thirty-one seminatural grasslands. They found low levels of congruence among taxa and did not believe that species richness in any taxon could be used as indicators of diversity in other taxa (Vessby et al. 2002).

The second approach to developing indicator relationships using species richness in various taxa is to select sites using one taxon as a potential indicator group (or conservation "umbrella") and applying a complementarity algorithm in order to efficiently include in the selected sites all species of the indicator group (see, for example, Ryti 1992). One then evaluates the degree to which species in other taxa are included in the sites. This approach potentially allows a large proportion of the *indicandum* (nonindicator) species to be covered in a reserve network, even when species richness values of the studied taxa are not highly congruent across sites. For example, the Greek conservation biologist Vassiliki Kati and colleagues studied the indicator properties of birds, woody plants, orchids, reptiles and amphibians, and the orthoptera (grasshoppers and crickets), using both complementary site selection and congruence approaches. Their results suggest that the complementarity approach might be a robust method for the development of indicator relationships and could function even when patterns of species richness are not congruent among taxa (Kati et al. 2004).

The US conservation ecologist Adam Lewandowski and colleagues addressed the relative effectiveness of the complementarity and congruency approaches. They reviewed 345 tests of surrogacy for species richness that were published in the peer-reviewed literature. Like others before them (Rodrigues and Brooks 2007), the authors found that studies were much more likely to find strong surrogate relationships using the complementarity approach than when the congruency approach was used (Lewandowski, Noss, and Parsons 2010). The complementarity approach is robust because it does not depend on site-by-site covariation in species richness among taxa. Instead, what counts is the overall number species of *indicandum* taxa that are "captured" by the chosen sites. Thus, the complementarity method can be an effective way to use indicator groups for determining the location of nature reserves or management priorities for sites.

Examining Endemic Species and Higher Taxa

One approach to developing indicators of species richness has been to examine the relationship between species richness and levels of endemism (the number of species with small ranges). In this approach, one compares the number of endemic species within a taxon to the species richness of one or more taxa across a set of sites. The focus on endemic species is notable because species with small ranges are often considered of high conservation value. The Brazilian ecologist Rafael Loyola and his co-authors discovered that when they selected priority ecoregions based on the total number of endemic species, the total number of vertebrates in the selected areas was greater than when the species richness of all vertebrates or any single class of vertebrates was used to choose the regions (Loyola, Kubota, and Lewinsohn 2007, 391). Nonetheless, a few studies have found that the richness of range-restricted (endemic) species in one taxon is not necessarily highly correlated with endemism or species richness in other taxa. Further study is necessary to determine the usefulness of this promising approach, where it works, and the best scale at

which to define units for analysis and conservation.

Given the complexities and cost of conservation research in the field, it would be advantageous if painstaking identification of species could be replaced by indicators that consist of the number of distinct species in a higher taxon, for example, a genus, family, or order. This approach simplifies data collection by entailing only the separation of species and their assignment to a genus or family, without continuing identification to the species level. The number of biotic families and genera (singular: genus) covaries in a positive way with the number of species in several studies (for example, Loyola, Kubota, and Lewinsohn 2007). Similarly, the Swiss biologist Peter Duelli and his colleagues have focused on developing indicators for aspects of biodiversity in agricultural landscapes (Duelli 1997; Duelli and Obrist 2003). In another example, the Polish biologist Grzegorz Mikusiński and co-authors reported that in three atlas datasets on bird species composition in Polish forests, the number of woodpecker species explained 53 percent to 78 percent of the variation in the total number of bird species (Mikusiński, Gromadzki, and Chylarecki 2001, 211). Depending on the requirements of an application, a figure of 78 percent could signify a useful relationship; however, caution is advisable. The Australian biologist John Hooper and his co-authors found that genus-level richness was a poor indicator of species richness in tropical marine sponges around the tropical Pacific Ocean and Australia (Hooper, Kennedy, and Quinn 2002). To some degree, this kind of relationship may depend on how readily taxonomists have split or lumped species into genera and families. Finally, rapid assessment of insect species richness in Europe relies on this kind of proxy method because of the difficulty of quickly identifying many insects to the species level (see Duelli 1997). This approach has thus gained a relatively high level of acceptance and application.

Model-Based Approaches

While most studies on species indicators have examined how species richness covaries among taxa, some studies have succeeded in making explicit statistical models of the relationship between indicators and species richness. With data on species composition and selected environmental variables, one can use statistical methods to describe the relationship between site-to-site variation in species richness, the presence of certain species, and certain environmental variables. If a selection of study sites, at which all these variables are measured, is representative of all sites within a region, generally achieved through a program of sampling at sites that are chosen at random, then these statistical models can predict the level of species richness at additional sites yet to be sampled. Sampling those sites and comparing the predictions to the new data can be used to validate or improve the original models.

Performance, Reliability, and Scale

As studies of biological indicators have accumulated, no key solution has emerged in the form of effective single species indicators for species richness. Indicators can be identified through which richness in a small group of species can indicate richness levels in a larger, more inclusive group of species. As such, focus on indicator species groups is a potentially useful approach to the evaluation of biodiversity patterns because it allows quicker, less expensive evaluation of trends, and it can be used to help prioritize sites for conservation attention. Some approaches to the use of indicators appear to be more robust than others, while some appear to be promising but require further study. Our current understanding suggests that confirmatory studies should likely be made in most cases, prior to committing a project to the use or application of any one particular indicator group or taxon.

The scale at which indicators are studied may play a major role in determining whether potentially useful indicator relationships are identified. It is possible that indicator relationships over large areas show greater congruence in species richness between taxa. This is because studies with large area extent could be more likely to include high-latitude and high-elevation areas, or simply larger environmental ranges, thus including conditions where most taxa tend to have low species richness. These shared areas of low species richness could reinforce positive covariation between taxa in regard to values of species richness, but this hypothesis is not always supported. Arizona State University biologists David Pearson and Steven Carroll used a type of spatial modeling to examine the performance of butterfly species richness as a predictor of bird species richness in grid cells distributed across western North America. They used a grid with cells of either small or large size (sides of 137.5 km or 275 km, respectively) (Pearson and Carroll 1999, 1081). They subdivided the grid into four smaller geographic areas but found that this change of grid extent did not affect the prediction accuracy of their models. Then the authors varied the number of small grid cells from which data were taken to determine how many cells would be necessary to reach the performance attained when using data from a fixed number of large grid cells. Equal performance was obtained with a greater number, but less total area, of small grid cells. This suggests that it would be less expensive to reach a given level of prediction performance using the smaller cell size than it would with data from a grid of fewer, larger cells.

Outlook

Indicator groups, when used in a complementarity analysis, provide an approach that can contribute to the establishment of conservation priorities and reserve selection. Similarly, it might be possible to identify areas or ecological regions in which richness at the genus or family level provides a reliable indicator of species richness in the genera and families themselves. Large databases of species occurrences, such as those provided by the Global Biodiversity Information Facility (GBIF, a network of fifty-seven countries and forty-seven organizations), could facilitate the application of model-based approaches that require extensive data. With regard to future development of biological indicators of species richness, the US biologist Jorie Favreau and colleagues suggested that the development of surrogate indicators might best proceed by considering the following research priorities: (1) develop measures of indicator effectiveness, (2) focus on areas with abundant data, (3) explicitly consider effects of spatial and temporal scale of study, (4) develop hypothesis-driven research, and (5) develop methods to monitor both indicator species and the relevant *indicandum* (Favreau et al. 2006). Finally, indices that use such factors as trends in population characteristics and levels of endangerment (e.g., IUCN's Red List Index) to monitor the global status of species will become more valuable as additional data accumulate and further analyses are conducted. These species indicators of the state of species richness do not depend on validation of surrogate relationships. The degree to which they accurately summarize, in an unbiased way, global and regional trends can be an additional topic of future research.

Peter B. PEARMAN and Niklaus E. ZIMMERMANN
Swiss Federal Research Institute WSL

See also Biological Indicators—Ecosystems; Biological Indicators—Genetic; Challenges to Measuring Sustainability; Fisheries Indicators, Freshwater; Fisheries Indicators, Marine; Global Strategy for Plant Conservation; Index of Biological Integrity (IBI); Intergovernmental Science-Policy Platform on Biodiversity and Ecosystem Services (IPBES); Species Barcoding

FURTHER READING

Butchart, Stuart H. M.; Akcakaya, H. Resit; Kennedy, Elizabeth; & Hilton-Taylor, Craig. (2006). Biodiversity indicators based on trends in conservation status: Strengths of the IUCN Red List Index. *Conservation Biology, 20*(2), 579–581.

Caro, Tim. (2010). *Conservation by proxy: Indicator, umbrella, keystone, flagship, and other surrogate species.* Washington, DC: Island Press.

Collen, Ben, et al. (2008). Monitoring change in vertebrate abundance: The Living Planet Index. *Conservation Biology, 23*(2), 317–327.

Duelli, Peter. (1997). Biodiversity evaluation in agricultural landscapes: An approach at two different scales. *Agriculture Ecosystems & Environment, 62*(2–3), 81–91.

Duelli, Peter, & Obrist, Martin K. (2003). Biodiversity indicators: The choice of values and measures. *Agricultural Ecosystems & Environment, 98*(1–3), 87–98.

Ellenberg, Heinz H. (2009). *Vegetation ecology of Central Europe* (Gordon K. Strutt, Trans.; 4th ed.). Cambridge, UK: Cambridge University Press.

Favreau, Jorie M., et al. (2006). Recommendations for assessing the effectiveness of surrogate species approaches. *Biodiversity and Conservation, 15*(12), 3949–3969.

Fleishman, Erica; Thomson, James R.; MacNally, Ralph; Murphy, Dennis D.; & Fay, John P. (2005). Using indicator species to predict species richness of multiple taxonomic groups. *Conservation Biology, 19*(4), 1125–1137.

Gregory, Richard D., et al. (2007). Population trends of widespread woodland birds in Europe. *Ibis, 149*(Suppl. 2), 78–97.

Hooper, John N. A.; Kennedy, John A.; & Quinn, R. J. (2002). Biodiversity "hotspots", patterns of richness and endemism, and taxonomic affinities of tropical Australian sponges (Porifera). *Biodiversity and Conservation, 11*(5), 851–885.

Kati, Vassiliki, et al. (2004). Testing the value of six taxonomic groups as biodiversity indicators at a local scale. *Conservation Biology, 18*(3), 667–675.

Landres, Peter B.; Verner, Jared; & Thomas, Jack Ward. (1988). Ecological uses of vertebrate indicator species: A critique. *Conservation Biology, 2*(4), 316–328.

Lewandowski, Adam S.; Noss, Reed F.; & Parsons, David R. (2010). The effectiveness of surrogate taxa for the representation of biodiversity. *Conservation Biology, 25*(5), 1367–1377.

Loyola, Rafael D.; Kubota, Umberto; & Lewinsohn, Thomas M. (2007). Endemic vertebrates are the most effective surrogates for identifying conservation priorities among Brazilian ecoregions. *Diversity and Distributions, 13*(4), 389–396.

Mikusiński, Grzegorz; Gromadzki, Maciej; & Chylarecki, Przemysław. (2001). Woodpeckers as indicators of forest bird diversity. *Conservation Biology, 15*(1), 208–217.

Paoletti, Maurizio G. (1999). *Invertebrate biodiversity as bioindicators of sustainable landscapes: Practical use of invertebrates to assess sustainable land use.* Amsterdam: Elsevier.

Pearman, Peter B., & Weber, Darius. (2007). Common species determine richness patterns in biodiversity indicator taxa. *Biological Conservation, 138*(1–2), 109–119.

Pearson, David L., & Carroll, Steven S. (1999). The influence of spatial scale on cross-taxon congruence patterns and prediction accuracy of species richness. *Journal of Biogeography, 26*(5), 1079–1090.

Pearson, David L., & Cassola, Fabio. (1992). World-wide species richness patterns of tiger beetles (Coleoptera: Cicindelidae): Indicator for biodiversity and conservation studies. *Conservation Biology, 6*(3), 376–391.

Prendergast, John R.; Quinn, Rachel M.; Lawton, John H.; Eversham, Brian C.; & Gibbons, D. W. (1993). Rare species, the coincidence of diversity hotspots and conservation strategies. *Nature, 365*(6444), 335–337.

Rodrigues, Ana S. L., & Brooks, Thomas M. (2007). Shortcuts for biodiversity conservation planning: The effectiveness of surrogates. *Annual Review of Ecology, Evolution, and Systematics, 38,* 713–737.

Ryti, Randall T. (1992). Effect of the focal taxon on the selection of nature reserves. *Ecological Applications, 2*(4), 404–410.

Vessby, Karolina; Söderström, Bo; Glimskär, Anders; & Svensson, Birgitta. (2002). Species-richness correlations of six different taxa in Swedish seminatural grasslands. *Conservation Biology, 16,* 430–439.

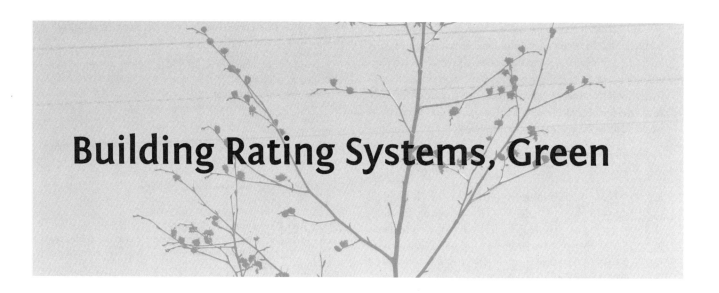

Building Rating Systems, Green

The use of rating systems to certify buildings as environmentally sustainable is making a significant contribution to the greening of the built environment. Green buildings have been shown not only to benefit the environment but also to enable lower operating costs, higher rental and capital values, and even higher productivity by building occupants.

Buildings are responsible for 40 percent of the world's energy use and more than a third of global greenhouse gas emissions. A report issued in 2007 by the Intergovernmental Panel on Climate Change (IPCC) estimated that, in 2004, buildings were responsible for 8.6 billion metric tons of greenhouse gas emissions, with this figure potentially doubling by 2030 (Levine et al. 2007). This means that the building industry has an unparalleled opportunity to substantially reduce the world's carbon emissions and mitigate climate change by way of a green built environment. The United Nations Environment Programme (UNEP) has argued that "no other sector has such a high potential for drastic emission reductions" (UNEP 2007a, 3).

The use of green building rating systems is arguably one of the most significant mechanisms for generating positive environmental outcomes and market transformation in the building sector. In markets where these systems have been established, there has been an increase in the environmental performance of buildings, through both direct and indirect influence. In some marketplaces, the widespread adoption of green building rating systems has also been perceived as increasing the monetary value of green buildings.

Since the introduction of the first green building rating system, the UK Building Research Establishment Environmental Assessment Method (BREEAM), in 1990, dozens of building evaluation tools focusing on

different areas of sustainable construction—from design to construction to performance—have been developed. These international rating systems are owned and operated by a wide range of private, public, and nonprofit organizations. The World Green Building Council (WorldGBC) does not endorse or promote rating systems but instead works with more than eighty established and emerging Green Building Councils to develop mechanisms relevant to each market that drive the adoption of green building practices.

Systems and Their Strategies

A green building rating system (also called a *rating tool*) is designed to quantify and certify the environmental performance of a building—that is, how well it performs against a range of criteria, including energy and water use, neighborhood integration, ecological improvement of its site, use of environmentally sustainable materials, reduction of transportation impacts associated with its use, and the minimization of pollutants both inside and outside of its walls.

Most rating tools follow a similar strategy for certifying a building as green. They put forth a wide range of environmental performance metrics that a building can achieve, allowing choice of those that are most appropriate for that building's function and location (buildings are not expected to meet all of the criteria). For each standard that is achieved, points are awarded to the project (the number of points varies in each system), and when a building reaches a given threshold of points set out by the system, it is certified as green.

Most systems have a tiered ratings program, so that increasing levels of green performance can be recognized. For instance the Leadership in Energy and Environmental Design (LEED) rating program from the United States Green Building Council (USGBC) awards certification at levels of Certified, Silver, Gold, and Platinum, whereas BREEAM awards ratings at Good, Very Good, Excellent, and Outstanding. The Green Star program used in Australia, New Zealand, and South Africa recognizes achievement by awarding a number of stars (e.g., a rating of four stars out of a possible six), and the Pearls Building Rating System in Abu Dhabi uses number of pearls (e.g., a rating of three pearls out of a possible five).

While their overall strategies are similar, rating systems use different means to assess the building performance and award certification. Some have a verification system through an expert who works closely with each project, others employ independent third-party assessment, and others may rely on self-assessment. Both the expert-based and third-party approaches require the generation of documentation demonstrating that the project has met the criteria put forth in the rating system, and these are generally seen as more reliable than self-assessment. A building may be claimed to be green, but it is only with third-party verification through a green building rating system that it can be credibly proven the building has the environmental performance that is claimed.

Rating systems are intended to evaluate a specific phase of the life cycle of a building, be it the design phase, construction or refurbishment, or the operations phase. A rating system may certify a building at any one or all of the phases. Tools that look at the design phase evaluate plans and specifications for the building as well as the commitments that the owner and the project team have made to implementing various strategies during construction. Certification at this stage allows the building to be marketed to potential tenants and owners as green. The vast majority of rating systems evaluate a building upon the completion of construction or major refurbishment. Certification at this phase means that the green features and strategies have been physically implemented, not simply designed or promised.

Since 2005, there has been an international push from governments and industry for certification of the ongoing environmental performance of building operations. Certification at the operational phase evaluates whether the building is functioning as designed and measures the environmental impacts associated with the ongoing use of the building. Certification of older, existing buildings is also promoted through, for example, the LEED for Existing Buildings Operations and Maintenance rating system.

In all stages, the impacts are assessed using quantifiable metrics wherever possible, although the indicators can be adapted depending on the life cycle phase. For instance, a design-stage rating would assess, among other things, the amount of construction waste the project promises to recycle or reuse; a construction-stage rating could look at the actual amount of construction waste that was recycled or reused; and an operations rating can evaluate how much waste is being recycled within the building during its ongoing operation.

Rating systems can transform the building industry by setting performance benchmarks and putting forth a common language for what it means, in a given market, that a building is green. The ratings then build on this foundation by recognizing and rewarding environmental leadership, raising consumer awareness of green building benefits, and stimulating green competition.

Development of Rating Tools

Green building rating systems can be either mandatory or voluntary. Mandatory tools tend to focus on one or two areas (such as energy, water, or waste) and are often used by governments to establish regulatory mechanisms. Voluntary tools, which tend to be broader in scope, are typically developed and managed by independent organizations, such as Green Building Councils, which are not-for-profit building industry bodies.

How a green building rating system is developed depends primarily on whether it is a mandatory program created by government or a voluntary system created by an independent body. Governments tend to create tools themselves, which then may be released for public comment or a pilot testing cycle before a final version is released. Voluntary programs usually employ the same comment, testing, and review periods, but they are often developed through a collaborative process with representatives from industry, government, and environmental interests.

The aim of rating tools is to go beyond the existing building code to set a new definition of standard practice in the industry. All of the criteria set forth in the tool must be applicable to the practices in a given market and have a range of performance requirements, some that can be readily met to encourage the uptake of the tool and some that are challenging to achieve in order to push projects toward better outcomes.

Rating systems are usually created for specific locations or regions, each of which has different environmental priorities. These differences are reflected in the types of initiatives and performance indicators and how much each initiative will contribute to a project's overall score. For instance, a country with potable water shortages may highly reward buildings that make a significant effort to reduce their potable water consumption. In contrast, a rating tool in a country with high rainfall (and therefore without potable water shortages) may only place a small emphasis on reducing potable water consumption. This same high-rainfall country may, however, have large areas with fragile ecosystems and reward projects for minimizing their ecological impacts.

Rating systems must evolve over time in order to stay ahead of the markets they seek to transform. Widely used commercial programs such as the LEED rating systems typically are revised every three years.

Green building rating tools are used in numerous countries around the world, in both developed and developing economies. The systems with the most widespread adoption and influence tend to be those that can be readily understood by a wide range of people within the industry, involve documentation that is already used by the industry, and have performance requirements that are appropriate for the given market.

The United States has the largest market for certified green buildings, and one of the most widely used green building rating systems is the LEED program, overseen by the USGBC. As of 2011, over twenty-eight thousand projects were registered for certification under LEED, and over seven thousand projects had already been assessed and certified under the program; the LEED system is becoming widely adopted internationally, with projects in 114 countries outside the United States, representing 27 percent of all LEED-registered building area (USGBC 2010).

In Singapore, the Green Mark program for rating buildings was launched in 2005 by the Singapore Building and Construction Authority (BCA) and serves as the core of the Singapore government's Green Building Masterplan. The government is looking to have 80 percent of the existing building stock Green Mark rated by 2030.

With a 10 percent per annum growth rate since 2000, India's construction industry has recognized the need for a focus on sustainability. By 2010, the India Green Building Council—which certifies green buildings under the LEED system as well as its own IGBC rating tools—had counted over 700 registered projects (over 40 million square meters of building area) and 112 certified projects around the country.

Cost of Green Certification

While evidence suggests that certified buildings involve only a small cost premium, it is a common misconception that green-rated buildings cost far more than comparable buildings without green credentials. Respondents to a 2007 survey by the World Business Council for Sustainable Development, for instance, said that a 17 percent premium on building costs was typical, despite evidence showing that less than 2 percent was more likely (WBCSD 2007).

A comprehensive international study of green buildings published in November 2008 analyzed 150 green buildings in ten countries. The results indicated that the cost premium to construct a green building rather than a conventional building ranged from 0–4 percent, and this increase was more often in the range of 0–1 percent (Kats et al. 2008).

The likely reason for this cost perception is that green building rating tools set high standards for performance that can require new ways of designing, constructing, and operating buildings. As with anything innovative, these new methods and materials can sometimes have a higher additional cost at first. As these practices and methods become more common, prices will tend to lower accordingly.

One cost associated with certified green buildings over other buildings, even others designed as green, is the cost of documenting that the building meets the criteria of the rating system. In order for a project to be assessed under a rating system, it has to submit considerable documentation, usually in the form of building specifications, architectural drawings, copies of legal documents, and documents verifying outputs from various building systems. While many of these documents are already generated as part of the design and building process, they must still be assembled and submitted to the certification body, an expense of effort that is in addition to the cost of the certification itself. A key component to the success of a rating tool in its market is achieving a balance between the need for a rigorous tool and assessment methodology with cost of achieving and demonstrating compliance.

Environmental and Financial Benefits

Green buildings offer a host of environmental benefits, from emissions and waste reduction to water conservation and recycling. One study found that green-certified buildings use 26 percent less energy than the average building and generate 33 percent fewer greenhouse gas emissions (Fowler and Rauch 2008).

According to the USGBC, green buildings can reduce energy consumption by 24–50 percent, reduce greenhouse gas emissions by 33–39 percent, reduce water use by 40 percent, and reduce solid waste by 70 percent (USGBC 2011).

The green building experience reveals a consistent pattern of higher rental yields and capital values, higher productivity by building occupants, and lower operating costs. These factors generate positive financial returns on capital costs. A study of 1,300 green-certified, Class A (or those buildings at the highest end of the market) office buildings (certified under the Energy Star and/or LEED programs) in the United States found that LEED-certified buildings had a 4.1 percent higher occupancy than non-LEED buildings. The study also found that LEED-certified buildings were renting for an average of US$122 per square meter more and selling for $1,900 per square meter more than uncertified buildings (Miller, Spivey, and Florence 2008).

Staff productivity gains are one of the frequently cited benefits of green buildings. The gains are complex to measure, but the number of studies continues to grow. A prominent example is Australia's first building to earn a six-star Green Star rating, Council House 2 (CH2) in Melbourne, which demonstrated that productivity of office building occupants can be enhanced through green building design and a high-quality, healthy, comfortable, and functional interior environment. A post-occupancy survey found that productivity had risen by an impressive 10 percent since staff moved into this green-rated office (Paevere and Brown 2008), and another study indicated that a conservative estimate of a 1 percent improvement in productivity at CH2 would result in a savings of over AU$350,000 annually (Lawther, Robinson, and Low 2005).

The use of green building rating systems is on the rise around the world. Continued progress in this direction will require that the systems adapt to market forces as much as they shape them.

Older Buildings: Retrofitting

Rating systems are most widely used to certify newly constructed buildings, which account for only 2 percent of all buildings. The greatest opportunity, then, to address the impact of buildings on the environment is to improve the existing building stock.

A well-known example of a green retrofit, rated under the LEED for Existing Buildings: Operations and Maintenance, is the iconic 102-story Empire State Building in New York City. This US$120 million renovation, which began in 2006, included $13.2 million for a range of green design features, with an emphasis on energy efficiency measures. These features are expected to reduce its energy use by 38 percent, resulting in a reduction of its carbon emissions by 105,000 metric tons over fifteen years and a savings of $4.4 million annually (Empire State Building 2009).

Future Trends

Most rating systems have addressed individual buildings, but tools are being created that look at entire communities or neighborhoods. As of early 2011, the LEED rating system has a Neighborhood Design (ND) rating system, Green Star is developing a Communities tool, and BREEAM has a Communities assessment system available. By their nature, such systems will have a broader environmental impact as well as a broader industry impact, enabling change on a scale greater than individual buildings alone.

The primary focus of rating systems has been on buildings' effects on the environment. Although some consideration has been given to how indoor environmental quality affects building occupants, the focus on environmental effects is why they are usually known as "green" building rating tools rather than "sustainable" building rating tools. True sustainability is widely seen as a balance between economic, social, and environmental interests. As rating systems continue to be adopted around the globe, particularly in developing countries, they will almost certainly need to address social and economic criteria in order to be relevant for those markets. The challenge will be in identifying quantifiable and verifiable socioeconomic metrics that can be demonstrated with the same level of rigor as the environmental metrics.

As green building rating systems have enhanced building performance in a number of markets around the world, governments have responded by increasing the requirements for buildings to meet their codes and standards. As of January 2011, buildings in the US state of California must meet the new California Green Building Standards Code (CALGreen), which has significantly raised the legal requirements for buildings across a broad range of criteria. Similarly, in May 2010, the International Green Construction Code Public Version 1.0 was released by the International Code Council, in conjunction with the American Institute of Architects and ASTM International (formerly known as the American Society for Testing and Materials), and is intended to create a consistent set of standards for green buildings that can be used by governments and other bodies.

Responsible for one-third of global carbon emissions, the building sector has a potentially significant role to play in carbon reduction policies and strategies around the world. Building rating systems can contribute, as they already require the quantification of a building's carbon savings. This verifiable figure can enable property owners and governments to use buildings as a means to demonstrate their carbon reduction efforts.

Jane HENLEY and Michelle MALANCA
World Green Building Council

See also Agenda 21; Business Reporting Methods; Carbon Footprints; Challenges to Measuring Sustainability; Cost-Benefit Analysis; Design Quality Indicator (DQI); Development Indicators; Life Cycle Assessment (LCA); Life Cycle Costing (LCC); Life Cycle Management (LCM); Regional Planning; Regulatory Compliance; Triple Bottom Line

FURTHER READING

California Building Standards Commission (BSC). (2010). *2010 California green building standards code (CALGreen): California Code of Regulations, Title 24, Part 11.* Sacramento: California Building Standards Commission.

Eichholtz, Piet, & Kok, Nils. (2009). *Doing well by doing good? An analysis of the financial performance of green office buildings in the USA.* London: Royal Institute of Chartered Surveyors.

Empire State Building. (2009). Case study: Cost-effective greenhouse gas reduction via whole-building retrofits: Process, outcome, and what is needed next. Retrieved January 10, 2012, from http://www.esbnyc.com/documents/sustainability/ESBOverviewDeck.pdf

Empire State Building. (2012). Sustainability & energy efficiency. Retrieved January 10, 2012, from http://www.esbnyc.com/sustainability_energy_efficiency.asp

Enkvist, Per-Anders; Nauclér, Tomas; & Rosander, Jerker. (2007). A cost curve for greenhouse gas reduction. *The McKinsey Quarterly, 1,* 34–45.

Fowler, Kim M., & Rauch, Emily M. (2008). *Assessing green building performance: A post occupancy evaluation of 12 GSA Buildings.* Washington, DC: US General Services Administration.

Kats, Greg, et al. (2008). Greening buildings and communities: Costs and benefits. Retrieved January 10, 2012, from http://www.goodenergies.com/news/-pdfs/Web%20site%20Presentation.pdf

Lawther, Peter; Robinson, Jon; & Low, Sowfun. (2005). The business case for sustainable design: The city of Melbourne CH2 project. *Australian Journal of Construction Economics and Building, 5*(2), 58–70.

Levine, M., et al. (2007). *Climate change 2007: Mitigation. Contribution of Working Group III to the Fourth Assessment Report of the Intergovernmental Panel on Climate Change.* Cambridge, UK: Cambridge University Press.

Miller, Norm; Spivey, Jay; & Florence, Andy. (2008). Does green pay off? Retrieved January 10, 2012, from http://www.costar.com/josre/pdfs/CoStar-JOSRE-Green-Study.pdf

Miller, Norm G.; Pogue, David; Gough, Quiana D.; & Davis, Susan M. (2009). Green buildings and productivity. *Journal of Sustainable Real Estate, 1*(1), 65–89.

Paevere, Phillip, & Brown, Stephen. (2008). *Indoor environment quality and occupant productivity in the CH2 Building: Post-occupancy summary.* Canberra, Australia: The Commonwealth Scientific and Industrial Research Organisation (CSIRO).

United Nations Environment Programme (UNEP). (2007a). *Assessment of policy instruments for reducing greenhouse gas emissions from buildings.* Paris: United Nations Environment Programme.

United Nations Environment Programme (UNEP). (2007b). *Buildings and climate change: Status, challenges and opportunities.* Paris: United Nations Environment Programme.

United States Green Building Council (USGBC). (2010). Presentations. About LEED. Retrieved January 10, 2012, from http://www.usgbc.org/DisplayPage.aspx?CMSPageID=1720

United States Green Building Council (USGBC). (2011). Presentations. Building impacts: Why build green? Retrieved January 10, 2012, from http://www.usgbc.org/DisplayPage.aspx?CMSPageID=1720

Building Research Establishment Environmental Assessment Method (BREEAM). (2011). FAQs. What is BREEAM? Retrieved January 10, 2012, from http://www.breeam.org/page.jsp?id=27#1

World Business Council for Sustainable Development (WBCSD). (2007). Energy efficiency in buildings: Business realities and opportunities. Retrieved January 27, 2011, from http://www.eukn.org/E_library/Urban_Environment/Environmental_Sustainability/Environmental_Sustainability/Energy_Efficiency_in_Buildings_business_realities_and_opportunities

World Green Building Council (WBCSD). (2010). Tackling global climate change, meeting local priorities. Retrieved January 10, 2012, from http://www.worldgbc.org/images/stories/worldgbc_report2010.pdf

Yudelson, Jerry. (2007). *Green building incentives that work: A look at how local governments are incentivizing green development.* Retrieved January 10, 2012, from http://www.naiop.org/foundation/greenincentives.pdf

Business Reporting Methods

Organizations and corporations around the world are increasingly reporting the status of their environmental, social, and governance initiatives, in addition to their financial reporting. As sustainability reporting has become more common, several standards for nonfinancial reporting have been promoted by organizations including the Global Reporting Initiative, AccountAbility, and the Copenhagen Charter. There are hopes for increased international harmonization of standards in the future.

The concept of sustainability in business and organizations is rooted in the wider notion of sustainable development. The foremost definition of sustainable development comes from the 1987 Brundtland Report of the World Commission on Environment and Development (WCED), published as *Our Common Future*: "development that meets the needs of the present without compromising the ability of future generations to meet their own needs." Incorporating sustainability into organizations requires radical changes in the way to do business. According to the International Federation of Accountants (IFAC), being sustainable asks an organization to think carefully about its environmental and social impacts on the Earth and its population. The Sustainability Framework developed by IFAC's Professional Accountants in Business (PAIB) Committee highlights the issues organizations must address to make sustainability an integral part of their business model, offering guidance on how to inject sustainability leadership into the management cycle, from making strategic decisions to reporting on their performance to stakeholders.

For an organization, sustainable development can be seen as a process of change in which the use of resources, the direction of investments, and the orientation of technological and social innovations are made consistent with future as well as present needs. Realizing sustainability requires a strong political will on the part of governments, organizations, and communities. Overall, it requires companies to take into account the consequences of economic decisions on the natural environment, on economic development, and on the social conditions in which people live and work.

A complementary concept of sustainability for organizations is that of corporate social responsibility (CSR). This concept helps to clarify how sustainability can be integrated into business strategies and decisions as well as into their interaction with stakeholders on a voluntary basis. Some organizations prefer the term *corporate citizenship* or *corporate responsibility*, as these capture a wider footprint, including ethical, economic, environmental, and social impacts and issues.

The World Business Council for Sustainable Development (WBCSD) supplies a platform for all organizations interested in investigating sustainable development issues and sharing not only knowledge and experience but best practices too. The WBCSD's three-pillar model of economic growth, ecological balance, and social progress is also a useful reference point for understanding sustainability: long-term environmental, social, and economic performance is linked to maximization of company shareholder value.

Reporting and Accountability

Investors, regulators, and the public are all increasingly demanding disclosure about corporate sustainability. Although several organizations have become active in reporting on initiatives undertaken to prevent these "externalities" of international trade and production, many studies indicate room for improvement (Kolk 2003).

Starting in the 1980s, organizations—especially energy-intensive businesses and those generating pollution—began publishing information and reports on the environmental impact of their activities, often for the purpose of green-washing their environmental performance corporate image. (Greenwashing refers to the practice of marketing a company or product as being "green" without actually making improvements—or making minimal improvements—to the company's or product's environmental footprint.) These disclosures represented early attempts to respond to pressing demands for "accountability," which over the years has been extended to social and ethical issues. Demands for disclosure and transparency have been even more pronounced in the aftermath of high-profile and large-scale financial scandals in the first decade of the twenty-first century.

With the growth of CSR, there has been a rise in non-financial reporting by many companies throughout the world, informing stakeholders about their performance with regard to social and environmental issues. There are several drivers of companies' auditing and reporting on their social performance:

- *Instrumental/economic reasons.* Social and environmental issues could pose a threat to the company's financial performance.
- *Political reasons.* Large multinational corporations are perceived as increasingly powerful institutions in society.
- *Integrating demand from stakeholders.* CSR reporting helps companies to improve their interaction with stakeholders.
- *Ethical reasons / responding to external pressure.* Companies face growing pressures from governments, investors, customers and competitors to live up to ethical standards.

As sustainability reporting became more common, a range of formats and voluntary socio-environmental accountability tools was used. Many organizations, companies, and investors soon recognized the need to standardize both performance measurement methods and their documentation, as is the case for financial reporting. There have been standardization initiatives on the part of groups of businesses operating in various sectors, such as the Public Environmental Reporting Initiative (PERI) and the Responsible Care Program of the European Chemical Industry Council (CEFIC). Others initiatives have been promoted by global organizations, such as the United Nations Environmental Program (UNEP), in order to reduce poverty and help meet Millennium Development Goals (MDG).

The Global Reporting Initiative (GRI), the Copenhagen Charter, and AccountAbility 1000 have issued widely used reporting frameworks. These can be classified as frameworks based on process standards and frameworks based on reporting standards. The former focus on methods for the compilation of documentation, a step-by-step process; the latter focus mainly on the format and content of documentation. Among the process-based reporting standards, the most noteworthy are those suggested by AccountAbility 1000 and by the Copenhagen Charter.

AccountAbility

AccountAbility 1000 (AA1000) is an international non-profit organization that provides tools for corporate responsibility and sustainable development, promoting accountability innovations. It encourages ethical behavior in business and the nonprofit world, promoting standards for measuring and reporting.

AA1000 aims to assist organizations in defining goals and targets, measuring progress made against these targets, auditing and reporting performance, and establishing feedback mechanisms. The core of its work is the AA1000 series of standards based on the principles of inclusivity (people should have a say in the decisions that have an impact on them), materiality (decision makers should identify and be clear about the issues that matter), and responsiveness (organizations should be transparent about their actions). It provides three sets of standards, on principles, assurance (reporting on sustainability issues), and stakeholder engagement.

The stakeholder engagement framework provides a step-by-step process for designing and implementing a quality stakeholder engagement process.

The steps in the framework for quality stakeholder engagement include the following:

1. Identify stakeholders
2. Initial identification of material issues
3. Determine and define engagement strategy, objective, and scope
4. Establish engagement plan and implementation schedule
5. Determine ways of engaging that work
6. Build and strengthen capacity
7. Engage with stakeholders in ways that increase understanding, learning, and improvement
8. Activate, internalize, and communicate learning
9. Measuring performance
10. Assess, re-map, and redefine

The Copenhagen Charter

The Copenhagen Charter, launched in 1999, is a management guide promoting dialogue with stakeholders while making reporting as credible as possible. This guide is divided into three sections. The first focuses on the value creation for the company and its key stakeholders as well as the effects of stakeholder reporting in terms of internal and external assessment. Value is realized if the processes are fully integrated into the organization's management and operation. The second section covers stakeholder dialogue and reporting principles and offers useful recommendations on how to manage the most important process elements, in relation to laying the groundwork, embedding the processes, and communicating the results. The third emphasizes three important elements of credibility: accounting principles, information relevance, and verification.

The framework of the Copenhagen Charter is based on a circular process of eight phases:

1. Top management commitment to company vision, strategy, and values
2. Identify key stakeholders, critical success factors, and values
3. Dialogue with stakeholders
4. Determine key performance indicators and adapt management information systems
5. Monitor performance and satisfaction with the company's values
6. Objectives, budget, and action plan for improvement
7. Prepare, verify, and publish report
8. Consult stakeholders about performance, values, and improvement targets

Global Reporting Initiative

Based on reporting standards, the model provided by the Global Reporting Initiative (GRI) is one of the most widely used frameworks. GRI is a major collaborative effort of large accounting firms, nongovernmental organizations, corporations, and universities, which seeks to establish a common framework for corporate social reporting worldwide. Its network of thousands of experts, in dozens of countries worldwide, comprises participants in GRI's working groups and governance bodies, users of the GRI guidelines to report or access information in GRI-based reports, or contributors to develop the reporting framework in other ways, both formally and informally.

GRI's vision is that disclosure of economic, environmental, and social performance should be as common as and comparable to financial reporting, and as important to organizational success. Its mission is to create conditions for the transparent and reliable exchange of sustainability information through the development and continuous improvement of the GRI Sustainability Reporting Framework. The foundation of GRI's efforts is the *Sustainability Reporting Guidelines,* the third version of which is known as *G3 Guidelines* (published in 2006).

The guidelines set out the principles and indicators that organizations can use to measure and report their economic, environmental, and social performance. They are in two parts. The first, related to the reporting principles and guidance, contains principles to define report content (materiality, stakeholder inclusiveness, sustainability context, and completeness); principles to define report quality (balance, comparability, accuracy, timeliness, reliability, and clarity); and guidance on how to set the report boundary. The second part concerns standard disclosures and comprises strategy and profile, management approach, and performance indicators. GRI has also published many sector supplements responding to the needs of particularly industries and economic sectors (mining and metals, electric utilities, automotive, apparel and footwear, food, construction and real estate, financial services, and others) that require specialized guidance in addition to the universally applicable core guidelines.

Outlook

Transparency and accountability have become the cornerstones for organizations to compete in all different arenas. Sustainability reporting demonstrates transparency and credibility in managing sustainability issues, documenting an organization's sustainability impact as well as management actions to improve sustainability performance. Sustainability reporting is an opportunity to account to stakeholders and to engender trust, which is likely to enhance reputation, increase value, and reduce uncertainty. A systematic reporting regime could also be a key driver in demonstrating transparency and accountability for sustainability activities and performance within an organization.

There are calls for organizations to provide "one report," which entails producing a single report that combines the financial information found in a traditional corporate annual report with the nonfinancial and narrative information (carbon emissions, water pollution, energy use, waste production, labor practices, occupational health and safety, product safety, etc.) found in a company's sustainability report. This presents challenges in implementing integrated reporting at the company level and in gaining broad adoption for it at the public level.

In order to move forward, however, advocates of sustainability reporting will need to agree on international standards and win acceptance for them from a wide range of constituencies. Besides AccountAbility, the Copenhagen Charter, and GRI, which representing the main frameworks recognized on an international level, many national organizations and institutions have developed specific tools often applicable to specific economic sectors or focusing on particular issues. There are moves, however, that indicate that international consensus is within reach.

At GRI's Third Amsterdam Conference on Sustainability and Transparency in May 2010, GRI announced its goal that by 2020 there should be an accepted international standard in widespread use to integrate financial reporting with environmental, social, and governance (ESG) reporting by all organizations. GRI and the United Nations Global Compact—a strategic policy initiative for businesses committed to aligning their operations with ten universally accepted principles in the areas of human rights, labor, environment, and anticorruption—will work toward an agreement to create a reporting framework so financial analysts and other stakeholders can better analyze and identify risks and opportunities as they relate to ESG issues.

Mario TESTA
University of Salerno

See also Agenda 21; Community and Stakeholder Input; Ecological Footprint Accounting; Ecological Impact Assessment (EcIA); Externality Valuation; Framework for Strategic Sustainable Development (FSSD); Global Reporting Initiative (GRI); International Organization for Standardization (ISO); Organic and Consumer Labels; Regulatory Compliance; Triple Bottom Line

FURTHER READING

AccountAbility. (2011). Homepage. Retrieved September 10, 2010, from http://www.accountability.org/home.aspx

Commission of the European Community. (2001, July 18). Green paper: Promoting a European framework on corporate social responsibility (COM [2001] 366 final). Brussels, Belgium: Commission of the European Community.

The Copenhagen Charter. (1999). *A management guide to stakeholder reporting.* Copenhagen, Denmark: Ernst & Young, KPMG, Pricewaterhouse Coopers, House of Mandag Morgen.

Crane, Andy; Matten, Dirk; & Spence, Laura J. (Eds.). (2008). *Corporate social responsibility: Readings and cases in a global context.* London: Routledge.

Eccles, Robert G., & Krzus, Michael P. (2010). *One report: Integrated reporting for a sustainable strategy.* Hoboken, NJ: John Wiley & Sons, Inc.

Global Reporting Initiative (GRI). (2011). Homepage. Retrieved January 20, 2011, from http://www.globalreporting.org/Home

Hinna, Luciano. (2005). *Come gestire la Responsabilità Sociale d'impresa* [How to manage corporate social responsibility]. Milan: Il Sole 24 Ore.

International Federation of Accountants (IFAC). (n.d.). IFAC sustainability framework. Retrieved October 1, 2010, from http://web.ifac.org/sustainability-framework/splash

Kolk, A. (2003). Trends in sustainability reporting by the Fortune Global 250. *Business Strategy and the Environment, 12*(5), 279–291.

Testa, Mario. (2007). *La responsabilità sociale d'impresa: Aspetti strategici, modelli di analisi e strumenti operative* [Corporate social responsibility: Strategic aspects, analytical models and operational means]. Turin, Italy: G. Giappichelli Editore.

World Business Council for Sustainable Development (WBCSD). (2011). WBCSD's 10 messages by which to operate. Retrieved September 10, 2010, from http://www.wbcsd.org

World Commission on Environment and Development. (1987). *Our common future.* New York: Oxford University Press.

Carbon Footprint

Carbon footprints represent the amount of greenhouse gases released into the atmosphere as a result of day-to-day activities such as driving, generating electricity, or manufacturing products. While footprinting methods continue to evolve, the indicator has value especially for monitoring activity and encouraging more sustainable behavior at all levels, from the individual to the global society.

A carbon footprint is an estimation of an entity's contribution of greenhouse gases (GHGs) to the global atmosphere. Carbon footprints can be estimated for individuals, cities, countries, products or processes, organizations, and ultimately, for the global population. The release of GHGs into the Earth's atmosphere is a primary driver of global climate change. Policy makers need a way to estimate human-caused GHG releases in order to assess progress toward climate stabilization goals, such as those stated in the Kyoto Protocol of 1997, and the concept of the carbon footprint serves that purpose.

Carbon footprint is used as shorthand for *greenhouse gas footprint* because many GHGs are carbon based, including carbon dioxide (CO_2), methane (CH_4), hydrofluorocarbons (HFCs), and perfluorocarbons (PFCs). For comparison and analysis, GHG releases are converted into equivalent quantities of carbon dioxide (CO_2e) using an estimate for each gas of its potential to cause global warming.

The footprint aspect of the term is derived from the ecological footprint, which measures the natural resources needed to sustain human activities. If our ecological footprint is larger than the stock of available resources, then our behavior is not sustainable over time. A similar premise applies to the carbon footprint; if GHG releases are more than the environment can absorb without fundamentally altering the global climate

system, then our behavior is unsustainable. A technical challenge lies in knowing what level of releases the environment can absorb without triggering catastrophic climate change, and at what level carbon footprints become unsustainable. For this reason, we tend to think simply: smaller is better.

Measurement Considerations

GHG releases are estimated from activities rather than directly observed by pollution monitors. Standardized protocols have been developed to estimate GHG releases for countries, leading to relatively comparable data by country. These protocols include the six major gases specified in the Kyoto Protocol, a standard procedure for converting GHGs to CO_2e, and a list of economic sectors and source activities that should be included in the assessments. The protocols are, however, based on estimates of activities and estimates of the releases from those activities, which are oversimplified reflections of reality.

To estimate the carbon footprint from driving a motor vehicle, for instance, one would estimate the amount of vehicle miles traveled (by vehicle type, such as passenger car, small truck, and large truck), estimate the amount of GHG released when driving (by vehicle type), and then multiply these amounts together (and sum across vehicle types) to get an estimate of GHG releases from driving. Both the estimation of vehicle travel and the estimation of emissions from vehicles are imprecise. Such imprecision compounds as footprints are calculated for multiple activities, including other types of energy fuel combustion, industrial processes and product use, agriculture, and waste disposal. As scientific knowledge improves, protocols must be updated and prior measurements recalculated, although the accuracy of estimates is always limited by data availability.

One consideration involves emissions from land-use change, such as the conversion of forest into agricultural or urban land. GHGs can be absorbed by the oceans and by vegetation on land. What is not absorbed by oceans or vegetation builds up in the atmosphere. A country's footprint can be adjusted downward to account for the extent to which available vegetation can absorb GHG releases, or adjusted upward if activities such as deforestation reduce the capacity of vegetation to absorb GHGs.

Many footprints entirely exclude emissions from land-use change, or report the footprints with and without land-use change. Data regarding emissions from land-use change tend to be available only for large geographies such as continents, be based on infrequent data collection, and contain substantial uncertainties when apportioned to smaller geographies. Available data suggest that tropical countries with extensive deforestation like Brazil and Indonesia release the majority of GHGs from land-use change. Alternatively, urbanizing countries like China and the United States have seen their vegetative capacity increase in recent years as agriculture is abandoned and the landscape transitions to denser vegetation. The inclusion of land-use change emissions opens the door to reduction strategies focused on reforestation.

Another consideration involves indirect emissions. The international protocol focuses on measuring GHG emissions where they are released, using "production-based" accounting. This approach is the easiest to accomplish given available activity data. An issue arises when releases within the country boundaries are related to production of goods or services consumed elsewhere. Much global industrial activity has moved to developing nations, even while most consumers of those industrial goods remain in developed nations. Similarly, disposal of waste has shifted to developing nations. Indirect GHG emissions associated with product consumption and waste disposal in developed nations may be substantially larger than is apparent from direct GHG releases within their borders.

For this reason, many scholars advocate using "consumption-based" accounting, in which the production-based footprint is (roughly) adjusted upward in high-consumption areas and adjusted downward in high-production areas. Calculation of consumption-based footprints requires analysis of environmental input and output or analysis of the life cycle of a product, tracking production, consumption, and disposal activities across spatial boundaries and over time. Data requirements are extensive. Advances have been made in calculating footprints of organizations and products using a life cycle approach, driven in large part by a desire to verify sustainable business practices. The methods are still being refined for countries and smaller geographies, especially to avoid double counting of GHG emissions at the point of production and the point of consumption, such as for electricity. Interim methods estimate a partial footprint associated with consumption from such activities as driving and heating homes.

The choice of production-based or consumption-based accounting has implications for policy. Assigning GHGs to the locations where they are released implicitly places responsibility for GHG reduction on producers, following the principle that the polluter pays, while ignoring consumer demand. This places the focus on obtaining reductions from the largest global contributors, such as China, the United States, Europe, Russia, and India. Given the spatial distribution of production activities, responsibility could fall on countries unable to afford reductions without compromising economic development, such as China and India. Policy makers question whether affluent areas like the United States and the European Union should shoulder more of the GHG reduction burden given their historical extensive releases and consumption activities, following a principle of shared responsibility.

A similar issue arises when calculating carbon footprints for urban areas, which have diverse combinations of production and consumption activities. Estimation of city footprints is complicated by the lack of a standard definition of *urban* and the lack of subnational data on activity and emission rates. As of 2011, most efforts focus on megacities, where data are more available, or on cities within single regions. Differences in methodologies make footprints difficult to compare across cities and over time.

Progress has been made at estimating consumption-based footprints for select global cities. A protocol for calculating carbon footprints of public sector organizations within the United States was released in 2010, following a similar approach (WRI and LMI 2010). According to the Greenhouse Gas Protocol, organizations are expected to report emissions from activities within their operational control and emissions from activities produced elsewhere but consumed within the organization's boundaries, such as purchased electricity. The organizations have discretion over including other emissions, such as for waste disposal and cross-boundary transportation, which can improve the comprehensiveness of the footprint but limit comparability across entities.

Estimates and Implications

The most widely available information on carbon footprints at the country level is production based. Footprints may be represented in three ways. (See table 1 below.) The broadest representation is in terms of a country's total GHG releases in a given year. A second figure is a country's footprint in terms of GHG releases per person per year, as a way to adjust for the size of a country; countries with larger populations are likely to have larger footprints. A third measurement is a country's footprint in terms of GHG releases per unit of economic output per year (known as emissions intensity), as a way to adjust for a country's development status; more developed countries are likely to have larger footprints, although their affluence may allow them to utilize low-carbon technologies and reduce their footprints.

China had the largest carbon footprint of the five areas listed in table 1, releasing nearly 20 percent of the global GHGs in 2005. The sheer size and rapid growth of emissions from China makes its footprint globally unsustainable. China's emissions were, however, spread across a population of nearly 1.3 billion residents, resulting in a much smaller footprint than, for example, the United States when viewed on a per person basis. Using the per person measure, which is most common for comparing footprints, it appears that Americans live much less sustainably than do residents of the Russian Federation, European Union, China, or India. Alternatively, when

using the emissions intensity indicator, it appears from the data in table 1 that the United States' footprint is more sustainable than that of India, China, or the Russian Federation but less sustainable than that of the European Union. Although the hope is to see all three footprint measures decline over time, total GHG releases matter most with regard to climate sustainability.

The three different approaches for representing footprints remind us that carbon footprints are determined by complex interactions of population, affluence, and available technology. Globally, rapid population growth and continued pressure to improve living standards are expected across much of the developing world, which will place upward pressure on footprints. Achieving climate stabilization goals thus requires focusing on reducing emissions intensity. Transitions to low- and no-carbon energy technology, including renewable fuels and nuclear power, could allow countries to develop economically while reducing their carbon footprint. Such transitions would be expensive and are a source of contention internationally, as nations such as China seek to utilize cheap, available, and carbon-intensive fuels like coal. In addition, technology improvements alone may simply increase the total amount of fuels consumed and carbon released unless they are coupled with other restraints on consumption. Reductions in consumption may be particularly important in high-income countries and cities, where affluence drives consumption and consumption dominates production.

Future Directions

The methods used to estimate carbon footprints are constrained by available data and rely on assumptions and aggregations that may not reflect reality well. Advances are needed in estimating releases for GHGs other than carbon dioxide, in estimating activity at smaller geographic scales, and in making adjustments to footprints

TABLE 1. Greenhouse Gas Releases for Selected Areas in 2005

	Total GHG Releases (million metric tons CO_2e)	GHG Releases Per Person (metric tons CO_2e)	Emissions Intensity (metric tons CO_2e per $GDP)
China	7,232.8	5.5	1,361.0
United States of America	6,914.2	23.4	559.2
European Union	5,043.1	10.3	382.5
Russian Federation	1,954.6	13.7	1,151.2
India	1,859.0	1.7	760.3

Notes: Higher values are less sustainable; emissions from land-use change and forestry are excluded.

Source: World Resources Institute (2011).

to reflect consumption behavior rather than production behavior. Differences in methodology make footprints difficult to compare across space and time.

Even without advances, the footprint concept has utility for policy makers for monitoring changes in behavior over time and examining the effectiveness of GHG reduction strategies in particular locations. The footprint concept also has financial utility for estimating the GHGs not released when reduction strategies are pursued, which can be bundled into credits and traded on a market. Measurement of one's carbon footprint by an individual or business also spreads awareness and signals a commitment to sustainable behavior, which can be a powerful force for curtailing GHG releases. For these reasons and more, the carbon footprint is likely to remain a popular indicator of climate sustainability for countries, cities, businesses and organizations, products and processes, and individuals.

Andrea SARZYNSKI
University of Delaware

See also Air Pollution Indicators and Monitoring; Computer Modeling; Ecological Footprint Accounting; Energy Labeling; Human Appropriation of Net Primary Production (HANPP); I = P × A × T Equation; Reducing Emissions from Deforestation and Forest Degradation (REDD); Regulatory Compliance; Shipping and Freight Indicators; Tree Rings as Environmental Indicators

FURTHER READING

Bader, Nikolas, & Bleischwitz, Raimund. (2009). Measuring urban greenhouse gas emissions: The challenge of comparability. *Surveys and Perspectives Integrating Environment and Society, 2*(3), 1–15.

Blake, Alcott. (2005). Jevons' paradox. *Ecological Economics, 54*(1), 9–21.

Brown, Marilyn A.; Southworth, Frank; & Sarzynski, Andrea. (2008). *Shrinking the carbon footprint of metropolitan America.* Washington, DC: The Brookings Institution.

Carbon Trust. (2010). Carbon footprinting: The next step to reducing your emissions. Retrieved November 14, 2011, from http://www.carbontrust.co.uk/Publications/pages/publicationdetail.aspx?id=CTV043

Dodman, David. (2009). Blaming cities for climate change? An analysis of urban greenhouse gas emissions inventories. *Environment & Urbanization, 21*(1), 185–201.

Hoffert, Martin I., et al. (1998). Energy implications of future stabilization of atmospheric CO_2 content. *Nature, 395,* 881–884.

Houghton, Richard. (n.d.). Data note: Emissions (and sinks) of carbon from land-use change. Retrieved November 14, 2011, from http://cait.wri.org/downloads/DN-LUCF.pdf

Intergovernmental Panel on Climate Change (IPCC). (2006). 2006 IPCC guidelines for national greenhouse gas inventories. Hayama, Japan: IPCC.

Kaya, Yoichi. (1989). *Impact of carbon dioxide emission control on GNP growth: Interpretation of proposed scenarios.* Hayama, Japan: IPCC.

Kennedy, Christopher A.; Ramaswami, Anu; Carney, Sebastian; & Dhakal, Shobhakar. (2009, June 28–30). Greenhouse gas emission baselines for global cities and metropolitan regions (paper, Proceedings of the 5th Urban Research Symposium). Marseilles, France.

Lenzen, Manfred; Murray, Joy; Sack, Fabian; & Wiedmann, Thomas. (2007). Shared producer and consumer responsibility: Theory and practice. *Ecological Economics, 61,* 27–42.

Levinson, Arik. (2010). Offshoring pollution: Is the United States increasingly importing polluting goods? *Review of Environmental Economics and Policy, 4*(1), 63–83.

Marcotullio, Peter J.; Sarzynski, Andrea; Albrecht, Jochen; Schulz, Niels; & Garcia, Jake. (2012). Assessing urban GHG emissions in European medium and large cities: Methodological issues. In Pierre Laconte (Ed.), *Assessing sustainable urban environments in Europe: Criteria and practices.* Lyon, France: Centre for the Study of Urban Planning, Transport and Public Facilities.

Satterthwaite, David. (2008). Cities' contribution to global warming: Notes on the allocation of greenhouse gas emissions. *Environment & Urbanization, 20*(2), 539–549.

Wackernagel, Mathis, & Rees, William F. (1996). *Our ecological footprint: Reducing human impact on the Earth.* Gabriola Island, Canada: New Society Publishers.

Wiedmann, Thomas, & Minx, Jan. (2008). A definition of "carbon footprint." In Carolyn C. Pertsova (Ed.), *Ecological economics research trends.* Hauppauge, NY: Nova Science Publishers.

World Resources Institute (WRI). (2011). Climate Analysis Indicators Tool (CAIT) version 8.0. Retrieved November 14, 2011, from http://cait.wri.org/

World Resources Institute (WRI) & Logistics Management Institute (LMI). (2010). The Greenhouse Gas Protocol for the US public sector. Retrieved November 28, 2011, from http://www.ghgprotocol.org/files/ghgp/us-public-sector-protocol_final_oct13.pdf

Challenges to Measuring Sustainability

Indices—measurements of movement toward or away from a goal—have proliferated in sustainability studies since the 1990s despite the following challenges faced by index developers: defining sustainability; balancing conflicting desires (i.e., technical rigor versus accessibility); incorporating ethical values; and connecting indices and policies. Progress toward sustainability may thus seem difficult to assess, but the problems of living unsustainably, such as climate change, will not go away if we refuse to monitor them.

Measurements and indicators of sustainability are increasingly important elements in sustainability scholarship and policy making. These indices enable people to articulate their vision of sustainability, determine the degree to which it is being achieved, and ideally, communicate this information clearly. Indeed, policy makers and the general public alike expect the use of indicators to assess policy effectiveness, allocate funds, and determine future actions. Yet, though sustainability indices are popular and proliferating, their creation and use come with challenges such as defining what sustainability is, balancing tensions such as the simultaneous desire for comprehensiveness and simplicity, determining how to incorporate ethical values into index formation, and connecting indicators and policies. Examining each of these challenges and common methods for resolving them will reveal the limitations of indicator use.

Before examining these challenges, it will be helpful to clarify terms. When people attempt to measure the sustainability of a system or action, the progress toward sustainability a system has achieved, or a policy's contribution to achieving sustainability, they use indices of sustainability—tools that compile data about a complex system into a relatively easy-to-understand output. Although the terms *index* and *indicator* are sometimes conflated in the literature, it is helpful to distinguish them by using *indicator* to denote one particular measurement or piece of data, and *index* to refer to a compilation of indicators. For example, a grade received at the end of a semester is an index of academic performance comprising multiple indicators (that is, the grades for individual assignments). A semester grade, like every index, is intended to aggregate a set of complex data in order to gain knowledge and aid decision making.

Defining Sustainability

Typically sustainability refers to the ability to simultaneously preserve ecosystems and human societies. Frequently society is emphasized in definitions of sustainable development such as "meeting the needs of the present without compromising the ability of future generations to meet their own needs" (WCED 1987, 8). Some definitions focus on particular aspects of sustainability, such as those related to agriculture, buildings, or energy—for example, explaining sustainable energy as "a dynamic harmony between the equitable availability of energy-intensive goods and services to all people and the preservation of the earth for future generations" (Tester et al. 2005, 8). Definitions, whether general or specific, may differ with respect to variables, including time frame and spatial scale, the weight placed on human society versus the rest of ecosystems, and the balance of technical and ethical criteria. Amid this diversity, consensus may be difficult to reach. Indeed, indices have proliferated. Other theoretical challenges to measuring sustainability exist, however, and deserve attention.

Balancing Polarities

Given the promise of indices to simplify data in order to learn about complex systems and help guide policy making, it is not surprising that many technical experts advocate the development and use of sustainability indices. To be most useful as guides for environmental decision making, indices must be relatively easy and inexpensive to calculate and measure, easily understood by decision makers so they are not ignored or accidentally misconstrued, scientifically sound so their results are meaningful and replicable, and adequately nuanced to discriminate between policy options. Constructing an index to meet these demands involves delicately compromising between at least three sets of technical polarities, including comprehensiveness and manageability, technical rigor and accessibility, and ideal and actual data.

Comprehensiveness versus Manageability

Since indices are intended to simplify the vast information associated with complex dynamic systems, some argue that a simple index focusing on the most important component of the system will be most appropriate. For example, a frequently used general indicator of anthropogenic contributions to climate change is the atmospheric concentration of carbon dioxide. As this number rises as a result of human activities, it is assumed that the effects of climate change will increase. Yet such simple indicators, while manageable, also come with limitations. Determining which factor most influences a system, and thus should be the *one* indicator of a complex phenomenon, can be quite challenging. Measuring the one supposedly simple data point—in this case, the average atmospheric concentration of carbon dioxide—can require a host of measurements, the development of new theories, and international cooperation about data collection. Furthermore, focusing on only one component of a system will draw attention away from the effects of other factors, on their own or in combination. For instance, carbon dioxide is not the only greenhouse gas; methane and nitrous oxide also contribute significantly to global warming. Additionally, other factors can dampen or intensify the greenhouse effect; ignoring them can skew understanding of climate change. The use of single-issue indicators can also distract from other environmental issues. Focusing solely on climate change could distract people from other environmental problems, such as nuclear waste.

To avoid some of the problems of simplistic indicators, some index developers aim to create a comprehensive list of indicators that assesses every part of the human–environmental system. Such a list may seem ideal, for it could grow to capture all important elements of the system. Such thinking was certainly behind the United Nations list of fifty-eight core indicators of sustainable development (United Nations 2001, 310). Yet comprehensiveness can be an obstacle to understanding and utilizing these indicators. Abundant information can easily overwhelm users as they struggle to recall what each indicator means, weigh the relative importance of the indicators, and gain an overall picture of sustainable development. Aggregating multiple indicators into a single index is a possible solution that comes with its own challenges: How should indicators with different units be aggregated? Should all indicators be given equal weights in the index, or are some more technically or morally important? Are any indicators correlated, a situation that could lead to overemphasizing an aspect of sustainability in the index as a whole? Additionally, amassing all of the data to compute an index with many indicators can be quite time-consuming and expensive; to do so year after year to gain a sense of progress toward or away from sustainability would be especially difficult.

Technical Rigor versus Accessibility

To be meaningful yet implementable, an index must balance the desire for technical rigor with a method accessible to the general public. Ideally, people who use an index would understand each detail of the index from data collection to calculation and the presentation of results. Such widespread knowledge could help reduce the use of indices out of context. It could also help ensure that indices are comprehensive; if people understand how an index is compiled, they will be able to assess whether anything important is left out. To achieve these ideals, the methods used for gathering and analyzing data as well as those used to construct the index must be "clear, transparent and standard" (Gallopin 1997, 25). Additionally, the data upon which the index is based must be observable in principle and preferably be a part of existing data sets. Realistically, however, most policy makers and average citizens do not want to take the time to learn about all of the details of an index; they desire a clear summary of the state or development of the system in question so they can decide how to act. On the other hand, technical experts want to ensure that their indices are rigorously constructed to withstand technical critiques.

To maintain the balance between technical rigor and accessibility, many indices are constructed in a hierarchical manner and explained at various levels of detail. First, data is collected and transformed through mathematical functions to form subindices that in turn are combined into one or a small number of high-level indices. The high-level indices—the final product—may be represented numerically or graphically so that policy makers have a clear, concise summary of the state of the system in question, leaving many of the technical details hidden in lower levels for experts to study. For example, twenty subindices, each of which may rely on numerous data points, are incorporated into two indices, the Human Wellbeing Index and the Ecosystem Wellbeing Index, which are graphically displayed in one diagram in Robert Prescott-Allen's *The Wellbeing of Nations* (2001).

To satisfy experts and ensure that indices are technically sound, the details of the data collection, the subindex calculations, and the process for combining the subindicators are usually described in detail in a long report. This report is generally summarized for laypeople and policy makers. Finally, the index is typically accompanied by a very brief interpretive statement. In this way both expert and lay requirements for the index can be met. A limitation of this summary approach, however, is that policy makers may not understand or recognize the assumptions or limitations of the index, conditions that provide a fertile ground for misinterpretation.

Employing gross national product (GNP) as an indicator of overall human well-being instead of just an economic indicator is a common but often critiqued extension of an index (Daly and Cobb 1994). Although higher GNPs can correlate with a higher material standard of living, GNP does not take into account the distribution of economic resources among a population, so a high GNP may benefit only a segment of society. Additionally, as GNP does not register the value of natural resources unless they are used and does register economic activity to clean up pollution, it can register the depletion of natural resources and increasing pollution as solely positive contributions to GNP, though many people find the disruption of their ecosystem to have negative consequences for their quality of life. Finally, as GNP is a monetary indicator, it cannot register aspects of a good quality of life that are not directly monetized, such as supportive family and friends.

Despite these limitations of GNP, it is often used as an overall indicator of quality of life, a situation that highlights the need for nonexperts to understand the proper application of indices.

Ideal versus Existing Data

The availability of data is also a considerable factor in index development. The desire for data sets that exactly correspond to what one wishes to measure must be balanced with the advantages of data that are already available or will be economically and politically feasible to obtain. Though data directly correlated to a topic is most desired, it is rarely available given budgetary, technical, and political constraints. For example, one may want to monitor the direct health impacts of pollution, but if data about direct health impacts is unavailable, one may need to settle for the number of days that air pollution levels are above the threshold deemed safe. In such cases, index developers must either determine what preexisting data can be used as a proxy for desired data or advocate for the collection of new data.

Using existing data sets can create biases in indices, because existing data may not include elements of the system deemed important by index users. For example, existing data on sustainability tend to include more economic than environmental data and more environmental data than data about the well-being of society (Burger, Daub, and Scherrer 2010; Pearsall 2010), even though societal well-being could be considered a critical component in monitoring sustainability. Additionally, data about industrialized countries tends to be more prevalent, potentially causing an index to be biased against the economies of less-developed countries.

Existing data, when incorporated into indices, can easily promote a nature-versus-humans mindset or, alternatively, one in which anything good for ecosystems is assumed to be good for humanity. Both assumptions are oversimplified. To avoid such biases, index developers need to assess all of the ramifications of using existing data sets and develop methods of overcoming their limitations in the construction, presentation, and use of indices.

As index developers aim to balance ideal data with actual data, technical rigor with accessibility, and comprehensiveness with manageability, they typically focus on quantified data and technical solutions. Indeed, many advocates of indices argue that reliable, accessible, appropriate index results are necessary to teach people about sustainability. These advocates tend to think that a lack of information is the greatest barrier to effective decision making (Hezri and Hasan 2004, 288; Inhaber 1976, 4, 162–163). While understanding a situation can help one to make effective decisions, information is not the sole influence on policy making, nor does it ensure that good decisions will be made. Preexistent values always influence the construction and use of indices and policies.

The Role of Values

Indeed, values—the ideas as well as physical and social conditions deemed important by a group—intersect with the development and use of sustainability indices in at least five ways: (1) in definitions of sustainability upon which indices are based, (2) in the decision to develop indices, (3) in the processes by which they are created, (4) in the particular decisions made during their creation, and (5) in the ways they are utilized after they are created. Since the role of values in index formation is often overlooked, these considerations deserve significant reflection.

Sustainability has many definitions, yet underlying all of them is both a technological aspect of sustainability (what can be sustained) and a normative aspect of sustainability (what people want to sustain). For instance, both *Our Common Future*, a report on sustainability commissioned by the United Nations, and Agenda 21, an international sustainability policy document, entail both inter- and intragenerational equity, as they emphasize that sustainable development should meet the needs of everyone in the present (intragenerational equity) and the needs of future generations (intergenerational equity). This focus on inter- and intragenerational justice is also found in religious and philosophical ethical systems around the world. Other normative elements common to sustainability discussions include responsibility (that is, humans taking responsibility for what they have done to the world and what they can do to change their actions) and farsightedness (that is, attention to the future

ramifications of actions and inactions). Yet sustainability indices do not embody all of these values equally. Responsibility and farsightedness shape indices much more than equity.

In addition, the decision to use quantifiable indicators to measure and monitor progress toward sustainability is a sign of the value that society places on quantification and the use of social indicators in general. We expect that policies will be evaluated for effectiveness, often assessed by basic measures of monetary gain or loss rather than the long-term societal consequences. The very decision to use indices thus reveals the value placed on the quantifiable, and often, the monetizable and short term.

Values also play a role in the methods used to create indices: do experts alone create the indices, or are they constructed through a participatory process involving laypeople from constituencies impacted by the index's use? Scholars increasingly argue that public participation is helpful in determining the goals of the index, its threshold levels (for example, how much pollution the community is willing to accept), and the ways in which indices influence policy. Such participation is intended to ensure that the index measures what is valued by the communities involved.

For instance, many studies of sustainability focus upon direct effects of pollution or environmental disruption on land, air, or water. Far fewer examine the simultaneous effects of multiple chemicals on human bodies (Fredericks 2011, 65). Even more rarely do studies monitor the complex psychological and social ramifications of environmental disruption, even though these impacts may be most valued by individuals and communities. For example, fishing and consuming local fish may be not only economically necessary to obtain protein for one's family but also central to one's culture and identity, as is the case with many Native American and Asian American populations. The value of living as one's ancestors did, of sharing rituals with one's present community, of providing food for one's family, and the psychological health that can come with cultural preservation, are not easily quantifiable. Nor are these values registered by simplistic quantifications of the presence of heavy metals and PCBs (polychlorinated biphenyls) in local waterways, common data points in sustainability assessments.

Some analysts try to monitor such cultural values by asking people what they would pay for the ability to catch clean fish or how much money they would accept to have polluted, uneatable fish (or other environmental destruction). Such studies can be critiqued because many object to monetizing something that has always been, and in their mind should be, free. Many people thus give very high or infinite monetary values for their willingness to accept environmental pollution, whereas their willingness to pay for clean water and fish is comparatively small. This discrepancy leads some economists to believe that laypeople are irrational and not to be trusted to establish values. Others see these results as true indicators of the value of ecosystems and the limits of quantifying and monetizing all things.

As people recognize the limitations of quantifying or monetizing value and focusing on environmental and economic data, they are emphasizing incorporating community input into sustainability indices. This may be done through surveys and interviews that record community members' perceptions of their quality of life. Such methods of data collection could chronicle what is important to locals, whether their goals change over time, and how their ability to achieve their goals has changed over time.

The US environmental philosopher Bryan Norton of the Georgia Institute of Technology suggests another approach to simultaneously monitor environmental, social, and economic ideals of sustainability. He maintains that conversations among stakeholders can reveal indicators that monitor multiple aspects of sustainability valued by different constituencies. He describes a potential sustainability indicator for Atlanta, Georgia, a place where people place significant cultural value on tall trees and where many trees are being cut to make way for suburban sprawl. Of course the trees also play a critical role in local ecosystems, as they provide habitat for animals, cleanse the air, control runoff, and lower local temperatures. Norton suggests that monitoring tree cover with satellite images could indicate the degree to which Atlanta's cultural and ecosystemic priorities are being preserved (Norton 2005, 391–392). This one indicator thus could register both normative and technical aspects of sustainability.

Regardless of the people involved in the construction of indices, values also influence the technical details of the index. For example, many indices separate economic and social dimensions of sustainability, implying that economic strength is valuable apart from what it can bring to society. Values also influence the way that indices are used. After all, if an indicator does not measure what people think is important, it may just sit on a shelf. Alternatively, indices that are perceived to monitor

something valued by the community (well-being) may be used frequently (GNP), even if the index does not necessarily correlate with the value. Cultural values and ethical priorities thus can influence indices at every stage from their initial development to use.

Disassociation from Policy Making

Challenges to implementing indices also arise when they are disassociated from policy making. Though many indices are constructed to monitor the connection between human societies and the environment in order to improve decision making, they may not be constructed with the users in mind. Index creators do not necessarily ensure that policy makers know about or understand the index in general or that they agree with its assumptions. Rather, they often expect that policy makers and the public will take their vision of sustainability as the objective truth, even though it involves normative judgments about what is important. Indeed, Robert Prescott-Allen, the developer of the *Wellbeing of Nations*, one of the most complex indices of sustainability, recommends developing policies only after examining the results of his indices (Prescott-Allen 2001, 289).

This common separation between policy makers and indices is troubling because many indicators are ostensibly created in order to effect policy, by increasing knowledge (Yale Center for Environmental Law and Policy 2010, 6; Fraser et al. 2006, 115). Yet, if the indicators are not developed with the needs of policy makers in mind, then they are likely to focus on aspects of sustainability that are not prioritized by the community; rely on data that is completely unavailable or that is monetarily, politically, or temporally prohibitive to collect; or yield a product that is cumbersome to use. Scholars are increasingly calling for the simultaneous development of policies and indices so that the indices are able to truly aid in the formation and assessment of policies (Hezri and Dovers 2006; Holden 2011, 319)

Similarly, index developers increasingly recognize the importance of collaboration between stakeholders, academic experts, and policy makers in the formation of indices, given the importance of local knowledge and values for human–ecosystem relations and the desire for people to participate in decision making that affects their lives. Such collaboration is particularly emphasized in the creation of local indices.

Those indices that are developed at a local level in conjunction with input from community members face another sort of problem: they are typically disassociated from regional and national indicators used by governments to assess the overall status of a country and to set national or international policy. For example, in a case study of quality-of-life indicators in Bristol, United Kingdom, the researcher Sarah McMahon identifies five levels of indicators: (1) indicators used across Europe, (2) national indicators, (3) indicators developed by stakeholders, (4) ward and city indicators, and (5) indicators specific to community groups. Though she notes that there are some common components of indicators at multiple levels—for example, national, stakeholder, and local indicators all include a measure of crime rate—lower-level data expressed in community-developed indicators are not integrated into higher-order indicators unless these variables are already a part of the indicator (McMahon 2002, 177). For example, the number of homeless households, road traffic casualties, reports of dog excrement in public places, the biological quality of local rivers, and the presence of local nature reserves are indicators that the people of Bristol identify as important to their quality of life, though these are not registered at higher political levels.

This disaggregation of data is probably due in part to the methodological challenges of aggregating information across scales and data types. How shall the data of any community be weighted against national indicators? Can some communities serve as representative examples? How can data of different units (species lost, concentrations of toxins) or different types (quantitative, narrative) be aggregated? To avoid these challenges and adhere to norms which expect quantifiable, numerical data, many index developers will focus on either the local or national scales.

While this lack of integration simplifies the process of index development, it has at least two important implications for use of indices. First, by ignoring community-based indicators, large scale or national indices may miss elements that are essential to the people. Second, by ignoring the assessment of community experience of sustainability, developers of national indices miss the opportunity to monitor the inequitable distribution of benefits or burdens by geographic location, race, class, or ethnicity within a country, even though intragenerational equity is an assumption of many definitions of sustainability. Admittedly, some of the prioritization of either national or community-based indicators is based on the necessary trade-offs involved in the creation of any indicator as discussed above. Yet the systematic disassociation of local and national-level indices hinders the development of new policies about sustainability that will require integrated indices for their implementation and evaluation.

Implications

After reviewing the challenges to measuring sustainability—defining sustainability, balancing polarities of indices, recognizing how values shape indices, and making indices relevant to policy makers—it may seem that these challenges are so large that no one should try to assess progress toward sustainability. Yet the problems of living unsustainably, such as climate change, will not go away if we refuse to monitor them. Additionally, it seems unlikely that the prioritization of quantifying progress toward goals such as sustainability will wane any time soon, and it seems unreasonable to avoid the benefits of monitoring sustainability just because there are limits to doing so. Rather, the best approach is to use indices carefully, remembering their limitations and striving to overcome them as much as possible in order to better articulate the goals of sustainability and to assess progress toward or away from it.

Sarah E. FREDERICKS
University of North Texas

See also Biological Indicators (*several articles*); Business Reporting Methods; Community and Stakeholder Input; Development Indicators; Environmental Performance Index (EPI); Genuine Progress Indicators (GPI); Global Environmental Outlook (GEO) Reports; Gross Domestic Product, Green; Gross National Happiness; International Organization for Standardization (ISO); Quantitative vs. Qualitative Studies; Sustainability Science; Systems Thinking

FURTHER READING

Azar, Christian; Holmberg, John; & Lindgren, Kristian. (1996). Methodological and ideological options: Socio-ecological indicators for sustainability. *Ecological Economics, 18,* 89–112.

Bell, Simon, & Morse, Stephen. (1999). *Sustainability indicators: Measuring the immeasurable?* London: EarthScan Publications.

Burger, Paul; Daub, Claus-Heinrich; & Scherrer, Yvonne M. (2010). Creating values for sustainable development. *International Journal of Sustainable Development & World Ecology, 17*(1), 1–3.

Corburn, Jason. (2005). *Street science: Community knowledge and environmental health justice.* Cambridge, MA: MIT Press.

Daly, Herman E., & Cobb, John B., Jr. (1994). *For the common good: Redirecting the economy toward community, the environment, and a sustainable future.* Boston: Beacon Press.

Davidsdottir, Brynhildur; Basoli, Dan; & Fredericks, Sarah E. (2007). Measuring sustainable energy development: The development of a three dimensional index. In Jon D. Erickson & John M. Gowdy (Eds.), *Frontiers in environmental valuation and policy* (pp. 303–330). Cheltenham, UK: Edward Elgar.

Failing, Lee, & Gregory, Robin. (2003). Ten common mistakes in designing biodiversity indicators for forest policy. *Journal of Environmental Management, 68*, 121–132.

Fraser, Evan D. G.; Dougill, Andrew J.; Mabee, Warren E.; Reed, Mark; & McAlpine, Patrick. (2006). Bottom up and top down: Analysis of participatory processes for sustainability indicator identification as a pathway to community empowerment and sustainable environmental management. *Journal of Environmental Management, 78*(2), 113–127.

Fredericks, Sarah E. (2011). Monitoring environmental justice. *Environmental Justice, 4*(1), 63–69.

Gahin, Randa, & Paterson, Chris. (2001). Community indicators: Past, present, and future. *National Civic Review, 90*(4), 347.

Gallopin, Gilberto Carlos. (1997). Indicators and their use: Information for decision-making, Part One: Introduction. In Robyn Matravers, Bedrich Moldan & Suzanne Billharz (Eds.), *Sustainability indicators: A report on the project on indicators of sustainable development* (pp. 13–27). New York: John Wiley & Sons.

Harner, John; Warner, Kee; Pierce, John; & Huber, Tom. (2002). Urban environmental justice indices. *Professional Geographer, 54*(3), 318–331.

Hezri, Adnan A., & Dovers, Stephen R. (2006). Sustainability indicators, policy and governance: Issues for ecological economics. *Ecological Economics, 60*(1), 86–99.

Hezri, Adnan A., & Hasan, M. Nordin. (2004). Management framework for sustainable development indicators in the state of Selangor, Malaysia. *Ecological Indicators, 4*, 287–304.

Holden, Meg. (2011). Public participation and local sustainability: Questioning a common agenda in urban governance. *International Journal of Urban and Regional Research, 35*(2), 312–329.

Inhaber, Herbert. (1976). *Environmental indices*. New York: John Wiley & Sons.

Intergovernmental Panel on Climate Change (IPCC). (2007). *Climate change 2007: The physical science basis: Summary report for policy makers*. Paris: Intergovernmental Panel on Climate Change.

Johansson, Per-Olov. (1999). Theory of economic valuation of environmental goods and services. In Jeroen C. J. M. van den Bergh (Ed.), *Handbook of environmental and resource economics* (pp. 747–754). Northampton, MA: Edward Elgar.

Kriström, Bengt, & Common, Mick S. (1999). Valuation and ethics in environmental economics. In Jeroen C. J. M. van den Bergh (Ed.), *Handbook of environmental and resource economics* (pp. 809–823). Northampton, MA: Edward Elgar.

Levett, Roger. (1998). Sustainability indicators—Integrating quality of life and environmental protection. *Journal of the Royal Statistical Society Series A (Statistics in Society), 161*(3), 291–302.

López-Ridaura, Santiago; Masera, Omar; & Astier, Marta (2002). Evaluating the sustainability of complex socio-environmental systems. The MESMIS framework. *Ecological Indicators, 2*(1/2), 135–148.

McMahon, Sarah K. (2002). The development of quality of life indicators- a case study from the city of Bristol, UK. *Ecological Indicators, 2*(1/2), 177–185.

Moldan, Bedrich. (1997). Box 2D: Values, services and goods of the geobiosphere. In Robyn Matravers, Bedrich Moldan & Suzanne Billharz (Eds.), *Sustainability indicators: A report on the project on indicators of sustainable development* (pp. 99–101). New York: John Wiley & Sons.

Norton, Bryan G. (2005). *Sustainability: A philosophy of adaptive ecosystem management*. Chicago: University of Chicago Press.

Obst, Carl. (2000). Report of the September 1999 OECD Expert Workshop on the Measurement of Sustainable Development. In Organisation for Economic Co-Operation and Development (Ed.), *Frameworks to measure sustainable development: An OECD expert workshop* (pp. 7–17). Paris: OECD.

Ott, Wayne R. (1978). *Environmental indices: Theory and practice*. Ann Arbor, MI: Ann Arbor Science Publishers Inc.

Pearsall, Hamill. (2010). From brown to green? Assessing social vulnerability to environmental gentrification in New York City. *Environment and Planning C-Government and Policy, 28*(5), 872–886.

Prescott-Allen, Robert. (2001). *The wellbeing of nations: A country-by-country index of quality of life and the environment*. Washington, DC: Island Press.

Taviv, Rina; Brent, Alan C.; & Fortuin, Henri (2009). An environmental impact tool to assess national energy scenarios. *Proceedings of World Academy of Science: Engineering & Technology, 39*, 612–617.

Tester, Jefferson W.; Drake, Elisabeth M.; Driscoll, Michael J.; Golay, Michael W.; & Peters, William A. (2005). *Sustainable energy: Choosing among energy options*. Cambridge, MA: MIT Press.

United Nations. (2001). *Indicators of sustainable development: Guidelines and methodologies*. New York: United Nations.

van den Bergh, Jeroen C. J. M., & Verbruggen, Harmen. (1999). Spatial sustainability, trade and indicators: An evaluation of the "ecological footprint." *Ecological Economics, 29*, 61–72.

Vatn, Arild. (2005). Rationality, institutions and environmental policy. *Ecological Economics, 55*, 203–217.

World Commission on Environment and Development (WCED). (1987). *Our common future: Report of the World Commission on Environment and Development*. New York: Oxford University Press.

Yale Center for Environmental Law and Policy & Center for International Earth Science Information Network. (2010). 2010 Environmental Performance Index. Retrieved November 17, 2011, from http://epi.yale.edu

Citizen Science

The concept of citizen science captures the relationships between science and the public and allows the relationships to be talked about and debated. It raises questions about what the public needs to know about science and how the scientific community can benefit from engagement with the public. Capitalizing on these ongoing debates may provide new avenues for scientific study, as well as socially robust ways to meet the pressing challenges of risk, environment, and sustainability facing societies today.

The relationships between science and the public are important features of contemporary life. Science can play essential roles in building an understanding of the world, in creating new technologies, in developing economies, and in improving health and social welfare. Science is more and more central to issues of risk, health, and the environment. It is a way to address these challenges, but it is also their potential source. Citizen engagement with science is an increasingly important part of the way we make sense of the world around us and create strategies for managing today's challenges into the future. How relationships between science and citizens are shaped and understood, however, are rarely straightforward, and often they are subjects of vigorous debate. The different meanings we give to "citizen science" are rooted both in how we ascribe roles to science in society and how we understand the value of public engagement with science. At the heart of the politics of scientific citizenship are critical debates about the authority of scientific expertise, trust in the wider scientific community, the value of public knowledge, and the sources of future prosperity, sustainability, and well-being in society.

Science, Progress, and Public Understanding

Much of the way society has historically thought about the relationship between science and the public is linked to the understandings of scientific progress that rose out of the Enlightenment in the eighteenth century. The term *science* itself has origins in the fourteenth century, when the word was used in a general way to refer to knowledge or theory. It was the writing of Enlightenment philosophers such as Francis Bacon and René Descartes, however, that shaped now familiar conceptions of science as a way to access rational and autonomous truths (free from subjective bias) about the world. This new approach to knowledge stood out in sharp opposition to the existing theologically oriented societies in which the ability to speak authoritatively about nature and society was linked to the transcendent appreciation of divinity. Since the Enlightenment, science has been characterized by optimism about the role of rational knowledge in contributing to the progress of society and the emancipation of humankind from ignorance, and as a source of knowledge that can be applied to tackling the material and social problems of that society. Across a terrain so broad as to include the economy, health, social welfare, government, and politics, people have tried to apply scientific rationality to achieve more, to develop further, and to foster the progressive advancement of society. For much of recent history, the scientific good and the public good have shared a close relationship.

This union of scientific and social progress has carried with it the responsibility for public citizens to embrace scientific knowledge and technological change. The attempt to develop widespread civic knowledge about science, for instance, through science education and science communication, has been one prominent expression of this responsibility. It is not necessary that everyone become a scientist, but a series of individual and social benefits can be obtained by participating in science and improving scientific literacy. Innovation and industry can be supported by knowledgeable workers and innovative researchers. The public is better positioned to understand and interpret government policy in areas where risks to health and the environment are being debated. And finally, the public is given the necessary intellectual tools for making personal choices and negotiating the increasing presence of science and technology in an individual's everyday life.

The Royal Society of London—one of the world's oldest and most preeminent scientific institutions—put forward these arguments in a report titled *The Public Understanding of Science* (Royal Society 1985). This report communicated a deep skepticism on the part of the British establishment about the ability of the country to fully participate in, and capitalize on, a modern world suffused with new knowledge and new technologies. In making its case, the Royal Society was replicating a view of the moral and social value of public education that had been repeated throughout the twentieth century in Britain. In 1959, the novelist C. P. Snow (1998), for example, made an impassioned argument for the reform of the education system in an influential lecture at Cambridge University. He called for the government and educators to include greater emphasis on teaching the sciences at all levels in a system that he saw as dominated by training in the classics. Snow saw such steps as necessary to ensuring Britain's global standing and the nation's position in relationship to its Cold War adversaries in particular. Thirty years before Snow's lecture, scholars and scientists were similarly involved in a campaign to advance public understanding of science, this time as a way to break down social class. Lancelot Hogben, the author of a variety of publically accessible scientific texts, saw civic participation in the natural sciences as necessary because, as he writes, "scientific discoveries affect the everyday lives of everyone. Hence science for the citizen must be science as a record of past, and as an inventory for future, human achievements" (Hogben 1938, i). He saw his writing as enabling *all of*

society to participate in a "genuinely constructive social project" for the *benefit of all.*

Each of these attempts to spread scientific knowledge shares the underlying idea that public understanding of science is a collective moral problem. It is the duty of scientists, educators, and other social elites to share their knowledge and raise the level of the intellect of the common layperson. Moreover, citizens are expected to cast off ignorance and take up this scientific expertise so as to fully incorporate scientific knowledge into their everyday lives. The failure of either the intellectuals to communicate the knowledge or the citizenry to incorporate it is perceived as damaging collective interests and hindering the progressive development of society.

Moving Toward New Approaches

The version of the public understanding of science outlined above may be among the most common expressions of citizen–science relationships in society; it has, however, attracted considerable critical attention. Scholars who study science, technology, and society have begun to carve out the basis for reimagining citizen–science relations as part of a wider critique of the progressive enlightenment associations drawn between science and society.

Central to these critiques has been the recognition of the necessarily unequal positions science and the public occupy in relation to each other. Those who have privileged access to understanding the world are seen as having power and authority, and the public that lacks this rational knowledge occupies a lower position. Writing about the role of science in creating new technologies, the sociologists Keith Grint and Steve Woolgar have observed that these hierarchies lead to a contradiction with social values of progress and democracy. "If democracy requires decision-making by roughly equivalent citizens, then the assumption that technology is beyond the wit of the majority necessarily impales the democrat on a technological horn" (Grint and Woolgar 1997, 61). It is in this sense that attempts to foster public understanding of science have come to be critically referred to as deficit models of scientific citizenship. Identifying an intellectual and rational deficiency on the part of the public makes it easy to justify the exclusion of public voices from conversations about the future of society.

The example of the way science and the public interact in the public press highlights existing unequal relationships. The US sociologist of science Dorothy Nelkin noted that journalistic coverage of science has by and large been uncritical of scientific activity. Instead of communicating balanced information to the public about science—including, for example, accounts of uncertainty and scientific disagreements—science journalism has tended to promote scientific progress to the public, Nelkin posited, through the creation of heroic storylines that announce discoveries and hype the promise of scientific advances. She saw this as a mutually reinforcing relationship where journalists are able to sell science, and in return for positive coverage, gain access to the popular stories necessary for selling media. Far from the value-neutral model of science journalism, which purports to communicate pure scientific reason for the benefit of all, for Nelkin, science communication speaks very clearly about some versions of science while potentially isolating the public from other, less heroic perspectives (Nelkin 1995).

The hierarchical approach to citizen–science relations has drawn particular criticism with regard to controversies about new technologies and risks. When new technologies are brought onto the market and into everyday citizens' lives, they are often heralded as in some way revolutionizing social experience. It is not uncommon, however, for the arrival of new technologies to also meet with public scrutiny and questions about their potential negative impacts. In the 1990s, for example, agricultural biotechnologies were heralded as revolutionizing productivity in ways that would improve the capacity of society to meet the nutritional needs of a growing society. At the same time, however, questions were raised about the negative impact of these new technologies across a diverse range of concerns, including potential impacts of genetically modified crops on human health and the biodiversity of the countryside. In many cases when such criticisms are raised, the initial reaction from the scientific community and science-based government and industry is to label public concerns ill-informed or irrational. The next impulse is often to seek to provide the public with the appropriate information to make rationally informed decisions about the risks and benefits of new technologies. Very often, the assumption is that simply providing the right information will make the public more likely to accept technologies such as biotechnology. In other words, people are not only being asked to become educated about science and technology but also to accept techno-scientific models of development and progress.

From a different perspective, it is possible to see public concerns about science and technology as having more to do with relevant concerns about the application of science in society than with lack of knowledge. In other words, there are good reasons to ask questions of science, and these questions suggest that the public is both informed and rational in raising concerns about the influence of science in their everyday lives. For instance, concerns about risk in the areas of health, the environment, and sustainability make up an increasingly important part of today's political discussions. As the influential German sociologist Ulrich Beck has noted, interpreting these risks involves coming to terms with the role of science in contributing to the creation of hazards and the uncertainties that come with them. The progress we associate with scientific invention, for example, is now tied to a vast array of environmental problems that challenge the sustainability of our societies. On another front, many critiques of science have called into question the autonomy of scientific knowledge—that is, knowledge free from subjective influence and necessarily beneficial for all. The production of scientific knowledge is now inseparable from economic development and business interests, however, and scientists and scientific institutions have developed considerable influence with government and public policy. Far from being a neutral actor, science has a considerable stake in society. In this sense, the preoccupation with the public understanding of science is less an indication of a moral problem in society, and more an indication of a sense of threat from the public challenge of the authority and influence of science in society. Alan Irwin and Brian Wynne, in their widely cited book *Misunderstanding Science?* (1996), provocatively suggest that the misunderstandings to be addressed by society are not those of what the public knows about science, but the ways in which science misunderstands the "public and itself."

A New Public Engagement

Critiques of deficit models of citizen science have led to calls for a reinvigorated and more balanced engagement between science and the public. Attempts have been made to shift communication from top-down, scientist-to-public models to dialogues that foster mutual understanding. First, engagement with science is seen as a way to grant a voice to the public in debates about science and in science-based decisions. Second, engagement may permit the public to participate in the creation of more socially robust ways of thinking about and applying scientific knowledge.

Particularly active and fruitful experiments in citizen–science engagement are occurring in decision making about environmental risks. Environmental policy makers may now find themselves involved with the public in any number of ways when considering a policy decision or the development of a policy direction. This could include canvassing public attitudes toward a policy, participating in a consensus conference where policy makers must negotiate a policy position in collaboration with both scientific and public members, or sitting on stakeholder working groups whose members represent a wide range of opinions in relation to a policy area.

These activities go against much historical experience in environmental regulation. As Harvard professor Sheila Jasanoff (1990) noted in a landmark study of scientific advisory committees in the United States, policy development throughout much of the twentieth century involved turning over policy decisions to legions of scientific advisors. She refers to this as the creation of a technocracy in US government; that is, governance by facts. While this process is often motivated by the need to improve efficiency and efficacy in public policy, the consequence is that technocracy isolates social and political debates from policy decisions made by experts. Engagement in environmental governance is one possible way to open up these processes.

What values could engagement bring to the environmental regulation, and what contributions can the public make in these venues? First, it is possible to see the public as knowledgeable actors. This is not to say that they have a mastery of scientific and technical knowledge, or even a related form of formal expertise (for example, social scientific or ethical expertise). The public can, however, provide alternative ways of thinking about issues that are useful in making policy decisions. For instance, in regulating the use of chemical pesticides and herbicides, farmers have experiential knowledge about the ways in which a chemical is applied, the conditions that impact its proper application, and how the use of the chemical deviates from the intended norms (Irwin 1995, 112–113). Second, public participation may be able to bring a greater degree of social accountability to the policy process. For example, in a study of the inclusion of laypeople on scientific advisory bodies conducted by Kevin Jones and Alan Irwin in Britain, committee members were found to value the roles of nonscientists as "public witnesses" to the application of science, or as a way to ensure that policy advice was not esoteric but was

grounded in the real world (Jones and Irwin 2010). And, third, public engagement is seen as a way to reframe policy approaches away from a technical focus on the possible risks and their management and toward the underlying social, moral, and political choices that may lead to the creation of hazards. Environmental policy is rarely based on absolutes but rather on balances between potential risks and potential benefits in very complex and uncertain contexts. The benefits of permitting an activity with uncertain environmental consequences (for example, genetic modification) are weighed against potential, equally as uncertain benefits to economic development and social prosperity. Technocratic approaches to regulation have by and large tended to support economic interests over precautionary approaches to risk. Public engagement is sometimes imagined as a way of rebalancing these types of debates.

It is difficult to assess whether experiments in public engagement represent a clear move away from deficit approaches to scientific citizenship. Critics argue that engagement has failed to fundamentally alter institutional and governmental approaches to scientific knowledge. More damning still, some commentators suggest that current engagement activities have actually further entrenched deficit approaches—by granting an aura of social legitimacy to what remain largely exclusionary policy systems, for example. Alan Irwin, a British-Danish sociologist who has written extensively on scientific citizenship and engagement, suggests that a fairer characterization is that policy systems blend both old and new thinking about the public (Irwin 2006). By outlining a model of scientific citizenship that is in a changing relationship with current policy practice, Irwin seeks to motivate scientists, governments, and the public to continue to experiment with imperfect forms of engagement to create the possibility for further change.

Outlook

Citizen science remains a relevant and essential way to engage the complex, difficult, and multifaceted challenges facing society. Although these relations have been bounded in the past by privileged visions of science based on the autonomy of knowledge, today opportunities for more balanced and meaningful engagements are opening up. The prospect of expanding citizenship is rooted in the recognition of the limits of science, as well as the strength of the public. What these openings mean for the future will depend on the ongoing commitments of both the public and scientists to engage each other and to construct shared understandings of the place of scientific knowledge in society.

Kevin Edson JONES
University of Alberta

See also Challenges to Measuring Sustainability; Community and Stakeholder Input; Environmental Justice Indicators; Focus Groups; Intergovernmental Science-Policy Platform on Biodiversity and Ecosystem Services (IPBES); New Ecological Paradigm (NEP) Scale; Participatory Action Research; Quantitative vs. Qualitative Studies; Regional Planning; Risk Assessment; Sustainability Science; Systems Thinking

FURTHER READING

Beck, Ulrich. (1992). *Risk society: Towards a new modernity.* London: Sage.

Beck, Ulrich. (1998). Politics of risk society. In Jane Franklin (Ed.), *The politics of risk society* (pp. 9–22). Cambridge, UK: Polity Press.

Giddens, Anthony. (1990). *The consequences of modernity.* Cambridge, UK: Polity Press.

Grint, Keith, & Woolgar, Steve. (1997). *The machine at work: Technology, work and organization.* Cambridge, UK: Polity Press.

Haldane, John Burdon Sanderson. (1941). *Science in everyday life.* London, Penguin.

Hogben, Lancelot. (1938). *Science for the citizen.* Woking, UK: Unwin Brothers.

Irwin, Alan. (1995). *Citizen science: A study of people, expertise and sustainable development.* London: Routledge.

Irwin, Alan. (2001). Constructing the scientific citizen: Science and democracy in the biosciences. *Public Understanding of Science, 10*(1), 1–18.

Irwin, Alan. (2006). The politics of talk: Coming to terms with the "new" scientific governance. *Social Studies of Science, 36*(2), 299–320.

Irwin, Alan, & Wynne, Brian. (Eds.). (1996). *Misunderstanding science? The public reconstruction of science and technology.* Cambridge, UK: Cambridge University Press.

Jasanoff, Sheila. (1990). *The fifth branch: Science advisers as policy makers.* Cambridge, MA: Harvard University Press.

Jones, Kevin E. (2004). BSE and the Phillips' Report: A cautionary tale about the uptake of "risk." In Nico Stehr (Ed.), *The governance of knowledge* (pp. 161–186). New Brunswick, NJ: Transaction Books.

Jones, Kevin E., & Irwin, Alan. (2010). Creating space for engagement? Lay membership in contemporary risk governance. In Bridget M. Hutter (Ed.), *Anticipating risks and organising risk regulation* (pp. 185–207). Cambridge, UK: Cambridge University Press.

Lezaun, Javier, & Soneryd, Linda. (2007). Consulting citizens: Technologies of elicitation and the mobility of publics. *Public Understanding of Science, 16*(3), 279–297.

Mulkay, Michael. (1976). Norms and ideology in science. *Social Science Information, 15*(4–5), 637–656.

Nelkin, Dorothy. (1995). *Selling science: How the press covers science and technology* (Rev. ed.). New York: W. H. Freeman & Company.

Nowotny, Helga; Scott, Peter; & Gibbons, Michael. (2001). *Re-thinking science: Knowledge and the public in an age of uncertainty.* Cambridge, UK: Polity Press.

Rothstein, Henry. (2007). Talking shop or talking turkey? Institutionalizing consumer representation in risk regulation. *Science, Technology and Human Values, 32*(5), 582–607.

Rowe, Gene, & Frewer, Lynn J. (2000). Public participation methods: A framework for evaluation. *Science, Technology and Human Values, 25*(1), 3–29.

Royal Society. (1985). *The public understanding of science.* London: Royal Society.

Snow, Charles Percy. (1998). *The two cultures.* Cambridge, UK: Cambridge University Press.

Stirling, Andy. (2008). Opening up and closing down: Power, participation, and pluralism in the social appraisal of technology. *Science, Technology and Human Values, 33*(2), 262–294.

Turner, Stephen. (2008). The social study of science before Kuhn. In Edward J. Hacket, Olga Amsterdamska, Michael Lynch & Judy Wajcman (Eds.), *The handbook of science and technology studies* (3rd ed., pp. 33–62). Cambridge, MA: MIT Press.

Williams, Raymond. (1976). *Keywords: A vocabulary of culture and society.* New York: Oxford University Press.

Wynne, Brian. (1992). Public understanding of science research: New horizons or hall of mirrors? *Public Understanding of Science, 1*(1), 37–43.

Wynne, Brian. (1996). Misunderstood misunderstandings: Social identities and public uptake of science. In Alan Irwin & Brian Wynne (Eds.), *Misunderstanding science? The public reconstruction of science and technology* (pp.19–46). Cambridge, UK: Cambridge University Press.

Wynne, Brian. (2001). Creating public alienation: Expert cultures of risk and ethics on GMOs. *Science as Culture, 10*(4), 445–481.

Wynne, Brian. (2006). Public engagement as a means of restoring public trust in science: Hitting the notes, but missing the music? *Community Genetics, 9*(3), 211–220.

Community and Stakeholder Input

In order for governments to manage their environments sustainably into the future, they require the integration of diverse knowledge. Involving communities in project management recognizes the value of different forms of knowledge, enabling a range of information, views, and experience to be incorporated into plans and increase long-term project success. For this reason, governments increasingly seek to embed community involvement in policy and decision making.

Managing ecosystems effectively is an information-intensive endeavor requiring an in-depth understanding of social–ecological interactions. It is therefore almost impossible for a small number of people to possess the depth of knowledge required to make effective and holistic management decisions. Instead, in order to draw on the diverse information needed, environmental managers must involve a complex mix of individuals and organizations that span society at different levels. Often this mix is referred to as "community" (defined here as a social group of any size with members residing in a specific locality, with common cultural and historical backgrounds) or "stakeholders" (defined here as people not directly doing the work of a project but who are affected by it, or can influence it).

Many sources show that an approach to sustainability that involves community input enables a greater depth and quality of information to be accessed and incorporated into environmental management plans. This in turn increases the sustainability of social–ecological systems, enabling them to better respond to change and stresses rapidly and effectively.

The success of sustainability initiatives is likely where there has been a transfer of discretionary powers from the government to local leaders to allow them to make meaningful decisions (Brechin et al. 2003). Involving and

empowering the community fosters a greater sense of ownership in environmental projects, which can have substantial benefits, particularly where members of local communities use or manage important habitats or sites. Community involvement can also lead to greater political and financial support for sustainability objectives (Weston et al. 2003). Projects involving the community create a sense of local and even national pride in areas where members of the public have worked together to conserve and restore (Giddings and Shaw 2000; Lane and McDonald 2005; Shi et al. 2005). Additionally, community input allows better community bonding and sense of belonging, increased self-esteem of participants due to improved knowledge about local habitats and species, and skill expansion (Giddings and Shaw 2000; Evely et al. 2010; Evely et al. 2011).

History

The involvement of local communities in environmental management has been embedded in policy for longer than many people realize. Government policy (and in some cases law) arising in the post-1987 era of sustainable development called for great participation of affected communities. In 1992 the UN Conference on Environment and Development stressed the importance of community involvement in environmental sustainability initiatives, and the need to decentralize decision making in order to find local-level solutions to environmental problems. As a result, 179 countries later accepted the Rio Declaration and its related plan of action, Agenda 21, which increased community participation in environmental decision making worldwide.

Definitions of community participation in environmental management have all included the notions of contributing, influencing, sharing, or redistributing power, and the control of resources, benefits, knowledge, and skills gained through involvement (Narayan-Parker 1996). Within this shared conceptual basis, community participation can be of two opposite types: top-down programs or bottom-up initiatives. The difference lies in who has overall control of the program—governments or implementing agencies, or the communities themselves.

The top-down model has a significant philosophical and practice history, predating the bottom-up model, and is structured around the use of externally provided professional leadership that plans, implements, and evaluates development programs. Community development programs using the top-down model typically focus on providing professional leadership to the development process, coupled with supportive concrete services.

Literature on top-down community participation states that the top (e.g., government) invites local people to become involved in projects (see Scoones and Thompson 1994; Rocheleau 1994). In general, this involvement is advocated for three reasons. The first is to increase project efficiency using local community participation to improve local support for the process and its outcomes (Beierle 2002; Richards, Blackstock, and Carter 2004). The second aims at empowerment and regards participation as a fundamental right of the community (Pretty 1995). The third is to access the local, tacit knowledge held by communities.

Practitioners using the bottom-up model, in which the community leads and develops the process, are informed by social development theory. Here, participation in community-wide discussions, improved opportunities to learn, and the sense of empowerment that comes with knowledge are the necessary precursors to accomplishing the stated and implied goals of community development.

Origins of Stakeholder Involvement

What is considered acceptable in terms of community involvement has changed over time. In the late 1960s, the focus was on raising awareness; then, in the 1970s, incorporating local views into data collection and planning became important. In the 1980s, a series of techniques were developed to better and more equally incorporate local knowledge into decision making. By the 1990s, community involvement had become an accepted item on the sustainable development agenda (Reed 2008).

Evaluation of past approaches has led to greater consensus on current best practices and approaches to community involvement. Yet, whether a top-down or bottom-up approach is taken has differed according to world context. Within the developed world, community involvement via public consultation (a more top-down approach) grew in popularity, whereas in the developing world, more action-oriented, site-specific bottom-up approaches were advocated (Lawrence 2006). Present approaches to community input see the developed world applying and learning from the participatory methods and approaches used by the developing world (Dougill et al. 2006; Stringer et al. 2006).

Controversies

Internationally, community involvement is increasingly sought and embedded into environmental decision-making processes, from local to governmental scales (e.g., Stringer et al. 2006). Participatory approaches in natural resource management can bridge knowledge systems (e.g., local ecological and scientific knowledge), enable knowledge to flow across scales, empower local people, speed adaptation, enhance human capital, and increase the likelihood of resource management goals being met (Chambers 2002; McAllister 1999; Ludwig, Mangel, and Haddad 2001; Folke, Colding, and Berkes 2003). The many claimed benefits of stakeholder participation have to an extent driven its widespread incorporation into national and international policy. At the same time, disillusionment has been growing among practitioners, stakeholders, and the wider public, who feel let down when these claims are not realized.

There is growing concern that stakeholder participation is not living up to many of the claims made. Stakeholder participation does not take place in a power vacuum: the empowerment of previously marginalized groups may have unexpected and potentially negative interactions with existing power structures (Kothari 2001). Community involvement can reinforce existing privileges, and group dynamics may discourage minority perspectives from being expressed (Nelson and Wright 1995), creating "dysfunctional consensus" (Cooke 2001, 19). Consultation fatigue may develop as a result of community members being increasingly asked to take part in poorly designed and executed processes, where involvement gains little reward or capacity to influence decisions (Burton et al. 2004; Wondolleck and Yaffee 2000). As a result, we may see declining levels of engagement as people question the credibility of processes. Likewise they may question the credibility of processes involving the community, as many stakeholders are without sufficient expertise to meaningfully engage in technical debates. Although community involvement may improve the quality of environmental decisions, the quality of a decision strongly depends on the quality of the process that leads to it.

Long-Term Outlook

People play an important role in nurturing or eroding sustainability, as they have the ability to learn from their own and others' experiences (Evely et al. 2011; Fazey et al. 2007; Reed et al. 2010). As a result, management strategies for environmental sustainability that are most likely to be durable in the long term are those that can accommodate both uncertainty and change. There is a growing body of literature that suggests that the combination of local and scientific knowledge may empower local communities to monitor and manage environmental change easily and accurately (e.g., Reed and Dougill 2002; Stringer and Reed 2007; Reed, Dougill, and Taylor 2007; Ingram 2008; Reed et al. 2010).

The durability of management decisions can be promoted through understanding ecosystem dynamics and integrating the knowledge of social and ecological scientists, local communities, and interest groups into management strategies. Strategies that remain flexible and open to knowledge integration and learning may build the adaptive capacity (i.e., the ability to deal flexibly with new situations) of both individual participants and projects as a whole. By combining the knowledge of a diversity of individuals, management can be improved even in the face of much uncertainty and limited information (Gunderson and Holling 2002; Kates et al. 2001). This is because within this diversity there exists greater understanding of the complex spatial and temporal links between ecological, social, and economic aspects of systems (Kates et al. 2001) than would be possible if the project was managed from a single discipline's perspective.

Learning may emerge as a result of a participatory process (Blackstock, Kelly, and Horsey 2007). Participation that has an iterative and interactive dimension is believed to have the most potential for learning among participants of very different world views (Reed

2008; Evely et al. 2011). By establishing common ground and trust, participants may learn to value the viewpoints of others, thereby transforming negative relationships into positive ones (Stringer 2006). Such learning may develop an individual's adaptive capacity and process of sense making (i.e., understanding of complex social–ecological systems and problems), which are essential features in the management of complex social–ecological systems (Evely et al. 2011).

Implications

Flexible approaches involving a diversity of individuals are better adapted for long-term sustainability than rigid approaches, because, through a greater focus on learning, management can influence slow-moving fundamental variables, such as the experience, memory, and diversity of both social and ecological systems, to better cope with change (Gunderson and Holling 2002; Holling 1978; Lee 1993). Learning is one of the major outcomes of knowledge integration by community involvement (Evely et al. 2011). It has been argued that those participating in the management of social–ecological systems may learn, and their adaptive capacity may increase, as a result of their involvement (Fazey et al. 2007; Folke et al. 2005). The more integrated the participants are with others and in management decisions, the more likely we are to see fundamental changes in how they view environmental management (as a complex process instead of a simple one), in their confidence to manage such systems, and in their understanding and respect for the views of others (Evely et al. 2011). In this way, taking a specific participatory approach over another type may be a means to change attitudes, behavior, and ultimately underlying philosophies more effectively than could otherwise be achieved.

Anna Clair EVELY
University of St. Andrews

See also Challenges to Measuring Sustainability; Citizen Science; Focus Groups; New Ecological Paradigm (NEP) Scale; Participatory Action Research; Quantitative vs. Qualitative Studies; Social Network Analysis (SNA); Systems Thinking

FURTHER READING

Beierle, Thomas C. (2002). The quality of stakeholder-based decisions. *Risk Analysis, 22*(4), 739–749.

Berkes, Fikret; Colding, Johan; & Folke, Carl (Eds.). (2003). *Navigating social-ecological systems: Building resilience for complexity and change.* Cambridge, UK: Cambridge University Press.

Blackstock, K. L.; Kelly, G. J.; & Horsey, B. L. (2007). Developing and applying a framework to evaluate participatory research for sustainability. *Ecological Economics, 60,* 726–742.

Brechin, Steven R.; Wilshusen, Peter R.; Fortwangler, Crystal L.; & West, Patrick C. (Eds.). (2003). *Contested nature: Promoting international biodiversity with social justice in the twenty-first century.* Albany: State University of New York Press.

Burton, Paul, et al. (2004). *What works in community involvement in area-based initiatives? A systematic review of the literature.* London: University of Bristol and University of Glasgow.

Chambers, Robert. (2002). *Participatory workshops: A sourcebook of 21 sets of ideas and activities.* London: Earthscan Publications.

Cooke, Bill. (2001). The social psychological limits of participation? In Bill Cooke & Uma Kothari (Eds.), *Participation: The new tyranny?* (pp. 102–121). London: Zed Books.

Dougill, Andrew J., et al. (2006). Learning from doing participatory rural research: Lessons from the Peak District National Park. *Journal of Agricultural Economics, 57,* 259–275.

Evely, Anna C., et al. (2010). Defining and evaluating the impact of cross-disciplinary conservation research. *Environmental Conservation, 37,* 442–450.

Evely, Anna C.; Pinard, Michelle; Reed, Mark S.; & Fazey, Ioan. (2011). High levels of participation in conservation projects enhance learning. *Conservation Letters, 4*(2), 116–126.

Fazey, Ioan; Fazey, John A.; & Fazey, Della M. A. (2005). Learning more effectively from experience. *Ecology and Society, 10*(2), Article 4. Retrieved June 27, 2011, from http://www.ecologyandsociety.org/vol10/iss2/art4/

Fazey, Ioan, et al. (2007). Adaptive capacity and learning to learn as leverage for social-ecological resilience. *Frontiers in Ecology and Environment, 5,* 375–380.

Folke, Carl; Colding, Johan; & Berkes, Fikret. (2003). Synthesis: Building resilience and adaptive capacity in social-ecological systems. In Fikret Berkes, Johan Colding & Carl Folke (Eds.), *Navigating social-ecological systems: Building resilience for complexity and change* (pp. 352–387). Cambridge, UK: Cambridge University Press.

Folke, Carl; Hahn, Thomas; Olsson, Per; & Norberg, Jon. (2005). Adaptive governance of social-ecological systems. *Annual Review of Environmental Resources, 30,* 441–473.

Forester, John. (1999). *The deliberative practitioner: Encouraging participatory planning processes.* London: MIT Press.

Giddings, Bob, & Shaw, Keith. (2000). Community regeneration projects in Britain. Retrieved November 13, 2011, from http://www.sustainable-cities.org.uk/db_docs/comregen.pdf Gittell, Marilyn. (1980). *Limits of citizen participation: The decline of community organizations.* Beverly Hills, CA: Sage Publications.

Gunderson, Lance H., & Holling, C. S. (Eds.). (2002). *Panarchy: Understanding transformations in human and natural systems.* Washington, DC: Island Press.

Holling, C. S. (Ed.). (1978). Adaptive environmental assessment and management. New York: John Wiley.

Ingram, Julie. (2008) Agronomist-farmer knowledge encounters: an analysis of knowledge exchange in the context of best management practices in England. *Agriculture and Human Values, 25*(3), 405–418.

Kates, Robert W., et al. (2001). Environment and development—Sustainability science. *Science, 292,* 641–642.

Kothari, Uma. (2001). Power, knowledge and social control in participatory development. In Bill Cooke & Uma Kothari (Eds.), *Participation: The new tyranny?* (pp. 139–152). London: Zed Books.

Lane, Marcus B., & McDonald, Geoff. (2005). Community based environmental planning: Operational dilemmas, planning principles and possible remedies. *Environmental Planning and Management, 48,* 709–731.

Lawrence, Anna. (2006). No personal motive? Volunteers, biodiversity, and the false dichotomies of participation. *Ethics, Place and Environment, 9,* 279–298.

Lee, Kai N. (1993). *Compass and gyroscope: Integrating science and politics for the environment.* Washington, DC: Island Press.

Ludwig, Donald; Mangel, Marc, & Haddad, Brent. (2001). Ecology, conservation, and public policy. *Annual Review of Ecology and Systematics, 32,* 481–517.

McAllister, Karen. (1999). *Understanding participation: Monitoring and evaluating process, outputs and outcomes.* Ottawa, Canada: International Development Research Centre.

Narayan-Parker, Deepa. (1996). *Toward participatory research.* Washington, DC: World Bank.

Nelson, Nici, & Wright, Susan. (1995). *Power and participatory development: Theory and practice.* London: Intermediate Technology Publications.

Pretty, Jules N. (1995). Participatory learning for sustainable agriculture. *World Development, 23,* 1247–1263.

Raskin, Paul, et al. (2002). *Great transition: The promise and lure of the times ahead* (Report of the Global Scenario Group, SEI PoleStar Series Report No. 10). Boston: Stockholm Environment Institute.

Raymond, Christopher M., et al. (2010). Integrating local and scientific knowledge for environmental management. *Journal of Environmental Management, 91*(8), 1766–1777.

Reed, Mark S. & Dougill, Andrew J. (2002) Participatory selection process for indicators of rangeland condition in the Kalahari. *Geographical Journal, 168,* 224–234.

Reed, Mark S.; Dougill, Andrew J.; & Taylor M. J. (2007). Integrating local and scientific knowledge for adaptation to land degradation: Kalahari rangeland management options. *Land Degradation & Development, 18,* 249–268.

Reed, Mark. S. (2008). Stakeholder participation for environmental management: A literature review. *Biological Conservation, 141*(10), 2417–2431.

Reed, Mark S., et al. (2010). What is social learning? *Ecology and Society, 15*(4), Response 1. Retrieved June 27, 2011, from http://www.ecologyandsociety.org/vol15/iss4/resp1/

Richards, Caspian; Blackstock, Kirsty L.; & Carter, Claudia E. (2004). *Practical approaches to participation* (SERG Policy Brief 1). Aberdeen, UK: Macauley Land Use Research Institute.

Rocheleau, Dianne E. (1994). Participatory research and the race to save the planet: Questions, critique, and lessons from the field. *Agriculture and Human Values, 11,* 4–25.

Scoones, Ian, & Thompson, John. (Eds.). (1994). *Beyond farmer first: Rural people's knowledge, agricultural research and extension practice.* London: Intermediate Technology Publications, Ltd.

Shi, Hua; Singh, Ashibindu; Kant, Shashi; Zhu, Zhilliang; & Waller, Eric. (2005). Integrating habitat status, human population pressure and protection status into biodiversity conservation priority setting. *Conservation Biology, 19,* 1273–1285.

Stringer, Lindsay C., et al. (2006). Unpacking "participation" in the adaptive management of socio-ecological systems: A critical review. *Ecology and Society, 11*(2), Article 39. Retrieved June 27, 2011, from http://www.ecologyandsociety.org/vol11/iss2/art39/

Stringer, Lindsay C., & Reed, Mark S. (2007). Land degradation assessment in southern Africa: Integrating local and scientific knowledge bases. *Land Degradation & Development, 18,* 99–116.

Weston, Michael; Fendley, Michael; Jewell, Robyn; Satchell, Mary; & Tzaros, Chris. (2003). Volunteers in bird conservation: Insights from the Australian Threatened Bird Network. *Ecological Management and Restoration, 4,* 205–211.

Wondolleck, Julia M., & Yaffee, Steven L. (2000). *Making collaboration work: Lessons from innovation in natural resource management.* Washington, DC: Island Press.

Computer Modeling

Computer simulation models that couple human and ecosystem systems provide a comprehensive and effective way to evaluate ecosystem services, sustainability, and human and social well-being from many different perspectives. Several modeling platforms focus on the field of sustainability. These computer models can provide predictive solutions to aid in sustainable management by balancing human use with ecosystem protection.

Computer simulation models, coupled with human and ecosystem indicators and measurements, provide researchers with the tools necessary to evaluate issues of sustainability. Several predictive models sustainably manage the balance between human use and ecosystem function and protection. These models incorporate advanced spatial technologies (computer programs that interact with actual geographic information) that provide a far more realistic view of ecosystem function and sustainable practices than their predecessors.

Functions

Models help ecologists understand complex problems such as deforestation or climate change through the identification of variables or external factors that affect the ecology of an area. Researchers can study the variables' interactions and relationships over time and space. Models help capture relationships and explore patterns of both existing and future conditions. Models are only a representation of real-world systems; they are a human construct to help researchers better understand those systems. The Belgian philosopher Robert Franck (2002) requires that models possess the following characteristics and/or perform the following functions:

- provide a simplified representation of the reality;
- represent what is considered to be essential to this reality;
- be testable;
- become the object of study (under the scientific approach);
- be conceptual;
- allow the possibility of measurement and calculation;
- allow explanation of the reality;
- be a fictive representation of the reality; and
- represent the functioning of real-world systems.

Computer models were once defined as simplifications of the real world. According to the Taiwanese ecologist Hsin Chi, "Oversimplified models will never represent real ecosystems" (Chi 2000, 164). As models constructed to derive sustainable solutions become more complex, ecologists, economists, conservation biologists, and many other economic, social, and landscape disciplines must cooperate. Models have played an important role in aiding decision making in the context of ecological problems in the past and will play an even more important a role as the twenty-first century unfolds (Chi 2000). There is a critical need to ensure that these complex models adequately address the integral connection between humans and their environments. Any model developed with sustainability as its goal must focus on the linkages between the economy, society, and the environment (i.e., ecosystem function).

Since 2000 there has been a dramatic increase in the use of a comprehensive set of models tackling this issue of sustainability. These models are spatially dynamic—that is, they focus on examining complex spatial dynamic patterns across a landscape. They evaluate human and landscape interactions over space and time. Through the testing of a variety of future scenarios, these models have also been used to assess sustainability and evaluate trade-offs that aid in decision making. As the British geographer Erik Swyngedouw notes, "As issues surrounding sustainability become of increasing concern, especially in the context of a changing climate, it becomes ever more important to understand how humans are affecting and responding to their environments" (Swyngedouw 2004, 41).

Although not all ecological problems require the integration of human-landscape interactions, those that fall within the realm of sustainability—complex problems such as fire dynamics or watershed management—are likely to be highly integrative (i.e., require input from a variety of disciplines), complex (i.e., some variables are difficult to measure), and nonlinear (i.e., the behavior of a system is dynamic and cannot be easily predicted). This scenario is especially true with problems where human decision making affects the landscape over time. The ecological community views the landscape as dynamic—changing over space and time—whereas they perceive humans as the agents that affect and change the landscape (Fox et al. 2003). Funding agencies around the globe and many in the ecological research community need to examine such complex, integrative issues of sustainability (such as fire management and restoration, human-wildlife interactions) with models.

New modeling techniques significantly improve decision making. They can be applied to complex, integrative problems to derive sustainable solutions. These models incorporate new methods, evolving technologies, and techniques for deriving spatial and temporal solutions to the problems of sustainability. Evolving technologies include the use of spatial agents (humans, cars, boats, etc.), remote sensing (using airplanes or satellites to gather information), geographic information systems (for gathering information about events on Earth), neural networks (statistical modeling tools based on biological models), Bayesian belief networks (statistical methods that assign probabilities before experimentation), and many others. Specifically, geographic information systems (GIS)

capture, store, manipulate, analyze, manage, and present all types of geographically referenced data. These systems coupled with an arsenal of techniques mentioned above have improved our ability to understand the simultaneous interactions between human and natural systems such as those with a focus on resilience (i.e., the ability of ecosystems to bounce back after disruption). Coupling these techniques has provided the research and decision-making community with a much more robust set of tools to examine problems of sustainability.

Spatial Agent–Based Modeling Approaches

Spatial-agent modeling is a form of modeling that represents such things as humans or cars as a set of individual agents that have rules that allow them to interact with a landscape (represented in GIS) and each other in space and time. Agents are surrogates for humans or other entities such as cars, boats, airplanes, and other mobile objects. They are represented as sprites that dynamically move around on the screen or raster cells that can change color in response to some set of conditions. Most agents exhibit spatial behavior, mobility, spatial learning, and adaptation. Models based on spatial-agent modeling can solve complex spatial dynamic problems such as understanding visitor behavior in protected areas, transportation systems, and fire management.

While much research focuses on spatial agent–based simulations (Gimblett 2002; Parker et al. 2003), two approaches dominate: agent-based models linked to land-use/land-cover change (LUCC) and agent-based models (ABM) linked to geographic information systems. Methods for collecting human or household data commonly link these approaches. Both approaches derive and implement behavioral rules (rules that determine how they act and interact with the landscape and with other agents). These rules can be imposed at multiple scales, such as a global scale (responding to a storm event) or at local scales (determining which direction to move along a trail). These are behavioral rules because the agents will move, interact, and change their behavior according to the situation they are in. For example, certain agents might modify their behavior if they encounter a certain level of other agents in a specific location by leaving and seeking a less crowded place. Their shared goal is to develop accurate simulations to allow managers and planners to make decisions. They provide the opportunity to model and test a variety of scenarios at many different space and time scales, making this model a flexible and powerful tool for decision making.

These modeling approaches differ, however, in the types of agents that researchers develop. For example agents can be autonomous where they move around on the GIS-represented landscape in a Pac-Man-type fashion: responding to rules, changing directions, or seeking out new locations. They can also be stationary, where the raster cells do not move but simply alter their color in response to changing conditions. For example, an agent cell might change its color from green while moving to red, indicating that it is resting; if the spatial location is vacated, it might turn white, indicating that it has changed its behavior. In addition, these models use GIS data structures that represent the landscape features captured in cells or pixels. The entire landscape that is being modeled is represented as a continuous surface or one large set of cells. The other data structure commonly used is a set of nodes and a topological (interconnected) network of linear elements. These linear elements could be roads, rivers, or trails, while the nodes along the network could represent such elements as campsites, seating areas, lookouts, and parking lots or spaces. Both of these model types use these data structures and agents to model ecosystem and human dynamics together. This integrative approach provides opportunities to examine ecosystem and human dynamics systems simultaneously and explore sustainable land management solutions.

Land-Use and Land-Cover Change Models

Land-use and land-cover change (LUCC) models emerged as a central controversy in the broader debate about global change, a debate that has its origins in the concerns about human-induced impacts on the environment and their implications for climate change.

Desertification, a land degradation problem common to the arid regions of the world, is a good example of human-induced impacts on the environment. Deterioration in soil and plant cover has adversely affected land cover as humans have mismanaged cultivated and range lands. Climate change dramatically increases this problem through continued drought and drying conditions. Land use and management practices drive land cover change. These practices are a function of environmental opportunities and constraints but also of a complex web of social, economic, and political processes. Researchers who work on large- and medium-scale land-cover conversions (for example, deforestation) in tropical ecosystems, have so far received the bulk of attention because of their prominent role in global biogeochemical cycling (a circuit or pathway by which a chemical element moves through an ecosystem), one of the "big issues" of land-use and land-cover change science (Skole et al. 1994). These models have been successfully used to improve our understanding of land-use and land-cover science.

The complexity inherent in the human-environment system and the diversity of real-world situations, even within a local setting, challenge modeling human-environment interactions and resulting land-cover changes. LUCC models that incorporate spatial agent–based models integrated with GIS and time-series remote sensing (repeat data collected remotely from satellites revolving around the Earth's surface that provide an opportunity to compare cells over time to detect changes) are subsequently used to model land-use and land-cover changes to assess the degradation or potential for regeneration. Vegetation change over time is a good example of a variable that would be measured using time-series data. Spatial agents representing individual landowners, households, or governing institutions embedded in an environment can aid in evaluating how land use changes have occurred. Researchers could examine farmers clearing vegetation from their land over decades, for example, to measure increased water runoff leading to sedimentation increase in nearby rivers. The spatial dimension provided by the remote sensing data and raster GIS datasets (a set of pixels or square cells that represent various features of a landscape, e.g., vegetation, topography, hydrology, etc.) allows the research community to ask the questions about why and how landscapes are changing and to evaluate the spatial location or proximity in which it is occurring. This information has many advantages when developing site-specific, long-term planning and monitoring strategies (Gimblett 2005).

The advantage of the LUCC approach is that researchers can assess the human dimension of land use, cover change, and degradation at the level of individual households as decision makers and at the level of the larger socioeconomic context in which these decisions are made. This approach to examining sustainability has succeeded in several settings. Researchers have examined the prospects for the prevention of deforestation in the Brazilian Amazon (Lim et al. 2002; Deadman et al. 2004). They have combined biophysical factors such as climate and topography in the context of deforestation with agent-based modeling to simulate land-cover change. This approach has proven valuable in examining sustainable land tenure, reducing deforestation, and improving the local way of life.

The US anthropologist J. Stephen Lansing (1996) examined a change in the traditional way of life of Balinese farmers. They have lived and grown rice sustainably for thousands of years. A new government ordered Balinese farmers to abandon their traditional water irrigation schedules in favor of a new approach using fertilizers and pesticides in an effort to increase rice production. After only a brief increase in productivity, crops dwindled drastically and fell prey to water shortages and vermin infestation. Lansing built and implemented an agent-based model to compare the old and new systems using historical rainfall data. He concluded that the traditional water irrigation schedules were far more effective than the government's policy. The government allowed Balinese rice farmers to return to the system that had served them well for over a thousand years. This result is an excellent demonstration of an integrated approach that links anthropological data into a more holistic, sustainable approach to ecological and agronomic problems

ABM-GIS Links on Linear Networks

Researchers using spatial agent–based models linked directly to geographical information systems using a topological data structure (connected linear networks and nodes) have successfully studied complex systems using agents that represent wildlife species to study population dynamics, vehicles to evaluate urbanization processes, and humans to evaluate human movement and behavior (Itami and Zanon 2003; Gimblett 2002; Batty, Desyllas, and Duxbury 2003). These simulations link the agents that represent the phenomenon being modeled

(i.e., humans, cars, animals, etc.) with landscape characteristics (i.e., roads, trails, and other linear networks such as patterns of human movement, etc.). Spatially explicit models employ autonomous agents that individually move around on the network. The US mathematician Stan Franklin calls spatially explicit agents "a system situated within and part of an environment that senses that environment and acts on it, over time, in pursuit of its own agenda and so as to affect what it senses (and acts on) in the future" (Franklin and Graessner 1996). Spatially explicit agents share the following attributes:

- They live in "geographic" space.
- They move according the principles of physics and physiology.
- They act on objects or other agents according to location, speed, or meaning.
- They realize objectives through spatial movement and location.
- They have rules that comprise triggers or events generated by changes in the internal state of the agent, changes in the network, or changes in global events.

Many of these simulations use behavioral data researchers collect in the field to generate agents from a variety of sources such as traffic and trail counters, global positioning systems, radio frequency technology (tagging an object and following it through radio frequencies), diaries, human observation, and local stakeholder knowledge. The researchers use the knowledge they gain from the models to frame both global and local rules that mimic human decision-making processes (Gimblett and Skov-Petersen 2008). Simulating existing baseline conditions using this type of field data allows the models to mimic patterns of human use across the landscape. Researchers enter data into the simulation. The model visualizes, measures, and assesses human use and interactions along linear networks and nodes. A database captures these dynamic interactions. Researchers then use time-series statistical approaches (specific statistical analysis procedures that evaluate space and time data such as spatial autocorrelation, a spatial measure of the degree of dependency among observations in a geographic space) to evaluate the data.

This simulation provides an opportunity for decision makers to explore the possible change of human patterns over time in different scenarios. It provides mechanisms to identify points of overcrowding, bottlenecks in circulation systems, peak periods of use, conflicts between different human user groups, and many other social or ecological indicators. Researchers can acquire a statistically representative sample of field data that captures both spatial and temporal variability of travel patterns. They can then develop simulations for making long-term, highly reliable predictions.

Since 1990, planners have used agent-based modeling to guide sustainability decision making and actions. The Australian environmental planner Robert Itami (2008) provides an elegant solution to a complex transportation problem in Melbourne, Australia. He combined the input of local users (stakeholders) with agent-based simulations to develop a vessel traffic management plan for the Yarra and Maribyrnong rivers in a busy, multiuse urban waterway. The plan accommodates the predicted increasing river traffic between 2013 and 2018. The plan maintains safety and a high quality recreational experience while it minimizes environmental and social impacts.

The Application of Sustainability Models

Researchers using models have incorporated spatial agent–based simulations with social science methodologies to engage stakeholders. They thus have developed a robust way to obtain insight into people's differing definitions of the quality of their experiences (such as experiencing nature, viewing wildlife, or simply walking along a trail), the impact of vessel traffic densities on their experience, and indications for sustainable management directions from them. The results of stakeholder workshops provide refined information that is useful for modeling and lend support to more traditional social science methodologies and provide strategic and tactical guidance to managers. By providing a strong user-based approach to capacity (understanding how many people are appropriate in a landscape without causing conflicts or irreversible impacts), planners can increase their understanding of scenario planning and gain constituent response and reaction. These applications have provided a transparent method for developing sustainable management strategies. This more collaborative nature of stakeholder involvement results in a more holistic and sustainable approach to land management. These applications put modeling and simulation into local action to solve complex social/ecological/economic problems and aid and inform decision making and the development of sustainable solutions.

The Future

In order to understand the ecosystem function and resiliency to human-driven change, computer models will continue to play a significant role in the future. Models that explore the coupling of human and natural systems using rules that govern land-use decisions and ecological models representing landscape change will ultimately lead to more informed decision making. Through a collaborative partnership with stakeholders, the modeling and implementation of alternative scenarios will result in a more holistic and sustainable approach to land management.

Randy GIMBLETT
University of Arizona

See also Challenges to Measuring Sustainability; Community and Stakeholder Input; Cost-Benefit Analysis; Ecological Impact Assessment (EcIA); Environmental Performance Index (EPI); Framework for Strategic Sustainable Development (FSSD); Geographic Information Systems (GIS); Land-Use and Land-Cover Change; *The Limits to Growth*; Regional Planning; Remote Sensing; Social Network Analysis (SNA); Sustainability Science

FURTHER READING

Batty, Michael; Desyllas, Jake; & Duxbury, Elspeth. (2003). The discrete dynamics of small-scale spatial events: Agent-based models of mobility in carnivals and street parades. *International Journal of Geographic Information Systems, 17*(7), 673–698.

Breshears, David; Lopez-Hoffman, Laura; & Graumlich, Lisa. (2011). When ecosystem services crash: Preparing for big, fast, patchy climate change. *AMBIO, 40*(3), 256–263.

Chi, Hsin. (2000). Computer simulation models for sustainability. *International Journal of Sustainability in Higher Education, 1*(2), 154–167.

Deadman, Peter; Robinson, Derek; Moran, Emilio; & Brondizio, Eduardo. (2004). Colonist household decision-making and land-use change in the Amazon Rainforest: An agent-based simulation. *Environment and Planning B, 31*(5), 693–709.

Fox, Jefferson; Rindfuss, Ronald; Walsh, Steven; & Mishra, Vinod. (Eds.). (2003). *People and the environment: Approaches for linking household and community surveys to remote sensing and GIS*. Boston: Kluwer Academic Publishers.

Franck, Robert. (Ed.). (2002). *The exploratory power of models*. Berlin: Springer.

Franklin, Stan, & Graessner, Art. (1996). Is it an agent, or just a program? A taxonomy for autonomous agents. In Jörg P. Müller, Michael J. Wooldridge & Nicholas R. Jennings (Eds.), *Intelligent agents 3: Agent theories, architectures, and languages: ECAI'96 workshop (ATAL), Budapest, Hungary, August 12–13, 1996, proceedings*. New York: Springer-Verlag.

Gimblett, Randy. (2005, December). Human-landscape interactions in spatially complex settings: Where are we and where are we going? In Andre Zerger & Robert M. Argent (Eds.), *MODSIM 2005 international congress on modelling and simulation* (pp. 11–20). Canberra, Australia: Modelling and Simulation Society of Australia and New Zealand.

Gimblett, Randy. (Ed.). (2002). *Integrating geographic information systems and agent-based modeling techniques for simulating social and ecological processes*. New York: Oxford University Press.

Gimblett, Randy, & Skov-Petersen, Hans. (Eds.). (2008). *Monitoring, simulation and management of visitor landscapes*. Retrieved December 13, 2011, from http://www.uapress.arizona.edu/onlinebks/Monitoring_Visitor_Landscapes.pdf

International Union for Conservation of Nature (IUCN). (2006, January 29–31). *The future of sustainability: Re-thinking environment and development in the twenty-first century* (Report of the IUCN Renowned Thinkers Meeting). Retrieved January 23, 2012, from http://cmsdata.iucn.org/downloads/iucn_future_of_sustanability.pdf

Itami, Robert M. (2008). Level of sustainable activity: Moving visitor simulation from description to management for an urban waterway in Australia. In Randy Gimblett & Hans Skov-Petersen (Eds.), *Monitoring, simulation and management of visitor landscapes* (pp. 331–347). Tucson: University of Arizona Press.

Itami, Robert M., & Zanon, Dino. (2003). *Visitor management model for Port Campbell National Park and Bay of Islands Coastal Reserve: Phase 2 simulation.* Victoria, Australia: GeoDimensions Pty Ltd.

Lansing, J. Stephen. (1996). Simulation modelling of Balinese irrigation. In Jonathan B. Mabry (Ed.), *Canals and communities: Small-scale irrigation systems* (pp. 139–156). Tucson: University of Arizona Press.

Lim, Kevin; Deadman, Peter; Moran, Emilio; Brondízio, Eduardo; & McCracken, Steve. (2002). Agent-based simulations of household decision making and land use change near Altamira, Brazil. In Randy Gimblett (Ed.), *Integrating geographic information systems and agent-based modelling: Techniques for simulating social and ecological processes.* (pp. 277–310). New York: Oxford University Press.

Liu, Jianguo, et al. (2007, September 14). Complexity of coupled human and natural systems. *Science, 317*(5844), 1513–1516.

Parker, Dawn; Manson, Steven; Janssen, Marco; Hoffmann, Matt; & Deadman, Peter. (2003). Multi-agent systems for the simulation of land-use and land-cover change: A review. *Annals of the Association of American Geographers, 93*(2), 314–337.

Skole, David; Chomentowski, Walter; Salas, William; & Nobre, Antonio. (1994). Physical and human dimensions of deforestation in Amazonia. *Bioscience, 44,* 314–322.

Scott, Christopher A., et al. (2010, October 17–19). Assessing resilience of arid region riparian corridors: Ecohydrology and decision-making in United States–Mexico transboundary watersheds (paper, Global Land Project—Open Science Meeting). Arizona State University, Tempe.

Swyngedouw, Erik. (2004). *Social power and the urbanization of water: Flows of power.* Oxford, UK: Oxford University Press.

Cost-Benefit Analysis

Cost-benefit analysis—which typically requires that pros and cons of a proposed policy be quantified in economic terms—is an increasingly central component of regulatory analyses worldwide. Cost-benefit analysis can improve transparency and aid decision making. But it does not address how environmental goods should be distributed across people, places, and time; it relies on meaningful quantification; and it provides little guidance in situations of uncertainty.

Cost-benefit analysis—or, as it is sometimes called, benefit-cost analysis—is a decision-making tool that compares the pros and cons of a proposed action. This comparison can be casual, as it often is in everyday life, or formalized, as it has become in most public policy applications. The use of formalized, quantified cost-benefit analyses to inform public policy decisions is a hallmark of the United States' approach to regulatory issues. In recent years, the approach has made substantial inroads into European, Canadian, and Australian regulatory decision making as well.

Overview of the Method

There are many different methods for comparing the pros and cons of a proposed policy, with varying levels and types of quantification. Such approaches include cost-effectiveness analysis, health-risk analysis, risk-risk analysis, and social-return-on-investment analysis. Some scholars have also argued that a form of cost-benefit analysis plays an important role in judicial decision making. For civil wrongs, for example, a common way to determine whether a defendant was negligent is to apply what amounts to a cost-benefit analysis: to determine whether the burden of an untaken precaution would have outweighed the probability of a harm, multiplied by its loss.

In public policy circles, however, cost-benefit analysis (CBA) has a particularized meaning, referring to a highly formalized and quantified type of analysis in which all the benefits and all the costs of the policy proposal are expressed as monetary values.

A public-policy CBA is typically performed as a multistep analytical procedure, which proceeds in the following order:

1. Identify a potential policy change.
2. Specify all relevant costs and benefits of the policy.
3. Determine the monetary value of those costs and benefits.
4. Adjust for the time-value of money by discounting future costs and benefits according to how far in the future they occur.
5. Come up with a final figure for net benefits or net costs, expressed as a present value.

The product of a CBA—the final figure representing net costs or net benefits—can then be used to inform a decision about whether the policy change is desirable.

Goals of Cost-Benefit Analysis

Advocates of CBA typically point to its usefulness as a decision-making method for allocating scarce resources among various options. The CBA procedure has several characteristics that help with this process.

The first is that CBA reduces diverse policy effects into the single metric of money. If all the effects of a policy are expressed in monetary terms, it is easy to see whether the benefits outweigh the costs or vice versa. In addition, by quantifying all costs and benefits in monetary terms, and then discounting future costs and benefits to present value, it is possible to see the net effects of a proposal in today's dollars. This makes it simpler to compare multiple policy proposals, both to each other and to the status quo.

This quantification process can have a secondary benefit of increasing transparency, insofar as CBA requires that each type of cost and each type of benefit be identified explicitly, prior to monetization. This forces the decision maker to be transparent both about what is valued in each decision and how it is valued compared to other goods. Transparency may improve accountability, which decreases the chance of error and increases opportunities for public and/or outside participation in the decision-making process. Because of greater oversight, transparency may also improve the quality of decision making.

Uses of Cost-Benefit Analysis

Quantified cost-benefit analysis became a central tool in US regulation in 1981, when President Ronald Reagan issued an executive order that directed all federal agencies to perform quantified cost-benefit analyses before undertaking any major actions. As it was applied in the early years, CBA often determined final policy choice: when an agency could not show that the quantified benefits of a proposed policy outweighed its costs, the agency was barred from promulgating the policy.

Subsequent US presidents have continued to require agencies to perform cost-benefit analyses, but the role has become increasingly advisory. Under President Barack Obama's order, agencies are still required to perform CBA on major federal actions, but they are directed to consider other decision-making factors—including "equity, human dignity, fairness, and distributive impacts" (White House 2011)—as well. In addition, agencies are directed to ensure that benefits "justify" (rather than exceed) costs.

Although CBA is often viewed as a touchstone of US regulatory policy, its use has also increased outside the United States. In 1999, Canada began requiring federal agencies to perform cost-benefit analyses prior to passing major regulations, and Australia has followed suit. The European Union, long a bastion of the precautionary principle, now requires CBA for environmental infrastructure projects over twenty-five million euros and for other projects over fifty million euros.

Controversies and Challenges

Despite its increasing use around the world as a guide to policy making, quantified CBA remains controversial for a number of reasons.

Difficulties in Quantification

Perhaps the primary objection to using CBA in policy contexts involves quantification itself. A CBA is only as accurate as the data plugged in to it, and inaccuracies can creep in from a number of sources.

The first of these is the monetization process itself. CBA requires that all the effects of policy decisions be expressed in monetary terms. But many policies have nonmonetary impacts, including important effects on human health and the environment. To express these goods in monetary terms, decision makers try to determine people's willingness to pay to secure those goods through the open market.

To do this, they use two kinds of evidence. The first looks at people's spending behavior in consumer and labor markets. Such studies show clearly where a policy intervention will affect deterioration of things that can be straightforwardly purchased with money, such as a boat dock or a sign. More controversially, these types of studies are also used to value mortality and health risks, most commonly by determining how much people get paid to work in risky conditions.

The second kind of evidence comes from contingent valuation studies, which rely on preferences elicited in studies. Contingent valuation studies are commonly—though not exclusively—used to value goods that are not traded in markets, such as preventing the extinction of a species or preventing the degradation of air quality.

The accuracy of these techniques has been criticized on a number of grounds. One ongoing concern is that they may be systematically biased against certain types of goods, such as those—like environmental goods or catastrophic risks—that are hard to value on the open market. Another source of potential inaccuracy comes from our inability to know the future. A CBA can incorporate known probabilities, but it has no mechanism to adjust for uncertainty, where no probabilities can be assigned.

These concerns about CBA accuracy are particularly piquant because the function of CBA—to quantify the effects of a policy decision—may give the approach a spurious image of accuracy, even when the component parts of the CBA are based on multiple controversial assumptions.

Commodification

Another objection to the use of CBA is that it commodifies diverse human goods. Under this view, expressing the value of a human life, or the existence of a species, in dollar terms is fundamentally incomplete, and possibly even harmful, in that it may cheapen the underlying good being valued. Some proponents of this view are more comfortable with less formal trade-off analyses that are based on metrics other than money.

Distribution

A third objection to CBA is that it is insensitive to distributional inequities. Public policy cost-benefit analyses are often performed based upon the Kaldor-Hicks approach to social welfare. Under this view, policy interventions are desirable when the money measure of gains exceeds the money measure of losses, because as long as the winners compensate the losers, everyone is potentially better off. This approach is insensitive both to initial distributional inequity and to the fact that—without supplementary incentives—winners rarely actually compensate losers. A simple Kaldor-Hicks analysis does not distinguish based on race, class, location, or position in time, and it therefore cannot identify the existence of inequity across any of these variables. As a result, using CBA alone as a guiding principle for regulation can lead to the creation of "hot spots," where a single part of the population ends up bearing a disproportionate portion of total risks. In support of this concern, environmental justice advocates often point to the fact that undesirable uses, such as the siting of waste dumps, end up disproportionately in areas near lower-income and lower-status communities. This distributional concern also arises in the context of intergenerational equity, where the concern is that the present generation may adopt policies based on CBA even when those policies disproportionately harm future generations.

Valuing Goods through Time

A final challenge for CBA is determining how to deal with costs and benefits that may be spread out across time. For cost-benefit analyses that use money as a metric, the widely accepted approach is to discount future monetary units back to present-day value, selecting a discount rate based on some measure of economic investment opportunities in economic markets. The choice of an appropriate discount rate remains highly controversial even among economists, and the issue is further complicated by the massive impact of discounting: through the power of compound interest, the choice of discount rate can easily swamp all other inputs in a CBA. Decision makers continue to struggle with these issues.

The Future of Cost-Benefit Analysis

Although it can provide substantial increases in the transparency of decision making, CBA as a decision-making framework provides limited guidance in solving many of the most difficult modern environmental issues, including how harms and benefits should be distributed across people and across time, and how regulatory systems should deal with scientific uncertainty and with catastrophic risks. Despite these challenges, the use of CBA continues to grow, and to grow increasingly quantified.

Arden ROWELL
University of Illinois College of Law

See also Community and Stakeholder Input; Computer Modeling; Ecological Impact Assessment (EcIA); Externality Valuation; Material Flow Analysis (MFA); Regulatory Compliance; Risk Assessment; Strategic Environmental Assessment (SEA); Triple Bottom Line

FURTHER READING

Ackerman, Frank, & Heinzerling, Lisa. (2004). *Priceless: On knowing the price of everything and the value of nothing.* New York: The New Press.

Baum, Seth D. (forthcoming 2011). Value typology in cost-benefit analysis. *Environmental Values.*

Boardman, Anthony E.; Greenberg, David H.; Vining, Aidan R.; & Weimer, David L. (2001). *Cost-benefit analysis: Concepts and practice.* Upper Saddle River, NJ: Prentice Hall.

Clowney, Stephen. (2007). Environmental ethics and cost-benefit analysis. *Fordham Environmental Law Review, 18,* 105–150.

Driesen, David M. (2006). Is cost-benefit analysis neutral? *University of Colorado Law Review, 77,* 335–405.

Farber, Daniel. (2009). Review essay: Rethinking the role of cost-benefit analysis. *University of Chicago Law Review, 76,* 1355.

Government of Canada. (2007). *Cabinet directive on streamlining regulation.* Retrieved January 6, 2011, from http://www.tbs-sct.gc.ca/ri-qr/directive/directive-eng.pdf

Hahn, Robert W., & Dudley, Patrick M. (2005). *How well does the government do cost-benefit analysis?* Washington, DC: AEI-Brookings Joint Center for Regulatory Studies.

Hammond, Richard J. (1966). Convention and limitation in benefit-cost analysis. *Natural Resources Journal, 6,* 195–222.

Kysar, Douglas A. (2010). *Regulating from nowhere.* New Haven, CT: Yale University Press.

Office of Regulation Review (ORR). (1998). *A guide to regulation* (2nd ed.). Retrieved January 5, 2011, from http://www.pc.gov.au/__data/assets/pdf_file/0006/66876/reguide2.pdf

Posner, Eric A., & Adler, Matthew D. (2006). *New foundations of cost-benefit analysis.* Cambridge, MA: Harvard University Press.

Posner, Richard A. (2004). *Catastrophe: Risk and response.* New York: Oxford University Press.

Revesz, Richard L., & Livermore, Michael A. (2008). *Retaking rationality: How cost-benefit analysis can better protect the environment and our health.* New York: Oxford University Press.

Rowell, Arden (2010). The cost of time: Haphazard discounting and the undervaluation of regulatory benefits. *Notre Dame Law Review, 85,* 1505–1542.

Sunstein, Cass R. (2005). Cost-benefit analysis and the environment. *Ethics, 115*(2), 351–385.

Sunstein, Cass R., & Rowell, Arden. (2007). On discounting regulatory benefits: Risk, money, and intergenerational equity. *University of Chicago Law Review, 74,* 171–208.

United States Environmental Protection Agency (EPA). (2000). *Guidelines for preparing economic analyses.* Washington DC: EPA.

The White House, President Barack Obama. (2011, January 18). Executive order: Improving regulation and regulatory review. Retrieved February 18, 2011 from http://www.whitehouse.gov/the-press-office/2011/01/18/improving-regulation-and-regulatory-review-executive-order

Wiener, Jonathan B. (2008). Benefit cost analysis in the United States and Europe. Retrieved December 1, 2010, from http://evans.washington.edu/files/bca_center/Weiner.pdf

Design Quality Indicator (DQI)

The Design Quality Indicator (DQI) was developed in the United Kingdom to evaluate building designs across a wide range of criteria and has been used in thousands of projects in the United Kingdom since its launch in 2003, as well as (more recently) in the United States. Although it was not conceived specifically as a sustainability assessment tool, its ease of use and its versatility have proven very useful in discussing sustainability issues with a range of stakeholders.

The Design Quality Indicator (DQI) is a web-based assessment tool for the evaluation of a wide range of criteria that define the design quality of a building, such as building character, performance in use, access, and urban integration. It was initially developed in the United Kingdom as a preconstruction tool to assess completed building designs but later was adapted for use throughout the entire briefing, design, and construction process for both new build and refurbishment projects. It is a straightforward tool that both professionals and laypeople can use readily with guidance and support from an experienced facilitator. While it does not claim to focus on sustainability, the range of issues covered in the DQI has made it appropriate for use as a framework within which sustainability issues can be evaluated and discussed openly and more sustainable buildings can be created.

The DQI is based on a questionnaire that is divided into three broad headings: impact, build quality, and functionality. These align with first-century Roman author Vitruvius's maxim *"utilitas, firmitas, venustas"* (commodity, firmness, and delight). The DQI contains ten subject groupings that are divided among the three headings. These are (1) character and innovation (visual impact and atmosphere), (2) form and materials (color, composition, and textures), (3) internal environment (light, air quality, and acoustics), (4) urban and social integration (fit in the neighborhood), (5) performance (operation, maintenance, and durability), (6) engineering (mechanical systems), (7) construction (methods of construction, design for recyclability, and climate change), (8) use (meeting needs of users), (9) access (parking and circulation), and (10) space (size and layout). Each of the ten subject groupings contains six to fifteen evaluative statements that are worded quite simply (e.g., "The layout allows for change of use" or "The engineering systems operate quietly."). The DQI is versatile in that the verb tense used in each statement changes from "should be" prior to design, to "will be" during design, and "is" postoccupancy.

Project stakeholders are asked to assign scores to these statements, a process explained later in this article. Representatives from both the supply side (architects, contractors, and engineers) and the demand side (client, users, and the public) are invited to participate in the scoring, which typically happens at five stages during a project's development (preparation, design, preconstruction, construction, and use). This enables the design team and building users to identify strengths and weaknesses in the building design and to monitor how well the evolving design is meeting their needs. For example, a statement such as "The circulation space works well," can be used to elicit feedback from stakeholders throughout the design development process and creates the opportunity to revise the building's layout if necessary. The experience of an expert DQI facilitator is also brought into the project through a series of structured workshops that occur at the five key stages in the design and construction process; these events are focused around the outputs from the DQI tool but also include extensive and wide-ranging discussion.

DQI's Development

Following calls for the UK construction industry to improve the ways in which it monitored performance and design quality, development of the DQI started in 1999 and continued until 2003, when it was formally launched. A pan-industry body, the Construction Industry Council, was responsible for the development process, which was supported by a number of UK government departments and other bodies such as the Commission for Architecture and the Built Environment. Importantly, a core group made up of several leading architecture and engineering practitioners together with academics from Imperial College London is credited with the intellectual development of the tool's content. It has been described as a "tool for thinking" and a way of arriving at a high-quality building that is not reliant on the opinions of experts—on decisions made behind closed doors—but rather on integrated outputs from a simple, flexible, and multipurpose tool that is open and transparent (Gann, Salter, and Whyte 2003).

The approach appears to have considerable merit; by 2005, over seven hundred projects (and over three thousand individual participants) were reported to be using the DQI. Additionally, a variant of the basic DQI—DQI for Schools—had also been devised in response to the UK government's program of school building. The DQI itself was updated in 2005 to extend its use throughout the entire briefing and design process, that is, to fully capture stakeholders' views preconstruction at key design stages. A comprehensive review of the 2005 version was undertaken by Imperial College London; its statistical analysis of the numerical data collated from individuals' scores showed that the DQI's content and process were extremely robust.

How the DQI Quantifies Sustainability

The DQI aims to evaluate, in general, the design and construction of new buildings and the refurbishment of existing buildings across the three headings of impact, build quality, and functionality, that is, the look, performance, and ease of use of a building.

To explain the scoring process in detail, at the briefing stage each user selects one of three levels (fundamental, added value, or excellent) for each evaluative statement; these values are applied to that user's scores whenever the DQI scoring is carried out, typically five times during a building project. At each of these iterations the respondents give their score for each evaluative statement, using a six-point scale from "strongly disagree" to "strongly agree." They then apply a weighting factor to each of the

ten groupings. For example, under the "impact" section, users are invited to allocate a total of twenty points between four groupings (character and innovation, form and materials, internal environment, and urban and social integration). They are able to spread the twenty points evenly or to allocate the majority of the twenty points to one category. When all users have completed their scoring, an algorithm interprets the subjective views to produce radar (spider) diagrams and bar charts that clearly display the overall scores for each statement and subject grouping.

The DQI was not designed to expressly address sustainable development objectives, but it does contain a number of criteria that relate directly to environmental, economic, and social goals, including the following:

- "The design minimizes carbon dioxide emissions."
- "The requirement for cooling is minimized by the design of the building."
- "The building stimulates social and economic regeneration."
- "The building caters for cyclists."
- "There is good access to public transport."
- "The building is designed for demolition and recyclability."
- "Future climate change has been considered in the design of the building."

While only about 20 percent of the ninety-one criteria statements relate overtly to sustainability, many others have indirect but meaningful relationships, notably to well-being and indoor comfort; these relate to the social dimension of sustainability in terms of human health. Furthermore, each individual user is able to attribute weightings to particular groupings of statements, so it is possible to give greater importance to groups of criteria that are more relevant to sustainability. Because this weighting is done on a user-by-user basis, however, there is no guarantee of consistency, so in this respect the DQI is perhaps too versatile to be fully classified as a sustainability indicator. Nonetheless, case studies suggest that the DQI can help project teams work toward other environmental assessment methods, such as BREEAM (the UK Building Research Establishment's Environmental Assessment Method), by highlighting important sustainability considerations relating to materials and energy use.

Applications and Benefits

The DQI is a tool for assessing the design quality of buildings with a range of stakeholders and project team members. Developed initially for the UK market, the DQI was made available in the United States in 2006, with an online version launched in 2008. The extent of its use in other countries is less clear. That said, it has been used in the United Kingdom to assess design quality on a wide range of projects such as the building and refurbishment of police stations, office buildings, college and university buildings, libraries, and other civic and private building projects. The DQI website (www.dqi.org.uk) includes a series of UK case studies that describe how the tool is applied and the benefits that can be gained from its deployment. A brief analysis of these case studies suggests that effective application of the DQI results in clearer expression of needs and priorities, open conversations between project stakeholders, a presentation of strengths and weaknesses in design that is visually accessible and reflects all stakeholders' priorities, and a structured forum to facilitate discussion among stakeholders, designers, and others as they move toward agreement upon common goals. All of these are helpful to the open and constructive discussion of sustainability objectives for a building project, making the DQI very attractive for a wide range of building clients and project types.

Challenges to the DQI

Critics argue that design quality remains hard to define and difficult to measure; some have described the DQI tool as a "delight detector," an attempt to quantify subjective responses rather than a robust arbiter of the quality of a building's design. Others also question whether the DQI should attempt to include both subjective aspects (such as "the building lifts the spirits") alongside technical or objective aspects like "there is a clear fire strategy," when the latter can be checked via compliance with building regulations (Markus 2003, 400). The DQI is praised for its iterative approach and interactive nature, but some argue that not all stakeholders are easily able to articulate their needs, values, and viewpoints, particularly when faced with ninety-one questions, each with a six-point scale response (Dewulf and van Meel 2004, 249). Moreover, there are calls for a thorough and independent statistical examination of the DQI data, now amassed from thousands of projects, to ascertain the effect of factors such as age and gender bias on its outputs (Markus 2003, 402). Another concern is that of sensible interpretation of results; here, the workshop facilitator must be diligent and sensitive when analyzing and communicating the DQI's outputs to the assembled stakeholders. Errors in interpretation—for example, if the facilitator fails to question any incongruous scores—could have dramatic effects on subsequent design decisions.

Despite these methodological concerns, critics recognize that the DQI was developed for "messy, pressured live project conditions" and its extensive use to date provides a strong indication of its utility and value to the design and construction community (Prasad 2004, 550).

Current Situation and Outlook

The DQI is certainly well established as a helpful and robust tool for the assessment of design quality in building projects, and it will likely continue to be utilized for some time. It has been developed carefully, and it has also been vigorously challenged. It has continually been improved to enhance its value to the building design and construction community. The DQI's focus on qualitative concerns satisfies a fundamental need to include and fairly represent the intangible elements of building design, which are often difficult to quantify. It also prevents measuring only the easy-to-quantify aspects of a building design, thus over-representing details that may be less important.

The DQI's recent introduction to the US market suggests a positive outlook in terms of its international presence. That said, as a sustainable building design assessment tool the DQI has only limited value; it lacks both depth and a sufficient number of sustainability-related indicators. It does, however, offer building teams an even-handed and accessible way to begin discussing sustainability with lay building occupants and users in particular. In this way, its original aim to be a "tool for thinking" is extremely valuable for those seeking to develop more sustainable building projects.

Jacqueline GLASS
Loughborough University

See also Building Rating Systems, Green; Community and Stakeholder Input; Life Cycle Management (LCM); Regional Planning; Sustainability Science; Triple Bottom Line

FURTHER READING

BREEAM. (2010). Homepage. Retrieved August 27, 2010, from http://www.breeam.org/

Design Quality Indicator. (2010). Homepage. Retrieved August 26, 2010, from http://www.dqi.org.uk/website/default.aspa

Dewulf, Geert, & van Meel, Juriaan. (2004). Sense and nonsense of measuring design quality. *Building Research & Information, 32*(3), 247–250.

Gann, David; Salter, Ammon; & Whyte, Jennifer. (2003). The Design Quality Indicator as a tool for thinking. *Building Research & Information, 31*(5), 318–333.

Markus, Thomas. (2003). Lessons from the Design Quality Indicator. *Building Research & Information, 31*(5), 399–405.

Prasad, Sunand. (2004). Clarifying intentions: The Design Quality Indicator. *Building Research & Information, 32*(6), 548–551.

Whyte, Jennifer, & Gann, David. (2003a). Design quality: Its measurement and management in the built environment. *Building Research & Information, 31*(5), 314–317.

Whyte, Jennifer, & Gann, David. (2003b). Design quality indicators: Work in progress. *Building Research & Information, 31*(5), 387–398.

Development Indicators

Indicators are variables designed to summarize complex data. They are widely used by nonexperts to measure progress in international development. Examples of development indicators include those associated with the Millennium Development Goals and those used in the human development index. Each set of indicators has advantages and limitations; foremost of the latter is that they are selected by human beings and subject to human bias.

The basic concept of international development, or human development as it is known today, arose in the years immediately following World War II. US president Harry Truman's 1949 inaugural address, known as the Four Point Speech, encapsulated the modernizing agenda of development. His fourth point is particularly relevant in that it introduces, in so many words, the indicators used to measure development:

> Fourth, we must embark on a bold new program for making the benefits of our scientific advances and industrial progress available for the improvement and growth of underdeveloped areas. More than half the people of the world are living in conditions approaching misery. Their food is inadequate. They are victims of disease. Their economic life is primitive and stagnant. Their poverty is a handicap and a threat both to them and to more prosperous areas. For the first time in history, humanity possesses the knowledge and skill to relieve the suffering of these people.

The four obstacles Truman lays out—inadequacy of food supply, disease, economic life, poverty—can all be described, or measured, with indicators, defined as "variables that summarize or otherwise simplify relevant information, make visible or perceptible phenomena of interest, and quantify, measure, and communicate relevant information" (Gallopín 1996, 108).

Indicators thus are a means of summarizing complexity, and we use them every day of our lives without even noticing. They are often thought of as being numerical: the ranking of a sports team in a league table is based upon points won after playing games with their competitors and indicates how good that team is. But there are also nonnumerical or qualitative indicators. For example, it is possible to "know" whether you are in a bad neighborhood by the signs (indicators) you see around you: the graffiti, trash in the street, and boarded-up houses and shops.

The topic of development indicators cannot be separated from the wider debate about what is meant by the term *development*. After all, the indicators reflect the changing perspectives of development and do not drive them (Morse 2004). Development indicators provide a summary of something that is far more complex, even if the persistent concerns over food supply, poverty, and so on provide a disturbing link between the past and the present. Unfortunately, despite the good intentions of Truman's speech, these obstacles to human development have not gone away. The UN's Millennium Development Goals (MDGs), aimed at eradicating extreme poverty, improving maternal health, halting the spread of disease, and providing universal primary education—goals that echo the themes of Truman's speech—each have a set of from three to nine indicators. A summary of some of these MDGs and their indicators appears in table 1 on page 76.

The purpose of the MDG indicators is to allow policy makers and others charged with achieving the goals to monitor progress.

Each of the indicators has its own set of assumptions and data requirements. For example, the poverty gap ratio (PGR) is found by multiplying the proportion of people in a population living below the poverty line by the average

TABLE 1. Some Millennium Development Goals and Associated Indicators

Goal	Indicator
Eradicate extreme poverty and hunger	Proportion of population below $1 purchasing power parity (PPP) a day
	Poverty gap ratio [incidence x depth of poverty]
	Share of poorest quintile in national consumption
	Prevalence of underweight children under 5 years of age
	Proportion of population below minimum level of dietary energy consumption
	Growth rate of GDP per person employed
	Employment to population ratio
	Proportion of employed people living below $1 (PPP) a day
	Proportion of own-account and contributing family workers in total employment
Achieve universal primary education	Net enrollment ratio in primary education
	Proportion of pupils starting first grade who reach the last grade of primary education
	Literacy rate of 15- to 24-year-olds
Promote gender equality and empower women	Ratios of girls to boys in primary, secondary, and tertiary education
	Share of women in wage employment in the nonagricultural sector
	Proportion of seats held by women in national parliament
Reduce child mortality	Infant mortality rate
	Under-5 mortality rate
	Proportion of 1-year-old children immunized against measles
Improve maternal health	Maternal mortality ratio
	Proportion of births attended by skilled health personnel
	Adolescent birth rate
	Antenatal care coverage (at least one visit)
	Unmet need for family planning
	Contraceptive prevalence rate
Combat HIV/AIDS, malaria, and other diseases	HIV prevalence among population ages 15 to 24 years
	Condom use at last high-risk sex
	Proportion of population ages 15 to 24 years with comprehensive, correct knowledge of HIV/AIDS
	Ratio of school attendance of orphans to school attendance of non-orphans ages 10 to 14 years
	Proportion of population with advanced HIV infection with access to antiretroviral drugs
	Incidence and death rates associated with malaria
	Proportion of children under age 5 sleeping under insecticide-treated bed nets
	Proportion of children under age 5 with a fever who are treated with appropriate antimalarial drugs
	Incidence, prevalence, and death rates associated with tuberculosis
	Proportion of tuberculosis cases detected and cured under directly observed treatment short course

Source: UN Millennium Development Goals (n.d.).

"depth" of poverty of those below that line. A key assumption in finding the PGR is the setting of the poverty line. For the sake of simplicity and allowing for international comparison, the poverty line is often assumed to be an absolute figure, such as US$1 or US$2 per day, but it will also vary across countries and even within a country depending upon the cost of accommodation and key consumables such as food and clothing. The poverty line can also change with time as a result of inflation. In other words the "purchasing power" of one US dollar is not the same everywhere and at all times, and that makes a difference as to how poverty is assessed.

How the selection of the poverty line influences the PGR is shown in table 2. Here there is a theoretical population of twenty people ranging in income from US$0.5 per day up

to US$4.0 per day. Also shown are two poverty lines: one set at US$2 per day and the other at US$1 per day. The higher poverty line of US$2 per day results in ten people, half the population, being classified as in poverty, while for the lower poverty line of US$1 per day the number classified in this way drops to five (one-quarter of the population). The average depth below the poverty line is also greater for the poverty line of US$2 per day compared to US$1 per day (US$0.34 per day and US$0.8 per day, respectively). Multiplying the proportion of the population below the poverty line against the average depth below that line yields values of the PGR of 0.085 and 0.4 for poverty lines of US$2 and US$1 per day, respectively. These values for PGR are very different; indeed one is forty-seven times higher than the other, yet it has to be stressed that the incomes for

Table 2. Theoretical Illustration of the Poverty Gap Ratio

| | | Depth Below Poverty Line ($US) | |
| | | --- | --- |
Person	Income/Day ($US)	Poverty Line = 1 US$/Day	Poverty Line = 2 US$/Day
1	4.0		
2	3.6		
3	3.5		
4	3.1		
5	3.0		
6	3.0		
7	2.8		
8	2.2		
9	2.1		
10	2.1		
11	1.9		0.1
12	1.9		0.1
13	1.9		0.1
14	1.8		0.2
15	1.2		0.8
16	0.8	0.2	1.2
17	0.7	0.3	1.3
18	0.7	0.3	1.3
19	0.6	0.4	1.4
20	0.5	0.5	1.5
Number of people below poverty line		5	10
Proportion of people below poverty line		0.25	0.5
Average depth below poverty line		0.34	0.8
Poverty gap ratio		0.085	0.4

Source: author.

Figures in the table are for a theoretical population of twenty people ranging in income between US $0.5 per day (minimum) up to US $4.0 per day (maximum) with two poverty lines; US $2 per day and US $1 per day. The poverty lines generate different proportions classified as being in poverty as well as different average depths below the poverty lines. Multiplying these values together generates Poverty Gap Ratios of 0.085 and 0.4 for poverty lines of US $2 and US $1 per day, respectively.

the population are exactly the same. All that has changed is the drawing of the poverty line. It should also be noted that the calculations in table 2, are dependent upon the availability of income data for the twenty individuals in the population. These may be available via, for example, tax returns (good quality data), but in many countries such required data sets are not readily available for the whole population, and estimates—sometimes quite rough in nature—have to be made to fill gaps (poor quality data).

Given the example of the PGR and how assumptions can make a big difference, it is perhaps understandable that people can and do debate each of the MDGs as well as the suitability of the selected indicators. For example, why assess the literacy rate and HIV prevalence only for fifteen- to twenty-four-year-olds? Why limit the list of diseases selected within the MDGs to malaria, HIV, and tuberculosis? Why not include cholera, typhoid, and measles, for example? These are judgment calls, and while a rationale is provided for each of the goals and indicators, there is inevitably room for disagreement, a point that will be returned to later.

Envisioning Development: Economics versus Humans

Development indicators have a long history. The reports of the International Bank for Reconstruction and Development (now called the World Bank) and International Monetary Fund (IMF) publish many indicators of economic development. Take, for example, the first *World Development Report*, published by the World Bank in 1978. At the end of the report, a series of eighteen tables rank nation-states in terms of their per capita income. Four of the tables focus on supply and demand, and seven present the "growth, structure and directions of trade, the balance of payments, capital flows, debt and aid" (World Bank 1978, 73). Twelve of the eighteen tables thus comprise economic indicators, including gross domestic product (GDP), the classic indicator of economic performance.

Before the establishment of the GDP, economic policy was based on stock price indices, rail freight figures, and similar fragments of information. For the Roosevelt administration, trying to pull the country out of the Great Depression, these "economic indicators" were only a little more useful than tarot cards. So the Department of Commerce called on Simon Kuznets of the National Bureau of Economic Research to develop a set of national economic accounts. By the early 1940s, gross national product numbers were figuring into the war effort.

In Australia, the economist Colin Clark saw that national accounts could be used to make comparisons between nations, and in 1940 he created one of the first such comparative tables, using income per capita adjusted for purchasing power (Clark 1940). A summary is presented in table 3, below, where annual per capita income is presented in terms of an artificial

Table 3. Country Ranking by Income

Average Yearly Income per Capita*	County/Region
1,300–1,400	United States, Canada
1,200–1,300	New Zealand
1,100–1,200	
1,000–1,100	Great Britain, Switzerland, Argentina
900–1,000	Australia
800–900	Holland
700–800	Ireland
600–700	France, Denmark, Sweden, Germany, Belgium, Uruguay
500–600	Norway, Austria, Spain, Chile
400–500	Czechoslovakia, Yugoslavia, Iceland, Brazil
300–400	Greece, Finland, Hungary, Poland, Latvia, Italy, Estonia, USSR, Portugal, "Rest of America," Japan, Palestine, Philippines, Algeria, Egypt, Hawaii, Guam
200–300	Bulgaria, Rumania, Lithuania, Albania, Turkey, Syria, Cyprus, South Africa, Morocco, Tunis
Under 200	China, British India, Dutch Indies, "Rest of Asia," "Rest of Africa," "Rest of Oceania"

Source: Clark (1940).

*Refers to the period 1925–1934. Artificial income unit has been adjusted for purchasing power (after Clark 1940, 54).

unit of currency and the nation-states are ranked by per capita income. In some cases a whole region rather than a nation-state is presented, such as "Rest of Africa" and "Rest of America."

It is hardly surprising that the World Bank favors economic development indicators, but not all development is solely economic. By the 1980s, some experts had begun to question the meaning of the term *development* and why economic measures should dominate the definition. For example, the Nobel Prize–winning economist Amartya Sen highlighted the importance of "capability" in development. He defined this as the availability of options and choice open to people to allow them to lead long and healthy lives. If capability is low then people will have fewer options to adapt to stress and improve their condition. But capability is more than just access to the financial resources stressed within economic development. It also includes access to social networks and physical assets (e.g., land) as well as skills and education. One outcome of this rethinking was the *Human Development Report* (*HDR*), published annually by the United Nations Development Programme (UNDP) beginning in 1990. The first of these reports set out the UNDP's vision of *human* development and how it differed from *economic* development:

> People are the real wealth of a nation. The basic objective of development is to create an enabling environment for people to enjoy long, healthy and creative lives. This may appear to be a simple truth. But it is often forgotten in the immediate concern with the accumulation of commodities and financial wealth. (UNDP 1990, 9)

The UNDP felt it necessary to create a new headline indicator—the human development index (HDI)—to counter the perceived dominance of GDP. The UNDP deemed three components to be important within its vision of human development, and these are set out in table 4, below. Because each of these three components is assessed by its own indicator, the HDI is a composite index.

The arithmetic used to combine the three HDI components does not need to be discussed here, but part of the process involves scaling (or standardization) to a value between 0 and 1, with an assumption that the higher the value (closer to 1), the better. The standardized values are then averaged to yield the HDI. The three components are equally weighted (Booysen 2002).

The UNDP also argued for a diminishing return in human development from income (measured as GDP per capita) to ensure that high incomes do not dominate the HDI. As a result, the GDP per capita is adjusted to reduce its relatively large variation across nation-states. In the first *HDR* (1990) the adjustment was made simply by taking the logarithm of the GDP per capita, but between 1991 and 1998 the more complex Atkinson formula was used. The effects of these two forms of transformation are different and reflect the views of the HDI's creators about how much GDP per capita should influence performance measurement. With the Atkinson formula, once the original GDP per capita reaches a predetermined point, the transformation forces the adjusted GDP per capita to level out. With the logarithmic-based transformation, the adjusted GDP per capita continues to increase (albeit more slowly) and never levels off completely. Since 1999 the UNDP has returned to the logarithmic method of adjusting GDP per capita because it was felt that the Atkinson formula was too severe on middle-income countries. In order to have the maximum impact on policy, the UNDP opted to follow the lead of others, such as the World Bank, and rank the countries based on their HDI. This league table style of presentation provides an element of "name and shame," whereby politicians and leaders in a country are encouraged to compare their national performance (HDI ranking) with that of their contemporaries.

In table 5, at the top of page 80, the HDIs appear as averages within each of the Clark categories set out in table 3. A cursory glance at table 5 reveals that even though the data are separated by some seventy years (the Clark data are for 1925–1934, and the HDI data are from 2007, published in the 2009 *HDR*) and measure different (but related) aspects of development, the ranking remains consistent. This relationship can be seen even more clearly in figure 1, at the bottom of page 80, where the HDIs are plotted against the midpoints of the Clark income–per capita categories of table 5.

Table 4. Three Components of the Human Development Index (HDI)

Goal	Indicator
Improve health care and living conditions	Life expectancy from birth (years)
Improve education	Adult (age of 15 and above) literacy rate (%)
	Gross enrollment ratio (primary, secondary, and tertiary education)
Improve income	Gross domestic product ($US) per capita

Source: author.

Table 5. Country Ranking by Income and HDI

Average Yearly Income per Capita*	County/Region	2009 HDI** (average across the countries/regions)
1,300–1,400	United States, Canada	0.961
1,200–1,300	New Zealand	0.950
1,100–1,200		
1,000–1,100	Great Britain, Switzerland, Argentina	0.924
900–1,000	Australia	0.970
800–900	Holland	0.964
700–800	Ireland	0.965
600–700	France, Denmark, Sweden, Germany, Belgium, Uruguay	0.941
500–600	Norway, Austria, Spain, Chile	0.940
400–500	Czechoslovakia, Yugoslavia, Iceland, Brazil	0.877
300–400	Greece, Finland, Hungary, Poland, Latvia, Italy, Estonia, USSR, Portugal, "Rest of America," Japan, Palestine, Philippines, Algeria, Egypt, Hawaii, Guam	0.848
200–300	Bulgaria, Rumania, Lithuania, Albania, Turkey, Syria, Cyprus, South Africa, Morocco, Tunis	0.793
Under 200	China, British India, Dutch Indies, "Rest of Asia," "Rest of Africa," "Rest of Oceania"	0.664

Sources: Clark (1940); UNDP (1990 and 2009).

*Refers to the period 1925–1934. Artificial income unit has been adjusted for purchasing power (after Clark 1940, 54).

**Human Development Index as published in the 2009 Human Development Report (UNDP, 2009)

Figure 1

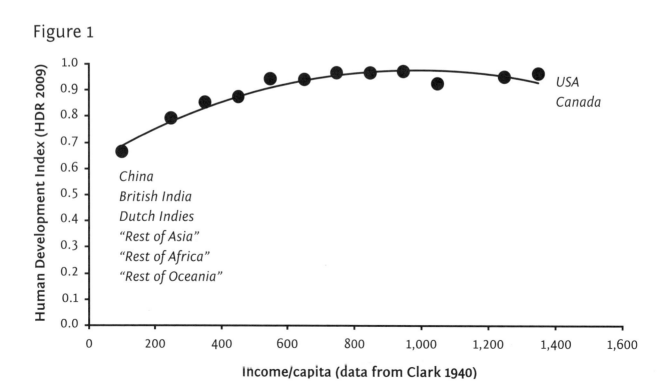

The line has been added to illustrate the form of a statistically significant relationship between these points.

While the HDI is the headline index of the *HDRs* and attracts the most attention, the UNDP has sought to create other indexes—such as the gender-related development index (GDI), the gender-empowerment measure (GEM), the human poverty index (HPI), and the technology achievement index (TAI)—to highlight other important aspects of human development. In each case the index has been created to reflect a dimension of human development that the UNDP sees as important; thus the index follows the vision—not the other way around.

Challenges: The Future of Indicators

The brief picture of development indicators presented here illustrates the various styles of indicator formulation and presentation, from a single (but widely used) indicator such as GDP to the suite of indicators in the MDGs and the HDI composite index. In each case the indicator must produce good quality data, or, no matter how well rationalized and constructed the indicator is, the results could be misleading.

It is also important to note that all indicators are value laden. This can be easy to miss given that indicators are typically numerical and derived from what are often complex methodologies. They feel technical, mechanical, and objective, remote from any potential for bias. Yet the decisions over which indicators to select (as with the MDGs), how they are to be constructed (as with the poverty gap ratio and income–per capita adjustments in the HDI), and how they are presented and interpreted are made by people, and no matter how well rationalized, their decisions are still nothing more than informed opinion. That is, anyone can select different MDG indicators and create a different HDI, provide their own rationale, and create very different pictures

of the progress toward human development. In practice, of course, indicators often emerge out of a process of consultation and are created by groups of experts with the knowledge, authority, and resources required.

Finally, but not least, there are the key questions as to how indicators and indices are to be used and by whom. In some cases this is relatively straightforward. For example, many governments use GDP when setting economic policy. In other cases, the rationale is not as clear, as when national and international agencies use MDG indicators to chart progress toward meeting a goal. Each MDG has a number of indicators associated with it, so when some of those indicators suggest a target has been met while others do not, the agency gets a somewhat muddy picture. Using the HDI presents even more difficulties. There are no defined goals with the HDI: the index suggests a direction of travel rather than a final destination. The extent to which HDI indicators should influence policy is a matter of much debate, and, perhaps surprisingly, has received very little attention within the research community.

Development indicators are useful tools for condensing complex information into digestible numbers. They are invaluable to the people charged with monitoring development because they provide a means by which progress can be charted. They also give nonexperts a way to promote their vision of development. But while all of this helps explain their popularity, development indicators do need to be handled with care. We must remember that all indicators are selected by people, who, even if they are experienced experts, are subject to human bias and the influence of others.

Stephen MORSE
University of Surrey

See also Agenda 21; Environmental Performance Index (EPI); Framework for Strategic Sustainable Development (FSSD); Genuine Progress Indicator (GPI); Global Environment Outlook (GEO) Reports; Gross National

Happiness; Human Development Index (HDI); Millennium Development Goals; Population Indicators; Sustainable Livelihood Analysis (SLA)

FURTHER READING

Booysen, Frederik. (2002). An overview and evaluation of composite indices of development. *Social Indicators Research, 59*(2), 115–151.

Clark, Colin. (1940). *The conditions of economic progress.* London: Macmillan.

Gallopín, Gilberto C. (1996). Environmental and sustainability indicators and the concept of situational indicators: A systems approach. *Environmental Modeling and Assessment, 1*(3), 101–117.

Morse, Stephen. (2004). *Indices and indicators in development: An unhealthy obsession with numbers.* London: Earthscan.

Sachs, Jeffrey D., & McArthur, J. W. (2005). The millennium project: A plan for meeting the millennium development goals. *The Lancet, 365*(9456), 347–353.

Sidanšek, Aleksander. (2007). Sustainable development and happiness in nations. *Energy, 32*(6), 891–897.

Truman, Harry S. (1949, January 20). Truman's inaugural address. Retrieved November 12, 2011, from http://www.trumanlibrary.org/whistlestop/50yr_archive/inagural20jan1949.htm

United Nations Development Programme (UNDP). (1990). *Human development report: Concept and measurement of human development.* Retrieved February 8, 2011, from http://hdr.undp.org/en/reports/global/hdr1990/

United Nations Development Programme (UNDP). (2009). *Human development report: Overcoming barriers: Human mobility and development.* Retrieved February 8, 2011, from http://hdr.undp.org/en/reports/global/hdr2009/

United Nations Millennium Development Goals (UN MDG). (n.d.) Homepage. Retrieved January 16, 2012, from www.un.org/millenniumgoals

World Bank. (1978). *World development report.* Retrieved February 8, 2011, fromhttp://econ.worldbank.org/external/default/main?pagePK=64165259&theSitePK=469072&piPK=64165421&menuPK=64166322&entityID=000178830_98101903334595

Ecolabels

Ecolabels are logos that inform consumers about a product's environmental features from production to disposal. Ecolabels may cover all attributes affecting the environment or a single one, such as organic production or energy efficiency. Many consumers will pay more for environmentally friendly goods if they can identify them easily and trustworthily. Understanding how that price premium works, however, it is not always a straightforward process.

An ecolabel is a specially designed, trustable logo that informs consumers about the environmental attributes and impacts of a product over its entire life cycle—the phases of production, consumption, and waste—which all affect the environment. Ecolabels can pertain to services, such as tourist accommodations, as well. They contribute to the efforts of making consumption patterns more sustainable. This process occurs in three stages.

First, we need to know and understand what unsustainable practices we want to change; second, we need a strong willingness to change habits; and third, we must be able to make changes happen. Ecolabels help by reducing the information asymmetry between buyers and sellers. This asymmetry arises because consumers cannot directly and easily identify a good's environmental attributes, while producers focus on communicating just its environmentally positive ones. In order to reduce this asymmetry, an ecolabel needs to make an adequate, reliable, and effective contribution to a producer's communication with consumers.

Ecolabels have a threefold purpose (Galarraga 2002):

1. To support more environmentally friendly consumption patterns by providing trustable, verifiable information that enables consumers to make an informed choice about products

2. To raise the environmental standards of the products or services produced by companies, governments, and other agents

3. To provide a competitive advantage over nonlabeled (or less environmentally friendly) goods and services

The labels themselves are divided into three types (OECD 1997).

Type I labels compare the environmental characteristics of a specific good with the rest of the goods in the same range, identifying the best in class through a special logo. These labels are usually granted by a third party based on independent expert assessments, and using them is voluntary. Although all environmental labels are often called ecolabels, Type I labels are the only ones that are officially referred to as such. Some well-known examples are the Blue Angel (Germany), the Nordic Swan (Nordic countries), the EU Ecolabel (European Union), and the NF-Environnement Mark (France).

Type II labels make one-sided claims by producers regarding a good's environmental attributes, for example, "CFC-free," "organic," or "carbon neutral." The relevant literature holds that third-party certification is not required for Type II labels, but nowadays most products bearing these logos do rely on some kind of authority that supports their claims. There is growing legislation in most countries to regulate this type of label in order to prevent fraud.

Type III labels use preset indices to provide quantified information about products. These labels also are based on independent, third-party verification. They are referred to as "environmental declarations" and are regulated by the International Organization for Standardization in ISO 14025.

Type I and Type II labels are referred to broadly as "ecolabels" or "environmental labels." Other label types cover attributes in addition to environmental ones, such as fair-trade labels.

Table 1, below, lists examples of existing ecolabeling initiatives. While this list is not exhaustive, it does represent a good sample of the most relevant labels. A complete list can be found at the Ecolabel Index website (www.ecolabelindex.com/ecolabels); it covers 378 ecolabels in 211 countries and 25 industry sectors.

Having a large number of competing labels in the market can generate confusion, so it is important for labeling organizations to clearly set out criteria, with some degree of convergence between different jurisdictions. Promoting environmentally friendly goods encourages the purchase of both private and public goods. (When consumers acquire an efficient appliance, they are buying a private good, at the same time generating what is known by economists as a public good—for the benefit of all—through the reduction of environmental impact.)

Labels can contribute to changing consumption habits and the ways that goods and services are produced.

Ecolabels can coexist with other policy instruments designed with similar purpose, such as environmental taxes, subsidies, ecocertification, or mandatory standards, and in some cases can be used to support these. For instance, subsidy programs to promote the use of certain environmentally friendly goods could be based on whether or not the goods have a label.

Although the idea of ecolabeling seems simple, there are some concerns related to the impacts of labeling policies, mainly (1) what is the market impact of using these labels and the consequent environmental impact? and (2) what impact will they have on international trade?

Numerous studies address market/environmental impacts in theoretical or quantitative terms (Delmas and Grant 2010; Crespi and Marette 2005; Galarraga and Markandya 2004). The main issues are the objectivity with which criteria are set up, the differences between goods in a given group (as two goods are unlikely to be exactly and easily comparable), the lack of information about demand for labels and willingness to pay for the

TABLE 1. Examples of Ecolabeling around the World

Country	Program	Starting Date	Type
Australia	Environmental Choice	1991	Abandoned in 1993 due to industry opposition
Canada	Environmental Choice	1988	Government sponsored
China	Green Label	NA	
European Union (EU):			
Austria	Hundertwasser Seal	1991	Government sponsored
France	NF-Environnement	1992	Government sponsored
Germany	Blue Angel	1978	Government sponsored
Netherlands	Stichting Milieukeur	1992	Government sponsored
Norway	Good Environmental Choice	1991	Privately sponsored
Scandinavia	Nordic Swan	1991	Government sponsored
Sweden	Good Environmental Choice	1988	Privately sponsored
Other countries	EU Ecolabel	1992	Most of the other countries plan to follow EU lead
India	Ecomark	1991	Government sponsored
Japan	Ecomark	1989	Government sponsored
New Zealand	Environmental Choice	1992	Government sponsored
Singapore	Green Label	1992	Government sponsored
South Korea	Ecomark	1992	Government sponsored
Taiwan	Environmental Seal	NA	
United States	Green Seal	1989	Privately sponsored
	SCS Claim Certification	1989	Privately sponsored

Source: Morris (1997).

attributes certified, how labeling programs are reviewed to ensure that the goods labeled remain among the most environmentally friendly (the attributes of other comparable goods might improve continuously), and whether labels might generate confusion among consumers.

There is no clear consensus on these topics, although there is general agreement that while sales have increased when labeling programs have been used, the labeling programs have failed to generate a significant market impact (OECD 1997; see Galarraga 2002 for a more detailed discussion of these issues). The Global Ecolabel Monitor (2010) provides an in-depth assessment of the programs based on questionnaires sent to 340 labeling programs worldwide. The main findings corroborate the need to improve transparency and accountability, the opportunities that collaboration among them can offer, and the need to measure and monitor the impacts of the programs.

With regard to impacts of ecolabeling on international trade, developing countries are becoming concerned that (a) environmental criteria represented by the logo might not be an important feature in the country of origin, (b) labels might be misused as some sort of trade barrier, and (c) they might have an important impact on competitiveness because of the higher costs that producers must incur in order to comply with requirements (see Zarrilli, Jha, and Vossenaar 1997 for an overview of international concerns).

Demand for Environmental Attributes

There is growing evidence of consumer willingness to pay for environmentally friendly goods or for product attributes that might be in line with their preferences. This information is essential for the design of effective labeling programs. One of the main challenges is to reduce the so-called intention-behavior gap between what consumers claim to be willing to pay and what they actually pay when they go to the market. Therefore, some studies (see, for example, Galarraga and Markandya 2004) focus mainly on what consumers actually pay rather than what they say they will pay.

Table 2, below, lists examples of the information available on demand for labels.

TABLE 2. Information on Demand for Labels

Country	Information	Study
Canada	64% of respondents willing to pay a 10% premium for a product bearing the Ecologo.	Quoted in Zarrilli, Jha, and Vossenaar (1997)
Europe	Consumers willing to pay a 5%–15% premium for sustainable timber products.	Varangis, Braga, and Takeuchi (1993)
Europe	37% of consumers would be prepared to pay a premium of 10% for bananas of equivalent quality produced according to fair-trade standards.	COM (1999)
Europe	70% of consumers who had already bought fair-trade goods would pay at least a 10% premium for fair-trade bananas.	COM (1999)
Germany	75% of people willing to buy environmentally friendly products at a higher price.	Robins and Roberts (1997)
Germany	50% of the people willing to buy environmentally friendly products at a higher price.	Robins and Roberts (1997)
Germany	50% of people ready to buy if clearly labeled.	Robins and Roberts (1997)
Germany	80% of people recognize and understand the Blue Angel label.	Robins and Roberts (1997)
Germany	The relevance of the class-A energy label attribute in the choice of five major household appliances was surveyed for Germany. They conclude that socioeconomic characteristics have little impact on appliance energy class choice. Regional electricity prices and residence characteristics do have an impact.	Mills and Schleich (2010)
Netherlands	Price for labeled flowers is about 30% higher.	Cited in Zarrilli, Jha, and Vossenaar (1997)

TABLE 2. *Continued*

Country	Information	Study
Singapore	5% premium for the Singapore Green label.	Jha, Vossenaar, and Zarrilli (1993)
Spain	The price premium paid on the market for dishwashers carrying an energy-efficient label is close to 15.6% of the final price. This percentage accounts for around 80 euros.	Galarraga, González-Eguino, and Markandya (2010)
Spain	The price premium paid for the highest energy-efficiency label (A+) in the refrigerator market in the Basque Autonomous Community (Spain) is 8.9% of the final price, or about 60 euros, which represents one-third of the energy savings that a consumer gets during the lifetime of a refrigerator with the highest energy-efficiency label.	Galarraga, Heres Del Valle, and González-Eguino (2011)
United Kingdom	67% of a sample of 1,000 adults stopped using (buying) products believed to be dangerous or environmentally harmful.	Smith (1990)
United Kingdom	25%–50% of Britons ready to pay up to 25% premium for (credible) goods with improved environmental performance.	Quoted in Peattie (1995)
United Kingdom	33% of the public surveyed is willing to pay an average 13% premium for sustainably produced timber.	Quoted in Zarrilli, Jha, and Vossenaar (1997)
United Kingdom	The presence of the "green" characteristic will increase the price of an average grade of coffee by 11.26%.	Galarraga and Markandya (2004)
United States	82% of consumers ready to pay a 5% premium for "greener" products.	Quoted in Levin (1990)
United States	Willingness to pay (WTP) for environmental/health attributes on food between 5%–7%.	van Ravenswaay and Hoehn (1991)
United States	34% of consumers surveyed willing to pay a 6%–10% price premium for sustainable wood.	Winterhalter and Cassens (1993)
United States	96% of consumers claimed to use environmental criteria in purchasing, at least occasionally.	Quoted in Peattie (1995)
United States	75% of consumers surveyed willing to pay a 1%–5% price premium for sustainable wood.	Quoted in Zarrilli, Jha, and Vossenaar (1997)
United States	60% of consumers willing to pay a 10% premium (or higher) for some "green" products.	Quoted in Morris (1997)

Source: Galarraga (2002) and authors.

Labeling Examples and Impacts

This section offers insights regarding some interesting labeling initiatives: the Energy Efficiency, EU Ecolabel, and organic and other food labels. These examples have been chosen to offer a wide view of some of the most predominant uses of labels. Specifically, energy-efficiency labels were chosen due to the growing importance they have on the context of climate policies; the EU Ecolabel is a well-known example of Type I labels; and finally food labeling was chosen due to the great attention that features such as "organic" or other directly/indirectly health-related attributes are attracting.

Energy-Efficiency Labels

The use of ecolabels to promote energy-efficient products is a fairly recent phenomenon, and there is a mixture of public and private programs running. Research suggests that government programs in general have been more successful than privately administered programs (Banerjee and Salomon 2003), and the key factors for success are government support and credibility, budget, publicity and partnerships, label clarity, targeted product category, legislative mandate, and incentives.

A study of five well-known US ecolabel programs for energy efficiency and sustainability (Green Seal, Scientific Certification Systems, Energy Guide, Energy Star, and Green-e) supports these findings, looking at consumer and manufacturer responses to the programs (Banerjee and Salomon 2003). An important feature of the programs is the method of establishing criteria for product category eligibility to use the label. Issues taken into account include ensuring that significant nationwide energy saving is achieved; product performance can be maintained or even increased with energy-efficiency improvements; payback times are adequate; the improved energy efficiency can actually be achieved by companies and is not limited by a technology not in general use for proprietary reasons; consumption and performance can be measured and checked; and consumers perceive labeled products as distinct from unlabeled products. With all these in mind, a list of potential products is prepared and prioritized, and then work begins with the industry and other stakeholders. In the case of the most significant energy labels, carbon saving is also an important criterion.

There is usually a trade-off between accuracy (and/or thoroughness) and readability when designing any label: a more complete label is less easy to read and more difficult to understand. The goal, therefore, is to achieve the optimum combination of information and comprehension. For energy-efficiency labels in particular, one additional feature deserves attention, that is, whether energy-efficiency savings can lead to greater energy demand and therefore to a "rebound effect" that could invalidate their advantages. No conclusive results are available with respect to this issue, as it depends on the consumers at whom the label is aimed and the particularities of different programs and consumer types (see, for instance, Howarth, Haddad, and Paton 2000).

In the European Union (EU), there is a mandatory EU appliance energy-consumption label that rates household appliances with a letter from A to G according to their efficiency (some new categories have been added, such as A+ and A++, to account for significant efficiency improvements in appliance production) so consumers can choose accordingly. Some authors have found that the tendency to buy "A" appliances increases with more favorable residence characteristics (such as the size, year built, or whether it is a detached house) and in some cases with regional electricity prices, but that socioeconomic characteristics have little impact on the choice (Mills and Schleich 2010).

Other research also studied voluntary labels in terms of simplicity of label design, the environmental standard chosen, the completeness of the assessment procedure, promotional effects, support from stakeholder groups, and acceptance/criticism (see, for instance, McWhinney et al. 2005 and Saidur, Masjuki, and Mahlia 2005). Again, the results are not conclusive.

The EU Ecolabel

The European Union Ecolabel is a voluntary program established in 1992 to promote environmentally friendly products and services. The EU Ecolabel covers a wide range of products that continues to increase. Groups include cleaning products, appliances, paper products, textile and home and garden products, lubricants, and services such as tourist accommodation. EU Ecolabel products can be sold in the European Union and the European Economic Area countries (Norway, Iceland, and Liechtenstein). The EU Ecolabel program is regulated by Regulation (EC) No 66/2010 of the European Parliament and of the Council (25 November 2009); the EU Ecolabel is part of a broader action plan on Sustainable Consumption and Production and Sustainable Industrial Policy adopted by the European Commission on 16 July 2008.

The EU Ecolabel illustrates just how many categories of goods and services can be included in an ecolabel initiative. It covers twenty-four product categories distributed across twelve groups: cleaning (five categories), clothing (two categories), do-it-yourself (one category), electronic equipment (three categories), floor coverings (three categories), furniture (one category), gardening (one category), household appliances (two categories), lubricants (one category), other household items (one category), paper (two categories), and services (two categories).

The EU Ecolabel criteria are based on the environmental performance of products over their whole life cycle, assessing their impact on climate change, nature and biodiversity, energy consumption and resources; and their generation of waste and hazardous substances, pollution, and emissions.

More than ten thousand companies had been awarded the EU Ecolabel by the start of 2010, at which point Italy (331) and France (203) had the most Ecolabel holders. Tourist accommodation accounts for 37 percent of the licenses.

Organic and Food Labels

Many labels can be included in this category, such as "dolphin-safe" labels for tuna; "organic" labels for foods, such as fruit, wine, vegetables, coffee, tea, and other products (cotton, for instance), as well as ecolabels for fish.

Some researchers have compared labeling for wine in California (Delmas and Grant 2010) and in Colorado (Loureiro 2003). All suggest that ecolabels are not sufficient per se to generate willingness to pay a premium unless they are associated with good quality. Unfortunately, not all labeled products are associated with better intrinsic quality. In fact, in the case of wine, a label stating the origin of the wine (e.g., Bourdeaux, La Rioja, or California) is usually more effective; however, this kind of label cannot be considered an ecolabel.

For organic products, associating the label with health benefits proves effective, as in the case of Patagonia organic cotton sportswear (Casadesus-Masanell et al. 2009). Consumers pay a significant price premium because of their perception of benefit. It should be noted, however, that there are at least two types of certification for organic products in general: "organic" itself and "biodynamic." The latter means that products are not only grown with no pesticides, hormones, or additives—thus causing a smaller environmental impact—but also help preserve a self-sufficient, healthy ecosystem. Other studies find a premium of around 11 percent for fair-trade and organic coffee (Galarraga and Markandya 2004).

Other labeled food products are available in many countries (for instance, the Netherlands, Germany, and the United States), although it is not always clear whether consumers are adequately informed about the real biological and environmental impacts of each product, mainly because it is difficult to trace the degree of producer compliance with program requirements: this information is not available to the public. The degree of trust that consumers place in the labeling body is therefore one of the crucial issues to be taken into account when discussing the effectiveness of programs.

The use of ecolabels for fisheries has been growing since 2000. These labels clearly state how, when, and where the fish were caught as proof of the sustainability of the fishing activity. Sustainable fishing should provide guarantees regarding the prevention of overfishing, depletion of the resource, and protection of the ecosystem.

The Future of Ecolabels

While the growing trend of ecolabels covering one or more characteristics of a product might seem positive, there is still a need for traditional ecolabels that assess a product's or service's overall environmental attributes. This is especially true for labeling programs that have built a good reputation for trustworthiness, provide access to significant amounts of relevant information, and have managed to keep numbers low. Regulating and controlling the use of confusing terms such as *bio* or

natural is also important. The way forward might lie in having a limited number of labels that are proven to enhance the protection of the environment in a quantifiable way. This would allow competition among labels to help reduce confusion and promote the survival of the most suitable.

In light of the need to embrace climate change policies at national and local levels, it seems clear that labels helping to identify energy-efficiency attributes, carbon footprint, and other relevant characteristics of goods and services are both appropriate and necessary. Focusing on single (or a few) attributes also helps minimize the problems that ecolabels face. Other issues, such as the impacts of labels on international trade, welfare, and competitiveness, will continue to be topics for in-depth discussion, as no clear consensus on them has yet emerged.

Ibon GALARRAGA and Luis María ABADIE
Basque Centre for Climate Change (BC3)

See also Advertising; Cost-Benefit Analysis; Energy Labeling; International Organization for Standardization (ISO); Life Cycle Assessment (LCA); Life Cycle Costing (LCC); Life Cycle Management (LCM); Material Flow Analysis (MFA); Organic and Consumer Labels; Supply Chain Analysis

FURTHER READING

Abadie, Luis María, & Chamorro, Jose M. (2010). Toward sustainability through investments in energy efficiency. In W. H. Lee & V. G. Cho (Eds.), *Handbook of sustainable energy* (pp. 735–774). New York: Nova Science Publishers.

Banerjee, Abhijit, & Solomon, Barry D. (2003). Eco-labeling for energy efficiency and sustainability: A meta-evaluation of U.S. programs. *Energy Policy, 31*(2), 109–123.

Blue Angel. (2011). Homepage. Retrieved March 24, 2011, from http://www.blauer-engel.de/en/blauer_engel/index.php

Casadesus-Masanell, Ramon; Crooke, Michael; Reinhardt, Forest; & Vasishth, Vishal. (2009). Households' willingness to pay for "green" goods: Evidence from Patagonia's introduction of organic cotton sportswear. *Journal of Economics & Management Strategy, 18*(1), 203–233.

Commission of the European Communities (COM). (1999, November 29). Communication from the Commission to the Council on "fair trade." Brussels, Belgium: Commission of the European Communities.

Crespi, John M., & Marette, Stéphan. (2005). Eco-labeling economics: Is public involvement necessary? In Signe Krarup & Clifford S. Russell (Eds.), *Environment, information and consumer behavior* (pp. 93–110). Northampton, MA: Edward Elgar.

Delmas, Magali A., & Grant, Laura E. (2010, March 11). Eco-labeling strategies and price premium: The wine industry puzzle. Retrieved February 21, 2011, from http://bas.sagepub.com/content/early/2010/03/04/0007650310362254.abstract

Ecolabel Index. (2011). All ecolabels. Retrieved February 19, 2011, from http://www.ecolabelindex.com/ecolabels/

Energy Star. (2011). Homepage. Retrieved February 19, 2011, from http://www.energystar.com/

European Commission. (2011a). Energy efficiency: Energy labelling of domestic appliances. Retrieved February 19, 2011, from http://ec.europa.eu/energy/efficiency/labelling/labelling_en.htm

Galarraga Gallastegui, Ibon. (2002), The use of eco-labels: A review of the literature. *European Environment, 12*(6), 316–331.

Galarraga, Ibon, & Markandya, Anil. (2004). Economic techniques to estimate the demand for sustainable products: A case study for fair trade and organic coffee in the United Kingdom. *Economía Agraria y Recursos Naturales, 4*(7), 109–134.

Galarraga, Ibon; González-Eguino, Mikel; & Markandya, Anil. (2010). Evaluating the role of energy efficiency labels: The case of dish washers (BC3 Working Paper Series 2010–06.) Bilbao, Spain: Basque Centre for Climate Change (BC3).

Galarraga, Ibon; Heres Del Valle, David; & González-Eguino, Mikel. (2011). Price premium for high-efficiency refrigerators and calculation of price-elasticities for close-substitutes: Combining hedonic pricing and demand systems (BC3 Working Paper Series.) Bilbao, Spain: Basque Centre for Climate Change (BC3).

Global Ecolabel Monitor. (2010). Towards transparency. Retrieved February 19, 2011, from http://www.ecolabelindex.com/downloads/Global_Ecolabel_Monitor2010.pdf

Gudmundsson, Eyjolfur, & Wessells, Cathy Roheim. (2000). Ecolabeling seafood for sustainable production: Implications for fisheries management. *Marine Resource Economics, 15,* 97–113.

Howarth, Richard B.; Haddad, Brent M.; & Paton, R. Bruce. (2000). The economics of energy efficiency: Insights from voluntary participation programs. *Energy Policy, 28*(6), 477–486.

Jha, Veena; Vossenaar, René; & Zarrilli, Simonetta. (1993). Eco-labelling and international trade (United Nations Conference on Trade and Development Discussion, UN Document 70). Geneva: UNCTAD.

Levin, Gary. (1990). Consumers turning green: JWT survey. *Advertising Age, 61,* 74.

Loureiro, Maria L. (2003). Rethinking new wines: Implications of local and environmentally friendly labels. *Food Policy, 28*(5–6), 547–560.

McWhinney, Marla, et al. (2005). ENERGY STAR product specification development framework: Using data and analysis to make program decisions. *Energy Policy, 33*(12), 1613–1625.

Mills, Bradford, & Schleich, Joachim. (2010). What's driving energy efficient appliance label awareness and purchase propensity? *Energy Policy, 38*(2), 814–825.

Morris, Julian. (1997). *Green goods? Consumers, product labels and the environment* (IEA Studies on the Environment No. 8). London: Institute of Economic Affairs (IEA).

Organization for Economic Co-operation and Development (OECD). (1997). Eco-labelling: Actual effects of selected programmes. Paris: OECD.

Peattie, Ken. (1995). *Environmental marketing management: Meeting the green challenge.* London: Pitman Publishing.

Potts, Tavis, & Haward, Marcus. (2007). International trade, eco-labelling, and sustainable fisheries—recent issues, concepts and practices. *Environment, Development and Sustainability, 9*(1), 91–106.

Robins, Nick, & Roberts, Sarah. (Eds.). (1997). *Unlocking trade opportunities: Changing consumption and production patterns.* London: International Institute for Environment and Development (IIED).

Saidur, Rahman; Masjuki, H. H.; & Mahlia, T. M. Indra. (2005). Labeling design effort for household refrigerator-freezers in Malaysia. *Energy Policy, 33*(5), 611–618.

Smith, Greg. (1990). How green is my valley. *Marketing and Research Today, 18*(2), 76–82.

Truffer, Bernhard; Markard, Jochen; & Wüstenhagen, Rolf. (2001). Eco-labeling of electricity-strategies and tradeoffs in the definition of environmental standards. *Energy Policy, 29*(11), 885–897.

van Ravenswaay, Eileen O., & Hoehn, John P. (1991). Consumer willingness to pay for reducing pesticides residues in food: Results of a nationwide survey. East Lansing: Department of Agricultural Economics, Michigan State University.

Varangis, Panos N.; Braga, Carlos Primo Alberto; & Takeuchi, Kenji. (1993). Tropical timber trade policies: What impact will eco-labelling have? *Wirtschaftspolitische Blatter, 3*(4), 338–351.

Winterhalter, Dawn, & Cassens, Daniel L. (1993). *United States hardwood forests: Consumer perception and willingness to pay.* West Lafayette, IN: Purdue University.

Zarrilli, Simonetta; Jha, Veena; & Vossenaar, René. (Eds.). (1997). *Eco-labelling and international trade.* London: Macmillan Press.

Ecological Footprint Accounting

Ecological Footprint accounting measures human demand on nature's resources, enabling a comparison to biocapacity, or nature's ability to renew resources. If the Footprint is larger than the available biocapacity, the result is a deficit. The deficit is compensated through ecological overshoot (extraction beyond regeneration) or net-import of biocapacity. Ecological overshoot, however, results in a depletion of ecological assets.

The Ecological Footprint emerged between 1990 and 1994 as the dissertation thesis of Mathis Wackernagel in collaboration with Professor William Rees, his thesis supervisor at the University of British Columbia. Acknowledging a primary challenge of sustainable development—to consume resources and energy within planetary constraints—Wackernagel and Rees wanted to translate these ecological limits into a measurable, observation-based concept that would overcome the somewhat relativistic definitions of sustainable development circulating in global policy debates at that time. The system they proposed was meant to allow researchers and analysts to assess, manage, and monitor the limitations of the Earth's biophysical resources.

Evidence of how such planetary restraints have been pushed to the limit (and often surpassed) surrounds us: When we catch more fish than waters can regenerate, fisheries eventually collapse. When we harvest more timber than forests can re-grow, we advance deforestation. When our modes of transport and methods of production emit more carbon dioxide than the biosphere can absorb, we increase the likelihood of global warming. This overuse of renewable resources is called "ecological overshoot." Simply put, the Footprint is an accounting system behind which stands an implicit warning that is also resonant in the theory of the Earth's limited carrying capacity: our failure to live within the budget of nature (i.e., to "overshoot"), will eventually lead to ecological—and economic—bankruptcy and collapse.

The Footprint accounting system aims to answer a basic question confronting sustainability researchers: how much of the planet's regenerative capacity does it take to support a particular human activity? The answer can be compared to the amount of materials and energy—such as food or fossil fuel and the resulting waste streams—that flow through ecosystems, from an individual or local level to a national or global scale. The question then becomes: how much regenerative capacity is required, using prevailing technology, to provide all the ecological services this population demands, including the resources it consumes and needs to absorb its waste?

Footprint accounts record "expenditure" and "income" entries on their "ledgers" and accordingly tally the actual amount of biological resources produced (and wastes absorbed) by the planet as well as how many resources humans extract and how much waste we generate. Another question thus arises when comparing both sides of the ledger: how much regenerative capacity (or biocapacity, for short) is available on planet Earth or in a particular region? In times of increasing ecological constraints, we need to assess and manage the human economy and humanity's demand on biocapacity by using an open, transparent, and scientific process applied in consistent and reproducible ways. The tools of the Footprint accounting system have this potential.

Ecological Footprint Accounts

In 2003 Mathis Wackernagel and Susan Burns founded Global Footprint Network as a home and global steward of Footprint methodology. (The organization has relied upon William Rees as a science and policy advisor from its inception.) Global Footprint Network's national and global accounts for 2010 show that in 2007, the most recent year for which data are available, humanity continued to overshoot renewable resources, demanding approximately 50 percent more than what the biosphere provided in that year.

The most detailed national Footprint accounts produced by Global Footprint Network use about 6,000 data points per country and year, and stretch back to 1961. The overwhelming majority of these data points are taken from official UN statistics such as the Food and Agriculture Organisation (FAO) or COMTRADE (UN Statistics' trade data base), or from leading intergovernmental agencies such as the International Energy Agency (IEA). Some data points stem from the UN or para-UN specialty literature such as Intergovernmental Panel on Climate Change (IPCC) reports.

If planetary limitations truly matter and if they are driving the global concern for sustainability, one may argue that understanding this relationship between human demand and biocapacity supply is as central for economies as it is for farmers to know the size of their farm. Whether their farmland extends over 5,000, 500, or 5 hectares makes a significant difference to the opportunities that are available to the farmer. The same "farmer logic" applies to any region or population. How can sustainability become operational or even tangible, one might ask, without understanding how much regenerative capacity is currently available, and what ecological constraints are affecting a particular region? The Footprint accounting system aims to address questions such as these, which are crucial to achieving sustainable development.

Calculating the Ecological Footprint

The Earth's surface space is the common platform for life, critical for obtaining inputs such as rainwater and sunlight. The underlying premise of the Footprint accounting system acknowledges that the ecological services demanded for human activities compete for space. Therefore, an Ecological Footprint is calculated as the biologically productive area (i.e., the space) necessary to sustain a population that uses a specified amount of resources.

This calculation is made by turning the formula for agricultural yield on its head. Since agricultural yield is defined as:

$$\text{Yield} = \frac{\text{Amount per year}}{\text{Area occupied}}$$

Algebraically, it follows that

$$\text{Area occupied} = \frac{\text{Amount per year}}{\text{Yield}}$$

Expressing the area results in hectares, however, can be deceiving because a typical hectare in Namibia is less productive than a typical hectare in France. In Footprint accounts, each hectare is adjusted for its respective biocapacity. These adjusted hectares are called *global hectares* and are the standard measurement units for both Footprint and biocapacity. Essentially, these global hectares represent a hectare with "world average" bioproductivity. This means that two actual hectares of land could be represented by vastly different amounts of global hectares—a highly productive hectare of cornfield in a soil-rich, moist, and climatically favorable area of the world may be worth over five global hectares, while a hectare of dry grassland may contain less than one-fifth of a global hectare's worth of bioproductivity. To refer to "one global hectare's worth of area" means that the unit should represent the same capacity to produce the same amount of biological regeneration, a proxy for overall ecological services. It is somewhat an approximation since the global hectares used in Footprint accounts are not exactly identical and do not provide identical services.

The Global Ecological Footprint

The distribution of natural resources and the consumption of materials are not evenly dispersed worldwide. Some countries make bigger footprints than their biocapacity allows. For instance, according to a Global Footprint Network Account based on data for 2007, ten countries generated about half of the Footprint that year, with the United States and China alone using 21 and 24 percent, respectively, of the Earth's biocapacity (Ewing et al. 2010, 18). Nations and regions run biocapacity deficits by net-importing biocapacity, by depleting their own ecological assets, or by using the global commons. The first two actions come at a cost. The latter, as in the example of fishing international waters or emitting carbon dioxide into the global atmosphere, is still predominantly payment free, but it nevertheless depletes resources. The national strategies (or at least unintended consequences of their strategies) of running ever larger biocapacity deficits are not globally replicable and therefore ever more risky to nations' own well-being.

On the other hand, some countries have an inherently larger biocapacity than others. Half of the world's biocapacity resides within the borders of eight countries. Brazil tops the chart followed in descending order by China, the United States, the Russian Federation, India, Canada, Australia, and Indonesia (Ewing et al. 2010, 18).

Human demand as a whole, however, has overshot what nature can renew since. Globally we are living "beyond the means of nature." (See figure 1 on page 93.)

Figure 1. Humanity's Ecological Footprint, 1961–2007

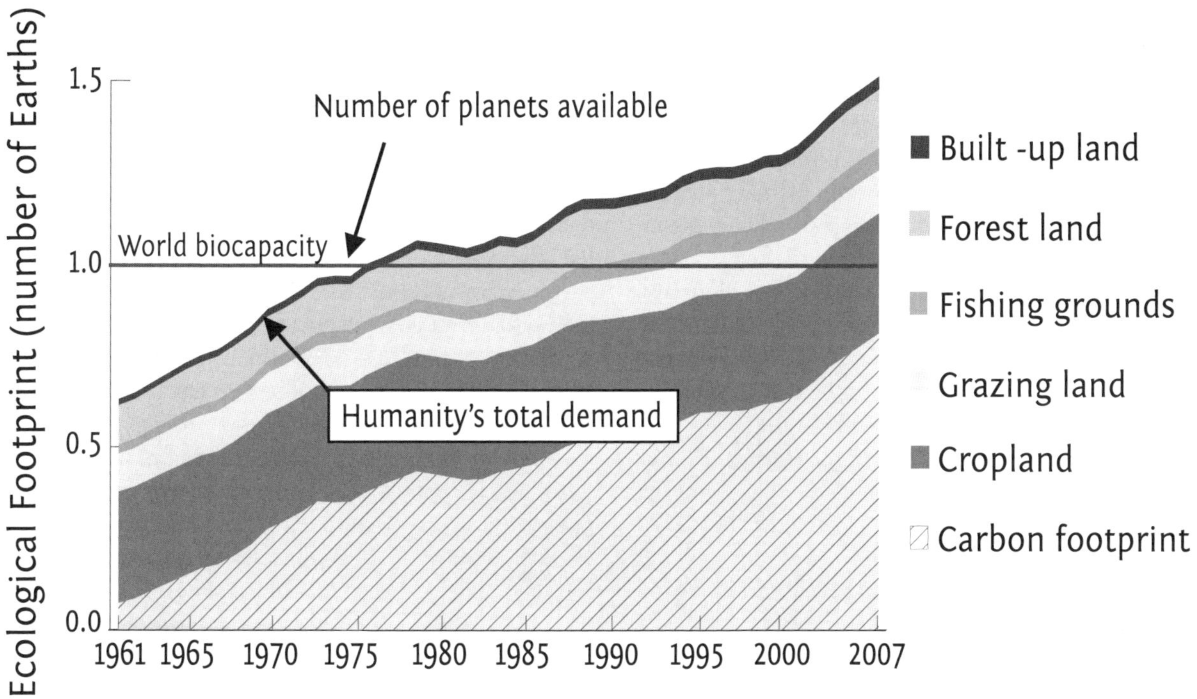

Source: Brad Ewing et al. (2010, 18).

This graph shows the ratio between human demand and the Earth's biocapacity, and the components of the human demand, from 1961 to 2007. Human demand can overshoot what nature can renew since it is possible to deplete stocks and fill waste sinks, thereby living "beyond the means of nature."

As the Footprint accounting system illustrates in figure 1, humanity did not start to draw down the principal of the planet's biocapacity until the 1970s and 1980s. Prior to that (as measured using data going back to 1961 by the Global Footwork), humanity was only spending the ecological interest. Figure 1 tracks six categories from 1961 to 2007: carbon footprint, forest, cropland, fishing grounds, grazing land, and built-up land.

Criticism, Assessments, and Responses

Criticism of the Footprint falls into three domains: skepticism about the usefulness of the research question, insufficient documentation and the quality of current results, and challenges to its methodology. In a few cases these criticisms overlap.

Several sources have challenged the Footprint accounting's viability in the context of policy making. For instance, the 2007 UK Department for Environment, Food, and Rural Affair (DEFRA) report, "A Review of Recent Developments in, and the Practical Use of, Ecological Footprinting Methodologies" (Risk & Policy Analysts Ltd. 2007), recommended that the UK

government not adopt the Footprint as a sustainability indicator. Basic reasons outlined in the report include: the unreliability of sub-national measurements due to the lack of specific data and inconsistent methodologies for collecting them (for example, input-output processes versus life cycle assessment processes); the Footprint assumption that expenditure reflects consumption; and the lack of empirical evidence that the Footprint can extend its capacity to raise consciousness and become a vehicle for changing behavior. And yet, as advocates of the Footprint accounting system point out, the United Kingdom has adopted no measure that gives them an even approximate answer to how much of the planet's regenerative capacity is demanded to support the nation, and how much of that capacity is available within the nation.

Global Footprint Network asserts that the DEFRA report was an example of a rather weak and biased assessment of the Footprint methodology, for which the ministry's consultants did not engage with the Footprint community to test their preconceptions; the network further asserts that the ministry did not show interest in soliciting input from the Footprint community for the report. In fact, after the first DEFRA assessment the ministry conceded soon after to redo the study. The same consultants produced the subsequent (2007) study referenced here, with the only input from Footprint experts conveyed to the consulting firm during a one-hour phone conversation. There was no provision made for the Global Footprint Network to fact-check a draft of the report. In contrast, the European Commission's assessment (European Commission—DG Environment 2008), far more inclusive, tested its assumptions with Footprint experts and generated a more meaningful and fair assessment of the Footprint's utility and scientific rigor.

Assuming that the Footprint's research questions are valid and relevant, and that the accounting system itself has the potential to be a valuable tool in sustainable development, some ask whether the Footprint method produces results that are sufficiently reliable and accurate for informing policy making. That question was raised in Eurostat's 2006 report "Ecological Footprint and Biocapacity: The World's Ability to Regenerate Resources and Absorb Waste in a Limited Time Period." The report stated that the Footprint concept "is a good tool for awareness rising" but that "current applications are too diverse and highly in-transparent" to be used among policy makers (Schaefer et. al [Eurostat] 2006, 4). While recognizing that the accuracy and detail of the results need further enhancement, Global Footprint Network maintains that the results are sufficiently strong to document a mismatch between human demand and nature's regenerative capacity. Also, to test the validity and transparency of the assessments, Global Footprint Network and its partners have encouraged a number of national governments to test the accounts, either independently, or if requested with technical assistance from Global Footprint Network. Over ten of those reviews have been completed and are available on the Internet (see a sampling in the Further Reading, under National and Regional Reports, below). For instance, the statistical office of the French Ministry of Sustainable Development reviewed the methodology and was able to regenerate the French Footprint and biocapacity time trend within 1–3 percent (Commissariat Général 2009, May).

If the foundations of the Footprint accounting system are accepted, then criticism of the methodology becomes relevant. Global Footprint Network's current development focuses on improvements in this area. To ensure that the Footprint accounting methodology is updated and improved in response to new scientific information—including data and the knowledge gleaned from a better understanding of geophysical processes—Global Footprint Network engages in ongoing internal and community reviews of its methodology through the activities of its National Accounts Review Committee. This committee, composed of representatives from the Network's partner organizations, is responsible both for suggesting methodological changes to the core National Footprint Accounts and for considering any changes suggested from external academics and reviewers. All changes to the calculation methodology are open for public comment before implementation, in accordance with the committee's charter, and external parties are encouraged to submit recommendations directly to Global Footprint Network for consideration by the committee. A complementary committee oversees the development of standards for Footprint accounting at all levels (Global Footprint Network 2012a).

Some criticism addresses the level of accuracy of current Footprint assessments, specifically that they exaggerate or underestimate actual overshoot. It is most likely true that current results more likely underestimate overshoot since the accounts are specifically designed to yield conservative estimates of human demand wherever data is inconclusive or issues are insufficiently documented. Ultimately, the accounts' purpose is to inform policy makers in each country about their particular risk exposure, and possible opportunities for their countries in a resource constrained world. Therefore, the accounts need to strive toward becoming reliable, well-documented, and simple to access. Hence it is essential for governments, as mentioned, to scrutinize the results posted on the Global Footprint Network (2012c) review page.

Eventually, advocates see Footprint assessments becoming part of a country's portfolio of measures, as have gross domestic product (GDP) accounts, unemployment statistics, or debt numbers. But until governments assume full financial and technical responsibility for implementing the measure, Global Footprint Network is providing its results with funds derived from donations made by foundations, individuals, and government agencies, as well as from data licensing. With this support, Global Footprint Network is also strengthening the robustness and accuracy of the accounts in the following ways, according to activities, resources, and research factors:

Trade

The current method utilizes estimated world average Footprint intensities for all traded goods and omits trade in services. By utilizing a global multiregional input–output model, the National Footprint Accounts will more comprehensively and consistently track energy and resource flows embodied in traded goods and services.

Equivalence Factors

Equivalence factors are central to Footprint analyses, as they provide the basis for consistent aggregation. They are key to translating a hectare into its respective global hectare value. The current equivalence factors are based on global-average agricultural suitability of various biomes. Proposed revisions to equivalence factors will include more in-depth and geographically specific assessments of the difference in the productivity of ecosystems across countries and across time, to factors that are important to consider separately.

Fisheries

The fishing grounds Footprint is currently under revision, with the aim of more explicitly incorporating estimates of sustainable yield, possibly even at the species level, and more geographically detailed catch and species range data. With fisheries being particularly complex due to the vast number of fish species being harvested, and the complexity and size of marine foodwebs, no global data set is yet available to help assess in somewhat accurate terms supply against demand in all of the globe's fishing grounds. In the interim, until better data sets are available through UN agencies, Global Footprint Network is using the data from the "Sea Around Us" project of the University of British Columbia, one of the most advance global fisheries data sets.

Carbon

Refinements are needed for specifying the biosphere's assimilative capacity for CO_2 emissions. Possible improvements include:

1. Define an explicit measure of the biocapacity available for carbon uptake, such that exceeding this capacity (measured in global hectares) results in an increase in atmospheric concentrations of CO_2.

2. Account for carbon uptake by multiple biomes, including narrowing our measure of marine carbon sequestration to encompass only biological fixation.
3. More explicitly include the latest scientific quantification of the fossil fuel driven as well as biotic carbon cycles, in order to more accurately gauge the flows between the human economy and the biosphere.

SEEA Compatibility

UN statistical agencies, supported by many national statistical offices, are driving the Integrated Environmental and Economic Accounting (SEEA) process, an effort to standardize environmental information across the globe to make it more relevant to economic decision making. The steering group is considering featuring the Ecological Footprint in Volume 3 of the SEEA documentation, the volume that will cover applications. At the same time, the National Footprint Accounts are being harmonized with the emerging SEEA standards, which in turn will improve the policy relevance and international utility of the National Footprint Accounts as it also will more easily allow Footprint analyses to be incorporated in economic decision making. One critical feature of this standardization is to ensure compatibility of categories, particularly when allocating national Footprint to consumption activities.

Sensitivity Analysis and Quality Assurance

A quantitative analysis of the National Footprint Accounts' sensitivity to inputs and assumptions will help guide future improvements to the source data and the calculation methodology.

Ongoing upgrades to the National Footprint Accounts' computational capabilities are improving data integrity and error checking, but also strengthening Global Footprint Network's governance structure, increasing the involvement of the committee in proactively selecting improvements to methodology and engaging with academic communities to resolve methodological issues.

Ideological Issues

Other themes and criticisms recurring in the literature address aspects that are not covered by the research questions or the actual results. For instance both the Stiglitz Commission (2007) report and the van den Bergh and Verbruggen (2007) article in *Ecological Economics* claim that Footprint accounting makes some normative assumptions that fail to take into account the diversity of peoples and environments on the planet and that Footprint accounting is anti-trade. In reality, trade is accounted for by allocating demand to the country that ultimately consumes these goods and services. This accounting reflects import and export flows, but makes no judgment regarding the benefits, disadvantages or fairness of trade. Studies have pointed out the risk of ecologically unbalanced trade, similar to the common understanding in economics that financially unbalanced trade poses risks. Therefore, Footprint supporters assert that this criticism does not really apply—Footprint accounts are merely a description of trade flows, not a prescription.

Footprint advocates address this criticism—that the Footprint accounting data mixes CO_2 emissions with resource generation—by asserting the following: the Footprint includes all competing demands on nature, and carbon sequestration does compete with many other human uses of the biosphere—hence the accumulation of CO_2 in the atmosphere. For instance, the primary lithosphere resource, fossil fuels, are constrained due to the biosphere's limited capacity to absorb waste, particularly CO_2 carbon dioxide emissions from burning fossil fuels.

Outlook for the Footprint

The verbal and general commitment to sustainable development as the common dream or necessary goal of humanity is ubiquitous in the global policy discourse. Still, few institutions or nations check the impact of their decisions, strategies or policies against the goal. Therefore, Global Footprint Network and its seventy partner organizations across the world aim at engaging business leaders and governments at all levels to track their demand on biocapacity and their resource availability.

For instance, to make progress in human development, project success should be measured against the project's ability to produce lasting progress for the project partners. Yet some analysts believe that the Millennium Development Goals for instance, without the necessary natural resources, are becoming unachievable, and current achievements may well erode. The United Nation's Development Programme is beginning to recognize this dilemma. UNEP's Green Economy is motivated by this recognition, and so is Vision 2050 of the World Business Council for Sustainable Development. All three build on Global Footprint Network's Human Development Index–Ecological Footprint framework, a measurement approach to track human development gains in the context of resource constraints.

Also, sustainable economics cannot succeed without bringing humanity back within the means of what planet Earth can renew. Therefore WWF International, one of the world's largest and most influential conservation organizations, has taken a lead role in promoting one-planet thinking, and is using the Ecological Footprint to do so. In fact, reducing humanity's Footprint to less than one planet has become one of their two main goals.

Mathis WACKERNAGEL
Global Footprint Network

See also Agenda 21; Business Reporting Methods; Carbon Footprint; Development Indicators; Fisheries Indicators, Freshwater; Fisheries Indicators, Marine; Genuine Progress Indicator (GPI); Global Environment Outlook (GEO) Reports; Global Reporting Initiative (GRI); $I = P \times A \times T$ Equation; *The Limits to Growth*; National Environmental Accounting; Triple Bottom Line

FURTHER READING

Chambers, Nicky; Simmons, Craig; & Wackernagel, M. (2000). *Sharing nature's interest: Ecological Footprints as an indicator for sustainability*. London: EarthScan.

Ewing, Brad; Moore, David; Goldfinger, Steven; Oursler, Anna; Reed, Anders; & Wackebagel, Mathis. (2010). *The Ecological Footprint Analysis 2010*. Oakland, CA: Global Footwork Network. Retrieved February 22, 2012, from http://www.footprintnetwork.org/images/uploads/Ecological_Footprint_Atlas_2010.pdf

Fiala, N. (2008). Measuring sustainability: Why the ecological footprint is bad economics and bad environmental science. *Ecological Economics, 67*, 519–525.

GIZ; Bayrischer Wald; & Global Footprint Network. (2009). A big foot on a small planet? Accounting with the Ecological Footprint; succeeding in a world with growing resource constraints. Retrieved February 19, 2012, from. http://www.conservation-development.net/index.php?L=2&ds=313

Global Footprint Network. (2012a). Application standards 2009. Retrieved February 16, 2012, from http://www.footprintnetwork.org/en/index.php/GFN/page/application_standards/

Global Footprint Network. (2012b). Data and results [2010 Data tables; Calculation methodology; 2008 National Footprint accounts guidebook]. Retrieved February 16, 2012, from http://www.footprintnetwork.org/images/uploads/Ecological_Footprint_Atlas_2010.pdf

Global Footprint Network. (2012c). National reviews. Retrieved February 22, 2012, from www.footprintnetwork.org/reviews

Grazi, F.; van den Bergh, Jeroen; & Rietveld, P. (2007). Spatial welfare economics versus ecological footprint: Modeling agglomeration, externalities and trade. *Environmental and Resource Economics, 38*, 135–153.

Kitzes, J. et al. (2009). A research agenda for improving national Ecological Footprint accounts. *Ecological Economics, 68*(7), 1991–2007. Retrieved February 16, 2012, from http://www.justinkitzes.com/pubs/Kitzes2009_EcoEco_Agenda.pdf

Kitzes, Justin; Peller. A.; Goldfinger, Steven; and Wackernagel, Mathis. (2007). Current methods for calculating national Ecological Footprint accounts. *Science for Environment & Sustainable Society* (Research Center for Sustainability and Environment, Shiga University), *4*(1).

Lenzen, M.; Murray, S.A. (2003). The Ecological Footprint—Issues and trends [ISA Research Paper 01–03]. Sydney: University of Sydney.

Moran, Daniel D. Moran; Wackernagel, Mathis; Kitzes, Justin A.; Goldfinger, Steven H.; & Boutaud, Aurélien. (2008). Measuring sustainable development—Nation by nation. *Ecological Economics, 64*(3), 470–474.

Rees, William E., & Wackernagel, Mathis. (1994). Ecological Footprints and appropriated carrying capacity: Measuring the natural capital requirements of the human economy. In AnnMari Jansson, Carl Folke, Monica Hammer, and Robert Costanza (Eds.), *Investing in natural capital.* Washington DC: Island Press.

Stake, Jeffrey E. (n.d.). How to protect from ranking-mania: The ranking game. Retrieved February 22, 2012, from http://monoborg.law.indiana.edu/LawRank/rankingmania.shtml

van den Bergh, Jeroen C. J. M.; & Verbruggen, Harmen. (1999). Spatial sustainability, trade and indicators: An evaluation of the "ecological footprint." *Ecological Economics, 29,* 61–72.

van Vuuren, D. P.; Bouwman, L. F. (2005). Exploring past and future changes in the ecological footprint for world regions. Ecological Economics, *52,* 43–62.

Venetoulis, J., & Talberth, J. (2008). Refining the ecological footprint. *Environment, Development, and Sustainability, 10,* 441–469.

Wackernagel, Mathis, and & Beyers, Bert. (2010). Die Welt neu vermessen [Ecological Footprint]. Hamburg, Germany: Europäische Verlagsanstalt.

Wackernagel, Mathis; Moran, Dan; & Goldfinger, Steven. (2006). Ecological Footprint accounting: Comparing Earth's biological capacity with an economy's resource demand. In Marco Keiner (Ed.) *The future of sustainability.* Berlin: Springer Verlag.

Wiedmann, Thomas, & Barrett, John A. (2010). Review of the Ecological Footprint indicator—Perceptions and methods. Sustainability, *2,* 1645–1693. doi:10.3390/su2061645

WWF International [World Wildlife Federation], Global Footprint Network, & Zoological Society of London. (2010). *Living planet report.* Gland Switzerland: WWF International.

National and Regional Reviews (sampling)

Commissariat Général Developpement Durable [Ministry of Sustainable Development] (2009, May). Une expertise de l'empreinte écologique [An expert assessment of the Ecological Footprint, No. 4, in French]. Retrieved February 22, 2012, from http://www.developpement-durable.gouv.fr/IMG/pdf/etudes_documents.pdf

European Commission—DG Environment (2008). Potential of the Ecological Footprint for monitoring environmental impact from natural resource use. Retrieved February 22, 2012, from http://ec.europa.eu/environment/natres/studies.htm

Federal Environment Agency [Germany/UMWETBUDESAMT]. Scientific assessment and evaluation of the indicator "Ecological Footprint." Research report 363 01 135. Retrieved February 18, 2012, from http://www.umweltdaten.de/publikationen/fpdf-l/3489.pdf

Risk & Policy Analysts Ltd. (2007). A review of recent developments in the use of ecological footprinting methodologies: A report to the Department for Environment, Food and Rural Affairs. London: DEFRA. Retrieved February 15, 2012, from http://www.rpaltd.co.uk/documents/J558Footprinting2Aug07.pdf

Schaefer, Florian; Luksch, Ute; Steinbanch, Nancy; Cabeça. Julio; & Hanauer, Jörg [Eurostat]. (2006). Ecological Footprint and biocapacity: The world's ability to regenerate resources and absorb waste in a limited time period. Luxembourg: European Communities. Retrieved February 21, 2012, from http://epp.eurostat.ec.europa.eu/cache/ITY_OFFPUB/KS-AU-06-001/EN/KS-AU-06-001-EN.PDF

Stigitz Commission. (2007). Report by the Commission on the Measurement of Economic Performance and Social Progress. Issues paper 25/07/08. Retrieved February 22, 2012, from http://www.stiglitz-sen-fitoussi.fr/documents/rapport_anglais.pdf

Ecological Impact Assessment (EcIA)

Ecological impact assessment (EcIA) is used to predict possible damage to biodiversity and ecosystems and identify the measures needed to avoid or reduce this damage when development is planned and implemented. It can be applied as part of broader impact assessment methods used to balance social, economic, and environmental concerns, such as environmental impact assessment (EIA), or it can be applied to wider land use plans or carried out independently.

Ecological impact assessment (sometimes abbreviated EcIA) is used to identify, predict, and evaluate the ecological consequences of new development, whether this is in the form of a localized, individual project or a wider-scale plan. It draws on ecological science to identify how living parts of the environment will be affected by a proposed activity and then applies more subjective methods to interpret the significance of the predicted ecological changes. The results are used to determine what actions should be taken to avoid adverse effects or to restore any damage (referred to as *mitigation*) (Treweek 1996). Doing this well requires interaction between those implementing a development project or plan, the ecological impact assessment practitioner, and those who are responsible for regulating the environment or making decisions about whether a proposed development should proceed.

Ecological impact assessment may be conducted as a stand-alone exercise or as part of impact assessments carried out to inform land-use planning (Wathern 1999). Impact assessment is used in many countries to provide land-use planners with the information they need to decide whether development should proceed from an environmental perspective and, if so, under what conditions. It is referred to as *environmental impact assessment* (EIA) when carried out for individual projects (such as new roads, hydroelectric power programs, mines) and *strategic environmental assessment* (SEA) when applied to policies, plans, or programs of development (a new transport policy, a regional transport plan, or a program of road development, respectively). Ecological aspects are just one of a whole suite of different environmental aspects that need to be addressed in impact assessment, but they are increasingly important because of the rate at which ecosystems and biodiversity (the richness and abundance of life in all its dimensions) are declining globally. Legal requirements to undertake ecological impact assessment vary between countries, as do the approaches and methods used, but most EIA and SEA systems include at least some requirement to address ecological impacts. Ecological impact assessment carried out as part of impact assessment provides an important opportunity to ensure that biodiversity and ecosystems are factored into or mainstreamed in development decisions.

Ecological impact assessment generally includes the following steps, though not necessarily in this order:

- Catalogue and understand the ecological dimension of the receiving environment (distributions, structure, and function) in the absence of the proposed development. This may be referred to as *baseline ecological assessment* and should include consideration of the changes that can be expected to occur anyway over time if the development does not occur.
- Identify the social, economic, and environmental changes that are likely to occur as a result of the development and define a "zone of ecological influence." This should include any changes that might be induced by the presence of the proposed development, or for which a clear causal link can be established, even if they might occur some distance away.

- Predict ecological responses to these changes and decide whether they are within the limits of baseline variation.
- Consider the ecological consequences of the changes that have been identified; for example, will any species suffer an irreversible decline toward extinction, or will a wetland ecosystem lose its water supply and disappear?
- Consider whether the ecological impacts that have been identified will be significant to anyone. Will people lose access to essential ecosystem services or will their well-being suffer because of the biodiversity decline? Establishing suitable criteria for evaluating significance is one of the more challenging tasks in ecological impact assessment.
- Identify measures to avoid or fix significant impacts (referred to as *mitigation*) and evaluate the ecological outcome with and without mitigation in place. Consider whether an acceptable outcome will be achieved given the criteria used to evaluate significance.
- Communicate the results, either as a stand-alone report or as part of a wider environmental statement or environmental impact report.

This should be followed by the important steps of monitoring and auditing to establish whether impacts were as predicted, whether mitigation measures worked, and whether a sustainable outcome was, in fact, achieved. In this context, a "sustainable outcome" is one in which affected ecosystems can be expected to remain in a healthy and viable state, and biodiversity can be expected to survive.

Origins and Development

First implemented in the United States in 1969, EIA has become an integral feature of planning systems in more than 120 countries and in many cases represents the only formal opportunity in the planning process for the ecological consequences of local development actions to be considered. Ecological considerations featured in EIA from its inception, but ecological impact assessment did not emerge as a specific discipline until the 1980s. A keynote paper by the Canadian environmentalists Gordon Beanlands and Peter Duinker in 1984 set out the scientific challenges inherent in applying ecology within the context of impact assessment, given its sociopolitical motivation. This catalyzed efforts to strengthen the scientific basis for ecological impact assessment, reflected in papers by Jo Treweek (1996) and Helen Byron (2000).

The United Nations Conference on Environment and Development (also called the Earth Summit or Rio Summit), which took place in Rio de Janeiro in 1992, resulted in the launch of the Convention on Biological Diversity (CBD). This reinforced the need to consider

impacts of development on biodiversity and resulted in a shift of emphasis in ecological impact assessment toward more explicit consideration of impacts on biodiversity and ecosystems. It also prompted renewed consideration of more strategic approaches to planning for biodiversity and a stronger emphasis on identification of alternatives that would result in reduced levels of ecological damage (Brownlie et al. 2005; Byron and Treweek 2005b).

The Millennium Ecosystem Assessment, published in 2000, further emphasized the need to include biodiversity in strategic planning and decision making because of its fundamental role in underpinning ecosystem services (the benefits that people get from ecosystems). Ecosystems directly support many livelihoods and provide essential goods and services to millions of people, but they are also being damaged by human activity at an unprecedented rate. The consequences and costs of this degradation are generally not accounted for in development planning because most of the services (for example, clean water, harvestable crops, fuel wood supply) are considered to be public goods. The fact expertise from the fields that there is no market value associated with them means they are typically under-priced or not priced at all. The internationally recognized study conducted by The Economics of Ecosystems and Biodiversity (TEEB) has further emphasized the growing costs of biodiversity loss and ecosystem degradation, as well as the need for closer integration of science, economics, and policy. The practice of ecological impact assessment has yet to respond to this challenge.

Application and Impact

Ecological impact assessment is now a well-established discipline, routinely used in many developed and developing countries either by itself or in conjunction with EIA and SEA to predict and evaluate ecological outcomes of new development (Byron and Treweek 2005a and 2005b). Many reviews of the environmental statements (ESs) produced to report the findings of EIA, however, have found the quality of ecological input to be particularly poor. Reviewers (see, for example, European Commission 1996; Mandelik, Dayan, and Feitelson 2005; Treweek 1996; Treweek and Thompson 1997, among others) have found poor impact prediction and lack of scientific rigor, although some improvement has been observed with time. The reasons cited are both technical and institutional and vary between countries. In Europe, the lack of a legal requirement to implement mitigation measures or to monitor their effectiveness has resulted in "paper promises" that are not delivered in practice. In many developing countries, quality of ecological impact assessment suffers from lack of reliable information that can be used to interpret impacts, but a more serious problem is the lack of regulatory capacity needed to influence the scope of ecological impact assessments and to enforce any conditions on development consent that might be required to achieve sustainable outcomes for ecosystems.

In many cases, ecological impact assessment has tended to focus solely on protected areas and species (Byron 2000) and has failed to give adequate consideration to the different levels of biodiversity (bioregions, landscapes, ecosystems, habitats, communities, species, populations, individuals, and genes); the structural relationships (e.g., connectivity, spatial linkage, fragmentation) and functional relationships (e.g., disturbance processes, nutrient cycling rates, energy flow rates, hydrologic processes) that are considered to be vital for thorough measurement of biodiversity (Noss 1990); sites or habitats that are not protected; or species that are not protected or included on listings of globally threatened species.

While the use of ecological impact assessment as a tool has grown steadily, many shortcomings remain. In particular, effective consideration of impacts on ecosystem services and the costs of ecological damage rarely takes place, despite growing awareness of the need for it.

International Agreements

Both EIA and SEA are recognized in the United Nations Convention on Biological Diversity (CBD) as important tools for identifying, avoiding, minimizing, and mitigating adverse impacts on biodiversity (CBD 1998, 2000, 2002, 2003, and 2006). Other biodiversity-related conventions such as the Convention on Migratory Species (CMS) and the Ramsar Convention on Wetlands also recognize the important role of impact assessment (as reviewed in Pritchard 2005).

The 1992 CBD requires its parties to consider biodiversity when they are planning development and sees EIA and SEA as important tools for achieving this. This is reflected in the CBD's Article 14 (CBD 1998), which relates specifically to impact assessment and states that each contracting party to the convention should introduce EIA and SEA into their planning systems if they do not have it already and that they should make sure

biodiversity and ecosystems are given full consideration. In effect, Article 14 of the CBD creates a requirement for "biodiversity inclusive" impact assessment. Guidance has been issued by the CBD and by the International Association for Impact Assessment to establish ground rules for how this can be achieved in practice (CBD 2006). Other guidance on how to integrate biodiversity with EIA following Article 14 has been issued by the US Council on Environmental Quality (1993), the Canadian Environmental Assessment Agency (1996), and the World Bank (1997).

These agreements establish a basis for national policies on biodiversity and ecosystems and a rationale for mainstreaming them. Within this context, national laws and regulations establish the requirement for ecological impact assessment to be undertaken. These are generally quite broad and are process based. In other words, there may be a legal requirement to undertake impact assessment and to include ecological considerations, but there is no legal requirement to deliver a sustainable outcome or demonstrate how it would be achieved. This remains a key shortcoming in how ecological impact assessment is applied.

Monitoring and Feedback

Ecologists have repeatedly emphasized the need to monitor both whether the impacts that actually occur match those that were predicted and whether the mitigation proposed to reduce ecological impacts to acceptable levels were effective. Without this information, opportunities to improve scientific knowledge, understanding, and predictive ability through the practice of ecological impact assessment will always be limited. Reviews of the effectiveness of EIA and ecological impact assessment have identified lack of monitoring and follow-up as a major barrier to improvement and adaptive management for at least twenty years, so we have to question why rigorous monitoring remains rare. Failure to monitor may result from lack of any legal requirement in EIA legislation to carry out monitoring or from lack of regulatory capacity and resources. It is hard to see why changes in legal requirements have not yet been made, despite obvious opportunities to do so when laws and policies are reviewed and updated.

Future Trends

Although ecological impact assessment has become widely used, the inherent complexity of ecosystems, lack of basic scientific knowledge, and limited resources restrict the ability to predict potential ecological impacts with certainty (Mangel et al. 1996).

Lack of monitoring and follow-up makes it difficult to establish how effective the use of ecological impact assessment has actually been in terms of delivering sustainable outcomes for biodiversity and ecosystems on the ground. There is, however, incontrovertible evidence that the world's biodiversity and ecosystems are continuing to decline, with increasing risks to human well-being due to loss of essential ecosystem services (pollination of food crops, carbon sequestration, water cycling, and so on). These risks are expected to be exacerbated by climate change, and ecological impact assessment must account for them more effectively if irreversible damage is to be averted. Unless there are stronger requirements to do so in law, however, little is likely to change in practice.

If it is to play an influential part in arresting ecosystem decline, ecological impact assessment will have to change from process-driven to outcome-oriented approaches. This is reflected in growing recognition of the need to consider the consequences of ecological change for people, through impacts on ecosystem services (Slootweg et al. 2010). Increasingly, international financial lending institutions are demonstrating leadership in this area and are making delivery of "no net loss" outcomes for biodiversity and ecosystem services a condition on loans. Similarly some international businesses and corporations are developing strong corporate positions on this issue and revising their ecological impact assessment procedures accordingly. In some countries, the need to deliver "no net loss" outcomes for biodiversity and for ecosystem services is now embedded in national policies and laws, prompting a stronger emphasis on ecological compensation (including biodiversity offsets) in cases where residual adverse impacts on biodiversity and ecosystems will remain after development.

Policies that reflect international agreements by requiring sustainable outcomes for biodiversity, together with laws requiring such outcomes to be delivered, can transform ecological impact assessment from a tool that merely identifies ecological risks into one that can ensure these risks are managed effectively.

JO TREWEEK
Treweek Environmental Consultants, United Kingdom

See also Cost-Benefit Analysis; Development Indicators; Ecosystem Health Indicators; Ecological Footprint Accounting; Externality Valuation; Land-Use and Land-Cover Change; Long-Term Ecological Research (LTER); Regulatory Compliance; Risk Assessment; Strategic Environmental Assessment (SEA)

FURTHER READING

Beanlands, Gordon E., & Duinker, Peter N. (1984). An ecological framework for environmental impact assessment. *Journal of Environmental Management, 18,* 267–277.

Brownlie, Susie, et al. (2005). Systematic conservation planning in the cape floristic region and succulent karoo, South Africa: Enabling sound spatial planning and improved environmental assessment. *Journal of Environmental Assessment and Planning, 7*(2), 20.

Byron, Helen. (2000). *Biodiversity and environmental impact assessment: A good practice guide for road schemes.* Sandy, UK: The RSPB, WWF-UK, English Nature and the Wildlife Trusts.

Byron, Helen, & Treweek, Jo. (Eds.). (2005a). Special issue on biodiversity and impact assessment. *Impact Assessment and Project Appraisal, 23*(1).

Byron, Helen, & Treweek, Jo. (Eds.). (2005b). Special issue on strategic environmental assessment and biodiversity. *Journal of Environmental Assessment Planning and Management, 7*(2).

Canadian Environmental Assessment Agency (CEAA). (1996). *A guide on biodiversity and environmental assessment.* Ottawa: Minister of Supply and Services, Canada.

Convention on Biological Diversity (CBD). (1998). Decision IV/10: Measures for implementing the Convention on Biological Diversity: C. Impact assessment and minimizing adverse effects: Consideration of measures for the implementation of Article 14. Retrieved December 29, 2011, from http://www.cbd.int/doc/quarterly/qr-04-en.pdf

Convention on Biological Diversity (CBD). (2000). Decision V/18: Impact assessment, liability and redress: I. Impact assessment. Retrieved October 12, 2011, from http://www.biodiv.org/decisions/default.aspx?dec=V/18

Convention on Biological Diversity (CBD). (2002) Decision VI/7: Further development of guidelines for incorporating biodiversity-related issues into environmental-impact-assessment legislation or processes and in strategic impact assessment. Retrieved October 12, 2011, from http://www.biodiv.org/decisions/default.asp?lg=0&dec=VI/7

Convention on Biological Diversity (CBD). (2003). Proposals for further development and refinement of the guidelines for incorporating biodiversity-related issues into environmental impact assessment legislation or procedures and in strategic impact assessment: Report on ongoing work. Retrieved October 12, 2011, from http://www.biodiv.org/doc/meetings/sbstta/sbstta-09/information/sbstta-09-inf-18-en.pdf

Convention on Biological Diversity (CBD). (2006). Voluntary guidelines on biodiversity-inclusive impact assessment. Retrieved October 12, 2011, from http://www.biodiv.org/doc/meeting.asp?lg=0&mtg=cop-08

European Commission (EC). (1996). *Evaluation of the performance of the EIA process.* Brussels, Belgium: European Commission.

Gontier, Michael; Balfors, Birgit; & Mortberg, Ulla. (2006). Biodiversity in environmental assessment—Current practice and tools for prediction. *Environmental Impact Assessment Review, 26*(3), 268–286.

International Association for Impact Assessment. (2005). *Biodiversity in impact assessment* (IAIA Special Publications Series No. 3). Retrieved

January 23, 2012, from http://www.iaia.org/publicdocuments/special-publications/SP3.pdf

Mandelik, Yael; Dayan, Tamar; & Feitelson, Eran. (2005). Planning for biodiversity: The role of ecological impact assessment. *Conservation Biology, 19*(4), 1254–1261.

Mangel, Marc, et al. (1996). Principles for the conservation of wild living resources. *Ecological Applications, 6*, 338–362.

Millennium Ecosystem Assessment. (2000). Homepage. Retrieved October 12, 2011, from http://www.maweb.org

Noss, Reed F. (1990). Indicators for monitoring biodiversity: A hierarchical approach. *Conservation Biology, 4*, 355–364.

Pritchard, David. (2005). International biodiversity-related treaties and impact assessment: How can they help each other? *Impact Assessment and Project Appraisal, 23*(1), 7–16.

Slootweg, Roel; Rajvanshi, Asha; Mathur, Vinod B.; & Kolhoff, Arend. (2010). *Biodiversity in environmental assessment: Enhancing ecosystem services for human well-being.* Cambridge, UK: Cambridge University Press.

The Economics of Ecosystems and Biodiversity (TEEB). (2010). *Mainstreaming the economics of nature: A synthesis of the approach, conclusions and recommendations of TEEB.* Retrieved February 14, 2012, from http://www.teebweb.org/LinkClick.aspx?fileticket=bYhDohL_TuM%3D

Tinker, Lauren; Cobb, Dick; Bond, Alan; & Cashmore, Mat. (2005). Impact mitigation in environmental impact assessment: Paper promises or the basis of consent decisions? *Impact Assessment and Project Appraisal, 23*(4), 265–280.

Treweek, Jo. (1999). *Ecological impact assessment.* Oxford, UK: Blackwell Science.

Treweek, Joanna R. (1996). Ecology in environmental impact assessment. *Journal of Applied Ecology, 33*, 191–199.

Treweek, Jo, & Thompson, Stewart. (1997). A review of ecological mitigation measures in UK environmental statements with respect to sustainable development. *International Journal of Sustainable Development and World Ecology, 4*, 40–50.

US Council on Environmental Quality. (1993). *Incorporating biodiversity considerations into environmental impact analysis under the National Environmental Policy Act.* Washington, DC: Council on Environmental Quality.

Wathern, Peter. (1999). Ecological impact assessment. In Judith Petts (Ed.), *Handbook of environmental impact assessment: Vol. 1. Environmental impact assessment: process, methods and potential* (pp. 327–346). Oxford, UK: Blackwell Science.

The World Bank Environment Department. (1997). Environmental assessment sourcebook update No. 20. Washington, DC: The World Bank.

Ecosystem Health Indicators

Improving the health of ecosystems is a long-term goal globally. Achieving this depends importantly on the establishment of meaningful ecosystem health indicators to identify critical drivers and pressures of ecological degradation and assess progress in addressing them. Indicators of ecosystem health and assessments based on them are essential to motivate both policy makers and the public to take the necessary actions to restore the health of the world's ecosystems.

Over the past half century, the concept of "health," long applied in reference to the vitality of individuals (humans as well as other species), has been extended to the higher levels of biological organization: populations, ecological communities, whole ecosystems, landscapes, and the biosphere. At each level, the metrics required to assess health differ. For example, the health of a population is not simply the summation of the health status of the individuals. New metrics are used that refer specifically to the status of an entire population. As for what constitutes ecosystem health, while there are a variety of definitions, nearly all of these comprise three basic elements: organization, vitality, and resilience. *Organization* refers to the structure of the ecosystem—the web of connections that link species with one another and with their environment. Loss of key structural properties of ecosystems—for example, disturbance to or removal of soil, coral, or stream bed—may cripple the ecosystem's capacity to maintain its biotic assemblage. *Vitality* refers to the overall metabolism of the ecosystem, that is, its capacity to maintain the flow of energy from primary producers (plants) to primary (herbivores) and secondary (carnivores) consumers, as well as its capacity to sustain the essential nutrient cycles. *Resilience* refers to the capacity of an ecosystem to recover from perturbations such as those caused by floods, fire, insect infestations, drought, and the like. While such perturbations cause short-term disruptions in community structure and ecological functions (drought, for example, may completely eliminate above-ground biota), healthy ecosystems are able to bounce back from these natural disturbances. For some perturbation-dependent ecosystems, natural disturbances such as forest fires or floods are an essential part of the dynamics to maintain the health of the system.

There is an ever-expanding list of metrics that are used to evaluate the health of ecosystems. Many of these are useful across the full range of the world's ecosystems. No single metric is adequate to evaluate health; rather, a suite of well-chosen indicators are employed. For indicators to be of service, it is necessary to establish the normal range of values for each indicator for the particular type of ecosystem under evaluation, for example, the normal range of primary productivity for grassland in a particular region, or the range of diversity of avian species in an old-growth temperate rain forest. Common indicators for a wide range of ecosystem health assessments include progressive dominance by opportunistic species, progressive invasion of nonlocal or non-native species, shifts in community structure, loss of substratum, disruption of nutrient cycling, and progressive loss of ecosystem services (attributes valued by humans) (Rapport and Whitford 1999, 193–203).

From Indicators to Indices

In descriptions of the overall condition of systems with large numbers of components, it is tempting to look for possibilities to create indices that aggregate information from individual indicators. Indices are valuable when they have a strong logical and scientific basis that allows for the amalgamation of disparate sets of data. This has been successful in certain social applications, such as the widespread use of a consumer price index, where the interpretation of the index is clear. Indices have been created for a variety of environmental applications (e.g., water quality, air pollution). In evaluating the health of ecosystems, there have also been attempts to amalgamate various considerations into a single index that would convey a general message on the health of the system. An example is the construction of a Forest Capital Index (Rapport and Ullsten 2006, 268–290). Such indices may give a crude overview of the health of a system, but they are often problematic as tools of communication. They are difficult to conceptualize if they combine many indicators related to different aspects of ecosystem health and the weighting (explicit or implicit) of the indicators that form the index heavily influences the message that the index conveys.

History of Indicator Development

The roots of indicator development are embedded in the history and prehistory of human culture. A remark attributed to Plato suggests that thousands of years ago people understood that certain modifications of agricultural drainage systems had adverse consequences for agricultural yields. Throughout the ages keen observers have taken note of correlations between human activity and ecosystem transformation. In the late seventeenth and early eighteenth centuries, when the rivers Thames and Rhine came under heavy stress from industrial waste, it was easy to recognize that foul smells, discolored waters, and local fish kills were a direct consequence of industrial activity.

In the twentieth century, the observations of naturalists, most notably those of Aldo Leopold in the 1940s, led to the realization that the consequences of human actions were rendering the land dysfunctional—resulting in what Leopold termed "land sickness." Among the worrisome signs Leopold observed in his native Wisconsin landscape were losses of native species; declines in biodiversity, soil fertility, and crop yields; reductions in biological productivity; increased presence of invasive species; and increased prevalence of diseases in both plants and animals. Several decades later, statistical agencies began to include the environment as part of their reporting functions, seeking a comprehensive framework that would relate human activities to environmental change. Statistics Canada's Stress-Response model provided a suitable template (Rapport and Friend 1979). Quickly adopted by the environmental secretariat of the Organization for Economic Cooperation and Development (OECD), this model, known today as the Pressure-State-Response (PSR) model, provides a taxonomy of anthropogenic stresses, ecosystem health indicators, and policy responses. Slightly modified, it is extensively used by the European Environment Agency for its state of environment reports.

A notable example of the application of the PSR model to assess ecosystem health is the retrospective assessment of the Baltic Sea undertaken by the Helsinki Commission (HELCOM 2010a). This report, *Ecosystem Health of the Baltic Sea*, is exemplary in showing the practicality of obtaining a suite of quantitative indicators of the health of a large-scale ecosystem and relating the state of health of this ecosystem to the suite of anthropogenic stresses impacting it. The value of this and many similar exercises—for example, evaluations of the health of the Laurentian Great Lakes (United States/Canada), Moreton Bay (Australia), Murray-Darling Basin (Australia), Bay of Fundy (Canada), Mesoamerican coral reefs, Florida Everglades—lies in providing a sound scientific basis for public policy geared to ameliorating environmental degradation.

Scale of Application

Indicators of the health of ecosystems may apply broadly across many ecosystems—or be more narrowly restricted to the characteristics of a particular ecosystem. For example, the prevalence of a particular forest insect pest, the mountain pine beetle, is a key indicator of the health of the coniferous forests of northern and central British Columbia, where an unprecedented outbreak (attributable to warmer winters and even age stands) has resulted in catastrophic loss of the forests of this region of Canada. This species, however, is specific to a particular ecological zone (mainly forests dominated by lodgepole pine, *Pinus contorta*). A more general indicator applicable to all forest ecosystems would be forest insect pest prevalence, without focusing on a specific species. Scaling up further, one could look at disease prevalence within an ecosystem. At this scale, the indicator could apply not only to forests but also to grasslands, lakes, marshlands, and so forth.

Scale is important in assessing ecosystem health. For example, monitoring the impacts of industrial sites is often limited to assessing the presence or absence of indicator species or potentially toxic compounds found in local biota. Such information may have little relevance beyond a very local domain. But when the pollution involves long-lived toxic substances that bio-accumulate in the food web, the consequences can eventually be reflected in ecosystem-wide degradation. Another example of widespread ecosystem-level impacts from industrial pollution is acidification of lakes and streams. In the 1970s, the sulfur dioxide emissions from a smelter near Sudbury, Ontario, were responsible for transforming a once-healthy mixed deciduous/coniferous forest to a virtual moonscape, eliminating forest cover and most vegetation on some 46,000 hectares, and in addition causing the acidification of more than seven thousand lakes in the region.

Quantitative Indicators for Ecosystem Health

An indicator is more than just the actual variable for which data is available. Massive algal blooms in a lake or a coastal area do not simply tell us that there are plenty of algae in the water; they also indicate that excessive nutrients are entering the water body due to either poor sewage treatment or unsustainable farming practices that waste nutrients. In a similar way, changes in bird populations can be linked with transformations in forests: the decline of species associated with old-growth forest indicates losses of particular habitats.

Why would one want to quantify the health of an ecosystem? Quantified or quantifiable measures of health and health change make it possible to evaluate actions that may improve or degrade health. By tracking the quantitative health estimate together with quantitative information on anthropogenic stresses, one may eventually be able to provide prescriptive information on what to do or not to do. For example, what intensity of fishing is compatible with sustaining the health of a lake or a sea area? What kinds of forestry practices are consistent with maintaining a healthy forest (that is, not just sustaining timber extraction)?

Traditional resource management has tried to approach these questions by examining each single exploitable resource as an independent entity for which it is possible to determine a maximum sustainable yield. This approach has proven to be inadequate in that, by focusing only on the resource, it neglects the interactions between different components of the ecosystem and thus falls short of assessing the overall health of the ecosystem. The maximum sustainable yield for a single species may actually be disastrous for the health of the whole ecosystem. Intense exploitation of forage fish may cause bird populations to decline; sustainable-yield harvesting of timber can lead to the demise of species dependent on dead wood.

A suite of quantitative indicators is required in order to cover the many facets of ecosystem health. For example, for the HELCOM retrospective assessment of the Baltic Sea, quantitative estimates of nutrient status, contaminant levels, state of fish stocks, and biodiversity were required. This allowed for the assessment of the overall ecosystem health of the Baltic, as well as the health of its sub-basins and regions. The value of such assessments lies in identifying critical issues that need immediate attention if the health of the ecosystem (upon which human well-being vitally depends) is to be improved. Similar approaches have been taken in North America's Laurentian Great Lakes, and yearly reports are published on a suite of ecosystem health indicators for each of the lake basins. These indicators and assessments provide guidance for both management and policy.

Monitoring Ecosystem Health

Monitoring the health of ecosystems requires not only careful selection of a suite of key indicators, but also attention to the practicality of gathering high-quality, reliable data on their status and trends, and the establishment of valid baselines (or normal ranges) in order to assess the health of the ecosystem. In some instances, this is relatively straightforward. For example, much can be learned about the health of the Baltic Sea from the abundance and distribution of an easily identified seaweed, bladderwrack (*Fucus vesiculosus*), found in the shallow waters of the Baltic Sea. The maximum depth at which this seaweed is found is limited by water transparency, and thus by the availability of light. Observing over time the depths at which this seaweed is found provides useful information on the overall eutrophic (nutrient) condition of the sea. Eutrophication (i.e., excess nutrients from sewage and agricultural runoff) is one of the main environmental issues in the Baltic. Monitoring for the bladderwrack serves double duty in that the seaweed provides habitat for many species, including many juvenile fishes. As its abundance increases, fish habitat improves, contributing to an improvement in the health of the entire ecosystem.

The baseline or reference level for each indicator is a crucial aspect of monitoring for ecosystem health. When it comes to anthropogenic synthetic pollutants such as polychlorinated biphenyls (PCBs), one can use zero as a reference level, but in addition one would also need to know the thresholds after which adverse effects begin to appear. The classical approach is to experimentally determine a dose-response curve; "no effect concentrations" can be estimated from the curve. These thresholds may provide guidance for monitoring ecosystem health, but one should be aware that the values commonly refer to laboratory tests using single substances, whereas ecosystems are subject to cumulative effects of multiple stressors. Thus the threshold levels for adverse effect may be significantly lower than in laboratory experiments. In some cases, different stressors may have antagonistic effects, and then the actual thresholds for adverse effects on the ecosystem may be higher than those anticipated in laboratory studies.

The baseline for variables such as species abundance or size distribution is more difficult to determine. In some cases it may be possible to derive an estimate of the conditions of the ecosystem when it was in a pristine state before significant human intervention. With the exception of some remote ecosystems, this approach is not practical, however, because many ecosystems have evolved in constant interaction with humans. Owing to such difficulties, often more pragmatic approaches are called into play in evaluating the health of ecosystems. In the European Union (EU), the Water Framework Directive and the Marine Strategy Directive (both legal documents) have created obligations to specify what constitutes "good ecological status" for different water bodies. This has led to identification of variables and thresholds that relate to ecological status (which in principle is closely related to health throughout Europe). The goal of these directives is to stimulate action plans that will result in restoring all water bodies to a healthy condition.

Trade-offs and Challenges in Ecological Monitoring

One of the major challenges in the development of ecosystem health indicators is finding indicators that can serve as "early warning" signals for ecosystem degradation. Too often these indicators are only discovered after the damage is done, and it is too late or economically impractical to reverse course. Generally, it is only in retrospect that changes in a seemingly insignificant part of the ecosystem might be linked to major ecosystem-wide consequences. For example, in the 1950s, mayflies (*Hexagenia* spp.), which became very abundant in spring breeding swarms along Lake Erie shores (United States/Canada), suddenly disappeared. While their disappearance did not go unnoticed (their swarming was always a nuisance to residents and resulted in slippery and thus hazardous driving conditions), the more far-reaching consequences for the health of Lake Erie were not immediately foreseen. Yet, in retrospect, the disappearance of mayfly larvae was one of the first signs of degradation of Lake Erie—for the disappearance of the larvae in the lake's bottom waters was due to nutrient loading and the creation of a seasonal dead zone in these bottom waters. In other situations, for example in lakes impacted by acidification, the earliest indicator that the level of acidification is negatively affecting the health of the lake might be found in altered behaviors of sensitive species. Yet, monitoring for behavioral changes in individuals or populations is extremely costly and generally impractical.

Another major challenge is the cost of acquiring synoptic data. With the rapid development of remote sensing imagery, and ever more numerous applications to ecosystem assessment, these costs are rapidly declining. Remote sensing is particularly well suited to spatial data on the extent of forest cover, forest tree composition, extent and location of wetlands, condition of grasslands, including surrogate measures for primary production, large-scale algal blooms, shoreline degradation, and the like. Yet for many variables that are essential in the evaluation of the health of ecosystems (such as fish stocks, water chemistry, soil biota, invasive species, disease prevalence, and so forth), remote sensing is of limited service. Intensive and often costly on-the-ground sampling is still required. In such cases, budgets require trade-offs among the number of variables being monitored, the frequency of data collection, and the intensity of the sampling design. All too often, such sampling results for large-scale ecosystems are far from ideal. Careful planning is therefore needed to combine different types of data collection so as to produce reliable indicators. It is particularly demanding to capture transient events that may reveal early stages of the degradation of the ecosystem health.

Outlook for the Coming Decades

The general goal to improve and secure the health of ecosystems has become widely accepted. For example, in the Helsinki Commission's first retrospective assessment of the state of the Baltic Sea, ecosystem health was the explicit focus. An emphasis on healthy ecosystems is also incorporated into the long term vision for the International Union for the Conservation of Nature, the strategy for 2009–2013 of the European Environment Agency, assessments of many large-scale ecosystems such as grasslands in Inner Mongolia, catchments in Australia, tropical reef ecosystems, and forest ecosystems. It has been implicitly and explicitly expressed for both aquatic and terrestrial ecosystems, and it has been included in legal documents. At the same time, it is obvious that this is a long-term goal. Many of the world's ecosystems display all of the signs of ecosystem distress syndrome, the result of decades—in some instances, centuries—of cumulative anthropogenic stress. In many cases, it is unlikely that the damage done can be quickly repaired. Yet these difficulties should by no means dissuade society from its efforts to improve the health of the world's ecosystems.

Ecosystem degradation has engulfed large areas of the planet. Researchers argue that we may already be well into the sixth mass extinction of life. Desertification has taken over once-productive grasslands; the world's oceans have been vastly depleted of their natural bounty of wild fish stocks; and whole ecosystems, including the world's tropical coral reefs (hot spots of biodiversity), have become endangered and are at risk of extinction within this century. The Aral Sea, once the world's fourth-largest lake, has practically disappeared and has left in its wake a highly toxic environment in which millions of people still reside. Many ecosystems such as the Great Lakes and the Baltic Sea remain highly degraded, despite decades of efforts to restore their health. Unless and until there is widespread recognition that the very foundations for sustaining human and other life on the planet are rapidly eroding, it seems unlikely that the will to change course will arise.

Indicators of ecosystem health are capable of providing a robust measuring rod for assessing in which direction we are heading. Such indicators are an essential ingredient for addressing the situation, as it is not possible to act responsibly without a clear picture of what the state of ecosystems actually is. The other indispensible ingredient, however, is the political and social will to act on the findings. Ecosystem health indicators and assessments based on them can help policy makers and the public see the need to act to maintain and restore the health of ecosystems.

David J. RAPPORT
EcoHealth Consulting

Mikael HILDÉN
Finnish Environment Institute (SYKE)

See also Biological Indicators (*several articles*); Computer Modeling; Ecological Footprint Accounting; Fisheries Indicators, Freshwater; Fisheries Indicators, Marine; Genuine Progress Indicators (GPI); Global Environmental Outlook (GEO) Reports; Human Appropriation of Net Primary Production (HANPP); Index of Biological Integrity (IBI); Land-Use and Land-Cover Change; Ocean Acidification—Measurement; Remote Sensing; Systems Thinking

FURTHER READING

Doren, Robert F.; Trexler, Joel C.; Gottlieb, Andrew D.; & Harwell, Matthew C. (2009). Ecological indicators for system-wide assessment of the greater everglades ecosystem restoration program. *Ecological Indicators, 9*(6, 1), S2–S16.

Helsinki Commission (HELCOM). (2010a). *Ecosystem health of the Baltic Sea.* Retrieved September 26, 2011, from http://www.helcom.fi/stc/files/Publications/Proceedings/bsep122.pdf

Helsinki Commission (HELCOM). (2010b). Homepage. Retrieved April 30, 2011, from http://www.helcom.fi/

Herrera-Silveira, Jorge A., & Morales-Ojeda, Sara M. (2009). Evaluation of the health status of a coastal ecosystem in southeast Mexico: Assessment of water quality, phytoplankton and submerged aquatic vegetation. *Marine Pollution Bulletin, 59*(1–3), 72–86.

Hildén, Mikael, & Rosenström, Ulla. (2008). The use of indicators for sustainable development. *Sustainable Development, 16*(4), 237–240.

Rapport, David J. (2007). Sustainability science: An ecohealth perspective. *Sustainability Science, 2*(1), 77–84.

Rapport, David J. (2010). How healthy are our ecosystems? In Bruce Mitchell (Ed.), *Resource and environmental management in Canada: Addressing conflict and uncertainty* (4th ed., pp. 69–96). Toronto: Oxford University Press.

Rapport, David J., & Friend, Anthony. (1979). *Towards a comprehensive framework for environmental statistics: A stress-response approach* (Statistics Canada Catalogue 11-510). Ottawa, Canada: Minister of Supply and Services Canada.

Rapport, David J., & Maffi, Luisa. (2011). Eco-cultural health, global health and sustainability. *Ecological Research, 26*(6),1039–1049.

Rapport, David J., & Singh, Ashbindu. (2006). An ecohealth based framework for state of environment reporting. *Ecological Indicators, 6*(2), 409–428.

Rapport, David J., & Ullsten, Ola. (2006). Managing for sustainability: Ecological footprints, ecosystem health and the forest capital index. In Philip Lawn (Ed.), *Sustainable development indicators in ecological economics* (pp. 268–290). Northampton, MA: Edward Elgar.

Rapport, David J., & Whitford, Walter G. (1999). How ecosystems respond to stress. *BioScience, 49*(3), 193–203.

Rapport, David J., et al. (Eds.). (2003). *Managing for healthy ecosystems.* Boca Raton, FL: CRC Press.

Wiegand, Jessica; Raffaelli, Dave; Smart, James C. R.; & White, Piran C. L. (2010). Assessment of temporal trends in ecosystem health using an holistic indicator. *Journal of Environmental Management, 91*(7), 1446–1455.

Energy Efficiency Measurement

Energy efficiency is easy to define but hard to measure. Indicators such as energy intensity are used as proxies for energy efficiency, but their results can be misleading. Efficiency improvements, mainly caused by stock turnover to more efficient products, are a normal by-product of economic growth and modernization. Government policies to promote energy efficiency have not led to reductions in national energy use, mainly due to rebound effects.

Energy efficiency is easy to define in theory but hard to measure in practice. At its simplest, it is defined as the ratio of the energy output to the energy input for a machine. For a boiler or an engine, the energy input (the fuel) and the output (the heat or power produced) thus can be measured fairly easily. For machines (or other devices) where the output is not simply energy but some form of energy service, however, measuring efficiency is more complex. For instance with a lightbulb, we are interested not in its heat output but its light output. The same with a refrigerator, an air conditioner, a car, or a computer—we are interested in the machine's ability to perform an energy service by cooling, transporting, or information processing. Evaluating the energy efficiency depends on defining the desired output: what aspect of the energy service are we really interested in—power, speed, reliability, or economy?

The more complex the energy system, the harder it is to agree on an output measure. How do you measure the output of a bakery, a restaurant, a hotel, a chemical factory, or an office? One approach has been to express energy efficiency in terms of energy intensity: energy input per unit of some (measurable) factor, such as physical or monetary output, number of workers, or floor area. When it comes to comparing industries, transport systems, or countries, the problems are immense. Measuring energy inputs is fairly easy—there are good energy statistics on national and sectorial energy production and on imports and exports—but what is the most suitable measure of industrial or national output? Is it some measure of monetary output or gross domestic product (GDP)? If so, we can then reach some trivial conclusions based on energy intensity: an investment firm's office is more efficient than a steel works; Denmark is a more efficient country than the United States. As a review of energy efficiency polices in International Energy Agency (IEA) countries admitted, "Trends in final energy intensity are often used to assess the extent to which energy efficiency is improving in countries. However, this can often be misleading as the ratio is affected by many factors such as climate, geography, travel distance, home size and manufacturing structure" (Taylor et al. 2010, 6468).

If our measure of transport efficiency is kilometers per liter, then a car is more efficient than a bus. If we account for the number of passengers, by using an index of passenger-kilometers per liter, this gives a better indication of efficiency; however, the efficiency measure now depends on the number of passengers on the bus (which depends on the time of day and route) and how often it stops. Similarly, trying to determine if it is more efficient to drive or fly requires making many assumptions, such as how full the car and plane are, the distance traveled, and even how people travel to and from the airport. Overall, however, a full plane or train is generally more efficient than a single-user car.

The challenge of trying to construct an energy efficiency index is that in a complex energy system there are so many variables that it is not possible to account for them all. For instance, a house can have a very efficient boiler but be ineffective overall in providing the standard of heating required by the occupants. This could be because the house is poorly insulated, so that much of the (efficient) heat produced by the boiler is lost through the walls, roof, and windows, or because there are few heating controls, so unoccupied rooms are heated. Similarly, a factory having very efficient equipment could be judged as inefficient overall if it is running at low capacity or produces poor-quality goods that fail to sell. It is not the owning of efficient machines that makes a factory (or a country) efficient, but how those machines are used. For example, exporting the most efficient machinery to developing countries is no guarantee of efficient industries or production.

Industrialization, through the use of modern energy efficient equipment, will undoubtedly lead to lower energy intensity, as it has done in China. But as the economy expands, energy consumption grows. This has only been considered a problem if energy consumption causes major environmental problems, such as local smoke or air pollution. Improved energy efficiency equipment can reduce these local problems, such as the replacement of open coal fires with gas central heating.

Technical Innovation

Changes in energy efficiency are an inevitable consequence of technical innovation and of manufacturers' desires to reduce costs of production through reducing material and energy inputs. Consumer choice of an energy-using product is seldom based on one attribute, such as energy efficiency; rather it is a compromise between price, performance, and operating costs. Designations of a product as "energy efficient," like labels such as "green," "powerful," or "glamorous," are advertising claims based on comparative measures. A modern compact fluorescent lightbulb (CFL) may be considered more energy efficient than the old incandescent bulb (in terms of light output per unit of electricity input), but they are not identical products. There are differences in purchase cost and lifetime, as well as consumer concerns about light color, performance, and suitability for certain fixtures. A subcompact car may be more efficient (in terms of kilometers per liter) than a large luxury sedan, but they are not similar vehicles in terms of size, power, or features. Technical innovation can produce more efficient products, but consumers will only buy them if they rate energy efficiency high among desirable attributes. Driven by the desire to cut (operating) costs or the perceived need to reduce energy use (due to national or global concerns), some consumers do place a high value on energy efficiency.

Environmental Interest

Until the mid-1970s, energy efficiency was a concept confined to the world of industrial engineers and factory managers and was closely allied to productivity concerns. It was then adopted by the emerging environmental movement and was heavily promoted by Amory Lovins in his book *Soft Energy Paths* (1977) as the alternative solution to nuclear power (and challenged by the British energy expert Len Brookes; see, for example, Brookes 2000). Lovins's argument was that consumers, by using more energy efficient equipment could get the same energy service for less fuel input, thus reducing national energy consumption (and the need to build new power plants). This new, or "soft," energy path, would involve the use of CFLs, condensing boilers, A+ rated refrigerators, and improved building insulation.

The simplicity and great appeal of this argument overlooked a key factor: the use of more efficient goods does not necessarily mean the consumption of less energy. A large refrigerator or house may be more efficient (in terms of energy use per unit of volume) than a smaller one, but it still uses more energy. A new car model may have a more efficient engine, but it also has more weight, power, and features, so it may end up using the same amount of fuel. A new house may have more insulation than an older one, but it is larger in area, and it has air conditioning. Furthermore, manufacturers and utilities have historically used increased energy efficiency to promote increased consumption. More energy efficient products and practices does not equate directly to lower (national) energy consumption, especially if the economy and the population are growing.

Nevertheless, environmentalists, followed by many governments and industry groups, promoted the efficiency message as a relatively painless and cost-effective way to solve the problems of energy supply, and, by extension, as the ideal solution to the problems of global warming. This argument rests on the belief that global or national energy use can be reduced by the sum of the millions of small energy savings by consumers through their adoption of energy efficient devices—that is, what is true at the micro (local) level is also true at the macro (national or global) level. At the micro level, energy efficiency does save energy (and the monetary savings are often used to cover the cost of investment), but the key question is whether these micro-level savings are cumulative or whether they get (re)spent and ultimately dissipated. Is energy saved never used, or is it merely diverted to another use? This is the rebound effect question.

Rebound Effect

Rebound effects, first identified by the nineteenth-century British economist Stanley Jevons, are normal occurrences in economic systems: as improvements in efficiency, due to technical change, make goods and services cheaper, we can and generally do buy more of them. If the cost of an energy service, such as heating, falls, we can afford to use more, by heating our rooms to higher temperatures, or for longer periods, or heating more of the house (a direct rebound effect). We could also use the money saved to buy other goods and services that use energy (an indirect rebound effect). For producers, more efficient production processes (e.g., in a steel industry) result in lower cost both for that commodity (cheaper steel) and for products made from that commodity (e.g., cars). Cheaper steel results in greater sales and hence more production;

cheaper cars result in more car sales and increased car travel. The end result is greater energy use in the long run that can outweigh the original efficiency saving.

When we save energy through improved efficiency but then consume only part of the saved energy, that is a rebound of less than 100 percent. If, however, that efficiency encourages us to consume more energy than we would have, that rebound of more than 100 percent is sometimes called a backfire effect. The rebound effect is linked to the major policy question: if energy use continues to grow despite large increases in energy efficiency, then is promoting greater energy efficiency a credible government policy to reduce national energy use, and hence carbon emissions?

Government Policy

The role governments should play in promoting energy efficiency is not at all clear. If the desire is to reduce energy use in the short term, perhaps due to some national crisis (such as the shortage of electricity in Japan after the devastating earthquake in March 2011), then regulations and social incentives can be used to change the behavior of consumers. Japan has a long history and culture of promoting energy conservation (or frugality), employing the cutting back and careful use of energy consumption as energy conservation measures. This was reinforced in 1979 by passage of the Law Concerning the Rational Use of Energy, which encouraged the development of more energy efficient appliances and industrial products and processes, with the overall aim of making Japan the world's most energy efficient nation.

Many Western governments have tried to influence their consumers to purchase more efficient products, through appliance subsidies and building regulations. It is not clear, however, whether this is good use of public money. Might people have bought the more efficient appliance without a subsidy? Should old, poorly insulated buildings be refurbished, or is it "better" to demolish them and rebuild with new, efficient buildings?

Energy efficiency policy, like all policy areas concerned with changing people's choices, is full of social and economic conflicts and can lead to unintended consequences. Chief among these is the rebound effect: greater efficiency lowers operating costs and opens up the market to more consumers. This is particularly the case where there is a large unmet demand for an expensive energy service (such as for air-conditioning, heating, or lighting) or where a technology or product is, or could be, widely used in industry or commerce (such as computers, electric motors, cement, or steel, so-called general purpose technologies).

The Chinese government set a goal in November 2005 to reduce its energy intensity (energy use per unit of GDP) by 20 percent between 2006 and 2010, a seemingly modest goal given that energy intensity had already decreased 5 percent annually between 1970 and 2001. This decline in intensity was due to the very rapid economic growth during these decades, which resulted in large increases in energy consumption (with the side effect that China overtook the United States to become the world's leading emitter of carbon dioxide in 2006). China's goal of improving its energy efficiency (as measured by declines in energy intensity) rests on a complex array of fiscal, pricing, and technical measures that affect all sectors of the economy. The most important is the Top-1000 Energy-Consuming Enterprises program, which targets the 1,000 largest industrial enterprises, accounting for a third of national energy consumption.

The goal of most national energy efficiency programs, however, is not to reduce absolute energy use or carbon emissions. Rather the goal is to reduce energy consumption below a projected forecast—that is, what the energy consumption would have been without the efficiency programs. The stated savings of most energy efficiency programs thus are hypothetical; energy use (at the macro level) usually increases even though the chosen indicators of energy efficiency, such as energy intensity, may show the desired decline.

Energy Sufficiency and Conservation

An alternative strategy to energy efficiency is energy conservation that seeks to cut energy consumption by decreasing levels of energy service, mainly through changes in behavior and lifestyle. This includes things like reducing heating levels, driving slower, using smaller appliances, and generally consuming less.

This strategy of consuming less is called "sufficiency," or in the United States, "simple living," "voluntary simplicity," or more generally, "downsizing," often done (voluntarily) through deciding to work and earn less. So how feasible is it to expand the idea of sufficiency to a national scale, by cutting consumption of energy-intensive goods and services like frozen foods or air travel? Furthermore, would the

widespread adoption of sufficiency have any impact on global resource or energy use? Once again the rebound effect has an impact, and the widespread impact of reducing demand for a commodity (like energy) results in lowering its global price and allowing greater consumption by marginal consumers.

So would our Western reduction of consumption merely allow poorer consumers elsewhere to enjoy a higher standard of living? Given the lower environmental standards in developing countries, a shift in energy demand from rich to poor countries could result in greater environmental pollution. If we use less electricity from our clean coal power stations, will China and India use more in their dirty ones? This is a complex debate that has only just started.

Outlook

Under conditions of economic growth, national energy use has historically increased despite big improvements in energy efficiency. Past attempts to promote energy efficiency as a means of reducing national energy consumption have proved futile. It has even been argued that promoting energy efficiency (like any other factor of production such as labor or resources) stimulates economic growth, and hence energy use. While improved energy efficiency, mainly brought about by stock turnover (the replacement of old, inefficient equipment by new, more efficient equipment) is good for the economy and for people's lives, it is unlikely to be a solution to the problems of energy shortages or climate change. Energy efficiency makes us richer, however, through lowering operating costs, and allows us (if we so choose) to invest our money savings in new or low-carbon energy sources. Energy efficiency is a means to a sustainable world, not an end in itself.

Horace HERRING
The Open University

See also Building Rating Systems, Green; Carbon Footprint; Computer Modeling; Development Indicators; Energy Labeling; Human Appropriation of Net Primary Production (HANPP); I = P × A × T Equation; International Organization for Standardization (ISO); *The Limits to Growth;* Material Flow Analysis (MFA); Shipping and Freight Indicators; Social Life Cycle Assessment (S-LCA); Supply Chain Analysis

FURTHER READINGS

Andrews-Speed, Philip. (2009). China's ongoing energy efficiency drive: Origins, progress and prospects. *Energy Policy, 37*(4), 1331–1344.
Balachandra, P.; Ravindranath, Darshini; & Ravindranath, N. H. (2010). Energy efficiency in India: Assessing the policy regimes and their impacts. *Energy Policy, 38*(11), 6428–6438.

Brookes, Len. (2000). Energy efficiency fallacies revisited. *Energy Policy, 28*(6–7), 355–366.

Calwell, Chris. (2010, March 22). Is efficient sufficient? The case for shifting our emphasis in energy specifications to progressive efficiency and sufficiency. Retrieved September 18, 2011, from http://www.eceee.org/sufficiency

Fouquet, Roger. (2008). *Heat, power and light.* London: Edward Elgar.

Herring, Horace, & Sorrell, Steve (Eds.). (2009). *Energy efficiency and sustainable consumption: The rebound effect.* Basingstoke, UK: Palgrave.

Jaccard, Mark. (2005). *Sustainable fossil fuels.* Cambridge, UK: Cambridge University Press.

Jackson, Tim. (Ed.). (2006). *The Earthscan reader in sustainable consumption.* London: Earthscan.

Jenkins, Jesse; Nordhaus, Ted; & Schellenberger, Michael. (2011). *Energy demand: Rebound and backfire as emergent phenomena.* Retrieved September 18, 2011, from http://thebreakthrough.org/blog/2011/02/new_report_how_efficiency_can.shtml

Lovins, Amory. (1977). *Soft energy paths.* London: Pelican.

Polimeni, John; Mayumi, Kozo; Giampietro, Mario; & Alcott, Blake. (2008). *Jevons' paradox and the myth of resource efficiency improvements.* London: Earthscan.

Smil, Vaclav. (2003). *Energy at the crossroads.* Cambridge, MA: MIT Press.

Stewart, Devin, & Wilczewski, Warren. (2009, February 3). How Japan became an efficiency superpower. Retrieved September 18, 2011, from http://www.policyinnovations.org/ideas/briefings/data/000102.

Taylor, Peter; d'Ortigue, Oliver; Francoeur, Michel; & Trudeau, Nathalie. (2010). Final energy use in IEA countries: The role of energy efficiency. *Energy Policy, 38*(12), 6463–6474.

Weizsacker, Ernst; Hargroves, Karlson; Smith, Michael; & Desha, Cheryl. (2009). *Factor five: Transforming the global economy through 80% improvements in resource productivity.* London: Earthscan.

Zhou, Nan; Levine, Mark; & Price, Lynn. (2010). Overview of current energy-efficiency policies in China. *Energy Policy, 38*(11), 6439–6452.

Energy Labeling

Recent awareness on process and product sustainability has brought about the diffusion of a wide range of tools to measure, evaluate, and compare energy performance. Energy labeling represents one of the most important systems in providing benchmarks for both sustainability performance and guidance in purchases models.

The increasing concern about business impacts on the environment and society has resulted in growing attention toward sustainable production and consumption models. Currently a wide range of tools providing significant benchmarks for sustainability product performance as well as guidance for consumers is available.

Energy labels are informative labels applied to manufactured products indicating data relative to energy performance, generally in terms of consumption, efficiency, cost, and so on. Consumers thus are provided with the necessary information for making more-informed choices.

Currently, three categories of energy labels are used in most countries: endorsement, comparative, and information only. Endorsement labels essentially offer a "seal of approval" that a product meets certain prespecified criteria. They are generally based on a "yes/no" procedure and offer little additional information. One example of an endorsement label for energy efficiency is the Energy Star label that is provided by the US Environmental Protection Agency (EPA).

Comparative labels are divided into two subcategories: one involves a categorical ranking system, and the other uses a continuous scale or bar graph to show relative energy use. The category labels use a ranking system that tells consumers how energy efficient a model is compared to others. The main emphasis is on establishing clear categories so that the consumer can easily understand, by looking at a single label, how an energy-efficient product compares relative to others in the market. The European energy label is an example of a category label. (See figure 1 on page 114.)

The other category of comparative label—continuous-scale labels—provide comparative information that enables consumers to make informed choices about products; however, they do not concern specific categories. The Canadian energy guide is an example of the continuous-scale label. (See figure 2 on page 114.)

Information-only labels provide data on the technical performance of the labeled product and offer no simple way (such as a ranking system) to compare energy performance between products. These types of labels are generally not consumer friendly because they contain only technical information. (See figure 3 on page 115.)

It is important to keep a consistent label style and format across product types; this makes it easier for consumers to understand individual types of labels to evaluate different products. Selecting a label to use is not always easy and usually depends on local consumer knowledge and attitudes. The endorsement label is quite effective, at least with consumers that are attentive to environmental issues. Categorical comparison labels provide more information about energy use and, if well designed and implemented, can provide a consistent basis that buyers can focus on when evaluating energy efficiency from one purchase to another. Continuous-scale labels can transmit more detailed information on relative energy use, but research has shown that this label format may be difficult for consumers to understand. Information-only labels are generally more effective for the most educated and economically and/or environmentally concerned consumers.

Figure 1. European Union Color Energy Label

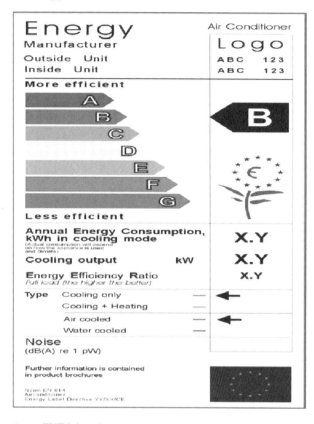

Source: ENEA (2004).

In this European Union label, the energy efficiency of an appliance, in this case an air conditioner, is rated in terms of a set of energy efficiency classes from A to G on the label, A (green) being the most energy efficient, G (red) the least efficient. The label also gives customers other useful information when choosing between various models.

Energy Labeling Overview

National energy labeling programs were developed at the beginning of the 1970s with the goal of controlling the confused overflow of "self-certified" private energy brands as well as for facilitating informed consumer choices. One of the first forms of these energy-efficiency labeling programs—obligatory for domestic-use refrigerators, freezers, and air-conditioners—dates to Canada's 1978 EnerGuide program, which was run by the government agency National Resources Canada. Subsequently a similar program was developed in the United States called Energy Guide, jointly managed by the Department of Energy (DOE) and the Environmental Protection Agency (EPA). In Europe, the Directive 79/530/CEE established that household energy consumption of electrical appliances had to be indicated. Unfortunately, this

Figure 2. Continuous-Scale Label (Canadian Energy Label)

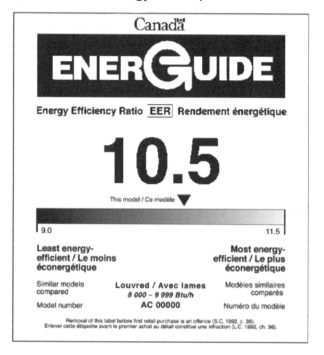

Source: Natural Resources Canada (2010).

Canada's black and white EnerGuide Label shows the average annual energy consumption of the appliance in kilowatt hours (kWh), energy efficiency of the appliance relative to similar models, annual energy consumption range for models of this type and size, type and size of the model, and model number.

never transposed because this directive was never implemented in all European countries. In Germany in 1986, the Blauer Engel plan considered marking boilers, while the Dutch program Milieuker began labeling light bulbs, computers, and televisions. The almost simultaneous 1986 diffusion of the Star Rating Scheme on the Australian continent was the outcome of the mandatory energy labeling of refrigerators, while in Canada the Environmental Choice Program (1988), an environmental excellence label, was envisaged for both domestic appliances as well as office equipment.

In the 1990s, following the success of previous initiatives, further energy labeling programs became widespread throughout the rest of the world. The European Union (EU) Directive 92/75/CEE relative to a mandatory energy labeling program provided energy consumption indications and supplementary information on how domestic appliances work. At the same time in the United States, in the light of previous experience in the household domestic appliances sector, an energy efficiency label—one of the most important on an international level—was applied to computers and computer

Figure 3. Information-Only Energy Label (US Energy Guide)

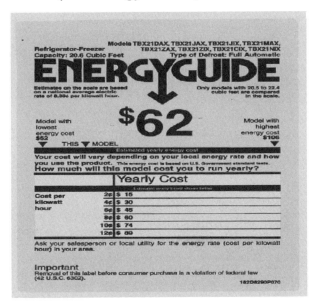

Source: Federal Trade Commission (2010).

The black and white US Energy Guide shows average energy consumption of the appliance in kilowatt hours (kWh); energy efficiency of the appliance; and the relative cost and energy consumption range for different models.

monitors (Energy Star Program) as well as an environmental excellence label (Green Seal) for light bulbs.

Energy Star is an international voluntary labeling mechanism introduced by the EPA in 1992. The agency's main aim was to promote the most energy-efficient products available on the market in order to facilitate energy saving as well as reduce climate-altering greenhouse gas emissions. The Energy Star label is currently the most widespread internationally and applies to over forty different types of products, including household electrical appliances (washing machines, refrigerators, dishwashers), office equipment (faxes, printers, scanners, computers), lighting products, home electronics, and more. The program merits particular attention as it enables the certification of buildings from an energy performance point of view (i.e., buildings with low energy consumption). During the late 1990s, the GEEA label was created in Switzerland by the Group for Energy Efficient Appliances (GEEA), a forum of government agencies from various countries including Denmark, Holland, and Sweden. The label—applied to computer appliances as well as to televisions, video recorders, DVD players, satellite receivers, audio systems, and more—has become widely used in the GEEA countries. The efficiency criteria—to which the appliance must conform—are far more restrictive when compared to the Energy Star label. In Sweden,

following several pioneering experiences within the certification sector, in particular regarding computer appliance safety, the Tjänstemännens Central Organization (TCO, or the Swedish Confederation of Professional Employees) label TCO'95 for cathode-ray tube monitors and computer keyboards was adopted. After several years, the program became more widespread—through the TCO'99 label—and was applied to liquid crystal monitors, printers, and laptop computers. The conforming criteria for label use include ergonomic aspects, radiation emissions reduction, low energy consumption, and appliance eco-efficiency.

Meanwhile in South America, the Programa Brasileiro de Etiquetagem, another type of energy labeling program, was set up and voluntarily applied to refrigerators and air conditioning by manufacturers. At the same time following the growth of the information and communication technology (ICT) sector, Asia implemented the Japanese environmental excellence label Eco Mark for photocopiers (1999), computers (2000), and printers (2001). The US government, one of the most attentive toward the competitive strategies being applied to its own market, adopted the International Energy Star program, followed closely by others including Japan (1995), Australia (1999), New Zealand (1999), the EU (2000), Taiwan (2000), and Canada (2001). The choice was based on bilateral agreements made with these countries. Subsequently, another environmental excellence label, the Good Environmental Choice, was applied to the computer sector in Australia.

The Swedish TCO had proposed the TCO'03 display label to be used specifically for computer monitors. TCO'03 not only represented an innovative generation of labeling programs, based on more restricting environmental and energy criteria than its predecessors, but it also envisaged the labeling of monitors that had superior performance qualities, such as color and image reproduction, low radiation emissions, safety, and energy efficiency. This could reduce the environmental impact during the product's life cycle, as evaluated through a life cycle assessment (LCA).

During the last decade, an agreement was signed between the US government and the European Union to coordinate the labeling programs relative to efficient energy use in office equipment. This resulted in the EU Directive of 8 April 2003 that definitively established the Energy Star program, which represents a decisive step toward harmonizing not only all the different types of energy consumption certification programs but also the diffusion of more energy efficient products. The European Union issued the Directive 2010/30/EU, which extends a new system of energy labeling to products that consume energy for commercial and industrial use, for instance television sets, decoders, fittings, refrigerators, and industrial machinery.

Implications

Energy labeling programs can realistically assume a driving force role in the transition process toward eco-sustainability only if their current critical elements are eliminated.

Without doubt, the main critical element is consumer disorientation that derives from the articulated range of energy labeling systems on the market. When the consumer is not always able to fully understand the information on the label, specific technical competence often is required. A further critical aspect involves the criteria adopted in the different programs, which at times is far too complex and on other occasions, too vague. The combination of these factors strongly limits the diffusion of energy-efficient products. Moreover, the price factor, which is generally higher than similar products, also represents a relevant barrier. In fact, the consumer is not always willing to pay a higher price for the purchase of energy-efficient goods.

No doubt, more widespread diffusion and development of energy labeling programs that are harmonized on a global level is desirable. Innovative solutions depend on consumer choices that are still based on price, without even considering socio-environmental advantages. The transition to a more eco-sustainable lifestyle and consumption model (both local and global) implies establishing agreements on various levels for the diffusion of standard programs, energy efficiency logos, and specific types of products, all capable of correctly informing the consumer on the economic, environmental, and social advantages of the product.

Ornella MALANDRINO
Salerno University

See also Building Rating Systems, Green; Ecolabels; Energy Efficiency Measurement; Organic and Consumer Labels

Further Reading

Agenzia nazionale per le nuove tecnologie (ENEA) [Italian National Agency for New Technologies]. (2004). *L'etichetta energetica* [The energy label] (Opuscolo no. 24 della Collana Sviluppo Sostenibile). Rome: ENEA.

Agenzia nazionale per le nuove tecnologie (ENEA) [Italian National Agency for New Technologies]. (2011). Homepage. Retrieved February 3, 2011, from http://www.enea.it/it

Energy Star. (2011). Homepage. Retrieved February 3, 2011, from http://www.energystar.gov

EU Energy Star. (2011). Homepage. Retrieved February 3, 2011, from http://www.eu-energystar.org

Europa: Il portale dell'Unione Europea [Gateway to the European Union]. (2011). Homepage. Retrieved February 3, 2011, from http://europa.eu/index_it.htm

Federal Trade Commission (FTC). (2010). Energy guidance: Appliance shopping with the Energy Guide label. Retrieved June 29, 2011, from http://www.ftc.gov/bcp/edu/pubs/consumer/homes/rea14.shtm

Harrington, Lloyd, & Damnics, Melissa. (2004). Energy labeling and standards programs throughout the world. Canberra, Australia: National Appliance and Equipment Energy Efficiency Committee (NAEEEC).

Mahlia, T. M. Indra. (2004). Methodology for predicting market transformation due to implementation of energy efficiency standards and labels. *Energy Conversion and Management, 45*(11), 1785–1793.

Mahlia, T. M. Indra, & Saidur, Rahman. (2010). A review on test procedure, energy efficiency standards and energy labels for room air conditioners and refrigerator-freezers. *Renewable and Sustainable Energy Reviews, 14*(7), 1888–1900.

Natural Resources Canada. (2010). Household appliances. Retrieved June 29, 2011, from http://oee.nrcan.gc.ca/residential/personal/appliances/energuide.cfm?attr=4#household

Proto, Maria; Malandrino, Ornella; & Supino, Stefania. (2007). Eco-labels: A sustainability performance in benchmarking? *Management of Environmental Quality: An International Journal, 18*(6), 669–683.

Environmental Justice Indicators

Environmental justice counters distributive and participatory injustice, in which certain demographic groups, generally people of color and the poor, are harmed by environmental burden without significantly benefiting from or participating in activities that caused the damage to environments, human bodies, and communities. As justice has long been central to sustainability, methods of monitoring environmental justice are critical to sustainability initiatives.

Environmental justice has been central to concepts of sustainability since the term first started to emerge as a way to link environmental, economic, and social factors. Sustainability advocates try to ensure that the needs of all living in the present as well as those of future generations can be met (that is to say, sustainability advocates are concerned with intra- and intergenerational justice). Efforts to monitor environmental justice thus are critical to monitoring progress toward sustainability and sustainable development. Understanding definitions of distributive, participatory, and restorative environmental justice; their connections to sustainability; and methods of monitoring environmental injustice will indicate the importance of environmental justice for sustainability initiatives and directions for future research to progress toward sustainability.

Defining Types of Environmental Justice

Some scholars, such as the US activist and historian Robert Gottlieb, trace the history of environmental justice movements back to public health initiatives of the late 1800s, the work of the United Farm Workers starting in the 1960s, and the activism surrounding Love Canal in the 1970s and 1980s (Gottlieb 1993). The term *environmental justice* and its relative, *environmental racism*, however, emerged in the 1980s out of the work of scholar-activists including Robert Bullard and those participating in the United Church of Christ's Commission on Racial Justice who documented trends in the racial and economic characteristics of communities in close proximity to toxic wastes: people of color disproportionately lived and worked near toxic waste facilities. With these studies and the conviction that all humans have dignity, worth, and the right to meet basic needs, environmental justice studies was born.

Environmental justice encompasses distributional, participatory, and restorative justice; it is typically defined as the opposite of environmental injustice. First, and most emphasized in the literature, are distributive injustices in which certain groups of people, usually people of color and the poor, are disproportionately impacted by environmental burdens. In other words, they are harmed by the effects of other humans' actions on the environment though they were not able to substantially gain from the activities that caused the environmental damage in the first place. If they are able to benefit a little from environmentally degrading activities, it is not to a degree that offsets the risks they face: the diminished health, limited economic opportunities, degraded ecosystems, and decreased cultural relationship to the environment that they actually experience. Meanwhile, those who did cause and/or benefit significantly from the environmental damage are able to circumvent its negative effects given their financial and political resources.

Long recognized by environmental justice advocates and increasingly in academic environmental justice literature, participatory justice is a second (and simultaneous) component of environmental justice. Participatory injustice occurs when certain groups of people are less likely to have the ability to participate in decision making that affects them because of overt prejudice or systematic conditions which hinder their participation. Certainly, participatory injustice is manifested when groups are formally barred from participating in decision making, such as when they are not allowed to vote and/or their desires are not considered by the government. Environmental justice advocates maintain that injustices also occur when people appear to be able to participate but systemic barriers effectively limit their ability to do so. For example, if interested communities are not informed of public hearings, or if the advertisements for public hearings and the information discussed during them is not communicated in the language the community speaks (e.g., if it's written in English for a Spanish-speaking neighborhood) or is written for a technical, not a lay audience, then the ability of community members to participate meaningfully in decision making will be hindered, if not thwarted. Participatory injustice can also occur when community preferences or knowledge about communities and ecosystems, based on decades or generations of experiential knowledge, is ignored when it comes time to actually make decisions. After all, when a group's knowledge and opinions are ignored they cannot actually contribute to the decision-making process. Distributional and participatory injustice often go hand in hand, since both focus on articulating past problems in the distribution of physical resources and political power, and since participatory injustice enables distributional inequities.

The emerging third type of environmental justice, restorative justice, focuses on the relationships between those most harmed by and those most benefiting from or causing environmental burdens. It aims at minimum to restore relationships to their status before the injustice occurred, though in practice it often aims to transform such relationships so they are better than they were previously in order to prevent future injustices. Restorative justice usually involves a significant commitment by all parties to articulate and understand the magnitude and scope of damage, compensate affected communities and individuals, make apologies where they are needed, and promise to change future behaviors (and follow through with such promises). Restoring environmental, economic, and cultural opportunities may also be a part of restorative justice. But creative solutions may be necessary where ecosystems and natural features are degraded beyond repair, as when a sacred mountain's top has been cut off to mine its coal or people have been killed by environmentally induced diseases.

Environmental Justice and Sustainability

All three types of environmental justice are connected to sustainability and sustainable development, though the connections are strongest with respect to distributional and participatory environmental justice because concepts and practices of restorative justice are still being developed. Illustrating these connections through a study of definitions of sustainable development and a theory of working toward sustainability will suggest that methods of monitoring environmental justice are critical to monitoring sustainability.

Definitions of sustainability and sustainable development inherently involve normative commitments, especially claims of justice. Consider, for example, the most widely known and influential definition of sustainable development, that articulated by the Brundtland Commission in 1987: sustainable development is "meet[ing] the needs of the present without compromising the ability of future generations to meet their own needs" (World Commission on Environment and Development 1987). Intergenerational justice, justice between generations, is a significant component of this definition of sustainable development and, indeed, is often emphasized by the sustainability movement. As this definition is also concerned with the ability of currently living people to meet their own needs, it is committed to intragenerational distributive justice, the type of justice most focused upon by the environmental justice movement, which wants to emphasize that environmental degradation and burdens have already contributed to injustices and significantly affected people. Environmental justice scholars and activists have contributed to the sustainability movement by expanding theoretical concepts of justice to environmental issues, maintaining that actions are not sustainable unless they foster justice, and chronicling the many ways in which environmental actions have been unjust in the past.

Sustainability initiatives also align with participatory environmental justice in that best practices for developing sustainability initiatives and indicators call for the involvement of people who will be affected by them. Involving communities in sustainability initiatives is commonly advocated for at least four reasons. First, a commitment to human rights and/or democracy, shared by many sustainability advocates, suggests that it is right, just, or fair to enable people to be involved in processes that will affect their lives. Secondly, it is recognized that groups of people may have significantly different values shaping their vision of sustainability such that it is necessary for them to participate in the process of articulating sustainability goals and policies if their visions are to have any influence on the process. Third, many sustainability advocates recognize that local people may have significant knowledge about ecosystems, weather patterns, or community behavior that will be critical to defining and moving toward sustainability in that location. Fourth, since people are more likely to follow new initiatives and encourage others to do so if they support the initiative, and since meaningful community participation in the creation of sustainability initiatives increases support for the initiative, sustainability initiatives will be more successful if conceived through a participatory community process. Theories of sustainability policy making and index development thus call for the involvement of local people and communities, conditions that have been implemented in the development of many sustainability initiatives, and enable participatory justice.

Restorative environmental justice also has a significant place in the sustainability movement as it can help determine how to proceed toward sustainability initiatives in the face of massive past environmental degradation and injustices. Theories and practices intentionally focusing on the restorative-justice aspects of sustainability are, however, still relatively new. In order to be widely implemented they need significant development to account for the widespread, often unconscious, responsibility for the types of environmental damage that may affect people who are significantly removed spatially and temporally from the initial action.

Given these realized and potential connections between environmental justice and sustainability, methods of monitoring environmental justice are vital aspects of monitoring sustainability.

Monitoring Environmental Justice

As people first started to explicitly monitor environmental injustice in the 1980s and 1990s, they faced many theoretical and practical challenges: they needed to determine how to define environmental justice, the best ways to monitor whether injustice was in fact happening, the types of groups affected and the ways in which they were affected, and whether such studies could be undertaken with existing data or if it would be necessary to collect significant amounts of new data. Unsurprisingly then, early studies of environmental injustice by the United Church of Christ and Robert Bullard's work significantly shaped the field for a number of years. Namely, the tendency to study environmental justice in localized areas, or to study injustices related to particular environmental problems—largely health risks from proximity to toxins—would pervade most early environmental justice studies. As evidence of environmental injustices became more widely available and accepted, studies of environmental injustices spread beyond toxic wastes to a multitude of environmental issues.

When members of the Commission for Racial Justice of the United Church of Christ, as well as Robert Bullard and others conducted research that informed the early literature about "environmental injustice" or "environmental racism," they examined the correlation between the location of community demographics and toxic wastes. They found that minority and low-income communities housed hazardous waste sites at far greater concentrations than white and high-income communities even though the communities with the hazardous waste storage and disposal facilities did not receive the majority of benefits from industries that produced this toxic waste (Bullard 1990, 1994b; Commission for Racial Justice United Church of Christ 1987; Goldman and Fitton 1994). Using the language of environmental justice studies, these communities are disproportionately burdened by the dangers of toxic waste, a distributional injustice (Figueroa and Mills 2001, 427).

While acceptance of environmental injustice as a problem grew throughout the 1990s, the academic community debated about the best way to assess the presence and significance of environmental injustice. Most studies at this time still focused on hazardous waste storage facilities, emitters of toxic wastes, or Superfund sites that were riddled with toxins. (Superfund sites are abandoned hazardous waste sites in the United States identified and cleaned up through the Superfund program, an environmental program established and funded by CERCLA—the Comprehensive Environmental Response, Compensation and Liability Act of 1980.) Researchers assumed that the closer one's home or business was to such toxins, the more likely that one would suffer adverse health effects. They thus counted the number of toxic waste sites within a community or within a certain radius from the community, often using geographic information system (GIS) tools to map such hazards. Researchers generally had to define neighborhoods based on census tracts or zip codes in order to access available demographic data. Limitations to such studies arise, of course, because hazards located just outside the boundary of a census tract or zip code may still affect the communities within those bounds, because demographic communities may not neatly follow zip code or census tract boundaries, because the scale of data available may reveal or conceal injustices, and because zip codes and census tracts can define communities so differently that they may yield contradictory results (Anderton et al. 1995; Bowen 2002; Taquino, Parisi, and Gill 2002). Furthermore, proximity to a potential harm does not necessarily correlate with a greater rate of harm. Some also questioned what the results of studies demonstrating correlations between race and toxic wastes actually indicated. Was it the case that the neighborhoods of people of color or the poor were targeted for toxic waste dumps and other environmental hazards, or was it the case that the presence of these environmental hazards and the accompanying lower housing costs attracted people who had few educational, financial, and political resources (Been 1995; Bullard 1994a; Mohai and Bryant 1995)? Are race, class, gender, or other demographic factors most related to environmental injustice (Mohai and Bryant 1995)?

Such questions and theoretical debates have prompted scholars to refine their methods of monitoring environmental injustice and conduct more longitudinal studies to explore its causes. Hundreds of studies focused on various communities and environmental issues throughout the world have demonstrated that communities of color and the poor are disproportionately targeted for environmental hazards, are less able to respond when they experience them, and sometimes, are forced into degraded areas for financial or political reasons. While environmental racism and injustice is not always intentional, its effects can be significant and are not limited to a community's proximity to toxic wastes.

For example, the US sociologist Sharon L. Harlan and colleagues maintain that the urban heat island effect is a significant environmental justice issue in Phoenix. The relative

lack of vegetation coupled with high concentrations of buildings and pavement in low-income Latino neighborhoods can lead to significantly higher temperatures:

> During a summer heat wave in 2003, average daily air temperature at 5:00 p.m. varied by as much as 13.5°F [7.6°C] . . . between an upper-income and lower-income neighborhood located 2.5 miles [4km] from each other in the city of Phoenix. On a "normal" summer day, the maximum difference of average daily temperature at 5:00 p.m. between the neighborhoods was 7.2°F [4.0°C]. (Harlan et al. 2008, 187)

Since high heat "cause[s] more deaths worldwide than all other extreme weather events combined" and the hottest neighborhoods are inhabited by people with the least ability to escape the heat through air conditioning, backyard pools, and community efforts, the higher temperatures have an even greater adverse affect than the thermometers would indicate (Harlan et al. 2008, 177, 191).

Environmental injustice also has been found to occur often when indigenous groups and more recent immigrants disagree about land use, as exemplified by relations between traditional inhabitants and Australian mining firms in Papua New Guinea (Low and Gleeson 1998) and Native American opposition to a proposed road through, nuclear waste storage on, or military activities on sacred land (Checker 2002; Martin 2002). Rising rates of asthma in inner-city children and the cultural and health impacts of subsistence fishing in polluted waters are also environmental justice issues (Corburn 2005). From time to time, studies of environmental justice have also found situations in which communities traditionally thought to experience only environmental injustice may experience disproportionate environmental benefits; in one study of the relationship between income level and proximity to outdoor recreation sites in the Chattahoochee National Forest, researchers found that people with lower incomes were more likely to live near the most desirable sites (Tarrant and Cordell 1999).

As environmental justice studies explored a more diverse range of issues they also increased the complexities of issues examined. The US researcher and professor Kristen Schrader-Frechette, for example, chronicled the multifaceted ethical and cultural dilemmas that occur within communities facing environmental damage largely made by others. Does one enable uranium mining or nuclear waste storage on the reservation for the promise of new jobs or cash payouts though it may damage religiously important sites and cause risks to ecosystems (Shrader-Frechette 2002)? Communities have been and often are divided on such issues, as people want what is best for their families and communities, both now and in the future.

Along with more-often examined factors of environmental justice (such as physical health risks and economic impacts), research and study in the field has begun to recognize and study the psychological and social effects for communities faced with difficult decisions, as well to address the sociocultural disruption from environmental degradation, including the loss of traditional food sources, ritual grounds, and green spaces, and the lack of ability to meaningfully participate in decision making about such issues. While psychological and social effects of environmental injustice can be difficult to quantify, surveys, oral histories, and other data collection methods are slowly being used to understand the extent of this damage.

Future Directions

Methods of monitoring environmental justice have broadened significantly in recent years, but more work is still needed. First, most studies still focus on several environmental justice issues in a particular place or a particular issue that may be distributed across several places. Certainly these methods of monitoring environmental injustice are significant in that they have chronicled the problems that exist, enabled community participation, and have been used to press for changes in industries and local policies. They also aid sustainability initiatives in that they help ensure that the environmental needs of current people are met. As they are so specific, however, more studies are needed to determine how to prioritize efforts to combat environmental injustice, to determine overall environmental justice goals for states or nations, and to determine the most effective ways of working toward them. This new research will certainly need to draw on existing work about distributive and participatory justice, but it will also need to involve restorative justice if all involved communities are to change to avoid future injustices. By doing so, environmental justice scholarship and activism can continue

to aid sustainability efforts as it works toward intra- and intergenerational justice regarding economic, social, and environmental factors.

Sarah E. FREDERICKS
University of North Texas

See also Citizen Science; Community and Stakeholder Input; Development Indicators; Environmental Performance Index (EPI); Focus Groups; Global Environment Outlook (GEO) Reports; Gross National Happiness; Human Development Index (HDI); Intellectual Property Rights; New Ecological Paradigm (NEP) Scale; Social Life Cycle Assessment (S-LCA); Supply Chain Analysis; Taxation Indicators, Green

FURTHER READING

Agyeman, Julian; Bullard, Robert D.; & Evans, Bob. (Eds.). (2003). *Just sustainabilities: Development in an unequal world.* Cambridge, MA: The MIT Press.

Anderton, Douglas L., et al. (1995). Studies used to prove charges of environmental racism are flawed. In Jonathan S. Petrikin (Ed.), *Environmental justice: At issue* (pp. 24–37). San Diego, CA: Greenhaven Press.

Arquette, Mary, et al. (2002). Holistic risk-based environmental decision making: A native perspective. *Environmental Health Perspectives, 110*(supplement 2), 259–264.

Been, Vicki. (1995). Market forces, not racist practices, may affect the siting of locally undesirable land uses. In Jonathan S. Petrikin (Ed.), *Environmental justice: At issue* (pp. 38–59). San Diego, CA: Greenhaven Press.

Bowen, William M. (2002). An analytical review of environmental justice research: What do we really know? *Environmental Management, 29*(1), 3–15.

Bullard, Robert D. (1990). *Dumping in Dixie: Race, class, and environmental quality.* Boulder, CO: Westview Press.

Bullard, Robert D. (1994a). A new chicken-or-egg debate: Which comes first—The neighborhood, or the toxic dump? *The Workbook, 19*(2), 60–62.

Bullard, Robert D. (1994b). *Unequal protection: Environmental justice and communities of color.* San Francisco: Sierra Club Books.

Checker, Melissa A. (2002). "It's in the air": Redefining the environment as a new metaphor for old social justice struggles. *Human Organization, 61*(1), 94–105.

Commission for Racial Justice United Church of Christ. (1987). *Toxic wastes and race in the United States: A national report on the racial and socio-economic characteristics of communities with hazardous waste sites.* New York: Commission for Racial Justice United Church of Christ.

Corburn, Jason. (2005). *Street science: Community knowledge and environmental health justice.* Cambridge, MA: MIT Press.

Elling, Bo. (2008). *Rationality and the environment: Decision-making in environmental politics and assessment.* London: Earthscan.

Figueroa, Robert M. (2006). Evaluating environmental justice claims. In Joanne Bauer (Ed.), *Forging environmentalism: Justice, livelihood, and contested environments* (pp. 360–376). New York: M. E. Sharpe.

Figueroa, Robert M., & Mills, Claudia. (2001). Environmental justice. In Dale Jamieson (Ed.), *A companion to environmental philosophy* (pp. 426–438). New York: Blackwell.

Fredericks, Sarah E. (2011). Monitoring environmental justice. *Environmental Justice, 4*(1), 63–69.

Goldman, Benjamin A., & Fitton, Laura. (1994). *Toxic wastes and race revisited: An update of the 1987 report on the racial and socioeconomic characteristics of communities with hazardous waste sites.* Washington, DC: Center for Policy Alternatives.

Gottlieb, Robert. (1993). *Forcing the spring: The transformation of the American environmental movement.* Washington, DC: Island Press.

Harlan, Sharon L., et al. (2008). In the shade of affluence: The inequitable distribution of the urban heat island. In Robert C. Wilkinson & William R. Fruedenburg (Eds.), *Equity and the environment: Vol. 15. Research in social problems and public policy* (pp. 173–202). Amsterdam: Elsevier.

Llewellyn, Jennifer J., & Howse, Robert. (1998). *Restorative justice: A conceptual framework.* Ottawa: Law Commission of Canada.

Low, Nicholas, & Gleeson, Brendan. (1998). Situating justice in the environment: The case of the BHP at the Ok Tedi copper mine. *Antipode, 30*(3), 201–226.

Martin, M. C. (2002). Expanding the boundaries of environmental justice: Native Americans and the South Lawrence trafficway. *Policy and Management Review, 2*(1), 62–85.

Mohai, Paul, & Bryant, Bunyan. (1995). Demographic studies reveal a pattern of environmental injustice. In Jonathan S. Petrikin (Ed.), *Environmental justice: At issue* (pp. 24–37). San Diego, CA: Greenhaven Press.

Shrader-Frechette, Kristin S. (2002). *Environmental justice: Creating equality, reclaiming democracy.* New York: Oxford University Press.

Taquino, Michael; Parisi, Domenico; & Gill, Duane A. (2002). Units of analysis and the environmental justice hypothesis: The case of industrial hog farms. *Social Science Quarterly, 83*(1), 298–316.

Tarrant, Michael A., & Cordell, H. Ken. (1999). Environmental justice and the spatial distribution of outdoor recreation sites: An application of geographic information systems. *Journal of Leisure Research, 31*(1), 18–34.

World Commission on Environment and Development. (1987). *Our common future: Report of the World Commission on Environment and Development.* New York: Oxford University Press.

Environmental Performance Index (EPI)

The Environmental Performance Index (EPI) ranks countries on twenty-five performance indicators spanning ten policy categories relating to both environmental public health and ecosystem vitality. The EPI's methodology facilitates country comparisons and analyses of how the global community is performing with respect to established environmental policy goals.

Environmental sustainability emerged in the first decade of the twenty-first century as a central policy issue and a topic of international debate. Governments face increasing pressure to explain, through quantitative metrics, their performance on a range of pollution control and natural resource management challenges. Researchers at Yale University and Columbia University collaboratively developed the Environmental Performance Index (EPI) in 2006 to respond to this growing need for more rigorous, data-driven environmental performance measurement. The 2008 and 2010 editions of the EPI brought various refinements to the methodology. The 2012 EPI will be the first edition to attempt to establish a stable index for tracking changes in performance over time.

About the Index

The 2010 EPI ranks 163 countries on twenty-five performance indicators in the following ten policy categories: environmental burden of disease, water (effects on humans), air pollution (effects on humans), air pollution (effects on ecosystems), water (effects on ecosystems), biodiversity and habitat, forestry, fisheries, agriculture, and climate change. (See figure 1 on page 124.) These policy categories are further aggregated into two broad policy objectives: environmental health (the first three)

and ecosystem vitality (the final seven). These objectives and the performance indicators are described on the 2010 EPI's website (EPI 2010), where the complete database and a detailed description of the methodology are available.

The EPI uses the best available data and practices in environmental health and ecological science. Some of the indicators represent direct measures of performance, while others are proxy measures that offer a rougher gauge of policy progress. In some cases (for example, with the water-quality index indicator), multiple imputation techniques were used to address problems with missing data. Each indicator has an associated long-term public health or ecosystem sustainability target. For each country and each indicator, the EPI calculates a proximity-to-target value based on the gap between the country's performance and the policy target. These targets were formed using input from four sources: treaties or other internationally agreed-upon goals; standards set by international organizations; leading national regulatory requirements; and expert judgment based on prevailing scientific consensus. The proximity-to-target scores are aggregated using weights that reflect their perceived relative importance within the two policy objectives. The environmental health and ecosystem vitality objectives are then each given 50 percent weight in the overall EPI.

The EPI provides a unique and simple framework for improved analytic rigor in environmental decision making. The EPI's development, however, has revealed severe global data gaps, weaknesses in methodological consistency in some policy areas, and the lack of a systematic process for verifying the environmental data reported by governments. The EPI's data sources are generally international organizations focused on researching specific policy issues, such as the World Health Organization, the UN's Food and Agriculture Organization, the World Resources Institute, and the International Energy

Figure 1. Indicators Used to Compute the Environmental Performance Index

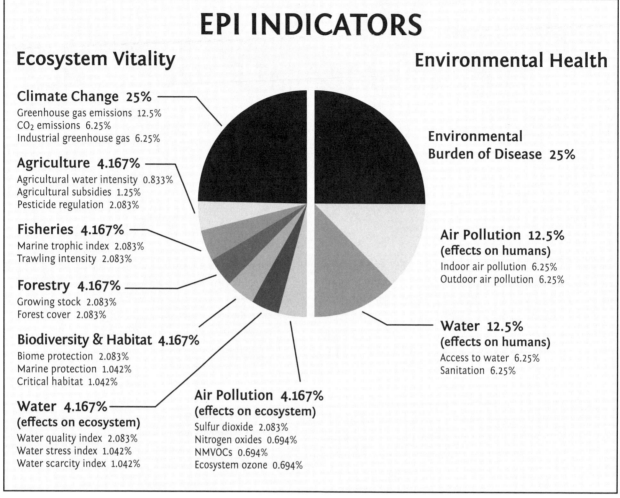

Source: EPI 2010.

The pie chart above shows the various indicators—such as agricultural water intensity, pesticide regulation, and forest cover—used to compute the Environmental Performance Index. A fully interactive version, showing the relative position of every nation on the planet, is available at http://www.epi2010.yale.edu/Metrics.

Agency. This informal array of data sources underscores the clear need for better global data collection, verification, review, and analysis in order to establish the trust required to support effective worldwide policy cooperation. The EPI provides a model for transparency in data and methodology, with all of the underlying data freely available online.

Policy Implications of the 2010 EPI

An examination of the 2010 EPI and the underlying indicators leads to several policy observations. Four are highlighted here. First, the 2010 EPI highlights the challenges due to gaps in data sources and methodological limitations; both hinder progress in data-driven

policy making. For example, the EPI has had to rely on imputed water-quality measures for a subset of countries with limited data. Second, policy makers need to push for better data collection, methodologically consistent reporting, and mechanisms for independent data verification; the international community currently lacks consensus on standards for all three elements of effective data acquisition. Third, wealth is correlated with the EPI in general and environmental health results in particular, although there is still a diversity of performance within every level of economic development. Statistical analysis also suggests that good governance may be associated with better environmental outcomes. Finally, environmental challenges come in several forms and vary with country wealth and development. Some arise from the resource and pollution impacts of industrialization, such as greenhouse gas emissions and rising levels of waste; these largely affect developed countries. Other challenges are commonly associated with poverty and under-investment in basic environmental amenities, such as access to safe drinking water and basic sanitation; these primarily affect developing nations.

One policy-relevant result of the EPI's emphasis on transparency is to encourage countries to improve data monitoring and reporting so as to avoid the stigma of low scores or exclusion from the EPI itself. For example, Singapore was excluded from the 2008 EPI because of insufficient water-quality data. Singapore remedied this data gap for inclusion in the 2010 EPI.

A more detailed discussion of policy implications appears in the full 2010 EPI report, which is available online (EPI 2010).

Future Work

The early editions of the EPI were limited in their ability to track changes in performance over time. Although the 2010 EPI included a pilot exercise focusing on time-series data for a small handful of indicators, further work and more complete data are needed. Plans for the 2012 EPI include increased attention to changes in environmental performance and a commitment to forming a stable index to facilitate tracking performance over time. In this way, policy makers can rely upon the EPI in their decision making and, in the future, as one measure of the success of their policy initiatives.

John W. EMERSON, Daniel C. ESTY, and
William E. DORNBOS
Yale University

Marc A. LEVY
Columbia University

See also Carbon Footprint; Development Indicators; Framework for Strategic Sustainable Development (FSSD); Genuine Progress Indicators (GPI); Global Environment Outlook (GEO) Reports; Global Reporting Initiative; Gross Domestic Product, Green; Gross National Happiness; National Environmental Accounting

FURTHER READING

Bandura, Romina. (2005). *Measuring country performance and state behavior: A survey of composite indices.* New York: United Nations Development Programme, Office of Development Studies.

Chess, Caron; Johnson, Branden B.; & Gibson, Ginger. (2005). Communicating about environmental indicators. *Journal of Risk Research, 8*(1), 63–75.

Emerson, John W., et al. (2010). *2010 Environmental Performance Index.* New Haven, CT: Yale Center for Environmental Law and Policy.

Environmental Performance Index (EPI). (2010). Environmental Performance Index 2010. Retrieved February 1, 2012, from http://www.epi2010.yale.edu/

Environmental Performance Index (EPI). (2012). Environmental Performance Index. Retrieved February 1, 2012, from http://epi.yale.edu/

Esty, Daniel C. (2002). Why measurement matters. In Daniel C. Esty & Peter K. Cornelius (Eds.), *Environmental performance measurement: The global 2001–2002 report.* New York: Oxford University Press.

Glasby, Geoffrey P. (2003). Sustainable development: The need for a new paradigm. *Environment, Development and Sustainability, 4,* 333–345.

Holmgren, Peter, & Marklund, L.-G. (2007). National forest monitoring systems: Purposes, options and status. In Peter H. Freer-Smith, Mark S. J. Broadmeadow & Jim M. Lynch (Eds.), *Forestry and climate change* (pp. 163–173). Wallingford, UK: CAB International.

Lumley, Sarah, & Armstrong, Patrick. (2004). Some of the nineteenth century origins of the sustainability concept. *Environment, Development and Sustainability, 6*(3), 367–378.

Niemeijer, David. (2002). Developing indicators for environmental policy: Data-driven and theory-driven approaches examined by example. *Environmental Science & Policy, 5*(2), 91–103.

Polfeldt, Thomas. (2006). Making environment statistics useful: A third world perspective. *Environmetrics, 17*(3), 219–226.

Wilson, Jeffrey; Tyedmers, Peter; & Pelot, Ronald. (2007). Contrasting and comparing sustainable development indicator metrics. *Ecological Indicators, 7*(2), 299–314.

Externality Valuation

Externality valuation is a method that assesses social costs caused by production or consumption activities. It is used for project and policy appraisal but also as a cornerstone of green national accounting, in which environmental assets are factored into national wealth. The concept of ecosystem services in conservation has enriched our understanding of externality valuation, promoting research on the appropriateness of monetary valuation for ecosystem sustainability performance.

An externality is a state of affairs in which the action of a person affects (positively or negatively) the production or consumption possibilities of another, without this action being mirrored in a corresponding financial compensation. The most widely publicized externalities of interest with regard to sustainable environments are of a negative nature: the smokestacks of industrial plants emitting smoke that reduces visibility and leads to cardiovascular diseases. These and many other externalities causing pollution, resource depletion, and global change are pervasive and subtle phenomena of today's societies. Externality valuation can be a useful approach in the consideration of environment and sustainability issues through the application of monetary values to economic benefits or losses deriving from changes in the natural environment.

By generating negative side effects that affect third parties but are not appropriately taken care of by its originator, an externality gives rise to social costs, such as the decrease in well-being caused to those affected by reduced visibility and health in the foregoing example. When production and consumption activities cause extensive social costs, the economy is not allocating its resources to the society's best advantage. The ensuing divergence between private and social cost is taken care of by the process of internalization of social cost—that

is, the adding-up of social and private cost components. Externality valuation is the identification of and assignment of monetary values to social costs and thus is the process by which monetary values are attached to the physical impacts of externalities.

Origins

Externality valuation originated in the efforts of the United States Corps of Engineers to manage navigation projects in the beginning of the twentieth century. In that early phase, the administrative bodies involved were explicitly seeking to quantify and value externalities "to whomsoever they may accrue" (Flood Control Act of 1936). The slowly emerging practice of externality valuation was in search of a solid analytical structure when, in the 1950s, specific methodologies for the valuation of nonmarket externalities began to emerge. The US economist Harold Hotelling proposed capturing nonmarket benefits of national parks in the United States through what has become known as the *travel cost method*. This method used direct and indirect expenses of visitors to a national park as a proxy for the value of the park. The approach has spawned the literature on revealed preferences that has dominated the estimation of nonmarket values for recreation sites in general (Shaw 2005).

Externality valuation received a methodological turn in the 1960s when the US economist John Krutilla introduced the concept of nonuse value. In his own words: "There are many persons who obtain satisfaction from mere knowledge that part of wilderness North America remains even though they would be appalled by the prospect of being exposed to it" (Krutilla 1967, 781). Krutilla's idea to disassociate the economic value of an object from its use has rendered revealed preference methods, such as travel cost, inadequate to capture the total economic value of natural environments because by definition nonuse values leave no behavioral traces to evaluate. Stated preferences have emerged in the 1970s as an alternative, promising avenue of an inclusive externality valuation (Smith 2000). Stated preferences approaches include mainly choice experiments (CE) and contingent valuation (CV), both survey techniques making use of structured questionnaires to elicit individual welfare measures of changes in the provision of environmental goods and services (Bateman et al. 2002). The CE method has been practiced widely in the marketing domain since the late 1950s, where it is known as conjoint analysis (Green, Krieger, and Wind 2001). In the early 1990s, CV gained world prominence when used in the litigation procedure that the State of Alaska and the US government filed against Exxon for the nonuse damages caused by the *Exxon Valdez* oil spill (Carson et al. 2003).

Besides ecosystem damages, another domain where externality valuation has been practiced is energy planning. Concern about negative environmental effects of electricity-generating technologies has prompted a number of externality valuation studies in the United States (OTA 1994), which have replaced the previously dominant analytical approach of comparative risk assessment of alternative electricity supply options (Stirling 1997). Externality valuation studies in the energy domain proliferated in response to the adoption of environmental adders (environmental cost values added onto the monetary costs of energy generation) in the 1990s by US public utility commissions aiming at internalizing external cost in the investment and pricing decisions of electricity firms (Harrison and Nichols 1996).

Applications

In spite of several applications to date in the United States and an ever-expanding literature worldwide, the impact of externality valuation on efforts to quantifiably measure sustainability remains limited. Nonetheless, externality valuation has played a role in quantifying sustainability on three different levels of policy making. Firstly, on the level of individual project appraisal, assessing the full cost of alternative investment options has been applied, for example, in the case of environmental adders in the US energy sector, or water-related projects as defined in the European Union's Water Framework Directive initiated in 2000. Natural resource damage assessment in the United States, however, has tended less toward externality valuation than toward promoting a physical (service-to-service) assessment of lost ecosystem services (e.g., habitat equivalency analysis) and only in special cases a monetary (service-to-value) valuation of damages (Jones 2000).

Secondly, on the level of policy assessment, externality valuation has been used to assess monetary cost and benefits of past and proposed environmental legislation. A prominent example is efforts by the US Environmental Protection Agency (EPA) to estimate the cost and benefits of the Clean Air Act of 1970 and its amendments (Yang et al. 2004). A similar approach for Europe has been presented by a group of Norwegian environmentalists (Tollefsen et al. 2009) and the ExternE project (Bickel and Rainer 2005). A growing domain of externality valuation is climate economics, where the global externalities caused by climate change are increasingly given monetary value in order to substantiate what has come to be called "the social cost of carbon" (Tol 2008).

Thirdly, externality valuation has been used to assess macroeconomic sustainability performance by providing national economic accounts with monetary figures for depreciation of natural capital (Nordhaus 2006).

Controversies and Debates

Externality valuation is the locus of both opportunity and controversy for conservation specialists. In the limited cases where externalities can be valued on the basis of market prices the analysis is straightforward. By their very nature, though, externalities are nonmarket, public-good phenomena, demanding the skills of both ecologists and economists to evaluate. Major debates today cluster around both the broad question of the appropriateness of individualistic, economic theory as analytical background of externality valuation as well as narrower technical questions on the robustness of specific nonmarket valuation approaches.

Referring to the former, it has been argued that individuals face trade-offs in uses of the natural environment not as self-centered consumers seeking to maximize private benefits but rather as pro-social citizens aiming at achieving broader, altruistic concerns (Sagoff 1988). Even if the citizens–consumers divide is ignored, though, the usefulness of economic externality valuation is contested on the basis of the complexity of the natural environment, the resultant unfamiliarity with the goods and services to be valued, and consequently the nonexistence of well-defined preferences. In that case, what is actually happening is not the elicitation of pre-existing values but rather the construction of new, artificial preferences through the elicitation mechanism (Gregory, Lichtenstein, and Slovic 1993).

Referring to technical questions regarding theory of choice, practitioners emphasize aspects such as preference reversal (Tversky, Slovic, and Kahneman 1990), the hypothetical and nonbinding nature of values elicited through questionnaire surveys (Murphy et al. 2005), the sensitivity of value estimates to the valuation format (Cameron et al. 2002), and the analytical rigor and policy usefulness of nonuse values (Kopp 1992).

Sustainability Performance

Research on sustainability is increasingly based on the concept of ecosystem services—flows of benefits accruing to humans through well-functioning ecosystems (MEA 2005). The consideration of ecosystem services in conservation and sustainability debates has enriched our understanding of externality valuation and boosted research on the appropriate links between nature and economy (Kontogianni, Luck, and Skourtos 2010).

Currently, three major areas of research are shaping future developments in the field: Firstly, a more realistic representation of individual motives and constraints is replacing the abstract notion of *homo economicus* (Shogren and Taylor 2008). Secondly, *spatial realism* through geographic information systems (GIS) techniques is infused into the description of externalities and affected populations (Boyd 2008). Thirdly, and as a direct consequence of the former trends, the method of transferring the externality valuation results from the original study site to further policy sites is refined (Navrud and Ready 2007).

Areti KONTOGIANNI
University of the Aegean

See also Business Reporting Methods; Carbon Footprint; Community and Stakeholder Input; Computer Modeling; Cost-Benefit Analysis; Environmental Justice Indicators; Geographic Information Systems (GIS); Human Appropriation of Net Primary Production (HANPP); *The Limits to Growth;* Risk Assessment; Strategic Environmental Assessment (SEA); Systems Thinking; Transdisciplinary Research; Triple Bottom Line

FURTHER READING

Bateman, Ian J., et al. (2002). *Economic valuation with stated preference techniques: A manual.* Cheltenham, UK: Edward Elgar Publishing.

Bickel, Peter, & Rainer, Friedrich. (Eds.). (2005). *ExternE. Externalities of energy. Methodology update.* Luxembourg: European Commission.

Boyd, James. (2008). Location, location, location: The geography of ecosystem services. *Resources, 170,* 11–15.

Cameron, Trudy A.; Poe, Gregory L.; Ethier, Robert G.; & Schulze, William D. (2002). Alternative non-market value-elicitation methods: Are the underlying preferences the same? *Journal of Environmental Economics and Management, 44,* 391–425.

Carson, Richard T., et al. (2003). Contingent valuation and lost passive use: Damages from the *Exxon Valdez* oil spill. *Environmental and Resource Economics, 25, 257–286.* Flood Control Act of 1936. 33 U.S.C. §701–709 (1936).

Green, Paul E.; Krieger, Abba M.; & Wind, Yoram. (2001). Thirty years of conjoint analysis: Reflections and prospects. *Interfaces, 31,* S56–S73.

Gregory, Robin; Lichtenstein, Sarah; & Slovic, Paul. (1993). Valuing environmental resources: A constructive approach. *Journal of Risk and Uncertainty, 7,* 177–197.

Hanemann, W. Michael. (2006). The economic conception of water. In Peter P. Rogers, M. Ramon Llamas & Luis Martinez-Cortina (Eds.), *Water crisis: Myth or reality?* (pp. 61–92). London: Taylor & Francis.

Harrison, David, & Nichols, Albert L. (1996). Environmental adders in the real world. *Resource and Energy Economics, 18,* 491–509.

Jones, Carol A. (2000). Economic valuation of resource injuries in natural resource liability suits. *Journal of Water Resource Planning and Management, 126,* 358–365.

Kontogianni, Areti; Luck, Garry W.; & Skourtos, Michalis. (2010). Valuing ecosystem services on the basis of service-providing units: A potential approach to address the 'endpoint problem' and improve stated preference methods. *Ecological Economics, 69,* 1479–1487.

Kopp, Raymond J. (1992). Why existence value should be used in cost-benefit analysis. *Journal of Policy Analysis and Management, 11,* 123–130.

Krupnick, Alan J., & Burtraw, Dallas. (1996). The social costs of electricity. Do the numbers add up? *Resource and Energy Economics, 18,* 423–466.

Krutilla, John. (1967). Conservation reconsidered. *American Economic Review, 57,* 777–786.

Millennium Ecosystem Assessment (MEA). (2005). *Ecosystems and human well-being: Synthesis.* Washington, DC: Island Press.

Murphy, James J.; Allen, P. Geoffrey; Stevens, Thomas H.; & Weatherhead, Darryl. (2005). A meta-analysis of hypothetical bias in stated preference valuation. *Environmental and Resource Economics, 30,* 313–325.

Navrud, Stale, & Ready, Richard. (Eds.). (2007). *Environmental value transfer: Issues and methods.* Dordrecht, The Netherlands: Springer.

Nordhaus, William D. (2006). Principles of national accounting for nonmarket accounts. In Dale W. Jorgenson, Dale W.; Landefeld, J. Steven; & Nordhaus, William D. (Eds.). *A new architecture for the U.S. national accounts* (pp. 143–160). Chicago: University of Chicago Press.

Office of Technology Assessment (OTA). (1994). *Studies of the environmental costs of electricity.* Washington, DC: US Government Printing Office.

Sagoff, Mark. (1988). *The economy of the Earth: Philosophy, law, and the environment.* Cambridge, UK: Cambridge University Press.

Shaw, W. Douglas. (2005). The road less traveled: Revealed preference and using the travel cost model to value environmental changes. *CHOICES, 20*(3), 183–188.

Shogren, Jason S., & Taylor, Laura O. (2008). On behavioral-environmental economics. *Review of Environmental Economics and Policy, 2,* 26–44.

Smith, V. Kerry. (2000). JEEM and non-market valuation: 1974–1998. *Journal of Environmental Economics and Management, 39,* 351–374.

Stirling, Andrew. (1997). Limits to the value of external costs. *Energy Policy, 25*(3), 517–540.

Tol, Richard S. J. (2008). The social cost of carbon: Trends, outliers and catastrophes. *Economics e-journal, 2,* 1–22. Retrieved October 13, 2011, from http://www.economics-ejournal.org/ej-search?SearchableText=tol

Tollefsen, Petter; Rypdal, Kristin; Torvanger, Asbjørn; & Rive, Nathan. (2009). Air pollution policies in Europe: Efficiency gains from integrating climate effects with damage costs to health and crops. *Environmental Science & Policy, 12,* 870–881.

Tversky, Amos; Slovic, Paul; & Kahneman, Daniel. (1990). The causes of preference reversal. *American Economic Review, 80,* 204–217.

Yang, Trend; Matus, Kira; Paltsev, Sergey; & Reilly, John. (2004). *Economic benefits of air pollution regulation in the USA: An integrated approach.* Cambridge, MA: MIT Joint Program on the Science and Policy of Global Change.

F

Fisheries Indicators, Freshwater

Freshwater fisheries exist among diverse ecosystems and fauna, provide societal benefits, and are influenced by human activities. Fisheries scientists assess the status and sustainability of fisheries by multiple approaches, including abundance and condition indices, population parameters, community indices, modeling, and surveys of habitat and human dimensions. The future sustainability of freshwater fisheries is limited not by available methods but by society's will.

Freshwater fisheries provide recreation, food, aesthetic values, and economic benefits to society. They are typically smaller in scale than marine fisheries but function through similar ecological processes and may thus serve as microcosms for larger fisheries. Activities and conditions on land, associated with the watershed and especially at the land-water interface (i.e., the riparian zone), strongly influence freshwater fisheries. Fisheries exist in a broad diversity of ecosystem types and corresponding fish fauna in freshwater environments, ranging from small streams to expansive lakes and the fishes supported in those systems. There is thus no single approach, method, technique, or tool best suited to assess freshwater fisheries. Fisheries scientists have developed over decades an extensive set of procedures to indicate the ecological state of freshwater fisheries.

Three primary, overlapping components constitute fisheries: (1) the fish or invertebrate organism, (2) the environment or the habitat for the resource, and (3) associated humans. Fishery assessment therefore often includes quantifying static or dynamic parameters of multiple fishery components. The associated methods, techniques, and indicators thereby may include aspects of biology, ecology, physiology, behavior, physical sciences, and socioeconomics. Thorough fishery assessment may require a multidisciplinary team.

There is no clear criterion for determining sustainability of freshwater fisheries. Freshwater fisheries worldwide receive varying levels of human management, usually by government agencies, nongovernmental organizations, or private landowners or consortiums. Scientists may consider even the most intensively managed fisheries (e.g., by fish culture, stocking, and harvest or habitat manipulations) sustainable as long as human intervention and resources are available. Some fisheries are self-sustaining, however (e.g., free-flowing rivers that are difficult to directly manipulate). Fisheries managers seek to achieve elements of self-sustainability in freshwater fisheries, but the nature of many fisheries (e.g., small ponds or urban community fisheries) may require continual intensive management to meet human resource demands.

A Rich History

Long ago, fisheries were considered abundantly endless food resources that could not be overexploited. With human population growth and modern interests in recreational fishing, it became clear that the productive capacity of freshwater ecosystems could not meet the demand for fisheries products in public waters. Scientists thus developed modern fisheries management and assessment over decades toward a goal to balance the supply and demand of fisheries. Modern conservation programs have further enhanced the movement. Achieving that supply–demand balance is an ongoing challenge, especially in densely populated areas of the world and in undeveloped countries, where food resources may be limited.

Many of the concepts and methods for fisheries assessment are rooted in ancient and historical fishing and early management efforts. Fish collection techniques have evolved over centuries with human desires to efficiently capture fish for food. Although many fisheries techniques existed in a rudimentary form earlier, North American and European fishery scientists developed fisheries techniques and analytical approaches during and since the latter half of the twentieth century, in what is considered the modern era of fisheries management.

Ecosystem and Faunal Diversity

Freshwater ecosystems and the aquatic fauna they support are tremendously diverse. Corresponding fisheries assessment approaches and techniques are thus similarly variable among ecosystems. Freshwater ecosystems generally divide between two categories based on geomorphology and hydrology. Lentic water bodies are standing or relatively still water and include lakes, reservoirs, ponds, and wetlands. Lotic waters are flowing streams, rivers, or springs.

The different physical and biotic properties and dynamic processes between lentic and lotic ecosystems warrant different conceptual and practical approaches to fisheries assessment. Overall, the spatial habitat patterns and dynamics of primary (plant photosynthesis) and secondary (animal tissue elaboration) production and associated fish population and community regulation mechanisms are rather distinct between the two types of water bodies. Density-dependent processes in both lentic and lotic systems regulate fish populations, for example, but density-independent factors (e.g., flooding, drought, temperature fluctuations) have a greater influence in the dynamic lotic environment. These ecological differences between system types have resulted in multiple approaches for fisheries assessment.

Within and among freshwater habitats, fishes have adopted a wide variety of morphological, life history, and behavioral patterns and adaptations to survive in specific aquatic habitats and changing environments, and to effectively utilize resources for ecological success. They have evolved a multitude of strategies and modes of feeding, reproduction, predator avoidance, habitat occupancy, and migration. This diversity in form, function, ecology, and behavior further complicates sampling and assessment of fish and fisheries.

Physical and Biotic Influences

A number of interacting natural and anthropogenic factors influence freshwater fish production, population dynamics, and sustainable exploitation rates. The physical setting of a freshwater ecosystem sets the framework in which biotic interactions occur to form the aquatic community. The latitude, climate, geology, geomorphology, water quantity and quality, and riparian and watershed attributes all interact at multiple scales to form the aquatic environment in which fish production occurs. Most of these factors are subject to human influences that can dramatically alter the aquatic environment and biotic community.

Ecological integrity of an ecosystem is the ability of its chemical, physical, and biological environments to exist and function similarly to that of a region's natural habitat. An ecosystem that human activities minimally influence has high ecological integrity, requires minimal direct management (other than protective measures), and is generally self-sustaining with regard to fisheries. Human global effects have both gradual and catastrophic impacts on biodiversity and ecosystem function at the local level of environments that support aquatic life, fish, and fisheries. Aquatic fauna thus are declining at a rapid rate globally and locally. Proximate effects of human activity on ecological integrity of aquatic systems include changes in land use in the watershed, stream channel modifications, point and diffuse chemical and thermal pollution, water impoundment and extraction, species introductions, fishing, and landscape development. (See figure 1 on page 132.) These activities act at multiple scales to transform the physical and biological components of aquatic systems from their original condition to altered states with reduced biological diversity and ecological function.

Figure 1. Physical and Biotic Factors Affecting the Ecological Integrity of Aquatic Systems and How Human Activity Alters Them

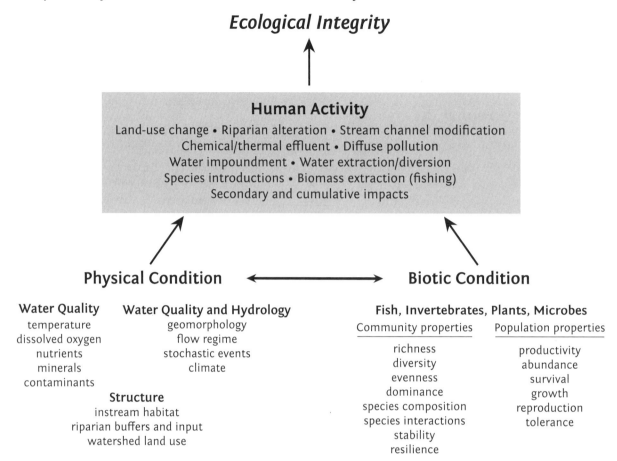

Source: Hubert and Quist (2010).

Fishery Assessment and Indicators

Fish abundance, age and size composition, and length and weight relationships are the primary parameters scientists require to describe the status of a fish population. In addition to static parameters (i.e., those at a single point in time), dynamic parameters that quantify rates of population processes, such as survival, growth, reproduction, and mortality, provide greater insight into a fish population's ecological state. Many management or policy objectives require assessment at the fish assemblage (or community) level, and parameters that describe fish assemblage composition can relate important ecosystem attributes. Exact measurement of most of these parameters is difficult, cumbersome, or impractical to conduct. Fishery scientists thus have developed methods to estimate these parameters without complete data, or have developed indices that describe attributes assumed to correlate with true parameters. An additional useful approach to understand population status or dynamics is

quantitative modeling to estimate parameters statically or over time. Physical surroundings and human interactions greatly influence the status of a fish stock or population. Managers thus find assessments of habitat and human dimensions associated with fisheries informative.

Sampling Considerations

Many different sampling gears (equipment and instruments) and techniques can sample freshwater fish. Electrofishing, angling, netting, seining (fishing with a net that hangs vertically in the water), and trawling have specific properties and biases for capturing fish that vary among fish species, sizes, and environments. Fish sampling gears are designed for, and most effective in, appropriate environments for target species and sizes. No single sampling technique can effectively sample the entire fish assemblage of an ecosystem; multiple gears are usually deployed for a more complete sample. Fish populations and assemblages vary over time and among sites within ecosystems. The spatial, temporal, and organizational scales of the sampling environment therefore are critical considerations in fishery assessment and monitoring. There is no standard procedure for sampling fish assemblages, but fisheries scientists have recognized the need to standardize sampling protocols and quantitative procedures for interpreting sampling results. Recent compendiums of standard methods for sampling freshwater fishes and analyses and interpretation of resulting data, published by the American Fisheries Society (Guy and Brown 2007; Bonar, Hubert, and Willis 2009), represent important advances toward common methods for freshwater fisheries.

Abundance and Condition Indices

Fish sampling is never complete (i.e., managers cannot sample all fish present), so scientists use actual catch or indices of catch to indicate relative population sizes to assess fish populations. Actual catch can be an indicative measure of fish population size, but it is highly variable and fluctuates with the amount of sampling effort expended. Scientists therefore most commonly apply catch per unit effort as an index that they assume to be proportional to population size. Catch is expressed as the number or total weight (i.e., biomass) of fish caught. Managers quantify effort as a standard time, space, or activity unit, depending on the gear and habitat fished. Sampling may be by a passive gear (e.g., trap or entanglement gear) or an active gear (e.g., seine net or electrofisher). Units of effort may include the time that a gear is set or actively fished, the linear distance, area, or volume of water sampled, or a standard sampling activity, such as a seine haul. Managers can also generate catch per effort data by conducting angler or commercial fisher surveys to estimate their catch and effort expended. Scientists may consider catch per effort indices a minimum estimate of, or proportional to, the true population abundance for assessment, but they are more useful as relative indices to compare over time or among sites or populations.

Fisheries science commonly uses the relationship of length and weight in individual fish within a population to indicate the condition (or plumpness) of individual fish as an index of their well-being. The condition of fish in a population may be estimated by graphing the curvilinear relationship of length–weight data and deriving the resulting mathematical equation. Scientists find indices of condition easier to interpret and routinely apply two common indices. Fulton-type condition indices are a scaled value of the quotient of a fish's weight and its length cubed. Relative weight is the ratio of a fish's actual weight to the expected weight of a fish that length. The expected weight is termed standard weight; scientists develop standard weight equations

for all sizes of a fish species to express the condition of a fish in good condition (often the 75th percentile of a large data set). Condition indices vary among species and are most useful for comparing populations or detecting length-related patterns or patterns over time within a population.

The size structure of a fish population is an important component of assessing population status. Length-frequency distributions are a simple but informative description of fish population dynamics. They are usually displayed as a histogram (bar graph) of fish numbers among size groups and incorporate information about reproduction, growth, and mortality. Imbalances in length-frequency histograms can indicate problems associated with reproductive failure, juvenile mortality, slow growth, or excessive exploitation or natural mortality. Stock density indices make further use of length-frequency distributions by expressing the proportion of catchable fish in a population (stock size) that are of a quality size or other specified length (e.g., preferred or trophy size). Deviations of stock density indices from expected ranges may indicate reproductive problems, overexploitation, or other causes for imbalance in the population size structure. The combination of relative weight indices and stock density indices can be extremely informative for assessing and managing exploited fish populations.

Population Parameter Estimates

In some situations, managers may require estimates of the true population density and biomass to guide management or policy decisions. Such procedures require additional cost and effort, compared to catch per effort indices. Scientists estimate the true abundance of freshwater fish populations using mark-recapture, removal, or surplus-production methods. Mark-recapture methods involve multiple sampling events where managers mark the fish and then resample them to detect the ratio of marked and unmarked fish to estimate the total population. Removal methods use repeated sampling without return to the population (temporarily or permanently) to detect the decrease in catch among samples to estimate the original population size. Scientists apply surplus-production methods to exploited fisheries to estimate population biomass from the pattern of yield (i.e., fish biomass harvested) and fishing effort over time.

Fish population abundance estimates are especially useful in freshwater fisheries to compare with rates of harvest to assess the sustainability of fishing. They also allow the estimation of population rate parameters. Population rate parameters, including reproduction, survival, and growth, are extremely helpful in understanding fish population dynamics toward effective management. Integrating these parameters also allows estimation of the annual rate of fish production or the total biomass of fish tissue produced by a population during a year. This integration is the ultimate parameter for assessing if a population is sustainably exploited.

Community Indices

In modern fisheries management, target game fish species are not managed in isolation of other fishes and aquatic organisms in their environment. Managers sample and consider the entire fish assemblage of an ecosystem in fishery assessments. Assemblage assessment may require additional effort, but assemblage attributes, such as species richness, are generally less variable than abundance estimates for individual species. Assemblage assessments thus usually require smaller sample sizes to obtain precise estimates and can ultimately be more cost-effective than single species approaches.

Ecologists have developed two primary approaches to quantify community structure and applied them to fish assemblages. They are the use of (1) community structural indices based directly on field samples and (2) biotic indices based on the relative abundance of indicator organisms. Both approaches are applicable to describing fish assemblage characteristics and may be related to environmental quality, but biotic indices are especially suited to quantifying ecological integrity. The relative abundance of species, other taxa (scientific classification), or other categorical attributes within an assemblage may be combined into a single measure to describe the status of the community. The most common of these measures is species diversity, which incorporates the number of species in an assemblage (species richness), as well as the relative abundance of those species (evenness). Scientists may develop fish biotic indices using indicator species or guilds (a group of species that use the same resources), which they may then incorporate into a single index. The most common fish biotic index is the Index of Biological Integrity, also known as the Index of Biotic Integrity. James R. Karr, a US ecologist and expert in fisheries, and his colleagues initially developed the index for warmwater stream ecosystems, but others have widely modified it and applied it in other systems. Scientists designed this fish community index to indicate biological integrity of aquatic ecosystems by integrating attributes of the fish assemblage, population, and individuals using relative abundance of species and condition of individuals. Developing an Index of Biological Integrity for fish within a region requires substantial effort, but scientists may use individual metrics of the index or related assemblage structural indices (e.g., richness, diversity, evenness) singly or in aggregate as quantitative characteristics for comparison and assessment.

Monitoring

Single static measurements of a fish population or assemblage are of limited value in fishery assessment, and monitoring the trend over time or spatial variation is more informative. Therefore, an optimal approach is to develop carefully designed monitoring programs to fully understand the dynamic processes and variation in an ecosystem and fishery. It is also beneficial to include standardized sampling over time and among sites and to consider multiple quantitative indicators in interpreting resulting data. Most fisheries resource agencies have adopted broad scale approaches to inform management decisions, and monitoring programs may include surveys of other fauna (e.g., aquatic macroinvertebrates), habitat conditions, and anglers and the nonfishing public.

Modeling Approaches

Fish population models estimate summary population characteristics by incorporating dynamic processes. These approaches are especially suitable to determine, forecast, and understand the exploitation and sustainability of fisheries, as they may include various ecological stressors and the projected population response. There are many modeling frameworks that may or may not include field data. A primary advantage of modeling approaches is that they can incorporate physical, biotic, natural, and anthropogenic factors and integrate their combined effects on a population or assemblage. Precise population prediction is not always the objective of modeling assessment; rather, scientists are primarily interested in the trends, relative sensitivity of influential factors, and the dynamic processes in understanding the ecology and sustainability of fisheries.

Habitat

Fish habitat includes all the physical, chemical, and biological attributes of the aquatic environment required to sustain a population. Natural and anthropogenic habitat alterations change the suitability of habitat for fish and other biota. Habitat monitoring is thus most informative in comparisons over time and among locations. Habitat monitoring is particularly important for quantifying gradual degradation over time or to assess restoration or other habitat management actions. Managers can measure individual parameters describing water quality, stream characteristics, or lake attributes by relatively standard procedures, and they may calculate and compare indices. Habitat assessment procedures generally are designed to describe the bank, riparian zone, and watershed characteristics of streams and rivers and the morphometrics, water quality, hydrodynamics, and trophic state of lakes and reservoirs. Geographic information systems and associated data sets allow approaches for habitat assessment at broad spatial scales. Scientists describe habitat at reach, segment, and basin scales and quantify riparian and watershed attributes from existing data layers. Many aquatic habitat processes act at broad scales and may be cumulative in nature; the ability to quantify watershed or riparian land cover and associated landscape parameters thus is an important advance.

The Human Factor

Humans manage fisheries because we exploit them for food or recreation. Our activities in the water and on land alter their environment. There are three primary reasons that humans exploit fisheries: subsistence fishers harvest fish to eat themselves, commercial fishers sell their catch, and recreational users fish for personal enjoyment. Along with the varied goals of these groups, their fishing techniques, habits, and attitudes differ as well. Managers frequently practice regulating or influencing people's behavior to indirectly manage the fishery resource. They thus need information about fishery constituents for effective management toward a sustainable harvest. Knowledge of fishery constituents and other human stakeholders of freshwater systems and their role in decision making is critical to allocating fishery resources, habitat management, policy and regulation development, and seeking stakeholder satisfaction with the fishery and their experiences.

Conservation and management decisions may require sociological, economic, legal, and political information. Scientists gather this information through document review; individual and group interviews; mail, telephone, and Internet surveys; and direct observation. Managers can then implement knowledge of the human factor into the management process to influence decisions on the exploitation and conservation of fishery resources.

Conflicting Goals

Management of aquatic systems for both fisheries and ecological integrity may be common goals in some systems but may also present a conflict. Fisheries management incorporates not only information about the biology and ecology of the resource, but also considers economics, aesthetics, human attitudes, and the interests of users and the general public. The values of direct fishery users (e.g., catch, harvest, fish quality) may conflict with those of indirect users or nonusers (e.g., aesthetics, existence value, ecological services), however. Fishery management goals, such as enhancing or maximizing fish abundance, population structure, catch, or harvest, therefore may be

contrary to those to maintain robust communities and natural self-sustaining habitat. As fishery managers seek to include multiple stakeholders and uses in management, they face a primary challenge to incorporate concepts and values of users and nonusers, as well as consumptive and nonconsumptive users, and to consider ecological services, function, and integrity as they manage the physical and biotic environments of fishes.

An Uncertain Future

Society has a growing interest in, concern for, and demand for the conservation and sustainable management of freshwater fisheries and ecosystems. Fisheries agencies are responding with action in many regions, but political and other societal pressures may limit their efforts. Progressive agencies are incorporating broad and holistic ecological and socioeconomic approaches into management. Integrating approaches, such as adaptive management and structured decision making, leads to improvement in the management process, results, and public support. The scientific tools and methods managers require for fishery assessment to guide conservation and management exist and are available to agencies worldwide, but the political will to employ them and consider the science in management and policy decisions is highly variable. The future sustainability of freshwater fisheries and ecosystems is uncertain and limited not by available methods or science but by the will of society.

Thomas J. KWAK
United States Geological Survey

See also Biological Indicators (*several articles*); Ecolabels; Ecosystem Health Indicators; Fisheries Indicators, Marine; Index of Biological Integrity (IBI); Ocean Acidification—Measurement; Organic and Consumer Labels; Remote Sensing; Species Barcoding

FURTHER READING

Bonar, Scott A.; Hubert, Wayne A.; & Willis, David W. (Eds.). (2009). *Standard methods for sampling North American freshwater fishes*. Bethesda, MD: American Fisheries Society.
Guy, Christopher S, & Brown, Michael L. (Eds.). (2007). *Analysis and interpretation of freshwater fisheries data*. Bethesda, MD: American Fisheries Society.
Hubert, Wayne A., & Quist, Michael C. (Eds.). (2010). *Inland fisheries management in North America* (3rd ed.). Bethesda, MD: American Fisheries Society.
Karr, James R., & Chu, Ellen W. (1999). *Restoring life in running waters: Better biological monitoring*. Washington, DC: Island Press.
Murphy, Brian R., & Willis, David W. (Eds.). (1996). *Fisheries techniques* (2nd ed.). Bethesda, MD: American Fisheries Society.

Fisheries Indicators, Marine

Modern indicators for evaluating marine fisheries sustainability are based on biological criteria that assume life history characteristics and ecological relationships can be accurately determined. If accurate measurements exist, they can be used to calculate the amount of commercially valuable marine life that can be harvested indefinitely, but it is better to incorporate ecosystem sustainability measures rather than rely solely on single species measurements.

The most important indicator for sustainability in marine fisheries, the point to which all other indicators contribute, is the *maximum sustainable yield* (MSY). The general concept is that the population growth for each species of fish varies according to several life history characteristics, including mortality rates, spawning stock, and the number of juvenile fish joining the stock, and that it can be optimized. In broad terms, a small population of any organism will have a small reproductive output, and a very large population that is near the carrying capacity of its environment will also have a small reproductive output. At an intermediate point, the maximum reproductive rate is achieved. If a population of fish can be kept at this point, then that reproductive rate can be harvested, and the population will continue producing at the same high rate year after year. In this situation, the harvest is sustainable at its maximum rate, hence the term *maximum sustainable yield*. In practice, biologists aim to calculate the *optimum sustainable yield* (OSY), sometimes called the *maximum economic yield* (MEY). The MEY maximizes the profitability of the fishery and is often a bit smaller than the MSY to take into account fluctuations and variations in the population. This approach has been used since the 1930s. It seems sound in theory, but in practice it has resulted in the collapse of many fisheries. Many researchers have concluded that most fisheries have been overexploited for many years (Jackson et al. 2001).

In the past, a far smaller human population and the use of simple, low-yield technologies meant that fishers had relatively little effect on their target populations. Since 1930, however, the efficiency of fishing methods has improved dramatically, and the number of fish caught has greatly increased around the world. As the number of fish taken increased, fishers and biologists recognized that fish stocks and yields actually varied significantly over time, and this realization led to agreement that it was important to manage fisheries to ensure that yields could be sustained and maximized.

Historically, the main indicator that fishers used (and still use) was simply whether the average amount of fish (or lobsters, mussels, etc.) they caught was the same as, or more, or less than they had caught in previous years. As catches started to decline, fishers started clamoring for local or national governments to intervene to reduce competition. One of the earliest documented cases of government intervention in fisheries occurred in 1816 in the form of a law that established territorial use rights over the Lofoten fishery in northern Norway (Hannesson, Salvannes, and Squires 2010; Jentoft and Kristofferson 1989). There were much older conventions, of course, which were not passed as formal laws. Conventions that have regulated artisanal fisheries in the Pacific have probably been in place for centuries (Johannes 1978). These determine, for example, who can and who cannot fish in a certain area; generally the rule is that a certain number of local villagers can fish in that area, and all others are forbidden to do so. Most of these rules or conventions are based on the observation that an increase in the number of fishers in an area leads to smaller catches overall in subsequent years. So the number of fishers is reduced in the hope that the catch will then improve.

This simple observation of whether or not fish catches are declining year to year has, in general, been a more accurate sustainability indicator than the complicated and time-consuming calculations for MSY or OSY, as the latter have been repeatedly shown to be incorrect (e.g., Larkin 1977; Walters and Maguire 1996). The explanation appears to be twofold. First, calculations for MSY have often been based on simplistic assumptions about the studied fish populations. This was compounded by the fact that most studies were based on a relatively small amount of data that was extrapolated incorrectly to make overly elaborate predictions. Second, the calculation of MSY is essentially a single-species model and does not acknowledge interactions between species, even though these interactions are critically important. Ideally, any calculation of MSY should include all the relevant life history data for the target species. That includes proper measurements of the average rate of growth, longevity, survivorship of each age class from year to year, rates of egg production of reproductively mature females of each age class, and even elements of social structure and mating systems. In practice, this kind of detailed information on marine species is hard to collect, because in most cases it is very difficult to observe a population directly. In fact, the primary source of information is usually the fish that are caught, and the way the fish are caught biases the sample in ways that may not be obvious. As a result, it is easy to make erroneous assumptions. One example of this problem occurred with the collapse of the fishery for the deepwater orange roughy (*Hoplostethus atlanticus*) in New Zealand beginning in the late 1970s. The MSY calculations and initial quotas were based on the assumption that the fish were short-lived, rapid breeders. Unfortunately, like many deepwater fish, orange roughy are actually long-lived and breed slowly, so the consequent fishing practices led to a near-complete collapse of fishing stocks. Catches have declined to less than 10 percent of peak levels in many places, and some fishing grounds are now closed completely (Francis and Clark 2005).

Part of the problem is that population dynamics models of marine species (and hence calculations of sustainability and MSY) are typically complicated models based on very limited data. Simpler models based on extensive and reliable data would provide more reliable

estimates (Bonfil 2005; Sparre and Hart 2002). The lack of accurate data has led to many damaging simplifications. For example, estimates of population sizes have been made without knowledge of age structure (Collie and Sissenwine 2011), which is needed to calculate population growth rates; measurements of a few tagged individuals are used in complicated equations to make generalizations about growth patterns for the whole species (Cope and Punt 2011); and size class distributions in fishnets are often assumed to represent the size class distribution of the species in the wild and to show survivorship of each age class from year to year (Rudstam, Magnuson, and Tonn 2011). This means that important conclusions are based on remarkably little fact, with much of the most essential data missing. Because the conclusions are faulty, MSY is frequently set at unsustainable levels.

Social and political factors can make the problem worse. Since biologists are aware that their data may not be accurate and that the resulting calculation of MSY might be wrong, a sensible conservative strategy would be to set the quotas well below the calculated MSY to provide a cushion allowing for error. In practice, fishers frequently lobby regulators to be allowed to increase their catches to the maximum extent. When quotas are set at this maximum level, any miscalculations of the MSY can then lead directly to dramatic population collapses. An example of this is the collapse of the five-hundred-year-old Atlantic cod (*Gadus morhua*) fishery on the Grand Banks of Newfoundland despite the fact that, at least in its later years, it was intensively managed by a large community of fisheries biologists and government regulators (Hutchings and Myers 1994).

Common fisheries practices often exacerbate the problems of inaccurate calculations of MSY. In most fisheries, for example, the normal procedure is to harvest the larger individuals, leaving the smaller individuals to grow, reproduce, and be harvested later. But in terms of maintaining sustainability, this is exactly the wrong approach, because for most marine species larger fish produce many times the numbers of eggs as smaller fish do. For example, the number of eggs produced by a single 61-centimeter female red snapper (*Lutjanus campechanus*) is the equivalent of the total egg output of 212 females that are 42 centimeters long; in other words a 45 percent increase in length results in an increase of about 2,000 percent in egg production (Birkeland 1997). Put another way, without reducing the total rate of egg production, up to 233 kilograms of the smaller size of red snapper could be harvested but only 12.5 kilograms of the larger size. Perhaps because this conclusion seems counterintuitive, the practice of harvesting larger fish continues.

Where fisheries management practices are based on good science and proper life history measurements, the consequent measurements of MSY and calculated quotas can be more truly reflective of reality, allowing for genuine sustainability. For example, well-managed quotas and releasing large male and female American lobster (*Homarus americanus*) in catches have led to an increase in stocks in the Gulf of Maine and Georges Bank. On the other hand, although the same practices are in place in southern New England, American lobster stocks are declining there (Steneck et al. 2011). This contrast demonstrates that the management requirements for individual fishing grounds can be very specific. The European Common Fisheries Policy, which does not take into account individual fishing grounds, has been heavily criticized for this reason (see Coffey 2000).

Since 2000, a few fish stocks are either being maintained or are actually increasing. Some of these are located in the northeastern Pacific and include Alaska plaice (*Pleuronectes quadritubercula-tus*), yellowfin sole (*Limanda aspera*), rock sole (*Lepidopsetta polyxystra*), and Greenland turbot (*Reinhardtius hippoglossoides*) (National Oceanic and Atmospheric Administration 2011). These species appear to be successfully managed using correctly calculated indicators. It is important to note, however, that (*a*) these are relatively young Pacific fisheries, and therefore these species do not have a history of uncontrolled exploitation, (*b*) life history characteristics are measured independently by regulatory bodies like the National Oceanic and Atmospheric Administration (NOAA), and therefore MSY/OSY calculations are more accurate, and (*c*) because northeastern Pacific fisheries occur in developed nations like Canada and the United States and involve large fishing vessels, regulation and enforcement of quotas can be (and up to now have been) more effective, and non-national fishing vessels have been kept out of the fishing grounds (historically this was not true of Atlantic fisheries until recently).

Up to this point, the measurements and calculations under discussion have been single species indicators, with little or no consideration for the effect on or by other species. But academics and fisheries biologists are coming to a consensus that the old standard of calculating MSY (or OSY or MEY) is fundamentally flawed, and researchers conclude that it would be much better to use ecosystem indicators, rather than single species indicators to calculate sustainable yields. For example, a "phase shift" in Caribbean coral reef ecosystems drastically changed many West Indian coral reef fish populations, due to a complex web of factors that included overfishing, pollution, storm damage, and the die-off of a critically important sea urchin species (Bruno et al. 2009; Haley and Clayton 2003; Hughes 1994). In many Caribbean locations, low diversity algae-dominated ecosystems have replaced high diversity coral-dominated systems, and hence the number and diversity of fish and other marine organisms found in those locations has changed (and, in general, been reduced). No measurements of life history characteristics or calculation of MSY for a single fish species would have been able to predict these changes. For this reason, any attempt to manage a fish species sustainably has to be based on an awareness of the health of the entire ecosystem.

Ecosystem indicators are also critically important in understanding the consequences of "fishing down the food web." In older established fisheries like those of the Atlantic, the tendency has been to switch to smaller species further down the food chain as it has become uneconomical to harvest the larger predatory fish species (Pauly and Watson 2005; Pauly et al. 1998). For example, as cod fishing became uneconomical on the Grand Banks, the focus changed to (among other things) capelin (*Mallotus villotus*), which are an important prey species for cod (Bailey et al. 2010). Harvesting the capelin may therefore impact the recovery of the cod fishery. Similarly, as whale stocks were overfished and international agreements banned most whale harvesting, a krill (*Euphausia superba*) fishery was established in its place. Krill is the main food source for many baleen whales, however, so the pressure on the whale population continued despite the ban on whale harvesting

(Nicol, Foster, and Kawaguchi 2011). In general, reducing the number of prey species severely limits the subsequent population sizes of their predators. It is unlikely, for example, that the cod population will recover to pre-fisheries levels even if no harvesting occurs for many years as long as their prey species, like capelin, are being harvested in large numbers.

Conversely, in some cases, reduction in one species may result in increases for another, particularly where those species are in competition within the same ecosystem. Many people suspect, for example, that the increase in the stocks of American lobster in the Grand Banks actually occurred primarily because of the depletion of cod stocks (Boudreau and Worm 2010).

The many positive and negative interactive effects point to the need for a much greater understanding of what is happening to an entire ecosystem to be able to assess whether catches are at sustainable levels. In general, most measurements of ecosystem health are based on measurements of biodiversity. Biodiversity indices vary considerably, from a simple count of the number of species present, to calculations that integrate the population sizes of each species with the number of species (an index variously referred to as the Shannon index or Shannon-Wiever or Shannon-Wiener index; see Spellerberg and Fedor 2003), to measurements of trophic (nutritional) complexity (for marine species the Marine Trophic Index is used; see Pauly and Watson 2005). Often other indicators that are different from, but related to, biodiversity are used; for example, the number of alien species present is also taken into account by many managers (see European Academy Science Advisory Council 2004 for this and other examples). Trained biologists can integrate the information provided by these indices into a comprehensive picture of ecosystem health.

An important difference between ecosystem indicators and the single species MSY calculations is that the ecosystem measures are all *comparative* indices, rather than stand-alone measurements. Unlike MSY calculations, which produce a number that can be (and usually is) used without reference to any other calculations, ecosystem measurements are only useful insofar as they can be compared to measurements in previous or subsequent years, so that it is possible to judge whether the ecosystem is improving, remaining stable, or degrading. In this sense, ecosystem indicators are similar to the simple historical artisanal assessments of whether fish catches are going up or down compared to previous years. The necessity for making comparisons over time is actually a strength, rather than a weakness, of this method of assessing sustainability; it takes longer but gives a much more useful and realistic picture. Widely adopting ecosystem indicators would provide for more effective fisheries management and allow fisheries to be operated sustainably.

Michael HALEY
EcoReefs Inc.

Anthony M. H. CLAYTON
University of the West Indies

See also Biological Indicators (*several articles*); Challenges to Measuring Sustainability; Computer Modeling; Ecosystem Health Indicators; Fisheries Indicators, Freshwater; Human Appropriation of Net Primary Production (HANPP); Index of Biological Integrity (IBI); Long-Term Ecological Research (LTER); Ocean Acidification—Measurement; Population Indicators; Systems Thinking

FURTHER READING

Bailey, Kevin M., et al. (2010). Comparative analysis of marine ecosystems: Workshop on predator–prey interactions. *Biology Letters, 6,* 579–581.

Birkeland, Charles. (1997). Implications for resource management. In Charles Birkeland (Ed.), *Life and death of coral reefs* (pp. 411–435). New York: Chapman and Hall.

Bonfil, Ramón. (2005). Fishery stock assessment models and their applications to sharks. In John A. Musick & Ramón Bonfil (Eds.), *Management techniques for elasmobranch fisheries* (FAO Fisheries Technical Paper 474; pp. 154–181). Rome: United Nations Food and Agriculture Organization.

Boudreau, Stephanie A., & Worm, Boris. (2010). Top-down control of lobster in the Gulf of Maine: Insights from local ecological knowledge and research surveys. *Marine Ecology Progress Series, 403,* 181–191.

Bruno, John F.; Sweatman, Hugh; Precht, William F.; Selig, Elizabeth R.; & Schutte, Virginia G. W. (2009). Assessing evidence of phase shifts from coral to macroalgal dominance on coral reefs. *Ecology, 90,* 1478–1484.

Coffey, Clare. (2000). Good governance and the Common Fisheries Policy: An environmental perspective. London: Institute for European Environmental Policy.

Collie, Jeremy S., & Sissenwine, Michael P. (2011). Estimating population size from relative abundance data measured with error. *Canadian Journal of Fisheries and Aquatic Sciences, 40,* 1871–1879.

Cope, Jason M., & Punt, André E. (2011). Admitting ageing error when fitting growth curves: An example using the von Bertalanffy growth function with random effects. *Canadian Journal of Fisheries and Aquatic Sciences, 64,* 205–218.

European Academy Science Advisory Council. (2004). A user's guide to biodiversity indicators. Retrieved November 4, 2011, from www.europarl.europa.eu/comparl/envi/pdf/externalexpertise/easac/biodiversity_indicators.pdf

Francis, Chris R. I. C., & Clark, Malcolm R. (2005). Sustainability issues for orange roughy fisheries. *Bulletin of Marine Science, 76*(2), 337–351.

Haley, Michael, & Clayton, Anthony. (2003). The role of NGOs in environmental policy failures in a developing country: The mismanagement of Jamaica's coral reefs. *Environmental Values, 12,* 29–54.

Hannesson, Rögnvaldur.; Salvannes, Kjell G.; & Squires, Dale. (2010). Technological change and the tragedy of the commons: The Lofoten fishery over 130 years. *Land Economics, 86,* 746–745.

Hughes, Terence P. (1994). Catastrophes, phase shifts and large-scale degradation of a Caribbean coral reef. *Science, 265,* 1547–1551.

Hutchings, Jeffrey A., & Myers, Ransom A. (1994). What can be learned from the collapse of a renewable resource? Atlantic cod, *Gadus morhua,* of Newfoundland and Labrador. *Canadian Journal of Fisheries and Aquatic Sciences, 51,* 2126–2146.

Jackson, Jeremy B. C., et al. (2001). Historical overfishing and the collapse of coastal ecosystems. *Science, 293,* 629–637.

Jentoft, Svein, & Kristofferson, Trond. (1989). Fisheries co-management: The case of the Lofoten fishery. *Human Organization, 48,* 355–365.

Johannes, Robert E. (1978). Traditional marine conservation methods in Oceania and their demise. *Annual Review of Ecology and Systematics, 9,* 349–364.

Larkin, Peter A. (1977). An epitaph for the concept of maximum sustainable yield. *Transactions of the American Fisheries Society, 106,* 1–11.

Nicol, Stephen; Foster, Jacqueline; & Kawaguchi, So. (2011). The fishery for Antarctic krill—recent developments. *Fish and Fisheries, 13*(1), 30–40. doi: 10.1111/j.1467-2979.2011.00406.x

National Oceanic and Atmospheric Administration (NOAA). (2011, September 22). Preliminary results from 2011 Bering Sea groundfish survey. Retrieved November 4, 2011, from http://alaskafisheries.noaa.gov/newsreleases/2011/beringsurvey092211.pdf

Pauly, Daniel; Christensen, Villy; Dalsgaard, Johanne; Froese, Rainer; & Torres, Francisco, Jr. (1998). Fishing down marine food webs. *Science, 279,* 860–886.

Pauly, Daniel, & Watson, Reg. (2005). Background and interpretation of the "Marine Trophic Index" as a measure of biodiversity. *Philosophical Transactions of the Royal Society, B, 360,* 415–423.

Rudstam, Lars G.; Magnuson, John J.; & Tonn, William M. (2011). Size selectivity of passive fishing gear: A correction for encounter probability applied to gill nets. *Canadian Journal of Fisheries and Aquatic Sciences, 41,* 1252–1255.

Sparre, Per, & Hart, Paul J. B. (2002). Choosing the best model for fisheries assessment. In Paul J. B. Hart, & John D. Reynolds (Eds.), *Handbook of fish biology and fisheries* (pp. 270–290). Oxford, UK: Wiley-Blackwell Publishing.

Spellerberg, Ian F., & Fedor, Peter J. (2003). A tribute to Claude Shannon (1916–2001) and a plea for more rigorous use of species richness, species diversity and the "Shannon-Wiener" Index. *Global Ecology and Biogeography, 12,* 177–179.

Steneck, Robert S., et al. (2011). Creation of a gilded trap by the high economic value of the Maine lobster fishery. *Conservation Biology, 25,* 904–912.

Walters, Carl, & Maguire, Jean-Jacques. (1996). Lessons for stock assessment from the northern cod collapse. *Reviews in Fish Biology and Fisheries, 6,* 125–137.

Focus Groups

Focus groups are best known as qualitative tools in marketing research but can be used in sustainability research to understand people's perceptions of risk and attitudes toward environmental issues, to help inform policy development, and to explore how people relate to place. When used properly, the method can open a window into the complexities of social dialogues around sustainability, enhancing understandings of social change dimensions.

A focus group is a research method that provides researchers with the opportunity to interact with a group of respondents who are "focused" on a particular topic. This qualitative method may be used in combination with quantitative methods. (See table 1 on the next page.) Typically, a focus group consists of six to twelve people brought together by a researcher for a one- to two-hour session in a comfortable setting to share their views on a particular subject through a discussion guided by a moderator (Krueger 1994, 6; Stewart and Shamdasani 1990, 10). People seeking to learn the focus group method can find detailed discussions in a number of how-to texts on focus groups (Krueger 1994; Stewart and Shamdasani 1990; Morgan and Krueger 1997), and they should be well read on the method and its challenges before carrying out focus group interviews.

Focus Group Features

Focus groups are characterized by the structured nature of discussion that takes place within them, the size and makeup of the group, and the number of groups employed in a project.

A Focused Discussion

The discussion in a focus group may be more or less structured, but the conversation must be focused. Typically the moderator is responsible for keeping the discussion on track using "pre-determined, open-ended questions. These questions appear to be spontaneous but are carefully developed after considerable reflection. The questions—called the questioning route or interview guide—are arranged in a natural, logical sequence" (Krueger 1994, 20).

Stimulus materials, such as accounts of "moral dilemmas" (Markovà et al. 2007, 79), card games (Kitzinger 1994, 107), or videos (Wilkinson 1998a, 116), can provide a shared foundation on which participants can build a focused interaction. For example, Jenny Kitzinger, a professor of Media and Communications Research at the University of Cardiff, describes the use of a card game in which participants were provided with a pack of cards with key statements written on them to sort into piles as a group; "the 'cards' can carry statements about opinions, descriptions of people, accounts of events or even pictures. The categories into which these cards are to be sorted may range from degree of agreement or importance, to the perceived health risk attributed to a certain activity" (Kitzinger 1994, 107). By observing the process and dialogue involved in sorting the cards, researchers may gain new insights into how participants understand and engage with the issue at hand.

Group Size

Ideally, a focus group should be small enough to enable all group members to actively participate in the dialogue while being sufficiently large to provide diversity of perceptions (Kruger 1994). The size of the group is ideally

Table 1. Using Focus Groups to Complement Quantitative Research

	Uses	Description
Pre-quantitative (research design phase)	Exploration	To search for new ideas among groups of interest for product, program, or research development; to obtain background information; to learn the language and concepts of target audience
	Pilot testing	To test hypotheses, survey instruments (wording, order, instructions); to diagnose problems
Mid-quantitative (in tandem)	Triangulation (using mixed methods to achieve a more detailed picture of the issue)	To address same issue from different angles for confirming or fleshing out findings, and to enhance research design through feedback loops
Post-quantitative (analysis or evaluation)	Post-evaluation	To aid in interpretation (asking groups about particular findings and getting feedback), so to add context or depth to findings
	Confirmation	To verify conclusions or test their "everyday" validity with target group

Sources: Calder 1977; Krueger 1994; Stewart and Shamdasani 1990.

determined by the complexity of the topic—the more complex the topic, the smaller the group should be to provide adequate time for individuals to develop their views. Groups that are too large tend to fragment. Smaller groups work better for sensitive topics that generate a lot of emotionally charged responses, whereas larger groups are better suited to the discussion of more neutral topics (Morgan 1996, 146).

Number of Groups

Focus groups are generally conducted in a series until the topics raised by participants have reached "saturation" (Morgan 1996, 144; Krueger 1994, 88), where most points have been repeated and new information is unlikely. Four to six groups are suggested as a rule of thumb (Morgan 1996, 144), though larger studies may run multiple series with different types of participant groups, in some cases running more than fifty groups (Kitzinger 1994, 104; Padel et al. 2007).

Homogeneity of the Group

Participants should be selected to facilitate and thus maximize participation. How comfortable participants feel about openly communicating their opinions is particularly affected by factors such as age, gender, and socioeconomic status (Stewart and Shamdasani 1990). It is thus important to compose the group to be homogenous with respect to key characteristics of the study. Even

when groups are selected to be homogenous along a particular dimension, it is important to recognize that the participants' interpretation of the focus group task will "bring out the multiplicity of their identities," and the positions they take may reflect viewpoints other than those assumed to fit them by the researcher (Marková et al. 2007, 104). For example, a woman included because she is a grandmother in her sixties may respond from the stance of her profession.

Familiarity

In the past, focus groups were made up of strangers to promote disclosure without the censure of continued interaction between participants outside the group, and to minimize the effects of relationships on the group (Krueger 1994, 18; Stewart and Shamdasani 1990, 34; Flick 2006, 198). As the use of focus groups has spread across different fields of inquiry, a more nuanced approach to the question of familiarity has developed. Preexisting groups, sometimes called "natural groups," are increasingly being used, as they may tap into collective memories, allow participants to elaborate and contextualize each others' responses, or to construct joint narratives (Kitzinger 1994, 105; Wilkinson 1998b, 191; Flick 2006, 201). As with other key decisions in focus group design, the question of familiarity between participants (or even with the researcher) needs to be decided on the basis of the research purpose.

Cautionary Notes

The method has developed into something of a jack-of-all-trade for qualitative studies, and in spite of the vast amount of well-written literature in the area, it appears as if researchers at times use focus groups without familiarizing themselves with best practices. Not conducting focus group studies properly entails two major risks. First, it is crucial to be aware that there are some situations in which focus groups should not be used. The University of Minnesota professor Richard Krueger (1994, 45) advises against the use of the method when the environment is emotionally charged or confrontational, the researcher has "lost control" over the study, statistical projections are needed, or other methods are better suited and more economical. Second, when analyzing and presenting the results it is important to be aware of the limits and applicability of focus group data, otherwise it is easy to overgeneralize the results, which might lead to serious misinterpretations and their associated consequences, especially when used as a basis for policy advice.

Origins of Focus Groups

Before the focus group came the focused interview. Most accounts of the history of focus groups begin with a retelling of how, in 1941, the sociologist Robert Merton came to work with his colleague Paul Lazarsfeld. Together, at Columbia University's Office of Radio Research, they collaborated to design new research methods aimed at understanding why audience members reacted positively or negatively to program content (Stewart and Shamdasani 1990, 9; Krueger 1994, 7; Lunt and Livingstone 1996, 5). The classic 1946 paper "The Focused Interview" by Robert Merton and Patricia Kendall outlines the focused interview method that was developed to explore the "subjective experiences" of individuals exposed to certain preanalyzed stimulus materials, for the purposes of testing "the validity of hypotheses derived from content analysis and social

psychological theory" and "to ascertain unanticipated responses" that could generate "fresh hypotheses" (Merton and Kendall 1946, 541).

Whereas the original focused *interview* is known to be developed by Merton and company, the origins of the focus *group* remain ambiguous (Reed and Payton 1997). We do know that until the late 1970s focus groups were mainly used in market research (Wilkinson 1998b, 183).

Curiously, as Merton himself points out, though he is credited as the founder of focus groups, he and his collaborators "never used the term," and they were unaware of both the conflation of the two methods and the widespread use of focus groups in marketing research until the 1980s (Merton 1987, 550 and 563). He concludes that "there is more 'intellectual continuity' between the focussed interview and focus groups than explicitly recognized historical continuity" (Merton 1987, 564). Differences include that the focused interview can be with an individual or a group, whereas focus groups are always groups; focused interviews explicitly use stimulus materials, which are optional in focus groups; and the focused interview is used in concert with quantitative methods, while focus groups can be used alone or alongside other quantitative or qualitative procedures. Nonetheless, it is fair to say that the focus group "evolved out of research methods designed by Paul Lazarsfeld, Robert Merton, and colleagues" (Kidd and Parshall 2000, 295). Regardless of its unclear history, the focus group flourished in the late 1980s and 1990s in a diverse range of fields, including public health, communication studies, education, political science, sociology, feminist research, anthropology, linguistics, and nursing (Morgan 1996, 132; Wilkinson 1998b, 183–184).

With this growth in popularity, the strengths of focus groups have been leveraged to various ends, although the method's weaknesses have sometimes resulted in misuse. Richard Krueger outlines some of the advantages and limitations:

> Focus groups offer several advantages. . . . The technique is a socially oriented research method capturing real-life data in a social environment, possessing flexibility, high face validity, relatively low cost, potentially speedy results, and a capacity to increase the size of a qualitative study. . . . Limitations include these: Focus groups afford the researcher less control than individual interviews, produce data that are difficult to analyze, require special skills of moderators, result in troublesome differences among groups, are based on groups that may be difficult to assemble, and must be in a conducive environment. (Krueger 1994, 37–38)

Focus Groups in Sustainability Research

The use of focus groups in sustainability research started to gain ground in the 1990s (e.g., Liebow, Branch, and Orians 1993; Macnaghten et al. 1995; Dahinden and Dürrenberger 1997; Myers 1998). Most commonly, focus groups have been used to understand people's perception of risk, their attitudes toward various environmental issues (such as waste incineration), or their acceptance of various policies. Focus groups are also used to explore environmental values, how people talk about environmental issues, and the complex relationships between identity and values and how people relate to place (e.g., Myers 1998; Burgess, Limb, and Harrison 1988; Cameron 2005).

Increasingly the method has been used to inform policy development, such as Susanne Padel's study on organic farming values that tested assumptions about national differences to guide development of organic regulations and standards in the European Union (Padel et al. 2007; Padel 2008). The use of focus groups as a participatory policy tool has grown almost to a separate field, in particular in the field of integrated assessment (Dürrenberger, Kastenholz, and Behringer 1999). The "Integrated Assessment Focus Group" variation on the method is presented in the edited volume *Public Participation in Sustainability Science: A Handbook*, which

combines focus groups with environmental modeling tools to get at the public's "mental maps" (perceptions of current problems and values) of sustainability issues (Kasemir et al. 2003, xx–xxi). Focus groups are also used to an increasing extent in eliciting or ranking sustainability indicators (e.g., King et al. 2000; Fraser et al. 2006).

Controversies

The focus group has developed into a ubiquitous qualitative research method. Not surprisingly, this diverse usage has resulted in diverse approaches to participant interaction, creating a debate over interaction that stretches the boundaries of our understanding of how and when to use focus groups. Participant interaction is said to be the hallmark of the focus group method, but a number of studies have pointed out that the defining feature of the method is virtually absent in most focus group research (Wibeck, Dahlgren, and Öberg 2007, 250; Webb and Kevern 2008, 7; Markovà et al. 2007, 35; Kitzinger 1994, 104). We conducted a review of this conflict (Belzile and Öberg 2012), which suggested that participants play different roles in different types of research, and that the absence of interaction data reflects a philosophical division between researchers who view the participants primarily as individuals sharing held truths and those who view them as social beings co-constructing meaning while in the focus group. We argue that the treatment of participant interaction should be a conscious design decision—one clearly rooted in a theoretical perspective and best suited to the research purpose.

The Method's Long-Term Utility

As outlined earlier in this chapter, focus groups are a powerful way of exploring social dimensions of issues that are complex and value-laden, which is true for most environmental subjects (Pielke 2007). We anticipate that focus groups will become increasingly relevant for answering questions where the use of science in policy is controversial, such as the production and use of GMOs, food security, climate change adaptation and mitigation measures, the relationship between environment and health, and controversies related to land-use and biodiversity. The use of focus groups is also likely to increase in addressing regional and local issues, such as community planning including for example transportation improvements, behavior change strategies and campaigns, and acceptability of alternative funding options (taxes, tolls, fines, etc.). To sum up, as it is increasingly recognized that environmental problems cannot be understood in isolation but must be viewed in light of social and economic perspectives, the utility of focus groups is likely to grow in the future.

Jacqueline A. BELZILE and Gunilla ÖBERG
University of British Columbia

See also Challenges to Measuring Sustainability; Citizen Science; Community and Stakeholder Input; New Ecological Paradigm (NEP) Scale; Participatory Action Research; Quantitative vs. Qualitative Studies; Social Network Analysis (SNA); Sustainability Science; Systems Thinking

FURTHER READING

Abrandt Dahlgren, Madeleine, & Öberg, Gunilla. (2001). Questioning to learn and learning to question: Structure and function of problem-based learning scenarios in environmental science education. *Higher Education, 41*(3), 263–282.

Agar, Michael, & MacDonald, James. (1995). Focus groups and ethnography. *Human Organization, 54*(1), 78–86.

Belzile, Jacqueline, & Öberg, Gunilla. (forthcoming 2012). Where to begin? Grappling with how to use participant interaction in focus group design. *Qualitative Research.*

Burgess, Jacqueline; Limb, Melanie; & Harrison, Carolyn M. (1988). Exploring environmental values through the medium of small groups: 1. Theory and practice. *Environment and Planning A, 20*(3), 309–326.

Calder, Bobby J. (1977). Focus groups and the nature of qualitative marketing research. *Journal of Marketing Research, 14*(3), 353–364.

Cameron, Jenny. (2005). Focussing on the focus group. In Iain Hay (Ed.), *Qualitative research methods in human geography* (2nd ed., pp. 83–102). Melbourne, Australia: Oxford University Press.

Catterall, Miriam, & Maclaran, Pauline. (1997). Focus group data and qualitative analysis programs: Coding the moving pictures as well as the snapshots. *Sociological Research Online.* Retrieved June 5, 2011, from http://www.socresonline.org.uk/2/1/6.html

Dahinden, Urs, & Dürrenberger, Gregor. (1997) Public participation in energy policy: Results from focus groups. In O. Renn (Ed.), *Risk perception and communication in Europe* (pp. 487–514). London: Society for Risk Analysis.

Dürrenberger, Gregor; Kastenholz, Hans; & Behringer, Jeannette. (1999). Integrated assessment focus groups: Bridging the gap between science and policy? *Science and Public Policy, 26*(5), 341–349.

Fraser, Evan D. G.; Dougill, Andrew J.; Mabee, Warren E.; Reed, Mark; & McAlpine, Patrick. (2006). Bottom up and top down: Analysis of participatory processes for sustainability indicator

identification as a pathway to community empowerment and sustainable environmental management. *Journal of Environmental Management, 78*, 114–127.

Flick, Uwe. (2006). *An introduction to qualitative research* (3rd ed.). London: Sage Publications.

Hydén, Lars-Christer, & Bülow, Pia H. (2003). Who's talking: Drawing conclusions from focus groups—Some methodological considerations. *International Journal of Social Research Methodology, 6*(4), 305–321.

Kasemir, Bernd; Jäger, Jill; Jäger, Carlo; & Gardner, Matthew. (Eds.). (2003). *Public participation in sustainability science: A handbook.* Cambridge, UK: Cambridge University Press.

Kidd, Pamela, & Parshall, Mark. (2000). Getting the focus and the group: Enhancing analytical rigor in focus group research. *Qualitative Health Research, 10*(3), 293–308.

King, C.; Gunton, J.; Freebairn, D.; Coutts, J.; & Webb, I. (2000). The sustainability indicator industry: Where to from here? A focus group study to explore the potential of farmer participation in the development of indicators. *Australian Journal of Experimental Agriculture, 40*(4), 631–642.

Kitzinger, Jenny. (1994). The methodology of focus groups: The importance of interaction between research participants. *Sociology of Health and Illness, 16*(1), 103–121.

Krueger, Richard A. (1994). *Focus groups: A practical guide for applied research* (2nd ed.). Thousand Oaks, CA: Sage Publications.

Liebow, Edward B., Branch, Kristi M. & Orians, Carlyn E. (1993). Perceptions of hazardous waste incineration risks: Focus group findings. *Sociological Spectrum, 13*(1), 153–173.

Lunt, Peter, & Livingstone, Sonia. (1996). Rethinking the focus group in media and communications research. Retrieved June 5, 2011, from http://eprints.lse.ac.uk/archive/00000409

Macnaghten, Phil; Grove-White, Robin; Jacobs, Michael; & Wynne, Brian (1995). *Public perceptions and sustainability in Lancashire: Indicators, institutions, and participation.* Lancaster, UK: Lancaster University.

Markovà, Ivana; Linell, Per; Grossen, Michèle; & Orvig, Anne Salazar. (2007). *Dialogue in focus groups: Exploring socially shared knowledge. Studies in language and communication.* London: Equinox.

McKenzie-Mohr, Douglas. (2009). *Fostering sustainable behavior: Community-based social marketing.* Gabriola Island, Canada: New Society Publishers.

Merton, Robert K. (1987). The focussed interview and focus groups: Continuities and discontinuities. *Public Opinion Quarterly, 51*(4), 550–566.

Merton, Robert K., & Kendall, Patricia L. (1946). The focused interview. *The American Journal of Sociology, 51*(6), 541–557.

Morgan, David L. (1996). Focus groups. *Annual Review of Sociology, 22*(1), 129–152.

Morgan, David L. & Krueger, Richard A. (1997). *The focus group kit* (Vols. 1–6). Thousand Oaks, CA: Sage Publications.

Myers, Greg. (1998). Displaying opinions: Topics and disagreement in focus groups. *Language in Society, 27*(1), 85–111.

Padel, Susanne. (2005). D21: Research to support revision of the EU regulation on organic agriculture. Aberystwyth, UK: University of Wales.

Padel, Susanne, et al. (2007). Balancing and integrating basic values in the development of organic regulations and standards: Proposal for procedure using case studies of conflicting areas (D2.3). Retrieved June 5, 2011, from http://www.organic-revision.org/pub/D_2_3_Integrating_values_final_2007.

Padel, Susanne. (2008). Values of organic producers converting at different times: Results of a focus group study in five European countries. *International Journal of Agricultural Resources, Governance and Ecology, 7*(1/2), 63–77.

Pielke, Roger A. (2007). *The honest broker: Making sense of science in policy and politics.* Cambridge, UK: Cambridge University Press.

Reed, Jan, & Payton, Valerie Roskell. (1997). Focus groups: Issues of analysis and interpretation. *Journal of Advanced Nursing, 26*(4), 765–771.

Sandelowski, Margarete. (2000). What ever happened to qualitative description? *Research in Nursing and Health, 23*(4), 334–340.

Smithson, Janet. (2000). Using and analysing focus groups: Limitations and possibilities. *International Journal of Social Research Methodology, 3*(2), 103–119.

Stewart, David W., & Shamdasani, Prem N. (1990). *Focus groups: Theory and practice* (Applied Social Research Methods Series, Vol. 20). Newbury Park, CA: Sage Publications.

Webb, Christine, & Kevern, Jennifer. (2008). Focus groups as a research method: A critique of some aspects of their use in nursing research. *Journal of Advanced Nursing, 33*(6), 798–805.

Wibeck, Victoria; Dahlgren, Madeleine Abrandt; & Öberg, Gunilla. (2007). Learning in focus groups: An analytical dimension for enhancing focus group research. *Qualitative Research, 7*(2), 249–267.

Wilkinson, Sue. (1998a). Focus groups in feminist research: Power, interaction, and the co-construction of meaning. *Women's Studies International Forum, 21*(1), 111–125.

Wilkinson, Sue. (1998b). Focus group methodology: A review. *International Journal of Social Research Methodology, 1*(3), 181–203.

Framework for Strategic Sustainable Development (FSSD)

The framework for strategic sustainable development is a methodology that helps decision makers, institutions, and society at large attain long-term goals that are informed by robust sustainability principles for the whole biosphere. The framework's unique qualities allow users to manage systems, rationally evaluate trade-offs, and calculate sustainable resource potentials. In conjunction with other tools, the framework can be applied worldwide in businesses, regional governments, and municipalities.

Strategic planning requires a robust and appropriate set of goals. It has been challenging, however, to develop such a set of goals for sustainability. As a result, one of the most pressing issues that businesses, governments, and other organizations and communities face is translating both broad sustainability concepts, such as the Brundtland Report's call for sustainable development, and more specific goals, such as carbon neutrality, into effective long-term strategic sustainability plans for cohesive actions.

The nongovernmental organization Natural Step was founded in 1989 to address this challenge, and since its inception, a network of scientists, business leaders, government officials, and private citizens has worked together to develop, apply, and assess a scientifically robust planning framework for sustainability. The framework is called the Framework for Strategic Sustainable Development (FSSD). The FSSD combines a general, five-level model for planning in complex systems with an approach known as backcasting from sustainability principles.

When using a backcasting approach, strategic planners first define the goal, and then work back from it to determine what should be done in the present time to maximize the chances of reaching the goal. The development of appropriate goals is therefore critical.

The definition of a sustainable goal should usually not be an exact, detailed description, because there will be many inevitable unforeseen changes over time (for example, technical and cultural developments) that will render such detailed plans less than optimal in the future. A good analogy for a suitable goal is to be found in playing chess; one employs rigorous strategic logic to arrive, step-by-step, at the goal of checkmate, while remaining flexible and adaptive regarding what each step should be. Successful strategy requires the player to reevaluate repeatedly, but the checkmate goal is not compromised in the process. The FSSD takes a similar approach to planning through the development and application of principles for sustainability.

The FSSD is designed to be a unifying framework for any planning project and also to support the synergistic integration of tools and concepts for sustainable development. Since 2000, a group of sustainability researchers and implementers has been exploring how best to integrate diverse sustainability-directed approaches. Concepts like ISO 14001 (a management system for administration), footprinting (data connected to specific locations), factor analysis (to monitor the reduction of material and energy throughputs), and others have been analyzed to determine which aspects of sustainability they cover and to identify what remaining aspects need to be addressed by other tools. When combined, and with the support of a strategic framework for sustainability such as the FSSD, individual tools and approaches can create a robust overview of sustainability that includes selection and integration of appropriate tools, evaluation, and adaptation (Robèrt et al. 2002).

Sustainability Principles

Work on the FSSD shows that in order to serve an integrating role, sustainability principles must exhibit the following characteristics:

- *Necessary* for global sustainability (but not more than necessary, to avoid imposing unnecessary restrictions and to avoid confusion over elements that may be open to debate)
- *Sufficient* to avoid gaps in thinking (to allow for development into higher order principles from a complete base)
- *General* to be applicable in any arena, at any scale, by any member of a team and all stakeholders, regardless of field of expertise, and to allow for cross-disciplinary and cross-sector collaboration
- *Concrete* to guide problem solving and redesign and a step-by-step approach to real-life planning
- *Non-overlapping* for clarity and to facilitate evaluation

With these requirements in mind, the researchers derived four sustainability principles for strategic planning by addressing the ways human actions negatively affect society and the environment. A myriad unsustainable impacts were aggregated into a few overriding mechanisms of ecological and social destruction. Thereafter, the word *not* was inserted into each statement to form four sustainability principles that define the goal of sustainability planning.

In the sustainable society, nature is *not* subject to systematically increasing (1) concentrations of substances extracted from the Earth's crust (such as fossil carbon or metals), (2) concentrations of substances produced by society (such as nitrogen compounds, chlorofluorocarbons, and endocrine disrupters), or (3) degradation by physical means (such as overharvesting of forests and overfishing).

Moreover, in such a (sustainable) society, people are *not* subject to conditions that systematically (4) undermine their capacity to meet their needs (such as from the abuse of political and economic power).

The Five-Level Model

The four sustainability principles are not sufficient for strategic sustainable development. The principles must be integrated with an organization's more traditional goals, such as profitability and social impact. To build such a general approach, the FSSD applies a five-level model for planning in any complex system.

1. The systems level. This level includes information on the system being studied, especially how it is constituted and its major functions. The description of the system must be detailed enough to inform the next four levels of the model. To apply an analogy, if the five-level model were used to analyze the game of chess, the systems level would contain the rules of the game, the pieces, and the chessboard. In the case of sustainability, the systems level includes an understanding of an organization or development project in the context of Earth's biosphere, human society, and their interactions, as well as knowledge of important stocks, flows, biogeochemical cycles, biodiversity, and resilience.

2. The success level. This level is where the planner defines the goal of the planning process. In the chess analogy, the goal is to checkmate the opponent, within the constraints of the game (described at level 1). When planning for global sustainability, the goal is an organization, topic, region, or society that is not contributing to violation of the four sustainability principles at the global level.

3. The strategic level. At this level, planners arrive at guidelines to approach the goal strategically. In chess, good moves serve as strategic steps to checkmate. Trade-offs are selected for their capacity to serve as platforms that move toward reaching the principles of success (level 2), rather than as choices between necessary evils. For sustainability, this implies a step-by-step approach that ensures that financial, social, and ecological resources continue to feed the process.

4. The actions level. The planner uses the knowledge from the first three levels of the model to inform every action that the organization, topic, region, or society could take to move strategically toward its goal. In chess, this level would include all the successively reevaluated strategic plans in the head of the player and the actual moves. In sustainability planning, it would include such plans and the concrete actions and investments taken toward a sustainable society.

5. The tools level. Tools are often needed to make sure that the actions a planner chooses (level 4) serve as

CASE STUDY: WHISTLER, BRITISH COLUMBIA

In 2000, the municipality of Whistler in British Columbia, Canada, had made some significant progress in committing to sustainable development and building community partnerships. Nonetheless, it was searching for a clearer way to plan and to communicate this new priority to the broader community and, in particular, to local businesses. As with most communities, the many diverging interests of various stakeholders presented a challenge to developing a common, strategic sustainability approach. To tackle this challenge, the municipality joined with key community stakeholders, called *early adopters,* to create a sustainability plan for the entire community based on the FSSD. The resulting plan, *Whistler 2020,* has won many awards since its completion in 2005, including the Federation of Canadian Municipalities national award for sustainable

community planning and the UNEP LivCom award for best long-range planning.

One concrete example of how the FSSD helped Whistler make more strategic sustainability decisions is related to the energy system that was built for the 2010 Winter Olympics. (Whistler hosted some of the events.) The local utility company offered Whistler a natural gas pipeline designed to have enough capacity to last for fifty years. To evaluate this proposal, the municipality backcast from the end goal of a sustainable energy system. As a result, Whistler turned down the offer and proposed a smaller pipeline. This decision reduced carbon dioxide emissions and freed financial resources to develop energy systems that were better in line with the principles of Whistler's sustainable vision, including renewable fuels and geothermal and district heating.

strategic platforms (level 3) to reach the goal (level 2) in the system (level 1). Some tools used in sustainability planning are life cycle assessment, sustainability indicators, and social and environmental management systems.

Organizations can map their current situations against the sustainability principles using the five-level model, identifying how they define themselves and their key efforts at each level. This analysis highlights overlaps and gaps between an organization's current context and its sustainability goals.

The ABCD Planning Process

Because planning for sustainability requires input from multiple perspectives and stakeholders, organizations that are implementing the FSSD also need an intuitive way to backcast from sustainability principles in a team setting. A four-step strategic planning approach, known as the ABCD process, has been developed to respond to this need. During the first step (A), participants discuss the topic or planning endeavor in the context of the sustainability principles offered by the FSSD. In the second step (B), participants list the ways in which the organization currently contributes to violations of its

own success principles and the global sustainability principles, as well as the assets available to move toward the goal of sustainability. In the third step (C), participants envision a future in which they are moving toward alignment with the principles of sustainable success and brainstorm possible actions they could take to move toward that goal.

In the final step (D), participants prioritize the action and investment ideas brainstormed in the previous step. Prioritized investments should fulfill three strategic guidelines. They should (1) provide a flexible platform for future investments toward sustainability, and in doing so they should strike a balance between (2) the direction and speed that the organization moves toward sustainability and (3) return on investment. If all three guidelines are not satisfied, the organization may run out of funding or other resources, diminish its competitive position, or choose easily implemented investments that actually lead to economic and sustainability-related dead ends.

Future Challenges

As with any pioneering effort in sustainability, the FSSD is continually applied, assessed, and revised. Challenges remain. For "unsustainable" institutions, successfully implementing the sustainability principles can seem extremely challenging. In addition, the large number of emerging sustainability approaches can often confuse decision makers and even appear to compete with rather than complement each other. Claims that several approaches can be integrated may be overstated.

Given these challenges, an important aspect of the FSSD is its collaborative partnerships and peer review of revisions. At the same time as it is used to help structure research into a step-wise approach toward the full scope of sustainability, the FSSD benefits from the opportunity to systematically scrutinize, test, and develop its principles. This is especially true of case studies in which universities cooperate with businesses and municipalities. The outcome is a new type of action research where methods, tools, concepts, modeling, and simulation emerge from flexible systems informed by a robust definition of success (rather than as attempts to deal with environmental impacts one by one). As the framework is applied, evaluated, and refined, it will become increasingly effective.

Karl-Henrik ROBÈRT and Göran BROMAN
Blekinge Institute of Technology

George BASILE
Arizona State University

See also Agenda 21; Community and Stakeholder Input; Development Indicators; Genuine Progress Indicator (GPI); Global Reporting Initiative (GRI); Gross Domestic Product, Green; Gross National Happiness; Human Development Index (HMI); I = P × A × T Equation; *The Limits to Growth;* Millennium Development Goals; Regional Planning; Sustainable Livelihood Analysis (SLA); Triple Bottom Line

FURTHER READING

Basile, George; Broman, Göran; & Robèrt, Karl-Henrik. (2011). A systems-based and strategic approach to sustainable enterprise: Requirements, utility and limits. In Scott McNall, James Hershauer & George Basile (Eds.), *The business of sustainability: Trends, policies, practices, and stories of success* (Vol. 1). New York: Praeger Publishers.

Broman, Göran; Holmberg, John; & Robèrt, Karl-Henrik. (2000). Simplicity without reduction: Thinking upstream towards the sustainable society. *Interfaces, 30*(3), 13–25.

Holmberg, John, & Robèrt, Karl-Henrik. (2000). Backcasting from non-overlapping sustainability principles: A framework for strategic planning. *International Journal of Sustainable Development and World Ecology, 7*(7), 291–308.

Missimer, Merlina; Robèrt, Karl-Henrik; Broman, Göran; & Sverdrup, Harald. (2010). Exploring the possibility of a systematic and generic approach to social sustainability. *Journal of Cleaner Production, 18*(10–11), 1107–1112.

Ny, Henrik; MacDonald, Jamie; Broman, Göran; Yamamoto, Ryoichi; & Robèrt, Karl-Henrik. (2006). Sustainability constraints as system boundaries: An approach to making life-cycle management strategic. *Journal of Industrial Ecology, 10*(1–2), 61–77.

Robèrt, Karl-Henrik. (2000). Tools and concepts for sustainable development, how do they relate to a general framework for sustainable development, and to each other? *Journal of Cleaner Production, 8*(3), 243–254.

Robèrt, Karl-Henrik, et al. (2002). Strategic sustainable development: Selection, design and synergies of applied tools. *Journal of Cleaner Production, 10*(3), 197–214.

Robèrt, Karl-Henrik, et al. (2010). *Strategic leadership towards sustainability.* Karlskrona, Sweden: Blekinge Institute of Technology.

Whistler 2020. (2007). Whistler 2020 vision document (2nd ed.): Moving toward a sustainable future. Retrieved April 11, 2011, from http://www.whistler2020.ca/whistler/site/gpage.acds?instanceid=1957300&context=1930607

Genuine Progress Indicator (GPI)

Indicators of the well-being of communities continue to evolve. First developed as measures of national economic activity and growth, indicators such as the genuine progress indicator have emerged that also consider social and environmental factors in order to allow a broader understanding of the welfare of the community. Studies suggest there exists a threshold for economic development beyond which well-being in fact declines.

For policy makers, determining whether the well-being of a community has improved is an important task. Making such a determination requires use of an indicator that considers the wide range of issues that impact upon well-being, which can include economic, personal, social, and environmental factors. A nation's standard national accounts, such as gross domestic product (GDP) or gross national income (GNI), have long been used to measure well-being, even though they were not designed for such a purpose (Kuznets 1941). From their inception in the early 1940s they have assumed this role both in economic literature and public debate (Beckerman 1974; World Bank 2011). Indeed, even before the formulation of these standard national accounts, estimates of nations' productivity were used as indicators of social well-being (Hicks 1940).

Standard national accounts are too narrow, however, and fail to consider many aspects of well-being, particularly environmental and social costs associated with economic expansion. In response to this shortcoming, calls were made in the 1960s for a new set of national accounts to be developed that included the costs and benefits of changes in environment. The US professor of economics Arnold Sametz called for leisure time, new products, nonmarketed goods, urbanization, and government expenditure to be considered in any measure of well-being. Sametz argued that "change in GNP over long periods of time is not a good measure of economic

growth or welfare" (Sametz 1968, 77). Recognizing the shortcoming of national accounts as an appropriate indicator of well-being occurred in the early 1970s, during a period of increasing debate surrounding the desirability of economic growth (Barkley and Seckler 1972; Meadows et al. 1972).

The US economists William Nordhaus and James Tobin first took an empirical approach to developing a revised GDP by addressing the inclusion and exclusion of certain disamenities that the national accounts did not correctly address (Nordhaus and Tobin 1973). A number of years later, the US ecological economist Herman Daly and Methodist theologian John Cobb developed the Index of Sustainable Economic Welfare (ISEW) (Daly and Cobb 1990). The ISEW was first applied to the United States but has now been applied to a range of developed and developing countries (see Lawn and Clarke 2008). The major question underlying the ISEW approach is whether an increase in economic growth "really reflects the true changes in welfare" (Brekke 1997, 158). The ISEW approach has evolved and has become most widely known as the *genuine progress indicator* (GPI), the underlying purpose of which remains evaluating whether economic growth truly benefits the well-being of a population, balancing beneficial growth against uneconomic or environmentally detrimental growth.

While the GPI is an alternative measure of a country's welfare, it still is rarely considered in wider reviews of well-being indicators (see McGillivray 2006 and McGillivray and Clarke 2006 as examples of this exclusion from mainstream surveys). Yet the GPI continues to attract interest and continues to be applied in an increasing number of countries.

The Australian researcher Phil Lawn and professor Matthew Clarke point out that, as with the ISEW, the GPI is "designed to ascertain the impact of a growing economy on sustainable well-being. Usually comprised of around twenty individual benefit and cost items, the GPI integrates the wide-ranging impacts of economic growth into a single monetary-based index. As such, the GPI includes benefits and costs of the social and environmental kind as well as those of the standard economic variety. Whilst the GPI embraces some of the national accounting values used in the computation of GDP, its calculation accounts for a number of benefits and costs that normally escape market valuation" (Lawn and Clarke 2008, 2). They go on to note that among the various GPI studies there are often variations in the adjustments included as well as the methodologies used to estimate these adjustments; this variability is largely related to the data available and limits the direct comparisons of well-being that can be made between countries. British lecturers at the London School of Economics Simon Dietz and Eric Neumayer have argued that without a standard set of adjustments and methodology, the construction of the GPI is subjective and lacks scientific rigor (Dietz and Neumayer 2006). While there is merit in this criticism, proponents of the GPI argue that flexibility can also be considered a strength, as it allows the GPI to take into account the unique circumstances of a given specific country (Clarke 2006).

There is variation among the empirically applied GPIs; however, it is instructive to identify some of the standard, most common adjustments made within a GPI. Each factor listed in table 1 either contributes to, as a plus, or detracts from, as a negative value, the general welfare.

Some examples of nonstandard adjustments that might be included, depending on the unique circumstances of the specific country, are the cost of commercial sex work, cost of corruption, cost of urbanization, or cost of commuting (Clarke 2006).

Personal consumption of basic needs—food, water, shelter, clothing—is the basis of the GPI. Not all personal consumption items are included, however, as much consumption is wasteful, conspicuous, or not welfare enhancing (as, for example, spending on tobacco products). Personal consumption that is rehabilitative or defensive expenditure is also excluded, such as expenditures on health and education (private and public), costs of vehicle accidents and insurance services (private consumption), and defense, environmental protection, and public order and security (public consumption). Much personal consumption includes expenditure on durable items. Calculation of GDP assumes that all the benefits of these purchases flow immediately and in total at the time of purchase; however, it is more likely that the benefits or services provided by these consumer durables continues over a period of time (and well outside the time limits of a normal GDP reporting period of a single year). To accommodate this, expenditure on consumer durables

is excluded from the GPI calculated, but services from accrued consumer durables (normally accumulated expenditure on consumer durables for the last ten years) are added back in. An index assessing changes in income distribution is then applied to this adjusted personal consumption figure.

The next three adjustments listed in table 1 explicitly acknowledge that well-being can be enhanced beyond simple increases in personal consumption. Public infrastructure, voluntary services, and unpaid household labor all enhance well-being and are therefore added to the GPI. Unlike in national accounts, explicit costs are associated

TABLE 1. Standard GPI Adjustments

Item	Welfare Contribution
Consumption (private and public) expenditure	+
Defensive and rehabilitative expenditures	−
Expenditure on consumer durables	−
Service from consumer durables	+
Distribution index	+/−
Welfare generated by publicly provided infrastructure	+
Value of unpaid household labor	+
Value of volunteer labor	+
Cost of unemployment and underemployment	−
Cost of crime	−
Cost of family breakdown	−
Change in foreign debt position	+/−
Cost of nonrenewable resource depletion	−
Cost of lost agricultural land	−
Cost of timber depletion	−
Cost of air pollution	−
Cost of wastewater pollution	−
Cost of long-term environmental damage	−

Source: author.

with an expanding economy and thus are subtracted from the GPI. Estimates of the costs of crime, unemployment or underemployment, and family breakdown are made and removed, as it is considered that an expanding economy can cause social pressures that exacerbate these social costs. It is assumed that less foreign debt enhances overall well-being for the country; therefore changes in foreign debt are reflected as either additions or subtractions from the GPI. Environmental costs are considered to include depletion of nonrenewable resources, timber reserves, lost agricultural land, and water and air pollution as well as long-term environmental damage. The GPI is therefore a constructed index of these adjustments.

The GPI has been empirically applied to a large number of developed and developing countries. The common finding across all these studies is that while economic growth (as measured by GDP) and GPI do track for a period of time, there is a point when additional increments in economic growth not only fail to deliver additional benefits in terms of increasing well-being but in fact reduce well-being. This divergence of economic growth and well-being (and often in developed countries a decline in real well-being) suggests that at a certain point—the *threshold point*—additional economic growth reduces well-being. In many developed countries this occurred in a period from the mid-1970s to the mid-1980s. In developing countries, the threshold point has been reached later but, importantly, at a lower level of national income. Lawn and Clarke label this the *contracting threshold point* and suggest that it signals the end of current neo-liberal market policies that seek to achieve economic growth at all costs (Lawn and Clarke 2010).

The GPI is a constructed number that is determined by the adjustments to personal consumption that are included and excluded. In this sense it is a subjective number that can be manipulated and thus can be criticized as being unreliable. It is important to remember, however, that the primary purpose for its initial construction was to challenge the hegemony of national accounts of economic growth as the sole indicators of well-being. The GPI may not be a precise measuring device, but for those who argue against conventional economic wisdom it is an important tool to challenge current policy makers. If countries are to sustain or improve their social, personal, economic, and environmental well-being, then the indicators employed must take into consideration social and environmental costs, not just economic growth.

Matthew CLARKE
Deakin University

See also Challenges to Measuring Sustainability; Computer Modeling; Development Indicators; Framework for Strategic Sustainable Development (FSSD); Gross Domestic Product, Green; Gross National Happiness; Human Development Index (HDI); I = P × A × T Equation; National Environmental Accounting; Regional Planning; Social Life Cycle Assessment (S-LCA); Sustainable Livelihood Analysis (SLA); Sustainability Science; Triple Bottom Line

FURTHER READING

Barkley, Paul W., & Seckler, David. (1972). *Economic growth and environmental decay: The solution becomes the problem.* New York: Harcourt Brace Jovanovich.

Beckerman, Wilfred. (1974). *In defence of economic growth.* London: Jonathan Cape.

Brekke, Kjell Arne. (1997). *Economic growth and the environment.* Cheltenham, UK: Edward Elgar.

Clarke, Matthew. (2006). Policy implications of the ISEW: Thailand as a case study. In Philip Lawn (Ed.), *Sustainable development indicators in ecological economics* (pp. 166–185). Cheltenham, UK: Edward Elgar.

Daly, Herman E., & Cobb, John B. Jr. (1990). *For the common good: Redirecting the economy toward community, the environment, and a sustainable future.* Boston: Beacon Press.

Dietz, Simon, & Neumayer, Eric. (2006). Some constructive criticisms of the Index of Sustainable Economic Welfare. In Philip Lawn (Ed.), *Sustainable development indicators in ecological economics* (pp. 186–206). Cheltenham, UK: Edward Elgar.

Hicks, John R. (1940). The valuation of social income. *Economica, 7,* 104–124.

Kuznets, Simon. (1941). *National income and its composition: 1919–1938.* New York: National Bureau of Economic Research.

Lawn, Philip, & Clarke, Matthew. (Eds.). (2008). *Sustainable welfare in the Asia-Pacific: Studies using the genuine progress indicator.* London: Edward Elgar.

Lawn, Philip, & Clarke, Matthew. (2010). The end of economic growth? A contracting threshold hypothesis. *Ecological Economics, 69,* 2213–2223.

McGillivray, Mark. (Ed.). (2006). *Human well-being: Concept and measurement.* New York: Palgrave-Macmillan.

McGillivray, Mark, & Clarke, Matthew. (Eds.). (2006). *Understanding human well-being.* Tokyo: United Nations University Press.

Meadows, Donella H.; Randers, Jørgen; Meadows, Dennis L.; & Behens, William W. (1972). *The limits to growth.* New York: Universe Books.

Nordhaus, William D., & Tobin, James. (1973). Is growth obsolete? In Milton Moss (Ed.), *The measurement of economic and social performance* (pp. 509–564). New York: National Bureau of Economic Research.

Sametz, Arnold W. (1968). Production of goods and services: The measurements of economic growth. In Eleanor Harriet Bernert Sheldon & Wilbert Ellis Moore (Eds.), *Indicators of social change: Concepts and measurements* (pp. 77–96). New York: Russell Sage Foundation.

World Bank. (1991). *World development report.* New York: Oxford University Press.

World Bank. (2011). *World development report.* New York: Oxford University Press.

Geographic Information Systems (GIS)

Geographic information systems (GIS) are an enabling computer technology for the collection and processing of geographic data. As a tool for representing geographic reality in the computer, GIS help us to compile, link, and query information about the state of the environment. Access to the information provided by GIS is a key element informing spatially aware decision making for sustainable development.

Geographic information systems (GIS) can be defined as a type of information technology (IT) used to collect, store, represent, query, process, analyze, and communicate any kind of data that bear a specific reference to a location on or near to the Earth's surface.

In the early twenty-first century, geographic information has become a widely used resource for decision making. This is particularly relevant when dealing with the environmental, economic, and social dimensions of sustainable development, which are inherently spatial in nature: understanding is increased when such dimensions can be visualized and analyzed as interrelated dynamic spatial patterns (e.g., the spatial distribution of resources or the spatial dynamics of social and economic processes).

Origins

Although early military GIS technologies were used in the 1950s, the first civil GIS were developed between the mid-1960s and mid-1970s as computational tools to support practical tasks of governmental agencies such as recording land or environmental resources inventories, automating the making and updating of maps, or linking geographic references to census data. The first industrial companies to develop GIS software, such as the Environmental Systems Research Institute (Esri) and

Intergraph, were formed in 1969. Since the mid-1980s in North America, Europe, and Australia, with the advances of computer technology and the subsequent reduction in hardware and software prices, the use of GIS started to spread in local governments, and most notably from the 1990s more widely in private enterprises. The use of GIS in academia started by the mid-1970s; at that time the first technical books were published, and the tool started being applied in such disciplines as cartography and geography, surveying and mapping, forestry, meteorology, biology and ecology, and urban and regional planning. In the late 1980s the debate started whether a new discipline called GIScience would have a role on its own in the scientific domain, and from the late 1990s universities began to offer on-site and online GIS and GIScience courses or full curricula worldwide.

Components

GIS are complex engineering artifacts that involve complex socio-organizational structures; their basic components include spatial data (or GI), hardware and software architectures, procedures, and users.

Geographic Data and Spatial Data Modeling

Geographic data describe objects or phenomena that can be observed and that can be measured or identified in geographic space (i.e., on or near the Earth's surface) at a given time, by a thematic and a spatial component. The thematic component of geographic data represents the values of attributes that measure any characteristic of interest of observed objects or phenomena, while the spatial component represents the location of objects (e.g., a set of buildings or parcels) on the Earth's surface, or the measured values of phenomena at a given location (e.g., the ground temperature or the elevation above sea level). Location is measured according to a defined spatial (geographic or projected) reference system.

As there may be more than a single way to represent the geographic objects or phenomena of interest, different data structures and digital formats, including both vector and raster formats, can be used to encode geographic data. Geographic data structures and models define both the thematic and the spatial dimensions of GI, and they can be considered as the templates used to represent objects or phenomena of a given type in a GIS application.

The process of data modeling defines how thematic and geographic measures will be recorded in the digital media by a series of steps that starts with the observation of the geographic reality and proceeds with the selection of the type of objects (e.g., buildings) and phenomena (e.g., temperature distribution) that will be represented in the database. Once the list of objects and phenomena is established, the next step involves the definition of the thematic (e.g., the height, age, architectural style for a building) and the spatial components for each class of objects or phenomena.

The vector format is often preferred for representing objects, and the raster format for representing phenomena as fields (e.g., the field of ground temperature variation in space). Most commonly used vector and raster data structures are 2-dimensional, meaning that the spatial component is given by the recording of a 2-tuple of coordinates (e.g., longitude x and latitude y, according to a geographic or projected reference system). Moreover, quite often both vector data structures, such as the triangulated irregular network (TIN) and raster data structures, such as the digital elevation model (DEM), are used to record a third coordinate (e.g., the elevation z). The resulting data structures are called 2.5-dimensional and represent surfaces in a 3-dimensional space. Three-dimensional data structures have also been developed to represent volumes in space, as well as 4-dimensional ones that include the temporal dimension (representing the variation of values of attributes over time), although they are not yet widely used.

Objects represented in vector format in two dimensions are commonly described as points, lines, or polygons—the geographic primitives. The point primitive allows recording of the coordinates of a single location, while the line and polygon primitives record 2-tuples of

coordinates for each node or vertex of lines or polygons, thus also describing geometrically the location of each object. The scale of observation and analysis influences the choice of a suitable primitive for a given set of objects during the data modeling process; for example in cartography, a city may be represented as a point at a continental scale but as a polygon at the regional scale.

Raster data models are structured according to a different approach, relying on a partition of space by a regular grid of cells. The position of each cell is recorded together with the value of one or more attributes for each cell (e.g., the average value of an attribute in the center of the cell, or the reflected radiation in case of remote sensing data) describing a phenomenon varying in space with a degree of continuity. The size of the cell defines the scale of the data.

Once the conceptual data model is defined, the logical data model is designed in order to implement the former in a given recording data structure and file format; then the physical datasets are created and populated with data. The population of an empty dataset can be done manually or automatically by means of peripherals and GIS functions.

Beginning in the 1990s, one of the most popular recording formats for geographic datasets was the commercial Shapefile developed by Esri Inc., which can still be considered a standard, although from the late 1990s, the trend became to migrate geographic data to the more efficient and robust structure of the relational database management systems (RDBMS). The most popular and widely used RDBMS offer sets of special functions for spatial data management and analysis (e.g., Oracle, MySQL, Postgres). With the developments in web technologies, geographic data are often encoded in GML (Geographic Markup Language, the XML specification for geo-spatial data) or KML (Keyhole Markup Language, a standard XML notation used by Google Maps/Earth) facilitating the exchange and exploitation of GI on the Web.

Several global and regional standards exist for spatial data and metadata (data describing the features of a geographic dataset), including the ISO/TC 211 Geographic Information/Geomatics of the International Organization for Standardization, and the standards and specifications of the Open Geospatial Consortium (OGC), a nonprofit, voluntary consensus standards consortium that includes members from commercial, research, governmental, and nongovernmental organizations worldwide. These standards are paving the way to GI sharing and exchange, fostering the exploitation of GI resources within the mainstream information communication technology (ICT) domain.

Software

The first forms of GIS software (SW) were developed for land mapping in the late 1960s. At that time a GIS SW was either based solely on the vector format or solely on the raster format. GIS SW development and use grew in the late 1980s in the most advanced countries, thanks to the growing use of personal computers. At that time many commercial companies started to develop SW able to work on and integrate both the vector and the raster formats, the so-called hybrid GIS. As of 2012, most commercial (e.g., Esri ArcGIS, Intergraph GeoMedia, MapInfo) and open-source (e.g., GRASS, gvSIG, Quantum GIS, MapWindow) GIS SW is of the hybrid type, although some others still use mainly one format.

GIS desktop SW tends to operate on the most common data formats and standards and feature functions for spatial data creation and management, visualization, processing and analysis (with a varying number of analysis tools), and communication. From the mid-1990s, client-server technologies were developed to implement Internet-based GIS applications, most of which have been widely used to distribute interactive maps on the Web. With the advances of Web 2.0 technologies in the early years of the twenty-first century, GIS SW modules have become available on the Web through application programming interfaces (API) such as the popular Google Maps API, which allows the seamless integration of geo-spatial functionalities (or services) within Web applications, further fostering the widespread diffusion of GI on the Web.

Hardware

GIS SW can run on a multitude of hardware (HW) technologies, including personal computers, mobile devices, and complex distributed architectures, and on top of the most diffused operating systems. GIS HW includes input (e.g., keyboard, pointing and measuring devices, networks) and output (e.g., monitors, printers, networks) peripherals, processors, and mass storage.

The basic HW elements can be integrated in a variety of simple or complex architectures. In desktop applications, data and SW are installed in a stand-alone personal computer; in enterprise applications, GIS runs on an intranet of computers, some of which may be used to perform specialized functions such as spatial data creation while others perform query or analysis; in an Internet-based system, both spatial data and processing services operate on a distributed network of computers and devices through the Internet infrastructure and technology; and mobile architectures are location-based services. As of 2012, most recent developments in geographic information technology include the use of a service-oriented architecture (SOA) and the move toward cloud computing.

Procedures

GIS allow simple and complex processing functions through user-friendly graphic interfaces. In GIS, data describing the sets of objects or phenomena that are of interest are conceived as layers. The overlay of different layers according to consistent spatial reference systems supplies a representation of the geographic space that allows description not only of the spatial distribution of features and properties but also of mutual topological relationships among objects and phenomena. The latter is a key element for the implementation of many geospatial functions.

The main categories of geo-processing functions include data creation, storage and management, spatial data query, visualization, and analysis. Spatial analysis includes simple tools (such as spatial data query and classification, overlay mapping, map algebra, geo-processing, or surface analysis) and more advanced functions (such as spatial statistics, spatiotemporal analysis, or exploratory spatial data analysis) that can be integrated in input-output chains as analytical models. The majority of professional GIS SW allow deploying new analysis tools and the implementing of new applications using most popular programming languages, including C++, Python, JAVA, .NET, and others.

The People Component

GIS should not be seen detached from their users—the people component. In the first decades of GIS development, until the mid-1990s, the systems were mostly used by experts, with relevant academic or professional background, involved in such tasks as dataset or database creation and maintenance, routine and application programming, or spatial analysis. In the first years of the twenty-first century, with the availability of Web 2.0 geo-browsers (Google Maps being one of the most popular), geospatial data and applications became a resource for the general population. Web users, even without being aware of what GIS are, take advantage of the availability of petabytes of geographic data and georeferenced multimedia collected by satellite or terrestrial sensors—or, thanks to mobile devices and cameras connected to the Global Positioning System (GPS), collected by Internet users and shared on the Web.

GIScience

Understanding the potential of GIS requires in-depth understanding of all the components introduced above. In addition, further work is needed to address some of the limitations of GIS, such as the difficulty of developing reliable spatiotemporal data structures, the issue of uncertainty, and the efficient management of huge volumes of data.

Interested scientists worldwide debate whether a new discipline, called GIScience, should be acknowledged to have a status comparable to that of other fundamental scientific disciplines, as noted by Professor Michael F. Goodchild (2010) from the University of California, Santa Barbara. It would be a multidisciplinary field involving geography, information theories, computer science, geodesy, management, cartography, among others. While debate continues on whether GIScience should be considered a fundamental discipline or a branch of engineering, scientists and researchers continue to produce promising results addressing scientifically fundamental questions related to all the components of GIS and their mutual relationships, including the issues of capture and collection, data structures, representation and geo-visualization, user interfaces, spatial analysis and statistics, and simulation, as well as managerial, ethical, and societal issues.

GIS and Sustainable Development

Geographic information is a key resource for the implementation of sustainable development principles, as acknowledged by Agenda 21, the action plan developed at the United Nations Conference on Environment and Development (chapter 40, "Information for Decision Making") (UN DESA 2009). GIS can represent a comprehensive support tool for assessment and decision making. Understanding the relationships between the Earth's environment and the nature and impacts of the anthropogenic processes requires up-to-date knowledge about the spatial distribution of resources, and the dynamics of the environmental, economic, and social processes affecting the sustainability of development.

The power of, and the need for, geographic information is repeatedly demonstrated when facing the most difficult challenges of our time, such as natural disasters, as explained by Russ Johnson (2000), Public Safety Industry Manager at Esri. The availability of GI that is continually updated through satellite, in situ, and mobile sensors enables us to monitor in real time such phenomena as natural hazards, spread of disease, or climate change, enhancing substantially our possibility for immediate responsive actions. To this end, at the global level the international Group on Earth Observations (GEO) is coordinating the creation of the Global Earth Observation System of Systems (GEOSS) to provide geographic information for the benefit of society, in such fields as disaster emergency management, natural resource and biodiversity protection, human health protection and quality of life improvement, and climate change monitoring.

GIS were born as tools available to only a few. The democratization of GI and GIS granted by the wider access to the data and reduction in technology costs since the 1990s has proven GIS can be a reliable tool supporting collaboration, public participation, and more socially inclusive decision making (the social dimension of sustainability).

Worldwide, there are ongoing policies and initiatives for the creation of spatial data infrastructures (SDI), which are frameworks of technology, policies, and standards that enable the access, use, and reuse of GI (Masser 2005). SDI are fostering accessibility to spatial data, supplying knowledge for more informed environmental decision making as well as for granting citizens the access to environmental information. One example is the Infrastructure for Spatial Information in Europe (INSPIRE), detailed in their Directive 2007/2/EC (EUR-Lex 2007). Successful SDI best practices demonstrate their benefits both in terms of economic savings in administration and better quality of services to citizens. Wider public access to geographic information is also seen as an opportunity for developing added value services to the private sector by supporting economic development.

At the same time, GI-enabled web technologies allow citizens to collect and share georeferenced information; this volunteered geographic information (VGI) is being used by people to describe whatever variegated phenomena interest them, from local weather conditions to the spread of a wildfire, from the spotting of rare animal species or waste dumping to reporting crime events or malfunctioning of urban public services.

SDI and VGI offer unprecedented availability of geographical information resources (official, provided by public authorities, and volunteered, provided by common citizens) which together increase our understanding and awareness, in real time, of phenomena affecting our quality of life and the current state of the environment. This is a socially inclusive and democratic construction of a "Digital Earth," as envisioned by the US vice president Al Gore in 1998 (Gore 1998). Many challenges remain in terms of the ability to manage the quantity of data and the computation intensity required to take full advantage of available information for sustainability goals. Nevertheless, the results achieved so far are promising.

Michele CAMPAGNA
University of Cagliari

See also Agenda 21; Challenges to Measuring Sustainability; Citizen Science; Computer Modeling; *The Limits to Growth;* Long-Term Ecological Research (LTER); Quantitative vs. Qualitative Studies; Remote Sensing; Risk Assessment; Social Network Analysis (SNA); Sustainability Science; Systems Thinking; Transdisciplinary Research

FURTHER READING

Burrough, Peter A., & McDonnell, Rachael A. (1998). *Principles of geographical information systems* (2nd ed.). Oxford, UK: Oxford University Press Inc.

Campagna, Michele. (2006). GIS for sustainable development. In Michele Campagna (Ed.), *GIS for Sustainable development* (pp. 3–20). Boca Raton, FL: CRC Press, Taylor and Francis Group.

Craglia, Max, et al. (2008). Next-generation digital Earth: A position paper from the Vespucci initiative for the advancement of geographic information science. *International Journal of Spatial Data Infrastructures Research, 3,* 146–167.

Craig, William J.; Harris, Trevor M.; & Weiner, Daniel. (Eds.). (2002). *Community participation and geographical information systems.* New York: Taylor and Francis.

de Smith, Michael J.; Goodchild, Michael F.; & Longley, Paul A. (2007). *Geospatial analysis: A comprehensive guide to principles, techniques and software tools* (2nd ed.). Leicester, UK: Matador, Troubador Publishing Ltd.

EUR-Lex. (2007). Directive 2007/2/EC of the European Parliament and of the Council of 14 March 2007 establishing an Infrastructure for Spatial Information in the European Community (INSPIRE). Retrieved January 18, 2012, from http://eur-lex.europa.eu/LexUriServ/LexUriServ.do?uri=CELEX:32007L0002:EN:NOT

Goodchild, Michael F. (2007). Citizens as voluntary sensors: Spatial data infrastructure in the world of Web 2.0. *International Journal of Spatial Data Infrastructures Research, 2,* 24–32.

Goodchild, Michael F. (2010). Twenty years of progress: GIScience in 2010. *Journal of Spatial Information Science, 1,* 3–20.

Gore, Al. (1998). The digital Earth: Understanding our planet in the 21st century. *Open GIS Consortium.* Retrieved September 7, 2011, from http://portal.opengeospatial.org/files/?artifact_id=6210

Longley, Paul; Goodchild, Michael F.; Maguire, David J.; & Rhind, David W. (Eds.). (1999). *Geographical information systems: Principles, techniques, applications and management* (Vols. 1–2, 2nd ed.). New York: John Wiley & Sons Inc.

Longley, Paul; Goodchild, Michael F.; Maguire, David J.; & Rhind, David W. (2010). *Geographic information systems and science* (3rd ed.). New York: John Wiley & Sons Inc.

Maguire, David J.; Goodchild, Michael F.; & Batty, Michael. (Eds.). (2006). *GIS, spatial analysis, and modeling.* Redlands, CA: Esri Press.

Malczewski, Jacek. (1999). *GIS and multicriteria decision analysis.* New York: John Wiley & Sons Inc.

Masser, Ian. (2005). *GIS worlds: Creating spatial data infrastructures.* Redlands, CA: Esri Press.

Nyerges, Timothy L., & Jankowski, Piotr. (2010). *Regional and urban GIS: A decision support approach.* New York: The Guilford Press.

Peng, Zhong-Ren, & Tsou, Ming-Hsiang. (2003). *Internet GIS: Distributed geographic information services for the internet and wireless networks.* Hoboken, NJ: John Wiley & Sons Inc.

Pickles, John. (Ed.). (1995). *Ground truth: The social implications of geographic information systems.* New York: The Guilford Press.

Johnson, Russ. (2000). GIS Technology for Disasters and Emergency Management. An Esri White Paper. Environmental Systems Research Institute, Inc. Printed in the United States of America.

Tomlinson, Roger. (2007). *Thinking about GIS: Geographic information system planning for managers.* Redlands, CA: Esri Press.

UN Department of Economic and Social Affairs (UN DESA). (2009), Division for Sustainable Development. Agenda 21, Section IV, Chapter 40. Information for Decision-Making. Retrieved January 19, 2012, from http://www.un.org/esa/dsd/agenda21/res_agenda21_40.shtml

Wise, Stephen, & Craglia, Max. (Eds.). (2008). *GIS and evidence-based policy making.* Boca Raton, FL: CRC Press, Taylor and Francis Group.

Worboys, Michael, & Duckham, Matt. (2004). *GIS: A computing perspective* (2nd ed.). Boca Raton, FL: CRC Press, Taylor and Francis Group.

Yang, Chaowei, et al. (2011). Spatial cloud computing: How can the geospatial sciences use and help shape cloud computing? *International Journal of Digital Earth, 4*(4), 305–329.

Global Environment Outlook (GEO) Reports

The Global Environment Outlook (GEO) is the flagship assessment through which the United Nations Environment Programme carries out one of its core functions: keeping the global environment under review. GEO's goal is to produce scientifically credible and policy-relevant assessment of the state of the global environment and to enhance the capacity of a wide range of actors to perform integrated environmental assessments.

Created as a result of the first United Nations Conference on the Human Environment held in Stockholm 1972, the United Nations Environment Programme (UNEP) is the leading global environmental authority that sets the global environmental agenda. UNEP holds the primary responsibility for keeping the world environmental situation under review and promoting the acquisition, assessment, and exchange of environmental knowledge and information. The Global Environment Outlook (GEO) is the landmark integrated environmental assessment that UNEP has published since 1997. The fifth GEO report will be published in mid-2012, in time for the UN Conference on Sustainable Development (Rio+20).

Unlike other international organizations such as the World Meteorological Organization or the World Health Organization, UNEP performs little direct monitoring and surveillance. Rather, it collects, collates, analyzes, and integrates data from UN agencies, other organizations, and national statistical offices to form broader environmental assessments. It engages a diverse range of experts from all regions and professions in the production process. The GEO assessments thus compile and interpret scientific findings on the causes and consequences of environmental change and provide policy options to help governments and organizations mitigate and adapt to the change.

The goal of the GEO reports and the process that produces them is to bridge the gap between science and policy by turning credible data into information relevant to environmental decision makers. The GEO reports have built a foundation of consistent data over the years on a set of global environmental concerns and have begun to identify possible policy responses.

Origins and Development

In 1995, at the eighteenth regular session of the UNEP Governing Council, governments requested the preparation of a comprehensive report on the state and trends of the global environment. In response, UNEP launched the Global Environment Outlook as part of implementing Principle 10 of the Rio Declaration, which concerns policy makers' access to appropriate information about the environment.

UNEP released the first GEO report in February 1997. Each GEO cycle develops the main report through a multi-stakeholder process that engages experts from around the world. The individual iterations have also resulted in the creation of related products, such as GEO assessments at regional, national, and city levels, and editions targeted at specific audiences, such as summaries for decision makers and GEO reports for youth. Most of the GEO products are available online at the UNEP website (United Nations Environment Programme 2011).

GEO has scheduled its fifth report (GEO-5) for 2012 to coincide with the Rio+20 Conference, the UN Conference on Sustainable Development held on the twenty-year anniversary of the 1992 Rio Earth Summit. All GEO reports to date have underscored three main themes: (1) persistent environmental problems significantly undermine human well-being, (2) environmental problems require urgent policy action, and (3) sustainable development can be attained only by moving the environment from the periphery to the core of decision making. The GEO reports have used an analytical framework known as DPSIR (Drivers-Pressures-State-Impacts-Responses) as an overall methodological tool. GEO-4 refined the DPSIR framework to highlight human well-being. Each GEO process has also used policy benchmarking against internationally agreed upon environmental goals as reference points for assessing progress in the environmental field. GEO-5 has made this benchmarking against goals more explicit.

The first GEO report, released in 1997, described the environmental status and trends in different regions. It concluded with a scenario projecting what could happen to the global environment if business as usual continued in an open-ended temporal assessment period. GEO-2, the second report, offered insights at both the regional and global scales over a hundred-year period. It concluded that excessive consumption by the minority of the planet's inhabitants and the persistent poverty of the majority are the two major causes of environmental degradation.

GEO-3 appeared in time for the World Summit on Sustainable Development in Johannesburg in 2002 and provided an overview of environmental change in the thirty years since UNEP's creation, from 1972 to 2002. This edition offered four scenarios of sharply contrasting futures for humanity in the year 2032 as a part of its outlook section. The report concluded that excessive consumption continued to cause environmental pressure and that the environment was still at the periphery of socio-economic development. The GEO-4 report's publication purposefully coincided with the twentieth anniversary of the launch of the 1987 Brundtland report, *Our Common Future*, which laid out the concept of sustainable development. GEO-4 highlighted the three themes of *Our Common Future*—environment, economics, and equity—and underscored that human well-being depends on the health of ecosystems.

Similar to previous iterations, GEO-5 provides an assessment of the state and trends of water, land, atmosphere, biodiversity, and chemicals and waste. It evaluates whether states are meeting the internationally agreed goals, set through legally or nonlegally binding multilateral environmental agreements, declarations, and guiding principles in each of these areas. Where governments and organizations have not met these goals, GEO-5 seeks to identify the causes, impacts on the environment, and consequences for human well-being. The report also evaluates successful environmental policies in the regions and their potential to speed up achieving internationally agreed goals. Building on GEO-4, GEO-5 uses scenarios to provide an outlook perspective for transformative policies. It outlines actions that can be undertaken at the global level to enable the adoption of transformative

policies and describes the legal, institutional, and policy frameworks required to make these policies successful. The most significant difference between GEO-5 and earlier GEO reports is that GEO-5 shifts the focus from identifying global priority problems to identifying global solutions that governments can then prioritize.

The Process: Consultation, Engagement, Capacity

In integrated environmental assessments such as the GEO, process is critical to the quality of the product. How the report authors conduct that assessment, and who participates and under what conditions significantly impact the ultimate results. Salience, credibility, and legitimacy are critical factors shaping the impact of scientific assessments (Cash et al. 2003). Salience means that scientific input is timely and focused and addresses issues of current importance to policy makers. Credibility refers to the adequacy of scientific evidence and arguments and to the credentials of the scientists involved. Legitimacy of scientific assessments requires that the processes be perceived as being free of bias, taking into account the views of stakeholders, and treating differing views fairly. The GEO strives to deliver across all three dimensions.

Each GEO cycle has employed a different approach to process design with an overall tendency toward greater consultation and engagement and increasing the capacity of the organizations involved. In its earliest stage, the GEO process involved a network of twenty Collaborating Centers and gathered data through regional policy consultations. The trend with each subsequent GEO report has been to increase the number of contributing organizations and individuals as authors, contributors to the methodology and process planning, and reviewers of multiple drafts. Government participation reached a new level in the process that led to GEO-4. A High-Level Consultative Group comprising member states and experts helped frame the report in a way responsive to policy needs. Governments also nominated experts for review and facilitated review meetings. By actively shaping the vision and process, these governments, member states, and experts transitioned from being a target audience to a functional stakeholder group.

The GEO-5 process builds on the model of engagement established during GEO-4. A multi-stakeholder consultative group agreed on the scope, objectives, and process for GEO-5. Governments nominated experts to serve as authors, reviewers, and members of advisory groups. A High-Level Intergovernmental Panel comprising nineteen high-level policy experts serving in their own expert capacities helped set the vision for GEO-5.

Such an approach increases the salience of GEO-5 significantly.

Government engagement often improves the policy relevance of scientific findings, ensures legitimacy, and facilitates broader use of scientific data and analysis in the decision-making process. That very engagement, some scholars note, could also lead to message dilution, politicization, and erosion of legitimacy in the eyes of the scientific community and the public when they perceive governments as meddling in science (Mitchell et al. 2006). Importantly, the tension between GEO's desire for governmental input and the fear of governmental involvement is present in other environmental impact assessment processes. In particular, the Intergovernmental Panel on Climate Change (IPCC) process and reports have been subject to such conflicting perspectives (InterAcademy Council 2010).

Another innovative design feature of the GEO-5 process is the establishment of a Science and Policy Advisory Board with researchers and scientists from a range of institutions; the mandate of the board is to provide expert guidance to all the report's chapters, and thus strengthen both the scientific credibility and the salience of the assessment.

Ultimately, evaluations of the GEO reports show that the participatory and consultative process gives GEO assessments scientific credibility, improves their accuracy and legitimacy, and earns them salience in a wide audience (UNEP/IUCN 2009).

Implementation and Impact

The GEO process's most important contributions have been developing capacity, raising broad awareness about global and international environmental issues, and fostering engagement and participation.

Developing Capacity

In the years since its inception, the GEO assessment process has become increasingly sophisticated in its inclusion of various scales of governance and the integration of concepts to inform capacity building (enhancing a region's or nation's ability to develop and implement programs with long-term sustainable results), data collection and analysis, and technology development and transfer. Regional governmental forums and national governments have also adopted the GEO methodology to produce and/or improve State of the Environment or Integrated Environmental Assessment reporting. In the spirit of the GEO methodology, the authors tend to structure these reports in a way that fosters stakeholder participation and with approaches that link knowledge and action (Pintér, Swanson, and Chenje 2007).

Raising Awareness

The GEO reports and associated outreach products offer distillations of the complex topic of global environmental change in a way carefully crafted to be accessible and useful for a broad range of audiences. In particular, the Summary for Policymakers has been a useful tool for delivering key messages to high-level policy makers. An evaluation of the GEO-4 report showed that it was particularly useful for policy makers in developing countries. The evaluation also noted that the launch of GEO-4 generated significant media attention; various news items and television documentaries either featured it or used it as a foundation. Academic and research institutions also state that GEO-4 was valuable for their work. These stakeholders' use of GEO-4 indicates that its messages are reaching the broader public.

Fostering Engagement and Participation

Environmentalists have hailed the bottom-up and consultative nature of the GEO process as a real strength (United Nations Environment Programme 2004). The range of stakeholders included in the process has increased its relevance by integrating various perspectives, priorities, and data sources. In addition, the structure has fostered ongoing inclusive dialogues between policy makers and stakeholders and has enhanced regional assessment processes.

Challenges and Limitations

Global environmental monitoring and assessment is complex and requires a dynamic approach. The breadth and scope of their coverage limits the GEO process and products. The GEO publications offer overarching trends by issue and geographic area; they do not provide comparative feedback to countries and regional networks on the policies' efficacy implementation. Other organizations have developed assessments and indices to fill this gap. Robust examples include the World Resources Institute's *EarthTrends Reports* and the 2010 *Environmental Performance Index*, a collaborative effort between Yale and Columbia universities and the World Economic Forum.

Further evidence that governments would value a tool that would enable direct comparison comes in the form of the Global Earth Observation System of Systems (GEOSS). Created in 2005 as a partnership among governments and intergovernmental organizations, GEOSS is intended to provide "comprehensive, coordinated and sustained observations of the Earth system" and "timely, quality long-term global information as a basis for sound decision making" (Global Earth Observation System of Systems 2005). Although GEO is intended to be an assessment process and GEOSS an observation system, the creation of GEOSS in the wake of the 2002 World Summit on Sustainable Development might indicate that governments found the UNEP data analyses and information function inadequate.

The Future

GEO-5's reception is likely to determine the scope and design of possible future GEO projects; UNEP has not planned a GEO-6 report as of 2012. If the five-year cycle were kept, GEO-6 would be published in 2017. Although the scope and design of the process and products are undetermined, the assessment landscape's current trends and government requests indicate that future global assessments will need to include workable solutions. There are several elements to be considered in this context.

National-scale data collection and analysis will continue to be vital for environmental policy making. In particular, GEO products can and should support the state of the environment assessment processes. Although the alternative indices could complement the GEO process, these initiatives have the potential to erode UNEP's status as the world's preeminent environmental authority. Because the GEO process involves active participation and consultation with government officials, the next GEO might well emphasize stronger collaboration with GEOSS or other groups of this nature, allowing the GEO process to evolve in a way that is complementary to related efforts.

The science-policy interface that current dialogues on environmental governance so strongly emphasize must integrate society. This integration requires that international environmental institutions develop new methods to bring in the views of society—both stakeholder groups and the general public—on science-policy issues important to them. They must disseminate scientific findings to society in understandable and useful ways, so that policy does not get too far "out in front" of society. In this context, the capacity building that the GEO process fosters is not limited to environmental monitoring and assessment. The knowledge and skills nurtured through these endeavors include research and analysis, website design, data processing, effective communication, and the organization of stakeholder processes.

The collaborative process of developing the GEO, which engages authors from around the world and from various organizations, is invaluable to the content of the GEO products. With each GEO, the contributing authors and reviewers have expanded significantly both in numbers and in a variety of expertise areas. The GEO-5 process has shown the need for a set of common standards to facilitate writing, review, and evaluation.

As the GEO products—national and regional outlooks, compendiums of datasets, online platforms, and the like—evolve to meet the increasingly urgent and complex challenges of global environmental governance, UNEP may have to update the process to enable a more dynamic approach to content development. Currently, authors compile their chapters in parallel over a period of about eighteen months. This system limits the depth of the content. Were the process to expand and become incremental, authors would more easily be able to cross-reference key concepts and could eliminate conclusions and redundancy.

The individual GEO reports and the associated production process have eclipsed their predecessors in sophistication, complexity, and utility for policy application. There is a fine line, however, between providing policy-relevant scientific recommendations and being policy prescriptive. As the GEO process evolves to meet a growing demand for policy solutions from policy makers and UN agencies, scientists engaged in the process will need to guard the GEO's scientific credibility and independence while offering visionary policy options and alternatives.

Maria IVANOVA
University of Massachusetts, Boston

Melissa GOODALL
Antioch University New England

The authors thank Sara Svensson for her assistance in the GEO-5 process and research for this chapter and Munyaradzi Chenje, Fatoumata Keita-Ouane, and Neeyati Patel for helpful comments on an earlier draft.

See also Agenda 21; Citizen Science; Community and Stakeholder Input; Computer Modeling; Environmental Performance Index (EPI); Externality Valuation; Genuine Progress Indictors (GPI); Global Reporting Initiative (GRI); Global Strategy for Plant Conservation;

Human Development Index (HDI); International Organization for Standardization (ISO); Long-Term Ecological Research (LTER); Millennium Development Goals; National Environmental Accounting; Strategic Environmental Assessment (SEA); Systems Thinking

FURTHER READING

Carr, Edward R., et al. (1997). Applying DPSIR to sustainable development. *International Journal of Sustainable Development & World Ecology, 14*, 543–555.

Cash, David W., et al. (2003). Knowledge systems for sustainable development. *Proceedings of the National Academy of Sciences, 100*(14), 8086–8091.

Global Earth Observation System of Systems (GEOSS). (2005). *The Global Earth Observation System of Systems (GEOSS) 10-year implementation plan.* Geneva: GEOSS.

InterAcademy Council. (2010). *Climate change assessments: Review of the processes & procedures of the IPCC.* New York: InterAcademy Council. Retrieved December 21, 2011, from http://reviewipcc.interacademycouncil.net/report.html

Kok, Marcel T. J., et al. (2009). *Environment for development: Policy lessons from global environmental assessments. Report for UNEP.* The Netherlands Environmental Assessment Agency. Retrieved December 21, 2011, from www.unep.org/dewa/pdf/Environment_for_Development.pdf

Mitchell, Ronald B.; Clark, William C.; Cash, David W.; & Dickinson, Nancy M. (Eds.). (2006). *Global environmental assessments: Information and influence.* Cambridge, MA: MIT Press.

Pintér, László; Swanson, Darren; & Chenje, Jacquie. (2007). *GEO resource book: A training manual on integrated environmental assessment and reporting.* Winnipeg, Canada: United Nations Environment Programme (UNEP) & the International Institute for Sustainable Development (IISD).

Potting, José, & Bakkes, Jan. (Eds.). (2004). *The GEO-3 Scenarios 2002–2032: Quantification and analysis of environmental impacts.* (UNEP/DEWA/RS.03-4 & RIVM 402001022). New York & Bilthoven, The Netherlands: United Nations Environment Programme (UNEP) & Netherlands National Institute for Public Health and the Environment (RIVM).

United Nations Environment Programme (UNEP). (2004). *Global environment outlook (GEO): SWOT analysis and evaluation of the GEO-3 process from the perspective of GEO collaborating centres.* New York: UNEP.

United Nations Environment Programme (UNEP). (2008). *Synthesis of global environmental assessment: Environment for development: Policy lessons from global environmental assessment.* (UNEP GC.25/INF/11). New York: UNEP.

United Nations Environment Programme (UNEP). (2011). Global environmental outlook. Retrieved December 21, 2011, from http://www.unep.org/geo

United Nations Environment Programme (UNEP), & the International Union for Conservation of Nature (IUCN). (2009a). *Findings of the GEO-4 self assessment survey.* http://www.unep.org/geo/Docs/Findings_GEO-4_Self_Assessment_Survey_lov.pdf

United Nations Environment Programme (UNEP), & the International Union for Conservation of Nature (IUCN). (2009b). *Review of the initial impact of the GEO-4 report.* Retrieved December 21, 2011, from http://www.unep.org/geo/docs/Review_Initial_Impact_of_the_GEO-4_Report_low.pdf

Woerden, Van. (Ed.). (1999). *Data issues of global environmental reporting: Experiences from GEO-2000.* (UNEP/DEIA&EW, TR.99-3 and RIVM 402001013). New York, & Bilthoven, The Netherlands: United Nations Environment Programme (UNEP) & Netherlands National Institute for Public Health and the Environment (RIVM).

Global Reporting Initiative (GRI)

The Global Reporting Initiative (GRI) offers the most prevalent standards for sustainability reporting. The first version of the GRI guidelines was published in 2000, and they have come to be used by more than 1,800 companies worldwide. They include economic, environmental, and social aspects and can be applied to all types of companies, irrespective of size or industry affiliation, although complementary sector supplements are available.

Reporting on sustainability issues can offer many advantages to companies. It is easier for a company to track progress if it has set and published specific environmental or social targets; also, publishing a sustainability report raises both internal and external awareness of the topic. Furthermore, the increased transparency not only gains credibility for the reporting company, but also offers reputational benefits (Kolk 2004).

Nevertheless, some companies hesitate to publish sustainability reports because doing so requires great time and financial efforts, mostly but not only due to difficulties in gathering data. And for some companies, publishing a sustainability report for the first time entails the notion of "waking sleeping dogs" and raising attention where attention might not be wanted (Kolk 2004).

The first separate environmental reports were published in the late 1980s (Kolk 2004). In 1997, the Coalition for Environmentally Responsible Economies (CERES, now Ceres), an American network of investors, labor, environmental, and other public interest groups, along with the Tellus Institute, an American nonprofit research and policy organization, and the help of the United Nations Environment Programme established the Global Reporting Initiative (GRI). Companies were facing increasing demands by various stakeholders to inform them about the company's environmental and social performance, which led many firms to publish inconsistent, incomplete, and precipitate reports on their activities. To prevent their stakeholders from "suffocating" from information overload, various national or industry-specific organizations attempted to coordinate their reports. Members of Ceres figured that an international, universally applicable standard was needed. In response, they published their first set of guidelines in 2000.

The GRI, a network-based organization, offers guidelines for companies on sustainability reporting, and finances itself by means of government or foundation grants, corporate sponsorship, and service provisions. Reporting on sustainability issues remains voluntary, contrary to financial reporting, whose international standards serve as a role model for sustainability reporting. The goal of the GRI guidelines is to provide a framework that matches financial reporting standards in terms of "rigour, comparability, auditability and general acceptance" (Willis 2003, 233). The GRI guidelines are the most prevalent sustainability guidelines worldwide, with any competing system lagging far behind in terms of scope and diffusion.

The guidelines have universal applicability in that they are valid for all types of companies, irrespective of size or industry affiliation. Yet these general guidelines do not account for the specific sustainability challenges experienced in different industries. Therefore, GRI working groups have created sector supplements, which are available for the energy utility, financial services, food processing, mining and metals, and nongovernmental organization sectors. These sector supplements do not substitute for the general guidelines but rather complement them with industry-specific aspects.

The GRI guidelines do not set performance goals; for instance, they do not state carbon dioxide emission values that companies must achieve. Rather, they lead to corporate transparency about what is being done, since generally set targets cannot apply to the diversity of companies using the GRI guidelines. It is up to each company's decision makers to define sustainability objectives. Report readers, however, could use lack of information about reduction targets as an indicator of a company's real commitment to sustainability.

The GRI guidelines support companies by answering two basic questions: what to report, and how to report.

The issue of what to report is solved by the reporting standards themselves and the sector supplements. A report that is produced in line with the GRI guidelines contains four main parts: a section on the company's sustainability vision and strategy, a corporate profile, a section on governance structures and management systems relevant to sustainability, and performance indicators.

The question of how to report is addressed by means of basic principles that companies need to follow, such as neutrality, comparability, completeness, and auditability. These make it possible to compare reports or achievements, respectively, across time and across organizations. The guidelines help firms make decisions about reporting content, the quality level of the information provided (e.g., whether to provide information on both achievements and drawbacks), and reporting boundaries.

The profile helps readers place the company and its sustainability activities in a context by providing general information about the company, such as size, products, markets, and operational structure. The description of the governance structure and the management systems explains how the sustainability vision is transformed into actual sustainable development by illustrating decision-making, controlling, and auditing processes and the location of responsibilities. Finally, the indicators expose the company's economic, environmental, and social performance.

The most recent version of the guidelines, referred to as the "Third Generation," or G3, covers more than 120 indicators relating to social, environmental, and economic aspects. These indicators range from material and water usage, emissions, and amount of waste, to net employment creation, average days of employee training, and workforce breakdown by country, region, and employment type (e.g., full-time and part-time).

Not all companies report to the same scope. Reports can be distinguished according to their application level, which can either be self-declared by the companies or determined by the GRI, which charges a fee. The levels ranging from A (the highest) to C (the lowest) indicate the number of indicators published and the scope of disclosure. A plus sign behind the level indication shows that the report content has been externally assured by a third party.

In 2010, more than 1,800 sustainability reports were designed in line with the GRI guidelines. Forty-five percent of these reports stemmed from Europe, followed by Asian reports at 20 percent, North and Latin America each at 14 percent, and Africa at only 3 percent. On a single-country basis, however, the United States led by accounting for 10 percent of the total number of reports. The leading European countries were Spain at 19 percent and Sweden at 10 percent of the total number of reports in Europe (GRI 2011).

Criticisms

The GRI standards are not without their critics. Most firms that follow the GRI do so in documents that are separate from their general economic annual report. This annual report is subject to control and certification by independent third-party agencies, whereas the sustainability report is not. A considerable number of firms integrate sustainability reporting into their annual reports to show their honest commitment to sustainability. This may deteriorate the transparency principle of the GRI, as such integrated reports cannot fully respect the GRI guidelines.

Another criticism relates to the principles themselves. In an academic article published in 2006, the Spanish researchers José Moneva, Pablo Archel, and Carmen Correa demonstrated that there is an overemphasis on the social dimension of sustainability, as 50 percent of all indicators are social indicators, followed by environmental (approximately 30 percent) and economic indicators (approximately 10 percent). To truly reflect a company's sustainability practices, these indicators should be more balanced; at the least, more indicators should be proposed for environmental sustainability.

Future of the GRI

In the future, the number of corporate sustainability reports is likely to increase. Compared to 2009, the number of reports in the United States has experienced steady growth, and the number in Brazil, for example, shows an extraordinary growth rate of almost 50 percent (GRI 2011).

The guidelines themselves are being continuously developed, and the Fourth Generation (G4) is slated for publication in 2013. Furthermore, so-called National Annexes are planned. As with the sector supplements, which are also being extended, National Annexes do not substitute for the reports but are used in addition to them and include specific country or regional issues or circumstances.

Anna GROBECKER and Julia WOLF
EBS Business School

See also Agenda 21; Business Reporting Methods; Challenges to Measuring Sustainability; Cost-Benefit Analysis; Human Development Index; Intergovernmental Science-Policy Platform on Biodiversity and Ecosystem Services (IPBES); International Organization for Standardization (ISO); Millennium Development Goals; National Environmental Accounting; Quantitative vs. Qualitative Studies; Reducing Emissions from Deforestation and Forest Degradation (REDD); Triple Bottom Line

FURTHER READING

Brown, Halina Szejnwald; de Jong, Martin; & Lessidrenska, Teodorina. (2007). The rise of the Global Reporting Initiative (GRI) as a case of institutional entrepreneurship (Corporate Social Responsibility Initiative, Working Paper No. 36). Cambridge, MA: John F. Kennedy School of Government, Harvard University.

Global Reporting Initiative (GRI). (n.d.). Homepage. Retrieved August 12, 2011, from http://www.globalreporting.org/

Global Reporting Initiative (GRI). (2007). Sustainability reporting 10 years on. Retrieved September 14, 2011, from http://www.globalreporting.org/NR/rdonlyres/430EBB4E-9AAD-4CA1-9478-FBE7862F5C23/0/Sustainability_Reporting_10years.pdf

Global Reporting Initiative (GRI). (2011). GRI sustainability reporting statistics: Publication year 2010. Retrieved September 14, 2011, from http://www.globalreporting.org/NR/rdonlyres/954C01F1-9439-468F-B8C2-B85F67560FA1/0/GRIReportingStats.pdf

Hartmann, Lauren, & Painter-Morland, Mollie. (2007). Exploring the global reporting initiative guidelines as a model for triple bottom-line reporting. *African Journal of Business Ethics, 2*(1), 45–57.

Kolk, Ans. (2004). A decade of sustainability reporting: Developments and significance. *International Journal Environment and Sustainable Development, 3*(1), 51–64.

Moneva, José M.; Archel, Pablo; & Corea, Carmen. (2006). GRI and the camouflaging of corporate unsustainability. *Accounting Forum, 30*(2), 121–137.

Sherman, W. Richard, & DiGuilio, Lauren. (2010). The second round of G3 reports: Is triple bottom line reporting becoming more comparable? *Journal of Business and Economics Research, 8*(9), 59–77.

Willis, Alan. (2003). The role of the Global Reporting Initiative's sustainability reporting guidelines in the social screening of investments. *Journal of Business Ethics, 43*(3), 233–237.

Global Strategy for Plant Conservation

The Global Strategy for Plant Conservation is recognized as a major step forward for universal plant conservation. Ratified in 2002 and implemented within the framework of the Convention on Biological Diversity, it acknowledges the importance of plants and the ecosystem services they provide for all life on Earth, provides a framework of sixteen measurable actions for all organizational levels, and promotes collaboration and networking.

When the Convention on Biological Diversity (CBD), an international treaty to sustain the diversity of life on Earth, came into effect in 1993, it was considered an important moment for nature conservation. A global consensus had been reached that biodiversity, the variety of life on Earth, mattered. But how was the implementation of this convention to be measured? How would people know if biodiversity conservation was actually occurring? Would that conservation effort be adequate to sustain life on Earth? In reality there were no internationally agreed measures with which to determine global effectiveness at conserving biodiversity. In fact indicators used by some nations subsequently showed that biodiversity declines continued unabated, long after the CBD was ratified and even in some of the world's most biologically diverse regions. As far as plants were concerned, by the year 2000 the planet was thought to be on the brink of a global crisis (Myers et al. 2000; Pimm and Raven 2000).

Origins of a Global Strategy

A global plant strategy, endorsed by the world's governments as part of their commitment to the CBD, may not appear to be an obvious mechanism to avert this global

plant conservation crisis or to monitor the effectiveness of conservation action. Yet that is exactly the route taken. A global strategy was first proposed at the XVI International Botanical Congress in St. Louis, Missouri, in August 1999. Thousands of botanists from more than one hundred countries adopted a resolution calling for an international strategy for plant conservation. In April 2000, Botanic Gardens Conservation International (BGCI), an international membership organization that is focused on the worldwide conservation of threatened plants, convened a follow-up meeting of botanists and plant conservation organizations. They issued the landmark Gran Canaria Declaration that called for a new and innovative global strategy to address the loss of plant diversity and to be implemented within the framework of the CBD (Wyse-Jackson and Kennedy 2009).

In 2002 the Global Strategy for Plant Conservation (GSPC) was ratified by 187 nations and sought to halt the continuing loss of plant diversity through sixteen measurable targets (CBD 2002). It also intended for human activities to support the diversity of plant life while ensuring prosperity for the civilizations it supported. Development of the GSPC meant governments and nongovernmental agencies had, for the first time, measureable and time-bound biodiversity targets, albeit for only one element of biodiversity: plants.

Importance of Plant Life

A key justification for the development of a global strategy specifically for plants was the universal acceptance that plants are a vital component of the world's biological diversity and an essential resource for humans and the planet. People use thousands of cultivated plant species for food, medicine, timber, fuel, and fiber. Many wild plants have great economic and cultural importance and potential as future crops, medicines, commodities, or even icons. Plants help maintain ecosystem integrity, provide habitat for animals, and deliver ecosystem services including oxygen production; carbon dioxide sequestration; the creation, stabilization, and protection of soils; the creation and protection of watersheds; flood attenuation; and the promotion of water infiltration and purification. This human dependence on plants is likely to increase as humans tackle the emerging challenge of global environmental changes including habitat modification and climate change.

Strategy Objectives and Targets

The GSPC had five major objectives that, in the first iteration of the strategy, were to be achieved by 2010:

- Objective I: Plant diversity is well understood, documented, and recognized.
- Objective II: Plant diversity is urgently and effectively conserved.

- Objective III: Plant diversity is used in a sustainable and equitable manner.
- Objective IV: Education and awareness about plant diversity, its role in sustainable livelihoods, and its importance to all life on Earth is promoted.
- Objective V: The capacities and public engagement necessary to implement the strategy have been developed.

Sixteen targets were developed to address these objectives. They were developed to guide and measure a country's ability to conserve threatened species and ecosystems, to guide policy, to set priorities for implementation, and to provide for sustainable cultural use of plants. They were designed to be "SMART" targets (which meant they would be specific, measurable, attainable, relevant, and time-bound) and were considered by many to be largely aspirational. They covered every aspect of plant conservation including conservation status assessments, networking, training, education, and in situ and ex situ (such as seed banks). (See table 1.)

TABLE 1. Global Strategy for Plant Conservation Targets, 2011–2020

Objective	Target	Measurement and Progress
I. Plant diversity is well understood, documented, and recognized	1. An online flora of all known plants	This was a clear target, albeit ambitious and one that is an open-ended, ongoing process rather than having a defined endpoint (Callmander, Schatz, and Lowry 2005). Regular assessments of the current number of plant species worldwide are critical for achieving this target and fundamental to plant conservation. Online working lists are available for more than 50 percent of all flowering plants (Paton et al. 2008).
	2. An assessment of the conservation status of all known plant species, as far as possible, to guide conservation action	Globally, more than 60,000 species have been evaluated for conservation status according to internationally accepted IUCN Red List criteria. Of these, 34,000 are classified as globally threatened with extinction. In some countries the IUCN's Red List criteria are not used, and so comparison of data between countries and collation of data worldwide is not possible. For vascular plants there is a better understanding of the patterns and extent of threat and therefore which species are most in need of recovery.
	3. Information, research and associated outputs, and methods necessary to implement the strategy developed and shared	This target does not provide a quantitative measure with which to measure against. For that reason those undertaking research and developing tools to implement that strategy merely have to continue to develop and share them. Further work is required to create a measurable indicator with which to monitor this target's implementation.

(*continued*)

Table 1. *Continued*

Objective	Target	Measurement and Progress
II. Plant diversity is urgently and effectively conserved	4. At least 15 percent of each ecological region or vegetation type secured through effective management and/or restoration	In general, forests and mountain areas are well represented in protected areas worldwide, while natural grasslands (such as prairies) and coastal, wetland, and estuarine ecosystems (including mangroves) are poorly represented. This target focuses attention on increasing the representation of different ecological regions in protected areas and achieving greater effectiveness of protection for them.
	5. At least 75 percent of the most important areas for plant diversity of each ecological region protected, with effective management in place for conserving plants and their genetic diversity	The most important areas of plant diversity can be identified by criteria such as endemism, species richness, uniqueness of habitats, presence of relict ecosystems, and the value of ecosystems services. Measurement within countries of this target is achievable, although consistent application of criteria for determining importance may differ between countries.
	6. At least 75 percent of production lands in each sector managed sustainably, consistent with the conservation of plant diversity	This target focuses on conservation of plant diversity that is integral to the production system itself (e.g., crop, pasture, or tree species). It also suggests the importance of protection of other indigenous plant species and ecological assemblages in the production landscape that are unique, threatened, or of particular socioeconomic value. Finally, the use of management practices that avoid significant adverse impacts on plant diversity in surrounding ecosystems is implied, for example, avoiding excessive release of agrochemicals and preventing unsustainable soil erosion. Worldwide there is increasing interest in integrated production methods in agriculture and forestry and on-farm management of plant genetic resources, although progress to achieve this target has been somewhat limited.
	7. At least 75 percent of known threatened plant species conserved in situ	This target provides a measurable step toward effective in situ conservation of all threatened species. Interpretation of the target does cause problems as "conservation in situ" can mean conserving one population out of many, or it can mean a single individual. Alternatively it may imply that the most significant genetic variation in the species is conserved.
	8. At least 75 percent of threatened plant species in ex situ collections, preferably in the country of origin, and at least 20 percent available for recovery and restoration programs	A clear target that has seen considerable progress mainly through a global network of seed banks, many of them in partnership with the Millennium Seed Bank in the United Kingdom. This has increased attention on the need for greater commitment to ex situ management of threatened plant species worldwide.

	9. 70 percent of the genetic diversity of crops including their wild relatives and other socioeconomically valuable plant species conserved, while respecting, preserving, and maintaining associated indigenous and local knowledge.	This requires that the genetic diversity of economically valuable plant species and their wild relatives are fully protected. This target will require much greater intersectoral cooperation.
	10. Effective management plans in place to prevent new biological invasions and to manage important areas for plant diversity that are invaded	This is a good quantitative target whose achievement can be monitored. Many alien species that threaten wild plant species and ecosystems are already subject to management in some parts of the world. Existing programs (such as weed control and biosecurity) are well developed in some countries (e.g., Chile, Australia, and New Zealand) and in some cases already subject to national strategies.
III. **Plant diversity is used in a sustainable and equitable manner**	11. No species of wild flora endangered by international trade	This is a clear, measurable target that will require continued vigilance over international trade in endangered plant species and monitoring of plant trade insofar as they relate to the Convention on International Trade in Endangered Species (CITES).
	12. All wild-harvested plant-based products sourced sustainably	Sustained management integrates social and environmental considerations, such as the fair and equitable sharing of benefits and the participation of indigenous and local communities. Global future markets may require more evidence and certification relating to export production, and this will include strong nature conservation and ecological sustainability criteria. How industry and producers at the farm and forestry gate will respond to these pressures is an unknown, especially for open-range grazing land. Monitoring and measuring this target will require greater intersectoral cooperation.
	13. Indigenous and local knowledge innovations and practices associated with plant resources maintained or increased, as appropriate, to support customary use, sustainable livelihoods, local food security, and health care	Plant diversity underpins livelihoods, food security, and health care, and this target is consistent with one of the widely agreed-upon international development targets, namely to "ensure that current trends in the loss of environmental resources are effectively reversed." Global measurement of this target has not been well coordinated.

(continued)

TABLE I. *Continued*

Objective	Target	Measurement and Progress
IV. Education and awareness about plant diversity, its role in sustainable livelihoods, and its importance to all life on Earth is pro- moted	14. The importance of plant diversity and the need for its conservation incorporated into communication, education, and public awareness programs	The target was not quantified, so monitoring its implementation was difficult. It is accepted that communication, education, and raising public awareness about the importance of plant diversity are crucial for the achievement of all the targets of the strategy. Not being a quantitative target, this is one that is achievable within the short term, but the spirit behind the target is much more ambitious.
V. The capacities and public engagement necessary to implement the strategy have been developed	15. Sufficient num- ber of trained people working with appropriate facilities (according to national needs) to achieve the targets of this strategy	This is a clear, measurable target. It is achievable through growth of national coordinating bodies such as national plant conserva- tion networks, botanic gardens, and governments that develop and implement training and development programs for volun- teers and community.
	16. Institutions, networks, and partnerships for plant conservation established or strengthened at national, regional, and international levels to achieve the targets of this strategy	Networks allow information exchange, development of common policies, coordination of effort among stakeholders, and can minimize duplication by optimizing efficient allocation of resources. There has been considerable progress with the establishment of national networks and partnerships. National and regional networks have been established worldwide, such as the Australian and New Zealand Plant Conservation Networks. Canada's botanical gardens formed the Canadian Botanical Conservation Network (CBCN) in 1995. Planta Europa is a Europe-wide network of independent organiza- tions, nongovernmental and governmental, working together to conserve European wild plants and fungi. Further world- wide network collaboration will be required to implement this target.

Source: author.

Application of the Global Strategy

The GSPC targets focused attention on priority con- servation activities to halt declines in the world's plant life. For that reason alone they were regarded as a major step forward for plant conservation worldwide. The mere existence of the targets meant that greater prog- ress was made than would have been had they never been adopted. In fact, the GSPC played a significant catalytic role in stimulating new programs and initia- tives worldwide and did result in many significant achievements.

Achievements

Ratification of the GSPC was the first time a series of internationally agreed, measurable targets had been devel- oped for biodiversity conservation under the CBD. For that reason the strategy was recognized as an innovative approach to target setting for the CBD, a model that could be used in other areas of biodiversity conservation.

The GSPC targets have since proved to be a useful reference point for monitoring progress and have helped rally public opinion behind priority conservation issues. A high level of commonality, at a broad program level, between the GSPC and many governmental conservation programs made implementation easier. The targets also stimulated new synergies and cooperation between multiple sectors. The GSPC was used as the basis for public awareness campaigns and as a lever to gain greater support for plant conservation from business partners and associates. In this way, increased pressure was exerted on those implementing the strategy, especially by nongovernmental organizations (NGOs). The GSPC stimulated the development of new projects and initiatives and the mobilization of resources for implementation of its targets. In general the GSPC was successful in stimulating the engagement of the botanical and plant conservation communities in the work of the convention through, most particularly, the establishment of national, regional, and global networks and increasing communication and collaboration. Implementation of the GSPC has seen considerable progress for eight of the sixteen targets. (See table 1 on pages 169–172.)

Limitations

The GSPC had several limitations. For example, no target was fully achieved by 2010, and most countries only recorded variable successes with many targets. Implementation of the strategy was not mandatory, and there were no penalties for failure to achieve the targets (except further erosion of the world's plant life). For that reason commitment from signatory countries was patchy.

Governments often saw the targets as aspirational rather than a statement of intent, and consequently, governments fell short in implementing several targets. In fact, some governments worked to limit liabilities and impacts on their existing programs. This was likely due to two main factors: firstly, the additional resourcing required; secondly, governments were wary of signing up to target commitments that did not align with existing in-country commitments.

In some cases the in-country leading role was unclear; in other cases the focus of government agencies was not aligned with the GSPC. Global coordination was limited until the 2004 development of the Global Partnership for Plant Conservation (GPPC) as a mechanism for coordinating work to achieve the targets. The GPPC was a consortium of international, regional, and national organizations that contributed to implementation of the strategy targets. Even after that responsibility for implementation largely fell to individual countries. There was also a lack of clarity over roles and responsibilities for implementing targets. For example, calls were made to implement the ambitious Target 2—a preliminary assessment of the conservation status of all plants—but it was never clear who should implement this or coordinate implementation (Callmander, Schatz, and Lowry 2005).

Limited progress was made on some targets, especially those where intersectoral cooperation was essential, including Target 2 (completion of preliminary conservation assessments), Target 4 (ecological regions conserved), Target 6 (conservation of biodiversity in production lands), Target 12 (sustainable use of plant-based products), and Target 15 (capacity and training for plant conservation) (CBD Secretariat and GPPC 2009).

For the first few years there was limited reporting about how well the strategy was being implemented. In addition, the scope of the targets and the development of subtargets and milestones for each target were not clarified. The GSPC would have benefited from development of national targets and regional components. A further problem was the limited baseline data in some parts of the world and few indicators to monitor progress toward achieving the targets. Baseline data and better indictors would have helped to monitor a country's effectiveness at achieving targets.

Monitoring Implementation of the Strategy

The GSPC was developed to have well-defined and achievable goals for integrated (ex situ and in situ) conservation of plant diversity, linked to targets for research, information management, public education, and awareness. Implementation of the strategy was monitored through the following four main methods.

Regular Reporting

The primary mechanism for monitoring implementation of the GSPC was through reports that were provided regularly by 190-plus parties to the CBD, which described the extent to which GSPC targets had been implemented. These reports are stored on the website of the CBD and provide summaries of work done by each country. These were high-level reports that were light on detail. Furthermore, no auditing was ever done in-country to assess their accuracy.

Global Partnership for Plant Conservation

Another primary mechanism used to help implementation of the GSPC, and thereby monitor and promote its effectiveness, was the Global Partnership for Plant Conservation (GPPC).

The GPPC was formed in 2004 and has since worked to support national implementation of the GSPC and provide tools and resources to help countries plan and act to achieve the targets. The partnership was included by the Convention on Biological Diversity as part of the flexible coordination mechanism of the GSPC and has played a role in monitoring and promoting its implementation. There are no formal reporting requirements for members of the partnership, but participating organizations are encouraged to provide relevant information regularly, especially existing or planned activities relevant to GSPC implementation.

National and Regional Strategies

Many countries published national strategies or responses to the GSPC, including South Africa, Mexico, Costa Rica, Ireland, Malaysia, United Kingdom, Seychelles, and Japan, among others. These national strategies provided a mechanism for countries to report on their implementation of the GSPC. For example, a national plant-conservation strategy in Ireland includes targets, actions, milestones, and indicators for Ireland to fulfill its obligations under the GSPC (National Botanic Gardens of Ireland 2005). In New Zealand an action plan was written based on plant conservation workshops held in 2003 (NZPCN 2003). Regional approaches to implementing the GSPC included the European Plant Conservation Strategy prepared by the Planta Europa Secretariat and the Council of Europe (Planta Europa Network 2008). In many parts of the world, however, no strategy was prepared, thereby limiting their ability to report on target implementation.

Progress Reviews

The *Plant Conservation Report* was a review of progress with implementation of the GSPC worldwide published in 2009. It was prepared by the Secretariat of the Convention on Biological Diversity in conjunction with the Global Partnership for Plant Conservation (CBD Secretariat and GPPC 2009). Regional reviews were also prepared. For example, the *First Asian Plant Conservation Report* was published in 2010 and outlines progress on plant conservation in Asia in fulfilling the targets of the GSPC (Ma et al. 2010). Scientific reviews of progress with some targets were also prepared. For example, a review of progress with global implementation of Target 1 (to prepare an accessible working list of all known plants) was completed in 2008 (Paton et al. 2008).

Where Next for the GSPC?

The GSPC highlighted the importance of plants and the ecosystem services they provide for all life on Earth. It provided a framework for actions at global, regional, national, and local levels and promoted collaboration and networking. It also recognized that effective, enduring conservation required a wide range of partners including governments, institutions, NGOs, and local communities.

Many countries implemented the GSPC through specific plant conservation activities, action plans, and national strategies as well as informally through existing biodiversity management programs. No government achieved all the GSPC targets by 2010, however.

This resulted in a renewed commitment to a revised strategy by the CBD at its Tenth Conference of the Parties in Nagoya, Japan, in 2010. The time frame for implementation was extended to 2020, perhaps recognizing the boldness of the initial 2010 date. Some have remained skeptical over whether the revised targets are achievable without substantial additional resourcing. The renewal was intended to sustain the momentum that the previous decade had generated and to keep the global plant conservation program focused on priority targets.

The GSPC provided a solid foundation for measuring plant conservation progress worldwide. Since its adoption, it has been implemented through an impressive combination of local, national, and international initiatives. Implementation has demonstrated the importance of diverse networks, collaborations, and the critical role played by cross-sectoral partnerships within the context of the Convention on Biological Diversity.

John William David SAWYER
Department of Conservation, New Zealand

See also Biological Indicators (*several articles*); Community and Stakeholder Input; Environmental Performance Index (EPI); Genuine Progress Indicators (GPI); Global

Environment Outlook (GEO) Reports; Intergovernmental Science-Policy Platform on Biodiversity and Ecosystem Services (IPBES); Reducing Emissions from Deforestation and Forest Degradation (REDD); Species Barcoding

FURTHER READING

Callmander, Martin W.; Schatz, George E.; & Lowry, Porter P. (2005, November). IUCN Red List assessment and the Global Strategy for Plant Conservation: Taxonomists must act now. *Taxon, 54*(4), 1047–1050.

CBD Secretariat & the Global Partnership for Plant Conservation (GPPC). (2009). *Plant conservation report: A review of progress in implementing the Global Strategy for Plant Conservation (GSPC).* Montreal: Secretariat of the Convention on Biological Diversity.

Convention on Biological Diversity (CBD). (2002, February 20). Global strategy for plant conservation of the Convention on Biological Diversity: Technical review of the targets and analysis of opportunities for their implementation (Paper UNEP/CBD/COP/6/12/Add.4). Retrieved June 28, 2011, from http://www.cbd.int/doc/meetings/cop/cop-06/official/cop-06-12-add4-en.pdf

Ma Keping, et al. (2010). *The first Asian plant conservation report: A review of progress in implementing the Global Strategy for Plant Conservation.* Beijing: Chinese National Committee for DIVERSITAS.

Myers, Norman; Mittermeier, Russel A.; Mittermeier, Cristina G.; da Fonseca, Gustavo A. B.; & Kent, Jennifer. (2000). Biodiversity hotspots for conservation priorities. *Nature, 403,* 853–858.

National Botanic Gardens of Ireland. (2005). *A national plant conservation strategy for Ireland.* Dublin: National Botanic Gardens of Ireland.

New Zealand Plant Conservation Network (NZPCN). (2003). *Global Strategy for Plant Conservation workshops: Summary report.* Wellington: New Zealand Plant Conservation Network.

Paton, Alan J.; et al. (2008). Target 1 of the Global Strategy for Plant Conservation: A working list of all known plant species—progress and prospects. *Taxon, 57*(2), 602–611.

Pimm, Stuart L., & Raven, Peter. (2000, February 24). Biodiversity: Extinction by numbers. *Nature, 403, 843–845.*

Planta Europa Network & Council of Europe. (2008). *A sustainable future for Europe: The European strategy for plant conservation 2008–2014.* Salisbury, UK: Planta Europa.

Wyse-Jackson, Peter, & Kennedy, Kathryn. (2009). The Global Strategy for Plant Conservation: A challenge and opportunity for the international community. *Trends in Plant Science, 14*(11), 578–580.

Gross Domestic Product, Green

Green gross domestic product incorporates the value of natural and social capital into calculations of the size of an economic system. A growing number of indices have been developed to measure this effect, but no one approach has been generally accepted and used consistently in an international setting. Many of these indices demonstrate that widespread environmental damage significantly offsets economic growth.

Gross domestic product (GDP) is a familiar economic index used to track the change in productivity of an economy from quarter to quarter or year to year. The index is an aggregation of productivity measures in many different sectors, such as natural resources, agriculture, manufacturing, and finance, and is restricted to those sectors and activities that are traded in markets. The use of GDP as an index of the health of an economy, or the welfare provided by it, has been generally called into question, commonly over two objections (Kulig, Kolfoort, and Hoekstra 2010). First, activities such as unpaid domestic work, volunteer work for the community, or other productive endeavors outside of markets are not taken into account, even though they may be centrally important to the productivity of households and communities. Second, of those activities that are included in GDP, all of them are treated as positive (that is, if they increase, they increase GDP), even if they affect productivity negatively in some sectors, and even though the society may consider these activities to be harmful or undesirable.

For example, in 2010 a catastrophe on an oil-drilling rig in the Gulf of Mexico resulted in the release of almost 5 million barrels of crude oil, along with 2 million gallons (7,600 cubic meters) of chemical dispersants (Khan 2010). The massive oil spill destroyed thousands of jobs in the fishing and tourism industries, and therefore reduced productivity in those sectors and decreased GDP. The spill, however, created numerous jobs related to the cleanup efforts, adding to GDP. Although the economic value of the fishing and tourism jobs lost is measurable (through unemployment claims), the values of the fish population, clean beaches, and unpolluted groundwater are not realized in traditional markets. Because there is no mechanism to subtract these losses from GDP, the true impact of the 2010 oil spill was not fully accounted for in the 2010 GDP estimate.

In response to the inability of GDP to account for the impact of environmental damage on long-term economic productivity (such as the loss of forests, fish populations, or clean water for future use), environmental economists have devised several different measures of "green GDP" that would bring these nonmarket values of ecosystem goods and services into the GDP accounting methodology. Ecosystem goods and services are tangible goods (such as food, fiber, and fuel) and intangible services (such as the protection of the atmosphere and filtering of fresh water) that are necessary to societies provided by healthy ecosystems. Although there are efforts underway to try to measure the natural capital, the economic value of these goods and services (Kareiva et al. 2011), many of them still exist outside of markets and are therefore not included in economic assessments of capital or productivity. Social scientists have also developed several indices that aim to incorporate social welfare issues into GDP measures, although the importance of characteristics such as happiness, freedom, good governance, and tolerance can be more difficult to quantify (Kulig, Kolfoort, and Hoekstra 2010).

Green GDP Indices

Efforts to include environmental damages (and therefore loss of natural capital) into the measurement of economic systems were spearheaded in the 1950s by Paul

Samuelson, the first US economist to win a Nobel Prize, and later with the US economist William Nordhaus. They defined environmental amenities such as clean air as "public goods," those that are often damaged or destroyed without proper compensation because their value is not typically captured in economic markets (Samuelson and Nordhaus 1995). Nordhaus (along with the US economist James Tobin) realized that GDP was only intended to measure the size of an economic system, not the welfare produced by it, and so they developed a measure of economic welfare (MEW) that tried to adjust GDP to consider welfare issues (Nordhaus and Tobin 1973).

Later, the US ecological economist Herman Daly developed the concept of uneconomic growth, which is economic activity or productivity that results in a decline in welfare or quality of life; environmental degradation and loss of natural capital are considered losses in current or future potential welfare. Daly questioned the physical possibility of an unlimited expansion of economic systems, as indicated by continuously increasing GDP (Daly 2005). Instead, he maintained that a useful GDP index should measure the development or qualitative improvement of economic conditions, which are not necessarily related to economic expansion and, in fact, may be damaged by it.

In response to these concerns, a variety of green GDP indices have been developed (Kulig, Kolfoort, and Hoekstra 2010). These indices make two adjustments: natural capital is given value and internalized into the accounting system; and economic system expansion is not required for the index to increase. Several of these indices have received more notice than others either due to the fame of the developer (Index of Sustainable Economic Welfare, Sustainable Net National Product), or to their ease of use for real economies (Genuine Savings Index, Sustainable National Income, Ecological Footprint Index).

Index of Sustainable Economic Welfare/Genuine Progress Indicator

Daly and Cobb (1989) modified Nordhaus and Tobin's MEW and renamed it first the Index of Sustainable Economic Welfare and later the Genuine Progress Indicator. (Around this time, Daly also proposed a Sustainable Net National Product). All of these indices use personal expenditure indicators that are adjusted for inequality in income and labor distribution; as wealthy people receive less welfare from an additional unit consumed than a poor person would, higher inequality results in lower overall welfare than the same level of consumption in a more equal society. Defense expenditures (actions that must be taken in

response to environmental damage, such as additional water filtration for degraded water supplies) and natural capital losses are then subtracted from these adjusted personal expenditures.

Genuine Savings Index

The Genuine Savings Index was a methodology developed by the World Bank to adjust net national income for environmental damage and depreciation of both human and natural capital (Hueting and Reijnders 2004). The index explicitly includes damages that result from carbon dioxide emissions (climate change), but otherwise it closely follows the United Nations' System of Integrated Environmental and Economic Accounting methodologies, allowing for consistent comparisons across countries.

Sustainable National Income

Headed by the Dutch economist Roefie Hueting, the Sustainable National Income index has been developed and modified by a multidisciplinary team at Statistics Netherlands (Hueting and Reijnders 2004). Unlike the other indices described here, Sustainable National Income uses a general equilibrium model to determine the income effects of matching consumption rates to available natural capital, and therefore a sustainable level of production (Gerlagh et al. 2002). In other words, the maximum size of the economy is determined by environmental constraints.

Ecological Footprint Index

Although this index has not been explicitly developed and advanced as a green GDP index, it functions in much the same way; it is a measure of the degree to which consumption is depleting available domestic supplies of natural capital (Rees 1992; Wackernagel et al. 2002). Developed and modified by the Canadian ecologist William Rees and the Swiss researcher Mathis Wackernagel, the index converts all resources available and consumed into hectare units, and then determines if the footprint of that nation is larger or smaller than the nation's biocapacity (or sometimes the world's biocapacity). The footprint is essentially the size of the economic system from the perspective of natural capital. A 2010 report by the World Wildlife Organization calculated that two Earths would be needed by 2030 to supply the ecosystem goods and services at current and projected rates of consumption (World Wildlife Fund 2010).

Present-Day Use

Although a few of these indices have been developed by international or national organizations, most of the continuous work of developing, updating, and measuring these indices has been performed by academic and professional researchers. In the few cases in which a national government has undertaken an analysis of green GDP, political pressure has prevented the analyses from continuing beyond a year or two.

US Integrated Environmental and Economic Analysis

In 1993, the US Department of Commerce's Bureau of Economic Analysis (BEA) developed an environmental accounting system called the "integrated environmental and economic analysis," with the intent to better understand the positive and negative impacts of extractive sectors (such as minerals mining) on the national economy (BEA 1994). At that time, there were plans to extend these efforts to other sectors (such as renewable natural resources) and environmental assets, but these efforts were never completed. These analyses would have formed an essential foundation for measuring the annual green GDP of the United States. In 1994, however, the US Congress ordered the BEA to cease the program until the approach could be reviewed by a panel of scientists (Nordhaus and Kokkelenberg 1999). Although the panel determined that the accounting practice would be an "important goal" and should be a "high priority for the nation," the efforts were not resumed (Irwin and Bruch 2002).

European Union

The European Union (EU) has several initiatives to increase the use of green GDP indices (not necessarily those described above) throughout the EU and in member countries. These initiatives include the GREENed National STAtistical and Modeling Procedures (GREENSTAMP) and the Green Accounting Research Project within the Eurostat agency (Lange 2003). The EU has also developed a common strategy for sustainable development policy that accesses a database of sustainable development indicators managed by the Statistical Agency of the EU, Eurostat (Kulig, Kolfoort, and Hoekstra 2010).

The Netherlands

While not an official government study, Reyer Gerlagh and his academic colleagues used the Sustainable National Income method to retroactively examine the sustainability of the Dutch economy in 1990. They found that, while the Dutch economy was sustainable (assuming that all trading partners with the Netherlands operate under similar sustainability policies, an arguably tenuous assumption), the most costly environmental problems were those related to climate change (Gerlagh et al. 2002).

China

Stemming from a directive from Chinese premier Wen Jiabao in 2004, the Chinese government began to calculate and report green GDP along with traditional GDP. The first accounting showed that environmental damage had caused economic losses equivalent to about 3 percent of the nation's traditional GDP (Sun 2007). In some provinces, economic growth was eclipsed by the costs of resulting environmental damages. The green GDP accounting program ended in 2007 under political pressure.

International Consistency

While several international organizations (such as Eurostat, the Organisation for Economic Co-operation and Development, the World Bank, and the United Nations) have developed databases and indicator sets that could be used to consistently calculate green GDP annually and across countries (Kulig, Kolfoort, and Hoekstra 2010), no international treaties, policies, or programs currently call for the calculation of any one index, making international comparisons over time very difficult. Furthermore, the use of multiple green GDP methodologies with substantially different assumptions (especially about the degree to which it measures welfare) makes their use for decision making and policy prescriptions problematic at best. Although there have been repeated calls for greater standardization in data collection, inclusion calculation, and use of green GDP indices, none of these calls has been heeded by international organizations, agreements, or treaties.

Audrey L. MAYER
Michigan Technological University

See also Agenda 21; Business Reporting Methods; Ecolabels; Ecological Footprint Accounting; Environmental Performance Index (EPI); Global Environment Outlook (GEO) Reports; Global Reporting Initiative (GRI); Gross National Happiness; Intergovernmental Science-Policy Platform on Biodiversity and Ecosystem Services (IPBES); International Organization for Standardization (ISO); Millennium Development Goals; National Environmental Accounting; Taxation Indicators, Green; Triple Bottom Line

FURTHER READING

Bureau of Economic Analysis (BEA). (1994). Integrated economic and environmental satellite accounts. Retrieved July 7, 2011, from http://www.bea.gov/scb/account_articles/national/0494od/maintext.htm

Daly, Herman E. (1996). *Beyond growth: The economics of sustainable development.* Boston: Beacon Press.

Daly, Herman E. (2005.) Economics in a full world. *Scientific American, 293*(3), 100–107.

Daly, Herman E., & Cobb, J. B. (Eds.). (1989). *For the common good.* Boston: Beacon Press.

Gerlagh, Reyer; Dellink, Rob; Hofkes, Marjan; & Verbruggen, Harmen. (2002). A measure of sustainable national income for the Netherlands. *Ecological Economics, 41,*157–174.

Hueting, Roefie, & Reijnders, Lucas. (2004). Broad sustainability contra sustainability: The proper construction of sustainability indicators. *Ecological Economics, 50,* 249–260.

Irwin, Frances, & Bruch, Carl. (2002). Public access to information, participation, and justice. In John C. Dernbach (Ed.), *Stumbling toward sustainability* (pp. 511–540). Washington, DC: Environmental Law Institute.

Kareiva, Peter; Tallis, Heather; Ricketts, Taylor H.; Daily, Gretchen C.; & Polasky, Stephen (Eds.). (2011). *Natural capital: Theory and practice of mapping ecosystem services.* Oxford, UK: Oxford University Press.

Khan, Amina (2010, September 4). Gulf oil spill: Effects of dispersants remain a mystery. Retrieved July 11, 2011, from http://www.latimes.com/news/science/la-sci-dispersants-20100905,0,6506539.story

Kulig, Anna; Kolfoort, Hans; & Hoekstra, Rutger. (2010). The case for the hybrid capital approach for the measurement of the welfare and sustainability. *Ecological Indicators, 10,* 118–128.

Lange, Glenn-Marie. (2003). Policy applications of environmental accounting (Environmental Economics Series, Paper No. 88). Retrieved July 7, 2011, from: http://siteresources.worldbank.org/INTEEI/214574-1115814938538/20486189/PolicyApplicationsofEnvironmentalAccounting2003.pdf

Nordhaus, William D., & Tobin, James. (1973.) Is growth obsolete? Retrieved July 7, 2011, from http://cowles.econ.yale.edu/P/cp/p03b/p0398ab.pdf

Nordhaus, William D., & Kokkelenberg, Edward C. (Eds.). (1999). *Nature's numbers: Expanding the national economic accounts to include the environment.* Washington, DC: National Academy Press.

Rees, William E. (1992). Ecological footprints and appropriated carrying capacity: What urban economics leaves out. *Environment and Urbanization, 4,* 121–130.

Samuelson, Paul A., & Nordhaus, William D. (1995). *Economics* (15th ed.). New York: McGraw-Hill.

Sun Xiaohua. (2007, April 19). Call for return to green accounting. Retrieved July 7, 2011, from http://www.chinadaily.com.cn/china/2007-04/19/content_853917.htm

Wackernagel, Mathis, et al. (2002). Tracking the ecological overshoot of the human economy. *Proceedings of the National Academy of Sciences USA, 99,* 9266–9271.

World Wildlife Fund. (2010). *Living planet report 2010: Biodiversity, biocapacity and development.* Retrieved July 11, 2011, from http://www.footprintnetwork.org/press/LPR2010.pdf

Gross National Happiness

The Himalayan nation of Bhutan has been a leader in devising and promoting an alternative development paradigm called gross national happiness. The king's statement "Gross National Happiness is more important than Gross National Product" arose from Buddhism, which recognizes the transitory nature of material satisfactions. This view, together with the findings of positive psychology, is encouraging Western nations to measure the full spectrum of human well-being.

In 1972, the fourth king of the Himalayan nation of Bhutan, King Jigme Singye Wangchuk, proclaimed, "Gross National Happiness is more important than Gross National Product"—a statement that challenged prevailing economic development theories around the world.

The proclamation was especially bold because tiny, mountainous Bhutan, wedged between India and China, was—at that time—one of the world's least-developed and most-isolated nations. Even today, it is among the least-developed countries in the world, according to the Office of the High Representative for Least Developed Countries, Landlocked Developing Countries and Small Island Developing States (OHRLLS) at the United Nations (UN DESA and OHRLLS 2011). Extreme topography and self-imposed isolationism kept Bhutan cut off from most visitors from beyond the Himalayan region until 1974, when foreign dignitaries arrived for the king's coronation. In the 1970s, more than 90 percent of Bhutan's populace lived in rural areas. Fewer than 1,200 kilometers of roads facilitated movement about the country. Villagers eked out subsistence livelihoods on the steep hillsides, without electricity, running water, or mechanized means of tilling their fields. How could a nation that sorely needed infrastructure and economic

development decide to put something as ephemeral as happiness first?

The king's statement signaled that Bhutan's development process would grow out of its own cultural context, including its ancient Vajrayana Buddhist traditions, rather than being imposed by foreign experts. Development would need to support the Buddhist quest for enlightenment for the good of all sentient beings—a quest associated with the development of enduring equanimity, compassion, and spiritual inspiration at the individual and collective levels.

Buddhist Roots

In articulating gross national happiness (GNH), the king drew on Bhutan's deep well of compassion for and nonviolence toward all sentient beings, based in its 1,200-year history of Buddhism. His statement connected with previous policies, also grounded in Buddhism. A 1675 Buddhist equivalent of a social contract declared that happiness of all sentient beings and the teachings of the Buddha are mutually dependent. In 1729, a Bhutanese legal code required that laws promote happiness of sentient beings.

Among the tenets of Buddhism are the ideas that all beings want to be happy, and that, while life is full of suffering, the cessation of suffering through guidance, practice, and attention is possible, leading to the achievement of enlightenment. Interdependent co-arising—the concept that there are no independently existing causes, identities, or egos—creates the impetus to protect life. The doctrine of karma teaches that one always reaps the benefits or harms of one's actions, which provides further incentive to treat other living beings compassionately and considerately. Within Vajrayana Buddhism, the figure of the bodhisattva (one who attains enlightenment but remains on the earthly plane to assist other sentient beings in their efforts toward enlightenment) is revered, indicating a cultural imperative to generate boundless compassion.

GNH and Gross Domestic Product

During the 1980s and 1990s, the king further elaborated on the concept of GNH as Bhutan's guiding development policy. He criticized standard socioeconomic development indicators for measuring means rather than ends, and indicated that happiness would be the goal of development in Bhutan. The king proclaimed that Bhutanese development would recognize the social, spiritual, and emotional needs, as well as the material needs, of the individual, instead of being based solely on economic measures and consumption. He recast "development" to mean the enlightenment of the individual through the creation a harmonious psychological, social, and economic environment that could lead to the blossoming of happiness. Measuring the country's consumption of goods and services would not reflect the paramount goal of spiritual development.

The king and his advisors further defined GNH as standing on four "pillars": sustainable and equitable socioeconomic development, environmental conservation, preservation and promotion of culture, and good governance, which guided development efforts in the late 1990s and early 2000s. These four pillars make it clear that socioeconomic development represents only one-quarter of the necessary conditions for the promotion of GNH. Economic development, rather than being a central metric for measuring progress, is part of a constellation of metrics.

In articulating this vision, the king and his advisors pointed out a well-recognized difficulty with standard measures of a country's development or success, such as gross domestic product (GDP). This measure reflects the economic value of all production of goods and services in a country during a given period and is typically seen as a proxy for standard of living, such that greater consumption of goods and services implies a higher material standard of living. As the Bhutanese have noted, however, after certain basic material needs are met, greater consumption of material goods does not guarantee greater happiness. Further, as ecological economists point out, the correlation between GDP and standard of living breaks down when a country increases its spending to combat social problems (see, for example, Daly and Cobb 1994; Norgaard 1994; Planning Commission, Royal Government of Bhutan 1999). In that scenario, GDP continues to rise, even as greater shares of resources are used to ameliorate drains on society, such as crime, natural disasters, chemical leaks, epidemics, or drug addiction. The GDP measures also ignore the externalities of industrial production, such as pollution, environmental degradation, and toxic waste, which have negative health and ecological effects over large areas. A more accurate accounting of the costs of production would subtract these social costs and make GDP more meaningful.

Table 1, on the next page, summarizes the primary concepts of GNH compared to established development measurement approaches.

Because GDP measures production, consumption must continually increase in order to raise production rates. Through increasing production, a nation may rapidly deplete its natural resources, which registers as an increase in GDP even as it drives down natural capital, the stock of resources available for the future. GDP thus can have an inverse relationship to GNH: as circumstances get worse, the economic standing of a nation rises. In contrast, GNH is inherently predisposed toward sustainability because it recognizes that material development is not the only valid measure of human progress, and it understands that declining natural resources are a drain rather than a boon to GDP.

GNH and Global Policy

With the introduction of GNH onto the global stage in 1998 at the Millennium Meeting for Asia and the Pacific in Seoul, South Korea, the concept began to gain international currency. *Gross National Happiness*, a book of discussion papers, was published in Bhutan on the occasion of the king's Silver Jubilee in 1999. In 2001, the Centre for Bhutan Studies co-hosted a seminar entitled "GNH—As Challenged by the Concept of Decent Society" in the Netherlands, with which Bhutan has a close aid relationship. In 2002, the South Asian Association for Regional Cooperation (SAARC) planning and economic ministers embraced GNH as a strategy for poverty reduction in southern Asia.

A series of conferences, begun in 2004 in Bhutan, has helped spread awareness of GNH, while supporting the Bhutanese government in creating tools to operationalize and eventually measure GNH. International experts in economics, psychology, policy, and other aspects of development were invited to deliberate on how Bhutan might use its development paradigm to guide international engagement and material improvements in the lives of local people. The conferences also introduced academics and policy experts from around the world to an alternative development paradigm, which many have worked to implement at various scales in their home countries. Conferences on GNH have since been held in

Table 1. Comparison of GNH and Traditional Development Paradigms

	GNH	UN Millennium Development Goals	Traditional Development
Seeks to maximize	Individual and national happiness	Social welfare	Strong economies (as measured by gross national product and gross domestic product)
Needs to be met	Material, spiritual, and emotional	Peace and security, human rights, and sustainable development, primarily through provision of education, health, and equality	Material, through international economic cooperation
Seeks to transform	Individual, within society	Society, global North–South relations	Economies
Success defined as	High level of happiness nationwide	Elimination of poverty, universal primary education, improvement of health indicators	Strong, stable economies, leading to high levels of material well-being
Based in	Buddhism	Humanitarianism	Economics
Societal sectors of concern	Human development, culture and heritage, balanced and equitable development, governance, and environmental conservation	Poverty and hunger, universal primary education, gender equality, health care, children, relation of rich and poor nations	Economy, trade, infrastructure, poverty eradication, employment, official development assistance, debt, global politics
Key institutions	Government of Bhutan, SAARC* nations	United Nations Development Programme and UN member states	World Bank, IMF,** WTO,*** individual national governments
Paradigm propounded	Since 1972	Since 2000	Since 1944

Source: Author

*South Asian Association for Regional Cooperation

**International Monetary Fund

***Word Trade Organization

Canada (2005), Thailand (2007), Bhutan (2008), and Brazil (2009). Bhutan organized a small international conference on Happiness and Economic Development in August 2011, with Bhutanese prime minister Jigme Thinley and Jeffrey Sachs, professor and director of the Earth Institute at Columbia University, as co-hosts.

Having generated global interest in the concept, Bhutanese officials then turned to efforts to incorporate GNH into international planning and policy. In July 2011, after ten months of lobbying by the Bhutanese delegation, the United Nations General Assembly adopted a nonbinding resolution calling on member nations to incorporate happiness into their development objectives. The resolution encourages UN member states to develop their own happiness indicators and contribute them to the UN's development agenda, framed as the Millennium Development Goals. The United Kingdom, one of the sixty-six co-sponsors of the UN resolution, is a leader in the effort to measure happiness and well-being through an initiative of its Office for National Statistics. Preliminary results are expected in July 2012.

Measuring Happiness

The Bhutanese concluded that they would need to measure GNH to ensure its improvement. The Centre for Bhutan Studies, a think tank, devised a series of nine

GNH variables, or "domains," comprising ecology, culture, good governance, education, health, community vitality, time use, psychological well-being, and living standards, each of which is further divided into numerous indicators that include everything from the amount of sleep last night to "frequency of feeling of compassion" and "freedom from discrimination." The indicators were developed from lengthy pilot surveys conducted around the nation in 2006–2007. A second, streamlined survey of 950 respondents was conducted in 2007–2008. Raw data from this survey is available on the website of the Centre for Bhutan Studies (2008a).

With the variables and indicators in place, all new projects and policies must pass muster with the GNH screening tool, developed by the Centre for Bhutan Studies, and the GNH Commission, formerly the Planning Commission of the Bhutanese government. As Bhutan works to implement GNH, other nations and communities have taken up the vision and its offer of an alternative to the unchecked consumption.

International Adoption of GNH Philosophy

Countries around the world, including the United States, have begun experimenting with their own ideas about GNH. While GNH arose from Buddhist roots in Bhutan, it aligns closely with the science of well-being, as well as recent studies of positive psychology and the economics of happiness.

Western European countries have led the international movement toward adopting GNH. In 2009, French president Nicolas Sarkozy announced a plan to make happiness a key indicator of growth, and requested that Nobel Prize–winning economists Joseph Stiglitz and Amartya Sen develop measures to incorporate well-being into national assessments. Following France's lead, British prime minister David Cameron called on economists and policy makers to focus on "GWB," or "general well-being," by polling 200,000 people about the state of their happiness. The results of this poll are scheduled for release in mid-2012.

In the Americas, GPI*Atlantic* of Nova Scotia, Canada, has been a leader since 1997 in identifying new measures of sustainability, well-being, and quality of life—called "genuine progress indicators"—that go beyond the unidimensional measures of GDP. Founder and executive director Ronald Colman attended the first two GNH conferences to advise the Bhutanese on developing GNH indicators.

Growing interest in GNH prompted Brazil to host the fifth GNH conference and establish diplomatic relations with Bhutan in 2009. Brazilian policy makers introduced a bill to amend Brazil's Constitution, making the quest for happiness an inalienable right, in early 2011.

Six residents of the US state of Vermont attended the fourth GNH conference in Bhutan and were inspired to launch Gross National Happiness USA (GNHUSA) in spring 2009. The group's initial work focused on raising awareness of GNH, gathering information, and connecting interested people. To kick off the national movement, GNHUSA held a conference in Vermont entitled "GNH 2010: Changing What We Measure from Wealth to Well-Being."

GNH: Values-Based Development Paradigm

Gross national happiness offers a way to understand national progress that incorporates an ethical function and values the intangible aspects of human life that are much of what provides vitality and well-being. It shifts consciousness away from the continual pursuit of more, bigger, and better—goals that are now well-known to be unsustainable and highly destructive to the surrounding environment—and toward goals that can satisfy human cravings for meaning, connection, value, and worth. In suggesting that happiness is more important than any product, GNH helps us consider what material goods might be enough, and what sufficiency rather than overabundance might mean for our lives, our homes, and our ecosystems.

As sustainability becomes an ever greater concern for citizens, nations, and the planet, GNH provides an important alternative to GDP as a measure of individual and national well-being. With the groundswell of interest in GNH that had built up by the end of the first decade of the twenty-first century, it is likely that more countries and institutions will seek to incorporate the promotion and measurement of happiness into their measures of well-being. The measurement of GNH may even prove to be a tool for sustainability, in that it will reveal the social, psychological, and emotional difficulties that led to unsustainable craving and overconsumption. If these difficulties can be identified and addressed, GNH may lead to a happier and more sustainable world.

Elizabeth ALLISON
California Institute of Integral Studies

See also Community and Stakeholder Input; Development Indicators; Environmental Justice Indicators; Genuine Progress Indicator (GPI); Gross Domestic Product, Green; Human Development Index (HDI); I = P × A × T Equation; *The Limits to Growth;* Millennium Development Goals; National Environmental Accounting; Population Indicators; Social Network Analysis (SNA); Taxation Indicators, Green; Weak vs. Strong Sustainability Debate

FURTHER READING

Acharya, Gopilal. (2004, February 21). Operationalising gross national happiness. Retrieved November 12, 2011, from http://www.kuenselonline.com/modules.php?name=News&file=article&sid=3765

The Earth Institute, Columbia University. (2011). Bhutan conference on gross national happiness, 2011. Retrieved February 13, 2012, from http://www.earth.columbia.edu/bhutan-conference-2011/?id=home

Centre for Bhutan Studies. (1999). *Gross national happiness.* Thimphu, Bhutan: Centre for Bhutan Studies.

Centre for Bhutan Studies, Gross National Happiness. (2008a). Homepage. Retrieved March 25, 2011, from http://www.grossnationalhappiness.com

Centre for Bhutan Studies, Gross National Happiness. (2008b). Results of GNH index. Retrieved on July 28, 2011, from http://www.grossnationalhappiness.com/gnhIndex/resultGNHIndex.aspx

Daly, Herman, & Cobb, John. (1994). *For the common good: Redirecting the economy toward community, the environment, and a sustainable future.* Boston: Beacon Press.

Dorji, Tshering. (2011, July 22). Global community embraces GNH, officially. Retrieved July 28, 2011, from http://bhutantoday.bt/index.php?option=com_content&view=article&id=616:global-community-embraces-gnh-officially

Gilbert, Daniel Todd. (2006). *Stumbling on happiness.* New York: Knopf.

Gross National Happiness USA. (2009). About GNHUSA. Retrieved March 25, 2011, from http://www.gnhusa.org/about-gnhusa

Kahneman, Daniel; Krueger, Alan B.; Schkade, David; Schwarz, Norbert; & Stone, Arthur A. (2004). Toward national well-being accounts. *American Economic Review, 94*(2), 429–434.

Kahneman, Daniel; Krueger, Alan B.; Schkade, David; Schwarz, Norbert; & Stone, Arthur A. (2006). Would you be happier if you were richer? A focusing illusion. *Science, 312*(5782), 1908.

Mancall, Mark. (2004). *Gross national happiness and development* (paper, First International Conference on Gross National Happiness). Thimphu, Bhutan.

Mydans, Seth. (2009, May 6). Recalculating happiness in a Himalayan kingdom. Retrieved March 25, 2011, from http://www.nytimes.com/2009/05/07/world/asia/07bhutan.html?pagewanted=1&_r=1

Norgaard, Richard. (1994). *Development betrayed: The end of progress and a co-evolutionary revisioning of the future.* Oxford, UK: Routledge.

Planning Commission, Royal Government of Bhutan, & Zimba, Lyonpo Yeshey. (1999). *Bhutan 2020: A vision for peace, prosperity and happiness.* Thimphu, Bhutan: Planning Commission Secretariat, Royal Government of Bhutan.

Plett, Barbara. (2011, July 21). Bhutan spreads happiness to UN. Retrieved July 28, 2011, from http://www.bbc.co.uk/news/world-14243512

Rogers, Simon. (2011, July 25). So, how do you measure wellbeing and happiness? Retrieved July 28, 2011, from http://www.guardian.co.uk/news/datablog/2011/jul/25/wellbeing-happiness-office-national-statistics

Sachs, Jeffrey. (2011). The economics of happiness. Retrieved Feb. 13, 2012, from http://www.project-syndicate.org/commentary/sachs181/English

Seligman, Martin E. P. (2002). *Authentic happiness: Using the new positive psychology to realize your potential for lasting fulfillment.* New York: Free Press.

Stratton, Allegra. (2010, November 14). David Cameron aims to make happiness the new GDP. Retrieved July 28, 2011, from http://www.guardian.co.uk/politics/2010/nov/14/david-cameron-wellbeing-inquiry

Tashi, Khenpo Phuntshok. (2000, May 27). The origin of happiness. *Kuensel: Bhutan's National Newspaper.*

Tashi, Khenpo Phuntshok. (2004). The role of Buddhism in achieving gross national happiness (paper, First International Conference on GNH). Thimphu, Bhutan. Retrieved February 13, 2012, from http://www.bhutanstudies.org.bt/pubFiles/Gnh&dev-25.pdf

Thinley, Lyonpo Jigmi Y. (1998). Values and development: Gross national happiness (keynote address, Millennium Meeting for Asia and the Pacific). Seoul, Republic of Korea. Retrieved April 20, 2011, from http://ndlb.thlib.org/typescripts/0000/0007/1548.pdf

Thinley, Lyonpo Jigmi Y. (2005). What does gross national happiness (GNH) mean? (keynote address, Second International Conference on GNH). Nova Scotia, Canada. Retrieved April 20, 2011, from http://www.gpiatlantic.org/conference/proceedings/thinley.htm

United Nations Department of Economic and Social Affairs (UN DESA) Statistics Division & Office of the High Representative for Least Developed Countries, Landlocked Developing Countries and Small Island Developing States (OHRLLS). (2011). *World statistics pocketbook 2010: Least developed countries.* Retrieved Feb. 13, 2012, from http://www.unohrlls.org/UserFiles/File/LDC%20Pocketbook2010-%20final.pdf

Ura, Karma. (2008). Explanation of the GNH index. Retrieved March 25, 2011, from http://www.grossnationalhappiness.com/gnhIndex/intruductionGNH.aspx

Wangchuk, Norbu. (2003, January). Gross national happiness: Practicing the philosophy. Retrieved November 12, 2011, from http://www.rim.edu.bt/Publication/Archive/rigphel/rigphel2/gnh.htm

Zencey, Eric. (2009, August 9). G.D.P. R.I.P. *New York Times.* Retrieved March 25, 2011, from http://www.nytimes.com/2009/08/10/opinion/10zencey.html?_r=1

Human Appropriation of Net Primary Production (HANPP)

Agriculture, forestry, settlements, and other human uses of the land alter stocks and flows of biomass in ecosystems. The human appropriation of net primary production (HANPP) is an aggregate measure of changes in net primary production and biomass availability in ecosystems resulting from land use. HANPP accounts can be used to derive indicators of land-use intensity and the scale of human activities in the biosphere.

The notion of "land use" encompasses a great variety of human activities. In terms of land area affected, the most important land uses are agriculture and forestry, in which humans intentionally alter terrestrial ecosystems to produce food, fodder, or fibers. In addition, humans also need land to host buildings and infrastructures, as living space (e.g., gardens, parks), for waste deposition, and for many other purposes.

Changes in land use have been recognized as pervasive drivers of global environmental change. Land-use change encompasses (1) the conversion of ecosystems, such as forests, grasslands, shrublands, or wetlands, into managed forests, settlement areas, and agro-ecosystems (cropland, rangelands, or meadows), and (2) changes of land management, such as the choice of plants that are grown, plowing, and machinery use, the amount and chemical composition of fertilizer or pesticides used, and so forth. Land-use change alters biospheric stocks and flows of essential elements, such as nitrogen and carbon, and affects water systems, soils, species composition, and biodiversity as well as many other important ecosystem attributes, including their stability and resilience.

Transitions toward more-sustainable land use need to be informed by data and indicators of the extent and intensity of land use. The human appropriation of net primary production, abbreviated HANPP, is an aggregate indicator that measures the changes in yearly biomass flows in ecosystems resulting from land use. It provides information both on the scale of human activities compared to natural flows and on the aggregate intensity of land use. HANPP and its components (e.g., biomass harvest) can be assessed in a spatially explicit manner and compared across locations and time.

Net Primary Production and Land Use

In the process of photosynthesis, plants convert radiant energy from the sun into energy stored in energy-rich materials, that is, biomass. They thereby convert inorganic substances—above all, carbon dioxide, water, and plant nutrients such as nitrogen, phosphorous, and potash—into organic materials. The amount of biomass produced by green plants per year, net of the plants' own metabolic needs, is denoted as net primary production (NPP). This process can be measured as yearly flow of dry matter biomass (in kilograms per year), as carbon flow (in kilograms of carbon per year), or as energy flow (in joules per year).

NPP results in organic material that either is accumulated by plants or in the soil (in this case, the stock of organic carbon in the ecosystem increases, i.e., the ecosystem acts as a carbon sink) or enters food chains (i.e., the biomass is used as food by animals, microorganisms, or fungi [heterotrophic organisms]). Because NPP is the ultimate food resource in ecosystems, it indicates the amount of trophic energy available in ecosystems, which is intimately related to many vital patterns and processes in ecosystems.

Humans affect the amount of NPP available in ecosystems through two closely related processes. First, by using the land, humans alter ecosystems, which mostly changes ecosystem NPP. For example, if natural vegetation is replaced with settlements, industrial areas, or infrastructures, sealed surfaces will have little, if any NPP, while adjacent land may often be highly productive (e.g., gardens, parks). The NPP of agro-ecosystems is often different from that of the natural ecosystems they replace. This process of direct human alteration of NPP is denoted as the change in productivity resulting from land conversion, abbreviated ΔNPP_{LC}.

Second, humans extract biomass from ecosystems for their own use, thereby rendering it unavailable to wild-living organisms. This process is denoted as the harvest of NPP, abbreviated NPP_h.

HANPP may be defined as the total of ΔNPP_{LC} and NPP_h (e.g., Haberl et al. 2007a); that is to say, HANPP equals the change in productivity due to land conversion plus the amount of biomass humans harvest from ecosystems. HANPP can be measured in the same units as NPP—that is, dry-matter biomass, carbon, or energy.

This basic concept of HANPP has been given different names and has been implemented using varying definitions. The first study of the magnitude of global human-related biomass flows to NPP (Whittaker and Likens 1973) only included selected components of NPP_h (e.g., human food supply) and did not consider ΔNPP_{LC}. In a seminal paper published in the journal *BioScience,* the US ecologist Peter Vitousek and colleagues (1986) used three different definitions to calculate the "human appropriation of the products of photosynthesis." The most restrictive definition included only biomass directly used by humans as "appropriated," whereas the least restrictive definition included not only human-induced changes in productivity (ΔNPP_{LC}) but also the total NPP of strongly human-managed ecosystems, such as croplands. The much-quoted result—global terrestrial HANPP amounts to almost 40 percent of the potential NPP of the terrestrial vegetation (Vitousek et al. 1986)—was based on the latter, most inclusive definition of HANPP. A subsequent study by the US biologist David H. Wright (1990) proposed yet another way to measure "human impacts on the energy flow through natural ecosystems": Wright's definition included ΔNPP_{LC} but not the total NPP of human-dominated ecosystems. The NPP_h concept proposed by Wright included biomass extracted from cropland and grazing land, but not timber harvest. The above-quoted HANPP definition (HANPP = $\Delta NPP_{LC} + NPP_h$) is currently used in many studies and also underlies the most recent spatially explicit global HANPP data

discussed below (Haberl et al. 2007a), wherein NPP_h was defined inclusively and encompassed all biomass extracted by humans or livestock, plants destroyed during harvest, and human-induced fires.

Another, complementary approach to estimating HANPP is based on human use of biomass-based resources instead of land use. This approach draws from consumption data and uses factors that are estimated with a life cycle analysis (LCA) approach to calculate HANPP. The first study based on this approach (Imhoff et al. 2004) derived LCA factors using the intermediate definition of Vitousek and his colleagues (1986). Later, this approach was denoted as "embodied HANPP," or eHANPP (Erb et al. 2009), and applied the same definition as the global HANPP study discussed below. Embodied HANPP can be used to map "teleconnections" (Haberl et al. 2009) between the places where biomass is produced and the places where it is consumed, thereby helping to better understand the ecological implications of urbanization processes or international trade.

Quantifying and Mapping Global HANPP

The calculation of global terrestrial HANPP by Vitousek and colleagues (1986) yielded three different estimates, depending on definition. According to the least inclusive definition, which considered only food, fodder, and wood, global HANPP amounted to only 3 percent of the (hypothetical) NPP of undisturbed vegetation (NPP_0). The intermediate definition excluded ΔNPP_{LC} but considered the total NPP of human-dominated ecosystems (e.g., croplands) as "appropriated." It yielded an estimated global HANPP of 27 percent. According to the most inclusive definition, which in addition considered ΔNPP_{LC}, global terrestrial HANPP was found to be 39 percent. This estimate pertained to the late 1970s and the early 1980s.

A more recent study by the Austrian human ecologist Helmut Haberl and colleagues (2007a) was based on spatially explicit databases for land use, country-level agricultural and forestry statistics, and a dynamic global vegetation model. According to this study, land use has reduced global terrestrial NPP by almost 10 percent. Note, however, that there are large spatial variations in ΔNPP_{LC}. For example, the NPP of irrigated areas often substantially exceeds the NPP of the natural vegetation it replaces. Global HANPP amounts to 24 percent of NPP_0—in other words, just one species (*Homo sapiens*) claims almost one-quarter of the total yearly potential biomass production of green plants on land for its own purposes.

Use and Interpretation of HANPP

HANPP calculations quantify human-induced changes in primary production, an important global ecological process, as well as changes in biomass availability in ecosystems. HANPP may be interpreted as an indicator of the scale of human activities compared to natural processes. The notion that HANPP was a straightforward measure of ecological limits to growth has lost credit, however, as several centennial-time series of HANPP revealed that HANPP can remain stable or even decline during transitions from agrarian to industrial society owing to improved efficiency of land-use systems.

Recent studies have focused on several other applications of HANPP. First, it has been used as an indicator of human domination of global ecosystems (Vitousek et al. 1997). Second, it indicates the aggregate intensity of land use, which can be used to quantify and map land-use intensity in a spatially explicit manner. (See figure 1 below.) Third, HANPP is a promising candidate as an indicator of human pressures on ecosystems and biodiversity (Haberl et al. 2007b). Fourth, HANPP has played a big role in understanding not only the magnitude and

ecological implications of global bioenergy potentials (Haberl et al. 2010) but also the interactions between bioenergy, food systems, and possible future impacts of climate change (Haberl et al. 2011).

With rising human population numbers and per capita resource consumption, there is a need to reorient global trajectories in a more sustainable direction. Approaches such as HANPP can help improve understanding of integrated socioecological (or human–environment) systems and thereby help forge a more sustainable future.

Helmut HABERL
*Alpen-Adria Universitaet Klagenfurt,
Wien, Graz (AAU), Office Vienna*

See also Biological Indicators (*several articles*); Computer Modeling; Development Indicators; Geographic Information Systems (GIS); I = P × A × T Equation; Land-Use and Land Cover Change; Long-Term Ecological Research (LTER); Material Flow Analysis (MFA); Population Indicators; Reducing Emissions from Deforestation and Forest Degradation (REDD); Remote Sensing

Figure 1. Global Terrestrial Human Appropriation of Net Primary Production (HANPP) in 2000.

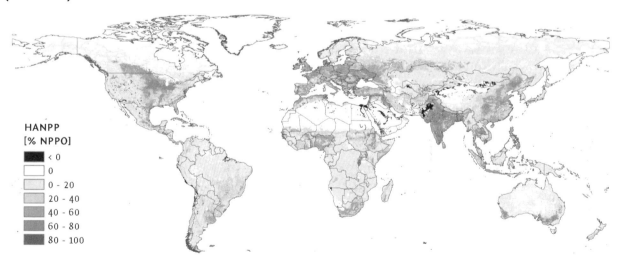

HANPP
[% NPPO]

< 0
0
0 - 20
20 - 40
40 - 60
60 - 80
80 - 100

Source: Redrawn using data of Haberl et al. (2007a, 12943).

The amount of biomass produced by green plants per year is referred to as net primary production (NPP). The grey scale denotes increasing intensity of human use (in terms of HANPP, low HANPP is light grey, high HANPP dark grey). These are areas of intensive agriculture and/or human habitation: India, eastern China, most of Europe, Nigeria, and the former prairielands of the United States and Canada. In the black regions, HANPP is negative. This occurs if NPP is raised above its natural potential, largely through fertilization and irrigation, and human harvest is smaller than the increase of NPP resulting from that. This generally occurs in arid regions which are irrigated, e.g. in the Gobi Desert, the deserts to the west of the Nile River valley, and portions of the Arabian peninsula.

FURTHER READING

Erb, Karl-Heinz; Krausmann, Fridolin; Lucht, Wolfgang; & Haberl, Helmut. (2009). Embodied HANPP: Mapping the spatial disconnect between global biomass production and consumption. *Ecological Economics, 69*(2), 328–334.

Haberl, Helmut et al. (2007a). Quantifying and mapping the human appropriation of net primary production in Earth's terrestrial ecosystems. *Proceedings of the National Academy of Sciences of the United States of America, 104*(31), 12942–12947.

Haberl, Helmut; Erb, Karl-Heinz; Plutzar, Christoph; Fischer-Kowalski, Marina; & Krausmann, Fridolin. (2007b). Human appropriation of net primary production (HANPP) as indicator for pressures on biodiversity. In Tomas Hak, Bedrich Moldan & Arthur Lyon Dahl (Eds.), *Sustainability indicators: A scientific assessment* (pp. 271–288). Washington, DC: Island Press.

Haberl, Helmut et al. (2009). Using embodied HANPP to analyze teleconnections in the global land system: Conceptual considerations. *Geografisk Tidsskrift [Danish Journal of Geography], 109*(1), 119–130.

Haberl, Helmut; Beringer, Tim; Bhattacharya, Sribas C.; Erb, Karl-Heinz; & Hoogwijk, Monique. (2010). The global technical potential of bio-energy in 2050 considering sustainability constraints. *Current Opinion in Environmental Sustainability, 2*(6), 394–403.

Haberl, Helmut, et al. (2011). Global bioenergy potentials from agricultural land in 2050: Sensitivity to climate change, diets and yields. *Biomass and Bioenergy, 35*(12), 4753–4769.

Imhoff, Marc L., et al. (2004). Global patterns in human consumption of net primary production. *Nature, 429*(6994), 870–873.

Vitousek, Peter M.; Ehrlich, Paul R.; Ehrlich, Anne H.; & Matson, Pamela A. (1986). Human appropriation of the products of photosynthesis. *BioScience, 36*(6), 363–373.

Vitousek, Peter M.; Mooney, Harold A.; Lubchenco, Jane; & Melillo, Jerry M. (1997). Human domination of Earth's ecosystems. *Science, 277*(5325), 494–499.

Whittaker, Robert H., & Likens, Gene E. (1973). Primary production: The biosphere and man. *Human Ecology, 1*(4), 357–369.

Wright, David Hamilton. (1990). Human impacts on the energy flow through natural ecosystems, and implications for species endangerment. *Ambio, 19*(4), 189–194.

Human Development Index (HDI)

The Human Development Index (HDI) is a primary tool for measuring progress toward sustainable human development. It was established in 1990 in the United Nations' first Human Development Report. The HDI uses easily available metrics to show broad comparisons about development on a nation by nation basis. Although it is open to criticism, it broke new ground by incorporating social factors into measurements of national development.

Throughout history, humans have relied on our unique ability to measure in order to overcome great challenges. The compass in navigation, the calendar in agriculture, and the development of economics and trade are examples of how applied metrics have shaped our world. In the quest for a sustainable standard of living, the challenge has been to measure the phenomenon of human development.

Establishing Criteria

The period after World War II saw increasing interest in the economic development and social growth of less-developed countries of the global South, under the assumption that more-developed countries would be better able to participate in the burgeoning world economy. During that period, the World Bank and the International Monetary Fund (IMF) were established as the principle lending institutions to less-developed countries, and the United Nations Development Programme (UNDP) was taking form. These new institutions faced a challenge establishing the criteria to measure levels of development.

Defining the variations in wealth between countries became a central focus of economists during the early

post-war period. A body of work called *development theory* combined ideas from many different disciplines and generated concepts for classifying rich and poor countries. The Argentinean economist Raul Prebisch introduced concepts such as "core," signifying rich countries, and "periphery," signifying poor countries. Other terminologies—such as global North and South, and first, second, and third World countries—entered into the language of global development.

For decades after World War II, measurements of human development were based on macroeconomic indices such as gross national product (GNP). Critics of such measurements cited many faults, particularly the assumption that the accumulation of wealth is the only road to sustainable human development. The country of Bhutan, for example, instituted the Gross National Happiness Index in 1972 and has since based some policy decisions on that index. The identification of non-monetary factors in measuring human development marked a turning point.

The Human Development Index

In 1990 the UNDP produced its first Human Development Report (HDR). A brainchild of the Pakistani economist Mahbub ul Haq and the Indian social economist and later Nobel laureate Amartya Sen, the HDR frames development from a social perspective and defines three goals that are essential to human development: to lead a long and healthy life, to acquire knowledge, and to have access to resources needed for an adequate standard of living. The absence of any of those criteria limits the ability to achieve human development. With the creation of the HDR came a set of standards for measuring development called the Human Development Index (HDI).

The HDI represents a country's development via three key indicators mentioned above: education, life expectancy, and gross national income (GNI), or the total amount of money a country produces after accounting for its expenditures. The developers of the HDI acknowledge that there are many other factors affecting human development that are not included in the calculation, such as economic and social freedoms and protection from violence. The three indicators selected for the HDI, however, are correlated with criteria not directly included in the measurement. For example, lower literacy rates are more likely when a population is experiencing prolonged violence.

HDI Composition

The method used to calculate the HDI standardizes country-level development by taking into account four factors: life expectancy at birth, mean years of prior schooling for adults aged 25 and older, expected years of schooling for school-aged youths, and gross national income per capita. The four factors are combined to create three indices, each of which can take values between 0 and 1.

The Life Expectancy Index (LEI) is calculated as follows:

$$\text{LEI} = \frac{\text{life expectancy at birth} - 20}{83.2 - 20}$$

This calculation is based on the maximum observed life expectancy at birth between 1980 and 2010 (from Japan, 83.2 years), and the assumption that all countries achieve at least a 20-year life expectancy.

The Education Index (EI) is calculated as follows:

$$\text{EI} = \frac{\sqrt{\dfrac{\text{mean years of schooling}}{13.2} \cdot \dfrac{\text{expected years of schooling}}{20.6}}}{0.951}$$

Although this appears quite complicated, it in fact follows the same principles as the calculation for the LEI. The geometric mean of the two measures of educational attainment is divided by the maximum such geometric mean. Between 1980 and 2010, the maximum observed mean years of schooling is 13.2 (United States, 2000), the maximum observed expected years of schooling is 20.6 (Australia, 2002), and the maximum observed combined education index is 0.951 (New Zealand, 2010). In all three cases, the minimum is taken as zero.

The GNI Index (GI) is measured in US dollars and is calculated as follows:

$$\text{GI} = \frac{\log(\text{GNP}) - \log(163)}{\log(108{,}211) - \log(163)}$$

Again, the equation is similar to the LEI. A per capita GNP of \$108,211 is the maximum observed per capita GNP between 1980 and 2010 (United Arab Emirates, 1980), and \$163 is the minimum observed per capita GNP for that time period (Zimbabwe, 2008). The logarithm function is used because the distribution of per capita GNPs across countries is clustered both at the low and high ends; taking the logarithm shrinks the size of the higher values, allowing the GI to be more evenly distributed between zero and one.

The final value for the HDI is then the geometric average of these three indices:

$$\text{HDI} = \sqrt[3]{\text{LEI} \cdot \text{EI} \cdot \text{GI}}$$

The UNDP's global Human Development Report has influenced the production of regional and national reports. The adaptability of the model combined with its simplicity makes it a valuable tool for policy makers at all levels. At the global level the HDI informs policy makers at international lending institutions and governments on allocating aid to countries in need. At the national level, policy makers use the human development reports to identify problem areas and allocate resources to enhance human development where those problems exist. Areas where the reports have influenced policy makers include strengthening of national institutions, modification of national economies, and identifying and developing approaches to combat human rights abuses, inequality, and enhance education.

Criticism of the HDI

Criticism of the HDI has mounted over the years, focused on several areas of concern. Some argue that the indicators used in the calculation do not sufficiently address levels of development. Others state that the HDI has strayed from its goal to put the human at the forefront of development. These criticisms result from the exclusion in the measurements of such factors as human happiness, quality of environment, mental well-being, cultural retention, and social inclusion. Other critics question the entire notion of ranking by performance, citing that the criteria used to judge good performance are biased toward the ideals of Western nations, and therefore performance scores only measure how a country conforms to Western standards. Technical criticisms cite the arbitrariness of assigning weights to the indicators; critics question the utility of equally distributing significance to each of the three categories used in the measurements, arguing that not all populations experience the same phenomena in the same manner. Critics also note that the HDI is very sensitive to small changes, meaning that countries can move up and down the rankings significantly as a result of a small change to only one component in the metric. Others cite the difficulty in collecting accurate data to update the indices for any country sufficiently, maintaining that any equation based on partial data is inherently flawed and works against the interests of populations most in need.

Implications

In spite of the criticisms, the HDI represents a reasonably impartial tool for measuring development. The creation of the HDI broke new ground in human development research and analysis by incorporating social factors into the measurements for ranking national development. Although the HDI does not capture all aspects of development that are important to measure, it does account for many factors indirectly. The simplicity of the measurement is perhaps its biggest asset, making measurements and predictions easier to manage. Because social problems related to human development are as relevant today as they were in 1990, tools such as the HDI serve to monitor progression toward the realization of sustainable development across the globe.

Juan Carlos ROSA and Jana ASHER
StatAid

See also Agenda 21; Development Indicators; Environmental Performance Index (EPI); Gross Domestic Product, Green; Gross National Happiness; *The Limits to Growth;* Millennium Development Goals; Regional Planning

FURTHER READING

Green, Maria. (2001). What we talk about when we talk about indicators: Current approaches to human rights measurement. *Human Rights Quarterly, 23*(4), 1062–1097.

Puri, Jyotsna, et al. (2007). *Measuring human development: A primer. Guidelines and tools for statistical research, analysis and advocacy.* Retrieved February 10, 2012, from http://hdr.undp.org/en/media/Primer_complete.pdf

Sagar, Ambuj D. (1998). The Human Development Index: A critical review. *Ecological Economics, 25*(3), 249–264.

Sen, Amartya. (2000). A decade of human development. *Journal of Human Development, 1*(1), 17–23.

ul Haq, Mahbub. (1999). Reflections on human development. New York: Oxford University Press.

United Nations Development Programme (UNDP). (1990). *Human development report 1990.* Retrieved February 10, 2012, from http://hdr.undp.org/en/reports/global/hdr1990/chapters/

United Nations Development Programme (UNDP). (2011). *Human development report 2011.* Retrieved February 10, 2012, from http://hdr.undp.org/en/reports/global/hdr2011/download/

I

I = P × A × T Equation

The I = P × A × T equation specifies that environmental impacts *are the multiplicative product of* population, affluence *(per capita consumption), and* technology *(impact per unit of consumption). Modifications and extensions of this equation have led to the ImPACT equation, the Kaya identity, and the STIRPAT model, all of which help predict the effects of human activity on the natural world.*

The I = P × A × T equation, also referred to as IPAT, specifies that *impacts* (I) on the environment are a multiplicative function of *population* (P), *affluence* (or per capita consumption, A), and *technology* (or impact per unit of consumption, T). The affluence factor can be defined in various ways, such as a monetary unit or a unit of consumption of a particular good or service. Technology is effectively defined as a residual term, being solved for based on observed values of the other factors: T = I/(PA).

The IPAT equation emerged in the early 1970s out of a debate between Barry Commoner, a prominent biologist and environmentalist, on one side, and Paul Ehrlich, ecologist and author of the renowned book *The Population Bomb,* and physicist John Holdren, on the other, over the causes of environmental problems. Ehrlich and Holdren were the first to conceive the idea of and the acronym for IPAT, while Commoner can be credited with the first four-factor algebraic formulation of the model and the first application of it to data analysis.

In a standard application of the logic of IPAT, Commoner in his book *Making Peace with the Planet* examines growth in pesticide use in the United States between 1950 and 1967. He notes that over this period pesticide use (an environmental impact [I]) for crop production increased 266 percent (i.e., the pesticide use in 1967 was 3.66 times what it was in 1950), while population (P) grew 30 percent (i.e., increased by a factor of 1.30)

and per capita crop production (affluence [A]) increased 5 percent (i.e., a factor of 1.05). These numbers can be placed into the IPAT formula to algebraically solve for technology (T):

$$3.66\ [I] = 1.30\ [P] \times 1.05\ [A] \times T,$$
$$\text{making } T = 3.66/(1.30 \times 1.05) = 2.68$$

Thus, pesticide use (T) increased by 168 percent (2.68 × 100 – 100). Using this type of analysis, one can assess how various factors contributed to changes over time in any particular environmental impact.

One can also use the formula in a similar fashion to compare nations (or other units) on the factors that contribute to a particular impact. For example, one could compare how different factors contribute to carbon dioxide emissions in the United States and China. Using 2006 data from the *International Energy Annual* produced by the Energy Information Administration, we see that China emitted 6.018 trillion kilograms of carbon dioxide (I), had a population (P) of 1.314 billion, and a gross domestic product (GDP) per capita (A) of US$1,607. Using the IPAT formula to solve for T, we can calculate that in China the impact intensity of consumption (T) was 2.85, measured in kilograms of carbon dioxide per US dollar of GDP:

$$6,018,000,000,000/(1,314,000,000 \times 1,607) = 2.85$$

The United States, during the same period, emitted 5.903 trillion kilograms of carbon dioxide (I), had a population (P) of 298 million, and a GDP per capita (A) of US$38,038, for an impact intensity of consumption (T) of 0.52:

$$5,903,000,000,000/(298,000,000 \times 38,038) = 0.52$$

Based on this calculation, we can see that, relative to the United States, China's higher carbon dioxide emissions were due to its larger population and larger impact intensity of consumption, despite its lower level of affluence.

An important aspect of the IPAT equation is that it implicitly recognizes that none of the factors leading to environmental impacts operates in isolation. Rather, each factor has its effects on impacts through interaction with the other factors. For example, the effect of population growth on the absolute size of any particular impact depends on the level of affluence (A) of that population and the type of production (T) used by that population. Therefore, modest population growth in a very poor nation typically will not have a large effect on the absolute amount of carbon dioxide emissions. Likewise, fairly small changes in affluence in a highly populous nation, like China, can have a large effect on the absolute amount of emissions. Due to this multiplicative interaction, one cannot say that a single factor is more important than any other, since in combination they produce impacts. Looking at changes over time, even if one factor doesn't change, it contributes to the overall scale of impacts. One can thus look at the relative contribution of each factor to *change* in impacts, as with the pesticide example above, but that does not indicate the relative importance of each factor to the *absolute size* of the impact. For practical purposes of curtailing environmental impacts, what is particularly important is the potential plasticity of each factor, in other words, how easily each factor can be changed via policy or other intentional action.

The IPAT formulation is appealing to environmental scientists because it incorporates variables whose contributions to environmental impacts are often asserted from first principles. The equation, nonetheless, has several limitations. Factors identified as driving the impacts, and the interactions among these factors, are assumed, rather than emerging from empirical investigation. Since the model is a mathematical identity (an accounting equation), and T is solved for based on the other factors, the validity of the model itself is asserted a priori and cannot be tested, since the equation can be solved for any values of I, P, and A that are put into it.

Because T is solved for based on the other factors, it not only incorporates the technologies of production, but also all factors other than population and affluence that affect impacts, such as social organization and biophysical context—making T a virtual black box of forces. Due to the T variable, the equation can obfuscate the qualitative trade-offs across various impacts. For example, if population growth increases demand for food, crop production could be increased by adding more chemical fertilizer to existing crop land and/or increasing the amount of land under production. If we focus on only one of these impact measures (fertilizer use or land under production), we could get starkly different estimates of the relative contribution of T to impacts. In *Making Peace with the Planet* Barry Commoner uses the pesticide example shown above to argue that changes in technology were the predominant force driving impact increases after the Second World War. However, since this was a period when crop production was increased primarily by intensifying production using chemical inputs (pesticides and fertilizers) rather than by increasing land area in crop production, using pesticides as the impact measure would suggest that T had increased dramatically (since pesticide use grew much faster than population and affluence), whereas using land area in production as the impact measure would suggest that T had decreased (since, despite substantial growth in population and affluence, land area in production did not increase substantially). The qualitative trade-offs among impacts can be partially overcome by using more-inclusive impact measures, such as the ecological footprint, which combines various types of impacts into a common metric.

There is also the consideration that each factor likely affects the other factors, and, therefore, indirect effects are made invisible in the IPAT equation. For example, it is well established that rising affluence is commonly associated with declining fertility rates; thus increases in A may ultimately suppress P. Likewise, the Jevons paradox highlights a common situation in which rising energy efficiency (i.e., declining T) can lead to an increase in energy use (I) because efficiency contributes to per capita economic growth (rising A). The Jevons paradox, which refers to situations where improvements in efficiency lead to more resource consumption, is named for William Stanley Jevons, who in the nineteenth century observed that the rise in the efficiency of coal use was associated with rising coal use, because improved efficiency made coal-powered machines more desirable to industrialists. In cases like this, it is inappropriate to use the "all else being equal" assumption that reducing, for example, T (improving efficiency) will reduce I, because all else will not be equal if T declines. Therefore, we should be cautious in talking about the effects of any one of the factors in isolation, recognizing that a decline in one, via its effects on the other factors, may actually lead to an increase in impacts, or vice versa.

The IPAT equation can be refined by breaking down the T factor into components. For example, the ImPACT model specifies that, similar to IPAT, $I = P \times A \times C \times T$, where the T variable from IPAT is broken into the C and T factors. Here, I, P, and A retain the meaning they have in IPAT, and C is consumption per unit of affluence, and T is the impact per unit of consumption. For example, using carbon dioxide as the impact measure, and GDP per capita as the affluence measure, C is energy consumption per unit of GDP (i.e., the energy intensity of the economy), and T is carbon dioxide emissions per unit of energy consumption (i.e., the carbon dioxide intensity of the energy supply). The Intergovernmental Panel on Climate Change uses a model like this—referred to as the Kaya identity, for the Japanese energy economist Yoichi Kaya—to generate its future emissions scenarios.

Despite their many worthwhile applications to assessment of environmental problems, the IPAT and ImPACT equations and the Kaya identity have certain limitations. Most important, these equations embed assumptions about the relationship among the factors a priori and do not allow for testing these assumptions with empirical analysis. The equations are based on assumptions not only about which factors drive impacts but also about the structure of the relationship between the driving forces and the impacts. In particular, IPAT assumes, for example, a proportional relationship between population and impacts—such as, if population doubles, all else being equal, then impact will double. These limitations are largely overcome with a stochastic reformulation of IPAT, called STIRPAT (stochastic impacts by regression on population,

affluence, and technology), which is amenable to hypothesis testing using standard statistical procedures, like ordinary-least-squares regression. The equivalent of an elasticity model, STIRPAT specifies:

$$I_i = aP_i^b A_i^c T_i^d e_i$$

in which "a" is a scaling constant; "b," "c," and "d" are the exponents of P, A, and T, respectively, that are to be estimated; and "e" is the error term standard to stochastic models that accounts for variance in I not explained by the other factors in the model. The subscript "i" indicates that these quantities (I, P, A, T, and e) vary across observational units (e.g., nations, counties, etc.). In the IPAT equation, proportionality is assumed, making $a = b = c = d = e = 1$, whereas in STIRPAT, these are coefficients to be estimated based on data. The coefficients can be estimated using an additive regression model by converting all variables into logarithmic form. Since T does not represent a single directly observable factor, but rather captures all factors other than population and affluence that influence impacts, it is typically incorporated into the error term, e (or assessed by adding new variables to the model—see below). These modifications yield the following basic STIRPAT model:

$$\log I = a + b(\log P) + c(\log A) + e$$

In this model, a and e are, respectively, the log of a and the log of e from the previously presented equation, and the subscript i is dropped to reduce clutter in the equation.

With STIRPAT, the effects of the independent variables on impacts are not assumed a priori, so that, for example, the assumption that population drives impacts is a falsifiable hypothesis. If population (or another factor) does not affect impacts, the estimated coefficient (b, in the case of population) would be 0 (or not be different from 0 in the statistically significant sense). The model can also assess whether a factor like population has a greater than proportional effect (coefficient greater than 1), a less than proportional effect (coefficient greater than 0, but less than 1), a proportionate effect (coefficient equal to 1), as assumed in the IPAT equation, or even an inverse effect (coefficient less than 0) on impacts. Importantly, other variables can be added to the model, opening up the black box that T serves in the IPAT equation. For example, variables like urbanization and industrialization, which serve as indicators of the technologies of production in a nation (or other unit), can be included in the model, which can then test whether these factors have a significant effect on impacts. Due to these features, STIRPAT helps overcome many of the limitations of the IPAT equation. The STIRPAT specification can also be used as part of a path model procedure, so that the effects of the right-hand-side variables on one another can also be estimated, although to date this approach has not been extensively explored by researchers.

Richard YORK
University of Oregon

See also Carbon Footprint; Challenges to Measuring Sustainability; Computer Modeling; Development Indicators; Human Appropriation of Net Primary Production (HANPP); *The Limits to Growth;* Population Indicators; Quantitative vs. Qualitative Studies; Sustainability Science; Systems Thinking; Taxation Indicators, Green

FURTHER READING

Commoner, Barry. (1971). *The closing circle.* New York: Knopf.

Commoner, Barry. (1972a). The environmental cost of economic growth. In Ronald G. Ridker (Ed), *Population, resources and the environment* (pp. 339–363). Washington DC: US Government Printing Office.

Commoner, Barry. (1972b). A bulletin dialogue on "The closing circle," response. *Bulletin of the Atomic Scientists, 28*(5), 17, 42–56.

Commoner, Barry. (1992). *Making peace with the planet.* New York: New Press.

Commoner, Barry; Corr, Michael; & Stamler, Paul J. (1971). The causes of pollution. *Environment, 13*(3), 2–19.

Dietz, Thomas, & Rosa, Eugene A. (1994). Rethinking the environmental impacts of population, affluence and technology. *Human Ecology Review, 1,* 277–300.

Dietz, Thomas, & Rosa, Eugene A. (1997). Effects of population and affluence on CO_2 emissions. *Proceedings of the National Academy of Sciences, 94*(1), 175–179.

Ehrlich, Paul. (1968.) *The Population Bomb.* New York: Ballantine.

Ehrlich, Paul, & Holdren, John. (1970, July 4). The people problem. *Saturday Review,* pp. 42–43.

Ehrlich, Paul, & Holdren, John. (1971). Impact of population growth. *Science, 171,* 1212–1217.

Ehrlich, Paul, & Holdren, John. (1972). A Bulletin dialogue on "the closing circle," Critique: One-dimensional ecology. *Bulletin of the Atomic Scientists, 28*(5), 16–27.

Jevons, William Stanley. (2001). Of the economy of fuel. *Organization & Environment, 14*(1), 99–104. (Original work published 1865)

Kaya, Yoichi, & Yokobori, Keiichi. (1997). *Environment, energy, and economy: Strategies for sustainability.* New York: United Nations University Press.

Waggoner, Paul E., & Ausubel, Jesse H. (2002). A framework for sustainability science: A renovated IPAT identity. *Proceedings of the National Academy of Sciences, 99*(12), 7860–7865.

York, Richard; Rosa, Eugene A.; & Dietz, Thomas. (2002). Bridging environmental science with environmental policy: Plasticity of population, affluence, and technology. *Social Science Quarterly, 83*(1), 18–34.

York, Richard; Rosa, Eugene A.; & Dietz, Thomas. (2003a). Footprints on the Earth: The environmental consequences of modernity. *American Sociological Review, 68*(2), 279–300.

York, Richard; Rosa, Eugene A.; & Dietz, Thomas. (2003b). STIRPAT, IPAT, and ImPACT: Analytic tools for unpacking the driving forces of environmental impacts. *Ecological Economics, 46*(3), 351–365.

Index of Biological Integrity (IBI)

Indices of biological integrity (IBI) or multimetric indices (MMI) incorporate variables such as species richness and evenness, relative abundance, migration, and age or size distribution. The metrics are scored relative to reference conditions, the scores are standardized to accommodate the differing ranges in variable raw values, and the variable scores are summed to yield an IBI score. IBIs can track changes in assemblages resulting from environmental improvements or degradation that lead to or detract from sustainability.

Scientists have employed pollution tolerance indices, diversity indices, or combined diversity/biomass indices for the past hundred years to assess the biological condition of aquatic ecosystems. Because those indices were based on only one or two ecological variables, such as the number of species or the presence or absence of particular indicator species (such as trout), the US ecologist James Karr proposed the Index of Biological Integrity, or IBI, a multimetric index (MMI). The IBI was first developed for assessing fish assemblage (the fish component of the community at a site) conditions of wadeable midwestern streams using twelve metrics. (See table 1 on the next page.) Since that time, the concept has been expanded to fish assemblages of large rivers, cold-water streams, and rivers with few fish species; lakes, estuaries, and coral reefs; benthic macroinvertebrates (large bottom-dwelling invertebrates) of streams and rivers; stream and river algae; riparian birds; and steppe vegetation. MMIs have been applied for assessing surface water quality by scientists in at least thirty-five countries (including Australia, Brazil, France, and India) and on all continents but Antarctica in a manner similar to the way economists assess the health of an economy through use of an index of leading economic indicators. To facilitate those applications, Karr's original IBI has been modified to include metrics such as those mentioned in table 1. MMIs have been used for assessing the status of individual rivers and river basins, ecoregions, multistate regions, the entire European Union, and the conterminous United States.

Controversies and Challenges

There are five major controversies or challenges concerning the IBI (or MMIs):

1. models predicting lists of common species from natural environmental variables
2. lack of scientific/statistical survey designs
3. lack of standard sampling methods
4. lack of rigorous metric definition calibration, selection, and scoring
5. profusion of IBIs for single basins, ecoregions, or states, often based on small numbers of ad hoc samples

Predictive Models

Predictive models of commonly occurring species have been proposed as less subjective and less variable alternatives to IBIs, but typically the number of commonly occurring fish species is too few for rigorous modeling. Instead, predictive model IBIs have been developed after calibrating metrics for natural environmental gradients, such as water body size, mean annual air temperature, channel slope, and geology. For example, more species and more piscivorous species are expected in water bodies that are naturally larger and warmer, and in those with lower slopes and more nutrient rich bedrock or soils. Metric expectations thus differ along differing natural gradients.

TABLE 1. Original IBI Metrics and Examples of Commonly Used MMI Metrics for Four Aquatic/
Riparian Assemblages

Original Fish IBI	Fish MMI	Macroinvertebrate MMI	Algae MMI	Riparian Bird MMI
# of species	# of native species	# of genera or families	# of species	# of native species
Presence of intolerant species	# of intolerant species	diversity	% sensitive individuals	% intolerant species
# of darter species	# of benthic species	% mayfly individuals	% heterotrophic individuals	% interior species
# of sucker species	% gravel spawning individuals	% stonefly individuals	% polysaprobic individuals	% nest sensitive species
# of sunfish species	# of water column species	% caddisfly individuals	% water column species	% ground gleaning individuals
% green sunfish	% tolerant individuals	% tolerant individuals	% tolerant individuals	% tolerant species
% top carnivores	% invertivore/ piscivore individuals	% shredder individuals	% chloride tolerant individuals	% foliage gleaning individuals
% insectivorous minnows	% invertivore individuals	% collector/gatherer individuals	% phosphorous tolerant individuals	% insectivorous individuals
% omnivorous individuals	% omnivorous individuals	% sand-preferring species	% nitrogen tolerant individuals	% omnivore/ granivore species
% hybrid individuals	% alien individuals	% non-insect individuals	% sediment tolerant individuals	% nest parasite individuals
% diseased	% diseased individuals	% individuals in 5 dominant taxa	% deformed individuals	% bark gleaning species
# of individuals	Catch per unit effort	# of individuals	% individuals in 5 dominant taxa	# of individuals
	% long-lived species	% long-lived individuals	% acid tolerant individuals	% warbler species
	% fast-water species	% fast-water species	% motile individuals	# of neotropical migrant species

Source: author.

Survey Site Selection

For many years political polls were conducted using biased survey techniques (such as interviews with wealthy voters only), achieving erroneous results. But in the past fifty years, political polls have been able to predict election results with error estimates of 2 or 3 percentage points. Similar to the earlier political polls, most ecological survey sites are selected in an ad hoc manner, meaning that the results cannot be extended with statistical rigor and known confidence limits or error estimates to a wider population of water bodies. This greatly restricts the usefulness of such surveys and means that many more sites must be sampled at great expense to provide convincing and correct information over large spatial extents. Development and implementation of probability (random) survey techniques by the US Environmental Protection Agency (EPA) and several states has improved this situation, but further adoption of probability sampling is needed to increase the cost-effectiveness of sampling and the ability to use inferential statistics. For example, Brazilian and Swedish scientists have used probability survey designs for selecting reservoir, lake, and stream sites for sampling.

Lack of Standard Methods

Although not specific to IBIs, the lack of standard sampling and sample processing methods hinders use of much of the assemblage data collected by biologists. The European Union (EU) has a standard fish sampling method, as does the EPA's EMAP/NARS (Environmental Monitoring and Assessment Program/National Aquatic Resources Survey); however, most biological surveys (including those of the EPA versus the EU) use differing sampling methods, making it difficult to ascertain whether the differences observed among sites and nations result from natural, anthropogenic, or sampling differences.

Metric Selection and Scoring

Karr used ecological theory to select and score twelve metrics, which was a major advance from using only one or two metrics for ecological assessment as was common at the time. Karr assumed that as the degree of environmental disturbance increased, the values for several metrics would decrease. For example, species richness and the number of intolerant species would decrease, whereas the percent of tolerant individuals and the percent of diseased individuals would increase with decreased environmental quality. Since then, however, many IBIs were developed without sufficient ecological knowledge and with little or no calibration for natural variability or evaluation of candidate metric scoring range, reproducibility, sensitivity to disturbance, or redundancy. Increasingly, monitoring and assessment programs and scientific journals have expected more rigorous metric selection and scoring, but many earlier IBIs are still being used without having been tested sufficiently.

Index Profusion

The popularity of MMIs and the recognition of local or basin faunal and floral differences have led to the development of dozens of different MMIs and the use of additional types of metrics believed useful for making ecological assessments. Although local MMIs tend to be more sensitive at discriminating local differences, they hinder making regional, national, and continental assessments via a consistent indicator, because it cannot be known if the differences observed result from environmental or index differences. Increased use of predictive modeling and the implementation of national and continental monitoring and assessment programs are likely to lead to fewer MMI metrics and fewer MMIs applied to larger areas.

Outlook

The IBI or a related MMI has persisted since 1981, evolved into many different forms, been applied to many different types of ecosystems and biological assemblages, and been adapted for use on all continents with freshwater—despite the existence of fundamentally different taxa in those places. This widespread use and applicability attests to its vigor and potential long-term usefulness. Further evidence of its long-term usefulness is its implementation by many different state and national agency monitoring programs.

Climate change, endocrine disrupting chemicals, persistent land use change, fundamental alterations of river flows and channels, and biological homogenization by alien invasive species—all spurred by economic and population growth—are becoming increasingly common globally. Such changes threaten the future existence of many species, especially aquatic species, making it ever more important to be able to track subtle temporal changes and local and widespread extirpations of sensitive species. Long-lived migratory species, species requiring unfragmented rivers for reproduction and growth, coldwater species, local endemic species, and species sensitive to toxic chemicals are especially at risk. IBI metrics that trace changes (especially reproduction, age structure, relative abundance, and distribution) in sensitive species as well as tolerant species will be especially important for aiding a concerned public toward making choices that are more likely to lead to sustainable environments, economies, and societies.

Robert M. HUGHES
Amnis Opes Institute & Oregon State University

See also Biological Indicators (*several articles*); Challenges to Measuring Sustainability; Ecosystem Health Indicators;

Fisheries Indicators, Freshwater; Fisheries Indicators, Marine; I = P × A × T Equation; International Organization for Standardization (ISO); Quantitative vs. Qualitative Studies; Strategic Environmental Assessment (SEA); Systems Thinking

FURTHER READING

Bonar, Scott A.; Hubert, Wayne A.; & Willis, David W. (Eds.). (2009). *Standard methods for sampling North American freshwater fishes.* Bethesda, MD: American Fisheries Society.

Comité Européen de Normalisation [European Committee for Standardization] (CEN). (2003). *Water quality: Sampling of fish with electricity* (European Standard—EN 14011:2003 E). Brussels, Belgium: CEN.

Dudgeon, David, et al. (2005). Freshwater biodiversity: Importance, threats, status and conservation challenges. *Biological Reviews, 81,* 163–182.

Hering, Daniel; Feld, Christian Karl; Moog, Otto; & Ofenböck, Thomas. (2006). Cook book for the development of a multimetric index for biological condition of aquatic ecosystems: Experiences from the European AQEM and STAR projects and related initiatives. *Hydrobiologia, 566,* 311–342.

Hughes, Robert M., & Oberdorff, Thierry. (1999). Applications of IBI concepts and metrics to waters outside the United States and Canada. In Thomas P. Simon (Ed.), *Assessing the sustainability and biological integrity of water resources using fish assemblages* (pp. 79–93). Boca Raton, FL: Lewis Publisher.

Hughes, Robert M., & Peck, David V. (2008). Acquiring data for large aquatic resource surveys: The art of compromise among science, logistics, and reality. *Journal of the North American Benthological Society, 27*(4), 837–859.

Hughes, Robert M.; Paulsen, Steven G.; & Stoddard, John L. (2000). EMAP-surface waters: A national, multiassemblage, probability survey of ecological integrity. *Hydrobiologia, 422/423,* 429–443.

Jelks, Howard L., et al. (2008). Conservation status of imperiled North American freshwater and diadromous fishes. *Fisheries, 33*(8), 372–386.

Karr, James R. (1981). Assessment of biotic integrity using fish communities. *Fisheries, 6*(6), 21–27.

Limburg, Karin E.; Hughes, Robert M.; Jackson, Donald C.; & Czech, Brian. (2011). Human population increase, economic growth, and fish conservation: Collision course or savvy stewardship? *Fisheries, 36*(1), 27–34.

Paulsen, Steven G., et al. (2008). Condition of stream ecosystems in the US: An overview of the first national assessment. *Journal of the North American Benthological Society, 27*(4), 812–821.

Pont, Didier, et al. (2006). Assessing river biotic condition at the continental scale: A European approach using functional metrics and fish assemblages. *Journal of Applied Ecology, 43*(1), 70–80.

Roset, Nicolas; Grenouillet, Gael; Goffaux, Delphine; Pont, Didier; & Kestemont, Patrick. (2007). A review of existing fish assemblage indicators and methodologies. *Fisheries Management and Ecology, 14*(6), 393–405.

Stoddard, John L., et al. (2008). A process for creating multi-metric indices for large-scale aquatic surveys. *Journal of the North American Benthological Society, 27*(4), 878–891.

Whittier, Thomas R., et al. (2007). A structured approach for developing indices of biotic integrity: Three examples from streams and rivers in the western USA. *Transactions of the American Fisheries Society, 136,* 718–735.

Intellectual Property Rights

Intellectual property rights are legal rights associated with human creativity. Sustainability issues focus on development of and access to clean technology and scientific information, trade in natural products, and agriculture. These rights can have positive and negative impacts, but these effects are complex and difficult to predict. Policy makers should design their intellectual property rules carefully and on the basis of objective evidence.

Business assets associated with inventions, artistic and literary works, designs, and signs fulfilling such criteria as novelty, originality, and distinctiveness are called *intellectual property.* The longest established categories are patents, which are for inventions, industrial designs for nonfunctional (aesthetic) designs, trademarks for signs used to distinguish between similar goods, and appellations of origin and indications of source. *Geographical indications* describes the last two types. Other types of intellectual property include trade secrets and special rights over plant varieties and layout designs of integrated circuits.

It is a confusing term: legally speaking, *intellectual property* should refer to the legal rights themselves rather than the invented products and processes, the designed and branded products, and the literary and artistic works to which the rights attach. In popular discourse, though, the term commonly applies to the physical and commercial expressions of these rights, and hence to the above-mentioned "things." Holders of the rights, as business assets that in the Anglo-American world are alienable property, are normally entitled to sell their patents, copyrights, designs, or trademarks or purchase the intellectual property

rights of others willing to sell them. They may also retain their rights but license them to third parties. Employees usually must assign their rights to their employers.

Intellectual property rights are negative rights—that is, rights to exclude others. A patent over a new medicine, for example, allows the patent holder to prevent others from making, using, selling, or importing the same product. Holders have no automatic right to make and sell the medicine to the public, however. The responsible government agency normally requires the holder to apply for regulatory approval. This process may take several years and entail extensive clinical trials that demonstrate safety and efficacy. Regulations unrelated to intellectual property rights such as those dealing with public health, safety, and environmental protection may govern the right to exploit a product in the marketplace. Patents, copyright, trademarks, geographical indications, and plant variety protection are the rights most relevant to sustainability.

To acquire a patent, applicants must disclose an invention to a government or other authority, such as the United States Patent and Trademark Office or the European Patent Office. The application consists of documentation comprising the title of the invention, an abstract, the specification, and the claims. The institution that is actually making the application also submits the names of the inventors. Employee-inventors usually are required to assign their property rights in their inventions to their employers.

The invention must pass four tests. First, it must be new; second, it must be unobvious to a person of ordinary skill in the relevant field of technology; third, it must have practical application ("utility" in United States patent law or "industrial application" in Europe). Mere discoveries, abstract theories, and laws of nature are not patentable. Fourth, the disclosure must be enabling, meaning that the specification should be sufficiently clear and thorough to enable the person having the relevant ordinary skill to practice the invention. The claims essentially define the scope of the legal monopoly the patent owners can enjoy in respect to the invention, which is to prevent others from making, using, offering for sale, selling, or importing the invention. In most parts of the world, the patent rights will last up to twenty years from the date of application, although this right is normally subject to the regular payment of renewal fees.

Copyright refers to rights to prevent unauthorized reproduction of artistic or literary works. The primary criterion is originality. The mere compilation of facts such as an alphabetical list of surnames with addresses and telephone numbers does not constitute an adequately creative work for protection. A database containing information presented or organized in an "original" way may form protectable subject matter. The law has an expansive conception of artistic and literary works and is thus able to accommodate new types of creative work such as computer programs (which, incidentally, can also be patented in the United States, although not everywhere else). Copyright does not protect ideas but merely the author's expression of those ideas. Whereas Isaac Newton could acquire copyright protection of *Principia,* he could claim no ownership of the universal law of gravitation he revealed and described in the book. International law forbids governments to impose conditions, such as entering the work on an official register, on the acquisition and exercise of the rights. The rights typically last for seventy years after the author's death.

Trademarks are distinctive signs that can graphically represent and distinguish the goods and services of one producer from those of any other. Words, images, shapes, sounds, and even smells may constitute marks. Bass, a British beer maker, developed the world's first trademark: a red triangle. The handwritten Coca-Cola logo and the shape of the glass bottles that carry the drink are among the best-known trademarks. Trademarks convey certain information about a good or service, such as its origins and qualities, that may interest consumers. Trademarks can last indefinitely, as long as they are kept in use.

The Agreement on Trade-Related Aspects of Intellectual Property Rights (TRIPS) of the World Trade Organization is the multilateral agreement that recognized geographical indications as an intellectual property category. The TRIPS Agreement defines them as "indications which identify a good as originating in the territory of a Member, or a region or locality in that territory, where a given quality, reputation, or other characteristic of the good is essentially attributable to its geographical origin" (Agreement on Trade-Related Aspects of Intellectual Property Rights 1994).

An indication of geographical origin, and the product so indicated, may be protected legally in diverse ways. Different countries may protect them under original and specific geographical indications laws. They may alternatively—or additionally—protect them largely or completely under an appellation (or designation) of origin regime (as with French wines), trademark law, or indirectly through unfair competition law.

Countries may in fact embed them within areas of law and regulation other than intellectual property according to the underlying purpose of protecting them, such as consumer protection rules relating to trade descriptions or food product labeling, cultural heritage regulations and policies, or rural development regulations and policies. Geographical indications thus are not a type of intellectual property right as is the patent, copyright, or trademark. Perhaps the term *geographical indications* is best regarded as a convenient catchall for a variety of mostly currently existing laws and regulations concerning products that are differentiated by possessing features or a reputation attributable to the place they come from.

Europe has the most sophisticated geographical indications system. Champagne and Scotch whisky are among the best-known indications. Producer groups intending to acquire an indication for their goods must provide a specification detailing such matters as the good's origin and the production methods. All producers using the indication must comply henceforward with the specification.

Plant variety protection, which is common in many countries, protects plants improved by scientific breeders.

Governments undertake certification tests to demonstrate that the new variety is distinct, uniform in its relevant characteristics, and genetically stable after repeated propagation. The term of legal protection is typically twenty to twenty-five years.

Sustainability

Any discussion on the relationship between intellectual property and sustainability needs to focus on four areas: (1) how patents affect the development and diffusion of new environmentally sound goods, manufacturing methods, and technologies; (2) the effects of copyright and copyright-based business models on access to relevant scientific knowledge and data; (3) the possible use of trademarks and geographical indications to certify goods produced sustainably, thereby promoting their production and sale; and (4) plant variety protection and its effects on biodiversity and the breeding decisions of private and public breeding institutions.

Patents and Environmental Technologies

The patent system legally protects inventions of all kinds including new environmentally sound goods, manufacturing methods, and technologies. It treats clean and environmentally friendly technologies the same as those that are not. Long-standing debates on whether the patent system facilitates or hinders technology transfer to developing countries also apply to green goods and technologies. Some member states of the United Nations Framework Convention on Climate Change have raised these concerns. On the one hand, patents may encourage investment in the development of environmentally sound goods and technologies where there is a demand for such products. Patents are especially valuable in areas where research and development is both risky and expensive. On the other, as some of these member states point out, patents can make it harder for others, especially developing countries, to access clean technologies.

A great number of economic studies have addressed the question of whether patents (and trade secrets) encourage or discourage foreign direct investment and technology transfer, especially to developing countries. Overall, the results are inconclusive. Few of these studies have considered specifically clean technologies. Those seeking to use certain key technologies very much need research relating to global patent information so that they may navigate paths through the patent "thicket" and avoid costly litigation from those claiming that their patents are being infringed. The issue of freedom to operate generates much discussion in this context. The freedom to operate refers to the availability of "space" to conduct research, development, and marketing beyond the reach of any patents. "Open source" licensing as in software production and, to a small but growing extent, in biotechnology is potentially relevant. Open source licenses are not alternatives to intellectual property rights; rather, they take advantage of the existence of intellectual property to promote and, if necessary, enforce open access and exchange.

Copyright and Access to Scientific Information

Most publishers depend on copyright to make a profit. Since copyright constrains people from reproducing works without permission, however, many scientists and planners, especially in the developing countries, lack access to up-to-date scientific information.

Copyright-protected journals and books publish a great deal of such information relevant to sustainability. These publications are often expensive, well beyond the budgets of many of the world's university libraries. Publishers as of 2011 often digitize their journal portfolios so that for a subscription fee—substantial but lower than the price of acquiring each journal separately—universities can make them available to students and academics. Even then, the price is still beyond the reach of many institutions. A scientific information divide consequently accompanies the global digital divide.

Scientists' dissatisfaction about publishers' closed-access business models has resulted in a backlash with a rapid increase in the number of open-access and delayed open-access journals. British BioMed Central and the US Public Library of Science (PLoS), which publish several science journals on an open-access basis, are among the best known initiatives. Authors or their employers or funders pay a fee to publish their work in a PLoS journal. In return, a Creative Commons license protects their rights of attribution and integrity.

The commercial viability of open-access journal publications nonetheless remains unproved. Many people in developing countries continue to lack access to the Internet, although the situation is certainly improving in some countries.

Trademarks and Geographical Indications

Labels and marks certifying that goods of natural origin are produced in a sustainable manner are commonly used, as one can notice in any good supermarket or grocery store. Trademarks are particularly relevant to sustainability when groups of producers are willing to cooperate to share their ownership. An association representing the producer group holds ownership to collective trademarks. Certification marks are somewhat different in that they keep apart ownership and right to use. A separate association will own a trademark but allow producers to use the mark subject to their compliance with regulations the association establishes. The certified characteristics must, of course, be ones favorable to consumers. Consumers may well be looking for products with high environmental or ethical standards, and labels and marks communicating such positive traits can be highly effective in directing consumers to such goods. There is no guarantee of success, however. There is a plethora of marks and labels in use, and their abundance can cause confusion. Moreover, unclear or misleading marks and labels may reduce consumer confidence.

Experience demonstrates that geographical indications have the potential to promote certain goods that can generate income for local communities and small-scale producers in developing countries while helping to conserve biodiversity. Such regimes can be complicated to manage, though. The production specifications are of vital importance to give consideration to the following: (1) the needs of local producers; (2) the importance of capturing as much of the production chain as possible in order to maximize the share of value retained within the region (taking into account possible capacity deficiencies); and (3) the vital need to maintain the integrity of the indication.

Plant Variety Protection and Sustainable Agriculture

Plant variety protection, common in many countries, protects plants that scientific breeders have improved ("modern varieties"). Protected varieties can be field crops for human or animal consumption or for other commercial uses such as the production of biofuels. Countries also commonly protect fruits, vegetables, and ornamentals.

Plant variety protection is a popular intellectual property system for commercial plant breeders who generally consider it more appropriate than patents. Commercial breeding has most commonly been dependent on breeders sharing a great deal of plant genetic material. Plant variety protection systems consequently tend to allow relatively free circulation even of protected varieties. Commercial breeders depend on their ability to provide seeds with traits that farmers need. They thus must be aware of shifts in demand. To the extent that plant variety protection genuinely attracts investment in research and development, there is good reason to expect plant variety protection to encourage the development and dissemination of varieties useful in mitigating the effects of climate change, such as different temperature and rainfall patterns.

Scientists' views on plant intellectual property are likely to be colored by their opinion as to whether the wholesale adoption of modern varieties in place of landraces (sometimes known as folk varieties) and traditional systems of agriculture is entirely a good thing or not. Those who hold that the radical shift from the traditional to the modern is likely to be socially disruptive and environmentally damaging often implicate intellectual property for promoting and accelerating this "harmful" trend. The reality is not quite so simple, however, because most of the first modern varieties were not legally protected.

Those with negative views on "old" varieties tend to be pro–intellectual property. They hold that the higher productivity of modern varieties can reduce pressure to expand cultivation into biologically diverse areas like rain forests and into other marginal, fragile environments such as in semiarid regions. Others favoring the spread of modern varieties instead point to the substantial productivity gains during a century of scientific breeding that mostly had little if anything to do with the availability of intellectual property protection. Some scientists may overstate the ability of plant variety protection to do good or harm.

The Future

In the context of sustainability, intellectual property rights can have both positive and negative effects. For intellectual property rights to operate effectively, policy makers should design their intellectual property rules on the basis of objective evidence. In addition, given the complexities involved and continued lack of certainty, planners need many more research results. Such research should be targeted to find the specific areas where the existence of intellectual property protection may unduly disrupt flows of environmentally sound goods, technologies, resources and practices, and the dissemination of the latest scientific information. Conversely, researchers need to work more to optimize the positive impacts of intellectual property rights in the interests of enhancing sustainability.

Graham DUTFIELD
University of Leeds

See also Advertising; Challenges to Measuring Sustainability; Ecolabels; Energy Labeling; Environmental Justice Indicators; International Organization for Standardization (ISO); Organic and Consumer Labels

FURTHER READING

Agreement on Trade-Related Aspects of Intellectual Property Rights (TRIPS). (1994). Retrieved November 5, 2011 from http://www.wto.org/english/tratop_e/trips_e/t_agm0_e.htm

Barton, John. (2007). *Intellectual property and access to clean energy technologies in developing countries: An analysis of solar photovoltaic, biofuel and wind technologies* (ICTSD Issue Paper no. 2). Geneva: International Centre for Trade and Sustainable Development. Retrieved October 25, 2011, from http://ictsd.org/i/publications/3354/

Dutfield, Graham. (2004). *Intellectual property, biogenetic resources and traditional knowledge*. London: Earthscan.

Dutfield, Graham, & Suthersanen, Uma. (2008). *Global intellectual property law*. Cheltenham, UK: Edward Elgar.

Maskus, Keith E., & Reichman, Jerome. (Eds.). (2005). *International public goods and transfer of technology under a globalized intellectual property regime*. Cambridge, UK: Cambridge University Press.

Rimmer, Matthew, & McLennan, Alison. (Eds.). (2012). *Intellectual property and emerging technologies: The new biology*. Cheltenham, UK: Edward Elgar.

Spence, Michael. (2007). *Intellectual property*. Oxford, UK: Oxford University Press.

Wong, Tzen, & Dutfield, Graham. (Eds.). (2011). *Intellectual property and human development: Current trends and future scenarios*. New York: Cambridge University Press.

Intergovernmental Science-Policy Platform for Biodiversity and Ecosystem Services (IPBES)

Since the 1990s, researchers and environmental groups have called for the establishment of a United Nations–sponsored organization to address scientific and policy concerns about biodiversity. In 2010, the United Nations General Assembly approved the creation of the Intergovernmental Science-Policy Platform for Biodiversity and Ecosystem Services (IPBES), which will regularly assess the state of the science and disseminate policy-relevant conclusions and tools to support sustainable development goals.

Leading up to the tenth Conference of the Parties to the Convention on Biological Diversity (CBD), delegates gathered at Busan, South Korea, in June 2010 and voted to establish the science-policy interface program known as the Intergovernmental Science-Policy Platform for Biodiversity and Ecosystem Services (IPBES). Approved by the United Nations General Assembly in December 2010, the independent platform will connect scientific knowledge on biodiversity and ecosystem services to government action worldwide, supporting the CBD and other multilateral environmental agreements. IPBES will prioritize scientific information needed for policy, assess existing knowledge on biodiversity and ecosystem services, disseminate policy-relevant tools and methodologies, and support capacity-building for policy makers (IPBES 2010).

The Long Road to IPBES

The Busan Outcome was the culmination of a process begun in the early 1990s by the United Nations Environment Programme (UNEP) and civil society to assess the state of biodiversity knowledge for creating policy to support the CBD. The urgency of the process heightened after 1999, when a number of leading research institutions and nongovernmental organizations (NGOs) developed a global assessment that became known as the Millennium Ecosystem Assessment (MA). Among other conclusions, the MA found that more than 60 percent of the services provided by ecosystems have been degraded, mostly during the past fifty years (MA 2005). Following the MA report, leading scientists and institutions called for further research into factors that affect biodiversity and ecosystem services and their relationship to human well-being (e.g., Carpenter et al. 2009).

A subsequent intergovernmental workshop on biodiversity in 2005 called for an international body to gather scientific evidence about services from biodiversity, identify global priorities for biodiversity conservation, and inform the CBD and other intergovernmental processes (see also Loreau et al. 2006). In response, CBD-affiliated scientists and agencies launched a two-year consultation called the International Mechanism of Scientific Expertise on Biodiversity (IMoSEB), which presented case studies on biodiversity science and policy in stakeholder meetings around the world. UNEP formally proposed a permanent, multistakeholder platform on biodiversity at the ninth CBD Conference of the Parties (COP) in May 2008.

The UNEP proposal was reviewed by government and civil society representatives over the following two years in a series of ad hoc multistakeholder and intergovernmental meetings. The 2010 UN General Assembly vote to establish the IPBES came as a result of the last of these meetings in Busan, South Korea, codified in the Busan Outcome, which endorsed six core findings of the UNEP

World Conservation Monitoring Centre (UNEP-WCMC 2009):

1. Though ad hoc, multiple science-policy interfaces exist, no mechanism yet exists for biodiversity.
2. These science-policy interfaces could be improved by increasing their independence and relevance for governance.
3. Despite an accumulation of knowledge in these interfaces, there are critical missing elements, including an understanding of relationships between drivers and outcomes for ecosystems and human well-being, a strategic guidance process to identify policy-relevant research, the incorporation of different types of knowledge and interdisciplinary approaches, ready access to data and effective use of existing data, and longitudinal studies.
4. The information available is not often presented in a policy-relevant way. For example, findings are sometimes contradictory, do not relate to policy alternatives, do not come from a shared framework or methodology, and have not come quickly for emerging issues of concern.
5. Existing coordinating bodies provide important lessons for a new coordinating authority to better align biodiversity research and capacity-building, reduce duplication and gaps in research, and increase relevance for governance.
6. For ecosystem services and biodiversity science to be used effectively in policy making, it is essential to build capacity in developing countries, in interdisciplinary approaches to producing new knowledge, and for appropriate use of knowledge in forming and implementing policy.

The first IPBES plenary was held in Nairobi, Kenya in October 2011.

The Mission of IPBES

IPBES was proposed to fill the gaps identified by UNEP-WCMC by bringing together relevant science and policy to support multilateral agreements and frameworks (IUCN 2012). Longtime IPBES supporters have characterized that role as "catalysing collaboration, strengthening existing scientific mechanisms, and making science more relevant by identifying priorities" (Larigauderie and Mooney 2010, 5). As approved in the Busan Outcome, the mission of IPBES is to create a science-policy interface for the conservation and sustainable use of biodiversity and ecosystem services, long-term human well-being, and sustainable development (IPBES 2010). Its principal functions are to identify gaps in the science, encourage and train researchers to fill those gaps, and translate research findings into actionable recommendations for policy makers at multiple levels.

IPBES is charged with performing impartial assessments of knowledge about biodiversity and ecosystem services as an independent body. It will play a coordinating role among relevant UN agencies and multistakeholder institutions, use its authority to support a research agenda that fills knowledge gaps, and address emerging concerns and policy questions. IPBES will build a repository of knowledge across fields, synthesize scientific evidence for policy makers, and describe the areas of consensus and controversy among scientists. Like the Intergovernmental Panel on Climate Change (IPCC), it will rely upon related mechanisms to perform primary research, conduct monitoring and observation, and establish multilateral policy related to biodiversity.

The Future: Opportunity and Challenges

The Busan Outcome acknowledged that global biodiversity and ecosystem services are suffering "significant loss," despite their critical importance for human welfare and poverty alleviation (IPBES 2010). To counter these losses, environmental conservation organizations have pushed for IPBES as a platform to stimulate national investment and action to protect biodiversity, particularly in developing countries. In 2012, the year IPBES is first fully operational, these decisions are still being solidified.

But concerns about sovereignty, rights, and ownership continue to affect the debate surrounding IPBES and related multilateral conventions. Developing countries have called for more financial support for their biodiversity conservation, payments for avoiding destructive activities, and a share in profits from exploiting genetic resources (Black 2010). Developed countries have urged stricter standards for species protection in the CBD and elsewhere. Meanwhile, environmental conservation organizations continue to push for action.

The debate is constrained by limited knowledge about how ecosystems work and how biodiversity relates to outcomes for human well-being. Future discussions are likely to focus on socioeconomic indicators related to ecosystem services and biodiversity, which have been identified collectively in the scientific literature as a gap in knowledge for policy making. Yet the necessary resources, determination, and coordination to tackle these scientific and policy concerns will depend in great part upon the establishment of IPBES and its approved functions, resource allocation, and composition.

Amy ROSENTHAL
Natural Capital Project at the World Wildlife Fund

See also Agenda 21; Citizen Science; Community and Stakeholder Input; Cost-Benefit Analysis; Framework for Strategic Sustainable Development (FSSD); Global Environment Outlook (GEO) Reports; Global Reporting Initiative (GRI); Millennium Development Goals; New Ecological Paradigm (NEP) Scale; Sustainability Science; Transdisciplinary Research

FURTHER READING

Black, Richard. (2010, October 21). Nature panel under threat as nations wrangle. *BBC News.* Retrieved December 11, 2010, from http://www.bbc.co.uk/news/science-environment-11595848

Carpenter, Stephen R., et al. (2009). Science for managing ecosystem services: Beyond the Millennium Ecosystem Assessment. *Proceedings of the National Academy of Sciences, 106*(5), 1305–1312.

Convention on Wetlands (Ramsar, Iran, 1971), 41st Meeting of the Standing Committee. (2010, April 26–May 1). Progress and advice on IPBES (Doc. SC41–27). Retrieved from http://www.ramsar.org/pdf/sc/41/sc41_doc27.pdf

Intergovernmental Science-Policy Platform on Biodiversity and Ecosystem Services (IPBES). (2010). 3rd meeting on IPBES. Retrieved November 12, 2010, from http://ipbes.net/3rd-meeting-on-ipbes.html?139181e9463c94a418d97a0a0634b1b9=95c414ef0fb89a13c545fe19e64df7b7

International Union for Conservation of Nature (IUCN). (2012). Intergovernmental Platform on Biodiversity and Ecosystem Services (IPBES). Retrieved February 22, 2012, from http://www.iucn.org/about/work/programmes/ecosystem_management/ipbes/

Larigauderie, Anne, & Mooney, Harold A. (2010). The Intergovernmental Science-Policy Platform on Biodiversity and Ecosystem Services: Moving a step closer to an IPCC-like mechanism for biodiversity. *Current Opinion in Environmental Sustainability, 2,* 1–6.

Loreau, Michel, et al. (2006, July 20). Diversity without representation. *Nature, 442,* 245–246.

Millennium Ecosystem Assessment (MA). (2005). *Ecosystems and human well-being: Synthesis.* Washington, DC: Island Press.

United Nations Environment Programme (UNEP). (n.d.). Homepage. Retrieved February 22, 2012, from http://www.unep.org/

United Nations Environment Programme World Conservation Monitoring Centre (UNEP-WCMC). (2009, August 19). Gap analysis for the purpose of facilitating the discussions on how to improve and strengthen the science-policy interface on biodiversity and ecosystem services (UNEP/IPBES/2/INF/1). Retrieved from http://www.ipbes.net/meetings/Documents/IPBES_2_1_INF_1%282%29.pdf

United Nations Environment Programme World Conservation Monitoring Centre (UNEP-WCMC). (2010). Intergovernmental Science-Policy Platform on Biodiversity and Ecosystem Services (IPBES). Retrieved November 7, 2010, from http://www.unep-wcmc.org/conventions/ipbes.aspx

International Organization for Standardization (ISO)

ISO, the abbreviation for the International Organization for Standardization, derives from the Greek word isos, meaning "equal." ISO, fittingly identified by the same three letters in all languages, is responsible for developing market-driven, voluntary standards or common language for products, services, and processes. From 1947, ISO gradually moved from product standards to process standards and, most recently, to social standards, reflecting global changes.

The International Organization for Standardization (ISO) is a multinational nonprofit organization based in Lausanne, Switzerland. ISO's goal is to create worldwide standards to assure the quality level of products and processes. ISO, rather than the obvious initialism IOS, comes from the Greek word *isos*, which means "equal." ISO creates equal standards that are used all over the world to produce quality products, services, and processes. ISO is the largest organization that creates international standards. Between its start in 1947 until the end of 2010, ISO has created more than nineteen thousand standards covering activities in all kinds of fields. Expert consensus sets the standards in any given field. These experts review the standards every five years to make sure they are up-to-date and address actual and relevant issues.

History

Two international organizations worked on creating standards: the International Federation of the National Standardizing Associations (ISA), which started in New York in 1926, and the United Nations Standards Coordinating Committee (UNSCC), which started its operations in 1944. These two organizations merged to form ISO. In October 1946 at the Institute of Civil Engineers in London, delegates from twenty-five countries created this new organization to coordinate industrial standards.

ISO developed only recommendations in the beginning. Manufacturers used its products to re-create national industries after World War II. In the early 1970s the organization decided that instead of making recommendations for national standards, they should create international standards addressing the growing needs of international trade. Because the organization's headquarters are located in Europe, however, most of the products applied only to Europe; local or regional organizations' standards applied in other parts of the world. In the early 1980s ISO began to focus on organizational practices and trade instead of the previous production focus. It created the ISO 9000 family of standards, which first standardized quality management terminology, then provided the requirements for quality management systems operated by organizations with different scopes of activity. Focusing on management quality standards increased the organization's impact and made ISO famous worldwide.

After the United Nations Conference on Environment and Development in Rio de Janeiro, Brazil, in 1992, ISO focused on finding solutions for global environmental challenges. The ISO 14000 family of standards for environmental management systems has become the most important and widely known ISO product in the early twenty-first century. It created the ISO 9001 and ISO 14001, which addressed organizational practices and trade, making ISO standards an essential for organizations in all sectors. By the end of 2011, ISO's 3,335 technical bodies had created 19,023 standards; the organization worked on 1,208 new standards in 2011 alone (ISO 2012a).

As a logical continuation of its new strategic focus, ISO began to concentrate on sustainability. The ISO 26000 standards, published in November 2010, provide guidance on social responsibility.

Costs and Benefits

The ISO standards' contribution to human evolution cannot be emphasized enough. Standards represent a common language to describe and ensure the desirable characteristics of physical products and services, known as *objects*. For example, ISO/TC 61 designates a technical committee working on the standardization of nomenclature, methods of test, and specifications applicable to materials and products in the field of plastics, while ISO 9001:2008 gives the requirements for quality management systems. In the process, standards reduce transaction costs by giving reliable information about the quality of the objects. ISO is responsible for most of the standards that benefit our everyday lives. When companies apply ISO 14000 standards, they implement an environmental management system by investigating all areas of activities that have an environmental impact. This system can save on waste management, energy, and material consumption, decrease distribution costs, and lead to a better corporate image. Researchers have offered a conceptual framework to improve environmental performance (Rondinelli and Vastag 2000; Vastag and Melnyk 2002), showing an illustrative example and results from a large-scale survey on the impacts of the ISO 14001 certification. A case study of Alcoa's aluminum ingot production facility in South Carolina revealed that "when corporations follow the spirit of the ISO 14001 guidelines, they can—as did Alcoa Mt. Holly—see attitudinal, managerial, and operational changes and their attendant benefits. The ISO 14001 standards can provide good 'common sense' guidelines for reducing the negative environmental impacts of industrial operations, thereby saving companies money from waste reduction and pollution prevention and at the same time contribute to the environmental quality of the communities in which they operate" (Rondinelli and Vastag 2000, 509).

Current Structure

By 2012 ISO had163 members of three kinds: member bodies (107), correspondent members (45), and subscriber members (11). A member body of ISO is the "most representative of standardization in its country" on the national level. There can be only one member body for each country. It is entitled to take part and have full voting rights on any ISO technical committee and policy committee. If an organization in a given country does not have a fully developed, representative national standards activity, it can be enrolled in ISO as a correspondent member. These members have the right to information about works of interest to them, but they do not have active voting rights in the committees. Subscriber membership enables smaller-nation economies to pay a reduced membership fee but still have some formal contact with the standardization ISO provides.

The General Assembly, the ultimate authority of ISO, meets once a year. The president, two vice presidents—one for policy and one for technical management—the treasurer, and the secretary-general are the principal officers. Member bodies nominate the delegates. Correspondent members and subscriber members may attend as observers. The General Assembly's agenda relates primarily to the ISO annual report, the *Strategic Plan*, and the treasurer's annual financial status report on the ISO Central Secretariat.

The ISO governing rules, the statutes, stipulate that its Council performs most of the operative and governance functions of ISO. The Council acts in accordance with the policy the member bodies have previously agreed upon. It meets twice a year. Its rotating membership ensures that all member bodies are equally represented over time. The different policy-development committees, which provide strategic guidance for the standards' development work on cross-sector aspects, belong to the council. They are the Committee on Conformity Assessment (CASCO), the Committee on Consumer Policy (COPOLCO), and the Committee on Developing Countries Matters (DEVCO). Member bodies and correspondent members both can take part in these policy development committees.

The main operational work is the task of the secretary-general, who reports to the Council. The Council's tasks include supporting ISO members, coordinating standards' development, publishing approved standards, and supporting the governing bodies.

The overall management of the technical work including the coordination of creating the strategy and the activities of the technical advisory groups is the duty of the Technical Management Board (TMB), whom the member bodies elect according to the Council's criteria.

Global Impact

The greatest international impact of ISO is through the application of standards in developing countries. The standards provide a development path for these countries regarding product, performance, quality, safety, and environmental issues. In the rebuilding period after World War II, the number of new ISO member bodies from the developing world increased enormously. Because most developing countries lacked an existing technological infrastructure and financial resources, they could not use ISO standards. In order to solve this problem, in 1968 ISO created the category of correspondent membership that involved developing countries in the work of ISO for a lower membership fee. Correspondent membership made it possible to design standards to meet the needs of developing countries. In order to expand the sphere of possible members to even countries with very small economies, in 1992 the organization introduced the subscriber member category, which enabled members to access the standards for a minimum fee.

The publication of the ISO 9000 family standard played an important role in globalization from the second part of the 1980s. It assisted multinational companies in bringing quality management systems to less developed countries, raising the level of performance in these countries. The ISO 14000 family standard, with its focus on environmental management, was also a major step toward fighting global environmental challenges such as excessive pollution, overuse of resources, and increasing waste production.

The ISO 14000 family proposed that companies organize their activities to minimize their impact on the environment. This family suggests that companies create an environmental policy, plan activities that influence the environment, implement and operate environmental management systems, check and correct actions that significantly impact the environment, and conduct management review of environmental management systems.

Monitoring and Developing New Standards

ISO starts developing new standards once stakeholders (such as industry and industry/trade associations, science and academia, consumers and consumer associations, governments and regulators, and societal and other interests, often represented by nongovernmental organizations) clearly formulate a need for them. The stakeholders take part in the technical work of ISO through national delegations that ISO member bodies (full members) appoint or, in the case of international organizations, through liaison organizations.

The first step of creating a new standard is to highlight the need for it. An industry sector or other stakeholder group to an ISO national member can bring forward the need. The member proposes the issue as a new work item to the relevant committee or, if a committee does not exist, to a new ISO technical committee whose duty it is to develop standards in that area. Organizations in liaison with the technical committees may also propose new work items for development. The new work item then needs to receive majority support from the participating members of the relevant technical committee. The members evaluate the new work item based on certain criteria. Because the organization's goal is to set global standards, a new work item must meet globally relevant standards. These items thus should respond to an international need, and they need to be able to be implemented worldwide.

If a specific field other than a certain industry sector requires standardization, policy development committees become involved in the standardization process for developing countries (DEVCO), consumers (COPOLCO), and conformity assessment (CASCO). These committees' standardization process is like that of the technical committees.

ISO creates technical committees for certain industrial, technical, and business sectors, and assigns experts in the field. Delegates of government agencies, associations, organizations, and science participate in the technical committees' standards development process. If a need for standards development arises and a new technological committee needs to form, the ISO asks all national member bodies to involve themselves in the process, either as participants or observers. The experts in the technical committees, selected by the national member bodies, participate as national delegations.

The Standard Development Process

Creating a proposal in a technical committee is the first step of the standards development process. If the majority of the committee member votes in favor of the new proposal and at least five members are willing to actively participate in the development of the standard, the new project is accepted. A working group of experts and stakeholders forms to create a draft document that the technical committee must accept. Committee members discuss, debate, and argue about the draft document until they reach a consensus. They then send the resulting document to all ISO member bodies as a Draft International Standard (DIS) for voting and comment. If the voting is in favor, the document becomes a Final Draft International Standard (FDIS) that includes all the suggested modifications. ISO puts it up to another vote from all ISO members. If the vote is successful, the FDIS becomes an international standard, and ISO publishes it. ISO reviews each standard three years after the publication and then in five years to make sure that the standard is still relevant.

If substantial technical development and debate occur during the work of the technical committee, they may submit the DIS for "fast track" processing. There is then no need for ISO members to vote a second time.

International Agreements

In May 1985, the European Council passed the New Approach Directives, the means by which open, voluntary standardization can support regulations concerning products on the European market. The directives defined "essential requirements" (e.g., related to health, safety, and environment) that products must meet before they can be placed on the European market. Europe already had voluntary standards that supported this legislation. The standards achieved the political objective of creating a single European market. This legislation boosted the growth of the European Committee for Standardization (CEN) and its programs. Because non-Europeans found it difficult to get information about European standardization activities, they approached ISO to take action. In the Lisbon Agreement of 1989, ISO and CEN agreed to provide each other full and mutual exchange of information. In 1991, ISO and CEN reached the Vienna Agreement. It went one step further and helped the integration of the European market into the global market. It made the European and other international standards compatible or even identical. ISO and CEN agreed to harmonize their activities because both organizations' processes required the use of expert resources.

Outlook

ISO started as an organization to create standards mainly for supporting international trade. When it published the ISO 9000 (1987) and later the ISO 14000 (1996), which dealt with management and environmental management issues, ISO became the world's largest organization dealing with standard development.

ISO has turned its focus on creating new standards that address worldwide issues. It published its ISO 26000 standard family (2010), which gives guidance on social responsibility as it becomes more and more important in international business. This new family, on the other hand, does not follow the management system model of previous standards because it is not a certification standard. As the number of ISO members continues to grow and globalization increases, the ISO will create and introduce more and more standards.

In 2012, twenty years after the United Nations Conference on Environment and Development in Rio de Janeiro, ISO's portfolio of standards provides solutions in all three dimensions of sustainable development—environmental, economic, and societal. In addition to ISO 14001, ISO offers twenty-four other standards covering specific challenges to the environment (e.g., environmental labeling, greenhouse gases). The economic benefits of standardization are well documented and may reach 1 percent of participating countries' gross domestic product. The public response to the new standard on social responsibility indicates a growing expectation that organizations take responsibility for their actions and act in a transparent and ethical manner.

Gyula VASTAG
Pannon University & Corvinus University of Budapest

Gergely TYUKODI
Corvinus University of Budapest

Áron ANTAL
Corvinus University of Budapest

See also Business Reporting Methods; Ecological Footprint Accounting; Energy Efficiency Measurement; Energy Labeling; Global Environment Outlook (GEO) Reports; Life Cycle Assessment (LCA); Life Cycle Costing (LCC); Life Cycle Management (LCM); Material Flow Analysis (MFA); National Environmental Accounting; Triple Bottom Line

FURTHER READING

International Institute for Sustainable Development (IISD). (1996). Global green standards: ISO 14000 and sustainable development. Retrieved February 6, 2012, from http://www.iisd.org/pdf/globlgrn.pdf

International Organization for Standardization (ISO). (2011). *Rio+20. Forging action from agreement: How ISO standards translate good intentions about sustainability into concrete results.* Retrieved February 12, 2012, from http://www.iso.org/iso/rio_20_forging_action_with_agreement.pdf

International Organization for Standardization (ISO). (2012a). About ISO. Retrieved February 17, 2012, from http://www.iso.org/iso/about.htm

International Organization for Standardization (ISO). (2012b). Discover ISO: What standards do. Retrieved February 17, 2012, from http://www.iso.org/iso/about.htm

Rondinelli, Dennis A., & Vastag, Gyula. (2000). Panacea, common sense, or just a label? The value of ISO 14001 Environmental Management Systems. *European Management Journal, 18*(5), 499–510.

Vastag, Gyula, & Melnyk, Steven A. (2002). Certifying environmental management systems by the ISO 14001 standards. *International Journal of Production Research, 40*(18), 4743–4763.

Whitelaw, Ken. (2004). *ISO 14001 environmental systems handbook* (2nd ed.) Burlington, MA: Butterworth-Heinemann.

Land-Use and Land-Cover Change

Land-use and land-cover change have significantly altered the Earth's surface. The current scientific understanding of these processes as a result of human-environment interactions is essential for evaluating their impacts on the environment and on sustainable development. Measurement methods include remote sensing and inventory data, which also are used to project potential future development in relation to global change.

Since the development of agriculture and a sedentary lifestyle, humans have continually changed the surface of the Earth to provide food, energy, and living space. The extent of these changes rose to an unprecedented level with the Industrial Revolution and population increase during the eighteenth century. Scientists have studied the impacts of land-use and land-cover change within their specific disciplines, such as forestry, agriculture, and ecology, over many decades. But land-use change as a general field of science that integrates human and environmental factors was established only as the dramatic loss of natural ecosystems through human expansion was recognized as a global problem beginning in the 1990s.

Understanding Land-Use and Land-Cover Change (LUCC)

The term *land cover* refers to the biophysical properties of the Earth's surface and its natural or human-made components. These properties include vegetation, fauna, soil, bodies of water, and other topographical features, as well as streets and structures in cities and towns. There is no standard classification of land-cover types. Global maps often apply the classification system developed by the International Geosphere-Biosphere Programme (IGBP)

that defines sixteen land-cover types, including various types of forest, grassland, and shrubland (Loveland et al. 2000). The Land Cover Classification System (LCCS) from the United Nations Food and Agricultural Organization (FAO) is more suitable for studying smaller geographical areas (Di Gregorio 2005). It provides a classification system that describes land-cover types hierarchically and can therefore be used to define regional land-cover patterns in a very detailed and consistent manner. *Land-cover change* happens either in the form of conversions or modifications (Meyer and Turner 1994). *Conversion* is a fundamental change of the Earth's biophysical properties, meaning that an existing land-cover type is replaced with a different one (e.g., forest is converted to cropland). On the other hand, *modification* is a change in the management of an existing land-cover type. Good examples of modification are logging management plans that affect the species and age distribution of trees in a forest.

The term *land use* refers to the way humans are using the land base or the existing land cover. Examples of land-use classifications are housing, crop cultivation, cattle grazing, and recreation. A particular type of land cover can be linked to different types of land use. For instance, forest as a land-cover type is characterized by the dominant presence of trees, but the forest can be used for wood production and/or can serve as a recreation area. Oftentimes land has multiple uses, although these may be difficult to discern from the appearance of the area (see Harrington 1996). For this reason, maps often combine land use and land cover, showing cover (generally based on satellite imagery) where use is not clear or takes multiple forms. Changing land use can cause either a conversion or a modification of land cover. Consequently, land use links human activities to the environment that is defined by the land cover.

Using a scientific approach to describe these interactions, researchers have proposed the concept of *land systems* as "coupled human-environment systems" (Turner, Lambin, and Reenberg 2007). In this context, a conceptual framework exists to describe and understand changes in land cover and land use, and it differentiates between proximate and underlying, or ultimate, causes of land-use change (see Meyer and Turner 1994; Geist and Lambin 2001). *Proximate causes* are human activities that lead to land-use change and as a result to a conversion or modification of land cover; they are more easily identified as a direct influence on LUCC. Examples include deforestation by slash-and-burn farming to create new cropland, application of fertilizer on a corn field, and the development of a new road network to provide improved regional transportation infrastructure. In contrast, *underlying causes* are a complex system of social, political, economic, technological, and cultural variables that are responsible for the emerging proximate causes. Social variables include the demographic development of a population as well as changes in personal lifestyle, expressed, for instance, in an increasing per capita demand for food and energy. Political variables include rural and urban development plans and the implementation of land-use restrictions within a nature conservation area. Economic variables include local and global economic growth and market mechanisms. Technological development includes scientific advances. In the agricultural sector, for example, this might mean increasing crop yields due to the breeding of new crop varieties and the development of improved cultivation methods. Finally, cultural variables include public attitudes, values, and beliefs, for instance, about environmental issues, as well as individual and household behavior.

Changes in the environment can influence the type and extent of land-use change within a region. Agriculture requires suitable soil and climate conditions, for instance, and the development of settlements might be restricted by terrain and/or topography. Climate change or the decline of soil fertility caused by erosion can have direct effects on land-use decisions (e.g., selection of crop type or fertilizer application rates). It is clear that the interdependencies between underlying and proximate causes on the one hand and environmental conditions on the other hand are very complex and variable in different parts of the world.

Measurement

The measurement of land cover is based on remote sensing techniques, such as aerial photography and satellite imagery. Prominent examples of satellite sensors that provide high spatial resolution land-cover data (about 10 m × 10 m to 30 m × 30 m) are LANDSAT TM (Thematic Mapper)

and SPOT (Systeme Pour l'Observation de la Terre) as well as the Indian Remote Sensing program (IRS). Additionally, data from commercial satellites with a spatial resolution of less than 5 m × 5 m, such as IKONOS or QUICKBIRD, are available. Medium-resolution data are used to develop globally consistent land-cover data sets. One of the first attempts to collect these data is the IGBP-DIS data set (Loveland et al. 2000), which maps global land cover with a spatial resolution of 1 km × 1 km. Later examples are the products based on data from the MODIS sensor (Friedl et al. 2002), with a resolution of up to 500 m × 500 m, and the GLOBCOVER project (300 m × 300 m). The second step in the analysis of land-cover data is to interpret the remote sensing raw data in order to define the land-cover class of each data point according to one of the accepted classification systems. Here, statistical techniques such as cluster analysis are applied. Nevertheless, two studies point out that the resulting global land-cover maps show significant differences depending on the satellite sensor and the approach used to interpret the data (Hannerz and Lotsch 2006; Giri, Zhu, and Reed 2005).

In order to generate information about land-cover change, it is necessary to monitor spatial land-cover distributions over a specific period of time. Consistent remote sensing data and classification methods must be used to ensure reliable interpretation. This type of analysis is often focused on a specific scientific question. Good examples are the monitoring of tropical deforestation during the 1990s by the TREES project (Mayaux et al. 2005), using LANDSAT data, and the study by Ruth DeFries and her colleagues (2002) using Advanced Very High Resolution Radiometer (AVHRR) data. Consistent time series data for land-cover distribution on the continental and global scale has been available only since about 2000. MODIS provides such products on the global level, while the CORINE Land Cover (CLC) data set covers the area of the European Union.

Data on land-use change is not usually accessible by satellite or airplane, and is therefore collected by censuses and surveys. This is typically done on the level of administrative units such as countries, districts, and towns or as surveys on the household or farm level. On the global level, the FAO is collecting statistical land-use data for all UN member countries, focusing on the agricultural and forestry sectors. While data for the agricultural sector is sampled at yearly intervals, the FAO Forest Resource Assessment (FRA) is updated at five-year intervals. In both cases, the inventories rely on national reporting, and as a result, their quality depends heavily on the accuracy of data collection within each country. Additionally, in countries such as the United States, Brazil, India, and Russia, as well as in the European Union, subnational inventories are available for land-use relevant variables such as population development, agricultural production, and forest management. As these inventories are updated regularly and historical data accumulate, they provide a valuable source of information.

Recently, several scientists have attempted to develop what are referred to as *spatially explicit land-use data sets* by combining remote sensing land-cover data and inventory data. This approach has been applied to various problems. One early project linked remote sensing data on nighttime light intensity with census data on gross domestic product (GDP) and population to generate population density maps and information on the spatial distribution of GDP (Doll, Muller, and Morley 2006). Other researchers developed global maps of crop distribution by merging census data and remote sensing land-cover data (Monfreda, Ramankutty, and Foley 2008; Ramankutty et al. 2008), and Georg Kindermann and his colleagues (2008) have published a global map of forest resources. Another approach is the global map of anthropogenic biomes, which describe the alteration of ecosystem structure and functions by human societies (Ellis and Ramankutty 2008). While each of these maps is specific to a single point in time, other researchers have aimed to identify global hot spots of rapid land-cover change (Lepers et al. 2005). This analysis combines remote sensing and inventory data to synthesize global maps of land-cover changes that have occurred since the 1980s. Some of the results are discussed below under the heading "Human Impact on LUCC: Outlook."

Impacts and Sustainability

Sustainable land use in the narrow sense can be defined as "the use of land resources to produce goods and services in such a way that, over the long term, the natural resource base is not damaged and that future human needs can be met" (Reid et al. 2006). In this context, the concept of *ecosystem services,* a scientifically well-established framework that describes the linkage between human society and the environment, is important. Different types of ecosystems and associated land-cover types provide different goods and services to society, including material resources such as food, energy, and space for living, but also processes such as climate regulation and water retention to avoid flooding (MEA 2005).

A depletion of these natural resources may imply negative consequences for human well-being (e.g., loss of forest recreation area or air pollution) and for the society's future social and economic development options (e.g., loss of genetic variability of plants or soil erosion that depletes soil fertility). Consequently, trade-offs are required to achieve a balance between the provision of essential material resources and the stabilization of other ecosystem services in the long run (Foley et al. 2005).

The importance of looking at these trade-offs can be illustrated with agriculture. In the past 150 years, two trends in agricultural development can be observed: expansion of cropland and pasture area and, since the 1960s, increase in crop yields per hectare (see Klein Goldewijk 2005). This became possible due to technological advancements, including the breeding of new crop varieties, application of mineral fertilizer, pesticides, and irrigation (e.g. via the Green Revolution). Although food security has not yet been achieved for all parts of the world, the total production of food (which is an important ecosystem service) has increased significantly due to these developments. But in turn, numerous negative effects on other services can be observed. Expansion of cropland, for instance, has been identified as a major factor in the loss of natural ecosystems. In particular, the loss of forest cover is an important driver for the release of carbon dioxide into the atmosphere (Achard et al. 2004), for changes in global water fluxes (Rockström et al. 1999), and for the decrease of biological diversity due to destruction and fragmentation of habitats (Sala et al. 2000). Intensification of agricultural management also adversely impacts ecosystems and human beings. For example, large cropland monocultures negatively affect biodiversity, while the excessive application of mineral fertilizer might alter the nutrient cycles within ecosystems. In addition, there may also be negative effects on human health, as might be caused by an improper application of pesticides, for example. With respect to global food security, the overarching question will be to identify ways to produce enough food for a growing world population, which may stabilize only after 2050, and to minimize the negative effects on ecosystem functioning. The scientific community is vigorously debating whether these aims might best be achieved by further agricultural intensification or by establishing larger but more extensively used cropping and grazing systems (Green et al. 2005; Power 2010). Another very important aspect of sustainability is the question of land tenure and, consequently, people's access to land and water resources. Competition for these resources can be observed both between nature conservation and agriculture and also among different human-influenced land uses. Examples include new settlement areas that encroach on fertile cropland and newly introduced energy crops that compete with food crops. Both developments might have negative consequences on food security of the local population, as land formerly available for food production is converted to another type of land use. The effect of the resulting "indirect land-use change" can be observed in a study of Brazil conducted by the ecologist David Lapola and his colleagues (2010). The study illustrates how replacing the cultivation of food crops with biofuel crops pushes grazing land farther toward the Amazon region, causing additional deforestation in that area; but it also highlights how these effects might be overcome by more effective pasture management.

Land-use change also affects water availability and accessibility of water resources. For instance, industry, households, and irrigated agriculture may compete for limited water within a region, and the emission of wastewater and nutrients can have an impact on water quality. A detailed introduction to these topics can be found in *Land-Use and Land-Cover Change: Local Processes and Global Impacts*, edited by Eric Lambin and Helmut Geist (2006).

Human Impact on LUCC: Outlook

Today more than 75 percent of the ice-free, terrestrial Earth's surface is influenced by human activities, with agriculture (cropland and grazing land) accounting for 40 percent of the land area (Ellis and Ramankutty 2008; Foley et al. 2005). Maps of rapid land-cover change summarize the most important developments since the 1980s (Lepers et al. 2005). These maps differentiate between changes in forest cover, agricultural land, urbanization, and land degradation. Deforestation can be observed mainly in the tropics, with hot spots in Southeast Asia and the Amazon. For humid tropical forests in Africa, the TREES project (Mayaux et al. 2005) quantifies the mean deforested area to about 7,000 square kilometers per year during the observation period 1990 to 1997. This equals a mean annual rate of deforestation of 0.36 percent. Agricultural area is expanding in many parts of the world, including Southeast Asia, eastern Africa, and the Amazon basin, while in some highly industrialized countries such as the United States and those of the European Union, exactly the opposite trend,

with decreasing area under cultivation, can be observed. As a result of unsustainable human activities, such as overgrazing, expansion of cropland into unsuitable regions, and uncontrolled wood extraction, the further degradation of arid lands is a global phenomenon. Sensitive regions are located on the Asian continent, eastern Africa, and the Mediterranean.

Future LUCC will be determined by the underlying and proximate drivers described earlier in this article. The dominant force will be the projected increase of human population up to about 9 billion people by the year 2050. This will lead to an increase in the demand for food and energy that will put further stress on land resources. Various scientists have used the available data to project future development pathways. Joseph Alcamo and colleagues (2006) found that during the next decade the current trends of urbanization and the expansion of agricultural area at the cost of natural land such as forest is very likely to continue. Pete Smith at the University of Aberdeen and his colleagues (2010) identify a growing competition among different land uses for available land resources. Against this future, the implementation of strategies and policies for sustainable management of land resources based on sound analysis of the available data is one of the major challenges for societies.

Rüdiger SCHALDACH
University of Kassel, Germany

See also Challenges to Measuring Sustainability; Computer Modeling; Ecological Footprint Accounting; Ecological Impact Assessment (EcIA); Geographic Information Systems (GIS); I = P × A × T Equation; New Ecological Paradigm (NEP) Scale; Reducing Emissions from Deforestation and Forest Degradation (REDD); Remote Sensing; Strategic Environmental Assessment (SEA); Systems Thinking; Transdisciplinary Research

FURTHER READING

Achard, Frédéric; Eva, Hugh D.; Mayaux, Philippe; Stibig, Hans-Jürgen; & Belward, Alan. (2004). Improved estimates of net carbon emissions from land cover change in the tropics for the 1990s. *Global Biogeochemical Cycles, 18*(2), Article GB2008. doi:10.1029/2003GB002142

Alcamo, Joseph; Kok, Kasper; Busch, Gerald; & Priess, Jörg A. (2006). Searching for the future of land: Scenarios from the local to global scale. In Eric F. Lambin & Helmut J. Geist (Eds.), *Land-use and land-cover change: Local processes and global impacts* (pp. 137–156). New York: Springer.

DeFries, Ruth S., et al. (2002). Carbon emissions from tropical deforestation and regrowth based on satellite observations for the 1980s and 1990s. *Proceedings of the National Academy of Sciences of the United States of America, 99*(22), 14256–14261.

Di Gregorio, Antonio. (2005). Land cover classification system. Classification concepts and user manual (Version 2) [Software]. Rome: Food and Agricultural Organization of the United Nations (FAO).

Doll, Christopher N. H.; Muller, Jan-Peter; & Morley, Jeremy G. (2006). Mapping regional economic activity from night time light satellite imagery. *Ecological Economics, 57*(1), 75–92.

Ellis, Erle C., & Ramankutty, Navin. (2008). Putting people on the map: Anthropogenic biomes of the world. *Frontiers in Ecology, 6*(8), 439–447.

Foley, Jonathan A., et al. (2005). Global consequences of land use. *Science, 309*(5734), 570–574.

Friedl, Mark A., et al. (2002). Global land cover mapping from MODIS: Algorithms and early results. *Remote Sensing of Environment, 83*(1–2), 287–302.

Geist, Helmut J., & Lambin, Eric F. (2001). *What drives tropical deforestation* (LUCC Report Series No. 4). Louvain-la-Neuve, Belgium: Land-Use and Land-Cover Change (LUCC) International Project Office, University of Louvain.

Giri, Chandra; Zhu, Zhiliang; & Reed, Bradley. (2005). A comparative analysis of the global land cover 2000 and MODIS land cover data sets. *Remote Sensing of Environment, 94*(1), 123–132.

Green, Rhys E.; Cornell, Stephen J.; Scharlemann, Jörn P. W.; & Balmford, Andrew. (2005). Farming and the fate of wild nature. *Science, 307*(5709), 550–555.

Gutman, Garik, et al. (Eds.). (2004). *Land change science: Observing, monitoring, and understanding trajectories of change on the earth's surface.* Dordrecht, The Netherlands: Kluwer.

Hannerz, Fredrik, & Lotsch, Alexander. (2006). *Assessment of land use and cropland inventories for Africa* (CEEPA Discussion Paper No. 22). Pretoria, South Africa: Centre for Environmental Economics and Policy in Africa (CEEPA), University of Pretoria.

Harrington, Lisa M. B. (1996). Regarding research as a land use. *Applied Geography, 16*(4), 265–277.

Kindermann, Georg, E.; McCallum, Ian; Fritz, Steffen; & Obersteiner, Michael. (2008). A global forest growing stock, biomass and carbon map based on FAO statistics. *Silva Fennica, 42*(3), 387–396.

Klein Goldewijk, Kees. (2005). Three centuries of global population growth: A spatial referenced population (density) database for 1700–2000. *Population and Environment, 26*(4), 343–367.

Lambin, Eric F., & Geist, Helmut J. (Eds.). (2006). *Land-use and land-cover change: Local processes and global impacts.* New York: Springer.

Lapola, David M., et al. (2010). Indirect land-use changes can overcome carbon savings from biofuels in Brazil. *Proceedings of the National Academy of Sciences of the United States of America, 107*(8), 3388–3393.

Lepers, Erika, et al. (2005). A synthesis of information on rapid land-cover change for the period 1981–2000. *BioScience, 55*(2), 115–124.

Loveland, Thomas R., et al. (2000). Development of a global land cover characteristics database and IGBP DISCover from 1-km AVHRR data. *International Journal of Remote Sensing, 21*(6–7), 1303–1330.

Mayaux, Philippe, et al. (2005). Tropical forest cover change in the 1990s and options for future monitoring. *Philosophical Transaction of the Royal Society B: Biological Sciences, 360*(1454), 373–384.

Meyer, William B., & Turner, Billie L., II. (Eds.). (1994). *Changes in land use and land cover: A global perspective.* Cambridge, UK: Cambridge University Press.

Millennium Ecosystem Assessment (MEA). (2005). *Ecosystems and human well-being: Vol. 2, Scenarios.* Washington, DC: Island Press.

Monfreda, Chad; Ramankutty, Navin; & Foley, Jonathan A. (2008). Farming the planet: 2. Geographic distribution of crop areas, yields, physiological types, and net primary production in the year 2000. *Global Biogeochemical Cycles, 22,* Article GB1022. doi:10.1029/2007GB002947

Power, Alison G. (2010). Ecosystem services and agriculture: Tradeoffs and synergies. *Philosophical Transactions of the Royal Society B: Biological Sciences, 365*(1554), 2959–2971.

Ramankutty, Navin; Evan, Amato T.; Monfreda, Chad; & Foley, Jonathan A. (2008). Farming the planet: 1. Geographic distribution of global agricultural lands in the year 2000. *Global Biogeochemical Cycles, 22*(1), Article GB1003. doi:10.1029/2007GB002952

Reid, Robin S.; Tomich, Thomas P.; Xu, Jianchu; Geist, Helmut J.; & Mather, Alexander S. (2006). Linking land-change science and policy: Current lessons and future integration. In Eric F. Lambin & Helmut J. Geist (Eds.), *Land-use and land-cover change: Local processes and global impacts* (pp. 157–172). New York: Springer.

Rockström, Johan; Gordon, Line; Folke, Carl; Falkenmark, Malin; & Engwall, Maria. (1999). Linkages among water vapor flows, food production and terrestrial ecosystem services. *Conservation Ecology, 3*(2), Article 5. Retrieved September 7, 2011, from http://www.consecol.org/vol3/iss2/art5/

Sala, Osvaldo E., et al. (2000). Global biodiversity scenarios for the year 2100. *Science, 287*(5459), 1770–1774.

Smith, Pete, et al. (2010). Competition for land. *Philosophical Transactions of the Royal Society B: Biological Sciences, 365*(1554), 2941–2957.

Turner, Billie L., II; Lambin, Eric F.; & Reenberg, Anette. (2007). The emergence of land change science for global environmental change and sustainability. *Proceedings of the National Academy of Sciences of the United States of America, 104*(52), 20666–20671.

Watson, Robert T., et al. (2000). *Land use, land-use change, and forestry.* Cambridge, UK: Cambridge University Press for the Intergovernmental Panel on Climate Change (IPCC).

Life Cycle Assessment (LCA)

Life cycle assessment plays a role as the environmental pillar within sustainability analysis. It provides a quantitative approach for developing sustainability indicators, analyzing the environmental and social impacts of a product or service from its inception to final disposal, or "from cradle to grave." The value and usefulness of LCA analysis heavily depend on the choices of methodologies made throughout the process.

According to the International Organization for Standardization (ISO), life cycle assessment (LCA) is the "compilation and evaluation of the inputs and outputs and the potential environmental impacts of a product system throughout its life cycle." The analysis begins when raw materials are acquired or generated from natural resources and ends with final disposal (ISO 2006a). Typically, LCA studies different options by linking changes in the production and disposal of goods and services to impacts on the environment (Wrisberg and Udo de Haes 2002), paying attention to the entire natural history of a product or system—from the extraction of raw materials to its final disposal, or "from cradle to grave."

LCA has its roots in the comparative study of environmental impacts of consumer products, which dates back to the 1960s and 1970s. One of several environmental management techniques, LCA plays a major role, at both the individual company and the institutional level, in supporting environmentally conscious decision making in business, and it has become a core element in guiding environmental policy and voluntary corporate behavior in the European Union and the United States, as well as other countries (Guinée et al. 2011).

An LCA study must be carried out in accordance with the technical norms established by the ISO (ISO 14040 and ISO 14044). It has four fundamental phases: goal and scope definition, inventory analysis, impact assessment,

and interpretation (ISO 2006a; ISO 2006b). The scope of an LCA study, defined in the first phase, affects the definition of the system boundaries and the level of detail. The primary function fulfilled by the product system under study must also be specified. The life cycle inventory (LCI) analysis phase involves the collection of the data on each stage of activity, especially regarding the environmental impacts. The life cycle impact assessment (LCIA) phase establishes a relationship between the quantified environmental impacts and the various impact categories they contribute to. Finally, the life cycle interpretation phase summarizes and discusses the results as a basis for conclusions, recommendations, and decision making. It is important to note that methodological assumptions made in each phase crucially affect the accuracy of the measures achieved as well as the value and utility of the final analysis and conclusions. Usually, LCA is conducted using dedicated software packages and datasets, the careful choice of which is key for achieving a useful analysis.

Preparing the Life Cycle Inventory

The inventory analysis phase is the empirical part of the evaluation. Because it is a comprehensive tool, LCA has a high data need, which can be met partly by collecting specific data on a case-by-case basis and partly by relying on databases. While gathering data for an LCI, no distinction is normally made for where and when emissions or extractions take place, thus making LCA site-independent and steady-state (Wrisberg and Udo de Haes 2002). Several measures to introduce a time dimension to LCA modeling have been proposed, which would make LCA dynamic, rather than steady-state. These measures, however, are controversial. Another sometimes controversial angle is the consequential approach, which emphasizes the consequences of changes caused by decisions or actions. This represents a way of conceiving LCA that also has consequences for many methodological choices.

Two issues that arise during the inventory phase can have a major impact on the final analysis; one concerns the allocation of environmental impacts to two or more products obtained by the same technological process. ISO recommends avoiding allocation when possible, either by dividing the unit processes into subprocesses and gathering the required environmental burden data, or by expanding the product system definitions. If allocation cannot be avoided, the environmental burdens of each product should be apportioned either according to their underlying physical relationships or to other relationships. This allocation process is among the most controversial issues in LCA (Suh et al. 2010; Guinée, Heijungs, and Huppes 2004; Weidema 2001; Heijungs and Fischknecht 1998).

Reuse and recycling scenarios are also problematic. There are several possible approaches (Fishknecht 2010). Under the recycled content, or cutoff, approach, environmental impacts are accounted for at the time they occur, so the second use of a material does not bear any environmental load from the primary material production activities. Alternatively, according to the end of life recycling, or avoided burden, approach, the amount of a given material that will probably be recycled in the future results in a reduction in primary material production; the avoided emissions must be credited to the product that delivers the scrap for recycling, thus reducing its environmental impacts substantially.

Life Cycle Impact Assessment

In the impact assessment phase, there is both an empirical and a normative component. The former consists of scientific information about several environmental effects. This information will be used to define the factors that provide quantifiable representations of environmental impact, including issues affecting the natural environment, human health, or resources. The normative component consists of information about the social values attached to the different impact categories, which can lead to the creation of a set of weighting factors.

Impact evaluation can be performed at any stage in the product life cycle, which starts from the first environmental interventions (emissions, extraction, land use); these impacts are quantified by impact indicators (such as climate change) that are responsible for certain types of damage (for example, value of lost land due to sea-level rise). The impact assessment takes place at either the midpoint or endpoint stage.

The main distinction between midpoint and endpoint indicators for a particular environmental impact category is that endpoint indicators are calculated to reflect differences between various stressors at an endpoint in a product life cycle, which may be relevant to society's understanding of the final effect. Midpoint indicators, on the other hand, provide parameters for potential impact rather than a final measurement. For example, global warming potential is a midpoint measure in the context of impacts to humans and ecosystems in the event of global warming, whereas the years of life lost (YOLL) due to ozone formation is an example of an endpoint indicator of human health impacts.

During the LCIA phase, the results are usually assigned to selected impact categories (classification). They are then converted to the common unit of the category indicator by means of available characterization factors (characterization). Additional nonmandatory steps may include the calculation of the magnitude of category indicator results relative to reference information (normalization), and weighting aggregate indicator results across impact categories based on social values.

Impact categories and characterization models change according to the methodology chosen. Practitioners have to select those that are relevant to the goal of their particular study. There are several relevant categories for which adequate baseline characterization methods are available (Guinée 2002):

- Depletion of abiotic resources: affected by LCI results such as the extraction of minerals and foil fuels, expressed in kilograms per functional unit (kg/functional unit). The typical category indicator is the depletion of the ultimate reserve in relation to annual use, and the characterization factor is the abiotic depletion potential (ADP) in kg antimony equivalents/kg extraction.

- Land competition: affected by LCI results such as the land use in square meters per year (m²/yr). The typical category indicator is land occupation.
- Climate change: affected by LCI results such as emissions of greenhouse gases (GHG) to the air in kg/functional unit. The typical category indicator is the infrared radiative forcing watts per square meter (W/m²), and the characterization factor is, for example, the global warming potential for a hundred-year time horizon (GDP_{100}) in kg carbon dioxide equivalents/kg GHG emission.
- Stratospheric ozone depletion: affected by LCI results such as emissions of ozone-depleting gases to the air. The typical category indicator is the stratospheric ozone breakdown, and the characterization factor is, for example, the ozone depletion potential in the steady state ($ODP_{steady\ state}$) in kg chlorofluorocarbon-11 equivalent/kg emission.
- Toxicity: affected by LCI results such as emissions of toxic substances to air, water, and soil (in kg). For human toxicity, the typical category indicator is the acceptable daily intake/predicted daily intake ratio, and the characterization factor is the human toxicity potential (HTP) in kg 1,4-dichlorobenzene equivalent/ kg emission. For ecotoxicity (including freshwater aquatic ecotoxicity, marine aquatic ecotoxicity, and terrestrial ecotoxicity), the typical category indicator is the predicted environmental concentration/predicted no-effect concentration ratio, and the characterization factors (freshwater aquatic ecotoxicity potential, or FAETP; marine aquatic ecotoxicity potential, or MAETP; and terrestrial ecotoxicity potential, or TETP) are also expressed in kg 1,4-dichlorobenzene equivalent/kg emission.
- Photo-oxidant formation: affected by LCI results such as emissions of volatile organic compounds and carbon monoxide to air in kg/functional unit. The typical category indicator is the tropospheric ozone formation, and the characterization factor is the photochemical ozone creation potential (POCP) in kg ethylene equivalents/kg emission.
- Acidification: affected by LCI results such as emissions of acidifying substances to the air in kg/functional unit. The typical category indicator is the deposition/ acidification critical load rate, and the characterization factor is the acidification potential (AP) in kg sulfur dioxide equivalents/kg emission.
- Eutrophication: affected by LCI results such as emissions of nutrients to air, water, and soil in kg/functional unit. The typical category indicator is the ratio between deposition and nitrogen/phosphorous in biomass, and the characterization factor is the eutrophication potential (EP) in kg phosphates equivalents/kg emission.

Outlook

The LCA process is continually evolving. One impact category that is gaining relevance is water use (Koehler 2008), and important improvements are being registered for human toxicity and freshwater ecotoxicity models (Rosenbaum et al. 2008). In the future, LCA's focus is expected to broaden, making LCA a broader life cycle sustainability analysis (LCSA) by including life cycle costing (LCC) and a social life cycle analysis (SLCA). In addition physical constraints, population dynamics, and rebound effects should be addressed (Heijungs, Huppes, and Guinée 2010).

Ettore SETTANNI, Bruno NOTARNICOLA, and
Giuseppe TASSIELLI
University of Bari Aldo Moro, Taranto, Italy

See also Carbon Footprint; Computer Modeling; Design Quality Indicators (DQI); Ecological Footprint Accounting; Ecological Impact Assessment (EcIA); Life Cycle Costing (LCC); Life Cycle Management (LCM); Material Flow Analysis (MFA); Shipping and Freight Indicators; Supply Chain Analysis; Triple Bottom Line

FURTHER READING

Bare, Jane C.; Hofstetter, Patrick; Pennington, David W.; & Udo de Haes, Helias A. (2000). Midpoints versus endpoints: The sacrifices and benefits. *International Journal of Life Cycle Assessment, 5*(6), 319–326.

Dreyer, Louise Camilla; Niemann, Anne Louise; & Hauschild Michael Z. (2003). Comparison of three different LCIA methods: EDIP97, CML2001 and Eco-indicator 99. Does it matter which one you choose? *International Journal of Life Cycle Assessment, 8*(4), 191–200.

Fischknecht, Rolf. (2010). LCI modeling approaches applied on recycling of materials in view of environmental sustainability, risk perception and eco-efficiency. *International Journal of Life Cycle Assessment, 15*(7), 666–671.

Guinée, Jeroen B. (Ed.). (2002). *Operational guide to the ISO standards. IIa: Guide.* Dordrecht, The Netherlands: Kluwer.

Guinée, Jeroen B., et al. (2011). Life cycle assessment: Past, present, and future. *Environmental Science and Technology, 45*(1), 90–96.

Guinée, Jeroen B.; Heijungs, Reinout; & Huppes, Gjalt. (2004). Economic allocation: Examples and derived decision tree. *International Journal of Life Cycle Assessment, 9*(1), 23–33.

Heijungs, Reinout, & Fischknecht, Rolf. (1998). A special view on the nature of the allocation problem. *International Journal of Life Cycle Assessment, 3*(5), 321–332.

Heijungs, Reinout; Huppes, Gjalt; & Guinée, Jeroen B. (2010). Life cycle assessment and sustainability analysis of products, materials and technologies: Toward a scientific framework for sustainability life cycle analysis. *Polymer Degradation and Stability, 95*(3), 422–428.

International Organization for Standardization (ISO). (2006a). *ISO 14040:2006: Environmental management—life cycle assessment— principles and framework.* Geneva: ISO.

International Organization for Standardization (ISO). (2006b). *ISO 14044:2006: Environmental management—Life cycle assessment— Requirements and guidelines.* Geneva: ISO.

Jolliet, Olivier, et al. (2003). IMPACT 2002+: A new life cycle impact assessment methodology. *International Journal of Life Cycle Assessment, 8*(6), 324–330.

Koehler, Annette. (2008). Water use in LCA: Managing the planet's freshwater resources. *International Journal of Life Cycle Assessment, 13*(6), 451–455.

Notarnicola, Bruno; Huppes, Gjalt; & van den Berg, Nico W. (1998). Evaluating options in LCA: The emergence of conflicting paradigms for impact assessment and evaluation. *International Journal of Life Cycle Assessment, 3*(5), 289–300.

Reap, John; Roman, Felipe; Duncan, Scott; & Bras, Bert. (2008a). A survey of unresolved problems in life cycle assessment. Part 1: Goal and scope and inventory analysis. *International Journal of Life Cycle Assessment, 13*(4), 290–300.

Reap, John; Roman, Felipe; Duncan, Scott; & Bras, Bert. (2008b). A survey of unresolved problems in life cycle assessment. Part 2: Impact assessment and interpretation. *International Journal of Life Cycle Assessment, 13*(5), 374–388.

Rosenbaum, Ralph K., et al. (2008). USEtox—the UNEP-SETAC toxicity model: Recommended characterization factors for human toxicity and freshwater ecotoxicity in life cycle impact assessment. *International Journal of Life Cycle Assessment, 13*(7), 532–546.

Schaltegger, Stefan. (Ed.). (1996). *Life cycle assessment (LCA)—Quo vadis?* Basel, Switzerland: Birkhäuser.

Suh, Sangwon, et al. (2004). System boundary selection in life-cycle inventories using hybrid approaches. *Environmental Science and Technology, 38*(3), 657–664.

Suh, Sangwon; Weidema, Bo; Hoejrup Schmidt, Jannick; & Heijungs, Reinout. (2010). Generalized make and use framework for allocation in life cycle assessment. *Journal of Industrial Ecology, 14*(2), 335–353.

Weidema, Bo. (2001). Avoiding co-product allocation in life-cycle assessment. *Journal of Industrial Ecology, 4*(3), 11–33.

Wrisberg, Nicoline, & Udo De Haes, Helias A. (2002). *Analytical tools for environmental design and management in a systems perspective.* Dordrecht, The Netherlands: Kluwer.

Zamagni, Alessandra, et al. (2008). *Critical review of the current research needs and limitations related to ISO-LCA practice* (CALCAS Project No. 037075 Rep.).

 Berkshire's authors and editors welcome questions, comments, and corrections. Send your emails about the *Berkshire Encyclopedia of Sustainability* in general or this volume in particular to: sustainability.updates@berkshirepublishing.com

Life Cycle Costing (LCC)

Life cycle costing (LCC)—an assessment of a product's cradle-to-grave costs—has its roots in management accounting. It has seen a renaissance in the twenty-first century in the environmental domain. Researchers usually combine LCC's outcomes with those of life cycle assessment to obtain eco-efficiency measures. Several aspects related to the methodology and implementation of LCC and its role within sustainability analysis remain open to discussion, however.

Life cycle costing (LCC) is a traditional method of calculating the total cost of some durable asset (e.g., equipment, vehicles, buildings) that one or more actors—mainly the owner and the manufacturer—incur throughout the asset's life cycle. The total costs include design, acquisition, operation, maintenance, and disposal (Dhillon 2010; Fabrycky and Blanchard 1991).

LCC usually applies when decision makers study different products and design trade-offs. Most applications of LCC are in the building and construction sector, in the energy sector, and in the public sector, mostly for procurement decisions (Korpi and Ala-Risku 2008; UNEP-SETAC 2009).

LCC has gained relevance in environmental management; researchers refer to it in that aspect as *environmental LCC*. Environmental LCC extends the traditional concept of LCC with environmental considerations by certain requirements. It must include (1) all the life cycle stages and actors (i.e., suppliers, manufacturers, customers, end users, and end-of-life actors); (2) externalities, that is, secondary or unexpected consequences that decision makers expect to internalize in the decision-relevant future, and (3) a complementary, nonmonetized life cycle assessment (LCA) (Hunkeler, Lichtenvort, and Rebitzer 2008; UNEP-SETAC 2009).

Environmental LCC therefore provides an economic counterpart to the environmental metrics obtained from an LCA. Many researchers give details about why environmental managers have adopted LCC (Fava and Smith 1998; Steen 2007; Weitz, Smith, and Warren 1994).

Although environmental LCC and LCA are distinct methodologies implemented in parallel, researchers understand them as logical counterparts forming, respectively, the economic and environmental "pillars" of sustainability assessments (Heijungs, Huppes, and Guinée 2010; Klöpffer 2008). Both take into account the full life cycle of a product—from raw material extraction to production to use and recycling or waste disposal—as a common basis for determining costs and environmental impacts, respectively.

Issues

Environmental LCC enriches the basic notion of LCC in some way, but how researchers actually accomplish this heavily depends on definitions. Some researchers have critiqued its role as a pillar for sustainability (Jørgensen, Hermann, and Mortensen 2010). The most authoritative viewpoint on the topic is that of the Working Group on LCC that operates within the Society of Environmental Toxicology and Chemistry (SETAC) Europe. The group mostly agrees that environmental LCC should summarize all costs, understood as real money flows, associated with the life cycle of a product—costs that one or more of the actors in that life cycle directly cover. Some definitions of environmental LCC also include the costs associated with environmental externalities—that is, the social costs borne by those suffering the adverse environmental impacts associated with production—for which a company, at a specified time, is not responsible if neither the marketplace nor regulations assign the firm such costs (White, Savage, and Shapiro 1996). Such costs can be included only if they are expected to be internalized (i.e., included in the cost structure of the polluter by means of environmental taxation or other economic measures adopted within some dedicated environmental policy) in the near future (Hunkeler, Lichtenvort, and Rebitzer 2008). Researchers envision environmental LCC as a complementary analysis to LCA, rather than as a stand-alone technique.

The literature gives many definitions of environmental LCC and often uses unclear terminology. Researchers view environmental LCC as either a way of incorporating costs into LCA (Ciroth 2009; Norris 2001; Shapiro 2001; White; Savage, and Shapiro 1996) or as a way of deriving the full environmental cost of products with the aid of LCA (Epstein 1996 and 2008; Schaltegger and Burritt 2000). Researchers have understood LCC, aside from any reference to LCA, as the projected financial consequences of environmentally relevant decisions throughout the product's life cycle (Burritt, Hahn, and Schaltegger 2002; Bennett and James 2000; Kreuze and Newell 1994). Products include train carriages, lightbulbs, washing machines, automobiles, and waste treatment, to mention but a few (Hunkeler, Lichtenvort, and Rebitzer 2008 includes extensive case studies.)

The environmentally relevant costs categories included in an environmental LCC may range from the internal (often potentially hidden) costs that one or more actors incur. Examples range from preventing pollutant releases or monitoring and treating pollution once it has been produced to the contingent, less tangible, and even external cost categories (US EPA 1995).

In practice, the approach that has prevailed so far is the combination of LCC and LCA as separate yet consistent tools, thus excluding any formal integration of the former into the latter. Decision makers therefore usually rank production alternatives in a number of ways based on independently calculated environmental and cost indicators. The measures thus obtained meet the definition of eco-efficiency, which researchers see as part of such a pragmatic, goal-driven set of tools that is sustainability accounting (Schaltegger and Burritt 2010).

To calculate the cost indicator to be combined with LCA, researchers use the traditional concept of LCC as a cash-flow analysis (Carlsson Reich 2005; Schmidt 2003; White, Savage, and Shapiro 1996). Researchers, however, often do not disclose the details about how they have performed LCC (see, for example, Early et al. 2009; Kicherer et al. 2007; Krozer 2008).

The Future

Critics charge that current environmental LCC practices suffer from limitations that undermine their potential as a support for decision making from the perspective of the individual firms involved in delivering a specific product (Settanni 2008). First, LCC is only a tool that supports investment decisions in durable goods. It thus may prove inappropriate for taking into account commodities other than durable assets (which can well be analyzed by LCA). Second, when it comes to assessing costs, the way researchers have collected, organized, and computed the underlying information about material flows may be poorer than in LCA. They need to emphasize what costs, even those that cannot be quantified easily, they are including in LCC. Third, although the inventory of physical flows to be set up in LCA provides a good basis for deriving the costs associated with material and energy (Rebitzer 2002), examples of LCA and LCC clearly combined through inventory are sparse. Researchers can address the above conceptual inconsistencies by adopting a new perspective on LCC as a process-oriented costing method—not only a cash-flow analysis—that adequately reflects the technology of the operations (Emblemsvåg 2003; Settanni, Tassielli, and Notarnicola 2011).

Ettore SETTANNI, Bruno NOTARNICOLA, and Giuseppe TASSIELLI
University of Bari Aldo Moro, Taranto, Italy

See also Business Reporting Methods; Design Quality Indicator (DQI); Energy Efficiency Measurement; Energy Labeling; International Organization for Standardization (ISO); Life Cycle Assessment (LCA); Life Cycle Management (LCM); Material Flow Analysis (MFA); Regulatory Compliance; Social Life Cycle Assessment (S-LCA); Supply Chain Analysis

FURTHER READING

Bennett, Martin, & James, Peter. (2000). Life-cycle costing and packaging at Xerox. In Martin Bennett & Peter James (Eds.), *The green bottom line* (pp. 347–361). Sheffield, UK: Greenleaf.

Burritt, Roger; Hahn, Tobias; & Schaltegger, Stefan. (2002). An integrative framework of environmental management accounting. In Martin Bennett, Jan J. Bouma, & Teun Wolters (Eds.), *Environmental management accounting: Informational and institutional developments* (pp. 21–35). Dordrecht, The Netherlands: Kluwer Academic Publishers.

Carlsson Reich, Marcus. (2005). Economic assessment of municipal waste management systems—Case studies using a combination of life cycle assessment (LCA) and life cycle costing (LCC). *Journal of Cleaner Production, 13*(3), 253–263.

Ciroth, Andreas. (2009). Cost data quality considerations for eco-efficiency measures. *Ecological Economics, 68*(6), 1583–1590.

Dhillon, Balbir S. (2010). *Life cycle costing for engineers.* Boca Raton, FL: CRC Press.

Early, Claire; Kidman, Tim; Menvielle, Michell; Geyer, Roland; & McMullan, Ryan. (2009). Informing packaging design decisions at Toyota Motor Sales using life cycle assessment and costing. *Journal of Industrial Ecology, 13*(4), 592–606.

Emblemsvåg, Jan. (2003). *Life cycle costing: Using activity based costing and Monte Carlo methods to manage future costs and risks.* Hoboken, NJ: John Wiley and Sons.

Epstein, Marc J. (1996). Improving environmental management with full environmental cost accounting. *Environmental Quality Management, 6*(1), 11–22.

Epstein, Marc J. (2008). *Making sustainability work: Best practices in managing and measuring corporate social, environmental and economic impacts.* Sheffield, UK: Greenleaf Publishing.

Fabrycky, Wolter J., & Blanchard, Benjamin S. (1991). *Life cycle costing and economic analysis.* Englewood Cliffs, NJ: Prentice Hall.

Fava, James A., & Smith, Joyce K. (1998). Integrating financial and environmental information for better decision making. *Journal of Industrial Ecology, 2*(1), 9–11.

Heijungs, Reinout; Huppes, Gjalt; & Guinée, Jeroen B. (2010). Life cycle assessment and sustainability analysis of products, materials and technologies: Toward a scientific framework for sustainability life cycle analysis. *Polymer Degradation and Stability, 95*(3), 422–428.

Hunkeler, David; Lichtenvort, Kerstin; & Rebitzer, Gerald. (2008). *Environmental life cycle costing.* Pensacola, FL: Society of Environmental Toxicology and Chemistry (SETAC) and CRC Press.

Jørgensen, Andreas; Hermann, Ivan T.; & Mortensen, Jørgen Birk. (2010). Is LCC relevant in a sustainability assessment? *International Journal of Life Cycle Assessment, 15*(6), 531–532.

Kicherer, Andreas; Schaltegger, Stefan; Tschochohei, Heinrich; & Ferreira Pozo, Beatriz. (2007). Eco-efficiency: Combining life cycle assessment and life cycle costs via normalization. *International Journal of Life Cycle Assessment, 12*(7), 537–543.

Klöpffer, Walter. (2008). Life cycle sustainability assessment of products. *International Journal of Life Cycle Assessment, 13*(2), 89–95.

Korpi, Eric, & Ala-Risku, Timo. (2008). Life cycle costing: A review of published case studies. *Managerial Auditing Journal, 23*(3), 240–261.

Kreuze, Jerry G., & Newell, Gale E. (1994). ABC and life-cycle costing for environmental expenditures: The combination gives companies a more accurate snapshot. *Management Accounting, 75*(8), 38–42.

Krozer, Yoram. (2008). Life cycle costing for innovations in product chains. *Journal of Cleaner Production, 16*(3), 310–321.

Norris, Gregory A. (2001). Integrating life cycle costing analysis and life cycle assessment. *International Journal of Life Cycle Assessment, 6*(2), 118–120.

Rebitzer, Gerald. (2002). Integrating life cycle costing and life cycle assessment for managing costs and environmental impacts in supply chains. In Stefan Seuring & Maria Goldbach (Eds.), *Cost management in supply chains* (pp. 127–142). Heidelberg, Germany: Physica-Verlag.

Schaltegger, Stefan, & Burritt, Roger. (2000). *Contemporary environmental accounting: Issues, concepts and practices.* Sheffield, UK: Greenleaf Publishing.

Schaltegger, Stefan, & Burritt, Roger. (2010). Sustainability accounting for companies: Catchphrase or decision support for business leaders? *Journal of World Business, 45*(4), 375–384.

Schmidt, Wulf-Peter. (2003). Life cycle costing as part of design for the environment: Environmental business cases. *International Journal of Life Cycle Assessment, 8*(3), 167–174.

Settanni, Ettore. (2008). The need for a computational structure of LCC. *International Journal of Life Cycle Assessment, 13*(7), 526–531.

Settanni, Ettore; Tassielli, Giuseppe; & Notarnicola, Bruno. (2011) An input-output technological model of life cycle costing. In Roger Burritt et al. (Eds.), *Environmental management accounting and sustainable supply chain management.* Dordrecht, The Netherlands: Springer.

Shapiro, Karen G. (2001). Incorporating costs in LCA. *International Journal of Life Cycle Assessment, 6*(2), 121–123.

Steen, Bengt. (2007). Environmental costs and benefits in life cycle costing. *Management of Environmental Quality: An International Journal, 16*(2), 107–118.

United Nations Environment Programme & the Society of Environmental Toxicology and Chemistry (UNEP-SETAC). (2009). *Life cycle management: How business uses it to decrease footprint, create opportunities and make value chains more sustainable.* Retrieved January 30, 2012, from http://www.unep.fr/shared/publications/pdf/DTIx1208xPA-LifeCycleApproach-Howbusinessusesit.pdf

United States Environmental Protection Agency (US EPA). (1995). *An introduction to environmental accounting as a business management tool: Key concepts and terms.* Washington, DC: United States Environmental Protection Agency.

Weitz, Keith A.; Smith, Joyce K.; & Warren, John L. (1994). Developing a decision support tool for life-cycle cost assessment. *Total Quality Environmental Management, 4*(1), 23–36.

White, Allen L.; Savage, Deborah; & Shapiro, Karen. (1996). Life-cycle costing: Concepts and applications. In Mary A. Curran (Ed.), *Environmental life-cycle assessment* (pp. 7.1–7.17). New York: McGraw-Hill.

Life Cycle Management (LCM)

Diverse international and national policies have been devised to promote sustainable consumption and production patterns in order to create innovative environmental, social, and economic paradigms. Among them, life cycle management stands out as a flexible framework of business techniques and tools adopted on a voluntary basis by all types of organizations to increase resource efficiency and reduce environmental and social impacts.

World economies share the challenge of decoupling economic growth and welfare from environmental harm, in order to increase resource efficiency and reduce pollution while promoting more-sustainable production and consumption patterns (European Commission 2005). Now that the need to adopt a more holistic view of economic, social, and environmental issues has been accepted globally (Elkington 1997), world summits have launched programs and action plans focused on innovative programs and tools for creating new environmental paradigms in production and consumer activities and promoting resource-efficient and ecofriendly products.

As well, consumers have become less willing to passively accept violations of both human rights and work-related health and safety, including environmental pollution—all linked to phases of the production chain. Consumers, in fact, have become increasingly interested in what happens beyond the products they buy (Porter and Kramer 2006).

The business community has responded by embracing the product life cycle concept, understanding that products themselves, not just manufacturing processes, can create environmental and social impacts during their distribution, use, and disposal. Organizations potentially gain more economic benefits, such as competitive advantage, by applying "green" and "ethical" principles along the supply chain, paying particular attention to improvements in a product's life cycle. Green and ethical supply-chain management applies across sectors such as manufacturing, services, energy, and government (Walker, De Sisto, and McBain 2008; Sarkis, Zhu, and Lai 2011). It improves efficiency, reduces risk, achieves lasting financial savings, and gains better relationships with stakeholders (Testa and Iraldo 2010).

The United Nations Environment Programme (UNEP) and the United Nations Department of Economic and Social Affairs (UN DESA)—along with national governments, development organizations, and civil societies—are the leading agencies of the Marrakech Process, a global multi-stakeholder program supporting the 10-Year Framework of Programmes (10YFP) on Sustainable Consumption and Production (SCP), whose main objective is promoting, at the regional and local levels, social and economic development, by de-linking economic growth from environmental degradation. The 10YFP on SCP was one of the themes taken up by the Commission on Sustainable Development-Nineteenth session (New York, 12–13 May 2011) in order to increase synergies among the multiple initiatives, strategies, and policies implemented (UN DESA 2011).

The concept of sustainable consumption and production (SCP), which embraces green consumption and production models as well as social issues, was first recognized as an urgent matter at the UN Conference on Environment and Development, held in Rio de Janeiro in 1992, and two years later at the Oslo Symposium on SCP it was defined by the Norwegian Ministry of Environment as "the use of services and related products which respond to basic needs and bring a better quality of life while minimizing the use of natural resources and toxic materials as well as the emissions of waste and pollutants over the life cycle of the service or product so as not to jeopardize the needs of future generations" (UNEP 2010).

Awareness has become widespread that products are characterized by their environmental and social impacts, as well as their use of resources. Quantifying them from manufacture to disposal, however, is a relatively new concept. UN agencies, regional and intergovernmental organizations, nongovernmental organizations, and businesses are engaged in making SCP a reality by taking a life cycle perspective. This means regional and global cooperation and engagement among policy developers, environmental managers, and product designers to improve their knowledge and use it to achieve socio-environmental and economic advantages.

The UNEP and the Society of Environmental Toxicology and Chemistry (SETAC), in collaboration with industry partners, promote sustainable development practice in production and general business strategies through the UNEP/SETAC Life Cycle Initiative, which was established in 2002. The initiative promotes life cycle thinking (LCT) and facilitates the exchange of knowledge among over one thousand experts worldwide and four regional networks on different continents. It fosters innovation and global trade along with the production of more-sustainable products by companies and their suppliers, and encourages the involvement of customers and value-chain partners and sponsors in the process.

Life cycle thinking aims to identify potential improvements to products and services linked to socio-environmental impact as well as to reduce the use of resources across all life cycle stages. The key concept is to minimize impact at one stage of the life cycle, in a specific geographic region or in a particular impact category, and avoid increases elsewhere. In LCT, everyone along the chain of a product's life cycle has a specific responsibility and a role to play (European Commission 2010a).

Life Cycle Management

In order to put the LCT approach in place, companies must adopt the life cycle management (LCM) system, which brings together best practices used around the world. Life cycle management is the application of LCT to business practices and includes a product sustainability model in company strategy and planning, decision making, and communication programs.

There is no universally accepted definition of LCM (Saur et al. 2003), and its prevalent domain is environmental impact assessment of products throughout their life cycle (Seuring 2004). In general, LCM is embodied by how businesses use management tools to reduce their resource consumption (material, energy, water, etc.) and improve their environmental, social, and economic performance in order to ensure a more sustainable value

chain (UNEP, SETAC, and Life Cycle Initiative 2009). Life cycle management integrates concepts, techniques, and procedures to form a flexible framework for implementing environmental and social improvement of both products/services and organizations (Hunkeler et al. 2004). It is the systematic implementation of the life cycle approach applied to the environmental, economic, technological, and social aspects not only of goods but also of organizations that voluntarily adapt it (Remmen, Jensen, and Frydendal 2007).

All business functions—from purchasing, production, and distribution to product development, sales, and marketing; from economy and finance to sustainability and stakeholder relations—are involved in implementing LCM and contribute to its success. The process focuses on continuous improvement by applying, for instance, the Deming cycle, a systematic approach that helps generate a vision through four key steps (Jensen and Remmen 2006):

- *Plan:* set policies and goals; organize commitment and participation; survey future prospects; select areas where the efforts will be addressed; draw up an action plan
- *Do:* make environmental and social improvements; put plan in action; report efforts and results
- *Check:* evaluate the experience and revise policies and organizational structures as necessary
- *Act:* set up new goals and actions, more detailed studies, and whatever else is necessary

Businesses can adopt different methods and instruments to implement LCM in their operations. Because of LCM's flexible nature, all types of organizations can use it to improve performance for economic, environmental, and social sustainability, employing tool sets that suit their character and circumstances (Cohen, de Bruyn, and Farole 2009).

The Three Pillars of LCM

Life cycle management is supported by three core practices: life cycle assessment, environmental life cycle costing, and social life cycle assessment.

1. *Life cycle assessment* (LCA) is an established technique, regulated by the International Organization for Standardization (ISO) through ISO 14040 and ISO 14044 standards for assessing environmental impacts associated with a product, process, or service. (The ISO is the world's largest nongovernmental organization and has developed over 18,500 international standards on subjects ranging from traditional and innovative activities to good management practices). To implement LCA, a company must draw up an

inventory of relevant energy and material inputs and environmental emissions, evaluate the potential impacts associated with those inputs and outputs, and interpret the results in order to lay the foundation for more-informed decision making.

2. *Environmental life cycle costing* (E-LCC) is a variant of life cycle costing (LCC), a traditional method of calculating all costs of a product/service throughout its life cycle, used for comparison, optimization, decision, design support, and other functions. Traditional LCC is confined to costs related to financial transactions, while E-LCC incorporates another aspect of sustainability, the environmental aspect, thereby providing information for management decisions in both monetary and environmental terms.

3. *Social life cycle assessment* (S-LCA), the least developed life cycle method, is a technique to assess the social and socioeconomic impacts of products or services, and their potential positive and negative effects, along their life cycle, encompassing extraction and processing of raw materials, manufacturing, distribution, use, re-use, maintenance, recycling, and final disposal.

Other tools exist to make the value chain more sustainable. Some are frameworks based on internationally accepted methodologies; for instance, the accounting framework for the Greenhouse Gas Protocol (for greenhouse gas emission reduction) developed by the World Resources Institute and the World Business Council for Sustainable Development, or the methodology developed by the UNEP/SETAC Water Assessment Project Group for the joint assessment of water use and water-quality degradation in corporations and the product value chain.

Still other tools offer different features and purposes, such as environmental management systems based on the ISO 14001 standard, which specifies criteria for minimizing an organization's environmental footprint, and the European Union's Eco-Management and Audit Scheme (EMAS) Regulation, which is used for evaluating and reporting. Further choices in the LCM toolkit include green procurement (public or private), ecodesign, ecolabeling, energy labeling, product-oriented environmental management systems, material and substances flow analysis, input-output analysis, and best practices such as auditing and benchmarking.

Conclusions

Life cycle management starts with qualitative and quantitative identification and assessment of the negative environmental and social impacts of using material and energy for production and consumption over the course of a product's or service's life. Measuring global and cumulative impacts throughout the product chain helps policy measures become more effective for both people and the environment, and it is more cost efficient for economic operators and public authorities (European Commission 2005).

As more products and services are traded regionally and globally, LCM is gaining use as an instrument to help businesses react to the challenges faced by the global marketplace (UNEP, SETAC, and Life Cycle Initiative 2009). In the European Union (EU), for example, a growing number of joint policies and instruments are operating, as evidenced by the integrated product policy (IPP), which is a framework based on a set of voluntary or mandatory tools, such as market-based instruments, technological innovations and design, environmental management systems, and restrictions on the use of hazardous substances. These minimize damage caused by goods, processes, and systems through more-effective actions on the part of industries, designers, retailers, and consumers.

Because there is no unique policy that encourages the greening of all products at all stages of their life cycles, a combination of instruments must be used jointly to reinforce effects. The IPP toolbox includes many such instruments and action plans, such as those cited above plus the EU's Environmental Technology Action Plan and the Sustainable Consumption and Production and Sustainable Industrial Policy Action Plan (European Commission 2010b). In the United States, many initiatives based on LCM are being implemented in both the private and public sectors to support environmental decision makers. Some of these are promoted by the US Environmental Protection Agency and apply to fuels and fuel additives, solid waste, plastics, nanomaterials, and electric and electronic products. In Canada, as in a growing number of countries, initiatives are being applied to packaging, waste reduction, and toxic substance management. In some developed countries, such as New Zealand, Japan, and Australia, LCM approaches are routine practice involving both traditional sectors (e.g., pharmaceuticals, food, and energy) and more-innovative sectors (e.g., mobility, logistics, and information and communications technology). In other countries, however, such as China, Thailand, and Malaysia, along with developing countries in Latin America and Africa, LCM is still emerging (European Commission 2010a).

Thanks to opportunities stemming from information sharing and networking, interesting advances are being made around the world. Businesses are using LCM more and more to achieve sustainable development, taking into account both short-term success and long-term value deriving from firm performance, corporate credibility, transparency, and the creation of shared value on local and global scales. In the future, the leading global companies will not only use cutting-edge technological and production innovation, but will also employ LCM to tackle the world's major challenges: poverty, climate change, resource depletion, water scarcity, globalization, and demographic shifts.

Maria PROTO
University of Salerno

See also Advertising; Community and Stakeholder Input; Cost-Benefit Analysis; Ecolabels; Ecological Impact Assessment (EcIA); Energy Labeling; International Organization for Standardization (ISO); Life Cycle Assessment (LCA); Life Cycle Costing (LCC); Material Flow Analysis (MFA); Shipping and Freight Indicators; Social Life Cycle Assessment (S-LCA); Supply Chain Analysis; Triple Bottom Line

FURTHER READING

American Center for Life Cycle Assessment (ACLA). (n.d.). International capability development activities on life cycle topics (presentations, Joint North American Life Cycle Conference).

Retrieved December 22, 2010, from http://www.lcacenter.org/LCA9/special/Capability.html

Cohen, Brett; de Bruyn, Michelle; & Farole, Tom. (2009). Mainstreaming sustainable consumption and production and resource efficiency into development planning. Paris: United Nations Environment Programme, Division of Technology, Industry and Economics (UNEP DTIE), Sustainable Consumption and Production Branch.

Elkington, John. (1997). *Cannibals with forks: The triple bottom line of 21st century business.* Oxford, UK: Capstone Publishing.

European Commission. (2005). Thematic strategy on the sustainable use of natural resources. Retrieved December 22, 2010, from http://ec.europa.eu/environment/natres/index.htm

European Commission. (2010a). *Making sustainable consumption and production a reality: A guide for business and policy makers to life cycle thinking and assessment.* Brussels, Belgium: European Commission Directorate-General for the Environment.

European Commission. (2010b). Integrated product policy toolbox. Retrieved December 22, 2010, from http://ec.europa.eu/environment/ipp/toolbox.htm

Hunkeler, David, et al. (2004). *Life-cycle management.* Pensacola, FL: Society of Environmental Toxicology and Chemistry (SETAC) Press.

Jensen, Allan Astrup, & Remmen, Arne. (Eds.). (2006). Background report for a UNEP guide to life cycle management: A bridge to sustainable products (Rev. ed.). Paris: United Nations Environment Programme, Division of Technology, Industry and Economics (UNEP DTIE).

Life Cycle Initiative. (2010). Homepage. Retrieved December 22, 2011, from http://lcinitiative.unep.fr

Porter, Michael E., & Kramer, Mark R. (2006, December 1). Strategy and society: The link between competitive advantage and corporate social responsibility. *Harvard Business Review.* Retrieved February 27, 2011, from http://hbr.org/2006/12/strategy-and-society/ar/1

Power, Winifred. (Ed.). (2009). *Life cycle management: How business uses it to decrease footprint, create opportunities and make value chains more sustainable.* Paris: United Nations Environment Programme, Society of Environmental Toxicology and Chemistry & Life Cycle Initiative.

Remmen, Arne; Jensen, Allan Astrup; & Frydendal, Jeppe. (2007). *Life cycle management: A business guide to sustainability.* Paris: United Nations Environment Programme, Division of Technology, Industry and Economics (UNEP DTIE).

Sarkis, Joseph; Zhu, Quingha; & Lai, Kee-hung. (2011). An organizational theoretic review of green supply chain management literature. *International Journal of Production Economics, 130,* 1–15.

Saur, Konrad, et al. (2003). Draft final report of the LCM definition study (Version 3.6). Paris: United Nations Environment Programme, Society of Environmental Toxicology and Chemistry & Life Cycle Initiative.

Seuring, Stefan. (2004). Industrial ecology, life cycles, supply chains: Differences and interrelations. *Business Strategy and the Environment, 13*(5), 306–319.

Society of Environmental Toxicology and Chemistry (SETAC). (2010). Homepage. Retrieved December 22, 2010, from http://www.setac.org

Testa, Francesco, & Iraldo, Fabio. (2010). Shadows and lights of GSCM (green supply chain management): Determinants and effects of these practices based on a multi-national study. *Journal of Cleaner Production, 18*(10–11), 953–962.

United Nations Department of Economic and Social Affairs (UN DESA). (2011). Commission on Sustainable Development. *Elements of 10-Year Framework of Programmes on Sustainable Consumption and Production.* Background Paper No.5. CSD 19/2011/BP5. Retrieved February 17,2012, from http://www.un.org/esa/dsd/resources/res_pdfs/csd-19/Background-paper-5-SCP-DSD.pdf

United Nations Environment Programme (UNEP). (2010). *ABC of SCP: Clarifying concepts on sustainable consumption and production.*

Towards a 10-Year framework of programmes on sustainable consumption and production. Retrieved April 4, 2011, from http://www.uneptie.org/scp/marrakech/pdf/ABC%20of%20SCP%20-%20Clarifying%20Concepts%20on%20SCP.pdf

United Nations Environment Programme, Division of Technology, Industry and Economics (UNEP DTIE). (2010). Homepage. Retrieved December 22, 2010, from http://www.unep.fr/en/

United Nations Environment Programme, Division of Technology, Industry and Economics (UNEP DTIE), Sustainable Consumption & Production (SCP) Branch. (2010). Life cycle & resource management. Retrieved December 22, 2010, from http://www.unep.fr/scp/lifecycle/

United Nations Environment Programme, Division of Technology, Industry and Economics (UNEP DTIE), United Nations Department of Economic and Social Affairs (UN DESA). (2010). *Marrakech Process on sustainable consumption and production: Project brief.* Retrieved December 22, 2010, from http://www.unep.fr/scp/marrakech/pdf/MP%20Flyer%2019.02.10%20Final.pdf

United Nations Environment Programme (UNEP), Society of Environmental Toxicology and Chemistry (SETAC) & Life Cycle Initiative. (2009). *Life cycle management: How business uses it to decrease footprint, create opportunities and make value chains more sustainable.* Retrieved April 4, 2011, from http://www.unep.fr/scp/publications/details.asp?id=DTI/1208/PA

Walker, Helen; Di Sisto, Lucio; & McBain, Darian. (2008, March). Drivers and barriers to environmental supply chain management practices: Lessons from the public and private sectors. *Journal of Purchasing and Supply Management, 1*(13), 69–85.

The Limits to Growth

The best-selling book The Limits to Growth *(1972), written by a team of scientists, described possible futures of the world economy and environment based on computer modeling. Many simulation scenarios resulted in the collapse of the economy, environment, and population in the twenty-first century, but alternative sustainable futures were also simulated. Though the work was much derided, the study's "standard run" scenario has accurately forecast decades of real-world trends.*

In 1972 a team of US computer scientists led by Dennis and Donella Meadows at the Massachusetts Institute of Technology published *The Limits to Growth* (sometimes referred to as *LTG*), a short book describing a computer model of the world economy and environment and many scenario simulations projected to the end of the twenty-first century. This work was sponsored by a group of wealthy entrepreneurs and intellectuals, gathering as the Club of Rome (named after their initial meeting place), who were concerned about the effects of growing global economic divisions and environmental pollution. Despite the technical nature of the research, which was based on groundbreaking "system dynamics" modeling pioneered by the computer scientist Jay W. Forrester, the book was a nontechnical account of the model and the scenario outcomes. It quickly became a best seller and was translated into more than thirty languages. One key message of the book was that a collapse of the economy and human population was likely in the twenty-first century if there was unconstrained growth in material-based lifestyles and if reliance on technological solutions to resource depletion and impacts of pollution continued. Another message was that radical changes in lifestyle and economic systems would be required decades ahead of time if such a collapse was to be avoided.

Early and widespread attention to these dire warnings coincided with environmental concern following seminal publications by biologists and ecologists, including Rachel Carson's *Silent Spring* (1962), Garrett Hardin's *The Tragedy of the Commons* (1968), and Paul Ehrlich's *The Population Bomb* (1968), which also warned of environmental catastrophe. Unlike these texts, however, *The Limits to Growth* brought the novel use of computer modeling to the study of complex interactions between the world economy and the environment. The LTG study thereby contributed more quantitative, reproducible, and transparent insights to the then nascent field of sustainability research.

Modeling and Outcomes

The computer model called World3, developed for the LTG study (following earlier "world" model versions), simulated numerous interactions within and among the key subsystems of the global economy: population, industrial capital, pollution, agricultural systems, and nonrenewable resources. For its time, World3 was necessarily coarse, for example modeling the total global population rather than separate regions or nations. In the system dynamics approach, causal links were made mathematically to reflect the influence of one variable on another (not necessarily in a linear fashion), both within and between various sectors of the global economic system. In this way, positive and negative feedback loops were established, where the outcome in one part of the system subsequently returns by a chain of influences to affect itself. When positive and negative feedback loops are finely balanced, a steady state outcome results (or oscillations about an average); however, when one loop dominates, an unstable state is the result, such as the simple case of exponential growth when there is a dominant positive feedback. A classic example is the accelerating growth of a biological population, such as bacteria, in which the birth rate at one point in time is proportional to the size of the population at that time.

The effect and control of these feedbacks depends on the presence of delays in the signals from one part of the world system to another. For instance, the effects of increasing pollution levels on human life expectancy or agricultural production may not be recognized for some decades after the pollution is emitted. This is important because unless the effects are anticipated and preventive action taken in advance, the increasing levels of pollutants may grow to an extent that prohibits correction. These are the dynamics that lead to "overshoot and collapse"—a concept emphasized in *The Limits to Growth* and subsequently commonly used in the environmental and sustainability movements.

The World3 model simulated a stock of nonrenewable as well as renewable resources. The function of renewable resources in World3, such as agricultural land and the environment, could erode as a result of economic activity, but they could also recover their function if deliberate action were taken or harmful activity reduced. The rate of recovery relative to rates of degradation affects when thresholds or limits are exceeded, as well as the magnitude of any potential collapse.

While the general dynamics operating in the World3 model were qualitatively explained in *The Limits to Growth*, the full details of the equations and data were provided in a larger technical report: *Dynamics of Growth in a Finite World* (1974). This report also documented numerous alternative scenarios, thereby examining the sensitivity of the model to possible alternative values of factors that were difficult to measure or quantify. This process established that the World3 model produced robust outcomes and was not sensitive to unknown factors. Nevertheless, the authors stressed that their modeling was not intended to make precise predictions or detailed forecasts, but rather to explore "the broad behavior modes of the population-capital system" (Meadows et al. 1972, 91) to improve understanding.

To depict this behavior, *The Limits to Growth* presented a dozen scenarios exploring the effects of various technological improvements and societal or policy changes. The scenario series started with a "standard run" that encapsulated business-as-usual values in the model for

the future. Parameter trends for this scenario were based on historical data and behavior (established to reproduce approximately the growth and dynamics observed from 1900 to 1970). This scenario displays further growth in global population and economic activity from 1970 to the early twenty-first century, but it subsequently leads to overshoot and collapse in the population and the economic system midway through the century. In this particular case, the cause of collapse is linked primarily to depletion of nonrenewable resources.

In additional scenarios, where pollution impacts and lack of arable land feature more prominently, the book explores a host of optimistic technological advances aimed at avoiding collapse, including virtually unlimited resources, widespread recycling, doubled agricultural yields, land rehabilitation, perfect contraception, and pollution control. With each technological introduction, a new challenge to global security emerges that causes collapse, and even with the full set of technological responses, collapse still occurs because the world system expands to levels that rapidly overcome the technological benefits. Collapse occurs because delays in the ultimate impacts of growth (e.g., of population, pollution, resource depletion) allow the world system to temporarily grow past sustainable limits—overshooting before collapsing.

Consequently, in the final set of scenarios, the book explores what societal changes employed in combination with a suite of technological advances lead to a stabilized world system that avoids overshoot and collapse. Some of the societal changes included were indirect constraints on population growth, preference for services over material consumption, capital directed to food production and healthy land, and excess capital used for consumption goods rather than industrial reinvestment. These changes support slower and diminishing growth in population and standard of living, which plateau within the twenty-first century and are maintained to 2100.

International Reaction

Following its first release and for decades thereafter, *The Limits to Growth* generated substantial interest and highly critical reviews. By the 1990s, however, the overwhelming reaction turned to one of derision, on the (erroneous) claim that, had the LTG study predicted correctly, resource depletion and collapse would have occurred already. Consequently there is a widespread myth that the LTG researchers, and the Club of Rome, were shown by history to be wrong. Ugo Bardi, the Italian physical chemist and commentator on the peak oil concept of limited fossil fuel resources, published *The Limits to Growth Revisited* in 2011. He has comprehensively recorded various efforts to discredit the LTG study and has drawn parallels with documented campaigns against the science of climate change and tobacco health impacts.

The earliest recorded discrediting of *The Limits to Growth* appears to be a 2 April 1972 review in the *New York Times Sunday Book Review* by three economists (Peter Passel, Marc Roberts, and Leonard Ross). While making unsubstantiated or false claims (e.g., "all the simulations based on the Meadows world model invariably end in collapse"), they also incorrectly claimed that the book predicted depletion of many resources by about 1990, which may have been inspiration for later attacks. Similarly, the noted US economist William Nordhaus joined the critics in 1973, making technically incorrect claims that demonstrate a misunderstanding of system dynamics (by focusing on isolated equations in World3 without considering the influence that occurs through the feedbacks in the rest of the model). In the same year an in-depth review and critique of the study, edited by the physicist Sam Cole and colleagues at the University of Sussex, was published; it contained both a technical review of the World3 modeling and essays focused on ideology that attacked the authors personally. The technical review largely proposed that the World3 model could not be validated from the perspective of simple linear modeling, according to Bardi (2011, 52–53). The review also established that the model could not run backward in time, though this is not necessary for the model to run forward properly. Criticism of the study continued for about two decades, including by other noted economists such as Julian Simon, along the vein of such misunderstandings and personal attacks.

For the last decade of the twentieth century, however, criticism of *The Limits to Growth* focused on the incorrect claim that the 1972 work had predicted resource depletion and global collapse. Ugo Bardi has identified a 1989 article titled "Dr. Doom" by Ronald Bailey in *Forbes* magazine as the beginning of this view. Since then it has been promulgated widely, including through popular commentators such as the Danish statistical analyst Bjørn Lomborg, and even in educational texts, peer-reviewed literature, and reports by environmental organizations.

Another rejection of the modeling and messages in *The Limits to Growth* has revolved around the question of technological progress. Critics suggest that such progress was not sufficiently incorporated in the model and that human ingenuity will ultimately overcome any of the constraints to growth found through the LTG simulations. The original LTG modeling did, however, explicitly incorporate technological advances across a wide range of sectors in the "comprehensive technology" and "stabilized world" scenarios, and the authors argued that the level of those advances was considerable and possibly overly optimistic. Subsequently, in the 1974 technical report (*Dynamics of Growth in a Finite World*), the authors pursued the modeling of technological progress by explicitly incorporating it within the model rather than having the researchers impose advances from outside the model. Within the model, technological solutions were automatically sought as modeled constraints to growth arose. The researchers were able to adjust the rate of technological advancement (e.g., how quickly efficiency increased per annum) as well as the delay (for research and development) before solutions were implemented. They found that only in one extreme case of innovation—when technologies where immediately available and progress rates were many times greater than historical rates—was collapse avoided and indefinite economic growth produced. In all other realistic settings, the outcome was overshoot and collapse.

Scenarios, Realities, and the Future

The critical reception of *The Limits to Growth* persisted in parallel with two revisions of the work some twenty and thirty years after the original publication, which produced little change in overall conclusions (Meadows, Meadows, and Randers 1992 and 2004). Since the beginning of the twenty-first century, however, several commentators have noted that the LTG standard run scenario appeared to corroborate key global trends. More specifically, using global data from 1970 to 2000, the Australian physicist Graham Turner (2008) has shown that the original standard run scenario of 1972 has accurately forecast the global data on population, resources, industrial output, food production, and persistent pollution. By contrast, the comprehensive technology and stabilized world scenarios depart substantially from most of the actual data.

This suggests that if the dynamics of the World3 model continue to reflect reality, then the beginning of global economic and environmental collapse is looming. The contemporary issues of peak oil and climate change are particularly relevant. The connection of oil supply constraints to food insecurity and economic downturn is reflected in the dynamics of resource-based collapse in the LTG world system. Similarly, the growing potential of dangerous disruptions to the climate system from increased emissions of greenhouse gasses aligns with LTG scenarios where collapse occurs through global pollution. Further, according to other LTG scenarios that examined the effect of delaying concerted actions until the year 2000, collapse would not be averted due to inherent lags in the world system. If this last scenario is playing out in actuality, then the decades since the warnings indicated in 1972 in *The Limits to Growth* will have been effectively squandered.

Graham M. TURNER
CSIRO Ecosystem Sciences

See also Agenda 21; Computer Modeling; Development Indicators; Framework for Strategic Sustainable Development (FSSD); Genuine Progress Indicator (GPI); Geographic Information Systems (GIS); Human Development Index (HDI); I = P × A × T Equation; Millennium Development Goals; Population Indicators; Remote Sensing; Sustainability Science; Systems Thinking

FURTHER READING

Bardi, Ugo. (2011). *The Limits to Growth revisited.* New York: Springer.

Carson, Rachel. (1962). *Silent spring.* New York: Houghton Mifflin.

Cole, H. S. D.; Freeman, Christopher; Jahoda, Marie; & Pavitt, Keith L. R. (Eds.). (1973). *Models of doom: A critique of* The Limits to Growth. New York: Universe Publishing.

Ehrlich, Paul. (1968). *The population bomb.* New York: Ballatine Books.

Hall, Charles A. S., & Day, John W. (2009). Revisiting the limits to growth after peak oil. *American Scientist, 97*(3), 230–237. doi: 10.1511/2009.78.230

Hamilton, James D. (2009). Causes and consequences of the oil shock of 2007–08. *Brookings Papers on Economic Activity, 1,* 215–283.

Hardin, Garrett. (1968). The tragedy of the commons. *Science, 162*(3859), 1243–1248. doi: 10.1126/science.162.3859.1243

Hardin, Garrett, & Berry, R. Stephen. (1972). Limits to growth: Two views. *Bulletin of the Atomic Scientists, 28*(9), 22–27.

Lomborg, Bjørn. (2001). *The sceptical environmentalist: Measuring the real state of the world.* Cambridge, UK: Cambridge University Press.

Lomborg, Bjørn, & Rubin, Olivier. (2002, November–December). The dustbin of history: Limits to growth. *Foreign Policy, 133,* 42–44.

McCutcheon, Robert. (1979). *Limits of a modern world: A study of the limits to growth debate.* London: Butterworths.

Meadows, Dennis L. (2007). Evaluating past forecasts: Reflections on one critique of *The Limits to Growth.* In R. Costanza, L. Grqumlich, & W. Steffen (Eds.), *Sustainability or collapse? An integrated history and future of people on earth* (pp. 399–415). Cambridge, MA: MIT Press.

Meadows, Dennis L., et al. (1974). *Dynamics of growth in a finite world.* Cambridge, MA: Wright-Allen Press.

Meadows, Donella H.; Meadows, Dennis L.; & Randers, Jørgen. (1992). *Beyond the limits: Global collapse or a sustainable future.* London: Earthscan Publications Ltd.

Meadows, Donella H.; Meadows, Dennis L.; Randers, Jørgen; & Behrens, William W. III. (1972). *The limits to growth: A report for the Club of Rome's project on the predicament of mankind.* New York: Universe Books.

Meadows, Donella H.; Randers, Jorgen; & Meadows, Dennis L. (2004). *Limits to Growth: The 30-year update.* White River Junction, VT: Chelsea Green Publishing Co.

Nordhaus, William D. (1992). Lethal model 2: *The Limits to Growth* revisited. *Brookings Papers on Economic Activity, 2,* 1–59.

Simmons, Matthew R. (2000). Revisiting *The Limits to Growth:* Could the Club of Rome have been correct, after all? An energy white paper. Retrieved November 16, 2011, from http://greatchange.org/ov-simmons,club_of_rome_revisted.pdf

Turner, Graham M. (2008). A comparison of *The Limits to Growth* with 30 years of reality. *Global Environmental Change, 18*(3), 397–411. doi:10.1016/j.gloenvcha.2008.05.001

Long-Term Ecological Research (LTER)

Long-term ecological research provides the opportunity to investigate important environmental questions that require long periods to resolve—from decades to centuries. Without established sites where observations can be made and experiments can be conducted for an extended time, it is difficult to identify the effects of long-term changes in climate, biodiversity, and ecosystem processes crucial for understanding and managing ecological sustainability.

Environmental change often happens slowly and can be difficult to detect until effects accumulate to the point that they become obvious, by which time they may be much more difficult to mitigate. Even when change happens quickly, it can be difficult to understand its importance to ecological sustainability unless there is a long-term, background record against which the change can be evaluated.

There are many examples of subtle environmental change that have required years of observation to detect. Global climate change is perhaps the best known and most widespread example: change has occurred slowly since the 1750s and has been difficult to detect against short-term variability, and solutions have become more difficult to attain with every passing year of inaction. Other examples of long-term change abound: acid rain, invasive pests including weeds that change grassland fire regimes, insects that kill specific types of trees, mussels that change freshwater lake quality, fisheries depletion, pollinator decline, and lake and coastal eutrophication, to name a few. All affect the habitability and sustainability of the ecosystems on which we depend.

Environmental change thus occurs within all ecosystems, from rain forests to tundra to oceans, and across all ecosystem levels, from communities and populations to the resources upon which they rely such as organic matter and nutrients. And change at every level can occur at different time scales, from slowly over decades to abruptly with little warning.

Without the opportunity to observe and experiment over time scales relevant to the organisms and systems they study, ecologists cannot fully understand the complex dynamics that play out in these systems. Processes that occur slowly over decades are hidden in the "invisible present" of short-term observations and experiments (Magnuson 1990). And change that occurs episodically can be missed if the period being studied doesn't happen to include the time that the change occurs. With short-term studies, then, ecologists risk missing change as it happens and therefore missing the opportunity to study many of the cause-and-effect relationships that are essential for understanding, predicting, and managing environmental change.

US Long-Term Ecological Research Network

To address this problem of the short-term observations and the invisible present, the US National Science Foundation established the US Long-Term Ecological Research (LTER) Network in 1980. The network has since grown to include twenty-six sites in many different biomes of North America and beyond. (See figure 1 on the next page.) At each site, scientists have the opportunity to ask questions not answerable through short-term research efforts alone.

Long-term research at these sites spans years to decades to a century or more, and it allows scientists to ask questions in the context of a wide range of environmental conditions; allows them to consider the occurrence of episodic events such as pest and pathogen outbreaks, the effects of which can last for decades; and

Figure 1. Map of the 26 US LTER Sites

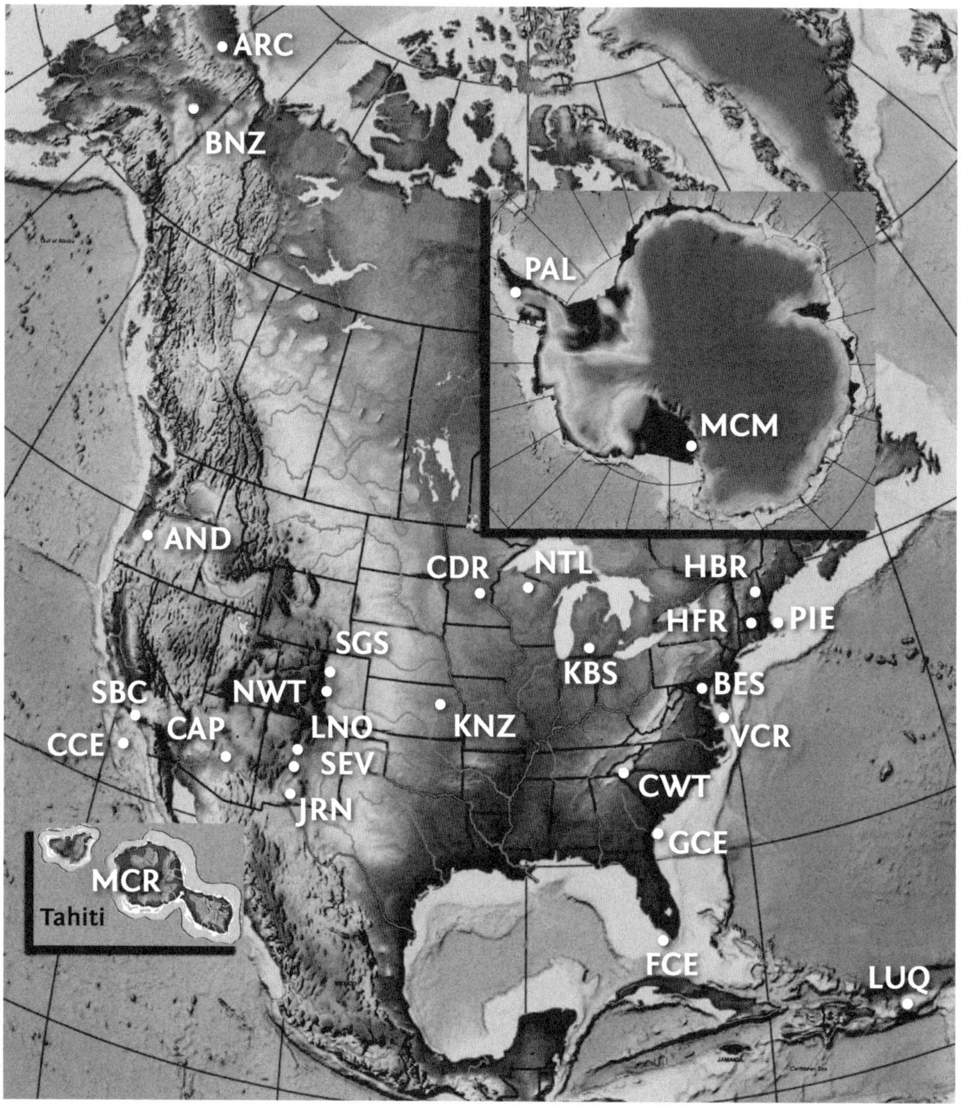

Note: See the LTER Network website (www.lternet.edu) for descriptions of the sites and data.

Source: LTER Network Office.

This map shows the locations of each research facility in the research network, across North America, in Antarctica, and in Tahiti. The table below lists ecosystems and the research facilities studying them.

Biome	Abbreviation
Antarctic	PAL, MCM
Arctic	ARC
Boreal Forest	BNZ
Coniferous Forest	AND
Eastern Deciduous Forest	CWT, HBR, HFR, LUQ
Tropical Wet Forest	LUQ
Alpine Tundra	CWT
Desert	JRN, SEV
Grassland	CDR, SGS, KNZ
Lake	NTL
Coastal Marine	PIE, VCR, GCE, FCE, SBC, CCE, MCR
Urban	BES, CAP
Agriculture	KBS

allows them to detect important but slow-acting phenomena such as changes in soil carbon, climate, and land use. Results also allow the most accurate calibration and validation of ecosystem models used to forecast ecological change (Hobbie et al. 2003).

For example, in the Antarctic, research includes questions about long-term changes in penguin populations as changing distributions of ice and krill push penguin populations poleward; in the Pacific Northwest, questions addressed include how and how much carbon is stored by old-growth and younger forests; in southern Florida, questions include how the Everglades removes phosphorus and other nutrients draining from agricultural areas to the north; in Puerto Rico, scientists ask how hurricanes influence the structure and function of wet tropical forests; and in Minnesota long-term questions include the role of plant biodiversity for maintaining ecosystem functions such as productivity and soil carbon accumulation. Such inquiries are common to every site as all address questions related to primary production; plant, animal, and microbial biodiversity; carbon and nutrient cycling; and natural and anthropogenic disturbance

Cross-Site Comparative and Experimental Research

Because LTER sites are part of a network, they provide a powerful context in which to ask comparative questions about how different ecosystems respond to common factors such as warmer winters, more-episodic precipitation, species introductions, nitrogen in rainfall, land use change, and other environmental factors that are likely to have different effects in different ecosystems. The geographic array of sites provides natural gradients such as temperature (from high to low latitudes), ecosystem type (from terrestrial to marine), aridity (from desert to rain forest), and human influence (from almost pristine to urban).

Common measurements among all sites provide a way to identify many of the differences that lead to compelling cross-site questions. While every site performs measurements important for addressing the scientific questions specific to its particular research theme, a set of common measurements is taken at all sites to ensure that comparative questions can be addressed. Thus at every site regular measurements are made of climate (e.g., rainfall, temperature, and precipitation chemistry), plant productivity (e.g., how much grass and tree and phytoplankton biomass are produced each year), populations of organisms important at that site (e.g., changes in the abundance and diversity of trees or penguins or bacteria or fish), carbon and nutrient reservoirs in soil and sediments, and major disturbances—whether natural, such as fire or insect outbreaks, or anthropogenic, such as species introductions or harvests. These common measurements provide not only a long-term record of background information for detecting change at a particular site but also a means for comparing changes across gradients.

Information Management and Education

Crucial to measuring environmental change is making measurements permanently and openly available to the scientific community and others with interests in tracking change. Every LTER site thus posts its data on a website that provides access to the data itself and to the metadata needed to interpret it. Information management is an important priority for network science: data must be curated and shared in ways that promote its long-term integrity and use.

Education is also an important component of LTER. Data from observations and experiments at long-term sites provide a means for K–12, undergraduate, graduate, and public audiences to better understand environmental change and what it means for their communities. LTER data posted on websites can be used for inquiry-based science instruction, and sites can be used for classroom experiments. Long-term ecological research sites are especially important for graduate training, wherein future environmental scientists gain a better understanding of long-term ecological processes and change in order to better inform their future professional activities.

International LTER

Stimulated by the success of the US LTER Network, similar networks have been formed in other countries and together make up the International LTER Network (ILTER); descriptions of the sites and data can be found on their website (www.ilternet.edu). The ILTER is a network of networks, comprising over forty networks devoted to long-term research around the world to help understand global environmental change. As in the US LTER effort, ILTER's focus is on long-term, site-based research.

Future Directions

Long-term ecological research has shown high value for documenting and understanding ecological change in and across a variety of ecosystems. For example, the effects of acid rain in the United States were first identified at the Hubbard Brook LTER site in New Hampshire. Decades of subsequent research have shown how rainfall acidity and nitrogen additions have altered forest productivity, stream chemistry, and various terrestrial and aquatic communities. Acid rain is but one example of how humans influence ecosystems, often unintentionally. Even ecosystems far afield are affected by atmospheric carbon dioxide fertilization and climate change, for example. In response to this influence, LTER research is now transitioning to a paradigm that more explicitly includes humans (Robertson et al. forthcoming 2012), blending the ecological and social sciences in order to better understand and forecast environmental change.

Socioecological questions are now important components of research in the US and European LTER networks (Collins et al. 2011). This approach will provide a better understanding of how humans perceive the services provided by nature at multiple scales, how these perceptions change behaviors and institutions, and how behavior and institutional changes in turn feed back to alter ecosystem structure and function—and the ability of ecosystems to continue to deliver services over the long term.

Of the environmental problems that challenge the sustainability of ecosystems—their current and future ability to provide the services on which we depend—there are few that can be adequately addressed with short-term study. Detecting population and ecosystem change, whether slow or episodic, often requires long-term observations, and fully understanding the causes and consequences of change often requires careful long-term experimentation. Long-term ecological research provides this essential context.

G. Philip ROBERTSON
Michigan State University

See also Biological Indicators (*several articles*); Challenges to Measuring Sustainability; Computer Modeling; Ecological Impact Assessment (EcIA); Ecosystem Health Indicators; Geographic Information Systems (GIS); Land-Use and Land-Cover Change; Remote Sensing; Strategic Environmental Assessment (SEA); Sustainability Science; Systems Thinking; Transdisciplinary Research

FURTHER READING

Callahan, James T. (1984). Long-term ecological research. *BioScience, 34*, 363–367.

Collins, Scott L., et al. (2011). An integrated conceptual framework for social-ecological research. *Frontiers in Ecology and the Environment, 9*, 351–357.

Hobbie, John E.; Carpenter, Stephen R.; Grimm, Nancy B.; Gosz, James R.; & Seastedt, Timothy R. (2003). The US long term ecological research program. *BioScience, 53*, 21–32.

International Long Term Ecological Research (ILTER). (2011). Homepage. Retrieved December 7, 2011, from www.ilternet.edu

Magnuson, John J. (1990). Long-term ecological research and the invisible present. *BioScience, 40*, 495–500.

Robertson, G. Philip, et al. (2008). Long-term agricultural research: A research education, and extension imperative. *BioScience, 58*, 640–643.

Robertson, G. Philip, et al. (forthcoming.) Long term ecological research in a human dominated world. *BioScience.*

US Long Term Ecological Research Network. (2011). Homepage. Retrieved December 7, 2011, from www.lternet.edu

M

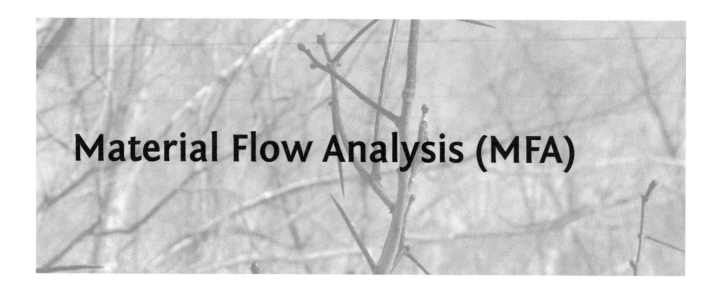

Material Flow Analysis (MFA)

Material flow analysis (MFA) is a method to describe and analyze the material and energy balance of a firm, a region, or a nation. It is based on the law of matter conservation and is defined by a geographic system boundary, a time span within which the analysis is performed, processes which depict human activities, and flows of goods, matter, or energy between these processes.

In the twenty-first century the material throughput of industrial societies (i.e., the amount of physical material moving through societies, and the energy expended to produce it) is not sustainable and cannot continue as such at a global level without causing severe damage to the life-sustaining functions of the ecosystem. Material flow analysis (MFA) is a method that provides an understanding of the underlying physical processes of the material and energy flows and supports the development of policies to minimize the key material and energy flows.

History

The origin of MFA can be traced to ancient Greece, where the law of conservation of matter (i.e., input into a process equals the output of the process) was first communicated more than two thousand years ago. The eighteenth-century chemical engineer Antoine Lavoisier was the first person to provide the experimental evidence for the conservation of matter in chemical processes. This knowledge was then applied in chemical engineering during the twentieth century.

Only in 1965 was MFA applied to larger systems such as cities. Since then MFA studies have been made at various scales, from businesses and firms to densely populated regions in developed countries, to entire nations. MFA has also been adapted to analyze environmental problems in developing countries and to trace pollutants through watersheds.

Methods

Two main types of MFA can be distinguished: economy-wide MFA (EMFA) and general MFA. EMFA studies the total material flows through a nation or a region. It provides an overview of all annual material inputs and outputs of an economy, including inputs from the national or regional environment, and outputs to the environment, as well as the physical amounts of imports and exports (Eurostat 2009). The accounting is made in physical units, usually tonnes per year. It includes "sectors" such as biomass, fossil fuels, construction materials, industrial materials and ores. A standardized methodology allows for historical and international comparisons.

General MFAs provide a more fine-tuned analysis categorized in terms of substances, materials, or goods through a firm, region, or nation. An analysis applied to a single material or substance is called a substance flow analysis (SFA) and uses the same key terms and components. The focus of an MFA thus involves optimizing the management of resources (e.g., wood or copper) within a country, region, or economic sector, or it involves reducing the flow of potentially harmful substances (e.g., heavy metals) to the environment. Thereby the pathways of the substances within the selected system are analyzed as well as their chemical, physical, and biological transformations. Both MFA and SFA are similar in that they define spatial and temporal system boundaries and that they consider the principle of conservation of mass or matter.

Economy-Wide Material Flow Analysis

The standardized methodology provided by Eurostat (2009) gives detailed instructions on how the system is defined, how stocks and flows are calculated, and which indicators can be derived from the stocks and flows.

The main variables considered (see also Eurostat 2001; Eurostat 2009) include the inputs, factors within the economy, and outputs:

Inputs

- Imports: Traded and imported commodities from basic commodities to processed products in tons.
- Domestic extraction (DE): Annual amount of solid, liquid, and gaseous raw materials (excluding water and air) extracted from the natural environment within the system boundaries, and used as material factor inputs in production.
- Input balancing items: Water and air, which have to be considered for the material balance.

Within the Economy

- Net Additions to Stock (NAS): Physical growth of the economy. NAS includes the amount of new construction materials used in buildings and infrastructure; material included in existing durable goods such as cars, household appliances, and furniture; and materials incorporated into new durable goods. In principle, old materials are disposed of and enter the DPO (domestic processed output; see next item), while new materials are consumed and enter the stock. Another factor is residence time, the amount of time in which a material or product remains in the system.
- Domestic processed output (DPO): Measures the total mass of waste materials generated along the value-added chain, including resource extraction, processing, manufacturing use, and waste management. DPO includes emissions to air, water, and landfill.

Outputs

- Exports: Traded and exported commodities, from basic commodities to processed products in tons.
- Output balancing items: Water and CO_2, which have to be considered for the material balance.

The national material balance equation is then defined as follows:

$$DE + Imports + Input\ Balancing\ Items$$
$$= Exports + DPO + Output\ Balancing\ Items + NAS$$

From the above measured variables several indicators can be defined (see Eurostat 2009). Here only a few are mentioned:

- Domestic material consumption (DMC): DMC relates to the material inputs into a region/nation that remain there until they are released to the environment. DMC "measures the annual amount of raw materials extracted in a national economy, plus all physical imports minus all physical exports" (Eurostat 2009). DMC is defined in the same way as other key physical indicators such as total primary energy supply (TPES). That implies that the term "consumption" as used in DMC relates to "apparent consumption" and not to "final consumption."
- Physical trade balance (PTB): PTB is calculated as physical imports minus physical exports. It is, thus, defined reverse to the monetary trade balance (which is exports minus imports), taking account of the fact that in economies money and goods move in opposite direction. A physical trade surplus indicates a net import of materials, whereas a physical trade deficit indicates a net export.

These indicators can be related to other indicators such as GDP (gross domestic product) and land area.

- Material intensity: The ratio of DMC to GDP.
- Area Intensity: The DE or DMC to total land area ratio. The ratio between material flows and total land area indicates the scale of the physical economy related to its natural environment.
- Domestic Resource Dependency (DE/DMC): The ratio of domestic extraction to domestic material consumption is an indicator for the dependence of the physical economy on domestic raw material supply (see Weisz et al. 2006).

MFA and SFA

Due to the diversity of questions that can be answered with MFA and SFA, no completely standardized methodology exists yet. The key terms and definitions for MFA, however, apply for almost any MFA or SFA performed. (See table 1 on the next page.) The balance time is usually one year, and the measured unit a physical mass unit.

Table 1. Key Terms Used in Material Flow Analysis

Key Terms	Definition	Graphical Representation	Mathematical Interpretation
Activity	Human actions to satisfy their needs (e.g., feeding, cleaning)		Functional subsystem of an MFA system
MFA system	Open system composed of processes and goods, through which material and energy flow		A specifically defined spatial and temporal unit in which the material and energy flows are measured
System boundary	Delimits the MFA system		Defines the MFA system geographically and within time
Process (stock)	Transport, transformation or depositing of elements and goods		Balance volume (a spatial unit which is balanced for a specific time period and for which mass conservation applies)
Good/Materials (flow)	Materials are used for activities valued by humans		Carrier of specific "matter"
Element	Chemical elements or compounds		Elements (i.e., components of materials)

Source: Adapted from Baccini and Bader (1996).

The key terms outlined for an MFA also apply to a substance flow analysis (SFA), which focuses on a single material or substance.

Furthermore, most researchers agree that an MFA consists of the following five iterative steps as proposed by Peter Baccini and Hans-Peter Bader (1996):

1. Definition of the system: In this step the system boundaries are set, that is the geographical space and the time span within which the analysis is performed are defined. Then the processes depicting the relevant transformation, transport and deposition processes within the system are defined, and the flows between the processes are identified. It is recommended that a graphical representation of the system is made. If stakeholders are included in a transdisciplinary process, they can be asked to validate the definition of the system.

2. Data collection or measurement: In this step the flows of goods/substances and the stock changes of processes are quantified. One common source is statistical data from government and multilateral agencies. Alternatively, specific flows of goods can be measured, for example with a household consumption survey (Binder et al. 2001). If environmental processes are included in the analysis, measurements within the environment might also be required, such as the concentration of elements in soil and water (van der Voet 1997).

3. Calculating the material or substance flows: In this step, based on the data obtained, the whole material flow system is calculated and, if possible, so are the critical flows validated through secondary calculations. As with the EMFA, the mass balance principle applies. That is: the output is equal to the input plus changes in stock.

4. For dynamic analyses the residence time in the stock has to be considered (Baccini and Bader 1996; Binder et al. 2001; 2004).

5. Representation and interpretation: In the final step the results are represented in a material flow diagram and interpreted with respect to the research question set in the beginning of the analysis. For the representation, open-source software STAN can be used (Tu Wien 2011). Alternatively, there are also some commercial software packages available, SIMBOX (EAWAG 2009) and GABI (PE International AG).

MFA and Life Cycle Assessment (LCA)

MFA and LCA are similar methodologies. Whereas MFA studies the material flows within a firm, region or nation, LCA studies the environmental impact of a

TABLE 2. Main Differences Between MFA and LCA

	MFA	LCA
Goal	Analyzes the flows of material and energy through a firm, region, or nation, and thus includes several products	Compares the environmental impact of different products through their whole lifespan
System boundary	Defined in geographic terms, and hence any materials and goods required for producing imported goods are not considered.	Defined through the functional unit as life span of a product, including the origin of its components. From cradle to grave.
Assessment	There is no specific assessment procedure included. Some authors favor the comparison of the anthropogenic flows to the geogenic flows. Others opt for comparing the change in material throughput over time.	LCA assesses the whole chain from the point of view of a functional unit. The process is divided into a LCI (life cycle inventory) without assessment and the assessment part. There are databases that support the assessment process (see ecoinvent 2012).

Source: author.

An MFA studies the material flows within a firm, region or nation, while an LCA studies the environmental impact of a specific product from cradle to grave.

specific product from cradle to grave. They differ in the goal setting, the system boundaries, and the assessment process. (See table 2 above.)

MFA and Sustainability

An MFA can contribute in different ways to a transition towards sustainability. First, it serves to identify the key flows originating from human activities and affecting the environmental issue at hand. It thus addresses the question: *how do different human activities affect the environmental problem to be solved?*

The answer to this question is a prerequisite for a development toward sustainability. If we do not understand which human activity contributes, and to what extent, to a certain environmental problem, we will not be able to develop sound measures that tackle the problem at its core. In particular, with respect to the following areas, MFA has been shown to provide significant inputs:

- Consumption: Researchers have shown that analyses of different activities regarding the consumption of resources such as water, energy, and materials provide specific knowledge on where the focus of sustainable measures to address overconsumption should be (Brunner and Baccini 1992; Daxbeck et al. 1997; Binder et al. 2004);
- Pollution: The key issue here is to identify the origin and to trace the pathway of pollutants through the whole system being analyzed. This is particularly

relevant when talking about water contamination, CO_2 emissions, and waste production (e.g., to trace pollutants through watersheds or urban regions). Another aspect to consider is the ratio between household and industrial pollution and regional assimilative capacity (Ayres et al. 1985; Lohm et al., 1994; van der Voet et al. 1994; Kleijn et al. 1994; Frosch et al. 1997);

- Optimization of industrial processes: Some authors have found that MFA allows for identifying the flows of energy and materials through all the industrial processes. The approach supports the analysis of trade-offs regarding the optimization of resources (e.g., energy, materials, water) and between resource optimization and economic optimization. Perhaps surprisingly, in most cases they found that both resource and economic improvements had been reached (Ayres 1978; Erkmann 2003; Henseler et al. 1995; Kytzia et al.);
- Global element flows: National and international flows of copper and zinc have recently been established. This provides the basis for planning against resource scarcity (Graedel et al. 2002; Gordon et al. 2003; Spartari et al. 2003).

A second way in which MFA contributes to a transition toward sustainability is as a precautionary tool. That is, MFA can be used to identify potential environmental problems before they escalate, which might occur if the current behavioral patterns continue or new ones are adopted, and to test potential measures to improve the situation. Hence a dynamic modeling approach is of special interest. The following research questions are addressed: *What are the potential environmental problems emerging from current or envisioned patterns of material use? What is the potential of (technical) measures for improving the current situation?*

Examples for the application of dynamic models include development of the photovoltaic market, building management, and cascade flows of used goods. The dynamic behavior of material or substance flows in human-environment systems can be simulated using mathematical models. These approaches have been applied in diverse fields by a number of researchers. Claudia R. Binder (1996), in solo research and again with her colleagues (Binder et al. 2001) modeled the dynamics of material use for different scenarios of furniture consumption. Daniel Beat Mueller (1998) analyzed the dynamics of forest and wood management for the lowlands of Switzerland. Marcus Georg Real (1998) developed a method for evaluating metabolism in the large-scale introduction of renewable energy systems. C. Zeltner and colleagues (1999) modeled the dynamics of copper flows in the USA; René Kleijn and colleagues (2000) looked at delayed behavior of PVC in durables related to waste production; and Ester van der Voet and colleagues (2002) used this model to predict future emissions.

Finally, MFA can be used to monitor the development of the system. This is done by calculating the MFA on a yearly basis. The following two-part research question is addressed: *How is the development of the system with respect to sustainable standards? To what extent has it been improving?*

The answer to this question is one area of application for the economy-wide MFA (EMFA). In this context, the DMC calculated with the EMFA methodology is viewed as the "material GDP" of a country (Eurostat 2009) and allows comparing countries with respect to their material intensity (Direct Material Consumption/GDP). When the material intensity decreases, it is a sign of de-materialization, or of

shifting material-intensive activities to other economies, especially rapidly developing ones such as China. Another important application for this methodology is development over time. Thereby one is able to track the material changes within specific transitions, such as from agricultural societies to industrial society (Fischer-Kowalski and Haberl 2007).

Linking MFA to Other Approaches

A significant number of approaches can be linked to MFA. Most of them stem from economics, as the structures of analysis of MFA and economic methodologies, such as input-output analysis and general equilibrium models, are quite consistent with each other. (For a review see Binder 2007a.)

In addition, a few approaches have been developed which link stakeholders/actors behavior to material flow analysis and provide information on how the material flows can be steered in the social system (Binder 2007b; Lang et al. 2006). They have been applied to the area of waste management (Lang et al. 2006; Binder and Mosler 2007), regional management of wood flow (Binder et al. 2004), and phosphorous management (Lamprecht et al. 2011) among others.

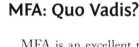

MFA: Quo Vadis?

MFA is an excellent tool in sustainability research: it provides an overview over the physical characteristics of a system. As the processes can be related to human activities, the results of an MFA can be linked to economics as well as actor-oriented analyses. This makes the tool particularly interesting for combined modeling endeavors in which changes in human behavior can be analyzed with respect to their environmental impact. For policy makers this tool is of relevance as it provides a base for designing policies, it supports the monitoring process, it is relatively easy to communicate, and it considers to a large extent the complexity of the system analyzed.

Claudia R. BINDER
University of Munich

The author thanks Christopher Watts for review and editing.

See also Agenda 21; Biological Indicators (*several articles*); Community and Stakeholder Input; Development Indicators; Ecosystem Health Indicators; Environmental Performance Index (EPI); Genuine Progress Indicator (GPI); Global Environment Outlook (GEO) Reports; Global Reporting Initiative (GRI); Human Appropriation of Net Primary Production (HANPP); I = P × A × T Equation; Land-Use and Land-Cover Change; Life Cycle Assessment (LCA); Life Cycle Costing (LCC); Life Cycle Management (LCM); National Environmental Accounting; Regional Planning; Systems Thinking

FURTHER READING

Adriaanse, Albert, et al. (1997). *Resource flows: The material basis of industrial economies.* Washington, DC: World Resources Institute.

Ayres, Robert U. (1978). Resources, environment and economics: Applications of the materials/energy balance principle. New York: Wiley.

Ayres, Robert U., & Simonis, Udo E. (Eds.). (1992). *Industrial metabolism e restructuring for sustainable development.* Tokyo: The United Nations University.

Baccini, Peter, & Bader, Hans-Peter. (1996). *Regionaler Stoffhaushalt: Erfassung, Bewertung und Steuerung* [Regional material management: Analysis, evaluation and regulation]. Heidelberg, Germany: Spektrum.

Bergback, Bo; Anderberg, Stefan; & Lohm, Ulrik. (1994). Accumulated environmental impact: The case of cadmium in Sweden. *The Science of The Total Environment, 145*(1–2), 13–28.

Binder, Claudia R. (2007a). From material flow analysis to material flow management part I: Social science approaches coupled to material flow analysis. *Journal of Cleaner Production, 15*(17), 1596–1604.

Binder, Claudia R. (2007b). From material flow analysis to material flow management part II: The role of structural agent analysis. *Journal of Cleaner Production, 15*(17), 1605–1617.

Binder, Claudia R.; Bader, Hans-Peter; Scheidegger, Ruth; & Baccini, Peter. (2001). Dynamic models for managing durables using a stratified approach: the case of Tunja, Colombia. *Ecological Economics, 38*(2), 191–207.

Binder, Claudia R.; Hofer, Christoph; Wiek, Arnim; & Scholz, Roland W. (2004). Transition towards improved regional wood flow by integrating material flux analysis with agent analysis: The case of Appenzell Ausserrhoden, Switzerland. *Ecological Economics, 49*(1), 1–17.

Binder, Claudia R., & Mosler, Hans-Joachim. (2007). Recycling flows and behavior of households in analysis for Santiago de Cuba. *Resources, Conservation and Recycling, 51*(2), 265–283.

Brunner, Paul H., & Baccini, Peter. (1992). Regional material management and environmental protection. *Waste Management & Research, 10*(2), 203–212.

Brunner, Paul H., & Rechberger, Helmut. (2004). *Practical handbook of material flow analysis.* New York: Lewis.

Daxbeck, Hans, et al. (1997). The anthropogenic metabolism of the city of Vienna. In Stefan Bringezu, Marina Fischer-Kowalski, René Kleijn & Viveka Palm (Eds.), *Proceedings of the ConAccount workshop* (pp. 247–252). Wuppertal, Germany: Wuppertal Institut für Klima, Umwelt, Energie.

EAWAG. (Eidgenössische Anstalt für Wasserversorgung, Abwasserreinigung und Gewässerschutz) [The Swiss Federal Institute of Aquatic Science and Technology]. (2009). Systemanalyse und modellierung SIMBOX [System analysis and modelling SIMBOX]. Retrieved November 10, 2011, from http://www.eawag.ch/forschung/siam/software/simbox/index

Ecoinvent. (2012). Homepage. Retrieved January 13, 2012, from http://www.ecoinvent.ch/

Erkman, Suren, & Ramaswamy, Ramesh. (2003). Applied industrial ecology: A new platform for planning sustainable societies. Bangalore, India: Aicra.

Eurostat (Statistical Office of the European Communities). (2001). *Economy-wide material flow accounts and derived indicators. A methodological guide.* Luxembourg: Eurostat. Retrieved January 13, 2012, from http://epp.eurostat.ec.europa.eu/cache/ITY_OFFPUB/KS-34-00-536/EN/KS-34-00-536-EN.PDF

Eurostat (Statistical Office of the European Communities). (2009). Economy-wide material flow accounts: Compilation guidelines for reporting to the 2009 Eurostat questionnaire. Luxembourg: Eurostat.

Fischer-Kowalski, Marina, & Haberl, Helmut. (Eds.). (2007). *Socioecological transitions and global change: Trajectories of social metabolism and land use.* Bodmin & Cornwall, UK: MPG Books Ltd.

Frosch, Robert A., et al. (1997). The industrial ecology of metals: A reconnaissance. *Philosophical Transactions of the Royal Society A, 335*(1728), 1335–1347.

Henseler, Georg; Bader, Hans-Peter; Oehler, Daniel; Scheidegger, Ruth; & Baccini, Peter. (1995). Methode und Anwendung der betrieblichen Stoffbuchhaltung: Ein Beitrag zur Methodenentwicklung in der ökologischen Beurteilung von Unternehmen [Method and application of substance bookkeeping in firms: A contribution to the development of methods for the ecological assessment of enterprises]. Zürich, Switzerland: vdf Hochschulverlag AG.

Kleijn, René; van der Voet, Ester; & Udo de Haes, Helias A. (1994). Controlling substance flows: The case of chlorine. *Environmental Management, 18*(4), 523–542.

Kleijn, René; Huele, Ruben; van der Voet, Ester. (1999, January 5). Dynamic substance flow analysis: the delaying mechanism of stocks, with the case of PVC in Sweden. *Ecological Economics, 32*(2), 241–254.

Kytzia, Susanne; Faist, Mireille; & Baccini, Peter. (2004, October–December). Economically extended MFA: A material flow approach for a better understanding of the food production chain. *Journal of Cleaner Production, 12*(8–10), 877–889.

Lamprecht, Heinz; Lang, Daniel J.; Binder, Claudia R.; & Scholz, Roland W. (2011). The trade-off between phosphorus recycling and health protection during the BSE crisis in Switzerland: A "disposal dilemma." *GAIA, 20*(2), 112–121.

Lang, Daniel J.; Binder, Claudia R.; Scholz, Roland W.; Schleiss, Konrad; & Stäubli, Beat. (2006, June). Impact factors and regulatory mechanisms for material flow management: Integrating stakeholder and scientific perspectives: The case of bio-waste delivery. *Resources, Conservation and Recycling, 47*(2), 101–132.

Moriguchi, Yuichi. (2002). Material flow analysis and industrial ecology studies in Japan. In Robert U. Ayres & Leslie W. Ayres (Eds.), *Handbook of industrial ecology* (pp. 301–310). Cheltenham, UK: Edward Elgar.

Mueller, Daniel Beat. (2002). *Modellierung, Simulation und Bewertung des regionalen Holzhaushaltes* [Modeling, simulation and evaluation of regional timber management] (PhD dissertation Nr. 12990). Zurich, Switzerland: Swiss Federal Institute of Technology.

Palm, Viveka, & Jonsson, Kristina. (2003). Materials flow accounting in Sweden: Material use for national consumption and for export. *Journal of Industrial Ecology, 7*(1), 81–92.

PE International, GaBi Software. (n.d.) Homepage. Retrieved November 10, 2011, from http://www.gabi-software.com/deutsch/index/

Real, Markus Georg. (1998). A methodology for evaluating the metabolism in the large scale introduction of renewable energy systems (PhD dissertation Nr. 12937). Zurich, Switzerland: Swiss Federal Institute of Technology.

Scholz, Roland W., & Tietje, Olaf. (2002). *Embedded case study methods: Integrating quantitative and qualitative knowledge.* Thousand Oaks, CA: Sage Publications.

Tu Wien. (2011). *Institut für Wassergüte, Ressourcenmanagement und Abfallwirtschaft:* STAN [Institute for water quality, resource management and waste management: STAN]. Retrieved November 10, 2011, from http://iwr.tuwien.ac.at/ressourcen/downloads/stan.html

van der Voet, Ester; Kleijn, René; Huele, Ruben; Ishikawa, Masanobu; & Verkuijlen, Evert. (2002, May). Predicting future emissions based on characteristics of stocks. *Ecological Economics, 41*(2), 223–234.

van der Voet, Ester; van Egmond, Lipkjen; Kleijn, Ruth; & Huppes, Gjalt. (1994). Cadmium in the European community: A policy-oriented analysis. Waste Management Resources, *12*(6), 507–526.

Weisz, Helga, et al. (2006). The physical economy of the European Union: Cross-country comparison and determinants of material consumption. Ecological Economics, 58(4), 676–698.

Wolman, Abel. (1965, September). The metabolism of cities. *Scientific American, 213,* 179–190.

Zeltner, C.; Bader Hans-Peter; Scheidegger, Ruth; & Baccini, Peter. (1999). Sustainable metal management exemplified by copper in the USA. *Regional Environmental Change, 1*(1), 31–46.

Millennium Development Goals

Eight Millennium Development Goals were established under the auspices of the United Nations in 2000 to combat poverty, inequality, and disease by working in a global partnership toward sustainable development. Based on the principles of economic security, strong institutions and governance, and social justice, the goals are monitored by indicators of achievement that assess the advancement of specific groups defined by ethnic origin, geographic location, gender, and other specific circumstances.

In September 2000, world leaders convened at the United Nations Millennium Summit to address ways in which a global partnership could simultaneously support growth, reduce poverty, and achieve sustainable development. As a result of those efforts, 189 countries adopted the Millennium Declaration. Through that declaration they committed themselves to alleviate extreme poverty and to tackle several deprivations, setting eight broad, quantifiable objectives encompassed in the Millennium Development Goals (MDGs), outlined in the next section, "MDGs and Their Targets." This coordinated political effort came about as a result of key debates during the 1990s, and it is founded on the notion that development objectives should be constructed on three main pillars: economic security, strong institutions and governance, and social justice (Hulme and Scott 2010).

The MDGs were conceived as the centerpiece of a strategy that understands public policy as an instrument to achieve universal basic rights. The MDGs are a benchmark for progress, individually and collectively construed in a multidimensional way. The goals can be understood from the perspective of human development, where social progress is defined not simply as economic growth but as a broader notion of individuals' quality of life and effective freedom.

The notion of human development is related to the capability approach proposed by the Indian economist Amartya Sen (1985). It conceptualizes *development* as centered on people and on the expansion of their choices to live meaningful and creative lives (Basu and Lopez-Calva 2011). Within this conceptual framework, *capabilities* refer precisely to the set of possibilities among which people are effectively free to choose. Capabilities are sets of *functionings*, which are made available by transforming an individual's access to goods and services into actual "beings" or "doings." Functionings encompass the possibility of living a long and healthy life or of attaining individually and socially valuable knowledge, but also other more complex options, such as an individual achieving self-respect, social integration, and participation in political processes. Those higher goals can only be achieved if basic conditions are met. The MDGs represent a fundamental political commitment to establish the universality of such basic conditions.

MDGs and Their Targets

Each of the eight MDGs specifies certain targets against which progress can be measured and monitored, working toward their achievement by the year 2015.

Goal 1: Eradicate Extreme Poverty and Hunger

- Target 1A: halve the proportion of people living on less than $1 a day.
- Target 1B: achieve decent employment for women, men, and young people.
- Target 1C: halve the proportion of people who suffer from hunger.

Goal 2: Achieve Universal Primary Education

- Target 2A: by 2015 all children can complete a full course of primary schooling.

Goal 3: Promote Gender Equality and Empower Women

- Target 3A: eliminate gender disparity in primary and secondary education.

Goal 4: Reduce Child Mortality

- Target 4A: reduce by two-thirds, between 1990 and 2015, the under-five mortality rate.

Goal 5: Improve Maternal Health

- Target 5A: reduce by three quarters, between 1990 and 2015, the maternal mortality ratio.
- Target 5B: achieve, by 2015, universal access to reproductive health.

Goal 6: Combat HIV/AIDS, Malaria, and Other Diseases

- Target 6A: have halted by 2015 and begun to reverse the spread of HIV/AIDS.
- Target 6B: achieve, by 2010, universal access to treatment for HIV/AIDS.
- Target 6C: have halted by 2015 the incidence of malaria and other diseases.

Goal 7: Ensure Environmental Sustainability

- Target 7A: integrate the principles of sustainable development into country policies.
- Target 7B: achieve, by 2010, a significant reduction in the rate of biodiversity loss.
- Target 7C: halve, by 2015, the proportion of the population without sustainable access to safe drinking water and basic sanitation.
- Target 7D: by 2020, to have achieved a significant improvement in the lives of at least 100 million slum dwellers.

Goal 8: Develop a Global Partnership for Development

- Target 8A: develop further an open, rule-based, trading and financial system.
- Target 8B: address the special needs of the Least Developed Countries (LDC).
- Target 8C: address the special needs of landlocked developing countries and small-island developing states.
- Target 8D: make debt sustainable in the long term.
- Target 8E: provide access to affordable, essential drugs in developing countries.
- Target 8F: make available the benefits of new technologies.

Each target within each of the MDGs has a series of indicators against which to assess progress. For instance, the indicators for Goal 7, "ensure environmental sustainability," include monitoring (1) the proportion of land area covered by forest; (2) carbon dioxide emissions (total, per capita, and per \$1 GDP (PPP); (3) the consumption of ozone-depleting substances; (4) the proportion of fish stocks within safe, biological limits; (5) the proportion of total water resources used; (6) the proportion of total marine and terrestrial area protected; and (7) the proportion of species threatened with extinction.

Policy Challenges

After the Millennium Declaration, the first challenge was to support governments in their efforts to adopt the goals seriously and incorporate them into their national development strategies. The idea was to use the indicators as relevant planning instruments. A second challenge was to mobilize civil society at the national and international levels so that nongovernmental actors supported the efforts to achieve the goals. Finally, a third challenge was to actually align policies to the MDG framework, using the goals in the implementation, monitoring, and evaluation of their government plans.

At the 2010 MDG Summit, the assessment showed a fundamental advancement in the attainment of the goals, although concern was raised regarding the MDGs whose achievement was lagging. For example, gender disparities in tertiary education were still present, child and maternal mortality rates were still high, and so were deaths attributed to malaria, as well as access to sanitation. In terms of the international commitment to development, important gaps persisted with regard to donor governments' funding commitments to the developing world.

In this context, the UN system launched the MDG Acceleration Framework (MAF), developed by the United Nations Development Programme (UNDP), which was intended to motivate the additional efforts required to step up initiatives and interventions toward the MDGs at the country level. The MAF provides a four-step methodology through which to (1) define the set of strategies that has the potential to accelerate progress toward targeted goals, which will help stakeholders determine—depending on governance challenges, political commitment, country capacity, and funding—more optimal solutions; (2) identify bottlenecks that are holding up a faster advance to the targets; (3) recommend comprehensive action based on prioritized areas; and (4) implement the strategies and monitoring of progress (UN 2011). This framework was developed to focus on goals and targets at risk of reversal as well as on those capable of producing positive spillover effects for advancing other goals and targets.

The MAF approach is based on the notion that the efforts to achieve the MDGs must overcome the constraints that are imposed by the local context and the institutional capacity in each country and, thus, can only be identified in conjunction with interested actors and communities. Intrinsically this approach is multidisciplinary, multisectoral, and multi-stakeholder.

It is also important to mention the specific emphasis on going "beyond averages," which means that indicators of achievement should be broken down to assess the advancement of specific groups defined by ethnic origin, geographic location, gender, and other specific circumstances—and not based on some generic "middle standard."

Multidimensional Measuring of Progress

The measurement of progress in achieving human development requires a multidimensional approach. Multidimensionality relates closely to the framework of *functionings* and *capabilities* proposed by Amartya Sen (1985). As described here in laymen's terms, Sen suggests that the assessment of individual welfare involves the analysis of a person's capability set, which encompasses all of the potential functionings that person can achieve (Kuklys 2005), and takes into account certain personal, social, and environmental factors. In this sense, a capability set represents the individual's effective choice set, taking account of nonmarket goods and services and nonmonetary constraints. The capability set becomes a metric of effective freedom—the whole set of options an individual is effectively able to choose from.

The basic dimensions in the MDG set are related to a capability failure, or a narrowing down of the set of available options. Policies must be comprehensive and consider the complementarities among dimensions. Sen (2004) has suggested the so-called Triple-R analysis, the *reach, range and reason* approach, which can be applied to the design of policies, as in UNDP (2010). In simple terms, this analysis implies that, first of all, public actions should reach the people, the households, and the communities for which they were designed (*reach*). Secondly, to be effective, these measures should be comprehensive; in other words, they should address all of the identified binding constraints (*range*). Lastly, these actions should

be consistent and should affect beneficiaries' aspirations, objectives, and autonomy, thus encouraging them to become active subjects and not passive recipients of development policies (*reason*). Only such an approach would result in sustainable policies.

Despite its conceptual value, translating the capability approach into an empirical setting is not always a straightforward task. A well-known example of a systematic attempt to capture multidimensionality at the aggregate, country, level, is the traditional Human Development Index (HDI) published by UNDP since 1990. This index itself is an aggregate of indices reflecting economic means (income), education, and health. Applications of the HDI at the household level are also possible, and the Global Human Development Reports have also introduced an inequality-sensitive HDI for international comparisons (UNDP 2010).

The attempts to bring multidimensionality into policy discussions have been enhanced by the formalization of multidimensional poverty indices as well. The design of better social policy for the achievement of the MDGs requires establishing a comprehensive view of poverty, relying on a robust methodology to identify those who are poor, and setting up a way to evaluate policy interventions rigorously, in ways in which the evaluation feeds back into policy design. A recent and innovative measure that addresses the identification and aggregation in an axiomatic way is the Alkire and Foster (2009) multidimensional poverty measure, applied to more than one hundred countries in the recent Human Development Reports UNDP (2010).

Countries have started to use a multidimensional approach to measurement and policy design in order to enhance their capacity to move toward the achievement of the MDGs under an integrated framework. Most likely, this type of comprehensive approach to social progress will be present in the future agenda beyond the 2015 deadline defined by the Millennium Declaration.

Rebeca GRYNSPAN
United Nations Development Programme

Luis F. LOPEZ-CALVA
The World Bank

Disclaimer: The authors collaborated with this volume on a personal basis. The content of this article does not reflect the official position of the institutions to which they are affiliated.

See also Agenda 21; Development Indicators; Environmental Justice Indicators; Environmental Performance Index (EPI); Framework for Strategic Sustainable Development (FSSD); Genuine Progress Indicator (GPI); Global Environment Outlook (GEO)

Reports; Global Reporting Initiative (GRI); Gross Domestic Product, Green; Human Development Index (HDI); I = P × A × T Equation; *The Limits to Growth;* Population Indicators; Social Life Cycle Assessment (S-LCA); Taxation Indicators, Green

FURTHER READING

Alkire, Sabina, & Foster, James. (2009). Counting and multidimensional poverty measurement (OPHI working paper 32). Oxford, UK: University of Oxford.

Basu, Kaushik, & Lopez-Calva, Luis F. (2011). Functionings and capabilities. In Kenneth J. Arrow, Amartya K. Sen & Kotaro Suzumura (Eds.), *Handbook of social choice and welfare* (Vol. 2) (pp. 153–187). London: Elsevier Science-North Holland Publishers.

Foster, James E.; Greer, Joel; & Thorbecke, Erik. (1984). A class of decomposable poverty measures. *Econometrica, 52*(3), 761–766.

Grynspan, Rebeca, & Lopez-Calva, Luis F. (2010). Multidimensional poverty: Measurement and policy. In Jose Antonio Ocampo & Jaime Ros (Eds.). *Handbook of Latin American economies.* Oxford, UK: Oxford University Press.

Hulme, David, & Scott, James. (2010). The political economy of the MDGs: Retrospect and prospect from the world's biggest promise. *New Political Economy, 15*(2), 293–306.

Kuklys, Wiebke. (2005). *Amartya Sen's capability approach: Theoretical insights and empirical applications, series: Studies in choice and welfare.* Berlin: Springer Verlag.

Sen, Amartya K. (1985). *Commodities and capabilities.* Amsterdam: North-Holland.

Sen, Amartya K. (2004). The three R's of reform. *Economic and Political Weekly, 40*(19), 7–13.

United Nations (UN). (2011). *MDG acceleration framework.* New York: United Nations.

United Nations Development Programme (UNDP). (2010). *Regional human development report for Latin America and the Caribbean 2010. Acting on the future: Intergenerational transmission of inequality.* San José, Costa Rica: Editorama.

National Environmental Accounting

National environmental accounting describes the interrelations between the economy and the environment at the country level in both physical and monetary terms. Environmental accounts are an extension of the standard national accounts. They provide a wide range of indicators that can be used to monitor green economy or green growth and, more broadly, sustainable development.

National environmental accounting (or environmental-economic accounting, or sometimes green accounting) refers to the activities undertaken by national statistical offices to compile statistics that describe the interrelations between the economy and the environment at the country level. Every economy depends on the environment for inputs of natural resources but also as a sink for outputs of production and consumption in the form of pollution and waste. The environment also produces various types of ecosystem services, such as enjoyable surroundings for leisure.

A concern with standard national accounting, which describes a country's economic activities (UNECE 2009), is that it does not properly take into account an economy's dependency on nature. For instance, if a country were to cut its entire tropical forest for harvesting timber within a single year, that would boost its gross domestic product (GDP), since no cost of depleting its natural capital is taken into consideration. This does not make sense from a sustainability point of view, as by depleting its natural capital base the country would jeopardize its future production possibilities.

Environmental accounting is based on a set of guidelines called the System of Environmental-Economic Accounts (SEEA). The SEEA is an extension of the national accounts designed as a multipurpose measurement framework from which a variety of indicators can be derived. These are relevant for monitoring green economics, green growth, and, more broadly, sustainability. Key examples are indicators of resource productivity and decoupling, extended measures of wealth, and environmental taxes and subsidies.

History

The origins of environmental accounting go back to the 1970s, when several European countries initiated work independently of each other (Hecht 2005, 9). In 1978, the Norwegian Environment Ministry commissioned Statistics Norway to develop natural resource accounts (NRAs) as a tool to better manage natural resources and the environment (Alfsen 1996, 5). This was due to growing environmental concerns about intensive expansion of hydropower, overexploitation of fish stocks, and the discovery of significant oil and gas reserves. In the 1980s, France developed an accounting system to assess, both quantitatively and qualitatively, the state and evolution of its "natural patrimony" (Vanoli 2005, 344). In the Netherlands, the economist

Roefie Hueting was influential in his ambitious efforts to estimate a sustainable national income that took into account depletion and degradation of the environment. His work triggered the development of physical flow accounts, or the national accounting matrix including environmental accounts (NAMEA), which present physical information alongside economic information to allow them to be compared (de Haan and Keunig 1996, 1). Another influential study was undertaken by the World Resources Institute (Repetto et al. 1989), which estimated the depreciation costs of Indonesia's natural resources and showed that this would lead to a significant downward adjustment of its growth rates.

The Earth Summit held in 1992 in Rio de Janeiro was a major stimulus for environmental accounting, as it called in its Agenda 21 for establishing "systems of integrated environmental and economic accounting" with "the main objective . . . to expand existing systems of national economic accounts in order to integrate environment and social dimensions in the accounting framework . . . in all member States at the earliest date" (UN DESA 1992, 8.41–8.42).

In parallel, several international conferences and workshops were organized by, among others, the United Nations Environment Programme and the World Bank. As a result, in 1993 the UN published the *Handbook of National Accounting: Integrated Environmental and Economic Accounting* (UNSD 1993). As its preface clearly states, the handbook was a work in progress, and there was a clear need to continue conceptual discussions. To this end, the statistical community established the London Group on Environmental Accounting, a forum for expert practitioners, from the increasing number of countries (both developed and developing) that started environmental accounting programs. This led in 2003 to publication of a revised *Handbook of National Accounting: Integrated Environmental and Economic Accounting 2003*, called the SEEA-2003

(United Nations et al. 2003), which was a major step forward but still fell short of the requirements of a statistical standard. A revised SEEA developed in 2011 is expected to be adopted as a statistical standard by the United Nations Statistical Commission in 2012 (UN DESA 2011).

Environmental Accounting in Practice

In practice, the work of an environmental accountant consists of integrating energy, water, land, and ecosystem statistics into economic statistics. In most countries, environmental accounting uses existing data, although occasionally separate surveys are run. Integration means adjusting data so that they match the concepts, definitions, and classifications of the national accounts. For instance, while an energy balance provides a technical overview of the energy use and transformation that occur within the geographical boundaries of a country, an energy account provides an economic picture of energy use by a country's residents.

The residency of a company or household is based on the territory with which it has the strongest connection. The national accounts focus on the activities of residents, regardless of whether these activities occur outside or inside a country's borders. Compiling an energy account may therefore result in large adjustments due to a different treatment of international tourism and transport. Similarly, while emission inventories used for reporting on the Kyoto Protocol exclude greenhouse gas emissions inherent in international aviation in the national totals, these emissions are included in air emission accounts in case the airline would be a resident of the country.

An energy account details the use of energy products by industrial activities, which allows for a direct comparison with an industry's production, value-added, or employment. One can compare, for instance, the energy efficiency of different industries.

The value-added of environmental accounting comes from the rigor of an accounting system, which may increase the reliability of estimates. Such accounting also ensures that resulting indicators are consistent. Critics of environmental accounting, however, point out that having separate statistics, such as an energy balance and an energy account, confuses users.

SEEA and Sustainable Development Indicators

The SEEA consists of several types of accounts.

The first category of SEEA accounts is *physical flow accounts*, which measure the use of the environment in terms of natural resource inputs and outputs of waste and emissions. Physical flow accounts can be expressed in different units, resulting in energy accounts (in joules), water accounts (in cubic meters), air emission accounts (in carbon dioxide equivalents), and material flow accounts (in tons). Due to their one-to-one relationship with monetary data, physical flow accounts allow the compilation of indicators of resource productivity or efficiency by industry. Physical flow accounts can be used to analyze the extent to which economic growth is being decoupled from resource inputs and pollution outputs. Figure 1, which contains an example from the Netherlands, demonstrates that despite strong economic growth of 53 percent that occurred between 1990 and 2009, the level of fine-dust emissions decreased almost 51 percent. This is an example of *absolute* decoupling. In contrast, net energy consumption increased during the period, although at a slower rate than economic growth, which is an example of *relative* decoupling. In order for

Figure 1

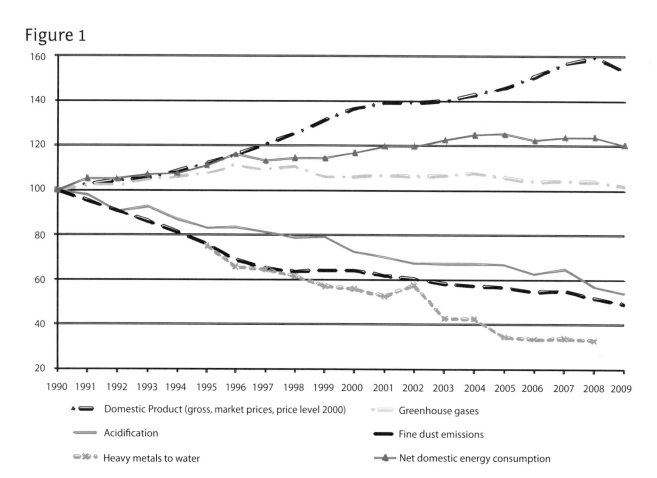

Source: Statistics Netherlands (2010).

The relationship between economic growth and resource inputs/pollution outputs shows decoupling.

a country to achieve sustainability, the absolute decoupling of environmental pressures from economic growth is considered a necessary condition by most researchers in the field.

The second category of SEEA accounts is *monetary accounts* that track environmentally related activities as well as policy instruments. Environmental protection expenditure accounts indicate how much a country spends on protecting or rehabilitating the environment. They also show what proportion of a country's investments has an environmental purpose (so-called green investments). Environmental goods and services accounts measure the scope of activities related to the environment and allow one to derive indicators of, for example, green jobs. Environmental tax accounts can be used to monitor whether a country's tax base is becoming more green. Accounts for emission permits allow the analysis of incentives that different industries face to reduce their greenhouse gas emissions.

The third category of SEEA accounts is *natural resource accounts* that describe a country's natural capital (both renewable and nonrenewable) in both physical and monetary terms. Analyzing a time series of stocks of timber, for instance, allows one to assess whether the natural capital base is being maintained in a sustainable manner. In monetary terms, natural resource accounts allow one to derive extended measures of wealth, such as that compiled by the World Bank (2011). Natural resource accounts also allow one to estimate the value of depletion of various types of natural capital. This enables the calculation of "green GDP" type of measures, which adjust common measures of production, income, and saving toward more sustainable measures by correcting for depletion and/or degradation of natural capital.

Country Impact

The development of environmental accounting is often guided by country-specific circumstances. For resource-abundant countries, natural resource accounts may have a higher priority, while in countries with high pollution rates, water or air emission accounts may be more policy relevant. Some countries focus on physical accounts, while others primarily have an interest in monetary data in order to estimate comprehensive wealth or a green GDP type of measure.

No single country compiles all types of environmental accounts, although some countries, such as Norway, come close. New possibilities and demands keep arising for environmental accounting, because environmental policy is continuously developing. For instance, accounts for carbon emission permits are being added to the environmental accountant's tool box.

Environmental accounting programs have been established in all regions of the world. In Europe, about ten countries have long-running accounting programs, focusing primarily on physical flow accounts and economic accounts. In 2011, a legal base for environmental accounting was adopted by the European Commission, which makes compilation of air emission, material flow, and environmental tax accounts compulsory (by 2013) for all European Union countries. Additional modules will be added in the future.

Outside Europe, Australia and Canada have had comprehensive programs since the early 1990s. The US environmental accounting activities, however, were stopped by political opposition shortly after their first publication in 1994. A panel was commissioned to review the work undertaken, which concluded that "extending the U.S. national income and product accounts (NIPA) to include assets and production activities associated with natural resources and the environment is an important goal" (Nordhaus and Kokkelenberg 1999). The report, however, did not change the situation.

In Asia, South Korea has a strong focus on wealth accounting, while Japan traditionally has had a large interest in material flow accounting.

Several developing countries such as Colombia, Mexico and South Africa have well-established programs that have been running since the 1990s. Many others have shown great interest in environmental accounting, although some have struggled to keep their programs running because of capacity constraints.

Green GDP has attracted controversy since its inception. For instance, in 2006, China published green GDP figures for 2004, which estimated damages at about 3 percent of GDP (Wang Jinnan et al. 2006, 11). These estimates were lower than expected and led to fierce debate. As a result, China seems to have reoriented its environmental accounting activities toward compiling individual accounts. Several European countries such as Germany and Sweden are opposed to estimating a green GDP due to a variety of reasons such as a lack of user interest or methodological concerns. By contrast, Mexico has good experiences with its green GDP indicator (or PINE, its Spanish acronym), which it is required by law to publish annually. In 2009, India announced that it is aiming for a green GDP alternative by 2015 (Mukherjee 2009).

Future Outlook

There appears to be increasing international recognition of the importance of environmental accounting as a framework for deriving indicators: for instance, indicators to measure societal progress as expressed by the economists Joseph Stiglitz, Amartya Sen, and Jean-Paul Fitoussi (2009, 66); indicators to measure sustainable development (UNECE 2009, 69); and indicators to assess green growth (OECD 2011, 13).

There is also a growing interest in consumption-based indicators, such as those showing carbon footprints, virtual water, or indirect resource use. Because the calculation of these indicators requires environmental data that is integrated with economic statistics, there is a growing demand for environmental accounting data.

So far, the use of spatially explicit data, such as remote-sensing data, within environmental accounting has been limited. This may change as land and ecosystem

accounting is an emerging area within environmental accounting. Measurement challenges remain for several types of ecosystem services when one tries to value them in monetary terms; several countries therefore have started pilot projects with a focus on physical descriptions.

Bram EDENS
Statistics Netherlands

See also Building Rating Systems, Green; Business Reporting Methods; Carbon Footprint; Cost-Benefit Analysis; Development Indicators; Ecological Footprint Accounting; Environmental Performance Index; Genuine Progress Indicator (GPI); Global Reporting Initiative (GRI); Gross Domestic Product, Green; Sustainability Science; Systems Thinking; Taxation Indicators, Green

FURTHER READING

Alfsen, Knut H. (1996). *Why natural resource accounting?* Oslo, Norway: Statistics Norway, Research Department.

de Haan, Mark, & Keuning, Steven J. (1996). Taking the environment into account: The NAMEA approach. *The Review of Income and Wealth Series, 42*(2), 131–148. doi:10.1111/j.1475-4991.1996.tb00162.x

Hecht, Joy E. (2005). *National environmental accounting: Bridging the gap between ecology and economy.* Washington, DC: Resources for the Future Press.

Mukherjee, Krittivas. (2009, October 13). India says aims for green GDP alternative by 2015. Reuters India. Retrieved March 29, 2010, from http://in.reuters.com/article/topNews/idINIndia-43127920091013

Nordhaus, William D., & Kokkelenberg, Edward C. (Eds.). (1999). *Nature's numbers: Expanding the national economic accounts to include the environment.* Washington, DC: National Academy Press.

Organisation for Economic Co-operation and Development (OECD). (2011). *Towards green growth: Monitoring progress; OECD Indicators.* Paris: OECD.

Repetto, Robert.; Magrath, William W.; Wells, Michael M.; Beer, Christine C.; & Rossini, Fabrizio F. (1989). *Wasting assets: Natural resources in the national income and product accounts.* Washington, DC: World Resource Institute.

Statistics Netherlands. (2010). *Environmental accounts of the Netherlands 2009.* The Hague, Netherlands: Statistics Netherlands.

Stiglitz, Joseph E.; Sen, Amartya; & Fitoussi, Jean-Paul. (2009). *Report by the commission on the measurement of economic performance and social progress.* Paris: Commission on the Measurement of Economic Performance and Social Progress.

United Nations, European Commission, International Monetary Fund, Organisation for Economic Co-operation and Development, & World Bank. (2009). *System of national accounts 2008.* New York: United Nations.

United Nations Department of Economic and Social Affairs (UN DESA), Division for Sustainable Development. (1992). *Agenda 21.* Retrieved October 18, 2011, from http://www.un.org/esa/dsd/agenda21/index.shtml

United Nations Department of Economic and Social Affairs (UN DESA). (2011). *SEEA revision. Draft chapters of the revised SEEA revision for global consultation.* Retrieved September 1, 2011, from http://unstats.un.org/unsd/envaccounting/seearev/

United Nations Economic Commission for Europe (UNECE). (2009). *Measuring sustainable development: Report of the Joint UNECE/OECD/Eurostat Working Group on Statistics for Sustainable Development.* New York: United Nations.

United Nations Statistical Division (UNSD). (1993). *Handbook of national accounting: Integrated environmental and economic accounting* (Series F, no. 61). New York: United Nations.

United Nations, European Commission, International Monetary Fund, Organisation for Economic Co-operation and Development & World Bank. (2003). *Handbook of national accounting: Integrated environmental and economic accounting 2003* (Series F, no. 61, rev. 1). New York: United Nations.

Vanoli, André. (2005). *A history of national accounting.* Washington, DC: IOS Press.

Wang Jinnan et al. (2006). A study report on China environmental and economic accounting in 2004. Retrieved October 18, 2011, from http://www.caep.org.cn/english/paper/China-Environment-and-Economic-Accounting-Study-Report-2004.pdf

World Bank. (2011). *The changing wealth of nations: Measuring sustainable development in the new millennium.* Washington, DC: World Bank.

New Ecological Paradigm (NEP) Scale

The New Ecological Paradigm scale is a measure of endorsement of a "pro-ecological" world view. It is used extensively in environmental education, outdoor recreation, and other realms where differences in behavior or attitudes are believed to be explained by underlying values, a world view, or a paradigm. The scale is constructed from individual responses to fifteen statements that measure agreement or disagreement.

The New Ecological Paradigm (NEP) scale, which is sometimes referred to as the revised NEP, is a survey-based metric devised by the US environmental sociologist Riley Dunlap and colleagues. It is designed to measure the environmental concern of groups of people using a survey instrument constructed of fifteen statements. Respondents are asked to indicate the strength of their agreement or disagreement with each statement. Responses to these fifteen statements are then used to construct various statistical measures of environmental concern. The NEP scale is considered a measure of environmental world view or paradigm (framework of thought).

History of the NEP

The roots of the NEP are in the US environmental movement of the 1960s and 1970s, inspired by the publication of Rachel Carson's *Silent Spring*. Social psychologists hypothesized that the prevailing world view of the population, called the dominant social paradigm (DSP), was changing to reflect greater environmental concern. Developing valid and reliable measures of the environmental world view would help scholars better understand the trajectory of these changes and their relationship to

demographic, economic, and behavior change in the US population.

Among the various efforts to measure such change, Riley Dunlap and colleagues at Washington State University developed an instrument they called the New Environmental Paradigm (sometimes called the original NEP), which they published in 1978. The idea was that this instrument could measure where a population was in its transition from the DSP to a new, more environmentally conscious world view, a change that the NEP scale developers thought was likely to happen. The original NEP had twelve items (statements) that appeared to represent a single scale in the way in which populations responded to them.

The original NEP was criticized for several shortcomings, including a lack of internal consistency among individual responses, poor correlation between the scale and behavior, and "dated" language used in the instrument's statements. Dunlap and colleagues then developed the New Ecological Paradigm Scale to respond to criticisms of the original. This is sometimes referred to as the revised NEP scale to differentiate it from the New Environmental Paradigm scale.

The revised NEP has fifteen statements, called items. (See table 1 on the next page.) Eight of the items, if agreed to by a respondent, are meant to reflect endorsement of the new paradigm, while agreement with the other seven items represents endorsement of the DSP. Using a Likert scale, a commonly used rating scale, respondents are asked to indicate their strength of agreement with each statement (strongly agree, agree, unsure, disagree, strongly disagree).

The authors asserted that the revised NEP had several strengths, making it a reliable and valid tool for measuring a population's environmental world view. In particular, they said the new scale was internally consistent

TABLE 1. Revised NEP Statements

1. We are approaching the limit of the number of people the Earth can support.
2. Humans have the right to modify the natural environment to suit their needs.
3. When humans interfere with nature it often produces disastrous consequences.
4. Human ingenuity will insure that we do not make the Earth unlivable.
5. Humans are seriously abusing the environment.
6. The Earth has plenty of natural resources if we just learn how to develop them.
7. Plants and animals have as much right as humans to exist.
8. The balance of nature is strong enough to cope with the impacts of modern industrial nations.
9. Despite our special abilities, humans are still subject to the laws of nature.
10. The so-called "ecological crisis" facing humankind has been greatly exaggerated.
11. The Earth is like a spaceship with very limited room and resources.
12. Humans were meant to rule over the rest of nature.
13. The balance of nature is very delicate and easily upset.
14. Humans will eventually learn enough about how nature works to be able to control it.
15. If things continue on their present course, we will soon experience a major ecological catastrophe.

Source: Dunlap et al. (2000).

The seven even numbered items, if agreed to by a respondent, are meant to represent statements endorsed by the dominant social paradigm (DSP). The eight odd items, if agreed to by a respondent, are meant to reflect endorsement of the new environmental paradigm (NEP).

(people who responded to some items in one pattern tended to respond to other items in a consistent manner) and that it represented a measure of a single scale (that it had unidimensionality).

Use and Critiques

The revised NEP is used widely in the United States and in many other nations. It is used in cross-sectional assessments of the relationship of environmental world views to attitudes on public policy, to recreation participation patterns, and to pro-environmental behaviors. It is also used in before-and-after studies of the effects of some intervention or activity, such as the impact of educational programs on environmental world views. It is probably the most widely used measure of environmental values or attitudes, worldwide.

The revised NEP scale has its critics. There are three broad categories of criticism. First is the assertion that the revised NEP scale is missing certain elements of a pro-ecological world view and thus is incomplete. Specifically, it is said that the scale leaves out expressions of a biocentric or ecocentric world view that comes from late twentieth-century environmental ethics literature.

A second line of criticism concerns the validity of the scale. This comes typically from researchers who have tried to document links between NEP scale results and

pro-environmental behavior. When links between NEP scale results and behavior are weak, some researchers suggest that the scale fails to measure a world view accurately. Tests of the NEP scale as a predictor of environmental behavior are part of extensive social-psychological research to explain the root causes of environmental behavior.

Finally, there is considerable debate about the dimensionality of the revised NEP scale. Dunlap and colleagues argued that the NEP in both of its iterations measures a single dimension, endorsement of a world view that could be measured simply by adding up the responses. Numerous studies have used a statistical technique called principal components analysis to test this. These studies had different results, suggesting that the NEP captured not one dimension but often three or more dimensions. This variability in results leads some to question both the NEP's validity (does it measure the phenomena it is claiming to measure?) and its reliability (does it measure those phenomena in the same way across different populations or across time?).

Future of the NEP Scale

Given its extensive use in many settings, the New Ecological Paradigm scale will continue to be used widely. Because no other instrument has been so extensively accepted as a measure of environmental world views, it will continue to be valuable, if for no other reason than it gives researchers comparisons to make across study types, population types, and time. The growing body of research will create additional opportunities to test the NEP for its reliability and validity.

More importantly, it is clear that underlying values will have significant effects on debates around sustainability. Advocates for the usefulness of the revised NEP scale believe that progress toward sustainability would be reflected in shifts in NEP scale scores in the general population from endorsement of the dominant social paradigm toward endorsement of a New Ecological Paradigm. As such, the revised NEP scale would be a fundamental metric of progress toward sustainability. In the same manner, public information or sustainability education campaigns would be deemed successful if they caused a similar shift. For the NEP scale to serve this function effectively, however, there will need to be greater acceptance of its validity and reliability as a metric of sustainability values.

Mark W. ANDERSON
University of Maine, Orono

See also Challenges to Measuring Sustainability; Citizen Science; Community and Stakeholder Input; Environmental Justice Indicators; Focus Groups; Participatory Action Research; Quantitative vs. Qualitative Studies; Sustainability Science; Transdisciplinary Research; Weak vs. Strong Sustainability Debate

FURTHER READING

Dunlap, Riley E. (2008). The new environmental paradigm scale: From marginality to worldwide use. *Journal of Environmental Education, 40*(1), 3–18.

Dunlap, Riley E.; Van Liere, Kent D.; Mertig, Angela G.; & Jones, Robert Emmet. (2000). Measuring endorsement of the new ecological paradigm: A revised NEP scale. *Journal of Social Issues, 56*(3), 425–442.

Hunter, Lori M., & Rinner, Lesley. (2004). The association between environmental perspective and knowledge and concern with species diversity. *Society and Natural Resources, 17,* 517–532.

Kotchen, Matthew, & Reiling, Stephen D. (2000). Environmental attitudes, motivations, and contingent valuation of nonuse values: A case study involving endangered species. *Ecological Economics, 31*(1), 93–107.

LaLonde, Roxanne, & Jackson, Edgar L. (2002). The new environmental paradigm scale: Has it outlived its usefulness? *Journal of Environmental Education, 33*(4), 28–36.

Hawcroft, Lucy J., & Milfont, Taciano L. (2010). The use (and abuse) of the new environmental paradigm scale over the last 20 years: A meta-analysis. *Journal of Environmental Psychology, 30,* 143–158.

Lundmark, Cartina. (2007). The new ecological paradigm revisited: Anchoring the NEP scale in environmental ethics. *Environmental Education Research, 13*(3), 329–347.

Shepard, Kerry; Mann, Samuel; Smith, Nell; & Deaker, Lynley. (2009). Benchmarking the environmental values and attitudes of students in New Zealand's post-compulsory education. *Environmental Education Research, 15*(5), 571–587.

Stern, Paul C.; Dietz, Thomas; & Guagnano, Gregory. A. (1995). The new ecological paradigm in social-psychological context. *Environment and Behavior, 27*(6), 723–743.

Teisl, Mario, et al. (2011). Are environmental professors unbalanced? Evidence from the field. *Journal of Environmental Education, 42*(2), 67–83.

Thapa, Brijesh. (2010). The mediation effect of outdoor recreation participation on environmental attitude-behavior correspondence. *The Journal of Environmental Education, 14*(3), 133–150.

Ocean Acidification— Measurement

Ocean chemistry is changing as a result of the uptake of carbon dioxide emissions, a process that oceanographers have directly observed since the 1980s. A consequence of increased carbon dioxide uptake is ocean acidification, which will likely have profound impacts on numerous marine organisms. Time series measurements have confirmed that changing seawater chemistry is occurring globally, and evidence is emerging of present-day ocean acidification impacts in vulnerable marine ecosystems.

The ocean and atmosphere are in contact with one another on 70 percent of the Earth's surface, resulting in gaseous exchanges between the two. Since the beginning of the Industrial Revolution in the mid-eighteenth century, human activities—such as the burning of fossil fuel and deforestation—have caused an increase in carbon dioxide (CO_2) concentrations in the atmosphere. Physical and chemical processes drive the surface seawater in contact with the atmosphere to remain at equilibrium by absorbing about a quarter of this anthropogenic (human-caused) CO_2 (Sabine et al. 2004; Le Quéré et al. 2009). This uptake of CO_2 has changed the chemistry of the ocean, a phenomenon referred to as "ocean acidification."

The oceans are a vast reservoir for carbon and hold approximately fifty times more CO_2 than the atmosphere (Sabine 2006). In the early stages of climate change research, scientists believed the oceans were well buffered and would be largely unaffected by CO_2 emissions. But as the understanding of carbon chemistry improved, and the number of ocean observations increased, oceanographers discovered that anthropogenic CO_2 was building up in the surface ocean and indeed was changing seawater chemistry (Feely et al. 2004; Orr et al. 2005). The ocean is now absorbing approximately 2.2 billion tons of

anthropogenic carbon per year—a net increase compared to the period between the end of the last ice age approximately ten thousand years ago and the beginning of the Industrial Revolution, when the flux into and out of the ocean was roughly equal (Sabine et al. 2004; Le Quéré et al. 2009). As a result, the modern surface ocean is experiencing altered acid-base chemistry and reduced availability of dissolved carbonate ions.

Ocean acidification has the potential to directly impact marine life sensitive to these changes in seawater chemistry. Calcifying organisms (i.e., organisms that build external skeletons and shells using dissolved calcium and carbonate ions) are likely to be most vulnerable to ocean acidification. Oysters, clams, sea urchins, shallow-water tropical corals, deep-sea corals, and calcareous plankton are some examples of marine calcifiers that may be affected by ocean acidification. Impacts to key organisms such as these can in turn influence the health of the marine ecosystems they inhabit. As ocean acidification progresses, there is also concern that changes in ocean carbon chemistry could alter important biogeochemical processes such as carbon and nutrient cycling and the chemical speciation of trace metals, nutrients, and toxic compounds (Hutchins, Mulholland, and Fu 2009).

The Chemical Reaction

When CO_2 gas from the atmosphere dissolves in the ocean,

Equation 1: CO_2 (atmosphere) $\rightleftharpoons$ CO_2 (seawater)

it reacts with water (H_2O) to form carbonic acid (H_2CO_3).

Equation 2: CO_2 (seawater) + H_2O $\rightleftharpoons$ H_2CO_3

Carbonic acid quickly dissociates and releases a hydrogen ion (H^+) and a bicarbonate ion (HCO_3^-).

$$\text{Equation 3: } H_2CO_3 \rightleftharpoons H^+ + HCO_3^-$$

One of the products of this reaction is H^+. Increasing H^+ in solution lowers the pH, resulting in a more acidic solution. This is one component of the chemistry of ocean acidification. The pH of a solution is the unit of measurement used to describe acidity, and it ranges from 0 to 14 (pH below 7 is acidic and above 7 is basic). Although the overall pH of the ocean is basic, acidification means the lowering of pH in a direction toward less basic, more acidic. Since the Industrial Revolution, the average pH of the ocean has decreased from 8.2 to 8.1 (Feely, Doney, and Cooley 2009). Like the Richter scale that measures the magnitude of earthquakes, the pH scale is logarithmic; therefore, this 0.1 decrease in pH represents a 26 percent increase in acidity of the oceans. The average pH of the surface ocean is now lower than it has been for approximately 20 million years (Pelejero, Calvo, and Hoegh-Guldberg 2010). Under the Intergovernmental Panel of Climate Change (IPCC) business-as-usual CO_2 emission scenario, ocean pH is predicted to decrease as much as an additional 0.3 units by the end of this century (Orr et al. 2005; Caldeira and Wickett 2005), which would mean an increase of approximately 150 percent in the acidity of oceans.

Some of the hydrogen ions released in equation 3 then react with carbonate ions (CO_3^{2-}) to produce additional bicarbonate.

$$\text{Equation 4: } H^+ + CO_3^{2-} \rightleftharpoons HCO_3^-$$

This is the other important component of ocean acidification chemistry. Calcifying marine organisms require free carbonate ions in seawater to form their calcium carbonate mineral skeletons and shells. This reaction consumes those free carbonate ions, making them less available to calcifying organisms. As a result of the uptake of anthropogenic CO_2, the average concentration of CO_3^{2-} in the surface ocean has decreased by approximately 16 percent compared to preindustrial times (Feely et al. 2009).

Another parameter that ocean scientists calculate when studying ocean acidification is the saturation state of calcium carbonate minerals. Saturation state is a way to describe the amount of calcium carbonate minerals expected in seawater based on the physical characteristics of that seawater (e.g., temperature, pressure, and salinity) and the solubility of that particular calcium carbonate mineral (e.g., aragonite and calcite, the two main forms of calcium carbonate minerals produced by marine calcifiers).

$$\text{Equation 5: } \Omega = [Ca^{2+}][CO_3^{2-}]/K'_{sp}$$

In this equation, Ω is saturation state, $[Ca^{2+}]$ is the concentration of calcium ions, $[CO_3^{2-}]$ is the concentration of carbonate ions, and K'_{sp} is a constant called the *apparent solubility product.*

When Ω in equation 5 is equal to 1, the concentrations of calcium and carbonate ions are equal to the apparent solubility product and the seawater is at equilibrium. When Ω is greater than 1, the seawater is considered saturated with respect to calcium carbonate minerals, meaning there are ample chemical building blocks for organisms to build and maintain their shells and skeletons. When Ω falls below 1, organisms typically have to expend more energy to extract those chemical building blocks from seawater, and, in some cases, the calcium carbonate mineral structures of organisms may begin to dissolve. Although Ω is a useful indicator, not all organisms respond in the same manner to varying saturation states. Many organisms require conditions well above saturation, at levels of 4 or 5 (e.g., tropical corals), and some organisms can maintain their structures in undersaturated waters, albeit at an energetic cost.

In general, as of the early twenty-first century, surface ocean waters are saturated with respect to aragonite and calcite minerals. Seasonal aragonite undersaturation has been documented in some areas of the surface ocean in upwelling regions (Feely et al. 2008) and in cold, high-latitude regions (Bates, Mathis, and Cooper 2009; Mathis, Cross, and Bates 2011), which has been attributed to the anthropogenic uptake of CO_2. Deep ocean waters are naturally undersaturated with respect to aragonite and calcite due to the products of respiration that build up in those waters since they were last in contact with the atmosphere. As a result, deep ocean waters are naturally high in CO_2 and low in pH and saturation state.

The depth in the ocean where saturated surface waters and undersaturated deep waters meet is called the *saturation horizon*. The aragonite saturation horizon has migrated 40–200 meters closer to the surface due to ocean uptake of anthropogenic CO_2 (Feely et al. 2004; Orr et al. 2005).

Monitoring the Changing Chemistry

More than three decades of observations have verified that ocean acidification is occurring. In the 1960s, the oceanographic community recognized the need to better understand ocean carbon in order to address the global-scale issue of climate change. At that time, scientists did not have coordinated international ocean-observing programs or standardized analytical techniques to measure ocean carbon parameters. Oceanographers knew the ocean was absorbing CO_2 from the atmosphere, but they were unclear about how much and where it was going. International efforts to coordinate research efforts and priorities, as well as to standardize analytical methods, began in the 1960s. By the early 1990s there were robust global ocean carbon surveys making highly accurate measurements of dissolved inorganic carbon (DIC) and total alkalinity (TA) from surface to deep waters in every ocean basin. Advances in technology now allow autonomous observation of a variety of chemical, biological, and physical parameters, including carbon system measurements such as pCO_2 (i.e., the partial pressure of CO_2) and pH. Today, scientists collect over 1 million measurements of ocean carbon every year through repeat hydrographic research cruises and autonomous instruments on buoys, gliders, research vessels, and commercial vessels. (See figure 1, below.) As a result, the understanding of

Figure 1

Source: Adrienne J. Sutton.

This photo shows a research vessel leaving port on an expedition to make high-quality measurements of ocean carbon along the west coast of the United States. The piece of equipment on the right is called a rosette, which is made up of numerous Niskin (i.e. sampling) bottles that collect seawater at different depths in the water column.

the chemical properties of the ocean carbon system and how it is changing over time has improved dramatically.

Ocean pH Time Series

One of the longest continuous ocean carbon time series is in the central Pacific Ocean off Hawaii. Oceanographers have been observing changes in surface ocean CO_2 and pH there since 1988 (Dore et al. 2009). Figure 2 (below) shows surface water pCO_2 increasing at approximately the same rate as CO_2 in the atmosphere and a steady decline in ocean pH since the beginning of the observations. This long-term trend in surface ocean pCO_2 and pH is similar to time series observations at other open ocean sites, such as the Bermuda Atlantic Time series Study and the European Time Series in the Canary Islands stations in the subtropical North Atlantic Ocean. These types of time series are critical to our understanding of long-term changes in ocean chemistry and are being replicated in other areas of the open ocean, in dynamic and productive coastal oceans, and in coral reef ecosystems.

Global Patterns

Ocean acidification will not manifest in a uniform way across the globe. There are physical, chemical, and biological factors that impact ocean uptake of CO_2 from the atmosphere. For example, CO_2 is more soluble in cold seawater; therefore, ocean acidification will be accelerated in colder regions of the surface ocean. Physical mixing of seawater, ocean circulation, and wind speed at the ocean–atmosphere interface can also affect ocean uptake of CO_2. Finally, biological production and respiration have large impacts on ocean carbon chemistry. In biologically productive regions of the ocean, like coastal oceans, estuaries, and shallow water coral reefs, daily cycles of carbon in surface waters are associated with daily cycles in biological activity. Large phytoplankton blooms can also cause large, episodic drawdown of CO_2 in surface ocean and coastal waters. These factors play a large role in causing some ocean ecosystems to be more vulnerable to ocean acidification than others.

Figure 2. Measurements of CO_2 and pH in Surface Ocean Waters

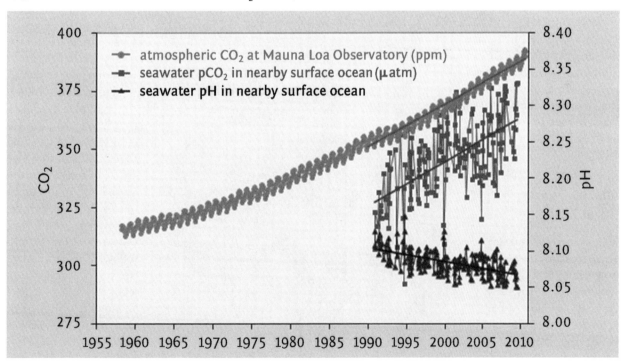

Source: Modified after Feely, Doney, and Cooley (2009). Data from the National Oceanic and Atmospheric Administration's Earth System Research Laboratory and the Hawaii Ocean Time-Series program.

Atmospheric CO_2 concentrations at Mauna Loa Observatory and changing seawater chemistry (pCO_2 and pH) observed in nearby surface waters north of Oahu, Hawaii, USA. Units of measurements are parts per million (ppm) for atmospheric CO_2 and micro-atmospheres (μatm) for seawater pCO_2.

High-Latitude Oceans

Ocean acidification occurs more rapidly in high-latitude oceans due to a variety of physical and chemical factors (Fabry et al. 2009). The surface waters of high-latitude oceans absorb more CO_2 than other regions because CO_2 is more soluble in lower-temperature surface ocean waters. A warming climate causes accelerated freshwater ice melt, exacerbating the changing chemistry associated with ocean acidification. In addition, persistent circumpolar winds further facilitate the exchange of CO_2 between the ocean and atmosphere in the Southern Ocean. Model projections based on IPCC business-as-usual CO_2 emission scenarios predict that the entire Arctic Ocean will be undersaturated with respect to aragonite by 2050 and the Antarctic by the end of the twenty-first century (Feely, Doney, and Cooley 2009).

Coastal Upwelling Systems

Upwelling is a natural process whereby surface waters are driven offshore by prevailing winds and are replaced by deeper waters naturally rich in CO_2 and low in pH and saturation state. This natural condition in coastal upwelling systems is exacerbated by the uptake of anthropogenic CO_2 at the surface. For example, in the coastal upwelling waters of the California Current Ecosystem, evidence suggests that the aragonite saturation horizon is now migrating toward the surface at the rate of 1–2 meters per year, making it more likely that undersaturated waters will reach the surface ocean during upwelling events (Feely et al. 2008).

Shallow-Water Coral Reefs

The presence of multiple stressors can also affect how ocean acidification will impact ocean ecosystems. Shallow-water coral reefs live in a thin band around the Earth where water clarity, temperature, nutrients, and the availability of aragonite are ideal for their growth. Projections indicate that by 2030 fewer than half of the

world's reefs will be in areas where aragonite conditions remain ideal, and by 2050 that number is further reduced to 15 percent (Burke et al. 2011). The stress of ocean acidification coexists with other stressors impacting coral reefs: warming ocean waters, overfishing and destructive fishing, coastal development, and pollution. The combination of these stressors create a significant threat to coral reefs and the estimated 1 million types of organisms—25 percent of the world's species—that live in coral reef ecosystems.

Biological Implications

The recognition that ocean acidification is occurring and that chemical changes may impact marine life has grown rapidly in the early twenty-first century, making this a burgeoning field of scientific research. Scientists have been interested in broadly understanding which organisms may be affected, and consequently much of the research on ocean acidification impacts has focused on short-term, single species experiments in the laboratory. In general, studies have shown that the rates of calcification (or shell-building) in calcifying organisms, such as coral and shellfish, are reduced in high-CO_2 seawater. Larval stages are particularly susceptible and in many cases have low rates of growth and survival in these types of experiments. Other potential direct impacts of ocean acidification on marine organisms include increased photosynthesis in phytoplankton, algae, and sea grasses; altered ability to regulate internal pH; hypercapnia; reduced olfaction (or sensory cues) in fish; and acoustic disruption due to a decrease in the sound absorption properties of seawater (see Fabry et al. 2008).

Humankind is also creating an experiment in our natural ocean ecosystems, where marine life in vulnerable ecosystems will be key indicators to the real-world impact of ocean acidification. Some organisms may already be showing signs of distress; a study on sixty-nine coral colonies in the Great Barrier

Reef has shown that coral calcification has already decreased 14 percent between 1990 and 2005, likely due to a combination of warming ocean waters and ocean acidification (De'ath, Lough, and Fabricius 2009). Other predictions indicate that by the middle of this century, coral erosion may be greater than growth for many tropical reefs, although this threshold is likely to vary greatly due to other factors, such as those described previously (Silverman et al. 2009).

In the Southern Ocean, there is evidence from sediment cores that the shell weight of planktonic foraminifera is negatively correlated with atmospheric CO_2 concentrations and that modern shell weight of one type of foraminifera is 30–35 percent less than during the Holocene (Moy et al. 2009). These calcifying plankton are important to the ocean carbon cycle, and a decrease in abundance could have significant implications to the transport of carbon to the deep ocean. Another key biological indicator in high-latitude oceans are pteropods, an important component of Arctic and Antarctic food webs. This is of concern because pteropods can reach densities of thousands of individuals per cubic meter, they are food for organisms ranging in size from krill to whales, and can be a primary food source for North Pacific juvenile salmon (Armstrong et al. 2005). In laboratory experiments, the thin shells of certain species of pteropods dissolve when exposed to seawater undersaturated with respect to aragonite, a condition expected throughout the Arctic Ocean by 2050 (Fabry et al. 2009). Due to their importance within these ecosystems and the relatively short food webs in the Arctic and Antarctic oceans, any impact to the pteropod population could threaten the health and abundance of other marine life in high-latitude oceans.

Another early indicator of the impact of ocean acidification is in the Pacific Northwest of the United States, where larval production in shellfish hatcheries plummeted for several years in the first decade of the twenty-first century. After many failed attempts to diagnose the problem and restore production levels, the shellfish industry partnered with local scientists to monitor hatchery intake waters used to raise larval oysters. They discovered that they were frequently drawing in high-CO_2 upwelled water to the hatchery, and when they did, they had low rates of larval survival. These shellfish hatcheries now monitor the intake waters and have changed their practices to adapt to the changing chemistry of the coastal ocean, resulting in increased larval survival. Shellfish and their predators (e.g., crabs) represent large fractions of United States (Cooley and Doney 2009) and international (Cooley, Kite-Powell, and Doney 2009) fisheries. Declining shellfish harvests could be one of the first direct impacts of ocean acidification on humankind.

Ocean acidification is a well-understood phenomenon that has been robustly documented using high-quality measurements. The chemistry of the ocean will continue to change in a predictable fashion as CO_2 continues to increase in the atmosphere. Biological implications to ocean acidification are likely beginning to manifest themselves in our ocean ecosystems, and they may become more common if CO_2 emissions continue unabated.

Adrienne J. SUTTON
NOAA Pacific Marine Environmental Laboratory

See also Air Pollution Indicators and Monitoring; Biological Indicators (*several articles*); Carbon Footprint; Computer Modeling; Ecosystem Health Indicators; Fisheries Indicators, Freshwater; Fisheries Indicators, Marine; Long-Term Ecological Research (LTER); Reducing Emissions from Deforestation and Forest Degradation (REDD); Remote Sensing

FURTHER READING

Armstrong, Janet L., et al. (2005). Distribution, size, and interannual, seasonal and diel food habits of northern Gulf of Alaska juvenile pink salmon, *Oncorhynchus gorbuscha*. *Deep Sea Research Part II: Topical Studies in Oceanography, 52*, 247–265.

Bates, Nicholas R.; Mathis, Jeremy T.; & Cooper, Lee W. (2009). Ocean acidification and biologically induced seasonality of carbonate mineral saturation states in the western Arctic Ocean. *Journal of Geophysical Research, 114*, C11007.

Burke, Lauretta; Reytar, Kathleen; Spalding, Mark; & Perry, Allison. (2011). *Reefs at risk revisited.* Washington, DC: World Resources Institute.

Caldeira, Ken, & Wickett, Michael E. (2005). Ocean model predictions of chemistry changes from carbon dioxide emissions to the atmosphere and ocean. *Journal of Geophysical Research, 110*, C09S04.

Cooley, Sarah R., & Doney, Scott C. (2009). Anticipating ocean acidification's economic consequences for commercial fisheries. *Environmental Research Letters, 4*, 024007.

Cooley, Sarah R.; Kite-Powell, Hauke L.; & Doney, Scott C. (2009). Ocean acidification's potential to alter global marine ecosystem services. *Oceanography, 22*(4), 172–181.

De'ath, Glenn; Lough, Janice M.; & Fabricius, Katharina E. (2009). Declining coral calcification on the Great Barrier Reef. *Science, 323*, 166–119.

Doney, Scott C.; Fabry, Victoria J.; Feely, Richard A.; & Kleypas, Joan A. (2009). Ocean acidification: The other CO_2 problem. *Annual Review of Marine Science, 1*, 169–192.

Dore, John E.; Lukas, Roger; Sadler, Daniel W.; Church, Matthew J.; & Karl, David M. (2009). Physical and biogeochemical modulation of ocean acidification in the central North Pacific. *Proceedings of the National Academy of Sciences, 106*, 12235–12240.

Fabry, Victoria J.; McClintock, James B.; Mathis, Jeremy T.; & Grebmeier, Jacqueline M. (2009). Ocean acidification at high latitudes: The bellwether. *Oceanography, 22*(4), 160–171.

Fabry, Victoria J.; Seibel, Brad A.; Feely, Richard A.; & Orr, James C. (2008). Impacts of ocean acidification on marine fauna and ecosystem processes. *International Council for the Exploration of the Sea (ICES) Journal of Marine Science, 65*, 414–432.

Feely, Richard A.; Doney, Scott C.; & Cooley, Sarah R. (2009). Ocean acidification: Present conditions and future changes in a high CO_2 world. *Oceanography, 22*(4), 36–47.

Feely, Richard A.; Sabine, Christopher L.; Hernandez-Avon, J. Martin; Ianson, Debby; & Hales, Burke. (2008). Evidence for upwelling of corrosive "acidified" water onto the continental shelf. *Science, 320,* 1490–1492.

Feely, Richard A., et al. (2004). Impact of anthropogenic CO_2 on the $CaCO_3$ system in the oceans. *Science, 305,* 362–366.

Feely, Richard A., et al. (2009). Present and future changes in seawater chemistry due to ocean acidification. In Brian J. McPherson and Eric T. Sundquist (Eds.), *Carbon sequestration and its role in the global carbon cycle* (pp. 175–188). Washington, DC: AGU Monograph.

Hutchins, David A.; Mulholland, Margaret R.; & Fu, Feixue. (2009). Nutrient cycles and marine microbes in a CO_2-enriched ocean. *Oceanography, 22*(4), 128–145.

Le Quéré, Corinne, et al. (2009). Trends in the sources and sinks of carbon dioxide. *Nature Geoscience, 2,* 831–836.

Mathis, Jeremy T.; Cross, Jessica N.; & Bates, Nicholas R. (2011). Coupling primary production and terrestrial runoff to ocean acidification and carbonate mineral suppression in the eastern Bering Sea. *Journal of Geophysical Research, 116,* C02030.

Moy, Andrew D.; Howard, William R.; Bray, Stephen G.; & Trull, Thomas W. (2009). Reduced calcification in modern Southern Ocean planktonic foraminifera. *Nature Geoscience, 2,* 276–280.

Orr, James C., et al. (2005). Anthropogenic ocean acidification over the twenty-first century and its impact on calcifying organisms. *Nature, 437,* 681–686.

Pelejero, Carles; Calvo, Eva; & Hoegh-Guldberg, Ove. (2010). Paleo-perspectives on ocean acidification. *Trends in Ecology and Evolution, 25,* 332–344.

Sabine, Christopher L. (2006). Global carbon cycle. In *Encyclopedia of life sciences*. Chichester, UK: John Wiley & Sons, Ltd. doi:10.1038/npg.els.0003489

Sabine, Christopher L., et al. (2004). The oceanic sink for anthropogenic CO_2. *Science, 305,* 367–371.

Silverman, Jacob; Lazar, Boaz; Cao, Long; Caldeira, Ken; & Erez, Jonathan. (2009). Coral reefs may start dissolving when atmospheric CO_2 doubles. *Geophysical Research Letters, 36,* L05606.

Organic and Consumer Labels

Consumer or product labels are the result of voluntary efforts by firms to make their products and production processes more sustainable and to communicate these efforts through information provided on the products they sell. Usually product labeling involves a thorough process of certification by an independent third-party institution. This vetting increases the reliability of product labels over firm-designed indicators. Product labels thus are an important instrument to promote sustainability.

More than five hundred years ago, Germany enacted the beer purity law (Reinheitsgebot) that precisely defined three ingredients to be used for beer production: water, barley, and hops. At the time, the government aimed to ensure availability of bread by keeping wheat out of beer, thus decreasing bakeries' competition for the grain. The objective of the law was to ensure long-term preservation of resources, and also to set German beer apart from international competition and to provide credible information to consumers about beer ingredients. Even today, beer producers claim to respect the purity law by providing corresponding information printed on their products. This is what in modern times is called "product labeling" by marketing experts.

One key objective of product labels is to set some products apart from others by promoting sustainability. Product labels are claims put forward by firms to inform customers about certain characteristics of their products. As Joop de Boer, a researcher from the Institute of Environmental Studies at the University of Amsterdam, puts it, in the case of sustainability, product labels serve to identify "ideal" sustainability goals to attain, or relevant "ills" to escape—for example, replacement of nonrenewable resources by renewable ones (de Boer 2003).

Product labels may also be "generic," identifying comparable levels of performance (e.g., a "fair trade" label reassures that revenues are distributed fairly across all parties involved in the production and delivery of a product; the label can be applied to any sort of product from food to complex goods such as vehicles), or they may be product "specific," recognizing particular characteristics of certain product categories (e.g., energy consumption labels that are applicable only to home appliances and other electronic goods). De Boer uses these two lines of reasoning to propose the classification of product labels shown in table 1, on the next page.

Some product labels target a specific consumer segment that is sensitive to sustainability. While the beer purity law allowed only specific ingredients in beer, product labels today provide information on inputs as well as on production, storage, and transportation processes. Organic labels, for example, are designed to reassure consumers that no synthetic and chemical materials are used as product inputs and in farmland treatment. The fair trade label is designed to promote a better distribution of revenues across the supply chain, in particular if suppliers from developing economies are involved. Energy efficiency labels inform consumers about expected energy consumption of home appliances such as refrigerators or washing machines. Product labels thus provide information about specific sustainability criteria. This information is designed to influence consumers' purchasing decisions.

Product labeling is related to one key sustainability strategy that may be adopted by manufacturing firms: product stewardship, or life cycle analysis. Product stewardship entails a thorough environmental and social analysis of all resources, parts, and components of a product and all production processes involved in manufacturing and delivering this product. It also involves reflections

TABLE 1. Categories of Product Labels

	Label as a Benchmark to Achieve Ideals	Label as a Bottom Line to Avoid Ills
Generic labels	EU Ecolabel	Organic label Fair trade label
Sector specific labels	Energy consumption label (home appliances)	"No sweat" label (apparel), indicating that sweatshop labor was not used

Source: de Boer (2003).

about possibilities for reuse and recycling of products at the end of their life cycle. Product stewardship, however, comes at a cost. For example, the replacement of a scarce resource by a widely available resource may lead to changes in production processes and technologies. The product label makes it possible for firms to communicate these efforts to consumers as they define and articulate preferable product characteristics. The communication of these efforts aims to ensure that investments made by firms to become more sustainable turn into economic profits.

Accreditation and Logos

Some firms design their own product labels that communicate their adherence to self-proclaimed sustainability standards. Although such labels may have some marketing benefits, they are based on noncomparable and opaque data and can cause confusion and distrust. Such labels continue to exist, but since the early 1980s, efforts have been made to create standards to make product labels more valid and comparable.

The best labels imply that the standards have been endorsed by multiple independent entities, compliance with accepted standards is verified by an independent entity, and the entity that is verifying compliance has been formally recognized by an authoritative body or accreditation institution.

Standardized product labels reflect clear expectations in terms of the conditions and processes under which a product is produced, stored, and shipped. An authorized institution will control whether a firm complies with the standards. In most cases, such control includes an on-site visit to the firm's production site. If the control process yields positive results, the authorized institution confers the right to the applying firm to use the product label. Normally, this allowance is restricted to a specific time period but can be renewed regularly.

Often consumer labels combine a picture (logo) with textual information. For example, the United States Department of Agriculture (USDA) issues an organic label in the form of a half-white, half-green circle with the inscription "USDA Organic." The European Union (EU) uses a green rectangular label with stars arranged in the form of a leaf to designate organic food.

The process for allocation of the EU's organic farming logo illustrates the accreditation process. In 1991, the EU adopted the EU Eco-regulation to specify how agricultural products should be grown and dealt with to deserve the designation "ecological." Refinements and supplements to this regulation led to the development of the organic farming label and corresponding standards used today. The regulation details the rules that need to be followed in order to be able to apply the label: products must contain at least 95 percent organic agricultural ingredients and no genetically modified organisms. Firms that want to use the label first undergo a conversion period of at least two years to adapt their production processes and to implement the regulation's rules. They are then subject to inspection by authorized institutions to ensure their compliance with regulations. After the conversion period and the successful implementation of the regulation, firms are granted EU organic certification, are allowed to label their products "organic," and are permitted to print the EU organic farming logo on their products. The logo on organic products guarantees to consumers that "at least 95 percent of the product's ingredients of agricultural origin have been organically produced; the product complies with the rules of the official inspection program; the product has come directly from the producer or preparer in a sealed package; the product bears the name of the producer, the preparer or vendor and the name or code of the inspection body" (European Commission 2011).

Costs and Benefits

The key benefit of defining general standards and issuing certifications by a third party is to increase the credibility and comparability of product labels. In fact, most customers feel reassured if they identify a sustainability label on a product they are already familiar with.

Such product labels are not without critics. First, while the labels assure that a product has been certified, they normally do not display the results of the certification process itself. Thus, consumers receive no information whether and to which extent the products offered by one firm exceed minimum expectations. The consumer does not receive any additional information or clear and comparable data or indicators that would serve as benchmark data to understand the extent to which the labeled product contributes to sustainability.

Second, many institutions that define labeling standards provide only superficial information on what they control. The European Union publishes the basic criteria to be met by organic products but does not provide access to the full documentation of the standards, such as the processes to be followed, the measures to be taken, or the indicators to be observed. This is for competitive reasons; product labeling is a business: firms pay for services of certification and for label usage. If information on certification details was publicly available, the process could be easily copied. Such practices foster a lack of transparency and seem to run counter to the product labeling ideals.

Third, product labels come at additional cost and in most cases will lead to higher product prices. This higher price may impede the diffusion of sustainability on a broader scale because not all consumers will be willing to pay higher prices for sustainable products. In fact, product labels address a very specific consumer segment. The question remains whether this segment will have the financial means and willingness to pay higher prices for a wide variety of products. It is possible that sustainability will be affordable for only a very small segment of high-income consumers. This will inhibit the solution of sustainability problems on a global scale because consumers from less-developed economies will not have the financial means to afford sustainable products. Globally, the share of consumers with high incomes is much lower than the share of consumers with low incomes. Therefore, the overall positive effect of product labels is open to question.

A fourth major criticism is the risk of increased consumer confusion because of the large variety of available product labels. In addition to labels attesting to fair trade, organic farming, and energy efficiency, there are many more addressing different aspects of sustainability but not sustainability as a whole. Energy efficiency labels account for energy consumption. Organic labels inform about the natural origins of food and beverage ingredients. Fair trade labels relate to the wage and income distributions of all entities in a supply chain. There is no label that integrates all these and other relevant sustainability elements into a single certification. Consumers are not always aware of these differences and may have difficulty in assessing the impact of the sustainability indicators represented by different labels. In addition, consumers will not always be capable of fully understanding the information provided with the labels.

Finally, labeling standards promote the achievement of only minimum standards. Once met, there is limited incentive for firms to exceed these minimum thresholds. Certification authorities would be in a better position to promote sustainability if they included mechanisms to ensure continuous improvement to meet sustainability targets.

Trends and Future Directions

Product labeling will change as key technologies evolve. Microelectronic devices, genetic markers, and bar codes such as radio-frequency information tags (RFID) that can be read by cell phones will change the nature of product labels. While traditional product labels provide binary information to consumers—either a product has a certain certification or it does not—these new technologies make it possible to provide information about the origins of a single product.

RFID tags communicate information through radio waves between a reader and a tag attached to a product. In the past, RFID has been used in inventory and transportation management to track and trace information on the product as it moves through a supply chain. First-generation RFID tags were thick and expensive to use. Therefore, their usage has been limited to a few business functions and for a few items. Today, RFID tags are smaller, cheaper, and more flexible to use. The tag can store data directly, and information provided on the tag can be updated as it moves through the supply chain. The tag can also provide unique identifier information that can be linked to data stored on the Internet. Combined with cell phones that can read RFID information and link it to web-based information, RFID tags make it possible for consumers to get any information on a specific product on demand.

A second major challenge will be to make product labels more uniform. Product labels today have different sustainability objectives. It will be a challenge to harmonize product labels, but this is important in order to increase transparency and reliability of the information provided.

Julia WOLF
EBS Business School

See also Advertising; Challenges to Measuring Sustainability; Design Quality Indicator (DQI); Ecolabels; Energy Efficiency Measurement; Energy Labeling; International Organization for Standardization (ISO); Shipping and Freight Indicators

FURTHER READING

de Boer, Joop. (2003). Sustainability labeling schemes: The logic of their claims and their functions for stakeholders. *Business Strategy & the Environment, 12*(4), 254–264.

European Commission. (2011). Consumer confidence. Retrieved June 27, 2011, from http://ec.europa.eu/agriculture/organic/home_en.

Fooducate. (2011, October). 1862–2011: A brief history of food and nutrition labeling. Retrieved June 27, 2011, from http://www.fooducate.com/blog/2008/10/25/1862-2008-a-brief-history-of-food-and-nutrition-labeling/

Hart, Stuart. (1995). A natural resource-based view of the firm. *Academy of Management Review, 20*(4), 986–1014.

Klimoski, Richard, & Palmer, Susan. (1993). The ADA and the hiring process in organizations. *Consulting Psychology Journal: Practice and Research, 45*(2), 10–36.

Koos, Sebastian. (2011). Varieties of environmental labeling, market structures, and sustainable consumption across Europe: A comparative analysis of organizational and market supply determinants of environmental-labeled goods. *Journal of Consumer Policy, 34*(1), 127–151.

Mackey, Mary A., & Metz, Marylin. (2009). Ease of reading of mandatory information on Canadian food product labels. *International Journal of Consumer Studies, 33*(4), 369–381.

Mihaela-Roxana, Ifrim, & Cho, Yoon C. (2010). Analyzing the effects of product label messages on consumers' attitudes and intentions. *Journal of Business & Economics Research, 8*(11), 125–136.

van der Merwe, Daleen; Kempen, Elizabeth; Breedt, Sofia; & de Beer, Hanli. (2010). Food choice: Student consumers' decision-making process regarding food products with limited label information. *International Journal of Consumer Studies, 34*(1), 11–18.

Participatory Action Research

Participatory action research (PAR) is an experimental method that involves close collaboration between researchers and participants, with a goal of long-term, sustainable social or environmental change within a community. PAR methodologies cover a broad spectrum with varying levels of participant involvement, but nearly all share a pattern of planning, research, action, and reflection.

The leadership styles of the twentieth century—command-and-control regulations, notice-and-comment rule-making procedures, and hierarchical leadership—are no longer appropriate for the challenges facing today's global community. Climate change, overpopulation, water scarcity, food shortages, and depleted natural resources demand more vital and effective strategies. Participatory action research (PAR) is designed to enable communities to work together by supporting sustainable decision making.

The most basic definition of PAR can be formulated by briefly elaborating on the essential elements of its name. *Participatory* indicates that researchers (sometimes called facilitators) and subjects (often called participants) collaborate on fairly equal footing to collect information. *Action* means that the goal of the research is to provide knowledge that can be acted on, producing real-world change. PAR has been called "a family of practices of living inquiry that aims, in a great variety of ways, to link practice and ideas in the service of human flourishing" (Reason and Bradbury 2008, 1). PAR differs from other research types by reframing questions to include how, by, and for whom research is taking place.

Methodologies

PAR methodologies cover a broad spectrum with varying levels of participant involvement, but nearly all share a pattern of planning, fact-finding, action, and reflection. Practitioners in the field have coined a number of names for these steps. Ernest Stringer (1999) calls them *look, think, and act;* Jill Grant, Geoff Nelson, and Terry Mitchell (2008) define iterative cycles of *research, learning, and action;* David Coghlan and Teresa Brannick (2005) describe cycles of *experiencing, reflecting, interpreting, and taking action;* and Stephen Kemmis (as cited in Herr and Anderson 2005) lays out a repeating pattern of *plan, act, observe, and reflect* that he calls the spiral of action.

Participant Involvement

PAR is a type of qualitative research in which participants may be involved in the design of, or even in control of, the research (Herr and Anderson 2005; Minkler 2004). PAR places more emphasis on process than on outcome, and the role of the researcher is often that of catalyst, facilitator, and participant (Cornwall and Jewkes 1995). That is, PAR is not the type of research where the investigator stands an arm's length from the "subjects" while remaining "objective." Quite the opposite: PAR encourages the researcher to become involved in the study along with participants.

PAR is also characterized as being a highly democratic process in which all participants have a voice, with the aim of enhancing community (Stringer 1999). In this way, PAR is focused not only on generating knowledge that can be applicable to scholarly settings, as traditional research is, but also on gathering information that can be used by participants to bring about social change (Herr and Anderson 2005).

Expert versus Community Knowledge

Participatory research can be differentiated from conventional research in part by the unusual alignment of power (Cornwall and Jewkes 1995). Because action research is grounded in social action, it can sometimes challenge expert knowledge and power. The use of scientific terms, academic titles, and institutional power can make the information and knowledge of certain groups appear more valid than the knowledge of others (Gaventa and Cornwall 2008, 174). This preference for the expert voice puts the community voice at a disadvantage and potentially limits public participation and indigenous knowledge. Participatory action research levels the playing field by providing opportunities for the public to research and discuss a problem along with the "experts." Because community members have helped to generate the knowledge, they can determine what future actions should occur.

Expanding the number of people involved in the knowledge creation potentially increases the diversity of voices brought into community decision making. Those who have never had a say, but who have knowledge to share (even unbeknown to themselves) can contribute valuable and even crucial information. For example, children may be brought into an age- and interest-appropriate PAR project. Giving children an opportunity to create an agenda, develop questions, and present their views—and having authorities respond—can make the project outcome more effective as it equalizes the balance of power (Hart 1997).

PAR has traditionally been used with disadvantaged communities as a catalyst for social change (Grant, Nelson, and Mitchell 2008). As such, a PAR project can upset the balance of power and shake up the status quo, threatening those with power and those without it. For this reason the academy often shies away, at the expense of its own effectiveness in working toward social change, from involvement in a form of research that empowers people and addresses community problems. Yet active participation is what allows the community to develop a sense of ownership, bringing with it the level of commitment that is needed for social change to occur.

Ethics

As with conventional research, elements of "do no harm," informed consent, and the safeguarding of rights, such as the right to privacy, all come into play with PAR. In addition, the unique nature of PAR requires ethical elements beyond the traditional.

One important component that addresses both the ethics and the quality of PAR is an understanding of "the sustainability and long-term consequences of the project" (Coghlan and Brannick 2005, 78). For facilitators of PAR, the "do no harm" axiom must include a way to sustain the changes that a project can bring about in a community. This might include appropriate, long-term funding and/or the social capital needed to make long-term sustainability possible.

Participatory action researchers need to keep in mind several points. First, the issue to be researched must be high on the community's agenda and not only the priority of outside corporations, institutions, or other interest groups who would profit from it. Second, researchers/facilitators need to listen openly, to let go of control, and to be sensitive to their own biases and the overt or implied prejudices within and around the community. Because many PAR projects focus on empowerment, they often involve groups that are at the receiving end of prejudices, such as minorities and the disabled (Minkler 2004).

In 1999 the Texas A&M University Center for Housing and Urban Development's Colonias Program and the Center for Environmental and Rural Health collaborated on a project aimed to reduce human exposure to pesticides in Cameron County, Texas, an unincorporated, socially and geographically isolated area lacking water and sewer services. Of its 99 percent Hispanic population, nearly 58 percent live below the poverty level, nearly a third are not US citizens, and another third are undocumented. Environmental monitoring programs indicate that intensive pesticide use in corporate-sponsored agriculture, the main industry in the region, has affected the land, indoor and outdoor air quality, and impaired the ground and drinking water. With a high level of poverty and low level of education, the community has little formal power or voice in these environmental issues.

Marilyn May and her research team chose PAR methodology to address challenges presented to the people of Cameron Park. The researchers understood that to gain the residents' trust—and to engage in dialogue, planning, and implementation of projects—they needed to partner with them and local organizations. *Promotoras* (translators and interpreters acting as liaisons between service providers and the residents) educated community members about environmental health issues. PAR methodology built on the strengths of community members, fostered relationships and dialogue to address communication and trust, and provided a way to integrate local experts and obtain local knowledge with "minimal distortion and/or reconstruction" (May et al. 2003, 1573).

A "train the trainer" seminar (developed with one co-investigator and two local staff members of the Colonias Program) involved the *promotoras* both in reviewing protocol questions and commenting on the relevancy. The *promotoras* were also trained in interview techniques and in sampling and developing research strategies, and thus became full collaborators in the project. Academic researchers functioned as the "trainers, confidantes, project managers, and sounding boards" (May et al. 2003, 1574).

Validity and Data Collection

Participatory action research requires its own quality criteria and should not be judged by the criteria of positivist science, which assumes that the researcher is an expert who is trained to be objective, uses a rigid scientific method of research, and has removed all that is personal or particular from the data, the context, and the analysis. Determining the validity of a project involves assessing cooperation between researcher and community members, iterative reflection, knowledge creation, community priorities, how the project can enhance the lives of the people who are engaged, and the project's sustainable outcome (Reason and Bradbury 2008; Stringer 1999).

To ensure validity, PAR requires the use of data streams, such as observation, interviews, and autobiographical information collected by journaling. Keeping a journal of

interpersonal and group processes is a vital component of a PAR project (Herr and Anderson 2005) and a good way for participants to develop reflective skills. As some see it, "action research is a messy, somewhat unpredictable process, and a key part of the inquiry is a recording of decisions made in the face of this messiness" (Coghlan and Brannick 2005, 78).

Environmental Sustainability Projects

Participatory action research is a natural fit with environmental sustainability issues and projects. Some examples of how it has been used in environmental arenas can help clarify PAR methodology.

Aerial Perspectives

Kalay Mordock and Marianne Krasny (2001) used PAR as a theoretical framework in an environmental science education program called Aerial Perspectives in the mid-1990s. The program trained educators in Rockaway, New York, to work with middle school students in comparing historic and current aerial photos, topographic maps, and historical documents to identify environmental changes such as vacant lots plagued by litter and illegal dumping.

The educators developed local programs in collaboration with students and adult participants that involved observation, open-ended interviews, and a review of the documents produced by the Aerial Perspectives collaboration. Each of the four case studies Mordock and Krasny followed had similar PAR elements: no formal academic researchers; teachers and nonformal educators facilitated the use of aerial photos and maps; youths were actively involved in field checking, gathering supplemental information, and talking with city officials. The results, which were given to the community in the form of a video, letter, or presentation at a daylong neighborhood conference, were used to bring about change within the community, including turning vacant lots into community gardens.

Community-Based Rangeland Management

The Tohono O'odham Nation of southern Arizona has a cultural tradition of communal land use and decision making. Like other Native American tribes, it seeks self-determination in all policies and programs. Today the Nation relies on cattle for food, cash, and cultural practices such as gift giving.

Aside from hunting and gathering, traditional Tohono O'odham subsistence was supplemented by seasonal agriculture in desert washes that stayed moist from spring floods. Migration was common, following the availability of water, plants, and animals; property boundaries did not exist. Family units came together and dispersed with seasonal cycles of food and social gatherings, which fortified community.

"In 1916 the U.S. Office of Indian Affairs divided the O'odham Nations land into 11 fenced grazing districts in anticipation of a permit system for livestock grazing" (Arnold and Fernandez-Gimenez 2007, 484). This policy exemplifies how government agencies frequently administer with no input from the people they impact. As expected, the action brought about anger and mistrust, negatively affecting the customary territories and previous cooperation that were part of O'odham culture. These grazing districts have not been used as intended, and resentment lingers.

Jennifer Arnold and Maria Fernandez-Gimenez used PAR-program strategies while working in partnership with the Tohono O'odham to create and implement a rangeland ecology and management curriculum. An advisory committee, comprised of natural resource representatives and livestock associations from the Nation, designed and piloted an eight-day, environmentally and culturally appropriate curriculum and helped with data collection, interpretation, and dissemination. The researchers "conducted in-depth semistructured interviews with seven core participants, including both O'odham and non-O'odham individuals from the Advisory Committee" (Arnold and Fernandez-Gimenez 2006, 485). They asked questions relating to the relevance, benefits, and limitations of the curriculum, conducted discussions and surveys, and queried individuals who led the pilot workshops about the success and limitations of the project.

Analysis of this project included coding notes from meetings, workshops, observations, and interview transcripts in order to identify emerging themes and patterns. The PAR curriculum project brought community members, political representatives, natural resource managers, and researchers together in an atmosphere that respected all knowledge holders. A new Agriculture and Natural Resource Program emerged from the curriculum, developed at the Tohono O'odham Community College.

Despite these outcomes, the authors acknowledge that their study was affected by a lack of participation from working-class groups and high attendance by others, such as natural resource professionals who could make attendance part of their workday. Only one-third of the participants were female. Ways to avoid such imbalances need to be addressed during the proposal stages of a PAR study. The authors state that "quality in participatory research is directly tied to who participates, how they contribute, and the enduring effects of their participation" (Arnold and Fernandez-Gimenez 2006, 492), and that as facilitators they worked very hard to expand the bounds of participation. "If we want to change the conversation," Margaret Wheatley (2002, 55) echoes, "we have to change who's in the conversation."

Identifying UK Environmental Inequalities

Research and political interest in the connection between environmental quality and social equality piqued in the United Kingdom with a call to action concerning environmental justice. The British researchers Helen Chalmers and John Colvin adopted methods that could "develop practical solutions to environmental inequalities by actively shaping the dialog around environmental equity with different research users and the policy community" (Chalmers and Colvin 2005, 340). Their cycle of inquiry included (1) framing the questions, (2) getting joint evidence, (3) making sense of the narrative, (4) seeking policy commitments, and (5) evaluation and new framings. This research included stakeholder discussions and a one-day workshop with agency staff as part of the action research paradigm.

Water Consciousness

Another example of participatory action research involved the weaving of disparate disciplines—art, water science, and community building—into a unified whole. Jill Jacoby (2009) brought together seventeen artists to participate in a PAR project with four study-circle sessions focused on water-related concerns, including the water quality of Lake Superior, water privatization in developing countries, the bottled-water industry, and spiritual aspects of water held by other cultures. The dialogue produced a rich tapestry of thoughts and ideas that collectively addressed the artists' awareness—how learning was internalized for each participant, how the process led to collaboration for some artists, and how the artists framed and/or reframed the water issues that concerned them—and also informed their art. Each artist created at least one work that was publicly exhibited as part of the Lake Superior Day activities held in Duluth, Minnesota. For example, concern about the plans of an energy company to discharge pollutants into a Minnesota mine pit lake called Canisteo—after iron ore is mined it results in an open pit that often fills with groundwater—prompted the creation of a fiber art "map" indicating the hydrology connections between Canisteo Lake and the surrounding communities, as well as the potential damage to aquatic and human health.

Jacoby's research was grounded in the urgent need to raise water literacy among the general population, along with the belief that artists are uniquely able to articulate social and environmental issues. As in any PAR project, participants shaped the agenda, in this case through the use of study circles as a means of dialogue about community water issues.

Community Partnerships and Sustainability

Many attributes of PAR interconnect with environmental sustainability and leadership. Marja Liisa Swantz's description that "action researchers are interested in walking shoulder to shoulder with ordinary people rather than one step ahead" (Swantz 2008, 31) defines the attribute of community empowerment as one reason why this methodology works well with environmental concerns. David Reason and Hilary Bradbury (2008, 8) speak directly to community partnerships in research and action:

An attitude of inquiry includes developing an understanding that we are embodied beings part of a social

and ecological order, and radically interconnected with all other beings. We are not bounded individuals experiencing the world in isolation. We are already participants, part-of rather than apart-from.

PAR methodologies break down the isolation that Reason and Bradbury describe, and help to harness collective intelligence to address social and environmental problems. It has been said that the environmental crisis stems from a human disconnection from not only our neighbors but from the web of life itself. If that crisis is to be resolved, humans need to recognize that they are but a strand in a very complex planetary network. PAR offers one way to do this.

JILL B. JACOBY
University of Wisconsin, Superior

See also Citizen Science; Community and Stakeholder Input; Environmental Justice Indicators; Focus Groups; Quantitative vs. Qualitative Studies; Social Network Analysis (SNA); Transdisciplinary Research

FURTHER READING

Arnold, Jennifer S., & Fernandez-Gimenez, Maria. (2007). Building social capital through participatory research: An analysis of collaboration on Tohono O'odham tribal rangelands in Arizona. *Society and Natural Resources, 20*(6), 481–495.

Chalmers, H., & Colvin, J. (2005). Addressing environmental inequalities in UK policy: An action research perspective. *Local Environment, 10*(4), 333–360.

Coghlan, David, & Brannick, Teresa. (2005). *Doing action research in your own organization* (2nd ed.). Thousand Oaks, CA: Sage Publications.

Cornwall, Andrea, & Jewkes, Rachel. (1995). What is participatory research? *Social Science Medicine, 41*(12), 1667–1676.

Gaventa, John, & Cornwall, Andrea. (2008). Power and knowledge. In Peter Reason & Hilary Bradbury (Eds.), *The Sage handbook of action research: Participative inquiry and practice* (pp. 172–189). Los Angeles: Sage Publications.

Grant, Jill; Nelson, Geoff; & Mitchell, Terry. (2008). Negotiating the challenges of participatory action research: Relationships, power, participation, change and credibility. In Peter Reason & Hilary Bradbury (Eds.), *The Sage handbook of action research: Participative inquiry and practice* (pp. 589–601). Los Angeles: Sage Publications.

Hart, Roger. (1997). *Children's participation: The theory and practice of involving young citizens in community development and environmental care.* London: Earthscan Publications.

Herr, Kathryn, & Anderson, Gary L. (2005). *The action research dissertation: A guide for students and faculty.* Thousand Oaks, CA: Sage Publications.

Jacoby, Jill B. (2009). Art, water, and circles: In what ways do study circles empower artists to become community leaders around water issues (Doctoral dissertation, Antioch University, 2009). Retrieved October 4, 2010, from http://rave.ohiolink.edu/etdc/view.cgi?acc_num=antioch1263579870

May, Marilyn L., et al. (2003, October). Embracing the local: Enriching scientific research, education and outreach on the Texas-Mexico border through a participatory action research partnership. *Environmental Health Perspectives, 111*(13), 1571–1576.

Minkler, Meredith. (2004). Ethical challenges for the "outside" researcher in community-based participatory research. *Health Education and Behavior, 31*(6), 684–697.

Mordock, Kalay, & Krasny, Marianne. (2001). Participatory action research: A theoretical and practical framework for environmental education. *The Journal of Environmental Education, 32*(3), 15–20.

Reason, Peter, & Bradbury, Hilary. (Eds.). (2008). *The Sage handbook of action research: Participative inquiry and practice.* Los Angeles: Sage Publications.

Stringer, Ernest T. (1999). *Action research* (2nd ed.). Thousand Oaks, CA: Sage Publications.

Swantz, Marja Liisa. (2008). Participatory action research as practice. In Peter Reason & Hilary Bradbury (Eds.), *The Sage handbook of action research: Participative inquiry and practice* (pp. 31–48). Los Angeles: Sage Publications.

Wheatley, Margaret J. (2002). *Turning to one another: Simple conversations to restore hope to the future.* San Francisco: Berrett-Koehler Publishers.

Population Indicators

Nearly 7 billion humans live on Earth, an indicator of our unprecedented success in mastering diverse environments. Yet ongoing population growth is also a force in environmental change and may threaten future well-being. Because population is a contentious topic and its environmental role is difficult to separate from other factors, its use as an indicator of sustainability remains imprecise and controversial.

In scientific terms, population refers to the number of living organisms occupying a specified place, area, or habitat. Although in common speech the word *population* sometimes identifies a particular group of human beings, this article limits the term to its scientific definition, focusing on the number of people on Earth. A variety of dynamics relating to the human population—changes in its size, age structure, and geographic distribution—can be seen as indicators relating to environmental sustainability. In most discussions of population and sustainability, however, population growth is the dominant indicator discussed, and it will be here as well.

A History of Concern

Discussions of population—and indeed presentations of population as a potential threat to nature and to human well-being—go back surprisingly far in the documented history of human thought. Clay tablets from 1600 BCE record a divine displeasure with the sound of multiplying humans that suggested the "the land was bellowing like a bull" (Cohen 1995, 5). The Hebrew god, Yahweh, commanded two censuses, recorded in a biblical book called Numbers. The biblical story of Genesis says—in what

may be the first statement of what later came to be called a Malthusian view of population (after Thomas Robert Malthus; see below)—that the followers of Abraham and Lot fought each other because "the land was not able to bear them . . . for their substance was great, so that they could not dwell together" (Genesis 13:6). Plato and Aristotle argued for small populations based on both ecological and governance grounds; Plato decried deforestation and degrading soils in ancient Greece, while Aristotle argued that large populations were more difficult to govern than smaller ones. Around 300 BCE, the Indian sage Kautilya and Chinese legal scholar Han Fei Tzu both decried the social and environmental impacts of large and growing populations. From late medieval times into the Renaissance and beyond, commentators debated whether large populations were a blessing or a curse, with a French writer going by the pen name of Fénelon arguing that "the Earth is inexhaustible and increases its fertility in proportion to the number of inhabitants who cultivate it" (Hutchinson 1967, 30).

Modern demography (derived from the Greek words for "people study") can be said to have begun with John Graunt, a low-level seventeenth-century London bureaucrat who took up what was then called "political arithmetic" as an avocation. Comparing records of London baptisms and burials, Graunt quantified the natural increase of the city's population and laid the groundwork for life tables. These are tabulations of people in different age groups that today form the basis of population projections. The much more famous Thomas Robert Malthus in 1798 brought a polemical edge to the nascent science of demography by arguing that the "geometric" (or exponential) growth of human numbers would inevitably outstrip the "arithmetic" (or incremental) increase in food production and bring famine, war, disease, and population decline. (Applied along similar lines to all organisms, this principle inspired Charles Darwin to work out his own ideas on natural selection and to develop the theory ultimately known as evolution.)

Malthus's characterization of the fundamental tension between population and natural resources, along with the contrary view that human beings endlessly find ways to exploit new resources when existing ones grow scarce, continues to dominate debates about the risks and benefits of population growth. While historians tend to accept a Malthusian depiction of human population dynamics as accurate prior to the Industrial Revolution, most join with contemporary economists in celebrating a presumed escape from Malthusian population declines with the marshaling of fossil fuels, steady advances in agricultural practices, and improvements in hygiene and human health. In fact, human population multiplied more than sevenfold after Malthus warned that world population must eventually decline due to food shortages, climbing from just under 1 billion people in 1800 to approximately 7 billion projected by the end of 2011. While he may have accurately analyzed historical interactions between population and its agriculture and natural resource base up to his own lifetime, Malthus failed to foresee the expansion of food production in Europe's colonial possessions in the nineteenth century and the epic increases in agricultural yields in the twentieth. This failure scarcely guarantees that his insight about the conflict between growth and a finite physical world is wrong for all time, however, only that such a conflict is not evident to most current commentators.

Counting Humanity

We know with some confidence what has occurred in human population since Malthus's time because of censuses, which began in their present form in 1703 in Iceland and spread from there to Sweden (1749), Spain (1787), and the newly independent United States (1790). The objective of a census is to document the precise number of people living in a particular country or other territory. Most countries have undergone several censuses over the last century or two, with a usual period of a decade between each. Some countries—Somalia is one example—have never had a proper census in modern times, and in other countries tabulation techniques are unsophisticated enough to raise questions about the accuracy of counts. Most demographers, however, argue that through multiple means of estimating population numbers (including, today, utilizing remote sensing of night lights and human infrastructure from space), the margin of error is insignificant for national and global population numbers. In practice, the assessment that approximately 7 billion human beings are now alive on

Earth (as of 2011) is not widely questioned by demographers or other experts.

In contrast, the common assertion that demographers expect world population to stabilize at 9 billion people at the middle of the twenty-first century is, in fact, inaccurate. Demographers do not so much forecast future population trends as *project* them, meaning they make conditional forecasts of what will happen if certain assumptions play out. Among the assumptions for the dominant current middle projection—so-called because low and high projections of future growth are also produced—are that fertility rates will continue to fall to the point where most countries have "replacement" fertility (a bit more than an average of two children per woman, leading eventually to a steady-state population absent net migration) by the mid-2000s. Yet it is not certain that governments and others will increase spending on contraceptive and family planning services sufficient to satisfy the needs of the growing population of reproductive-age people (whose numbers are expected to rise from 3.5 billion worldwide in 2010 to more than 4 billion in 2050). In fact, spending by wealthy countries on family planning assistance to developing countries (where all the growth of this subpopulation is now occurring) has been decreasing since 2000. Moreover, there is no guarantee—especially given predicted impacts of climate change and other ecological disruptions in coming decades—that life expectancy for humanity as a whole will continue to lengthen as it has for the last century. In all, it will be interesting and relevant to sustainability to monitor population numbers and to probe whether changes in birth or death rates are responsible for any future changes in population size.

Numerous demographic indicators may relate to sustainability issues. Conventionally, population density— the number of people living in a specific area per square mile or kilometer of land—has often been noted and compared between places and times. In recent years, however, attention has begun to swivel to more-precise ratios of human beings to the natural resources on which they rely. Scientific journals and even the news media increasingly offer details on per capita flows of renewable freshwater, per capita availability of arable land, or per capita emissions of greenhouse gases. Such measurements necessarily combine population data with other data related to natural resource production, consumption, and disposal.

Growth and Natural Resources

Trends in ratios of population to specific natural resources often have direct relevance to environmental sustainability; for example, freshwater and cropland become more scarce for each individual as populations grow. In the early 1990s, the Swedish hydrologist Malin Falkenmark developed an indicator of freshwater scarcity, arguing that when countries have less than 1,000 cubic meters of renewable freshwater per person per year, as measured chiefly by river flows through national territory, it becomes next to impossible for them to advance through key development transitions. Falkenmark's scarcity benchmark—especially translated into how many people live or are projected to live in countries with less than the minimal amount of freshwater—has gained wide attention and use in analysis and negotiations around freshwater availability.

As suggested by indicators of population exposure to natural resource scarcity, population distribution also has important connections to the discussion of environmental sustainability. Sometime in 2007, according to United Nations Population Division calculations, the world's population for the first time in history became half urban—that is, more people lived in metropolitan than rural areas. This spurred considerable discussion over whether urban dwellers have smaller environmental "footprints" than rural dwellers, especially in relation to climate change but also in terms of impacts on water, forests, and biological diversity. Recent estimates that large proportions of the world's population live near a seacoast has engendered similar debates, especially given scientific agreement that significant increases in sea levels and storm intensities are among the certain impacts of climate change.

Climate change itself increases the relevance of population as a sustainability indicator. The Intergovernmental Panel on Climate Change (IPCC) has noted that population growth is among the four drivers of increasing greenhouse gas emissions. (The other three are economic growth, changes in the energy intensity of economies, and changes in the carbon intensity of energy; this relationship is known as the Kaya identity, named after the Japanese energy economist Yoichi Kaya.) Climatologists are beginning to refine projections of future emissions with different projections of population growth as independent variables. Population is relevant to more than emissions, however. The governments of numerous less-developed countries have stated in climate adaptation planning reports to the United Nations that population growth, density, or

pressure constrains their capacity to adapt to the impacts of climate change.

Using population dynamics as indicators of sustainability is complicated by their enormous diversity around the world as well as by debate on precisely how population numbers matter to sustainability. Population growth rates range from over 3 percent in some countries in sub-Saharan Africa and western Asia to less than zero—that is, modest annual declines—in Japan, Germany, and several eastern European countries. In general, higher population growth rates correlate positively with low per capita income. That correlation contributes to arguments that population is less relevant than consumption in the matter of sustainability, based on the presumption that people in wealthy countries have greater environmental impacts than people in poor countries because they consume more resources per capita. The examples of China, India, and the United States demonstrate, however, that population and consumption growth can be out of sync and yet still combine powerfully over time to affect the environment. In the United States, for example, population grew throughout most of nineteenth century at annual rates comparable to those characterizing the populations in many developing countries today. US consumption of fossil fuels was minimal during this century-long growth spurt, only becoming an issue of global importance in the twentieth century when US population growth rates had declined significantly. A similar progression of rapid population growth followed by rapid consumption growth characterized China a century later. Most countries grow more rapidly while incomes and consumption are low (US population grew at 3 percent a year, for example, throughout much of the nineteenth century) but may subsequently boost per capita consumption levels dramatically against the backdrop of large and still-growing populations.

Age structure, too, enters into the discussion of population and sustainability. Populations vary significantly in their proportions of young and old people, with rapidly growing populations generally younger, and declining or slowly growing populations generally older. Whether older people consume or otherwise affect the environment differently than young people—and, if so, to what extent—remains uncertain. Therefore, the implications of population age structure for sustainability are not clear.

Along with the IPCC authors, scientists generally consider the size and growth of the world's human population to be among the handful of critically important factors in sustaining stable civilizations. In a joint statement in 1993, representatives of fifty-eight national scientific academies stressed the complexities of the population–environment relationship but nonetheless concluded, "As human numbers further increase, the potential for irreversible [environmental] changes of far-reaching magnitude also increases. . . . In our judgment, humanity's ability to deal successfully with its social, economic, and environmental problems will require the achievement of zero population growth within the lifetime of our children" ("Science summit" 1994, 234–235). In 2005, the United Nations Millennium Ecosystem Assessment identified population growth as a principal indirect driver of environmental change, along with economic growth and technological evolution.

Some commentators disagree, arguing that other factors, such as consumption and particular policies or uses of technology, dwarf the importance of human numbers. In fact, scholars have often found it difficult and frustrating to separate out the independent impacts of all these factors on sustainability, making the task not worth pursuing. Since no specific environmental problem correlates neatly and directly with absolute population numbers, some commentators argue that population is not really a sustainability indicator at all. Others argue that population numbers and growth rates are among the most important sustainability indicators of all, given population's importance as a scale factor in essentially all environmental problems.

Implications

Despite the controversy, few experts argue that population dynamics are irrelevant to environmental sustainability. Most agree that the scale of living human beings uniquely influences the entire range of environmental changes and types of degradation that challenge human and natural well-being. Some argue that this is more the case, rather than less, when population is considered in conjunction with per capita consumption levels and the use of environment-altering technologies, from internal combustion engines to bottom-trawl fishing equipment. These factors, in this view, are more multipliers of each other than independent forces to be compared to each other.

Indeed, one equation often used to describe the way such forces act on the environment is

$$I = P \times A \times T \text{ (or } I = PAT, \text{ pronounced "eye-pat")}$$

where I stands for the environmental impact, P for population, A for affluence (or consumption), and T for technology. While the equation oversimplifies the relationships among these factors and the environment, it does convey that they all interact, with none operating alone.

To capture even a fraction of how population undermines or supports sustainability requires monitoring of multiple factors: population numbers and growth, geographic and age structure, rates of migration between rural and urban areas and across international borders, and birth and death rates. Of particular interest is total fertility—the average number of live births to women over their lifetimes—as this has the greatest impact on contemporary population growth. (Although millions of people die each year well before what most of us would consider old age, life expectancy at birth is unprecedentedly high, sixty-eight years and rising for the species as a whole.) Demographic indicators must be carefully combined with data on various kinds of consumption, greenhouse gas emissions, energy and material flows, land use, and plant and animal species counts in order to develop usable measures of what might be sustainable population dynamics.

Development of such measures is rarely encouraged, owing to global political and social uncertainty about what actions could—or should—be taken to influence population dynamics, especially to slow the growth of human numbers. For many experts and much of the public, the idea of "population control" raises imagery of coerced use of contraception and abortion to stem birthrates. For that and other reasons, the more neutral concept of population policies and programs has little appeal. There is little public awareness that the majority of family planning programs around the world have been based on choices individuals make about their health, well-being, and options in life, rather than childbearing targets imposed by governments. The halving of fertility rates since about 1970 is in large part the outcome of the global spread of inexpensive and safe contraceptives, which are today used by most couples of reproductive age to avoid unintended pregnancy. Yet unintended pregnancy remains common in most countries, developed as well as developing. Approximately 40 percent of pregnancies and at least 21 percent of births result from pregnancies that women and their partners did not seek or want to have.

These numbers suggest that making universal access to safe and effective contraception would significantly slow global population growth. Based on a considerable body of research, this positive impact on demographic sustainability could be enhanced further by raising the education level of girls and women and to bring women to equality with men in health, economics, and political participation.

Robert ENGELMAN
Worldwatch Institute

See also Agenda 21; Development Indicators; Framework for Strategic Sustainable Development (FSSD); Human Development Index (HDI); I = P × A × T Equation; Land-Use and Land-Cover Change; *The Limits to Growth;* Millennium Development Goals; Regional Planning; Weak vs. Strong Sustainability Debate

FURTHER READING

Cohen, Joel E. (1995). *How many people can the Earth support?* New York: Norton.

Ehrlich, Paul R., & Holdren, John P. (1971). Impact of population growth. *Science, 171,* 1212–1217.

Engelman, Robert. (2008). *More: Population, nature, and what women want.* Washington, DC: Island Press.

Engelman, Robert. (2009a). Population and sustainability: Can we avoid limiting the number of people? *Scientific American Earth 3.0, 19*(2), 22–29.

Engelman, Robert. (2009b). *State of world population 2009: Facing a changing world: Women, population and climate.* New York: United Nations Population Fund.

Engelman, Robert. (2011, April). An end to population growth: Why family planning is key to sustainability. *Solutions, 2*(3). Retrieved December 7, 2011, from http://www.thesolutionsjournal.com/node/919

Falkenmark, Malin, & Widstrand, Carl. (1992). *Population and water resources: A delicate balance.* Washington, DC: Population Reference Bureau.

Hutchinson, Edward P. (1967). *The population debate: The development of conflicting theories up to 1900.* Boston: Houghton Mifflin.

Malthus, T. Robert. (1926). *First essay on population* (Rev. ed.). London: Macmillan. (Original work published 1798)

O'Neill, Brian C., et al. (2010). Global demographic trends and future carbon emissions. *Proceedings of the National Academy of Sciences, 107*(41), 17521–17526.

Pearce, Fred. (2010). *The coming population crash and our planet's surprising future.* Boston: Beacon Press.

Reid, Walter V. R., et al. (2005). *Millennium Ecosystem Assessment: Ecosystems and human well-being—synthesis.* Washington, DC: Island Press.

Rockström, Johan, et al. (2009). A safe operating space for humanity. *Nature, 461,* 472–475.

Rogner, Hans-Holger, et al. (2007). *Climate change 2007: Mitigation of climate change. Contribution of Working Group III to the Fourth Assessment Report of the Intergovernmental Panel on Climate Change.* Cambridge, UK: Cambridge University Press.

Satterthwaite, David, & Dodman, David. (2009). The role of cities in climate change. In Robert Engelman, Michael Renner & Janet Sawin (Eds.), *State of the world 2009: Into a warming world.* New York: Norton.

"Science Summit" on world population: A joint statement by 58 of the world's scientific academies. (1994). *Population and Development Review, 20*(1), 233–238.

United Nations Department of Economic and Social Affairs (UN DESA), Population Division. (2009). World population prospects: The 2008 revision population database. Retrieved March 4, 2011, from http://esa.un.org/unpp

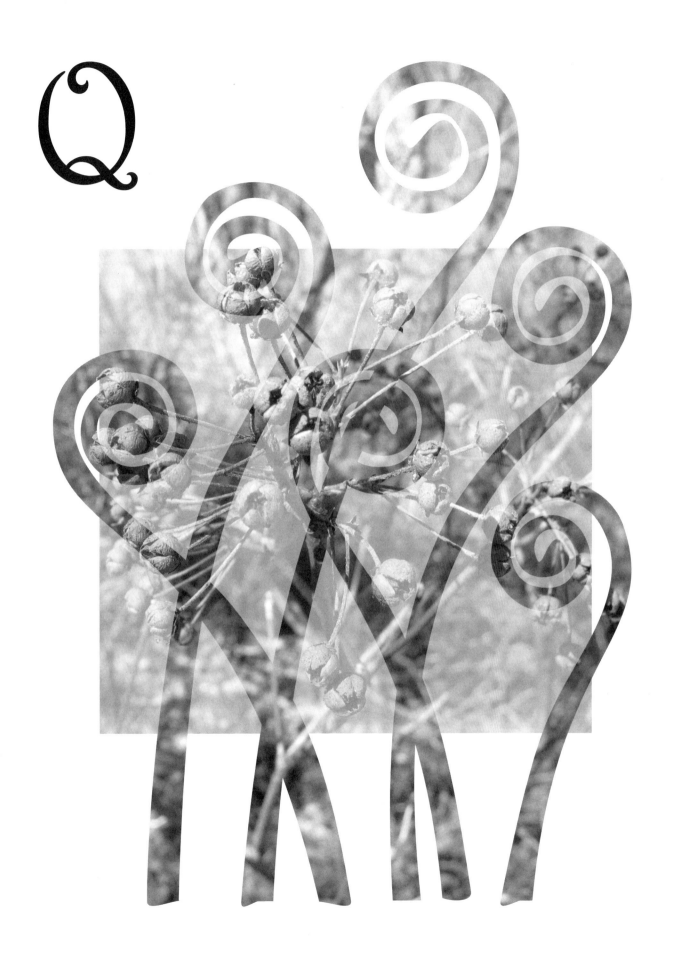

Quantitative vs. Qualitative Studies

In general terms, quantitative research methods involve measurements while qualitative methods address questions of how and why. Both methods have strengths and weaknesses, and different disciplines prefer one to the other. As rigorous mixed-methods studies become increasingly valuable in sustainability research—where facts often are uncertain, values are in dispute, stakes are high, and decisions are urgent—scholars must be trained to develop an acute awareness of the possibilities and limitations of qualitative and quantitative methods.

The words *quantitative* and *qualitative* have different meanings in different disciplines, which complicates cross-disciplinary collaboration. Generally speaking, *qualitative* studies aim at answering questions such as "how" and "why," and deal either with issues that cannot be quantified or issues where quantification has no meaning. For example, "Why do many people prefer driving to biking, even in cases when the latter is faster, cheaper, and healthier?" Qualitative methods are commonly used in sustainability studies that draw on disciplines such as philosophy, sociology, analytical organic chemistry, political science, taxonomy, ecology, and history. *Quantitative* studies focus on measuring things and aim at answering questions such as "how much," "how fast," and "how long." For example, "How large a percentage of the population drives short distances, even in cases when biking would be faster, cheaper, and healthier?" Quantitative methods are commonly used in sustainability studies that draw on disciplines such as economics, hydrology, chemistry, physics, sociology, biogeochemistry, geography, and political science.

Students interested in sustainability studies commonly propose research projects that require using both quantitative and qualitative methods. Few professors, unfortunately, are able to provide equally rigorous supervision,

since it is uncommon to be trained in both methods. This may change with a new generation of scholars, but most academic programs in 2012 are still run by professors who have a strong background in quantitative *or* qualitative research. Far too often, mixed-methods quantitative/qualitative studies will either contain quantitative elements of questionable quality or nonrigorous qualitative elements. For instance: scholars with poor or no qualitative training unilaterally supervise interviews or surveys, even though they have no deeper knowledge of qualitative methods; and scholars with poor or no quantitative training unilaterally conduct studies that require statistical analysis, even though they have no deeper knowledge of statistics.

Rigorous Quantitative Studies

When quantitative studies are of poor quality, it is often a question of not understanding what statistics can and cannot be used for. A common mistake is to believe that a bad study design can be fixed with advanced statistics. This is not possible. When planning a study, it is crucial to think carefully about data collection and anticipate the types of statistics required. Statistics textbooks often seem overly complicated, and many are not aimed at the type of (fairly simple) statistics normally needed for most types of sustainability studies. Several straightforward and user-friendly publications are available, however, including *Statistical Methods in Water Resources* by the environmental statisticians Dennis Helsel and Robert Hirsh (2002). It is generally wise to consult with a statistician to discuss sample size and time-scale and sampling regime when attempting to determine if "something" has increased or decreased (such as mercury in mussels in the Philippines, the number of people traveling by car in Canada, the land area used to grow biofuels in Brazil, or the per capita use of household water in China).

Before addressing the statistical questions, however, the student researcher needs to determine the research question—noting that they are never the same. The research question, for example, may be "Is the concentration of mercury in the mussels people eat approaching a deleterious level?" One might use statistics to answer the question (in lay language): "What is the likelihood that the concentration of mercury in these mussels has increased over the given time period?" One cannot, however, use a statistical analysis of the given data set to figure out what a "deleterious level" is. To make this determination, one needs to draw on information from other disciplines, such as (eco)toxicology and epidemiology.

Rigorous Qualitative Social Science and Humanities Studies

When qualitative studies dealing with human or social issues are of poor quality, it is often a question of basic methodological ignorance: a surprising number of researchers who are trained in engineering, the natural sciences, and medicine carry out interviews, surveys, and document studies without even having opened a book on the procedures in question. Work conducted without proper methodological competence generally produces questionable results when examined according to basic criteria for good scholarly work. There are numerous good introductory texts on qualitative methods, such as, for example, *Designing and Conducting Mixed Methods Research* by the University of Nebraska-Lincoln professors John W. Creswell and Vicki L. Plano Clark (2011). Serious interdisciplinary studies must be rigorous and based on sound methodology.

Methodological Awareness

Students who wish to combine qualitative and quantitative methods need to acquire a strong methodological awareness. Education in the humanities and many of the social sciences usually emphasizes the need to acquire this awareness, which fosters the ability to reflect upon how the subtleties of context influence the outcome of a study. When dealing with sustainability issues, where facts often are uncertain, values are in dispute, stakes are high, and decisions are urgent, a deep understanding of the knowledge-producing process will prevent the researcher from becoming an unconscious advocate for one side of an issue. An easy-to-read introduction to the challenges related to knowledge production in the sustainability field is *The Honest Broker* by Roger Pielke Jr.

Textbooks on qualitative social science research procedures generally explain the strengths and weaknesses of qualitative methods clearly, whereas textbooks geared toward natural science studies generally focus on technicalities and rarely touch on the strengths and weaknesses of the general approach. As a result, many natural science students (and scholars) have a rather rudimentary understanding of the knowledge-production process and its context dependence.

Many of the questions that are discussed in the social science and humanities methods literature are general in nature and many of the issues discussed are highly relevant for all types of student researchers. A few simplified examples illustrate that the choice of research topic depends on political, cultural, and historical context: desalination is primarily studied in dry countries with coastal access, such as Saudi Arabia, Israel, Singapore, and Australia; studies in alternative energy increased dramatically after the oil crisis in 1973; acupuncture was considered a pseudoscience until about thirty years ago, while racial biology was a highly regarded discipline until the mid-1950s.

It may seem tautological to point out that data is only available in fields that have been studied, but this fact further illustrates the subtleties of the context dependence of knowledge: available data invites us to draw certain conclusions, while the lack of other data dissuades us from other possibilities. For example, the fact that the meteorological and climatic networks are denser over Europe than anywhere else in the world led to the assumption that the little ice age in the eighteenth century was a global phenomenon. Controversy surrounding the implications of this assertion in 2009 had both global political and scientific consequences because it involved the post–2012 Kyoto Protocol discussions and called into question the trustworthiness of the climate science society.

It is crucial to be aware that "objective and value-free data" do not exist when dealing with sustainability issues. Even the most exact and utterly correct findings do not have a meaning in a complex field if they are not put into context.

Summing Up

Increasing the awareness of methodology is usually beneficial—whether conducting qualitative, quantitative, or mixed-methods studies. The following questions can serve as a guide or checklist for students and/or experienced researchers in many disciplines: Is a qualitative or a quantitative study the goal, or does the study perhaps contain elements of both? Has the study design been thought through and discussed carefully with a supervisor before starting to gather data? Is the supervisor sufficiently familiar with the proposed methods, or will it be necessary to consult other experts? How familiar are the general and specific strengths and weaknesses of the methods to the researcher who plans to conduct the study? If the study contains quantitative elements: is a statistician available to consult and communicate with, and has the research question and the statistical question(s) tied to it been formulated? If the study contains qualitative elements: does the researcher have sufficient training in the methods he or she plans to use, and if not, is there someone who does, and who is willing to help with the design and interpretation of the study?

Quantitative and qualitative studies have different strengths and weaknesses. If we are to move toward a sustainable society, we need scholars with deep methodological awareness and the ability to carry out rigorous mixed-methods studies that are carefully designed to draw on the strengths of both qualitative and quantitative methods. Such scholars, of course, must be cautiously aware of the weaknesses of both approaches.

Gunilla ÖBERG
University of British Columbia

See also Challenges to Measuring Sustainability; Citizen Science; Focus Groups; Participatory Action Research; Sustainability Science; Systems Thinking; Transdisciplinary Research

FURTHER READING

Creswell, John W., & Plano Clark, Vicki L. (2011). *Designing and conducting mixed methods research.* Thousand Oaks, CA: SAGE.

Fleck, Ludwik. (1981). *Genesis and development of a scientific fact.* Chicago: University of Chicago Press. (Originally published in German in 1935)

Haraway, Donna. (2007). *When species meet.* Minneapolis: University of Minnesota Press.

Helsel, Dennis R., & Hirsch, Robert M. (2002). Statistical methods in water resources. In United States Geological Survey, *Techniques of water resources investigations. Book 4, Chapter A3.* Reston, VA: USGS. Retrieved December 27, 2011, from http://www.practicalstats.com/aes/aesbook/files/HelselHirsch.PDF

Kuhn, Thomas. (1996). *The structure of scientific revolutions.* Chicago: University of Chicago Press.

Latour, Bruno. (1988). Science in action: How to follow scientists and engineers through society. Cambridge, MA: Harvard University Press.

Öberg, Gunilla. (2010). *Interdisciplinary environmental studies: A primer.* Hoboken, NJ: Wiley and Blackwell.

Pielke, Roger A., Jr. (2007). *The honest broker: Making sense of science in policy and politics.* Cambridge, UK: Cambridge University Press.

Reducing Emissions from Deforestation and Forest Degradation (REDD)

Reducing emissions from deforestation and forest degradation (REDD) *is the collective term for a series of measures that use financial incentives in order to reduce the emission of greenhouse gases from deforestation and forest degradation in developing countries. "REDD+" refers to REDD projects that provide additional benefits such as biodiversity conservation. Successful implementation of REDD has a number of methodological and legal challenges that are not yet fully resolved as of 2012.*

REDD (reducing emissions from deforestation and forest degradation) is a mechanism that enables developing countries to better protect, manage, and sustainably use their forest resources. REDD creates financial incentives for developing countries to leave their forests standing, instead of cutting them down, by attributing a financial value to the carbon stored in trees. In the initial stages of a REDD program, project managers assess and quantify carbon. Developed countries then pay developing countries "carbon offsets" for their standing forests. In return, developed countries receive "carbon credits." The carbon credits generated by REDD projects are then used by developed countries to meet internationally agreed targets. Carbon credits may also be traded within the carbon markets. REDD+ projects—those REDD projects that provide additional benefits such as biodiversity conservation—may enhance forest values as well as facilitating better environmental protection. REDD thus has the potential to extend beyond climate change mitigation and involve the full range of forest goods and services such as the conservation of forest biodiversity and enhancement of forest carbon stocks. The project-based REDD approach may, however, significantly increase transaction costs.

REDD programs thus have the potential to extend beyond climate change mitigation and involve the full range of forest goods and services such as the conservation of forest biodiversity and enhancement of forest carbon stocks. The project-based REDD approach may, however, significantly increase transaction costs.

One of REDD's significant applications is in progress in the Democratic Republic of Congo (DRC) in central Africa, home to the world's second-largest tropical forest. That forest has been particularly vulnerable to deforestation as a result of several combined factors: the country's high level of poverty and its weak rule of law have contributed to the high commercial value of forestland for harvesting timber. In March 2011 the country launched a DRC National Programme to develop a national strategy. In November 2011, the DRC received World Bank assistance for its program, and pilot projects have begun in several locations.

REDD and Climate Change Negotiations

REDD is an important issue in international climate change negotiations because forest ecosystems, which cover approximately one-third of the Earth's surface, provide for the storage of carbon. Deforestation and forest degradation reduce the carbon storage capacity of forests and result in the emission of GHGs into the atmosphere. Approximately 20 percent of annual global anthropogenic carbon emission is caused by deforestation and forest degradation (UN REDD 2011). Deforestation in tropical rain-forest countries is now recognized as a significant contributor to global climate change, demanding the attention of scholars from a wide range of disciplines. The conversion of forests to nonforest uses currently contributes around 12–17 percent of annual GHG emissions, and in some countries, deforestation may cause as much as 85 percent of annual anthropogenic GHG (UN REDD 2011). International attention is now focusing on the incentives that may be offered to tropical rain-forest countries for reducing emissions from deforestation and degradation through REDD+, a strategy that fosters other sustainable development practices. REDD+ projects seek both to reduce GHGs by establishing carbon-trading projects and also to achieve other benefits, such as biodiversity conservation.

This raises several key legal questions. Jurisdictions that have established emissions trading programs, or are proposing to do so, must determine, for example, whether to permit liable entities to rely on forestry offsets to meet their legally binding carbon abatement obligations. Since the adoption of the Bali Action Plan in 2007 by the Conference of the Parties (COP) of the United Nations Framework Convention on Climate Change (UNFCCC), the parties to that international treaty have recognized the crucially important role that REDD+ can play in reducing global greenhouse gas emissions. As a result, REDD+ is now high on the agendas of many international treaty secretariats.

International REDD Initiatives

There are several international REDD+ initiatives. The United Nations (UN) REDD Programme, launched in 2008, is the largest REDD initiative globally. Bringing together the technical expertise of the UN Food and Agriculture Organization (FAO), the United Nations Development Programme (UNDP), and the United Nations Environment Programme (UNEP), the UN REDD Programme aims to assist countries to prepare and implement national REDD+ strategies. As of 2012 it supports activities designed to prepare countries for REDD+ mechanisms in thirty-five partner countries in Africa, Asia-Pacific, and Latin America. Other international REDD+ initiatives include the Forest Carbon Partnership Facility (FCPF) and the Forest Investment Program (FIP), hosted by the World Bank. The UN REDD Programme works with the FCPF and the FIP to provide unified support for national REDD+ strategies in developing countries. Other UN REDD partners include the UN Forum on Forests (UNFF), the Global Environmental Facility (GEF), the UN Framework Convention on Climate Change (UNFCCC), and the International Tropical Timber Organization (ITTO).

The UN REDD Programme is governed by a policy board comprising representatives from the FAO, UNDP, and UNEP, from partner countries, donors to the Multi-Partner Trust Fund, members of civil society (as distinct from government and business), and indigenous peoples. The secretariat, based in Geneva, coordinates the work of the policy board. At the international level, the UN REDD Programme aims to build consensus and knowledge about REDD+ and facilitate dialogue between government, technical experts, and civil society in order to ensure that REDD+ projects are scientifically based, provide opportunities for the engagement of participants at all levels (e.g., governments, scientists, forest dwellers), and ensure that forests continue to provide multiple benefits. The UN REDD Programme seeks to develop common approaches, analyses, methodologies, tools, data, and guidelines that facilitate REDD+. Its work is divided into seven areas: measurement, reporting, and verification; multiple benefits; knowledge management; coordination and communication; national REDD+ governance; equitable benefit sharing systems; and sectoral transformation.

Implementation of REDD

Full implementation of REDD+ requires three stages. First, a REDD strategy is developed, often with the support of external funding agencies. Second, the REDD+ strategy is implemented. This strategy will include capacity-building measures. Third, following initial implementation, REDD+ strategy is refined in the context of low-carbon development of the broader economy, and payments continue for verified emission reductions and removals. These payments may provide incentives for changes in land use or better forest stewardship and so contribute to the development of low carbon economies.

The development of cost-effective, robust, and compatible measurement, reporting, and verification (MRV) systems is central to the effectiveness of REDD+. These systems are designed to use field inventory data, in conjunction with data from satellite systems and other technologies, to produce inventories of GHGs and so to establish reference emission levels. Most international REDD+ initiatives provide assistance to partner countries to enable them to strengthen their technical and institutional capacity in order to develop national MRV systems.

Good governance and the rule of law are important prerequisites for successful REDD+ projects. This is because effective implementation of REDD+ requires transparency and accountability in MRV systems and the corresponding allocation of payments. If, for example, the distribution of benefits is unpredictable or if MRV standards are not enforced uniformly, stakeholders are unlikely to engage fully with REDD+. Similarly, if the business environment is insecure and is not uniformly regulated, investors are unlikely to invest in new initiatives or technologies that might lead to low carbon economies.

The enforcement of any international agreements and domestic legislation, which may be enacted by REDD countries, will rely on the ability of developing countries to monitor rates of deforestation for compliance with, and enforcement of, those laws. Carbon credits, whether they are generated by a national government or on a project basis, will depend for their legitimacy and commercial viability on the proper monitoring of rates of deforestation against the baselines and reference scenarios. Without this, the credits are unlikely to satisfy any rules and modalities that might be developed by the UNFCC COP.

Methodological Challenges

Although REDD countries are now establishing national GHG inventories, fewer than 20 percent of countries have fully developed inventory, and in about 50 percent of countries, inventories are less than 50 percent complete (UN REDD 2011). Consequently, the majority of countries in which REDD+ projects are to operate cannot yet provide a complete and accurate estimate of GHG emissions and forest loss. Furthermore, very few REDD countries report on soil carbon, even though emissions from deforested or degraded peatlands may be a significant proportion of overall emissions. This will prove problematic if it is agreed that the soil carbon pool is to be included in a country's strategy to receive REDD credits for reducing emissions from forestlands.

Even if methodological shortcomings can be rectified, one of the biggest challenges for REDD is determining the means by which benefits may be distributed in a just and equitable manner. Three categories of issues are relevant. First, the participation of indigenous peoples and forest-dependent communities in the design, implementation, and monitoring of REDD activities is important. Second, there is a risk that while forests may be protected on REDD sites, deforestation will simply move to other non-REDD sites, so strategies to prevent "carbon leakage" (i.e., the movement of GHG emissions from one site to another) are important. Third, the accrual of multiple benefits (e.g., biodiversity conservation, ecosystem

services, and social benefits) will make REDD projects more complex and more difficult to manage, so care must be taken to ensure that projects remain focused on the primary objective.

Because REDD is still at a relatively early stage of development, a number of issues have yet to be fully resolved. One of the biggest challenges is the fact that there is not yet an agreed definition of forest degradation, so different REDD organizations may be using different baselines. This may lead to inconsistency in project design, implementation, and outcomes. It is also not yet clear whether REDD projects will rely on current or historic emissions levels and deforestation rates. Another challenge arises from the risk that corporations in developed countries may simply purchase REDD credits from suppliers in developing countries, instead of reducing their own GHG emissions. Linking REDD to a broader system of carbon trading could allow developed countries to offset their own emissions and meet emissions reductions targets. Some developing countries, however, including Brazil and China, have argued that developed countries must commit to genuine emissions reductions, independent of any offset mechanism.

An important issue in designing a REDD+ strategy is the need to understand the cost of REDD+ at local and national levels. One important cost component is the economic trade-offs of deforestation: for instance, by conserving forests, forest owners forego the benefits that may arise from other (and potentially more lucrative) uses of the land on which forest is located.

REDD may be one of the most cost-effective ways of stabilizing atmospheric concentration of GHG emissions, and REDD is an important aspect of the climate change solution, but the implementation of REDD and REDD+ alone will not be sufficient to mitigate climate change. A range of other strategies, including a significant reduction in emissions in both developed and developing countries, will be required.

Catherine P. MacKENZIE
University of Cambridge

See also Agenda 21; Ecosystem Health Indicators; Land-Use and Land Cover Change; Millennium Development Goals

FURTHER READING

Freestone, David, & Streck, Charlotte. (2005). *Legal aspects of implementing the Kyoto Protocol mechanisms: Making Kyoto work.* New York: Oxford University Press.

Freestone, David, & Streck, Charlotte. (2009). *Legal aspects of trading carbon: Kyoto, Copenhagen and beyond.* New York: Oxford University Press.

Global Canopy Programme. (2008). *The little REDD+ book.* Oxford, UK: Global Canopy Programme.

Helm, Dieter, & Hepburn, Cameron. (2009). *The economics and politics of climate change.* New York: Oxford University Press.

Her Majesty's Stationery Office (HMSO). (2008). Climate change: Financing global forests: The Eliasch Review. London: HMSO.

Lyster, Rosemary. (2011). REDD+, transparency, participation and resource rights: The role of law. *Environmental Science & Policy, 14*(2), 118–126.

Lyster, Rosemary. (2010). Reducing emissions from deforestation and degradation: The road to Copenhagen. In Rosemary Lyster (Ed), *In the wilds of climate law* (pp. 91–142). Bowen Hills, Australia: Australian Academic Press.

Lyster, Rosemary. (2009). The new frontier of climate law: Reducing emissions from deforestation (and degradation. *Environmental and Planning Law Journal, 26*(6), 417–456.

Meridian Institute. (2009). *Reducing emissions from deforestation and forest degradation: An options assessment report.* Dillon, CO: Meridian Institute.

Porter, Gareth; Bird, Neil; Kaur, Nanki; & Peskett, Leo. (2008). *New finance for climate change and the environment.* London: ODI.

United Nations Collaborative Programme on Reducing Emissions from Deforestation and Forest Degradation in Developing Countries (UN REDD). (2011). *UN REDD Programme Strategy 2011–2015.* Washington, DC: FAO, UNDP, and UNEP.

United Nations Collaborative Programme on Reducing Emissions from Deforestation and Forest Degradation in Developing Countries (UN REDD). (2012). Homepage. Retrieved February 21, 2012, from http://www.un-redd.org/Home/tabid/565/Default.aspx

World Bank Institute. (2010). *Estimating the opportunity costs of REDD+.* Washington, DC: World Bank Institute.

Regional Planning

Regional planning develops and coordinates concepts, programs, policies, projects and other actions for the benefit of a specific region. It is a "political project" because it carries numerous normative images of how the region should develop in the future. The notion of sustainability is translated into numerous planning concepts and strategies.

Regional planning creates policies and policy tools to guide development of specific regions. The characteristics of the region—its environmental, social, and economic context, including connections to other places—create the conditions to which planning responds. Numerous rationales; laws, administrative rules, procedures, concepts, and normative images shape planning.

Tasks and Scope

Regional planning is concerned with the future of a specific spatial entity, or "'the region." The area may be municipal, regional, or even (trans)national. Patsy Healey, one of the world's most influential planning scholars, uses the term *spatial planning* when she refers to "self conscious collective efforts to re-imagine a city, urban region or wider territory and to translate the result into priorities for area investment, conservation, measures, strategic infrastructure investments and principles of land use regulation" (Healey 2004, 46).

Spatial or regional planning coordinates and moderates the different interests of individuals and of public and private organizations. It addresses specific sectoral issues such as space for transportation, recreation, services, and housing. Planners inform citizens and communicate the potential impacts of planning actions, including land-use changes. A public planning agency normally carries out these tasks. (See sidebar on planning in Stockholm County, Sweden on page 297.)

Regional planning integrates objectives and basic principles from various levels of government, including national-level policies. The planners' main instrument is the regional plan.

Major Development Phases

Spatial planning in general—urban, regional, or otherwise—divides into three phases in Europe and North America. The UK scholar Nigel Taylor summarizes this transition from planner as creative designer, to planner as a scientific analyst and rational decision maker, to planner as manager and communicator. The first phase dates to the European Renaissance and lasts until around the 1960s. Its roots are in architecture. Spatial planning, particularly urban planning, was viewed as an applied art or a creative activity (Taylor 1999, 330–331).

The second phase, characterized by the zeitgeist of modernism, particularly from the 1950s to 1970s, marked a radical departure from the prevailing model. Cities or regions were socioeconomic systems, and planning itself was a process for rational decision making. This shift emphasized controlling social and economic activities and their spatial interrelations rather than focusing on the static and design-based built environment prevalent during the first phase (Taylor 1999, 332).

In the third phase, starting during the late 1970s or early 1980s and continuing to the present, the planner has transformed from a dedicated technical expert to a process facilitator or manager. Many different strategies, goals, and interests vie for the planner's attention. As a result of the range of influences on a city or region, planning focuses, in particular, on moderating and mediating between different

REGIONAL PLANNING IN STOCKHOLM COUNTY, SWEDEN

Sweden has a three-tiered administrative system with national, regional (county), and municipal levels. The municipalities play the strongest part in regional planning. There is no national spatial planning as such, but the national government plays an important role in providing infrastructure (roads, rail, university facilities, etc.) and in setting the legal framework for spatial planning (e.g., the Planning and Building Act of 1987 and the Environmental Code of 1999). There is no national formalized planning, but it is left up to each county. The strongest regional planning system is found in Stockholm County.

In the early 1950s regional planning was institutionalized in Stockholm County. The comprehensive and explicitly strategic character of planning here is an exception in Sweden. Its main instrument, the regional development plan (*regional utvecklingsplan*) is designed to guide municipal planning. The regional development plan is process oriented, allowing for informal coordination and networking. The municipalities—of which there are twenty-six in the Stockholm region—are obliged to make long-term municipal comprehensive plans (*översiktsplan*), which should be aligned to the regional development plan. They are not legally binding but do form the basis of decisions on land- and water-area use. They serve as guidelines for the development of detailed development plans and building permits, which are legally binding (*detajlplan*). Any change to the land use must be based on a municipal plan. With few exceptions, the national state cannot decide on a change of land use.

The Office of Regional Planning develops non-binding regional plans, which go through several stages of negotiations and participation with all municipalities and other relevant stakeholders. The Stockholm County Council is, in this sense, a designated regional planning authority—its operational organ is the Office of Regional Planning. The regional development plan must be developed in cooperation with the County Administrative Board, which is a state agency that examines, for instance, municipal planning decisions and building permits in appeal cases. It retains certain rights to intervene and guarantees that national interests and laws are sufficiently considered. The regional development plan must be adopted by the county council, the democratic counterweight to the County Administrative Board, in order to take effect.

The existing plan, approved in 2010, identifies several long-term objectives for 2030, such as general land-use structure, infrastructure, energy supply, economic development, and environmental protection. It is a cross-sectoral, comprehensive development program for Stockholm County.

For many decades, the interplay among enlarging housing and labor markets and the regional transportation system has been the central issue in the regional planning discourse. In this respect, the Stockholm regional plan 2010 underlines the approach of its forerunner, the regional development plan from 2001, which introduced for the very first time the concept of polycentricity at the city-regional level. The region is structured by eight "regional urban cores" located fifteen to forty kilometers from the central core (that is the inner city of Stockholm and some adjacent central urban areas).

The rationale is that the central core must be released from strong developmental pressure. The regional urban cores shall build up a robust polycentric structure supported by corresponding transportation service. The development of the selected regional urban cores will be promoted by distinct investments in the transport system, by increasing the density and compactness of energy-efficient settlements, by improving the urban environment, by creating competitive milieus, and finally by providing the multiple cores with distinct urban functions (such as more diversified workplaces, higher education and health care facilities, better urban flair through cultural and dining provisions) (Office of Regional Planning 2009 and 2010). In other words such "cores" serve as "territorial anchors" to concentrate land developments, as well as to accommodate distinct urban functions to follow up the intended gradual transformation of a monocentric urban configuration into a polycentric one. It remains to be seen if such a planning concept will combat urban sprawl and will have a positive effect on climate change.

stakeholders and potential conflicts through intentional interventions such as programs, strategies, or projects. This ensures that the planning process is more communicative, collaborative, transparent, consensual, and finally democratic (Forester 1999; Innes and Booher 2010).

Spatial Scope

The spatial aspect of regional planning is a multifaceted—and to a large extent arbitrarily used—term. Transnational areas like Europe, North America, or Asia are often called "regions'" in different contexts, but the subnational level is most often in focus in regional planning. A region covers an area that is larger than the local level; it might stretch over the boundaries of more than one city or municipality. Los Angeles County is an example of regional planning, as are western Saxony in Germany, which includes Leipzig and some adjacent counties, and the Kinki region in Japan, including the cities of Osaka, Kobe, and Kyoto.

As the examples indicate, planning regions are a specific administrative-political layer within a country and can include numerous municipalities, counties, or districts. In many cases, defining the borders of these planning regions can be one of the central challenges. The borders may not necessarily represent a functional spatial image of the region, defined by, for example, the labor market or a commuting area. The relevant political stakeholders are, however, bounded by their specific territories, such as the politico-administrative boundaries of municipalities, provinces, or counties and districts, and their inherent institutional restrictions. This leads at times to conflicts and difficulties integrating a diverse range of interests in regional planning. Regional delimitations are always compromises and are thus contested, as they are inevitably built on a variety of perspectives about what the region is and what the best geographic delimitation for regional planning should be.

Processes and Instruments

A public planning agency carries out the regional planning agenda. It is the central node in the web of relations between stakeholders and organizations. Because different countries and regions have different administrative-political systems, cultures, and practices, regional planning systems differ a lot when viewed from an international perspective. It can also vary significantly even within a country, as is the case, for instance, in Germany and the United States.

The planning process serves to inform about development potentials and objectives (e.g., in terms of infrastructure development, new spaces for housing and industries, nature conservation); to communicate any impacts, restrictions, or other impacts that planning decisions could have on the people and organizations concerned; and, finally, to mobilize their active participation. As such it is part of the political decision-making process.

A regional plan functions as the central guiding principle, and it is renewed approximately every ten years. The plan is based on analyses and expertise on issues such as urban sprawl, reduction of carbon dioxide emissions, restructuring of the regional economy, and potential locations for wind turbines. It is frequently developed from previous plans and uses a variety of methods and data collection tools including opinion polls, satellite imagery or aerial photography, field surveys, census data, environmental impact assessments, physical planning proposals, and finally geographic information systems (GIS), which are designed to capture, analyze, manage, and present data that are referenced by spatial coordinates.

Based on past plans, new data, and consultations with the regional and local/municipal political bodies, the regional planning agency develops a draft proposal. Normally, a regional plan identifies and describes intended land uses and related activities, including settlement areas and open space; places with specific socioeconomic functions, such as centers for commerce or industrial sites; and areas for water protection or the utilization of a particular natural resource. Additionally, it may indicate the locations and layouts of transportation infrastructure, supply units for energy, waste disposal, and other systems.

Subsequent to preparation of a draft plan, often including several options for the future, the public is involved through hearings, exhibitions, and/or web-based surveys. Comments and criticism can be integrated into a revised plan (again, often including several options) discussed by political bodies and eventually followed by a second round of public participation. After that, the appropriate government body approves the regional plan. The application of the regional plan is in the center of the planning process; evaluations follow, and, if necessary, plans are updated or even realigned. The regional plan is very often complemented by further policy documents that depict current and future regional development objectives, such as a spatial vision for the next thirty years, large-scale flagship projects, regional retail concepts, or specific plans for nature conservation. It is important to emphasize once again the fact that regional planning varies greatly, in terms of its influence, legal rigidity, or implementation, among countries and regions.

Regional Planning and Sustainability

Sustainability is a key normative concept found in almost any national, regional, or municipal spatial plan today in the Western world. In particular, at the regional level planners are addressing various aspects of sustainability. First to be mentioned is relative long-time horizon of regional planning, as the plan should ideally serve as a kind of road map for regional development in the next ten years or so. Aspects of social cohesion, such as the quest to minimize social segregation or to support socially deprived neighborhoods, are often found on regional planning agendas. Other examples strive for more resource-efficient urban forms by proposing cognate planning concepts such as "compact cities" (which suggest to develop a better functional mix in urban quarters in order to promote shorter distances to work, services, etc.) or "transit-oriented development" (which aims at a better integration of high-density development with high quality public transport access).

The Future

The monocentric model, in which central city locations are considered the sole functional focal point for all types of social and economic activity, is no longer the norm in evolving spatial patterns across Europe, North America, and increasingly in Asia. Cities, or even clusters of proximate cities, are integrating more and more with their hinterlands to form multicentered functional regions. A wider array of economic functions leads to a broad variety of new centralities, peripheries, and intermediate zones. The restructuring process can not necessarily be described only as an extension of the urban fabric; it can be also caused by a kind of "perforation" of the urban form in shrinking regions. These spatial dynamics often are not a

result of planning, but rather of multiple decision makers working in a weak planning context.

Nonetheless, land use fragmentation challenges different aspects of regional planning, in general, and the political vision to strive for more sustainable development, in particular. Urban areas play a key role in climate change mitigation strategies. What the urban form's impact on sustainability will be is a central question that planners will need to address.

Peter SCHMITT
Nordregio (Nordic Centre for Spatial Development)

See also Agenda 21; Building Rating Systems, Green; Citizen Science; Community and Stakeholder Input; Design Quality Indicator (DQI); Focus Groups; Geographic Information Systems (GIS); Human Development Index (HDI); Land-Use and Land-Cover Change; *The Limits to Growth;* Participatory Action Research; Social Network Analysis (SNA); Sustainable Livelihood Analysis (SLA)

FURTHER READING

American Planning Association (APA). (2011). About APA. Retrieved October 18, 2011, from http://www.planning.org/aboutapa/

Birch, Eugéne L. (Ed.). (2009). *The urban and regional planning reader.* London: Routledge.

Forester, John. (1999). *The deliberative practitioner: Encouraging participatory planning processes.* Cambridge, MA: MIT Press.

Hall, Peter, & Tewdwr-Jones, Mark. (2010) *Urban and regional planning* (5th ed.) London: Routledge.

Healey, Patsy. (2004). The treatment of space and place in the new strategic spatial planning in Europe. *International Journal of Urban and Regional Research, 28,* 45–67.

Healey, Patsy. (2007). *Urban complexity and spatial strategies: Towards a relational planning for our times.* London: Routledge.

Innes, Judith E., & Booher, David E. (2010). *Planning with complexity: An introduction to collaborative rationality for public policy.* London: Routledge.

METREX—the Network of European Metropolitan Regions and Areas. (2011). Homepage. Retrieved October 18, 2011, from http://www.eurometrex.org/

Office of Regional Planning and Urban Transportation, Stockholm County Council (RTK). (2009). *Regionala stadskärnor* (Rapport 1:2009). Stockholm: Office of Regional Planning, Stockholm County Council.

Office of Regional Planning [Regionplanekontoret]. (2010). *RUFS 2010—Regional Utvecklings-plan för Stockholmsregionen 2010* [Regional development plan for the Stockholm region] (Rapport 1:2010). Stockholm: Office of Regional Planning, Stockholm County Council.

Sustainable Urban Metabolism for Europe (SUME). (n.d.). Welcome to the SUME project! Retrieved October 18, 2011, from http://www.sume.at

The Regional Plan Association (RPA). (2011). Homepage. Retrieved October 18, 2011, from http://www.rpa.org/

Taylor, Nigel. (1999). Anglo-American town planning theory since 1945: Three significant developments but no paradigm shifts. *Planning Perspectives, 14,* 327–345.

Regulatory Compliance

Regulatory compliance involves conforming to applicable laws and regulations. Compliance activities range from installing and maintaining pollution control equipment to compiling data and submitting reports to federal, state, and local regulatory agencies. Each facility is responsible for its own compliance, and noncompliance often stems from lack of commitment or lack of resources. Increasing facility staff commitment to environmental performance and regulatory factors can often improve compliance.

Regulatory compliance refers to the extent to which entities engaged in regulated activities conform to applicable laws and regulations. Federal, state, and local regulatory agencies implement and enforce environmental regulatory programs. In some cases, multiple agencies regulate different aspects of the same activity. For example, one agency may have authority for issuing permits while another has authority for inspections and enforcement.

In the United States, an adversarial approach to regulation and enforcement, rather than a cooperative approach, is the norm. US regulation also frequently emphasizes use of approved waste treatment and pollution control technologies rather than an outcome-based emphasis on decreasing actual environmental impacts. In other cultures and under other models of regulatory enforcement and agency–industry interaction, the dynamics of regulatory compliance may vary considerably. What does not vary, however, is the need to identify effective solutions to noncompliance in order to protect human and environmental health and create a sustainable future. In all cases, this requires understanding the broader context of forces that influence regulatory compliance and the complex interactions among them.

The organizations governed by environmental laws and regulations engage in a variety of actions that pose ongoing or potential risks to human health and environmental quality. Examples include public and private sector activities such as manufacturing, mining, logging, agriculture, fishing, construction, electric power generation, and operation of hospitals, jails, sewage treatment plants, dams, and golf courses. Even public high schools that generate hazardous waste in their chemistry labs pose a risk.

A description of regulatory compliance for all types of regulated activities is beyond the scope of this article. Here the focus will be on manufacturing facilities, although regulatory compliance and the set of factors influencing it are substantially similar for all types of regulated facilities and activities.

In the United States, environmental regulatory compliance is required under several laws, such as the Clean Air Act (CAA), Clean Water Act (CWA), Resource Conservation and Recovery Act (RCRA), Emergency Planning and Community Right-to-Know Act (EPCRA), and Magnuson Fishery Conservation Act (MFCA). Activities like installing and maintaining pollution control equipment, meeting discharge limits established in regulations and permits, monitoring processes and wastes, submitting reports to regulatory agencies, labeling equipment and containers, and training staff may all address compliance issues. Different laws and regulations emphasize different types of regulatory compliance activities. For example the CWA stresses pollution control technologies, whereas the EPCRA focuses on record keeping and reporting, and the MFCA prioritizes limits on access to, and total amounts of, marine resources that may be harvested.

Some regulatory compliance activities, such as proper management of hazardous wastes as required by the

RCRA, have direct impacts on human and environmental health that the laws were written to protect. These are commonly referred to as substantive regulatory compliance. Regulatory compliance activities without direct impacts on human and environmental health, such as labeling and reporting, are forms of procedural regulatory compliance.

Causes of Noncompliance

Noncompliance is possible wherever regulatory requirements exist. Levels of regulatory compliance can range from a high of "beyond compliance" for facilities that not only meet but exceed the regulatory requirements, to a low of total noncompliance. Noncompliance can be accidental or deliberate and can result from ill- or well-intentioned actions. Common forms of noncompliance include "exceedances," which occur when a facility emits more waste into the environment than a regulation or permit allows; pollution control equipment failures due to problems with design, installation, maintenance, or operation; submitting incomplete or inaccurate reports to regulatory agencies; and failure to keep records in accordance with regulations. Usually, industries themselves have control over compliance factors, but regulatory agencies, the language in laws and regulations themselves, contracted service providers, and in some cases, the relationships among these parties also have an effect.

Intent is a key factor in noncompliance. Accidentally filing paperwork late and intentionally releasing large amounts of hazardous waste to surface waters are both forms of noncompliance, yet they differ substantially in motive and effect. Intentional noncompliance can stem from principled disagreement with laws and regulations, such as a fisher who believes that the only things limiting a catch should be luck and ability, or a facility manager who believes it should be allowable to make a modification to a production line that will have no environmental impacts without waiting weeks or months for the regulatory agency to approve a minor modification to the production facility's Title V operating permit under the CAA. Real or perceived procedural injustice, as occurs when agencies inconsistently enforce laws and regulations, can also result in intentional noncompliance, because people are less likely to comply when they believe they are being treated unfairly.

Internal Causes

How committed facility managers are to regulatory compliance is often at the root of compliance or noncompliance. Facility managers vary significantly in their commitment to human and environmental health, the level of resources they can commit to regulatory compliance at any given time, their knowledge of laws and regulations, their level of truthfulness, and the degree to which they are proactive or reactive with respect to laws and regulations. The attitudes of the managers, in turn, affect the likelihood that their staff will have developed written operating procedures, attended trainings, and be able to commit the time necessary to comply. Failure to follow appropriate operating procedures, conduct routine site and equipment checks, and maintain records is more likely in cases where facility staff lack expertise, experience, or awareness of applicable laws and regulations, do not understand the regulatory policies due to language barriers or lack of technical knowledge, or simply lack the resources necessary to comply.

Facility size also contributes to regulatory compliance. Noncompliant facilities are disproportionately represented by small ones, which often lack the resources to comply with even moderately complex regulatory frameworks or solve technical problems when they arise. In contrast, those facilities that go beyond compliance are usually large ones that have more resources committed to complying and are often covered under multiple environmental laws and regulations.

External Causes

External contributors to noncompliance include inadequate regulatory agency implementation and enforcement capacity, regulatory agency corruptibility, equipment vendors, waste haulers, other contracted service providers, deterrence failure, and public levels of concern over perceived risks to health and the environment associated with a facility or sector's operation.

Problems stemming from regulatory agencies include complex, ambiguous, or inconsistently interpreted and enforced laws and regulations, absence of clear technical guidance documents and facility staff training opportunities, poor communication, and lack of provision of technical assistance. Such problems are more likely to contribute to noncompliance at facilities that do not have access to third-party information providers like industry trade associations and environmental consultants.

Some regulated groups have enough political influence to affect policy formation, implementation, and enforcement. Some can even influence agency funding. Reduced funding can cause or exacerbate agency understaffing, which in turn reduces the agency's ability to function at all levels, including its ability to provide information to regulated parties. Industry efforts to weaken proposed regulations can also result in ambiguity in policy language, making compliance more difficult.

In jurisdictions with weak or easily corruptible regulators, regulatory compliance is often lacking.

In such cases, increased agency transparency and decreased inspector and agency discretion are appropriate. In addition, where government capacity is weak or lacking, top-down regulatory models are prone to failure. In such cases, alternatives like community-based resource management or local community monitoring with publicly available results may be more effective.

Ideally, the regulatory framework is designed and implemented in such a way that regulatory compliance, rather than noncompliance, is a rational choice. Deterrence failure can occur when noncompliance is both unlikely to be detected and highly advantageous, or when penalties for noncompliance are too low. Even more fundamentally, regardless of all other factors, when there is no credible threat of sanctions, regulation is ineffective.

Improving Regulatory Compliance

Regulatory compliance can be improved through actions taken by several sources—most importantly, the noncompliant facility staff. Actions taken by the regulatory agency, industry trade groups and vendors, and local citizen groups are also potentially effective.

Facility Actions

Facilities can improve regulatory compliance through a clear, articulated, and ongoing commitment to environmental quality on the part of management. This commitment might include employee training, development or acquisition of supporting resources like internal inspection checklists, and conducting self-audits to identify the direct and underlying causes of noncompliance events. Participation in some voluntary programs, such as ISO 14000 and the Natural Step, can improve regulatory compliance. These programs require facility staff to develop a comprehensive understanding of and engage in ongoing tracking of all aspects of a facility's environmental impacts, educate many employees not traditionally considered relevant to regulatory compliance, and continuously improve facility environmental performance. Such actions fundamentally and broadly enhance a facility's capacity for regulatory compliance.

Regulatory Agency Actions

Regulatory agency actions like consolidation of overlapping regulatory requirements, improved coordination among federal, state, and local agencies, and improved communication between agency and facility staff—especially where laws and regulations are ambiguous or inconsistent—may also improve compliance. Guides that explain laws and regulations in plain language are also highly valued by facility staff. Rewards for highly compliant facilities, such as expedited permit processing, reduced frequency of inspections, penalty relief, and public recognition, can also serve as potent incentives for improved regulatory compliance.

Information Provision

Should problems arise, returning to regulatory compliance often depends on the facility's ability to access technical expertise and legal resources. These may be part of a facility's existing staff or may be available through paid consultants, equipment vendors, and industry trade groups. Small facilities or those with limited financial resources may not have or be able to afford needed technical and legal resources. In the absence of low-cost technical assistance, their return to regulatory compliance can become more difficult and time consuming.

The responsibility for providing this technical information is sometimes debated. Regulated facility staff often claim that the regulatory agency should provide the information, since it is requiring compliance. Others argue that costs associated with regulatory compliance are reasonable costs of doing business and do not justify taxpayer-funded government assistance. They claim that if a company cannot afford to comply with applicable laws and regulations, then it cannot afford to be in business.

Citizen Action

Historically, local community watchdog groups have been effective at reducing noncompliance, especially at facilities with chronic problems. Among other things, such groups are able to monitor and document a variety of activities such as illegal air and water emissions and waste disposal. They also have the advantage of being able to monitor during nights, weekends, and storm events, when many intentional violations occur. Local groups can also influence facilities by increasing public pressure through demonstrations, community meetings, and the many forms of social, public, and private media. In addition, the citizen suit provision in nearly all US environmental statutes enables local groups and individuals to pursue legal remedies directly if regulatory agency enforcement is absent or ineffective.

Dee EGGERS
University of North Carolina at Asheville

See also Agenda 21; Building Rating Systems, Green; Business Reporting Methods; Citizen Science; Community and Stakeholder Input; Externality Valuation; Reducing Emissions from Deforestation and Forest Degradation (REDD); Shipping and Freight Indicators; Social Life Cycle Assessment (S-LCA); Supply Chain Analysis; Taxation Indicators, Green; Triple Bottom Line

FURTHER READING

Andrews, Richard N. L. (2006). *Managing the environment, managing ourselves: A history of American environmental policy.* New Haven, CT: Yale University Press.

Ayres, Ian, & Braithwaite, John. (1992). *Responsive regulation: Transcending the deregulation debate.* New York: Oxford University Press.

Bardach, Eugene, & Kagan, Robert. (1982). *Going by the book: The problem of regulatory unreasonableness.* Philadelphia: Temple University Press.

Burby, Raymond J.; May, Peter J.; & Paterson, Robert G. (1998). Improving compliance with regulations: Choices and outcomes for local government. *Journal of the American Planning Association, 64*(3), 324–334.

Fiorino, Daniel. (2006). *The new environmental regulation.* Cambridge, MA: MIT Press.

Durant, Robert F.; Fiorino, Daniel J.; & O'Leary, Rosemary. (Eds.). (2004). *Environmental governance reconsidered: Challenges, choices, and opportunities.* Cambridge, MA: MIT Press.

Kagan, Robert A. (2000). Introduction: Comparing national styles of regulation in Japan and the United States. *Law and Policy, 22*(3 & 4), 225–244.

Kagan, Robert, & Axelrod, Lee. (Eds.). (2000). *Regulatory encounters: Multinational corporations and American adversarial legalism.* Berkeley: University of California Press.

Kagan, Robert A., & Scholz, John T. (1984). The criminology of the corporation and regulatory enforcement strategies. In Keith Hawkins & John M. Thomas (Eds.), *Enforcing regulation* (pp. 67–95). Boston: Kluwer-Nijhoff.

Kenny, Charles, & Soreide, Tina. (2008). *Grand corruption in utilities* (Policy Research Working Paper 4805). The World Bank. Retrieved July 17, 2011, from http://www-wds.worldbank.org/external/default/WDSContentServer/IW3P/IB/2008/12/30/000158349_20081230224204/Rendered/PDF/WPS4805.pdf

May, Peter J., & Winter, Søren. (1999). Regulatory enforcement and compliance: Examining Danish agro-environmental policy. *Journal of Policy Analysis and Management, 18*(4), 625–651.

May, Peter J., & Wood, Robert S. (2003). At the regulatory front lines: Inspectors' enforcement styles and regulatory compliance. *Journal of Public Administration Research and Theory, 13*(2), 117–139.

Scholz, John. (1984). Voluntary compliance and regulatory enforcement. *Law and Policy, 6,* 385–405.

Scholz, John. (1991). Cooperative regulatory enforcement and the politics of administrative effectiveness. *American Political Science Review, 85,* 115–136.

United States Environmental Protection Agency. (1999). *EPA/CMA root cause analysis pilot project* (EPA-305-R-99-001). Washington, DC: US Government Printing Office.

Vig, Norman J., & Kraft, Michael E. (Eds.). (2009). *Environmental policy: New directions for the twenty-first century* (7th ed.). Washington, DC: CQ Press.

Zaelke, Durwood; Kaniaru, Donald; & Kružíková, Eva. (Eds.). (2005). Making law work: Vols. I & II. *Environmental compliance & sustainable development.* London: Cameron May.

Remote Sensing

Remote sensing generally refers to the gathering of information about the Earth from satellites. It has provided broadscale views of our planet since the 1970s. Due to the consistency, uniqueness, and repeatability of the imagery provided, coupled with ever-increasing spatial, spectral, and temporal resolutions, remote sensing provides a particularly valuable contribution to monitoring trends that may indicate shifts toward or away from sustainable conditions.

R emote sensing is the means by which a target of interest on the Earth's surface (or in its atmosphere) can be studied using a device separated from it by some distance. It is an increasingly important approach to studying the Earth's environment, as robust decision making toward more sustainable conditions and healthy environments benefits greatly from the assimilation of geospatial information. After careful processing of the data, remote sensing affords a continuous record of our environment that is consistent and can be more accurate than that derived through the interpolation of limited field observations. Remote sensing is based on light, a naturally occurring medium of electromagnetic radiation, which carries information about our environment that, when collected by remote sensing devices, can be interpreted to provide information for assessing sustainability.

Electromagnetic Radiation

Electromagnetic radiation (EMR) can be thought of as time-varying electric and magnetic fields that are orthogonal to each other, which travel through space and media in the form of a wave at the speed of light (2.998×10^8 meters per second, or m s^{-1}). These waves can be short or long in length, with an associated high or low energy,

respectively. These properties are described by the electromagnetic spectrum, which is commonly divided into regions for convenience, the main regions, or wavebands, being *visible* (short wavelengths of 0.4 to 0.7 μm); *near infrared* (NIR; 0.7 to 1.50 μm); *middle infrared* (MIR; 1.5 to 5.0 μm); *thermal infrared* (TIR; 5.0 to 15 μm) and *microwave* (long wavelengths of 3 to 300cm). (The symbol μm stands for micron or micrometer—one-millionth of a meter.) The length, and thus energy, of the electromagnetic waves principally determines how the radiation interacts with targets in the environment and thus allows us to distinguish between the properties of our environment that vary not only by geography but also by time.

All things having a temperature above absolute zero (−273°C, 0K) emit electromagnetic radiation. In remote sensing, the sun is the most obvious source of natural EMR (solar radiation). Generally speaking, solar-emitted EMR is used for remote sensing at visible to MIR wavelengths, and Earth-emitted EMR is used for remote sensing at wavelengths beyond the middle MIR region of the electromagnetic spectrum. This natural phenomenon (referred to as passive remote sensing) is exploited by remote sensing and, once the sensor is deployed, represents the least costly approach per unit area for measuring and monitoring the environment and its properties.

Active Remote Sensing

The energy of the EMR from both the sun and the Earth is so low that to use these wavelengths for remote sensing can be problematic. Therefore, in many instances, it is more effective to use active remote sensing, in which EMR is produced artificially by the sensor rather than by natural sources. Two common approaches are the use of *radio detection and ranging* (radar) and *light detection and ranging* (lidar). Microwaves are capable of penetrating the atmosphere under almost all conditions and therefore are used if the atmosphere is prone to clouds, light rain, or smoke. The intensity of the echoes from targets on the Earth's surface is determined by both the features of the radar system (i.e., wavelength, polarization, and geometrical characteristics) and the characteristics of the Earth's target (i.e., terrain geometry, surface roughness, and complex dielectric constant of the surface).

Lidar systems are similar to radar systems in their principles. Remote sensing using lasers is a rapidly growing technology, particularly small-footprint lidar systems that are mounted on helicopters or aircraft. Other systems have been used on terrestrial and satellite mounts. The rotation and position of the sensor is continuously recorded as it moves along a flight path, using an inertial measurement unit (IMU) and a global positioning system (GPS). Integration of all of these measures allows the construction of a georeferenced three-dimensional point cloud from which geospatial products can be constructed, such as digital terrain models (DTM), digital surface models

(DSM) in vegetated environments, canopy height models (CHM), and building height models in urban areas.

Understanding Place from Space

Once emitted from its source, radiation can interact with matter in a number of ways, depending on its wavelength and the properties of the matter. A wide variety of properties of the environment can be measured by remote sensing using the main wavebands of the spectrum. (See table 1 below.) Having thus measured these properties, scientists can indirectly infer related properties and extrapolate over time and place to keep a watchful "eye" on our environment. By sensing that which is not visible (i.e., is beyond the visible spectrum), satellites have provided us with the first large-scale maps of vegetation health, atmospheric pollutants, weather patterns, rock types, soil moisture, sea temperatures, ice packs, and more.

The information that remote sensing provides regarding sustainability can be used to inform policy making or to

TABLE 1. Properties of Environmental Components Measured by Remote Sensing

Environmental Component	Electromagnetic Spectrum Wavebands				
	Visible (0.4–0.7 μm)	Near infrared (0.7–1.5 μm)	Middle infrared (1.5–5.0 μm)	Thermal infrared (5.0–15.0 μm)	Microwave (3–300 cm)
Rock and Soil	Iron-bearing minerals Texture/structure Soil moisture Organic matter	Iron-bearing minerals Texture/structure Soil moisture Organic matter	Texture/structure Soil moisture Organic matter Carbonates Sulfates	Temperature	Surface soil moisture Texture/structure
Vegetation	Chlorophyll	Physiological structure Protein Lignin Oil	Water content Nitrogen Lignin Sugar Cellulose	Temperature	Canopy structure and roughness
Snow and Ice	Snow depth Snow grain size	Snow water Snow grain size	Water/ice differentiation Cloud/ice differentiation	Temperature	Snow depth
Water	Organic matter Suspended sediments Chlorophyll			Surface temperature	Surface roughness
Atmosphere	Aerosol properties Cloud thickness Aerosol optical thickness	Water vapor Cloud top height Aerosol optical thickness Precipitable water	Cloud particle radius Aerosol optical thickness	Cloud temperature	

Source: Based on P. J. Curran. (1994). Imaging spectrometry. *Progress in Physical Geography, 18,* 247–266.

assist in policy implementation. A picture (or rather a remotely sensed image) is indeed worth a thousand words. Seeing is believing, and building up a story over time with a series of remotely sensed images affords a deep understanding of how the environment is changing locally, regionally, and globally. One such example is knowledge gained about ice sheet mass balance and dynamics. Only through remote sensing were observers able to follow the disintegration on the Larsen Ice Shelf in Antarctica.

Due to its frequent observations, the EOS (Earth Observing System) MODIS (Moderate Resolution Imaging Spectroradiometer) satellite sensing system was able to capture the loss of more than 2,000 square kilometers of ice. (See figure 1 below.) Knowing about an event such as the melting of an ice shelf is important for predicting future rise of sea level, which has significant implications for the roughly 10 percent of the global population currently living in low-lying areas. Since the beginning of the twenty-first

Figure 1. A Temporal Series of EOS-1 MODIS Images Capturing the Disintegration of the Larsen Ice Shelf in Antarctica

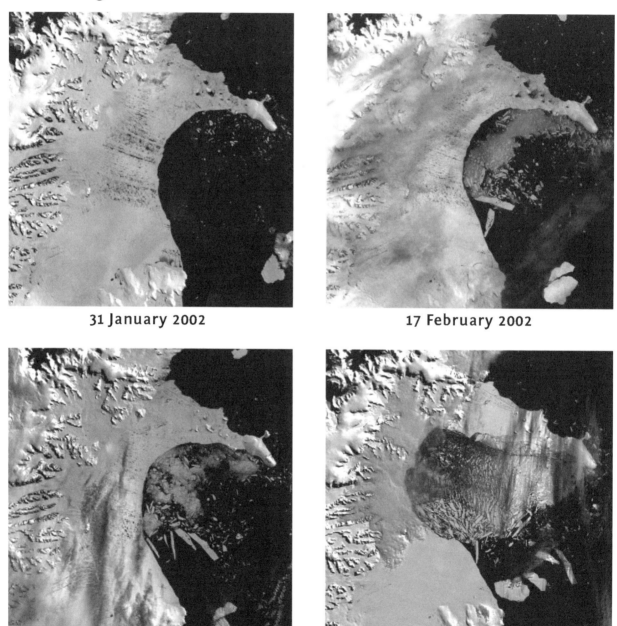

31 January 2002

17 February 2002

23 February 2002

5 March 2002

Source: J. Dozier. (2009). Remote sensing of the cryosphere (in Warner, Nellis, and Foody 2009, 397–408). Photos used by permission of SAGE.

EOS MODIS imagery showing the disintegration of the Larsen Ice Shelf in Antarctica over a five-week period in early 2002.

century there has been a wealth of remote sensing studies that provide data, such as ice sheet thickness, that is required for planning what the future might be for those people.

Remote sensing has assisted the United Nations Collaborative Programme on Reducing Emissions from Deforestation and Forest Degradation (REDD), which compensates countries for their carbon emissions reductions. This creation of a financial value for the carbon stored in their forests requires that accurate data on forests be provided quickly, accurately, and systematically, which remote sensing does. Other information on forests provided by satellite remote sensing includes the dates of green-up or leaf-fall; multitemporal records of satellite sensor data (phenological profiles) are constructed, and key phenological event information is extracted and related to climatic variations.

Other uses of remote sensing in sustainability studies include the measurement of what are called urban heat islands, demonstrating the effect that urbanization has on air temperature and therefore on meteorological events, such as increased precipitation, as well as on energy demands, environmental quality, and the long-term sustainability of local environments.

A Variety of Systems

Remotely sensed records for the study of the Earth's environment are currently available from a plethora of sensing systems that are continually evolving with respect to their size, sensing capabilities, platform type, and costs. The Landsat Observatory of satellites and sensors was first launched by the United States in the early 1970s and continues to set the standards for other systems. The forty years following saw the launch of numerous other remote sensing systems; as of 2011, there were more than 150 in orbit, including the European Space Agency's (ESA) Envisat and the National Aeronautics and Space Administration's (NASA) Earth Observing System platforms, both of which carry a suite of sensors designed for integrated Earth observation. As of 2011, the trend is toward smaller, less expensive national satellites, with more than twenty countries currently developing or operating remote sensing satellites.

The various remote sensing systems differ in their characteristics. They measure radiation at different pixel sizes (the spatial resolution), wavebands (spectral resolution), and temporal frequencies (temporal resolution). Much remote sensing uses sensors that are on satellite platforms and can provide a global perspective on the environment (e.g., the Landsat satellite, which carries the Enhanced Thematic Mapper sensor). Other platforms, including airplanes, helicopters, or unmanned aerial vehicles (UAVs), may be used to acquire a very detailed perspective on a particular locality. The deployment of different remote sensing devices on these various platforms ensures that our environment can be measured at the appropriate scale for the phenomenon under investigation.

As improvements in technology continue, researchers will design remote sensing devices that can provide ever-more accurate and precise information about our environment, allowing better-informed decision making. Given the commitment indicated by countries around the globe to remote sensing programs, the future looks promising for continued movement in this direction.

Using the Data

Remote sensing agencies increasingly are facilitating the use of their data by producing higher-order geospatial datasets, which can more easily be integrated for decision making about our sustainable futures. As such, remote sensing is now able routinely to produce a wide range of geospatial products about the environment that can be used to answer sustainability questions.

Doreen S. BOYD
University of Nottingham

See also Challenges to Measuring Sustainability; Computer Modeling; Ecosystem Health Indicators; Geographic Information Systems (GIS); Land-Use and Land-Cover Change; Long-Term Ecological Research (LTER); Millennium Development Goals; Ocean Acidification—Measurement; Reducing Emissions from Deforestation and Forest Degradation (REDD); Regional Planning; Systems Thinking

FURTHER READING

European Space Agency (ESA). (2011). Homepage. Retrieved October 26, 2011, from http://www.esa.int/esaEO/index.html

Faculty of Geo-Information Science and Earth Observation (ITC) of the University of Twente. (2011). ITC's database of satellites and sensors. Retrieved October 26, 2011, from http://www.itc.nl/research/products/sensordb/searchsat.aspx

Gibson, Paul J., & Power, Clare H. (2000). *Introductory remote sensing: Digital image processing and applications.* London: Routledge.

Jensen, John J. (2007). *Remote sensing of the environment: An Earth resource perspective* (2nd ed.). Upper Saddle River, NJ: Prentice-Hall.

Lillesand, Thomas; Kiefer, Ralph W.; & Chipman, Jonathan. (2009). *Remote sensing and image interpretation* (6th ed.). New York: John Wiley and Sons.

Liverman, Diana; Moran, Emilio F.; Rindfuss, Ronald R.; & Stern, Paul C. (Eds.). (1998). *People and pixels.* Washington, DC: National Academy Press.

National Aeronautics and Space Administration (NASA). (2011). Earth: Your future, our mission. Retrieved October 26, 2011, from http://www.nasa.gov/topics/earth/index.html.

Tatem, A. J.; Goetz, S. J.; & Hay, S. I. (2008). Fifty years of Earth-observation satellites. *American Scientist, 96,* 390–398.

Warner, Timothy A.; Nellis, M. Duane; & Foody, Giles M. (2009). *The SAGE handbook of remote sensing.* London: SAGE.

Risk Assessment

Risk assessment is a process for analyzing data to determine whether an environmental hazard might cause harm to exposed persons or ecosystems. It is often the first step in both public and private risk analyses, and it serves a central role in US environmental regulation. The process is gaining popularity worldwide.

R isk assessments come in many varieties and are performed by many different decision makers. Private companies, academics, and even individuals may all perform informal risk assessments on everything from financial risk to human health risk to ecological risk. When used in public policy contexts, however, risk assessment has developed into a highly technical process for analyzing and quantifying the type, magnitude, and probability of harm that may be caused by exposure to environmental hazards. Quantitative risk assessment of this kind has played a central role in US environmental regulation since the 1980s and has increasing popularity worldwide.

Development of Quantitative Risk Assessment

Quantitative risk assessment as it is used today developed out of several events in the United States in the 1980s. The first was the US Supreme Court's decision in *Industrial Union Department, AFL-CIO v. American Petroleum Institute* (commonly called "the benzene case"), where the Court struck down regulations promulgated by the Occupational Safety and Health Agency for failure to demonstrate the existence of a significant risk to human health from occupational exposure to benzene, which was a known carcinogen. This decision surprised many regulators at the time and left them scrambling to find new ways to ensure that their regulations were based on verifiably "significant" risks.

Around the same time, there was substantial controversy regarding what was seen as the increasing politicization of the US Environmental Protection Agency (EPA), under Reagan-appointed director Anne Gorsuch, who implemented a series of policies to shrink the size of the agency and to lessen environmental burdens on businesses. These policies were exceedingly controversial, and Gorsuch was forced to resign in 1983 amid a Congressional inquest and a citation for contempt of Congress.

William Ruckelshaus, who had been the founding director of the EPA in 1970, was asked to step in after Gorsuch's resignation. Ruckelshaus saw quantitative risk assessment as a tool for combating the kind of overt politicization of the regulatory process that had taken place under Gorsuch. Accordingly, he advocated for sharp distinctions between the scientific risk assessment process and the more political decision making inherent in decisions about risk management.

In response to the perceived need for this distinction between risk assessment and management, in 1983 the National Academy of Science developed *Risk Assessment in the Federal Government: Managing the Process*, more commonly called the Red Book for the original color of its cover. This document became the basic source book for quantitative risk assessment and is still widely relied upon despite the issuance of the National Resource Council's *Science and Decisions: Advancing Risk Assessment*, known as the Silver Book, in late 2008.

Quantitative Risk Assessment as Methodology

The initial edition of the Red Book was focused particularly on human health risks from carcinogens. Accordingly, it adopted a set of methods borrowed from toxicology, which is the study of poisons. This methodology continues to provide the basis for US federal environmental regulation, although it has been somewhat modified over the years to apply to other types of health risk and to risk to the environment as well as to humans. The US EPA currently applies two related but distinct methods for quantitative risk assessment: one for human health risks, and the other for ecological risks.

Human Health Risk Assessments

A human health risk assessment addresses the probability and extent of adverse health effects in humans who are exposed to environmental stressors like hazardous chemicals.

The Red Book identifies four distinct processes necessary for quantitative risk assessment: hazard identification, dose-response assessment, exposure assessment, and risk characterization.

Hazard Identification

Hazard identification is an assessment of whether an environmental stressor has the potential to be hazardous to human health. Particular attention is paid to toxicodynamics (the effect the substance has on the human body) and toxicokinetics (how the body absorbs, distributes, metabolizes, and eliminates the substance). Although statistically controlled clinical studies on humans are considered the gold standard for linking a stressor to adverse health impacts, these are often not available because of concerns about testing dangerous stressors (like poisons) on people. Consequently, environmental risk assessors must often extrapolate from two kinds of second-best data: epidemiological studies, which look at statistical evaluations of human populations to see if there is an apparent association between exposure to the stressor and adverse health effects; and animal studies, which test the health impacts of environmental stressors on animals.

Dose-Response Assessment

Dose-response assessment, also called hazard characterization, seeks to establish the "dose" of a stressor that causes measurable harm to human health, and the way in which changing a dose will affect the likelihood or magnitude of that harm. With most (but not all) stressors, the adverse effects of the stressor increase with the dose. Assessors try to draw a dose-response curve to represent just how quickly adverse effects worsen.

Dose-response assessment analysis requires detailed knowledge of clinical, epidemiological, and toxicological studies on how the risk of toxic effect changes with dose. As with hazard identification, there are uncertainties involved in extrapolating from epidemiological and animal studies. These uncertainties are only exacerbated by the possibility of significant interpersonal differences in how people respond to toxins.

Another continuing controversy in dose-response assessment is what assessors should assume about the dose-response curve when information is limited, as it often is at very small doses. For many substances there are levels of exposure for which current science cannot establish any negative effects. Should assessors assume that there really are no negative effects from that substance at those levels? Should they extrapolate the dose/response curve, and, if so, with what shape? This inquiry is further complicated by the fact that some substances (like vitamins) exhibit "hormetic" dose-response curves, which means that they have positive effects at low levels, even though they are toxic in larger quantities.

Exposure Assessment

Exposure assessment is the process of determining the magnitude, frequency, and duration with which humans are exposed to an environmental stressor. Because exposure to stressors often varies widely across the population, a challenge in exposure assessment is determining the population whose exposure will be measured. Typically, assessors try to describe the size, nature, and types of humans exposed to the stressor, as well as the different exposure

pathways (the course a stressor takes from its source to the person being exposed) and exposure routes (the means of entry into the body) through which people can be exposed. Assessors attempt to quantify exposure using three different approaches: point of contact measurement, scenario evaluation, and reconstruction. Assessors also attempt to adjust for variable exposure across individuals.

Risk Characterization

The final step in an assessment of environmental risks to human health is meant to integrate the three prior steps. At this point, the assessors are supposed to know the potential health effects of the substance (from hazard identification), how the risk of those effects changes with the dose (from dose-response assessment), and how and how much the target population is likely to be exposed to the substance (from exposure assessment). To characterize the risk, assessors set the dose incurred by the target population against the hazard and dose-response data available for the substance. This characterization typically includes a detailed explanation of the nature of the hazard, its seriousness, and how likely it is to occur.

Ecological Risk Assessments

An ecological risk assessment is a process for estimating the probability and extent of adverse ecological effects as a result of exposure to environmental stressors, including hazardous substances, invasive species, land change, and climate change. Like human health risk assessment, ecological risk assessment is designed to lead to risk characterizations, which can then inform policy decisions. For ecological risk assessments, risk characterization is typically preceded by two information-gathering steps: problem formulation and analysis.

Problem Formulation

In the problem formulation, assessors gather information to determine what plants and animals might be at

risk. A key initial portion of the formulation is determining which ecological entities should be protected, and at what level of generality. For example, a formulation might choose to focus on a particular species; a group of species; a specific lake, river, or other ecosystem; or a type of ecosystem to be protected. Once the assessor has identified the relevant entity, the next step is to determine the attributes of the entity that need protection. These two aspects together—the choice of entity and the attributes to be protected—are sometimes called the "assessment endpoints."

The assessment endpoint might be an endangered species, a commercially important fishery, aesthetic air quality in national parks, or a general ecosystem function such as nutrient cycling. There is substantial discretion for an assessor choosing an assessment endpoint, and the choice of endpoint is frequently treated as a political decision rather than a scientific one.

Once an assessor has chosen assessment endpoints, the assessor pulls together what information can be found on the hypothesized relationships between the relevant ecological entities and environmental stressors, and attempts to create some kind of model representing those relationships. The information often includes data about the source of the stressor, the stressor itself, potential exposure, and the predicted effects on the ecological entity.

Analysis of the Problem

In the analysis portion of an ecological risk assessment, assessors determine the degree to which plants and animals are exposed and whether that level of exposure is likely to cause harm. The goal of this phase is to create a model for predicting or determining the ecological response to the relevant stressors. The specifics of the model vary widely based on the assessment endpoints. Typically they include a hazard quotient, which provides a quantifiable measurement of a risk, and some parameters for determining the levels at which the assessment endpoint is exposed to the stressor. The goal is to have a quantifiable measure for how the endpoint is being affected by exposure.

Risk Characterization of Ecological Risks

In an ecological risk assessment, the risk characterization provides an estimate of the risk posed to ecological entities. The characterizations are often split into two components: risk estimation and risk description. Risk estimation is an integrated measure of the effects and likely magnitude of exposure. Risk description identifies the level at which harmful effects are likely to arise.

Uses and Applications of Risk Assessment

For environmental risks, the goal of risk assessment is typically to integrate scientific data about hazardous chemicals and other environmental stressors into risk characterizations, which exhibit the nature and extent of the risks that the stressors pose to human health and the environment. These risk characterizations are then used to inform risk communication (how risk analysts convey their assessments to stakeholders) and risk management (how decision makers choose how to manage the risk).

In the public decision-making realm, risk assessment continues to be integral to the United States' approach to risk policy, which is highly quantified in comparison to environmental regulatory approaches in most of the rest of the world. In the United States, the federal EPA performs a wide variety of environmental risk assessments, analyzing both human and ecological risks. Regulators at many other agencies, including the Food and Drug Administration (FDA) and the US Department of Agriculture (USDA), also perform environmental risk assessments, and many state environmental protection agencies incorporate risk assessment into their regulatory processes as well. Indeed, quantified risk assessments are typically thought to be required prior to regulation in light of the Supreme Court's decision in the benzene case.

Europe's approach to environmental risk has become increasingly quantified since the 1990s, and as European countries struggle to harmonize their environmental laws, centralized environmental risk assessment may prove a promising starting point.

Controversies and Challenges

Although it can highlight the need for additional scientific research, risk assessment is limited in that it does not create any new information: it is entirely dependent on existing research. To the extent that current knowledge about the effects of toxic substances is incomplete or even wrong, the risk assessment process offers no solution.

Indeed, because risk assessment requires assessors to extrapolate beyond existing data, it has been criticized as having the potential to exacerbate existing uncertainties. Even when research is relatively accurate or complete within the context in which it was gathered, the purpose of risk assessment is to help decision makers generalize beyond the observations in the initial studies. There can be real challenges in extrapolation, however, as the conditions under which the studies were run were almost certainly not identical to the conditions under which actual people, animals, and ecosystems will be exposed to the environmental stressor. This is particularly true when exposure to a stressor is intermittent or comes in combination with exposure to other stressors, when there may be substantial variability in the sensitivity of various subpopulations, and when there may be differences in the way that humans and nonhuman animals respond.

A final objection to quantitative risk assessment is that it throws a mantle of objectivity over what are essentially subjective decisions about the seriousness of environmental risks. The public is often concerned with risks that appear slight under quantitative risk assessment—such as risks from toxic waste dumps and nuclear power plants—and it may be that a democratic society should respect public prioritizations, even where they are unsupported by quantitative analyses.

These criticisms have been addressed by the risk assessment community with attempts to develop more integrated approaches to risk assessment. The most visible—and potentially most influential—movement in this direction came in the US National Resource Council's Silver Book, which explicitly criticized many of the Red Book processes, not least because of the Red Book's attempt to bifurcate the quantitative decisions in risk assessment from the more political decisions inherent in risk management.

Risk assessment thus has an uneasy position within environmental policy. While it was originally conceived of as a tool to depoliticize decisions about environmental regulation, it allows for significant and potentially political judgment calls in the face of uncertainty, and it has traditionally assumed that the magnitude of a risk can be quantified without reference to public preference. Nevertheless, it continues to be used as a critical tool for informing regulatory decisions about risk.

Arden ROWELL
University of Illinois College of Law

See also Citizen Science; Community and Stakeholder Input; Cost-Benefit Analysis; Ecological Impact

Assessment (EcIA); Externality Valuation; Quantitative vs. Qualitative Studies; Regulatory Compliance; Sustainability Science

FURTHER READING

Breyer, Stephen. (1993). *Breaking the vicious circle: Toward effective risk regulation.* Cambridge, MA: Harvard University Press.

Mazurek, Janice V. (1996). *The role of health risk assessment and cost-benefit analysis in environmental decision making in selected countries: An initial survey.* Washington, DC: Resources for the Future.

National Research Council. (1983). *Risk assessment in the federal government: Managing the process.* Washington, DC: National Academy Press.

National Research Council. (1994). *Science and judgment in risk assessment.* Washington, DC: National Academy Press.

National Research Council. (1996). *Understanding risk: Informing decisions in a democratic society.* Washington, DC: National Academy Press.

National Research Council of the National Academies. (2008). *Science and decisions: Advancing risk assessment.* Washington, DC: National Academies Press.

Paustenbach, D. J. (Ed.). (2002). *Human and ecological risk assessment: Theory and practice.* New York: John Wiley & Sons.

Rodricks, Joseph. (2007). *Calculated risks: The toxicity and human health risks of chemicals in our environment.* (2nd ed.). Cambridge, UK: Cambridge University Press.

Rosenthal, Alon; Gray, George; & Graham, John. (1992). Legislating acceptable cancer risk from exposure to toxic chemicals. *Ecology Law Quarterly, 19,* 269–362.

Sunstein, Cass. (2004). *Risk and reason: Safety, law and the environment.* Cambridge, UK: Cambridge University Press.

Ruckelshaus, William D. (1984). Risk in a free society. *Risk Analysis, 4*(3), 157–162. doi: 10.1111/j.1539-6924.1984.tb00135.x.

US Environmental Protection Agency (EPA). (2000). *Science Policy Council handbook: Risk characterization.* Retrieved April 13, 2011, from http://www.epa.gov/spc/pdfs/rchandbk.pdf

US Environmental Protection Agency (EPA). (2010a). Planning an ecological risk assessment. Retrieved February 15, 2012, from http://www.epa.gov/risk_assessment/planning-ecorisk.htm

US Environmental Protection Agency (EPA). (2010b). Planning a human health risk assessment. Retrieved February 15, 2012, from http://www.epa.gov/risk_assessment/planning-hhra.htm

US Environmental Protection Agency (EPA). (2010c). Risk assessment. Retrieved February 15, 2012, from http://www.epa.gov/ncea/risk/index.htm

US Environmental Protection Agency (EPA), Office of the Science Advisor. (2004). Risk management: Principles & practices. Retrieved February 15, 2012, from http://www.epa.gov/osa/pdfs/ratf-final.pdf

Industrial Union Department v. American Petroleum Institute, 448 US 607 (1980).

Berkshire's authors and editors welcome questions, comments, and corrections. Send your emails about the *Berkshire Encyclopedia of Sustainability* in general or this volume in particular to: sustainability.updates@berkshirepublishing.com

Shipping and Freight Indicators

Marine transportation occurs within fragile ecosystems. Environmental performance indicators measure the impact of shipping operations on the biosphere, the atmosphere, and the hydrosphere. With growth in world traffic, however, the development of indicators must consider transportation service worldwide through systems combining port and ship transportation, integrating technical and policy innovations to permit shipping to exploit its sustainability assets as competitive advantages.

Growth in the volume of merchandise carried by sea is one of the major phenomena of world trade. Seaborne trade amounts to more than 30 trillion ton-miles, accounting for 90 percent of world trade. Day-to-day maritime transport operations founded on ship movements and maintenance have significant impact on ecosystems. Shipping freight indicators refer to a range of measures used to assess the effectiveness of the shipping industry's environmental management program. Such a program requires the adoption of practices and technologies that allow the achievement of high environmental quality standards.

Environmental Issues of Shipping

The main environmental issues pertaining to maritime shipping relate to water quality, air quality, and waste management.

A wide range of shipping activities can modify water quality, such as disposal of ballast water and wastewater from ships. All ships use ballast water, which is pumped on board to ensure stability at sea for the safety of crew, freight, and vessel. Ballast water helps control a ship's stability and draft and modify its center of gravity in relation to the cargo carried and variance in weight distribution. Ballast water acquired in one region may contain aquatic species that, when discharged in another region, may thrive in a new marine environment and disrupt the natural marine ecosystem.

Wastewater, also generated by all ships, comes from galleys, showers, kitchens, medical facilities, animal waste disposal, and bilge waters from machinery and auxiliary systems. The discharge of wastewater that is biologically or chemically active also can damage marine life. An average 250,000-ton bulk carrier can take between 75,000 and 100,000 tons of ballast water on a single trip. The ship's thirty crew members will generate approximately 10,000 liters of wastewater.

The average distance covered in maritime trade is rising, which reflects the expansion of Latin American and west African commerce in east Asia. Long-haul trade of commodities is creating a demand for additional tonnage in the world carrier fleet and increasing traffic on the world oceans. The resulting increase in emissions negatively affects the atmosphere. Vessels can release toxic pollutants from fuel combustion, container and cargo refrigeration, insulation around pipes, air-conditioning, and onboard incinerators. Some activities produce greenhouse gases that prevent the wavelengths of electromagnetic radiation from leaving the Earth's surface and thus contribute to global warming. A ship affects climate principally through its emissions of carbon dioxide (CO_2), nitrogen oxide (NO_x), sulfur dioxide (SO_2), and particles.

Other forms of waste follow the growth in maritime trade. A vessel's daily operations at sea or in ports might discharge organic matter and plastic materials containing high levels of bacteria that are harmful to human health and to marine ecosystems, thereby creating or exacerbating serious environmental problems.

Environment as a Competitive Factor

Environmental problems are eroding the income of shipping lines and preventing them from benefiting from the increased demand for maritime transport. For instance, a series of tanker accidents during the 1960s and 1970s led to major oil spills and compelled vessels to change routes, leading to loss of productivity and flexibility. The rising average temperature of the Earth's surface has reduced snow cover of the polar regions, with the melt contributing to sea level rise and greater ocean heat content, both of which affect navigation routes. Some navigation channels have been adversely affected by changes in coastal ecosystems caused by invasive species. As well, smog has impeded visibility and downgraded the quality of life on board ships; and submerged, floating plastics, metals, or wood debris hamper ship movement at sea as well as in berthing operations. In 2011, major shipping lines were rerouted in the South Pacific after the Greek container-ship *Rena* ran aground on a reef off New Zealand and spilled hazardous materials.

Growing awareness of the impact of environmental problems on shipping safety and profitability led to the adoption of various international conventions in terms of responsibility and compensation. These conventions represent an important breakthrough in terms of environmental protection norms against pollution by ships from operational or accidental causes. The main reference is the International Convention for the Prevention of Pollution from Ships (the MARPOL Convention).

The International Maritime Organization (IMO) is the primary entity responsible for providing regulation and practices related to all technical aspects involving shipping. Since 1958, the IMO has adopted over forty conventions and more than eight hundred rules, codes, and recommendations concerning marine safety, marine pollution prevention and control, and related issues.

The implementation of international quality standards forces marine carriers to redesign their fleets and network in order to promote environmental innovations and to adopt a series of metrics for assessing their environmental performance related to vessel movement, ship engine-room activities, and loading and unloading operations. In 2010, Maersk, the world's leading container shipping line, placed orders for up to twenty so-called EEE (environment, economies, efficiency) container ships. These vessels focus on fuel efficiency, bunker savings per container carried, reductions in carbon dioxide, and on the fact that the vessels will be designed for slow steaming, effecting fuel savings and environmental impact.

Quantifying Shipping Freight Sustainability

A range of measures is used to quantify shipping freight sustainability, depending on the nature of the environmental issue(s) identified by shipping lines. Measures for water quality, for example, may include salinity, temperature, suspended solids, and oxygen level. Air quality might be assessed by amount of carbon dioxide, methane, nitrous oxide, sulfur oxide, and particulate dust. Waste measurement can include volume of nonbiodegradable marine debris, while habitat and ecosystems may be measured in terms of range of biodiversity. Reduction in consumption of water, electricity, fuel, or chemicals can be reported as indicators of performance.

A grid system is the most commonly used method of assessing environmental responsibilities and establishing benchmarks for environmental performance concerning shipping and ship-related issues. The grid approach has found application in Canada, the United States, Australia, and the European Union. Under this method, each indicator is defined by a grid composed of several levels. The criteria applicable to each level are specific to an environmental issue. Table 1 (below) summarizes the actions corresponding to a five-level grid system used by Green Marine, an initiative between the United States and Canada to manage

TABLE 1. Shipping Corporate Actions and Performance Indicators

Level	Criteria
1	Compliance with environmental legislation
2	Systematic use of a definite number of best practices
3	Integrating best practices within corporate strategies
4	Introduction of new technologies
5	Excellence and leadership

Source: Green Marine (2010).

shipping-related environmental issues in North America. In this system, the criteria of a previous level must be fulfilled before advancing to the next level, so that shipping firms will establish continuous improvement of their environmental performance. This type of measurement system allows progress to be observed and assessed while comparing environmental performance to other industry stakeholders.

Monitoring Changes

Enforcing environmental management systems for shipping comes up against three difficulties. First, data on the results of efforts to meet environmental obligations are often incomplete. Second, monitoring is subject to national legal systems. Third, international convention provides few mechanisms to enforce environmental legislation.

Environmental monitoring programs for the shipping industry include industry self-regulation and control imposed by a coastal state, by a ship's flag state, or by a port state. Organizations such as Lloyd's Register of Shipping in Britain and Bureau Veritas in France offer services in risk assessment and management, with a view toward improving standards for environmental quality. Countries with coastline have the right to take legal action to protect their waters and ecosystems from substandard ships. Countries participating in international environmental conventions are required to enforce the controls of the conventions on ships that bear their flag. Port authorities within states that are signatories to the various international environmental conventions have the right to inspect for environmental compliance any ship entering the port, regardless of its flag. These measures testify to efforts to enforce international environmental conventions. While these enforcement measures can be improved in terms of legal obligations and fines, they represent the most efficient method to constrain marine transport operations to conform to local, national, and international regulations.

Varied Conditions

The environmental strategies pursued by the shipping industry are molded by three primary elements and processes. First, shipping firms are exposed to different environmental forces and will behave differently; for instance, shipping in the Arctic encounters geographical and weather conditions far different from the Caribbean Sea. Second, globalization has given rise to a complex web of stakeholder relationships, and ships are open systems influenced by changes in world trade. The physical handling of commodities links ocean transport, ports, and hinterland transportation units, so that any environmental initiative undertaken by one component of the transportation chain affects the others. Third, the financial market has integrated environmental performance into its assessment of shipping enterprises, with banks implementing credit programs that charge different interest rates in relation to environmental performance and insurance companies fixing premiums according to a vessel's green certification. Lloyd's Register of Shipping, the marine insurance company, is lowering premiums for shipping companies that possess a recognized environmental management certificate. In the charter market, a well-maintained ship is easier to place and is often requested for the movement of high-value goods. The shipping companies Leif Höegh of Norway and Wallenius Lines of Sweden, use silicone-based paints. These coatings are more expensive than other types of anti-fouling paints, but they keep the hull free from organisms and enable the carriers to reduce the consumption of fuel oil, consequently reducing the amount of air pollutant emissions.

Controversies and Challenges

Maritime transport has an impact on the environment as a result of rising technical capacities to improve navigation. The effects of engineering works, such as dams, dredging, breakwaters, and seawalls, are often irreversible. Some of the most vulnerable ecosystems have been transformed or destroyed, others have appeared, some have even been artificially created to such an extent that it is extremely difficult to identify a pristine reference. In Japan, there are more than 9,000 kilometers of artificial coasts built by reclamation techniques, along the Inland Sea and in the Tokyo, Ise, and Osaka Bays. Construction of the Three Gorges Dam project in Sichuan Province, China, has flooded 1,000 square kilometers, raised the water level on the upper Yangzi River by 200 meters, and created a new inland lake 700 kilometers long. This allows strings of barges totalling 10,000 deadweight tons to reach the port of Chongqing, which is located 2,500 kilometers from the sea.

All coastal communities are confronted with a dilemma: either the oceans offer an enormous resource potential that must be exploited to answer global demand for water, energy, and fishing products, or they act as a climate regulator maintaining the natural equilibrium of the planet and thus require protection. The answer to this dilemma is inscribed technically in planning practices compatible with marine ecosystems, and politically in the search for compromise between protection and planning that often implies a modification of the ecological order. The best practices are founded on the rehabilitation of contaminated sites and on the creation of new ecosystems. The construction company Gammon from Hong Kong, China, has undertaken site remediation of a former shipyard on northern Tsing Yi island in Hong Kong. The project has been permitted to extract heavy metals and to reduce the amount of money spent on cement by 30 percent. The port authority of Montreal has increased the ecological potential of selected islands on the Saint Lawrence River. The objective is to use the improvement of these environmental areas as compensation for future port development.

Extended Impact

The adoption of environmental management approaches by the shipping industry is leading to innovative development of new indicators, advanced ship design, and complex environmental adaptation rationales. Leading international manufacturers and retailers such as Ikea, Walmart, Nike, and the Home Depot are requesting shipping lines to include environmental performance of product transport into their corporate footprint. Adopting environmentally sustainable policies is becoming an advantage in stock market capitalizations where shareholders are seeking shipping lines that realize economies by becoming more environmentally compatible. In addition, the aging of the world fleet raises the issue of ship recycling. A ship's hull may contain hazardous substances, such as asbestos, heavy metals, hydrocarbons, and products known to deplete the ozone layer. This requires an assessment of risk presented by substandard ships and on the importance of the legal responsibilities of shipowners. The best practices focus on the establishment of a ship quality index, increasing the number of ship inspections in ports of call, and the construction of quality ships so as to facilitate safe and environmentally sound recycling. Companies that respect the directives on ship recycling can obtain a Green Passport from the IMO. (A Green Passport was created by the IMO's guidelines on ship recycling; it is a document that lists all potentially hazardous materials used in a ship's construction, updated with any subsequent changes in materials or equipment, and delivered with the vessel to the recycling yard.)

The quality of ships in operation is becoming a more important competitive factor on global markets, leading to the development of new indicators, as well as policies and programs relating to coastal erosion, noise, antifouling paints, and dredging. Work is being carried out to develop atmosphere and ocean free-emission vessels. This is being addressed by various shipping yards where new designs include ballast-free ships equipped with sails made of photovoltaic panels, in which a constant flow of seawater flows through a network of pipes running from bow to stern below the waterline, and power comes from the sun, wind, and waves. Technological innovators are seeking recyclable lightweight composite materials to counter different wear-and-tear challenges, reduce maintenance costs, improve ship efficiency, and ensure optimum environmental protection. In terms of policy orientation and practice, the results of shipping indicators permit critical assessment of two major tendencies: the adoption of naval technology compatible with the environment and human modification of the genetic material of different marine plants with a view to increase their resistance to changing environmental conditions.

Future Outlook

As commercial exchange continues to grow worldwide, the maritime transport system will quickly become highly solicited. But environmental challenges are determining factors in the process of globalization, and regions that have environmental problems are not competitive at the global scale. The operations of ships and ports will become increasingly affected by countries implementing complex systems of differential charging for environmental purposes, such as congestion fees as well as fines and fees for polluting emissions, waste management, and energy efficiency—all of which will be built into shipping costs. Nonetheless, shipping remains the most ecological mode of transport, and to exploit its sustainability assets as competitive advantages, it must continually integrate technical and policy innovations into its blueprint.

Claude COMTOIS
Université de Montréal

See also Air Pollution Indicators and Monitoring; Carbon Footprint; Energy Efficiency Measurement; Life Cycle Assessment (LCA); Life Cycle Costing (LCC); Life Cycle Management (LCM); Social Life Cycle Assessment (S-LCA); Supply Chain Management; Triple Bottom Line

FURTHER READING

Comtois, Claude, & Slack, Brian. (2007). Sustainable development and corporate strategies of the maritime industry. In James Wang, Daniel Olivier, Theo Notteboom & Brian Slack (Eds.), *Ports, cities, and global supply chains* (pp. 233–245). Aldershot, UK: Ashgate.

Corbett, James J., & Fischbeck, Paul S. (2000). Emissions from waterborne commerce vessels in United States continental and inland waterways. *Environmental Science and Technology, 34*(15), 3254–3260.

Freimann, Juergen, & Walther, Michael. (2001). The impacts of corporate environmental management systems: A comparison of EMAS and ISO 14001. *Greener Management International, 36,* 91–103.

Green Marine. (2010). *Self-evaluation guide: Green marine environmental program: Shipowners.* Quebec City, Canada: Société de développement économique du Saint-Laurent (SODES).

Harrison, David, Jr.; Radov, Daniel; & Patchett, James. (2004). *Evaluation of the feasibility of alternative market-based mechanisms to promote low-emission shipping in the European Union sea areas: A report for the European Commission, Directorate-General Environment.* London: NERA Economic Consulting.

Kågeson, Per. (1999). *Economic instruments for reducing emissions from sea transport* (Air Pollution and Climate Series No. 11, T&E report 99/7). Solna, Sweden: The Swedish NGO Secretariat on Acid Rain, the European Federation for Transport and Environment (T&E), and the European Environmental Bureau (EEB).

Kolb, Alexander, & Wacker, Manfred. (1995). Calculation of energy consumption and pollutant emissions on freight transport routes. *Science of the Total Environment, 169*(1–3), 283–288.

Ringbom, Henrik. (1999). Preventing pollution from ships: Reflections on the "adequacy" of existing rules. *Review of European Community and International Environmental Law, 8*(1), 21–28.

Wooldridge, Christopher F.; McMullen, Christopher; & Howe, Vicki. (1999). Environmental management of ports and harbours: Implementation of policy through scientific monitoring. *Marine Policy, 23*(4–5), 413–425.

Social Life Cycle Assessment (S-LCA)

Social life cycle assessment is a product assessment technique for evaluating the social and socioeconomic aspects, as well as their potential positive and negative impacts, throughout a product's life cycle—from extraction and processing of raw materials, through manufacturing, distribution, use, reuse, maintenance, and recycling, to final disposal. Because the technique is still in its infancy, however, it requires further development in methodology and operations.

The global economic scenario has been in a phase of continuous change, owing to the deterioration of ecological balance, the spread of social inequalities around the world, and the controversial effects of growth and related production and consumption models.

The guiding principle of sustainable development has shifted from a focus on the environment to a broader and more complex dimension. Sustainable development has come to be considered a vector of environmentally and socially desirable objectives, such as increasing real income per capita, creating more-equitable income distribution, enabling broader access to resources, maintaining and increasing environmental quality, improving public health and education, ensuring the basic freedoms, and establishing social equity and cohesion.

In terms of the business community, sustainability implies an ongoing commitment to promoting corporate social responsibility by integrating environmental and social issues into long-term company strategies.

The implications for the twenty-first century are that the profit motive is not sufficient as a goal: economic systems should be based on socially responsible firms that address their strategies and operations toward all pillars of sustainable development, taking into consideration the triple bottom line: economy, society, and environment.

In this scenario, life cycle approaches for product and process assessment play a key role in achieving sustainability in all its dimensions through the implementation of life cycle management (LCM), an integrated concept for managing the total life cycle of goods and services toward more-sustainable production and consumption models. The basic tool for supporting the integration of LCM into business management is environmental life cycle assessment (E-LCA), normally referred to as life cycle assessment (LCA). This standardized methodology evaluates the environmental impacts of a product generated over its entire life cycle, from raw material acquisition or natural resource production to the disposal of the product at the end of its life. Therefore, criteria rated in the traditional LCA consider only environmental aspects of a product's life cycle, as compared to addressing possible trade-offs between environmental protection and both economic and social concerns (Dreyer, Hauschild, and Schierbeck 2006).

The economic counterpart of LCA is environmental life cycle costing (E-LCC), a newer tool used for assessing all costs, internal and external, related to a product during its entire life cycle, from production to use, maintenance, and disposal. It addresses the economic impact of a product whose environmental performance is analyzed using LCA.

Social life cycle assessment (S-LCA), the least developed life cycle method, is an assessment technique for evaluating the social and socioeconomic aspects of products and their possible positive and negative impacts, encompassing the extraction and processing of raw materials, manufacturing, distribution, use, reuse, maintenance, recycling, and ultimate disposal (UNEP/SETAC 2010).

Social life cycle assessment complements E-LCA and LCC with social and socioeconomic features. Their integration provides a more comprehensive profile of product sustainability through different perspectives on its life cycle impacts, and by offering a system-oriented toolbox for the LCM approach.

The S-LCA Framework

Researchers and policy makers have been conducting studies on the development of S-LCA in order to discuss and define methodologies for assessing a product system, taking into account social criteria (Fava et al. 1993; Klöpffer 2003; Dreyer, Hauschild, and Schierbeck 2006; Griesshammer et al. 2006; Hunkeler 2006; Jorgensen et al. 2008; Klöpffer 2008).

In 2009, an important step forward in methodology development and standardization came with the publication of the *Guidelines for Social Life Cycle Assessment of Products* by the United Nations Environment Programme (UNEP), the Society of Environmental Toxicology and Chemistry (SETAC), and the Life Cycle Initiative. The methodological framework provided in these guidelines closely follows the LCA method, as described by the International Organization for Standardization (ISO) in its standard ISO 14040 (ISO 2006). Both LCA and S-LCA present similarities and significant differences. Their object of study is the same—the product life cycle—but while LCA is concerned with the evaluation of environmental impacts, S-LCA assesses social and socioeconomic impacts. Another important difference concerns the type of impact: environmental impacts tend to be negative, whereas impacts in the social sphere may be either negative or positive. As concerns application, both S-LCA and LCA can be used during product design, product comparisons, marketing and reporting, procurement considerations, and supplier evaluations.

The essence of S-LCA is the information describing the product life cycle, the processes involved, and the focus on the participation and involvement of stakeholders. The latter play a core role in the S-LCA framework and may be classified in five main categories:

1. workers/employees
2. local community
3. society (national and global)
4. consumers (covering end consumers as well as consumers who are part of each link in the supply chain)
5. value chain actors

Additional categories of stakeholders (e.g., nongovernment organizations, public authorities, and future generations) as well as a further list of subcategories are envisaged and recommended in the guidelines.

The S-LCA process draws on the same four main phases used in LCA:

1. definition of goal and scope
2. life cycle inventory (LCI) analysis
3. impact assessment (IA)
4. interpretation

The first phase describes the study by defining the goal and scope pursued, the system boundaries, the functional unit, and the reference flows.

In the LCI analysis, data are collected, and a hot-spot assessment is carried out. The latter provides information on where the most relevant potential social impacts—in terms of risk or opportunity—may be located within the product life cycle. Life cycle inventory is one of the most demanding aspects of S-LCA, particularly as it relates to the lack of databases for hot-spot screening.

In the IA phase, inventory information is translated into impact categories using a four-step approach: classification, characterization, normalization, and valuation. Many methodological approaches are available for IA, characterized by significant differences with respect to their design and, consequently, their outcomes (Hunkeler 2006; Weidema 2006; UNEP/SETAC 2010). Accordingly, these approaches represent an open field for future research on information for inventory and impact assessment.

Finally, the interpretation phase summarizes and discusses the results obtained as a basis for conclusions, recommendations, and decision making relative to the goal and scope of the study.

As evidenced, S-LCA methodology substantially reflects the LCA framework, adapted principally to the following aspects: greater importance to geographical location and the relevant use of site-specific data; integration of management practices assessment; a more prominent use of subjective data; and qualitative and semiquantitative—which are often more meaningful than quantitative—indicators and methods (Benoît and Vickery-Niederman 2010).

Outlook and Implications

Because S-LCA is still in its infancy, it requires further improvements in methodology. Although the UNEP/SETAC/Life Cycle Initiative *Guidelines* provide a well-articulated procedural framework and practical guide to all the steps of S-LCA, considerable research is still needed in order to develop more-systemic and more-standardized pathways.

Consequently, in order for S-LCA to be used for promoting in-depth knowledge, informed decision making, and improved social conditions in the product life cycle, it is essential to unravel the critical and unresolved issues that comprise this assessment technique. Some of these issues still negatively affect mainstream LCA, the only ISO-standardized tool in life cycle methodologies.

A potential road map to follow that will facilitate the widespread use of S-LCA should privilege the definition of generally accepted indicators, the development of scoring and weighting systems, the improvement and integration of existing databases, and, above all, practical applications in empirical case studies.

Stefania SUPINO
Salerno University

See also Business Reporting Methods; Design Quality Indicator (DQI); International Organization for Standardization (ISO); Life Cycle Assessment (LCA); Life Cycle Costing (LCC); Life Cycle Management (LCM); Material Flow Analysis (MFA); Social Network Analysis (SNA); Supply Chain Analysis; Taxation Indicators, Green; Triple Bottom Line

FURTHER READING

Bauer, Ramond A. (Ed.). (1966). *Social indicators*. Cambridge, MA: MIT Press.
Benoît, Catherine, et al. (2010). The guideline for social life cycle assessment of products: Just in time! *International Journal of Life Cycle Assessment, 15*(2), 156–163.
Benoît, Catherine, & Vickery-Niederman, Gina. (2010). *Social sustainability assessment literature review* (White Paper No. 102). Retrieved December 7, 2011, from http://www.sustainabilityconsortium.org/wp-content/themes/sustainability/assets/pdf/whitepapers/Social_Sustainability_Assessment.pdf
Benoît, Catherine, & Mazijn, Bernard. (Eds.). (2009). *Guidelines for social life cycle assessment of products*. Nairobi, Kenya: United Nations Environment Programme/Society for Environmental Toxicology and Chemistry.
Dreyer, Louise Camilla; Hauschild, Michael Z.; & Schierbeck, Jens. (2006). A framework for social life cycle impact assessment. *International Journal of Life Cycle Assessment, 11*(2), 88–97.
Fava, James, et al. (1993). A conceptual framework for life-cycle impact assessment (Workshop Report). Pensacola, FL: Society for Environmental Toxicology and Chemistry (SETAC).
Griesshammer, Rainer, et al. (2006). *Feasibility study: Integration of social aspects into LCA*. Freiburg, Germany: Öko-Institut.
Hunkeler, David. (2006). Societal LCA methodology and case study. *International Journal of Life Cycle Assessment, 11*(6), 371–382.
International Organization for Standardization (ISO) 14040. (2006). *Environmental management—Life cycle assessment—Principles and framework*. Geneva: International Organization for Standardization.
Jorgensen, Andreas; Le Bocq, Agathe; Nazarkina, Liudmila; & Hauschild, Michael Z. (2008). Methodologies for social life cycle assessment. *International Journal of Life Cycle Assessment, 13*(2), 96–103.
Klöpffer, Walter. (2003). Life-cycle based methods for sustainable product development. *International Journal of Life Cycle Assessment, 8*(3), 157–159.
Klöpffer, Walter. (2008). Life-cycle sustainability assessment of products. *International Journal of Life Cycle Assessment, 13*(2), 89–94.
Swarr, Thomas E. (2009). Societal life cycle assessment—Could you repeat the question? *International Journal of Life Cycle Assessment, 14*(4), 285–289.
United Nations Environment Programme (UNEP), Society for Environmental Toxicology and Chemistry (SETAC) & Life Cycle Initiative. (2009). *Guidelines for Social Life Cycle Assessment of Products*. Retrieved December 7, 2011, from http://www.unep.fr/shared/publications/pdf/DTIx1164xPA-guidelines_sLCA.pdf
United Nations Environment Programme/Society for Environmental Toxicology and Chemistry (UNEP/SETAC). (2010). Methodological sheets for 31 sub-categories of impact: For consultation. Retrieved December 8, 2011, from http://lcinitiative.unep.fr/default.asp?site=lcinit&page_id=A8992620-AAAD-4B81-9BAC-A72AEA281CB9
Weidema, Bo P. (2006). The integration of economic and social aspects in life cycle impact assessment. *International Journal of Life Cycle Assessment, 11*(Special issue 1), 89–96.

Social Network Analysis (SNA)

Social network analysis (SNA) studies relations between persons, organizations, or other social groups, mapping and measuring them in order to better understand human behavior. SNA has increasingly been applied to understanding how knowledge is shared among groups involved in managing ecosystems such as fisheries, nature reserves, and urban parks. For practical managers, SNA helps identify knowledgeable people to include in resource management discussions.

How people are organized into groups, communities, and nations influences their abilities to sustainably use nature and the environment. Social network analysis (SNA) supplies a tool that measures the network of relations between people and organizations that are linked to a natural resource, be it fish, crops, or an urban park. By analyzing the network, one can not only identify how groups can contribute to the management of a resource but also start understanding how certain communities can take action toward protecting nature and using resources more sustainably. While traditional resource theories treated people as detached economic agents or analyzed rules outside their social context, SNA's main contribution lies in depicting and analyzing the complexity of social relations in connection to natural resources. SNA is mainly a researcher's tool, but there are efforts underway to adapt it to use in practice by conservation and resource managers.

Historical Background

Since the rise of the Internet, Twitter, and Facebook, social networks and networking have rapidly been popularized. The formal study of social networks can be traced to 1932, however, when the US-based social psychologist Jacob Moreno and his colleague Helen Jennings studied runaways from a girls' school in upstate New York. They concluded that their actions had less to do with the girls' individual attributes and personalities than with their friendship ties, which had been mapped by Moreno and Jennings. Who they were friends with, and who they were not friends with, established their position in the social network and "provided channels for the flow of social influence and ideas among the girls in a way that even the girls themselves may not have been conscious of" (Borgatti et al. 2009, 892).

Application to Environmental Management

Three key assumptions are necessary in every SNA study: what is an actor (or node), what constitutes a tie (or link), and what is the boundary of the system (network). Moreno, for instance, drew a boundary around the school, excluding the girls' relations to parents and friends outside the school and relations to adults working at the school. In environmental studies, a researcher typically composes a list of all actors linked to a natural resource, for instance fishers that use a certain fishing area. Columns for relations are then added so that each actor can indicate its relations to all others on the list. In gathering this data, a matrix can be created that describes the relations between all actors being studied (as in figure 1, on page 323, on the left). Descriptive data (called attributes) are also added, like gender or the number of years of fishing. The selection of studies below describes how researchers have dealt with these assumptions and how networks are analyzed at different levels. The examples also demonstrate SNA's general applicability in marine, terrestrial, and urban resource systems, and on various continents and under various climate conditions.

Figure 1. Representations of Social Network Analysis Measurement

Matrix of relations

Visualization of a social network

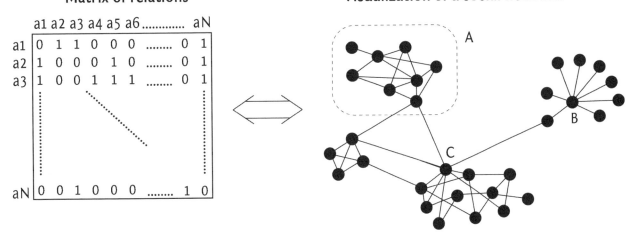

Source: author.

Social network analysis (SNA) is used to visualize and analyze relations between humans and organizations. The systematic recording of relations into a square matrix, as shown on the left, often comes from interviews or archival data. Based on graph theory from mathematics, software programs measure properties of the resultant network pattern, as shown on the right. Those actors or nodes with more relations to each other make up (A) cohesive subgroups, which could indicate they have a shared understanding of the world. Those with many ties, being "popular," have (B) high degree centrality, with increased ability to influence others. Those placed on network paths in between many others have (C) high betweenness centrality, with increased potential to control information flow in the network beyond their immediate social surrounding. These are just a few among many different measurements used in SNA.

A long-standing problem of natural resource management is how to avoid the tragedy that occurs when those depending on the same resource each take out more than the resource can replenish (Ostrom 1990). SNA can bring a fresh view to understanding why this happens. The Swedish system ecologists Beatrice Crona and Örjan Bodin used SNA to study the case of fish resource depletion in a coastal village in Kenya, Africa. Visiting 80 percent of all 206 households and using a village map to facilitate data generation, they measured the network of information sharing about marine and fish resources. Their result demonstrated that those using the same fishing method communicated more with each other (forming cohesive subgroups) and shared a similar knowledge about the resource (Crona and Bodin 2006). Consequently, while older resource theories have depicted communities as being homogeneous, this study demonstrated the complexity by which a network of users interacts with a common resource. In using SNA further, they also concluded that the group of migrant deep-sea fishermen was placed most centrally in the network. Crona and Bodin suggested that although most groups recognized resource depletion, their inability to take action against it was partly due to the reality that the group in the most influential network position had the least sense of community, and they had tools and methods that made them less dependent on the local resource. SNA allowed researchers to systematically visualize and understand the community structure and, from there, inform interventions.

Urban parks and woodlands are crucial resources in many cities, as they bring recreational space, improve air quality, and provide habitat for animals. With pressure to develop houses, roads, and shopping centers, however, there is a continual struggle to sustain parks as urban public resources. The Swedish urban social ecologists Henrik Ernstson, Sverker Sörlin, and Thomas Elmqvist used SNA to study how civic groups could achieve the collective power to protect a large urban park area in Stockholm, Sweden. They sent out a survey to generate data on collaborative ties among forty-seven civic organizations that had successfully protected a vast park landscape. From this pattern of ties, they deduced that the network consisted of a small core of six organizations plus forty-one user groups more loosely tied to each other in a peripheral position; the latter included boating clubs, riding clubs, and community gardeners (Ernstson, Sörlin, and Elmqvist 2008). SNA revealed that collective power resides in the network itself, since the network structure helped the civic groups to divide tasks and coordinate effectively. While the core group, who had learned about the intricate details of urban planning, could stop big exploitation plans, the periphery's user groups, who spent time in the park almost daily, could detect smaller exploitation threats, like the building of a car park. SNA demonstrated that the ability to protect the park was not held by single organizations or leaders, as is often portrayed, but by how the network was "wired." Importantly, as with any network structure, this one was not designed by a single actor but had emerged through a myriad of interactions that over time had produced network-level mechanisms.

While the above two examples demonstrate SNA as a device for the scholar, the US and European sociologists Christina Prell, Mark Reed, and Klaus Hubacek have put forward SNA as a practitioner's tool to identify knowledgeable resource users to include in so-called stakeholder dialogues. Measuring a communication network around the Peak District National Park in the United Kingdom, they identified eight persons, from over sixty names, who could contribute most to a dialogue being planned. They based this on two criteria for which SNA was crucial: on one hand, these eight persons enhanced the diversity of users to enrich deliberations of how to use the Peak District in ways most users could agree upon; on the other hand, these persons tended to have a network position in between various groups and thus would be the most effective to spread their experience of the dialogues throughout the whole network. Prell, Hubacek, and Reed (2009) argue that this brings out a practical value of SNA: it helps to select persons to enrich dialogues while spreading experiences across a wide range of user groups. This improves the condition of learning about a resource beyond those individuals participating in dialogues, which in turn could facilitate a mutual understanding of a resource system and mitigate conflicts, reaching a more favorable use of resources for different users.

An important effort to expand SNA into the environmental sciences is toward social-ecological network analysis (SENA), where humans and ecological entities can be analyzed as part of a single network (Cumming et al. 2010). Initial efforts attempt to record relations of how civic actors protect certain urban parks, or fishers select certain fishing sites.

There are a growing number of empirical SNA studies, several gathered in *Social Networks and Natural Resource Management* (Bodin and Prell 2011) and in a special issue in the free online journal *Ecology and Society* (Crona and Hubacek 2010). Studies include marine social networks from Loreto Bay in Mexico, Chesapeake Bay in the United States, and coastal Chile; agrarian advice networks in Ghana; watershed governance networks in Tanzania; inland fisheries networks in northern Sweden; forest management networks in British Colombia, Canada; and urban civic networks in Chicago, Illinois. A further resource is the online e-community NASEBERRY.

Validity, Controversies, and Variations

Although many real situations can be coded into actors, ties, and networks, it is important to be cautious. First, what the analyst considers an actor or node needs to be stable; for instance an organization that is only short-lived does not make a stable collector of ties and cannot serve as a unit for analysis. Second, when it comes to ties or links, it is worth remembering why researchers think networks matter; while Moreno posited that they conveyed influence, in an early study of environmental management, the professor of political science Mark Schneider and colleagues argued that since networks span organizational boundaries, they provide details of what works and does not work in different organizations (Schneider et al. 2003). Consequently, those involved in a network will presumably learn about and negotiate more effective ways to coordinate organizations to carry out joint action than if a network did not exist. Importantly, the network's effects, such as coordination and learning, hinge on an assumption that networks are the result of repeated and local interaction among pairs of actors. Importantly, any relation recorded as a tie in the network matrix should not be transient or momentary but should be persistent enough to be able to carry information that both actors can understand, and from which they can learn and co-create a joint behavior. For the empirical researcher, and for practitioners venturing to use SNA, this forms a rule of thumb that increases the validity of the method: relations should have left traces, either in historical archives (the documentation of collaborative projects, attendance lists at meetings, co-authorship of reports, etc.), or in persons' memories that can be assessed in interviews using a prepared list of actors as described above.

Impact and Long-Term Development

Two developments will most probably increase the use of SNA for studying environmental management: the increasing human pressure on Earth's ecosystems, from local fishing pressure to global carbon dioxide emissions, and the recognition by ecologists that ecosystems are not like static machines but are complex, interlinked, and continuously changing. This increases the need for humans to collaborate and learn more about the natural world. No longer can environmental management be handled by hierarchical state agencies alone; rather, more participatory arrangements that facilitate learning need to be nurtured. SNA can be used to prepare and analyze such attempts and at the same time assist with interventions, for instance in identifying knowledgeable users. While network analysis is further pursued in various fields, from sociology and biology to computer modeling and physics (Borgatti et al. 2009), tools and methods within SNA are bound to evolve as one field borrows from another. For sustainability science, three developments seem crucial: studying how network structures change over time (Frank 2011), understanding how to arrange management for larger geographical entities (Ernstson et al. 2010; Newig, Günther, and Pahl-Wostl 2010), and development of the SENA approach, which by analyzing social and ecological nodes in the same network seems especially promising for clarifying how humanity and ecosystems are interwoven.

Henrik ERNSTSON

University of Cape Town & Stockholm University

See also Citizen Science; Community and Stakeholder Input; Computer Modeling; Ecosystem Health Indicators; Fisheries Indicators, Freshwater; Fisheries Indicators, Marine; Focus Groups; Geographic Information Systems (GIS); Long-Term Ecological Research (LTER); Sustainability Science; Systems Thinking; Transdisciplinary Research

FURTHER READING

Belaire, J. Amy; Dribin, Andrew K.; Johnston, Douglas P.; Lynch, Douglas J.; & Minor, Emily S. (2011). Mapping stewardship networks in urban ecosystems. *Conservation Letters, 4*(6), 464–473. doi:10.1111/j.1755-263X.2011.00200.x/full

Bodin, Örjan, & Crona, Beatrice. (2009). The role of social networks in natural resource governance: What relational patterns make a difference? *Global Environmental Change, 19,* 366–374.

Bodin, Örjan, & Norberg, Jon. (2005). Information network topologies for enhanced local adaptive management. *Environmental Management, 35*(2), 175–193.

Bodin, Örjan, & Prell, Christina. (Eds.). (2011). *Social networks and natural resource management: Uncovering the social fabric of environmental governance.* Cambridge, UK: Cambridge University Press.

Borgatti, Stephen P.; Mehra, Ajay; Brass, Daniel J.; & Labianca, Giuseppe. (2009). Network analysis in the social sciences. *Science, 323*(5916), 892–895.

Crona, Beatrice, & Bodin, Örjan. (2006). WHAT you know is WHO you know? Communication patterns among resource users as a prerequisite for co-management. *Ecology and Society, 11*(2), 7.

Crona, Beatrice, & Hubacek, Klaus. (2010). The right connections: How do social networks lubricate the machinery of natural resource governance? *Ecology and Society, 15*(4), 18. Retrieved January 4, 2012, from http://www.ecologyandsociety.org/vol15/iss4/art18/

Cumming, Graeme S.; Bodin, Örjan; Ernstson, Henrik; & Elmqvist, Thomas. (2010). Network analysis in conservation biogeography: Challenges and opportunities. *Diversity and Distributions, 16,* 414–425.

Emirbayer, Mustafa, & Goodwin, Jeff. (1994). Network analysis, culture and the problem of agency. *American Journal of Sociology, 99,* 1411–1454.

Ernstson, Henrik; Barthel, Stephan; Andersson, Erik; & Borgström, Sara T. (2010). Scale-crossing brokers and network governance of urban ecosystem services: The case of Stockholm. *Ecology and Society, 15*(4), 28. Retrieved January 4, 2012, from http://www.ecologyandsociety.org/vol15/iss4/art28/

Ernstson, Henrik, & Sörlin, Sverker. (2009). Weaving protective stories: Connective practices to articulate holistic values in Stockholm National Urban Park. *Environment and Planning A, 41*(6), 1460–1479.

Ernstson, Henrik; Sörlin, Sverker; & Elmqvist, Thomas. (2008). Social movements and ecosystem services: The role of social network structure in protecting and managing urban green areas in Stockholm. *Ecology and Society, 13*(2), 39. Retrieved January 4, 2012, from http://www.ecologyandsociety.org/vol13/iss2/art39/

Frank, Ken. (2011). Social network models for natural resource use and extraction. In Örjan Bodin & Christina Prell (Eds.), *Social networks and natural resource management: Uncovering the social fabric of environmental governance* (pp. 180–205). Cambridge, UK: Cambridge University Press.

Hanneman, Robert A., & Riddle, Mark. (2005). *Introduction to social network methods.* Riverside, CA: University of California. Retrieved January 4, 2012, from http://faculty.ucr.edu/~hanneman/

Maiolo, John R.; Johnson, Jeffrey; & Griffith, David. (1992). Applications of social science theory to fisheries management: Three examples. *Society & Natural Resources, 5*(4), 391–407.

Marín, Andrés, & Berkes, Fikret. (2010). Network approach for understanding small-scale fisheries governance: The case of the Chilean coastal co-management. *Marin Policy, 34*(5), 851–858.

Mendeley. (n.d.). NASEBERRY—network analysis in social-ecological studies. Retrieved February 15, 2012, from http://www.mendeley.com/groups/1306083/naseberry-network-analysis-in-social-ecological-studies/papers/

NASEBERRY: A community for "Network Analysis in Social-Ecological Studies." (n.d.). Homepage. Retrieved February 10, 2012, from http://www.naseberry.org

Newig, Jens; Günther, Dirk; & Pahl-Wostl, Claudia. (2010). Neurons in the network: Learning in governance networks in the context of environmental management. *Ecology and Society, 15*(4), 24. Retrieved January 4, 2012, from http://www.ecologyandsociety.org/vol15/iss4/art24/

Ostrom, Elinor. (1990). *Governing the commons: The evolution of institutions for collective action.* Cambridge, UK: Cambridge University Press.

Prell, Christina; Hubacek, Klaus; & Reed, Mark. (2009). Stakeholder analysis and social network analysis in natural resource management. *Society & Natural Resources, 22*(6), 501–518.

Schneider, Mark; Scholz, John; Lubell, Mark; Mindruta, Denisa; & Edwardsen, Matthew. (2003). Building consensual institutions: Networks and the National Estuary Program. *American Journal of Political Science, 47*(1), 143–158.

Scott, John. (2012). *Social network analysis. A handbook* (3rd ed.). London: Sage Publications.

Snijders, Tom A. B. (2001). The statistical evaluation of social network dynamics. *Sociological Methodology, 31*(1), 361–395.

Stein, Christian; Ernstson, Henrik; & Barron, Jennie. (2011). A social network approach to analyzing water governance: The case of the Mkindo catchment, Tanzania. *Physics and Chemistry of the Earth, 36,* 1085–1092.

Wasserman, Stanley, & Faust, Katherine. (1994). *Social network analysis: Methods and applications.* Cambridge, UK: Cambridge University Press.

Species Barcoding

For as long as scientists have measured DNA, it has been used to identify species, museum specimens, and other types of biological tissues. Recently, the use of shorter, standardized DNA sequences has increased the efficacy of this approach. But standardized genetic markers, such as DNA barcodes, depend on the existence of a library of reference sequences in order to be meaningful.

The number of named species—from plants and animals to fungi and protists—has been estimated at more than 1.7 million worldwide (IUCN 2011). The actual number of species, however, is likely to range from 3 million to 100 million (Gaston and Simon 2007).

Our ability to rapidly and accurately identify, measure, and monitor aspects of species population and diversity faces four challenges:

1. The actual number of species is not known, to within an order of magnitude (Gaston and Levin 2007).
2. Rates of species extinctions are higher than they have been at any time outside of the previous five mass extinction events (Barnosky et al. 2011).
3. Human-mediated species translocations will occur more frequently in a global economy (Lockwood, Cassey, and Blackburn 2005).
4. Taxonomists (the biologists who describe species diversity) are not being trained and replaced as quickly as they are retiring, which has resulted in a global phenomenon called the "taxonomic impediment." This term has been applied both to the shortage of taxonomic knowledge (as pertains to the undescribed or unrecognized portion of global diversity in nature) and also to the shortage of taxonomists and funding for taxonomy (House of Lords 2008).

Meeting these four challenges requires the integration of traditional and modern means of species identification. Using DNA as a tool for species and specimen identification is an important part of that modern tool kit.

DNA Barcode

A DNA barcode is a short, standardized DNA sequence used for the identification of specimens and species, as well as a tool for the discovery of previously unappreciated provisional species that are often morphologically cryptic (Floyd et al. 2002; Hebert et al. 2003). Where traditional sources of taxonomic knowledge exist, the DNA barcode can be used in concert with them (although it is not a replacement for such systems) and also as a transparent first-pass survey of a system or taxa where there is a paucity of other knowledge sources (Smith et al. 2009).

DNA barcode information, as characters or as distances, can help identify known species, perhaps from trace amounts of tissue, or a taxonomically nonlabile life history stage; also, it can be part of a suite of characters used for the discovery and description of new species, and the flagging of otherwise cryptic diversity.

Barcode Gap

Critical to successfully establishing a standardized marker for species identification was the selection of a gene or gene region that displayed low within-species (intraspecific) variation and larger between-species (interspecific) variation. Some have called the difference between these two types of variation the "barcoding gap." Calculating intraspecific variation requires the collection and analysis of multiple specimens from a single species across the range of the species. Failure to account for this potential geographic structuring of intraspecific variation (phylogeography) can lead to misidentification of an artificially large barcode gap.

Animal DNA Barcode

The standardized barcode region for animals is part of the cytochrome *c* oxidase 1 (CO1) mitochondrial gene. The efficacy of this gene was initially tested using diverse arthropod groups (Hebert et al. 2003). The CO1 barcode region fit the requirements of containing a region of sufficient variability (to discriminate even recently evolved species) that was flanked by relatively conserved regions (to enable the design of polymerase chain reaction primers that can be used across a wide taxonomic breadth). Selecting CO1 from among the other thirteen protein-coding mitochondrial genes was at least partially pragmatic, since many of the other markers would work; however, at the time (2002–2003) there were more arthropod CO1 sequences in GenBank than any of the other thirteen protein-coding mitochondrial genes. (See Library Creation and Analysis, below, for more about GenBank.)

Early thinking suggested that this arthropod CO1 stockpile would accelerate the completion of the library in one of the most diverse groups of metazoans. It was learned very quickly that the agreed-upon data standards by the barcoding community were high enough to prevent the inclusion of most of this early parcel of data.

The use of mitochondrial DNA (mtDNA) as a DNA barcode has led to some criticisms based on the mode of inheritance. Mitochondrial DNA is maternally inherited, and therefore if the species hybridizes, or has experienced introgression or incomplete lineage sorting, a mtDNA barcode would produce an erroneous answer—in the former case, the maternal species, and in the latter, an alternate or ancestral species.

Uses

The animal DNA barcode has several practical applications:

- It prevents consumer market fraud that occurs when a product is labeled incorrectly and the consumer is charged a higher price. If the product is biological, DNA barcodes can be used to monitor and test identifications; as when, for instance, the labeled ID of more than 30 percent of fish samples was contradicted by DNA barcoding, which raised both economic and health concerns (Lowenstein, Amato, and Kolokotronis 2009).

- It monitors the commercial trade of endangered species, particularly when the products are processed (Eaton et al. 2010).
- It ensures that we understand who eats whom in a pragmatic and repeatable fashion, which allows moving toward easily identified food web units (Smith et al. 2011).

Plant DNA Barcode

For plants, the search for a standardized region took longer to complete. The mtDNA marker selected for animals, CO1, does not possess sufficient nucleotide variation to identify most species. Botanists therefore searched for another marker, or small number of markers, that would permit a similarly precise and accurate standardized system of species and specimen identification. The botanical community has converged on a two-gene solution based on recoverability, sequence quality, and capacity for species discrimination (Hollingsworth et al. 2009). Like the animal marker, the two-loci combination of *rbcL*+*matK* is non-nuclear—and so is exposed to the same theoretical concerns regarding inheritance, in that a species and a single gene have not necessarily experienced the same types of selection and do not necessarily reveal the same answer.

Library Creation and Analysis

To facilitate the creation, curation, and analysis of various DNA barcoding loci, the barcoding community uses both the Barcode of Life Datasystem (BOLD) (Ratnasingham and Hebert 2007) and the more general, public genetic repository GenBank. A DNA-barcode-specific database, BOLD is an online workbench for DNA barcoding that is designed to aid in the collection, management, analysis, and use of DNA barcodes and associated metadata (e.g., photographs, GPS). As of 2011, BOLD contained more than 1.3 million specimens representing nearly 110,000 species. As total global diversity likely exceeds this total by one or two orders of magnitude, the creation of this critical reference library is not at the beginning of the end, but it is, perhaps, the end of the beginning.

GenBank created a restricted keyword—Barcode—to be used when a sequence meets the minimum data standards associated with a DNA barcoding initiative, such as the International Barcode of Life project (iBOL 2011). These standards, established by the Consortium for the Barcode of Life (CBOL 2011) and the National Center for Biotechnology Information (NCBI 2011), require that the sequence be from a community-agreed-upon gene locus (e.g., CO1 in eukaryotic animals or *rbcL* and *matK* in plants), that they trace files and specimen collection locality, and that they be of a minimum length (500 base pairs) and quality (fewer than 2 percent ambiguous bases).

Criticisms

Since the publication of the first DNA barcoding papers in the early twenty-first century, there have been criticisms of the efficacy of such an approach. Researchers using DNA barcodes were warned not to use the standard sequence typologically but rather as part of an integrative taxonomy. Concerns were also raised regarding the non-nuclear basis of both the animal and the plant barcodes—and how this would particularly bias species discovery by incorrectly labeling species that possess deep intraspecific variation as de novo species. In addition, worries about the effects of hybridization and introgression on these mitochondrial and plastid barcoding regions were raised. Hybridizing species and those possessing introgressed DNA are a challenge to nuclear or mitochondrial DNA-based identification systems—and indeed an integrative approach is necessary in order to capture the philosophical "fuzziness" (i.e., a non-Aristotelian definition) of what a "species" is. Others have asked why the apparently reductionist nature of the DNA barcoding endeavor (using one single gene or a small number of genes) would be pursued in an era when we expect the cost of sequencing entire genomes to continue to decline dramatically.

Future

Even though the cost of DNA sequencing will fall, it is likely that using a single, or a small number of, barcoding sequence(s) to identify specimens—and subsequently selecting from which of these to sequence entire genomes, when and if that is desirable—will stay the standard practice as sequencing costs for small fragments will remain comparatively more affordable. The key original elements remain critical: standardized selection of loci and the existence of a reference library of identified specimens.

M. Alexander SMITH
University of Guelph

See also Biological Indicators (*several articles*); Ecosystem Health Indicators; Fisheries Indicators, Freshwater; Fisheries Indicators, Marine; Global Strategy for Plant Conservation; Index of Biological Integrity (IBI);

Intergovernmental Science-Policy Platform on Biodiversity and Ecosystem Services (IPBES); Land-Use and Land-Cover Change

FURTHER READING

Barnosky, Anthony D., et al. (2011). Has the Earth's sixth mass extinction already arrived? *Nature, 471*(7336), 51–57.
Consortium for the Barcode of Life (CBOL). (2011). What is CBOL? Retrieved August 28, 2011, from http://www.barcodeoflife.org/content/about/what-cbol
Eaton, Mitchell J., et al. (2010). Barcoding bushmeat: Molecular identification of central African and South American harvested vertebrates. *Conservation Genetics, 11*(4), 1389–1404.
Floyd, Robin; Abebe, Eyualem; Papert, Artemis; & Blaxter, Mark. (2002). Molecular barcodes for soil nematode identification. *Molecular Ecology, 11*(4), 839–850.
Gaston, Kevin J., & Levin, Simon Asher. (2007). Global species richness. In Simon Asher Levin (Ed.), *Encyclopedia of biodiversity* (pp. 1–7). New York: Elsevier.
Hebert, Paul D. N.; Cywinska, Alina; Ball, Shelley L.; & deWaard, Jeremy R. (2003). Biological identifications through DNA barcodes. *Proceedings of the Royal Society—Biological Sciences, 270*(1512), 313–321.
Hollingsworth, Peter M., et al. (2009). A DNA barcode for land plants. *Proceedings of the National Academy of Sciences of the United States of America, 106*(31), 12794–12797.
House of Lords. (2008). Systematics and taxonomy: Follow-up (HL Paper 162). Science and Technology Committee, 5th Report of Session 2007–08. London: The Stationery Office Limited.
International Barcode of Life (iBOL). (2011). What is iBOL? Retrieved August 28, 2011, from http://ibol.org/about-us/what-is-ibol/
International Union for Conservation of Nature and Natural Resources (IUCN). (2011). The IUCN red list of threatened species (Version 2011.1). Retrieved August 4, 2011, from http://www.iucnredlist.org
Lockwood, Julie L.; Cassey, Phillip; & Blackburn, Tim. (2005). The role of propagule pressure in explaining species invasions. *Trends in Ecology & Evolution, 20*(5), 223–228.
Lowenstein, Jacob H.; Amato, George; & Kolokotronis, Sergios-Orestis. (2009). The real *maccoyii*: Identifying tuna sushi with DNA barcodes—contrasting characteristic attributes and genetic distances. *PLoS ONE, 4*(11), Article e7866. Retrieved August 4, 2011, from http://www.plosone.org/article/info:doi%2F10.1371%2Fjournal.pone.0007866
National Center for Biotechnology Information (NCBI). (2011). About NCBI. Retrieved August 28, 2011, from http://www.ncbi.nlm.nih.gov/About/index.html
Ratnasingham, Sujeevan, & Hebert, Paul D. N. (2007). BOLD: The barcode of life data system (www.barcodinglife.org). *Molecular Ecology Notes, 7*(3), 355–364.
Smith, M. Alex, et al. (2011). Barcoding a quantified food web: Crypsis, concepts, ecology and hypotheses. *PLoS ONE, 6*(7), Article e14424. Retrieved August 4, 2011, from http://www.plosone.org/article/info%3Adoi%2F10.1371%2Fjournal.pone.0014424
Smith, M. Alex; Fernandez-Triana, Jose; Roughley, Rob; & Hebert, Paul D. N. (2009). DNA barcode accumulation curves for understudied taxa and areas. *Molecular Ecology Resources, 9*(s1), 208–216.

Strategic Environmental Assessment (SEA)

Strategic environmental assessment (SEA) identifies the environmental impacts of policies and plans, with the aim of minimizing the plans' negative impacts. SEAs have led to many changes in plans, but are limited by the fact that they are decision-informing rather than decision-making tools and that they normally test whether the plan is as good as it can reasonably be, rather than whether it is truly sustainable.

Strategic environmental assessment (SEA) proposes to make policies and plans "greener" by identifying their environmental impacts and minimizing the negative impacts. SEA is like environmental impact assessment (EIA) but applied to policies and plans rather than large development projects.

Policies and Plans

Government bodies prepare policies and plans, which can also be called "programs," "strategies," and the like. National energy policies, for example, state how energy will be produced and used in the future; regional transport programs list roads that government intends to build; and local development plans explain how housing, employment, and infrastructure will be developed. All of these plans will have environmental impacts. The national energy policy could have noise and visual impacts if it promotes wind farms, or cause air pollution if it promotes coal-burning power stations. A road-building program could increase air pollution and noise and affect animals and their habitats. This kind of information, which is the outcome of the SEA process, can help planners choose between alternatives (more wind farms versus more coal-burning power stations) and fine-tune the plan (no wind farms in areas of particular

natural beauty). Table 1, on the next page, summarizes differences between SEA and EIA, which in turn are linked to the differences between the strategic nature of policies and plans and the more detailed nature of projects.

Practice

SEA practice started in the United States in the 1970s, became more widely applied in the 1990s, and leaped forward in the 2000s with the adoption of the European SEA Directive of 2001 and the United Nations Economic Commission for Europe SEA Protocol of 2003, each of which applies to multiple countries. Other countries with formal SEA legislation include China and Canada, and many others have SEA guidelines.

A typical SEA involves (1) preparation of an SEA report, (2) consultation with environmental bodies and the public on the SEA report and draft plan, (3) decision makers taking account of the SEA report and consultation findings when making their planning decisions, and (4) monitoring the actual environmental impacts of the plan.

In turn, a typical SEA report includes a description of the following:

- the emerging plan, and how it affects (and is affected by) other plans, projects, and environmental objectives
- the current environment, existing environmental problems, and likely future changes to the environmental situation if there was no plan ("business as usual")
- possible alternatives to the emerging plan
- several rounds of assessment, for instance, identifying the environmental impacts of the plan objectives, plan alternatives, draft plan, and final plan

Table i. SEA versus EIA

	SEA	EIA
Decision-making level	Policy → Plan → Program	→ Project
Nature of action	Strategic, visionary, conceptual	Immediate, operational
Output	General	Detailed
Scale of impacts	Macroscopic, cumulative	Microscopic, localized
Time scale	Long to medium term	Medium to short term
Type of data	More qualitative	More quantitative
Alternatives	Areawide, political, regulative, techno-logical, fiscal, economic	Specific locations, design, construction, operation
Rigor of analysis	More uncertainty	More rigor

Source: Fischer (2007).

- for each round of assessment, identification of ways that the plan/alternative's negative impacts can be minimized and its positive impacts enhanced
- a description of how the assessment was undertaken and any problems faced

SEAs aim to inform decision makers while they are preparing their plan, rather than acting as a post hoc "environmental check." The government body preparing the plan or consultants to these planners carry out the SEA.

Strengths and Weaknesses

SEAs often trigger changes to plans that make the plans more environmentally sustainable. Examples of these include the following:

- removal of proposed projects that would have unacceptable environmental impacts (e.g., a waste-composting facility near a sensitive water body)
- establishment of rules for new projects (e.g., energy-efficiency targets for new homes)
- requirements for infrastructure to reduce environmental impacts (e.g., new wastewater treatment stations)
- requirements for additional impact studies at a lower level of planning

In some cases, an SEA may lead to a completely different approach to plan making. For instance, it may emphasize reducing the need to travel rather than providing more transport infrastructure.

SEAs deal with strategic-level issues that would otherwise not be dealt with through project-level EIA, such as climate change, tranquility, and equity between different social groups. They can help to narrow the focus of project EIAs by dealing with some issues at the plan level. SEA's public consultation requirements (where they exist) have increased the transparency of plan making and public accountability of planners. Surveys of planners (e.g., Therivel and Walsh 2006) also suggest that SEA helps planners better understand their plan and the principles of sustainable development.

That said, most of the changes to plans triggered by SEA are minor: changes to individual words rather than to broad policy directions. Because SEAs are typically carried out by the planners or their consultants, they may not be fully independent and critical. SEA is most effective, however, if it is carried out alongside the plan-making process rather than acting as a post hoc "environmental check," so it is difficult to see how this could be improved.

SEA is often long-winded and expensive. A typical SEA might take forty to eighty person-days and cost about $100,000 (European Commission 2009). Studies of SEA effectiveness and efficiency (European Commission 2009; Smith, Richardson, and McNab 2010) suggest that SEAs as currently practiced may not provide value for the money. Most SEAs also do not test whether the plan is truly sustainable in the sense of staying within environmental limits, but rather whether it is as sustainable as it reasonably can be. Interviews with English planners in 2008 (Therivel et al. 2009) suggested that even after SEA, most plans still promote social and economic objectives to the detriment of the environment. The SEA process helps to make the plans more balanced and sustainable, however.

Despite these limitations, SEA makes planners think more carefully about the impacts of their plans, generally improves plans' environmental performance, and provides information to the public about how planning decisions have been made.

The Future

If SEA follows the model of project EIA, it will be used in more and more countries, first through pilot applications and then through legislation. Future SEAs are likely to be more focused on key issues of concern ("scoping"), have closer links between the plan alternatives and provision of data about environmental conditions, and include formal statements from planners about how they have taken the SEA findings into account.

Riki THERIVEL

Levett-Therivel Sustainability Consultants, United Kingdom

See also Agenda 21; Building Rating Systems, Green; Cost-Benefit Analysis; Design Quality Indicator (DQI); Ecological Impact Assessment (EcIA); Framework for Strategic Sustainable Development (FSSD); International Organization for Standardization (ISO); Regional Planning; Risk Assessment

FURTHER READING

European Commission. (2001). Directive 2001/42/EC of the European Parliament and of the Council of 27 June 2001 on the assessment of the effects of certain plans and programmes on the environment, Brussels. Retrieved July 13, 2011, from http://eur-lex.europa.eu/LexUriServ/LexUriServ.do?uri=CELEX:32001L0042:EN:NOT

European Commission. (2009). Study concerning the report on the application and effectiveness of the SEA Directive (2001/42/EC): Final report. Retrieved July 15, 2011, from http://ec.europa.eu/environment/eia/pdf/study0309.pdf

Fischer, Thomas. (2007). *Theory and practice of strategic environmental assessment.* London: Earthscan.

Sadler, Barry, et al. (Eds.). (2011). *Handbook of strategic environmental assessment.* London: Earthscan.

Smith, Steven; Richardson, Jeremy; & McNab, Andrew. (2010). Towards a more efficient and effective use of strategic environmental and sustainability appraisal in spatial planning: Final report. Retrieved July 13, 2011, from http://www.communities.gov.uk/documents/planningandbuilding/pdf/1513010.pdf

Therivel, Riki. (2010). *Strategic environmental assessment in action* (2nd ed.). London: Earthscan.

Therivel, Riki, & Walsh, Fiona. (2006). The strategic environmental assessment directive in the UK: 1 year onwards. *Environmental Impact Assessment Review, 26*(7), 663–675.

Therivel, Riki, et al. (2009). Sustainability-focused impact assessment: English experiences. *Impact Assessment and Project Appraisal, 27*(2), 155–168.

Supply Chain Analysis

Supply chain analysis is the study of quantitative models that help reduce waste and optimize performance of a supply chain. An increase in the disclosure of environmental and social performance metrics, global reporting initiatives, and a deeper understanding of a supply chain performance have made this analysis more dynamic. These measures are reducing the risks and associated environmental impacts of many consumer products.

Firms today are focused on shareholder value and customer value while they maximize the velocity of information transfer, reduce waste in the system, and minimize response time. Supply chain analysis, also called supply chain optimization, involves managers working across multiple enterprises or companies to remove waste and shorten the supply chain time in the delivery of goods and services to the consumer. Until recently, supply chain analysis has overlooked opportunities for systems thinking. It has not had the ability to include forward-looking strategies for firms and their supply chains that involve the primary elements of sustainability. Sustainability in this sense means the ethical management of social, environmental, and economic resources so firms can better measure and manage this "triple bottom line" (Savitz and Weber 2006).

A supply chain is a firm's customer relationship, order fulfillment, and supplier relationships processes. It also includes interconnected linkages between the services, materials, and information suppliers and the customers of the firm's services or products. Supply chain managers are the people at various levels of an organization responsible for managing supply and demand both within and across business organizations. These professionals need measurement tools and models to understand the current state of operations and to make decisions. These tools

allow them to predict the strategic opportunities that come from measuring new performance metrics, sustainability reporting, and levels of transparency. Life cycle assessment is a primary enabler of this measurement and visibility into a product and its supply chain.

The overlay of sustainability within supply chain analysis applies the emerging measurement tools and quantitative models that characterize various relationships and economic trade-offs in the supply chain. Supply chain analysis has made significant strides in both theoretical and practical applications of waste reduction. The application of a sustainability lens to analysis results in an unprecedented mixture of prescriptive, descriptive, and predictive models, global reporting initiatives, life cycle assessment, and the ability to quantify environmental costs of operations, products, and supply chains.

Life Cycle Assessment

Life cycle assessment (LCA) measures and tracks a product's resource use and impacts from cradle to grave, from raw material extraction to end-of-life processes. This tool is essential for managing sustainability risks and waste reduction and discovering opportunities to create environmentally and socially driven value. An established approach to a macro level of analysis involves systems thinking. This holistic approach to analysis focuses on the way that a system's constituent parts interrelate and how systems work over time and within the context of larger systems (Meadows 2008). Conducting an LCA is one way to understand interconnected supply chain systems of products and services.

In the 1970s companies in both the United States and Europe performed comparative life cycle inventory analyses. Inventory analysis is an objective, data-based process of quantifying energy and raw material requirements, air emissions, waterborne effluents, solid waste, and other environmental releases incurred throughout the life cycle of a product, process, or activity. Publicly available government documents or technical papers provided much of the data; specific industrial data were not available. A resource and environmental profile analysis, as practiced in the United State and called ecobalance in Europe, quantified resource use and environmental releases. The Russian American economist Wassily Leontief theorized and developed economic input-output life cycle assessment (EIO-LCA) in the 1970s. The primary focus of this early period was the development of a protocol or standard research methodology for conducting these studies.

Life cycle inventory analysis continued through the early 1980s. Studies focused on energy requirements improved the methodology. As interest in all areas affecting resources and the environment grew, researchers further refined and expanded the methodology beyond the life cycle inventory to impact. Impact assessment is the phase of an LCA that deals with the evaluation of environmental impacts (e.g., climate change and toxicity) of products and services over their whole life cycles.

During the 1990s, false claims of environmental product attributes along with pressure from environmental organizations to standardize LCA methodology led to the development of the LCA standards in the International Organization for Standardization (ISO) 14000 series. Researchers at the Green Design Institute of Carnegie Mellon University, with the help of sufficient computing power, operationalized Leontief's EIO-LCA method in the mid-1990s. This model is still available online (Carnegie Mellon 2011). A manager can take the EIO-LCA method and transform it into a tool available to evaluate quickly a commodity or service as well as its supply chain.

After the turn of the century, the United Nations Environment Programme joined forces with the Society of Environmental Toxicology and Chemistry to launch the Life Cycle Initiative, an international partnership. The initiative's programs put life cycle thinking into practice and improved the supporting tools through better data and indicators. The Life Cycle Inventory program improves global access to transparent, high-quality life cycle data by hosting and facilitating expert groups whose work results in web-based information systems. The Life Cycle Impact Assessment Programme increases the quality and global reach of life cycle indicators by promoting the exchange of views among experts whose work results in a set of widely accepted recommendations (Scientific Applications International Corporation 2006). Several proprietary software solutions help make LCA a reality.

Integrated Supply Chain Management

Despite ongoing attempts to analyze supply chains, the organization of data required for effective analysis and an understanding of sustainability issues and opportunities overwhelms many individuals and teams. Supply chain analysis and optimization give firms a competitive advantage. Supply chain and sustainability professionals can now understand and leverage the emerging research methods and tools. Successful supply chain management analysis requires communication and trust because information exchange is essential for supply chain members to understand each other, share common goals, and make mutually beneficial decisions. As Michael Senge, a US scientist and founding chair of the Society for Organizational Learning, and his colleagues found, meeting the challenges of sustainability "writ large" will require not only supply chain integration, but also cross-sector collaboration for which there is no real precedent (Senge et al. 2007).

Successful analysis requires supply chain visibility leveraging information systems and data sharing with supply chain members. Managers need to see into any part of a supply chain to access data on inventory levels or the status of shipments. This visibility within supply chains is growing more expansive for both social and environmental metrics. These metrics are now included in firm performance and solicited as part of supplier assessment programs and audits (Wal-Mart n.d.).

Performance metrics are an important part of any analysis. They are necessary to confirm a supply chain is functioning as planned and to identify opportunities for improvement. Managers use reliability, asset utilization, costs, quality, and flexibility, among traditional measures. Performance metrics involving sustainability are gaining prominence now, more than at any previous time in history, as stakeholders including supply chain customers ask for disclosure of social, governance, and environmental information. The pressure to measure and disclose provides a proving ground for new and innovative ways to analyze the performance of a firm or a supply chain along multiple dimensions of sustainability.

Measurement Tools and Research Methods

The environmental health and safety (EH&S) function within firms historically has managed the environmental performance metrics as the firms remain in compliance with occupational safety and environmental laws. The EH&S function has evolved over time to provide support for quality management and total quality environmental management initiatives as well as for oversight of environmental management systems. EH&S personnel have transitioned in many cases into new functional roles as sustainability coordinators and sustainability professionals. They work in this role with cross-functional teams, including supply chain managers and designers, to find solutions to emerging sustainability opportunities while utilizing tools such as LCA and supply chain analysis.

LCA quantifies the environmental impacts at each step of a product's life cycle. LCA sustainably designs products and even supply chains so that they have the least negative environmental and social impact (Ehrenfeld 2008). Life cycle management (LCM) is the application of life cycle thinking to modern business practice. LCM aims to manage the total life cycle of an organization's product and services toward more sustainable consumption and production (Jensen and Remmen 2006). LCM is an integrated framework of concepts and techniques to address environmental, economic, technological, and social aspects of products, services, and organizations.

To support LCM, environmental management systems and the International Organization of Standardization 14001 set standards for these systems and provide research showing positive impacts on design, waste reduction, and recycling (Sroufe 2003). The benefits from these systems include proactive environmental management, resource and cost efficiency, enhanced reputation, and improved communication (Curkovic and Sroufe 2011). LCA-specific standards include ISO 14040 to 14044. They describe the primary principles and framework for life cycle assessment, which include the following:

1. a definition of the goal and scope of the assessment
2. the life cycle inventory analysis phase
3. the life cycle impact assessment phase

4. the life cycle interpretation phase, reporting and critical review of the assessment, limitations, and relationships between the four primary assessment phases

Economic input-output life cycle assessment uses aggregate sector (industry) level data quantifying how much environmental impact each industry directly contributes to the economy and how much each industry purchases from other industries in producing its output. EIO-LCA analysis traces the various economic transactions, resource requirements, and environmental emissions required for producing a particular product or service. Results from using EIO-LCA provide guidance on the relative impacts of different types of products, materials, services, or industries with respect to resource use and emissions throughout the supply chain (Cicas et al. 2007).

LCA Impacts

An LCA allows a decision maker to study an entire product system and supply chain to avoid the suboptimization that could result if the study focused on only a single process. For example, Electrolux wanted to improve environmental performance of its products. They examined their washing machines to find out where in the life cycle their products had the most impact (i.e., manufacturing, transportation, or disposal). Based on the LCA they found (much as the manufacturers of other consumer electronics products have) that most of the impact was in the product's use, the years of laundry loads, using upward of 151 liters of water and often energy-intensive hot water. This analysis led to the development of front-load washers that use a fraction of the water traditional machines need. The new design reduced energy use and extended the laundered clothing's useful lifetime. The innovation provided early access to a burgeoning Chinese market and the status of having environmentally preferable products. There are further examples of LCA insight and impacts:

• Stonyfield Farms in New Hampshire conducted an LCA on their yogurt product-delivery system to compare options for containers. They found that the size of the container and the distance to retailer were important impacts on the environment. If they sold all their yogurt in 32-ounce (0.95 liter) containers, they could save the equivalent of 11,250 barrels of oil per year. Transportation to the retailer represented about a third of their products' energy impact (Branchfeld et al. 2001).

• Timberland conducted an LCA for a leather boot and calculated emissions at all stages of the value chain, including subsuppliers like the cattle industry that provided the leather. Surprisingly, leather use was responsible for most of the emissions, at around 80 percent of the boot's greenhouse gas burden. Timberland now knows that reducing the amount of leather per boot will shrink its climate-change impact far more than reducing energy use at assembly plants or distribution centers.

- Data from companies such as Trucost enable organizations to identify, measure, and manage the environmental risk associated with their operations, supply chains, and investment portfolios. Quantifying environmental risks and a price for these risks is key to their approach. Trucost provides a systematic approach to managing supply chain environmental impacts through its data to quantify the environmental costs of suppliers, including carbon, water, waste, and air pollution (Trucost 2011).

Supply chain and procurement managers can request LCA data from vendors. Some firms are already releasing environmental product disclosures. Given the complexity of establishing the goal and scope of the assessment, it is important to know how this data-intensive tool can be leveraged in supply chain analysis. Managers can conduct a simplified life cycle review focused on key "hot spots," or they can conduct a more sophisticated, data-intensive LCA with primary data collection for carbon, water waste, and other stakeholder impacts.

Issues and Challenges

Researchers at Carnegie Mellon's Green Design Institute leveraged an EIO-LCA model to estimate greenhouse gas emissions including supply chains (Matthews, Weber, and Hendrickson 2008). They combined this existing information with industry-specific data to obtain estimates of both direct and indirect carbon emissions. Results show that an organization's direct emissions are on average only 14 percent of total supply chain greenhouse gas emissions. Direct and electrical use emissions are on average only 26 percent of the total. Firms that estimate impacts using limited LCA scope and goals may make shortsighted decisions about cost-effective sustainability and supply chain strategies. Managers who use any analysis tool will always need reliable sources of consistent data with clear goals and scope of analysis.

Performing an LCA can be resource and time intensive. The information developed in an LCA study should be used as one component of a more comprehensive decision process. Managers need to assess the trade-offs with cost and performance, for example, against life cycle management and supply chain analysis.

Opportunities

At 3M the protocol for new product development now includes assessment of environmental, health, and safety issues at suppliers, within 3M, and with the customer. This approach to understanding full-system impacts of its products gives 3M a foundation for building strategies leveraging an eco-advantage. Companies such as DuPont, Bayer Material Science, and Alcoa are taking similar initiatives. Teams of LCA experts now connect with cross-functional teams in design and supply chain management. Resource efficiency and LCA have become tools for pollution reduction and waste minimization, allowing managers to better understand where they can most affect a design, process, and supply chain.

Forward-thinking managers scan their external environment. They look at the eco-consequences of their products all along the value chain, upstream and downstream. These supply chain analysis tools and methods to integrate sustainability are most effective when they rest on a foundation of good data, careful planning, and an environmental management system. Companies now manage worldwide databases of sustainability performance metrics. Establishing key metrics that track results on energy use, water and air pollution, waste generation, and compliance helps decision makers benchmark performance, optimize supply chains, set goals, and monitor progress.

The exponential growth in sustainability reporting and the integration of financial and sustainability reports will increase in the development of materials databases that include information on a given product's suppliers and the location of all components and parts. Increased supply chain transparency has already led to open source (free to anyone) online LCA collaboration platforms such as Sourcemap.org. Anyone can see exactly where a product comes from and what environmental impacts materials have from extraction, to transportation to the retail location, and delivery to your home.

Robert P. SROUFE
Duquesne University

See also International Organization for Standardization (ISO); Life Cycle Assessment (LCA); Life Cycle Costing (LCC); Life Cycle Management (LCM); Material Flow Analysis (MFA); Organic and Consumer Labels; Shipping and Freight Indicators; Social Life Cycle Assessment (S-LCA); Triple Bottom Line

FURTHER READING

Branchfeld, Dov, et al. (2001). *Life cycle assessment of the Stonyfield product delivery system.* Ann Arbor: University of Michigan, Center for Sustainable Systems.
Carnegie Mellon. (2011). EIO-LCA: Fast, free, easy life cycle assessment. Retrieved November 13, 2011, from http://www.eiolca.net/
Cicas, Gyorgyi; Hendrickson, Chris T.; Horvath, Arpad; & Matthews, H. Scott. (2007). Development of a regional economic and environmental input-output model of the US economy.

International Journal of Life Cycle Assessment. Retrieved April 12, 2011, from http://dx.doi.org/10.1065/lca2007.04.318

Curkovic, Sime, & Sroufe, Robert P. (2011). Using ISO 14001 to promote a sustainable supply chain strategy. *Business Strategy and the Environment, 93,* 71–93.

Ehrenfeld, John. (2008). *Sustainability by design.* New Haven, CT: Yale University Press.

Electrolux. (n.d.). Environmental product declarations for products. Retrieved April 12, 2011, from, http://www.laundrysystems. electroluxusa.com/Files/pdf/Environmental%20decl_eng_low.pdf

International Organization for Standardization (ISO). (2009). Environmental management: The ISO 14000 family of international standards. Retrieved April 12, 2011, from http://www.iso. org/iso/theiso14000family_2009.pdf

Jensen, Allan Astrup, & Remmen, Arne. (Eds.). (2006). *Background report for a UNEP guide to life cycle management: A bridge to sustainable products.* Retrieved April 12, 2011, from http://lcinitiative.unep.fr/ includes/file.asp?site=lcinit&file=86E47576-EC54-4440-99B6-D6829EAF3622

Matthews, H. Scott; Weber, Christopher; & Hendrickson, Chris T. (2008). The importance of carbon footprint estimation boundaries. *Environmental Science & Technology, 42,* 5839–5842.

Meadows, Donella H. (2008). *Thinking in systems: A primer.* White River Junction, VT: Chelsea Green Publishing.

Savitz, Andrew, with Weber, Karl, (2006). *The triple bottom line.* San Francisco: Jossey-Bass.

Scientific Applications International Corporation (SAIC). (2006, May). Life cycle assessment: Principles and practice. Retrieved May 13, 2011, from http://www.epa.gov/nrmrl/lcaccess/ pdfs/600r06060.pdf

Senge, Peter M.; Lichtenstein, Benyamin B.; Kaeufer, Katrin; Bradbury, Hilary; & Carroll, John S. (2007). Collaborating for systemic change. *MIT Sloan Management Review, 48*(2), 43–53.

Sourcemap. (2011). Homepage. Retrieved April 12, 2011 from http://www.sourcemap.org/

Sroufe, Robert P. (2003). Effects of environmental management systems on environmental management practices and operations. *Production and Operations Management, 12*(3), 416–432.

Trucost. (2011). Homepage. Retrieved April 12, 2011 from http://www. trucost.org/

US Environmental Protection Agency (EPA). (n.d.). Life cycle assessment. Retrieved November 14, 2011, from http://www.epa.gov/ nrmrl/std/sab/lca/

US Environmental Protection Agency (EPA). (n.d.). LCA 101. Retrieved April 12, 2011, from http://www.epa.gov/nrmrl/lcaccess/lca101.html

Wal-Mart. (n.d.). Sustainability supplier assessment. Retrieved April 12, 2011, from http://walmartstores.com/sustainability/9292.aspx

Berkshire's authors and editors welcome questions, comments, and corrections. Send your emails about the *Berkshire Encyclopedia of Sustainability* in general or this volume in particular to: sustainability.updates@berkshirepublishing.com

Sustainability Science

Sustainability science is a new field of research focused on advancing understanding of social and environmental conditions and relationships, and appropriate technologies, in order to move toward a sustainability transition. It involves research in the social sciences, the physical sciences, and engineering and technology, often in interdisciplinary or transdisciplinary contexts. Sustainability science is explicitly represented in the scientific literature and has been growing globally in prominence.

Sustainability science refers to the general pursuit of knowledge related to sustainable development, or strengthening societal transformation to more sustainable conditions. Like sustainable development concepts (or simply "sustainability"), sustainability science recognizes various spheres of interest, including environmental sustainability, economic development, human development, and cultural sustainability. Although science, broadly speaking, has traditionally avoided applications of value judgments, sustainability science developed with explicit recognition that sustainability involves choosing among what people may judge to be better or worse outcomes, and that the alternatives among which we choose are judged on the basis of human (and environmental) well-being. As noted by the Harvard professor of international science, public policy, and human development William C. Clark (2007), "Sustainability science is a field defined by the problems it addresses rather than by the disciplines it employs."

Conceptual Development

The term *sustainability science* was suggested by the US geographer Robert Kates and others in 2001 in the journal *Science*. (An earlier version of this suggestion appeared as a report from Harvard's Kennedy School of Government/Belfer Center for Science and International Affairs in 2000.) The suggestion evolved from work on *Our Common Journey* (National Research Council 1999), a US National Academy of Sciences follow-up report based on the UN-commissioned *Our Common Future* ("The Brundtland Report" from the World Commission on Environment and Development, 1987), the oft-cited source of widespread adoption of the term *sustainable development*. *Our Common Journey* was subtitled *A Transition toward Sustainability*, reflecting emphasis on the process of creating more sustainable conditions both socially and environmentally. This view also considers increasing sustainable conditions as an ongoing process, rather than the achievement of a clear end product or status. *Our Common Journey* also included preliminary suggestions for sustainability science (NRC 1999, 10–11).

In calling for development of "sustainability science," Kates and his coauthors (2001, 641) described it as science that "seeks to understand the fundamental character of interactions between nature and society. Such an understanding must encompass the interaction of global processes with the ecological and social characteristics of particular places and sectors." Authorship of the National Research Council report and the *Science* article overlapped. The authors' key motivation seemed to be development of a branch of research or science that would focus on critical issues related to sustainability and would integrate basic and applied science with the admittedly normative goals of sustainable development.

Through much of the history of modern Western science, complete objectivity—a lack of value judgments—has been the hoped-for norm. In more recent decades, science has recognized that decisions that may be shaped to a greater or lesser degree on values guide scientific endeavors. Some branches of science are clearly oriented to the pursuit of what we see as good or beneficial. Medical research, for example, is pursued based on the desire not only to understand disease, but to reduce suffering. Likewise, any science labeled as "applied" is assumed to help create better conditions in some area that people have judged to be important, or at least to provide understanding that will aid creation of better conditions. Basic science is oriented toward improved understanding (and may or may not have any discernible applications).

Decisions related to what basic understanding scientists want to build can also be related to what science has judged significant. William Clark described the new field of sustainability science as neither pure basic science (focused specifically on building fundamental understanding) nor pure applied science (addressing questions with a focus on the usefulness of the work). It occupies the area that concerns both basic questions and applications (Clark 2007).

The pursuit of sustainability or sustainable development means that people must choose what is to be sustained. It requires "normative" decision making (Clark, Crutzen, and Schellnhuber 2004; Kemp and Martens 2007; Parris and Kates 2003a). Normative decisions are based on what decision makers see as good or bad, or desirable versus undesirable. Although the idea of sustainable development generally recognizes environmental, social, and economic needs, emphasis varies on "what is to be sustained" and "what is to be developed" (Kates, Parris, and Leiserowitz 2005; NRC 1999).

Trends in academic publishing indicate that sustainability science is a growing area of study, with some variation on "sustainable," "sustainability," "sustainable development," or "sustainability science" appearing in the title or subtitle of a variety of newer journals. A journal specifically entitled *Sustainability Science* was established in 2006. As would be expected given the definition of sustainability science above, this journal is highly international in content, frequently publishing research on conditions and change relevant to sustainability in specific countries of Africa and Asia, for example, as well as in larger world regions. In the same year, the *Proceedings of the National Academy of Sciences* (*PNAS*), the weekly journal of the US National Academy of Sciences, added a section specifically entitled "Sustainability Science." Most sections are discipline identified, but in contrast to the long-term traditions of *PNAS*, sustainability science might be considered interdisciplinary.

Papers published under the sustainability science heading focus on a broad range of topical or disciplinary areas of research. Their key component is a contribution to basic and/or applied science topics and approaches relevant to sustainability. The *PNAS* Sustainability Science section has become an important outlet for researchers concerned with sustainability. It has included featured sets of papers organized around specific themes of concern, including climate change and water in the North American Southwest, climate mitigation and food production in the tropics, ecosystem services, tipping elements in Earth systems, and others (see, e.g., Daily and Matson 2008; DeFries and Rosenzweig 2010; MacDonald 2010; Schellnhuber 2009). Articles may focus on particular broad issues, specific world regions, or smaller areas.

Questions and Approach

Sustainability science was—and is—envisioned as focused on understanding "the dynamic interactions between nature and society" (Kates et al. 2000; Kates et al. 2001). The team proposing establishment of sustainability science as a new field also identified four research strategies: to span the range of spatial scales between diverse phenomena; to account for both temporal inertia and urgency; to deal with functional complexity; and to recognize a wide range of outlooks regarding what makes knowledge usable (Kates et al. 2001).

Kates and his collaborators also recommended a number of core questions upon which sustainability science could initially focus. In abridged form, they include the following (Kates et al. 2000; Kates et al. 2001):

1. How can nature-society interactions be better incorporated in models and conceptualizations integrating the Earth system, human development, and sustainability?
2. How are long-term trends reshaping nature-society interactions in ways relevant to sustainability?
3. What determines the vulnerability or resilience of the nature-society system in particular kinds of places and for particular concerns?
4. Can scientifically meaningful limits to human-environment systems (beyond which there are risks of serious degradation) be identified?
5. What systems of incentive structures can guide nature-society interactions toward more sustainable trajectories?
6. How can environmental and social monitoring and reporting systems be made to provide more useful guidance for sustainability?
7. How can research planning, monitoring, assessment, and decision support be better integrated into adaptive management and societal learning systems?

Altogether, the proposed creation of sustainability science and suggestions for its initial development through the recommended research strategies and core questions are part of social and scientific moves to transition society toward more sustainable conditions.

Sustainability science addresses a breadth of questions about connected human-environmental systems, as well as occupying the overlap area of basic and applied science. It is by its nature multidisciplinary (involving a number of academic disciplines or specialties) or even transdisciplinary (transcending traditional divisions among academic specialties, weaving ideas and approaches together). Of course, many of the research projects pursued and published under the heading of sustainability science take a single discipline's approach to contribute to the core questions of sustainability science and to sustainability and sustainability science goals. Sustainability science involves approaches to the social sciences, the physical or natural sciences, engineering, and technology.

Measurement

Measurement concerns and efforts relevant to sustainability science range broadly: essentially, any move to assess or measure any aspect of Earth conditions—social and/or environmental—relevant to human-environment systems operations or status and playing a potential role in moving conditions toward greater sustainability would be relevant to sustainability science. The breadth of the core questions and other descriptions of sustainability science concerns and approaches are indicative of this. One might take some of the work done by researchers who originated the idea of sustainability science as suggestive of broader conceptual measurements and indicators in the rapidly growing field. The assessment of trends and of conditions that might be indicative of transitions toward greater sustainability or sustainable development are of particular concern (Kates and Parris 2003; Parris and Kates 2003a and 2003b); an ability to assess conditions at different scales also is desirable (see, e.g., Graymore, Sipe, and Rickson 2008).

Outlook

Sustainability science encompasses most research—at least most meaningful research—relevant to the pursuit of increased sustainability, or the sustainability transition. It has become a key organizing realm for scientists dealing with sustainability issues, and particularly for those integrating basic and applied science (see Clark 2007) and researchers developing approaches that pull together knowledge and approaches from multiple disciplines to speed along a sustainability transition. Although these outlets for sharing the science of sustainability originated in this new millennium, explicit recognition of sustainability science through establishment of a journal of the same name and of a *Proceedings of the National Academy of Sciences* section will help strengthen the field and add to its stature.

Lisa M. Butler HARRINGTON
Kansas State University

See also Challenges to Measuring Sustainability; Citizen Science; Community and Stakeholder Input; Focus Groups; *The Limits to Growth;* Participatory Action Research; Social Network Analysis (SNA); Systems Thinking; Weak vs. Strong Sustainability Debate

FURTHER READING

Clark, William C. (2007). Sustainability science: A room of its own. *Proceedings of the National Academy of Sciences of the United States of America, 104*(6), 1737–1738.

Clark, William C.; Crutzen, Paul J.; & Schellnhuber, Hans Joachim. (2004). Science for global sustainability: Toward a new paradigm. In Hans Joachim Schellnhuber, Paul J. Crutzen, William C. Clark, Martin Claussen & Hermann Held (Eds.), *Earth system analysis for sustainability.* Cambridge, MA: MIT Press.

Daily, Gretchen C., & Matson, Pamela A. (2008). Ecosystem services: From theory to implementation. *Proceedings of the National Academy of Sciences of the United States of America, 105*(28), 9455–9456.

DeFries, Ruth, & Rosenzweig, Cynthia. (2010). Toward a whole-landscape approach for sustainable land use in the tropics. *Proceedings of the National Academy of Sciences of the United States of America, 107*(46), 19627–19632.

Graymore, Michelle L. M.; Sipe, Neil G.; & Rickson, Roy E. (2008). Regional sustainability: How useful are current tools of sustainability assessment at the regional scale? *Ecological Economics, 67*(3), 362–372.

Kates, Robert W., & Parris, Thomas M. (2003). Long-term trends and a sustainability transition. *Proceedings of the National Academy of Sciences of the United States of America, 100*(14), 8062–8067.

Kates, Robert W.; Parris, Thomas M.; & Leiserowitz, Anthony A. (2005). What is sustainable development? Goals, indicators, values and practice. *Environment: Science and Policy for Sustainable Development, 47*(3), 8–21.

Kates, Robert W., et al. (2000). Sustainability science: Research and assessment systems for sustainability (Program Discussion Paper 2000–33, Belfer Center for Science & International Affairs and John F. Kennedy School of Government, Harvard University). Retrieved July 23, 2011, from http://ksgnotes1.harvard.edu/BCSIA/sust.nsf/pubs/pub7/$File/2000-33.pdf

Kates, Robert W., et al. (2001). Sustainability science. *Science, 292*(5517), 641–642.

Kemp, René, & Martens, Pim. (2007). Sustainable development: How to manage something that is subjective and never can be achieved? *Sustainability: Science, Practice, and Policy, 3*(2), 5–14.

MacDonald, Glen M. (2010). Water, climate change, and sustainability in the Southwest. *Proceedings of the National Academy of Sciences of the United States of America, 107*(50), 21256–21262.

National Research Council (NRC), Board on Sustainable Development. (1999). *Our common journey: A transition toward sustainability.* Washington, DC: National Academy Press.

Parris, Thomas M., & Kates, Robert W. (2003a). Characterizing and measuring sustainable development. *Annual Review of Environment and Resources, 28,* 559–586.

Parris, Thomas M., & Kates, Robert W. (2003b). Characterizing a sustainability transition: Goals, targets, trends, and driving forces. *Proceedings of the National Academy of Sciences of the United States of America, 100*(14), 8068–8073.

Schellnhuber, Hans Joachim. (2009). Tipping elements in the Earth system. *Proceedings of the National Academy of Sciences of the United States of America, 106*(49), 20561–20563.

World Commission on Environment and Development (WCED). (1987). *Our common future.* Oxford, UK: Oxford University Press.

Sustainable Livelihood Analysis (SLA)

Sustainable livelihood analysis (SLA) is a methodological approach to understanding the activities that households engage in. The methodology is applicable in any context, rural or urban, and is founded upon an appreciation of available capitals (resources), as well as their vulnerability and institutional context. SLA is used especially by researchers and policy makers who are interested in improving people's lives.

The word *livelihood* is a commonly employed one in English with old origins. The *Oxford English Dictionary* (OED) defines it as "a means of securing the necessities of life." It is derived from an Old English word *līflād*, "way of life," and *hood*, meaning "person, condition, quality." In this sense, all human beings have a livelihood, the condition of their way of life, irrespective of where they live, although the form that livelihood takes can be very different in different places and indeed over time in the same place. Life, on the other hand, is much more than just livelihood. The OED describes life as the "state of being alive as a human; the experience and activities that are typical of all people's existences." Clearly, to live, people have to have enough food, water, and so on, but to have a livelihood is to have experience and activities beyond just the consumption of such necessities. Sustainable livelihood analysis (SLA) explores the complexity of human activity, often with the goal of improving its quality and viability.

Understanding Livelihoods

Understanding livelihood in any particular place and time presents a significant challenge. One definition that attempts to capture the complex concept was suggested early in the development of the field by the British ecologists Robert Chambers and Gordon R. Conway. They suggest that a person's livelihood consists of the capabilities, assets, and activities for a way of living and that it is sustainable when it can recover from stresses, maintain itself, and provide opportunities for future generations:

> A livelihood comprises the capabilities, assets (stores, resources, claims and access) and activities required for a means of living; a livelihood is sustainable which can cope with and recover from stress and shocks, maintain or enhance its capabilities and assets, and provide sustainable livelihood opportunities for the next generation; and which contributes net benefits to other livelihoods at the local and global levels and in the short and long-term. (Chambers and Conway 1992, 7)

Diana Carney, at the time a research fellow at the Overseas Development Institute in London, further refined the definition of SLA to include the statement that "a livelihood is sustainable when it can cope with and recover from stresses and shocks and maintain or enhance its capabilities and assets both now and in the future, while not undermining the natural resource base" (Carney 1998, 4).

According to these definitions, livelihood has to both maintain and enhance its capabilities into the future and be able to recover from stresses and shocks. A central element in this resilience to stress and shocks is often assumed to be the diversification of elements that comprise livelihood, that is, the livelihood includes a variety of activities. A livelihood founded on just one activity, such as agriculture, is assumed to be more vulnerable to shocks (drought, flooding, and pest attack, for example) than a livelihood that encompasses agriculture alongside a number of nonagricultural activities such as tailoring, carpentry, trading, and even paid employment.

Assessing Livelihoods

SLA is often used by development economists and policy makers as the basis for interventions that might improve peoples' lives. There is certainly logic to beginning any development intervention, be it a policy or indeed a specific project, by examining the way those meant to be helped currently earn their living. This overt focus on what people do to get by, however, often misses the richness that comprises the people's lives. Leisure, for example, is obviously important to people, yet rarely does it appear in any analysis undertaken as a prelude to a development intervention. Some researchers point out that such structural economic approaches to livelihood neglect the fact that households are sources of identity and social connections, not just places to live, eat, and work:

> The major shortcoming of structural-functional and economic approaches to the household is the neglect of the role of ideology. The socially specific units that approximate "households" are best typified not merely as clusters of task-oriented activities that are organized in variable ways, not merely as places to live/eat/ work/reproduce, but as sources of identity and social markers. They are located in structures of cultural meaning and differential power. (Guyer and Peters 1987, 209)

Unfortunately, the important ideas like identity, social fabric, and cultural meaning are subjective. So it is perhaps not unreasonable for policy makers to focus on the more tangible, task-oriented activities that can be seen and measured. Even this one-dimensional way of looking at households does shed some light on what people do and why they do it, as well as provide insight into interventions that might improve matters.

The Department for International Development (DFID) in the United Kingdom has developed one framework for analyzing sustainable livelihood. (See figure 1 on the following page.)

At the center of the DFID analysis is *capital,* or assets owned or accessible to the social unit such as a household. There are five types of capital (Carney 1998):

1. *Natural,* including natural resource stocks (soil, water, air, genetic resources, etc.) and the environmental services they provide
2. *Human,* including skills, knowledge, and labor, as well as good health and physical capability
3. *Economic,* including cash, credit and debt, savings, and other economic assets
4. *Physical,* including human-made infrastructure (buildings, roads), production equipment, and technologies
5. *Social,* including social networks, social claims, social relations, affiliations, and associations

Information has been suggested as a sixth form of available capital (Odero 2006). Once the assets of a particular household have been identified and assessed in terms of the contribution they make (or could make) to livelihood, sustainable livelihood analysis takes into account the vulnerability of the system: what are the shocks and pressures that might impact the different capitals? This can be assessed in part by exploring historical trends with such stresses (drought, for example) and how people have responded (perhaps by migration or investment in infrastructure). Shocks and stresses may have different effects on each of the types of capital. For example, in the short term, an increasing likelihood of drought or flooding as a result of climate change will be a shock to natural capital such as land and vegetation (including crops) but may have little or no effect on physical capital such as road and rail. In the longer term, however, a continuous cycle of ever more intense droughts and flooding (a pressure) can have severe impacts on many capitals, including social capital. Making reliable predictions about the long-term effects of such pressures on the range of livelihood capitals is not easy.

The policy and institutional context within which the livelihood capitals exist must also be taken into account. Relevant authorities may be able to act to limit damage from certain short-term shocks. For example, government agencies may take action to reduce the impact of flooding on natural or economic capital. Similarly, publicly funded information services may be available to provide information and advice. Nongovernmental organizations (for example, charities) or even private agencies (for example, banks and insurance companies) may also provide support for livelihoods. The larger legal framework in which all of these organizations operate, and the limits on their available resources, also affect the way pressures and shocks impact households. All these factors have to be taken into account to develop strategies that enhance livelihood, perhaps by making it more resilient to shocks and pressures.

Critiques of Sustainable Livelihood Analysis

The SLA of the Department for International Development has attracted some criticism, which highlights opportunities for further research. Some of these are outlined in the following paragraphs.

SLA can become a rather mechanical and quantitative cataloging of capitals exercise (a task that is relatively straightforward), with less emphasis on the more qualitative aspects, such as vulnerabilities and institutional contexts. In effect, the complexity of households can become reduced to a few tables and graphs, and the people themselves can

Figure 1. Some Components of the DFID Sustainable Rural Livelihoods Framework

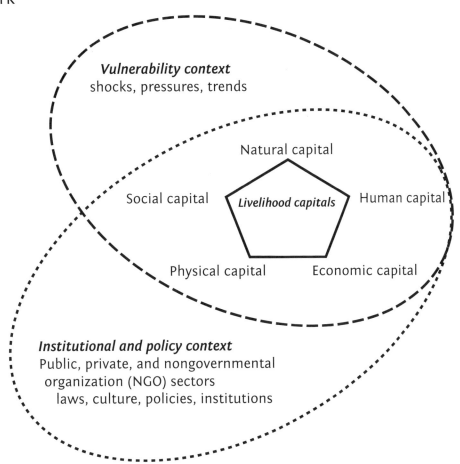

Source: after Carney (1998).

Figure 1 shows the United Kingdom's Department for International Development's Sustainable Rural Livelihoods Framework. At the center of the DFID analysis is capital, or assets owned or accessible to the social unit such as a household. The five types of capital include natural capital (natural resource stocks), human capital (skills, knowledge, and labor), economic capital (cash, credit and debt, savings, and other economic assets), social capital (social networks, etc.), and physical capital (human-made infrastructure). The policy and institutional context within which the livelihood capitals exist must also be taken into account.

become invisible. Quantification certainly resonates with reliance on numbers and statistics in thinking about social policy (Neylan 2008), but reducing the complexity of people's livelihoods, let alone their lives, to a set of numbers can be the basis for a dangerous oversimplification.

It can be difficult to observe all the relevant capitals that make up a livelihood. For example, in rural areas it seems reasonable to assess land available to a farming household as one of the natural capitals, but a household may own many irregular parcels of land that can be located far from the place of residence. Cataloging all the plots and the quality of the land in each is time consuming. If plots are rented on a seasonal basis rather than owned, there can be significant variation in this capital over time.

SLA relies on the cooperation of the households being assessed, but declaring ownership of assets can be sensitive

for all sorts of reasons. For example, a household might choose to understate how much land it owns or other physical assets during interviews to avoid documenting the assets and having to pay taxes on them, and as a result that household's capital may be grossly underestimated.

Assessing vulnerability presents another difficulty, because the process is complicated and unreliable. Researchers rely on historical trends, if data is available, and on computer modeling. But models themselves rely on high quality data, and they are often designed for large areas and time spans rather than the smaller scales of village or farm that SLA addresses. Of course, unexpected shocks and pressures will certainly arise. An example would be a change in government as the result of a coup d'état or perhaps a major civil disturbance. The banking crisis in the first decade of the twenty-first century is another such shock, one that had a major impact on the livelihoods of many people throughout the globe in both urban and rural areas. Another unpredictable shock in the same decade is the so-called Arab Spring, a wave of astonishing political upheavals in North Africa and the Middle East that began in late 2010.

Because these factors contribute a large degree of uncertainty, it is important to recognize that any assessment of livelihood is a complex task and that any one snapshot in time may be misleading.

Challenges: The Future of Livelihood

For all the criticisms it faces, SLA represents a significant step forward. It does consider multiple factors, and this helps avoid any narrow single-sector perspective that may (inadvertently) be adopted by experts who are specialists in a particular sector. Considering multiple factors also brings into perspective the interactions and trade-offs that are central to sustainability. An attempt to enhance one capital, perhaps by reducing its vulnerability to shocks, may have both positive and negative repercussions for the other capitals. Investment in erosion prevention, for example, could significantly diminish the economic and human resources available for other income generating activities. Change can, and often does, come at a cost. Finally, SLA reinforces the understanding that livelihoods are dynamic rather than static. Not only do capitals change with time, partly as a result of the pressures at play, but so to do the institutional and policy contexts within which the livelihoods are embedded.

What is the future for SLA? Although many researchers are working on the topic, much of the research takes the form of case studies, which are place and time specific, and it is distributed in working papers and project reports. Moving forward, policy makers and economists will have to develop ways to evaluate the qualitative aspects of livelihood, rather than focus on thinking about livelihood capitals in purely utilitarian terms. The British geographer Anthony Bebbington has pointed out that

"people's assets are not merely means through which they make a living: they also give meaning to the person's world" (Bebbington 1999, 2022).

Social capital is particularly important in this regard. Interactions with other people are not solely a means to generate income, but they are also a means by which people influence other communities, institutions, and politicians. In an era of rapid global communication, social capital provides a way for people to engage with the world (or perceive to engage) even if this has no obvious or immediate impact on their livelihood. There is still much scope for refining and expanding on the basic understanding of SLA and developing more effective ways to use those understandings to improve people's lives.

Stephen MORSE
University of Surrey

See also Agenda 21; Community and Stakeholder Input; Development Indicators; Environmental Justice Indicators; Genuine Progress Indicator (GPI); Global Environment Outlook (GEO) Reports; Global Reporting Initiative (GRI); Gross National Happiness; $I = P \times A \times T$ Equation; *The Limits to Growth*; Population Indicators; Regional Planning; Social Network Analysis (SNA); Sustainability Science; Taxation Indicators, Green

FURTHER READING

Bebbington, Anthony. (1999). Capitals and capabilities: A framework for analyzing peasant viability, rural livelihoods and poverty. *World Development, 27*(12), 2021–2044.

Carney, Diana. (Ed.). (1998). *Sustainable rural livelihoods: What contribution can we make?* London: Department for International Development.

Chambers, Robert, & Conway, Gordon R. (1992). *Sustainable rural livelihoods: Practical concepts for the 21st century* (IDS Discussion Paper No. 296.) Brighton, UK: Institute of Development Studies.

Guyer, Jane I., & Peters, Pauline Elaine. (1987). Introduction: Conceptualizing the household: Issues of theory and policy in Africa. *Development and Change Special Issue, 18*(2), 197–214.

Neylan, Julian. (2008). Social policy and the authority of evidence. *The Australian Journal of Public Administration, 67*(1), 12–19.

Odero, Kenneth K. (2006). Information capital: 6th asset of sustainable livelihood framework. *Discovery and Innovation, 18*(2), 83–91.

Berkshire's authors and editors welcome questions, comments, and corrections. Send your emails about the *Berkshire Encyclopedia of Sustainability* in general or this volume in particular to: sustainability.updates@berkshirepublishing.com

Systems Thinking

In systems thinking, entities are viewed primarily as connected, mutually interacting parts of some larger whole, such as an ecosystem, an economy, or an organization. The systems approach complements the reductionist approach, which typically analyzes entities and problems individually. Systems thinking can support better decision making and reduce the risk of unintended consequences and is thus relevant to sustaining the biosphere.

Systems thinking and reductionism are often contrasted with each other, but they are actually complementary, and it is usually necessary to use both approaches to understand complex, dynamic phenomena. The various impacts of the 7 billion humans currently alive include the loss of biodiversity, depletion of Earth's natural resources, and pollution of water, air, and land. One approach to managing and reducing these impacts is to analyze individual issues and then to try to find solutions to each problem separately. This reductionist approach has much to offer, and it is possible that the most useful approaches to increasing sustainability will be developed in this manner. But it is also clear that the patterns of stresses on ecosystems, physical systems, and human systems are deeply interconnected, and that it may not be possible to understand or solve some of the great problems of our time if we treat each issue in isolation. For example, if we try to solve our energy problem by converting food plants into ethanol, we might help to offset demand for oil but precipitate an immediate food shortage, followed by an increased loss of biodiversity as agriculture expands into unconverted land. In such cases, we have to try to solve more than one problem at the same time so that we actually reduce impacts instead of just displacing them.

Reductionism

Reductionism attempts to explain the behavior and properties of larger, more complex systems in terms of interactions of smaller or simpler components. This reductionist approach has been exceptionally successful, producing clear predictions that can be tested by experiments. For example, Newton's Law of Universal Gravitation says that in order to understand the gravitational influence that bodies exert on each other, we need only know their masses; details of their composition, shape, and appearance do not matter. In this sense, we can *reduce* a set of bodies to their masses, with no significant loss of information. Newton's law explains very precisely how an apple falls to Earth and allows us to predict the orbits of planets.

The success of reductionism has led some people to think that reductionism is synonymous with science, and that we will (eventually) be able to explain all higher-level phenomena in terms of lower-level components. It is not known whether this is true in principle, but it is certainly the case that many large, complex systems exhibit behaviors that are not easily understood by decomposing the system and analyzing its parts in isolation. In such cases, better scientific predictions can usually be made by describing components at a higher level of organization, sometimes in terms of behavior that might not be apparent or even exist at the lower level. For example, the behavior of a flock of birds cannot be predicted from studying one bird in isolation (or the cells that make up the bird, or the molecules that make up the cells), because the way the flock wheels through the sky requires each bird to keep a certain distance and bearing from the other birds.

The importance of overall organization is particularly clear in living systems, where it is reflected in the hierarchy of organizational structures and control processes from atoms, chemicals, molecules, cells, organs, organisms, social groupings, and species. Behavior at each lower level cannot be easily explained without reference to organizing functions at higher levels. The precise arrangement of the organic bases in DNA, for example, is crucial in biological terms, although many possible arrangements would be compatible with the laws of physics and chemistry. Thus, a reductionist approach alone will not enable a full understanding of biological phenomena.

The Systems Perspective

Thermodynamics provides an example of the complementary qualities of the systems perspective and reductionism. The laws of thermodynamics were first developed through macroscopic analysis of entire physical systems and were only later shown to be deducible from a lower-level mechanical formulation based on individual particles.

Scientific methodology and definitions of proof, however, cannot be uniformly applied throughout the spectrum from physics to economic behavior. Situations appear to become more variable, less controllable, and less predictable as complexity increases. The response of an individual human operator in an economic system, for example, is less predictable than the response of a given molecule in a chemical reaction. One practical problem is that events in the social world do not replicate exactly. There are patterns of events that may appear to replicate, but this claim calls for some degree of judgment as to what degree of overlap constitutes a genuine replication.

This degree of uncertainty has led some people to conclude that holism must be incompatible with reductionism, but this too is incorrect. The world is vast and complex, and the human ability to process information is limited. All models of the world are reductionist in that loss of information must be accepted in order to gain simplicity and clarity. The need is for an intelligent and sophisticated reductionism.

General systems theory was developed in response to this need. It provides a unifying analytical and explanatory framework throughout the hierarchy of nature. This framework allows the contributions of different perspectives and disciplines to be integrated into a coherent analysis. A systems approach usually involves invoking general principles concerning systems to make inferences about likely and actual interactions between the specific systems being studied.

A system is a set of components that interact with each other so that changes in one component can induce changes in another component. Some of these interactions are relatively simple, causal, and directional, but, particularly in a larger system, many such interactions can be linked together in complex chains of causal relationships. A given component can sometimes operate both in a control function (causing change in another) and in a dependent function (being changed by another), so chains of cause and effect relationships can intersect. In practice, a component can start a sequence of causes and effects that eventually loops back, so that each of the components in the loop indirectly influences itself. This is called a feedback loop. A feedback loop is called positive when the input makes the original component more likely to initiate another event sequence, and negative when the input makes the original component less likely to initiate another event sequence. A system can contain more than one feedback loop, and it is also possible for some of these loops to intersect each other. The behavior of a given component can then be the outcome of multiple competing factors, some positive, others negative.

An important characteristic of many systems is that they exhibit nonlinear behavior. In general, we expect that small changes in inputs will lead to small changes in outputs. This, however, is not always true. Sometimes, small changes in inputs can trigger phase transitions, when the system changes its behavior dramatically. For example, an elastic band will stretch in proportion to the pull until it reaches its breaking point. At that stage, a tiny increase in the tension will cause the band to snap. An example of nonlinear behavior in systems occurs when small, simultaneous changes to several inputs trigger disproportionately large consequences, much bigger than would have resulted from changing each input separately. For example, the complex ecology of coral reefs can be impacted by overfishing, pollution, turbidity, sea temperature, storms, or disease. Reefs are usually capable of dealing with one or two of these factors at a time, but they are not capable of dealing with many of them simultaneously. An apparently minor increase in just one factor when the reef is already stressed may thus have far more serious consequences than when the reef is not stressed.

One consequence of nonlinearity is that in some circumstances it can be difficult to predict the behavior of even well-understood systems. This may be the result of the starting condition of the system or of the combination of multiple inputs, or because the precise location of the phase transition is not known, and a tiny change to a system near its critical threshold can result in dramatically divergent behavior (such as living or dying).

Open and Closed Systems

To conceptualize complex systems involving life and ecosystems, one must understand the distinction between open and closed systems. This distinction depends on the second law of thermodynamics, which states that without some input of energy, all systems tend to degrade from organized to disorganized states. For example, of all the possible ways of arranging the components of a tree or a computer, very few configurations will produce functioning systems; most possible arrangements will be just a jumble of parts. Because only a few configurations are viable, any random change is more likely to leave the system less ordered than it was before, rather than more. This is the reason things disintegrate, decay, and die. The amount of disorder in a system can be measured and is called the entropy of the system.

Closed systems have unchanging components. They will eventually arrive at equilibrium and tend to move toward a state of higher entropy (disorder). This means that a closed system usually reaches a point at which no further change is possible in the system.

Open systems exchange flows with their environment. These flows can consist of materials, energy, or information. Open systems can reach a steady state, which depends on maintaining continuous exchanges with their environment. This continuous input allows some open systems to create and maintain a state of low entropy and to retain their integrity as systems.

All living systems are open systems. Life itself is an entropy-decreasing process. Living systems build, reproduce, and create order. The open system that is life on Earth functions because the Earth continually receives energy from the sun. This solar energy is the essential input that allows entropy on Earth to decrease rather than increase; it allows flowers to grow, people to build computers, and order to be created out of disorder.

Of course, the environments that living systems inhabit are themselves never completely stable, so living systems need to obtain reasonably stable flows from sources that may change over time or be able to adapt along with the changes that do occur. That environments change requires living systems to have effective processes of communication and control so that they can monitor, respond to, and resist the changes in those real-life environments. This does not have to be a conscious process. Darwinian evolution is an example of a blind, unconscious system response that allows living organisms to adapt over time to their environments.

Applying Systems Thinking

This understanding of the nature of life, and the crucial importance of inputs of energy and other resources, underpins the systems perspective on sustainable development. One of the core tasks is to ensure that human social, economic, and political systems can distribute energy and other resources as efficiently as possible. Unlike other species, however, humans can analyze and improve their solutions and thereby try to ensure that essential resources remain available indefinitely.

The Earth is an open system, bathed in a continuous flow of energy in the form of sunlight. In spite of this thermodynamic abundance, most energy is currently derived from fossil hydrocarbons, a finite source, with a range of serious potential environmental consequences, including climate change, rising sea levels, and changes in weather patterns. These could in turn mean the loss of areas of coastal settlement and infrastructure, reduced agricultural productivity in many regions, the loss of biodiversity, and the spread of insect-borne diseases, followed by large-scale migration as people relocate from the worst-affected areas.

This highlights two serious failings in most current political and economic decisions. The first is the typical assumption is that the systems affected will respond in linear rather than nonlinear fashion. Awareness of the implications of long-term gradual change is often imperfect, and system elements are often treated discretely, instead of as parts of a system. This can be seriously misleading, however, when dealing with nonlinear systems, as even small differences in the starting conditions, or in the pattern of interaction of multiple inputs, can result in dramatically different outcomes. A systems approach will usually focus on these nonlinear problems.

The second is that political and economic decisions are made with little understanding about how different objectives may conflict. One important basis of systems thinking is the general principle that every decision implies a trade-off (in the example above, this would be cheap energy today at the cost of the loss of coastal cities later this century). It would be better if these trade-offs were taken explicitly into account in the decision-making process. This would represent a significant improvement over much current practice, which often reduces problems to nominal monetary inputs and outputs in a cost-benefit equation.

A systems approach involves first thinking about possible connections and implications, and then looking for the optimal multidimensional solution, which usually involves trying to solve several problems at the same time. This approach might suggest looking for a third- or fourth-generation biofuel, for example, that did not compete directly with the production of food and the maintenance of biodiversity.

The most important roles of systems thinking, therefore, are to help people to make better decisions, improve the chances of long-term success, and reduce the risk of unintended consequences, all of which are particularly relevant in areas that are crucial to the future of humanity.

Anthony M. H. CLAYTON
University of the West Indies

Nicholas RADCLIFFE
Stochastic Solutions Ltd. & Edinburgh University

C. Andrea BRUCE
University of the West Indies

See also Challenges to Measuring Sustainability; Intellectual Property Rights; New Ecological Paradigm (NEP) Scale; Quantitative vs. Qualitative Studies; Social Network Analysis (SNA); Sustainability Science; Transdisciplinary Research; Weak vs. Strong Sustainability Debate

FURTHER READING

Ackoff, Russell L. (1970). *Redesigning the future: A systems approach to societal problems.* New York: Wiley.

Checkland, Peter. (1981). *Systems thinking, systems practice.* New York: Wiley.

Clayton, Anthony, & Radcliffe, Nicholas J. (1998). *Sustainability: A systems approach* (2nd ed.). London: Earthscan.

Costanza, Robert, & Wainger, Lisa. (Eds.). (1991). *Ecological economics: The science and management of sustainability.* New York: Columbia University Press.

Daellenbach, Hans G. (1994). *Systems and decision making: A management science approach.* Chichester, UK: Wiley.

Gell-Mann, Murray. (1994). *Part IV of the quark and the jaguar: Adventures in the simple and the complex.* New York: Henry Holt.

Gharajedaghi, Jamshid. (1999). *Systems thinking: Managing chaos and complexity. A platform for designing business architecture* (2nd ed.). Woburn, MA: Butterworth-Heinemann.

Lewin, Roger. (1993). *Complexity: Life at the edge of chaos.* London: JM Dent.

Meadows, Donella; Meadows, Dennis; & Randers, Jorgen. (1992). *Beyond the limits.* London: Earthscan.

Pratt, Julian; Gordon, Pat; & Plamping, Diane. (1999). *Working whole systems: Putting theory into practice in organizations.* London: Kings Fund.

Senge, Peter. (1990). *The fifth discipline: The art and practice of the learning organization.* London: Century Business.

Sigmund, Karl. (1993). *Games of life: Explorations in ecology, evolution and behaviour.* New York: Penguin.

Waldrop, Mitchell. (1993). *Complexity: The emerging science at the edge of order and chaos.* New York: Simon & Schuster.

Taxation Indicators, Green

Green taxes are becoming an increasingly important means by which governments can try to achieve environmental sustainability. Their indicators do not measure the environmental problem but assess the policy instrument itself. They focus on the extent to which governments are using tax measures and the effectiveness of those measures.

Although tax systems are designed primarily to generate funding for government, they can also incorporate provisions that encourage sustainability. For example, tax systems can contain environmental taxes, such as taxes on the carbon content of fossil fuels that encourage energy conservation or the use of renewable energy. Tax systems can also provide special tax benefits for people who engage in environmental friendly activities, such as using the sun to generate electricity or conserving important wildlife habitat. These tax benefits are often called environmental "tax expenditures" because they provide the equivalent of government expenditures but do so through the tax code rather than direct government spending programs. This article uses the term *green tax measures* to refer to both environmental taxes and environmental tax expenditures.

Indicators for green tax measures can focus on various issues—where, how, and how often they are used; their fiscal impact, which also reflects the extent to which they are used; and their environmental effectiveness. This article reviews different approaches to green tax indicators and describes some of the databases that are available.

Use as an Indicator

One way to measure green tax measures is to look at how often they are used, in which countries, and at which level of government. Information about their use can provide an indication of the extent to which countries are looking to tax codes to achieve sustainability and which types of tax instruments they are choosing.

The Organisation for Economic Co-operation and Development (OECD) and the European Environment Agency (EEA) were early leaders in compiling information about green tax measures. They currently maintain a very useful electronic database of environmental taxes, fees, subsidies (including tax expenditures), and other market-based instruments used in the European Union, OECD countries, and selected other countries (OECD and EEA 2012). Through the website one can tailor a search of the database to specific countries, environmental issues, and types of measures. The data include brief descriptions of the measures and the level of government, as well as other information where possible, such as the date of enactment. Individual countries also maintain databases on specific issues. For example, the federal government in the United States provides funding for the web-based Database of State Incentives for Renewables and Efficiency, which provides information about state tax incentives and other types of incentives on a state-by-state basis.

Revenue Impact as an Indicator

Green tax measures can also be evaluated by the revenue they generate, in the case of green taxes, or the revenue they lose, in the case of green tax expenditures. Because green tax measures are part of the tax system, they will have a direct impact on the flow of funds into government coffers. The fiscal impact provides an indication of the extent to which government is looking to its tax system to send price signals that will encourage environmental sustainability.

The OECD/EEA database described above provides statistics and figures showing the percentage of revenue that the OECD and European countries received from environmentally related taxes since 1994. For example, the weighed average for thirty-four countries was 5.66 percent in 2009, and the country percentages ranged from a low of 1.4 percent in Mexico to a high of 14.22 percent in Turkey (OECD and EEA 2012). The higher the percentage, the more the country is relying on environmentally related taxes to generate its revenue. The database's historical figures allow one to track trends over time.

The OECD/EEA database also evaluates the revenue as a percentage of each country's gross domestic product (GDP), as does the European Commission's Eurostat office. As Eurostat explains, considering revenue from environmental taxes as a percentage of GDP provides a perspective on the tax burden of environmentally harmful products and activities. Eurostat reports that the €287 billion that European countries received in revenue from environmental taxes in 2009 were the equivalent of 2.43 percent of GDP. Environmental taxes were the equivalent of over 4.79 percent of GDP in Denmark, the highest percentage among the twenty-seven member states in the European Union (Eurostat 2012). The OECD/EEA database reports a weighted average of 1.66 in 2009 for thirty-four countries it covers, and it provides data back to 1994.

Larger percentages for either revenue or GDP may mean that a country is using a large number of green taxes, that it is applying its green taxes to an economically pervasive activity that provides a broad tax base (such as use of fossil fuels), and/or that it is using a high tax rate (such as a high tax on gasoline). Hence, it is useful to cross-reference the data about which green taxes are used (the "use indicators") to develop a clearer picture of the extent to which different types of taxes are playing a role generating the revenue. The OECD/EEA database and Eurostat provide some useful cross-referencing analysis. The OECD/EEA database indicates how tax revenues are allocated among energy taxes, vehicle taxes, and other types of environmentally related taxes. Eurostat provides statistics on the amount of revenue from various types of environmental taxes and from different sectors, including manufacturing, transport, and households.

Governments that use environmental tax expenditures may calculate what the tax measures cost in terms of foregone tax revenue. Providing tax benefits in the form of exemptions, deductions, tax credits, or reduced tax rates means that government will receive less revenue. Calculations of the foregone revenue help provide an indication of the extent to which taxpayers have claimed these tax benefits (ex post) or are projected to claim them (ex ante). Hence, they are a useful measure of the level of government investment in specific environmental issues and the degree of response. For example, the federal congressional staff in the United States each year prepares a tax expenditure budget that projects the revenue impact of all federal tax expenditures, including environmental tax expenditures, for the next five years. Its 2012 report projected that taxpayers will claim $6.8 billion in tax credits for the production of electricity from wind farms between 2011 and 2015 (Staff of the Joint Committee on Taxation 2012, 33). The analysis does not indicate the number of taxpayers receiving the benefit, but the aggregate figures provide a good view of the level of support the government is delivering through the tax code.

Environmental Impact as an Indicator

From an environmental perspective, one ideally would develop a consistent international or national system for periodically measuring the actual environmental impact of each green tax measure, such as the carbon dioxide avoided as a result of a carbon tax or a tax credit for wind farms. It is often difficult, however, to measure the environmental impact of tax measures. Because they are market-based instruments, they operate in the private-sector decision-making realm where people are influenced by a green tax measure's price signal as well as a number of other factors. Ideally the influence of the tax should be isolated from other factors. In addition, not everyone will react the same way, unlike an environmental regulation that requires all covered entities to meet a certain standard. As a result, calculations of the anticipated (ex ante) or actual (ex post) environmental impact should determine the extent to which the environmental benefit arose just from the tax measure, how many people changed their behavior as a result, and how much environmental benefit occurred as a result. The data and economic assumptions will change from tax measure to tax measure and from country to country.

The complexity of these calculations means that there currently is no systematic, international assessment that yields comprehensive data on the environmental impact of green tax measures. Information about the environmental impact tends to be sporadic and depends on government, nongovernmental organization (NGO), or academic initiatives that focus on evaluating specific tax measures. For example, some valuable studies that use sophisticated economic modeling have provided assessments of the impact of environmental taxes, such as the impact of energy tax reforms in Europe on the consumption of fossil fuels (e.g., Andersen and Ekins 2009). The United States is evaluating the federal tax code's impact on greenhouse gas emissions, and a report from the National Academies is due in late 2012.

More simplified assessments of the environmental impact can provide a less refined sense of the scope of the environmental impact. Sometimes organizations collect data that can serve as a rough proxy, such as the number of acres conserved through voluntary donations of land or conservation restrictions to land trusts that qualify for a tax benefit. Although the number of acres conserved does not precisely indicate the extent to which the decisions were linked to tax benefits, it provides a sense of the relative magnitude of activity.

Evaluations of effectiveness can also consider cost-effectiveness. For instance, congressional staff in the United States has evaluated a number of environmental tax credits in terms of the tax cost for displacing fossil fuels. Although this approach does not determine the precise behavioral impact of the tax expenditures, it offers a useful perspective on the relative value of different measures, combining the factors of revenue impact and environmental impact. The study concluded, for example, that the tax credit for the production of electricity from wind power implicitly costs $2.25 cents for each million BTUs of displaced fossil fuel, whereas the tax credit for ethanol costs $5.92 cents per million BTUs of displaced fossil fuel (Staff of the Joint Committee on Taxation 2011, 26).

In some instances, environmental taxes are enacted primarily to generate funding to address an environmental problem. The tax rates are not high enough to adjust behavior, but the tax revenue can be earmarked for related environmental problems. For example, the federal government in the United States imposes a small tax on oil to fund federal efforts to clean up oil spills. In this instance, the environmental impact arises more from the use of the funds than the mere existence of the tax. Its effectiveness, therefore, would be measured in terms of the environmental benefits of the use of the funds, such as funds used to help respond to the BP oil spill in the Gulf of Mexico in 2010.

Indicators of Environmentally Damaging Tax Measures

The discussion above focuses on environmentally positive tax measures. Tax systems, however, often contain benefits for activities that are environmentally damaging, such as the production of fossil fuels that, when burned, will generate carbon dioxide and contribute to climate change. Governments are increasingly becoming aware of the need to evaluate these tax benefits. The G-20 negotiations in 2009 resulted in a commitment to phase out inefficient fossil fuel subsidies that "undermine efforts to deal with the threat of climate change" (Pittsburgh Summit 2009, 3). A growing number of studies evaluate the amount that governments are spending in subsidies, including tax benefits, for various types of fossil fuels. They can also present the dollar amount of environmentally damaging subsidies in relation to spending on renewable energy. For example, in a global survey the International Energy Agency (IEA) estimated that subsidies for fossil fuel totaled $409 billion in 2010, compared to $66 billion for renewable sources. It projected that phasing out fossil fuel subsidies by 2020 would reduce carbon dioxide emissions by almost 6 percent in 2035 (IEA 2011, 507.) Another study estimated that the United States federal government spent $72 billion on fossil fuel subsidies from 2002 to 2008, compared to $29 billion for renewable fuels during the same period (Environmental Law Institute 2009, 3). These studies can serve as an important indicator of government investment in environmentally damaging activities and government's relative commitment to more environmentally sustainable initiatives. A joint report by the IEA, OPEC, OECD, and the World Bank in 2010 describes the state of data collection for a broad range of green and environmentally damaging energy subsidies.

The Path Forward

As indicated above, there are multiple ways to assess green tax measures, each of which provides a different perspective on governments' use of their tax codes to promote sustainability. The mere existence of a measure indicates a policy choice to use the tax system to achieve environmental protection. Revenue impact indicates the fiscal benefit or cost to government of this policy approach and the size of the price signal flowing through the tax code. The environmental impact measures the extent of environmental improvement. Other indicators could be developed, such as ones showing when and how green tax measures relate to other policy approaches, including regulations, spending programs, and other market-based instruments.

The indicators described above may be different from sustainability indicators for other policy instruments in some respects. First, because green tax measures are built into the tax code, their linkage to the government budget is more pronounced than for many other policy instruments. Revenue impact therefore becomes a distinctive characteristic and indicator. This strong linkage may provide opportunities for green tax measures: the demand for new revenue may cause governments to consider green taxes or to repeal environmentally damaging subsidies. It may also create barriers: government may not be able to afford green tax expenditures in times of budget deficits.

Second, unlike command-and-control regulations, green tax measures do not require a certain level of compliance, so evaluating them is challenging. One cannot measure effectiveness based on an explicit regulatory standard or the number of violations of that standard. Instead, their effectiveness is the result of many private-market decisions and depends on the aggregate effect of those dispersed decisions. For both regulation and tax measures, one might measure, for example, the avoided greenhouse gas emissions, but the methodology for measuring them is quite different.

It will be important in the future to continue to build the databases and methodologies for these and other possible indicators. More information will allow policy makers and other interested individuals to develop a better understanding of the extent to which governments are using tax measures, and at which levels of government. It can offer examples of techniques that other countries' might consider adopting. It can provide assessments of the extent to which the measures are advancing sustainability.

Developing this information, however, will require a commitment on the part of governments, institutions, and academia. The efforts of organizations such as the European Environment Agency, OECD, and International Energy Agency to date have been pivotal to developing a better global and country-specific understanding of the role of environmental taxation. Initiatives at the individual country level can further enhance an individual country's understandings and contribute to a stronger international assessment. A continued, sustained commitment of talent and resources is essential to building and refining the indicators of use and revenue impact over time.

In addition, determining the actual environmental impact of different green tax measures will require significant commitments. Given the sophisticated economic models needed to do the task and the individualized characteristics of each tax measure and the setting within which it operates, studies are time consuming, complex, and tax specific. Nonetheless, it is important to continue to refine the art of ex ante and ex post studies and to apply it to as many tax measures as possible to determine the actual environmental impact. From a sustainability perspective, indicators of environmental impact represent the ultimate test for the greenness of tax measures. Again, governments and other institutions will need to play a significant role and commit to this investment in order to systematically analyze the effectiveness of green tax measures.

Janet E. MILNE
Vermont Law School

See also Building Rating Systems, Green; Business Reporting Methods; Gross Domestic Product, Green; National Environmental Accounting; Regulatory Compliance; Triple Bottom Line

FURTHER READING

Andersen, Mikael Skou, & Ekins, Paul. (Eds.). (2009). *Carbon energy taxation.* Oxford, UK: Oxford University Press.

Database of State Incentives for Renewables & Efficiency (DSIRE). (2012). Homepage. Retrieved January 24, 2012, from http://www.dsireusa.org/

Environmental Law Institute. (2009). Estimating US government subsidies to energy sources: 2002–2008. Washington, DC: Environmental Law Institute.

Eurostat. (2012). Total environmental tax revenues as a share of total revenues from taxes and social contributions. Retrieved January 24, 2012, from http://epp.eurostat.ec.europa.eu/portal/page/portal/product_details/dataset?p_product_code=TEN00064

Eurostat, Energy. (2011). *Transport and environment indicators* (2011 ed., Chap. 4.6). Luxembourg: Publications Office of the European Union.

International Energy Agency (IEA). (2011). *World energy outlook 2011* (Chap. 14). Paris: IEA.

International Energy Agency (IEA), Organization of the Petroleum Exporting Countries (OPEC), Organisation for Economic-Cooperation and Development (OECD) & the World Bank. (2010). Joint report: Analysis of the scope of energy subsidies and suggestions for the G-20 initiative. Paris; Vienna, Austria; & Washington, DC: IEA, OPEC, OECD & the World Bank.

Milne, Janet, & Andersen, Mikael Skou. (Eds.). (2012). *Handbook of research on environmental taxation.* Cheltenham, UK: Edward Elgar.

Organisation for Economic-Cooperation and Development (OECD). (2012). Inventory of estimated budgetary support and tax expenditures for fossil fuels. Paris: OECD.

Organisation for Economic-Cooperation and Development (OECD) & European Environment Agency (EEA). (2012). OECD/EEA database on instruments used for environmental policy and natural resources management. Retrieved January 24, 2012, from http://www2.oecd.org/ecoinst/queries/index.htm

Pittsburgh Summit. (2009, September 24–25). Leaders' statement: The Pittsburgh Summit. Retrieved January 24, 2012, from http://ec.europa.eu/commission_2010-2014/president/pdf/statement_20090826_en_2.pdf

Staff of the Joint Committee on Taxation. (2011). Present law and analysis of energy-related tax expenditures and description of the revenue provisions contained in H.R. 1380, the New Alternative Transportation to Give Americans Solutions Act of 2011. Washington, DC: Joint Committee on Taxation.

Staff of the Joint Committee on Taxation. (2012). Estimates of federal tax expenditures for fiscal years 2011–2015. Washington, DC: US Government Printing Office.

Berkshire's authors and editors welcome questions, comments, and corrections. Send your emails about the *Berkshire Encyclopedia of Sustainability* in general or this volume in particular to: sustainability.updates@berkshirepublishing.com

Transdisciplinary Research

When stakeholders collaborate with researchers in developing solutions to societal problems, high-quality and implementable solutions can result. Transdisciplinary research allows researchers, experts, decision makers, and citizens to contribute to solution-oriented research. This research is particularly suitable for complex sustainability challenges, which affect the public and require collective problem-solving efforts. Transdisciplinary research's wider adoption depends on the willingness to secure resources, expertise, and institutional support.

Transdisciplinary research is a particular mode of research in which researchers, experts, policy makers, business leaders, and citizens collaborate in developing solution options to complex societal problems such as a lack of sustainability.

Definitions

In his 2011 book *Bird on Fire*, Andrew Ross, a professor of social and cultural analysis at New York University, draws "lessons from 'the world's least sustainable city,'" referring to Phoenix, Arizona. Ross's insights provide an overview of well-known urban challenges that have accumulated and deteriorated over the past two decades—ranging from overuse of water resources and energy-intense urban development (sprawl) to economic disparities (poverty), public health issues (obesity), and social tensions (immigration). These challenges do not fall into a particular societal sector but pertain to the entire society and thus require new, collaborative ways of problem solving, one of which is *transdisciplinary research*.

Ross provides examples of collaborative efforts such as community-based water management and local food initiatives. The administration of the city of Phoenix formed another recent initiative (not mentioned in the book). Increasingly aware of and concerned about the aforementioned challenges, the Phoenix Planning Department reached out to Arizona State University's School of Sustainability in 2009. The intent was simple and straightforward: urban challenges require innovative solutions and structural changes. What better place to look for new insights and ideas than at a university unit that specializes in sustainability? After several months of deliberation and negotiation with an extended network of stakeholder groups, the groups forged a partnership that set off a series of collaborative research projects to create urban solution strategies that are both scientifically credible (evidence based) and practically applicable. This particular research practice is labeled *transdisciplinary research*. Research in this mode goes beyond (hence the prefix *trans*) disciplinary research and interdisciplinary research, which are in origin and use primarily confined to academia.

Disciplinary research refers to a single academic discipline; *multi*disciplinary research follows an additive or sequential model of combining concepts or methods from different disciplines; *inter*disciplinary research refers to a more integrated blending of concepts or methods from different disciplines. It is important to note that the term *transdisciplinary research* is not always used the way we present it here. It is also used to denote an advanced form of interdisciplinary research, which has a distinctly different meaning. (For more details on these definitions, see Pohl and Hirsch Hadorn 2007; Scholz 2011.)

Before introducing detailed features of transdisciplinary research, it might be beneficial to first explore what transdisciplinary research is not. It is not a new research paradigm; it is not unique to a particular field of applications; it is not a singular research approach; and it is not a specific research method.

First, transdisciplinary research has no clear origin as a phenomenon, unlike the term, which different researchers coined and introduced in the 1970s (Thompson Klein 2004). In fact, it originates from various strands of research that pursued both developing solutions to societal problems and expanding the general (scientific) knowledge base. In this respect, transdisciplinary research differs from applied sciences, which primarily focus on practical applications.

Second, several fields have adopted transdisciplinary research practices in one form or the other, including sustainability science, environmental sciences, agricultural science, health sciences, social work research, and urban planning and design research. In short, fields that address broader societal challenges use it widely.

Third, transdisciplinary research shares common principles with *participatory* (Blackstock, Kelly, and Horsey 2007), *community-based* (Savan and Sider 2003), *boundary* (Clark et al. 2011), *interactive* (Talwar, Wiek, and Robinson 2011), and other collaborative research approaches (Lang et al. 2012)—all of which provide templates for researchers, experts, decision makers, and citizens to participate in and contribute to problem-driven and solution-oriented research. Transdisciplinary research can, therefore, be used as an umbrella term for all these approaches. This pragmatic description does not do justice to the particularities of the respective approaches; however, the focus on similarities should enhance the wider understanding and acceptance of the basic principles.

Fourth, there is neither a single nor an exclusive set of *methods* for transdisciplinary research. Experts best describe transdisciplinary research as a *setting* in which they can apply a broad variety of methods. The method of scenario analysis, for example, is not per se a transdisciplinary method; in fact, experts have widely applied scenario analysis in purely disciplinary, multidisciplinary, and interdisciplinary settings (using researchers' expertise from one or more academic disciplines). Researchers apply scenario analysis in a *transdisciplinary* setting only if they conduct it in a particular way, primarily allowing different stakeholders (academics and nonacademic stakeholders such as government representatives or citizens) to collaboratively engage in a problem-driven and solution-oriented research process. As a setting (or frame), defined through principles or guidelines, it prescribes particular features the research needs to comply with in order to qualify for the distinction of *transdisciplinary research*.

Characteristics

Three key characteristics of transdisciplinary research apply (Bergmann et al. 2005; Blackstock, Kelly, and Horsey 2007; Lang et al. 2012; Pohl and Hirsch Hadorn 2007; Scholz 2011; Scholz et al. 2006). First, it is *problem driven;* there is reciprocal interest in addressing an agreed-upon problem that is both societally and scientifically relevant. Second, it involves *collaborative research.* Experts conduct research jointly across different disciplines and different stakeholder groups that have a legitimate stake. The research encompasses mutual as well as joint learning and capacity building. Third, it is *solution oriented.* Research results in solution options that both apply to the problem situation and are generalizable into the body of scientific knowledge. It is thus transferable to similar problem constellations (the latter is considered a key difference from the applied sciences). Each of these characteristics allows researchers to demarcate transdisciplinary research from other, seemingly similar types of research—from action research, which addresses societally relevant problems but often less scientifically relevant ones; from conventional social sciences research, which entails some level of engagement with individuals or groups but is extractive (eliciting information); from decision science research (decision support systems), which often provides scientifically sound solution options but often fails to consider practical applicability, feasibility, and efficiency (Talwar, Wiek, and Robinson 2011).

Transdisciplinary research is particularly suitable for sustainability challenges, which researchers recognized early in the evolution of sustainability science (Kasemir et al. 2003; Kates et al. 2001; Thompson Klein et al. 2001; van Kerkhoff and Lebel 2006) and have reiterated since then (for a summary see Lang et al. 2012). Systemic failures often cause sustainability problems. These problems have broad-scale effects, are highly complex, and are urgent because they are approaching tipping points (Jerneck et al. 2011). Sustainability problems exceed conventional cognitive, emotional, and organizational capacities. They call instead for new and enhanced forms of societal intelligence, affection, and structure built up through concentrated, constructive, and coordinated inputs from various sources and stakeholder groups. This framework is even more relevant when we transition from understanding sustainability problems to actually crafting solution options (Wiek et al. 2012). The requirements are daunting: solution-oriented sustainability research requires a sophisticated mix of analytical, normative, anticipatory, and instructional knowledge, ultimately providing evidence-based guidance for complex transition and intervention strategies (Pohl and Hirsch 2007; Wiek 2007). And finally, elevated levels of ownership, commitment, and accountability related to both the problem as well as the developed solution options are particularly critical as path dependency, inertia, and resistance continue to obstruct transition pathways to sustainability. With the outlined key characteristics, transdisciplinary research can positively contribute to meeting all the outlined requirements.

The Practice

The practice of transdisciplinary (sustainability) research can best be described by following the actual research process and highlighting design principles where they apply (for details see Lang et al. 2012, based on the following resources: Bergmann et al. 2005; Blackstock, Kelly, and Horsey 2007; Pohl and Hirsch Hadorn 2007; Stauffacher et al. 2008; Talwar, Wiek, and Robinson 2011). The process of transdisciplinary research integrates societal problem solving and scientific inquiry. The following three phases structure the process. In the first phase researchers and stakeholders build a collaborative research team, collaboratively define (identify, frame) the sustainability problem they want to address, and design a methodological framework for collaborative knowledge production and integration. They define the problem as a "boundary object" that reflects both societal needs and scientific interest, and thus allows for coproducing practically applicable and scientifically credible knowledge (Clark et al. 2011). The second phase is the core research phase, in which researchers and stakeholders coproduce solution-oriented and transferable knowledge through applying and adjusting integrative research methods and transdisciplinary settings. In the third phase researchers and stakeholders apply the created knowledge (implementing solution options), as well as reintegrate it into and thereby expand the body of scientific knowledge (comparing, transferring, generalizing insights). The third phase also comprises the evaluation of scientific and societal impacts (from short term to long term) (Walter et al. 2007).

Transdisciplinary research encounters various challenges and requires particular expertise and experience in order for researchers to successfully navigate through the field of potential pitfalls (Bergmann et al. 2005; Lang et al. 2012; Wiek 2007). Researchers face a general challenge that they cannot conduct transdisciplinary research by simply following a generic recipe. They instead need to contextualize the research, accounting for particularities of stakeholders' problem perception, interests, capacities, and preferences and the available resources. Specific challenges play out differently in the three phases, of which three are exemplarily described in the following. The first flaw concerns the selection of stakeholders. Researchers often over rely on the "usual suspects," that is, stakeholders who nominate themselves and involve themselves in many different public issues. Also, researchers often do not know who the legitimate stakeholders are. Finally, at least some of the key stakeholders often lack the interest, capacity, or resources to participate. Second, researchers are pressured to succeed. Researchers thus often retreat to pre-packaged (technical) solutions without allowing for in-depth collaborative knowledge production because of tensions in the team or external pressures (e.g., deadlines). Researchers also often produce results that are publishable (and rewarded in academia) but continuously postpone the generation of real solution options (knowledge-first trap). The third exemplary problem concerns the tracking of scientific and societal impacts; "contextualized results" are often not only more difficult to publish compared to conventional research, but they are also more difficult to track because societal impacts become visible only with delay and through indirect causal relations that are hard to back up with empirical evidence (Walter et al. 2007).

The Future

Despite these challenges, transdisciplinary research has moved a good way toward becoming an established research practice for sustainability. Job profiles, promotion and tenure policies, peer-review guidelines, and requests for proposals increasingly reference or request this type of research. Transdisciplinary research is now widely considered an important practice that, in conjunction with disciplinary or interdisciplinary research, can play a critical role in addressing the sustainability challenges of the twenty-first century. Transdisciplinary research's wider success depends on society's willingness to build and secure a broader financial resource base because transdisciplinary research requires additional initial costs. Transdisciplinary research also requires profound collaborative (interpersonal) expertise, which calls for specific educational programs (Wiek, Withycombe, and Redman 2011). Transdisciplinary researchers finally need innovative institutional support structures, namely, incentives and reward systems that reflect the specific features and goals of transdisciplinary research, including extended peer review of societal impacts (Talwar, Wiek, and Robinson 2011; Walter et al. 2007). When these criteria are met, transdisciplinary research is poised to become an important tool for developing solution options to sustainability challenges.

Arnim WIEK
Arizona State University, United States

Daniel J. LANG
Leuphana University of Lüneburg, Germany

See also Challenges to Measuring Sustainability; Citizen Science; Community and Stakeholder Input; Cost-Benefit Analysis; Intellectual Property Rights;

Participatory Action Research; Quantitative vs. Qualitative Studies; Social Network Analysis (SNA); Sustainability Science; Systems Thinking; Weak vs. Strong Sustainability Debate

FURTHER READING

Bergmann, Matthias, et al. (2005). *Quality criteria of transdisciplinary research: A guide for the formative evaluation of research projects* (ISOE-Studientexte, No. 13). Frankfurt am Main, Germany: Institute for Applied Ecology.

Blackstock, K. L.; Kelly, Gail J.; & Horsey, B. L. (2007). Developing and applying a framework to evaluate participatory research for sustainability. *Ecological Economics, 60*(4), 726–742.

Clark, William C., & Dickson, Nancy M. (2003). Sustainability science: The emerging research program. *Proceedings of the National Academy of Sciences USA, 100*(14), 8059–8061.

Clark, William C., et al. (2011). Boundary work for sustainable development: Natural resource management at the Consultative Group on International Agricultural Research (CGIAR). *Proceedings of the National Academy of Sciences USA, Early Edition, 8.* doi:10.1073/pnas.0900231108

Jerneck, Anne, et al. (2011) Structuring sustainability science. *Sustainability Science, 6*(1), 69–82.

Kasemir, Bernd; Jäger, Jill; Jaeger, Carlo C.; & Gardner, Matthew T. (Eds.). (2003). *Public participation in sustainability science: A handbook.* Cambridge, UK: Cambridge University Press.

Kates, Robert W., et al. (2001, April 27). Sustainability science. *Science, 292*(5517), 641–642.

Lang, Daniel J., et al. (2012). Transdisciplinary research in sustainability science: Practice, principles and challenges. *Sustainability Science, 7*(Suppl), 25–44.

Pohl, Christian, & Hirsch Hadorn, Gertrude. (2007). *Principles for designing transdisciplinary research: Proposed by the Swiss Academies of Arts and Sciences.* Munich, Germany: Oekom Verlag.

Ross, Andrew. (2011). *Bird on fire: Lessons from the world's least sustainable city.* New York: Oxford University Press.

Savan, Beth, & Sider, David. (2003). Contrasting approaches to community-based research and a case study of community sustainability in Toronto, Canada. *Local Environment, 8*(3), 303–316.

Scholz, Ronald W.; Lang, Daniel J.; Wiek, Arnim; Walter, Alexander I.; & Stauffacher, Michael. (2006). Transdisciplinary case studies as a means of sustainability learning: Historical framework and theory. *International Journal of Sustainability in Higher Education, 7*(3), 226–251.

Scholz, Roland W. (2011). *Environmental literacy in science and society: From knowledge to decisions.* Cambridge, UK: Cambridge University Press.

Stauffacher, Michael; Flüeler, Thomas; Krütli, Pius; & Scholz, Roland W. (2008) Analytic and dynamic approach to collaborative landscape planning: A transdisciplinary case study in a Swiss pre-alpine region. *Systemic Practice and Action Research, 21*(6), 409–422.

Talwar, Sonia; Wiek, Arnim; & Robinson, John. (2011). User engagement in sustainability research. *Science and Public Policy, 38*(5), 379–390.

Thompson Klein, Julie. (2004). Prospects for transdisciplinarity. *Futures, 36*(4), 515–526.

Thompson Klein, Julie, et al. (Eds.). (2001). *Transdisciplinarity: Joint problem solving among science, technology, and society; An effective way for managing complexity.* Berlin: Birkhäuser.

van Kerkhoff, Lorrae, & Lebel, Louis. (2006). Linking knowledge and action for sustainable development. *Annual Review of Environment and Resources, 31,* 445–477.

Walter, Alexander I.; Helgenberger, Sebastian; Wiek, Arnim; & Scholz, Roland W. (2007). Measuring societal effects of transdisciplinary research projects: Design and application of an evaluation method. *Evaluation and Program Planning, 30*(4), 325–338.

Wiek, Arnim. (2007). Challenges of transdisciplinary research as interactive knowledge generation: Experiences from transdisciplinary case study research. *GAIA—Ecological Perspectives for Science and Society, 16*(1), 52–57.

Wiek, Arnim; Ness, B.; Brand, F. S.; Schweizer-Ries, P.; & Farioli, F. (2012). From complex system analysis thinking to transformational change: A comparative appraisal of sustainability science projects. *Sustainability Science, 7*(Suppl), 5–24.

Wiek, Arnim; Withycombe, Lauren; & Redman, Charles L. (2011). Key competencies in sustainability: A reference framework for academic program development. *Sustainability Science, 6*(2), 203–218.

Tree Rings as Environmental Indicators

Tree rings, the concentric circles visible in tree-trunk cross sections, record ecosystem events like fire, insect outbreaks, and logging. We study and date them (in the process called dendrochronology) to understand how ecological processes have worked in the past and how they might work in the future. As more tree-ring studies are done around the world, we will be better able to answer questions about sustainability that affect us all.

Trees and tree growth can be useful indicators of processes and events that occur in the natural environment. This is particularly true in climates with distinct seasons, where the annual growth rings of trees, as seen in tree-trunk cross sections, are easy to distinguish from each other. (See figure 1 on page 360.) As a tree grows, it forms a new layer of woody tissue each year. This growth occurs in a thin layer of cells, called the *vascular cambium*, located just inside the bark. In temperate regions, most trees break from winter dormancy and use nutrients stored during the previous year to produce cells. In conifer trees, cells created during the spring are less dense and thin-walled, forming a light-colored zone called *earlywood*. Toward the end of the growing season, smaller and thicker-walled cells are produced in a darker-colored zone called *latewood*. Together, the earlywood and latewood zones of wood are considered the annual growth ring. The science of studying tree rings to learn something about changes in the environment is called *dendrochronology*, and it can be used to analyze patterns of processes and events in the natural, physical, and cultural sciences. Since the growth rate of a tree is sensitive to both natural and human-induced events, conditions during a given year will be either favorable or unfavorable for tree growth, resulting in a variation in ring widths from year to year throughout the life of a tree. This pattern of wide and narrow growth rings can serve as an indicator to monitor environmental processes in most regions around the world.

Origins of Dendrochronology

The ancient Greeks, and later Leonardo da Vinci, recognized that trees form new rings of growth each year, but the modern development of dendrochronology is credited to Andrew E. Douglass. In the early 1900s, Douglass, an astronomer at the University of Arizona, was interested in studying the relationships between sunspot activity and the Earth's climate. Because he knew that plant growth was affected by changes in climate, he thought that the size of a tree's growth rings would change as cycles of sunspot activity affected weather conditions. Before long he showed that there was a link between tree-ring widths and climate, and he then developed a technique for matching patterns of wide and narrow growth rings between trees and between locations within a geographic region. This technique, known as *crossdating*, is the most fundamental principle of dendrochronology and is crucial in nearly every application of the science.

Applications of Dendrochronology

The science of dendrochronology is conducted primarily in temperate and subpolar regions, where most trees produce a single growth ring each year in response to seasonal changes in some aspect of the environment. Since its development, dendrochronology has become a useful tool that bridges a wide range of environmental disciplines. These include biogeography (the study of

Figure 1. Annual Growth Rings of a Douglas Fir (*Pseudotsuga menziesii*) Tree

Source: authors.

As seen in this photo of a douglas fir's tree rings, growth rates are sensitive to both natural and human-induced events, leading to variability in tree growth. This results in a variation in ring widths from year to year throughout the life of a tree. This pattern of wide and narrow growth rings can serve as an indicator to monitor environmental processes in most regions of the world.

the geographical distribution of animals and plants), climatology (the study of climate), hydrology (the study of water), geomorphology (the study of land formations), and ecology (the study of the relationship between organisms and their environments). Climatology and hydrology, for example, use dendrochronological techniques to examine past environmental conditions in order to help evaluate the future sustainability of different aspects of the environment. Scientists start by creating a model based on data that describes certain environmental variables (such as precipitation, temperature, drought, carbon dioxide, and other climatic factors) for a particular time period (the twentieth century, for instance). Information about tree-ring widths (or other physical and chemical properties) is added to the model so that the other variables can be reconstructed back in time for the length of the tree-ring record. Information about trees growing in a watershed that are sensitive to precipitation, for example, can be compared with information from river gauging stations (locations that scientists use to collect data about water) and used to model streamflow (the flow of streams, rivers, etc.) back in time long before streamflow records were ever kept. These longer-term perspectives of streamflow can then be compared to water levels during the twentieth and twenty-first centuries and used to create water management policies that promote greater sustainability of this ever-dwindling resource.

Tree rings also can be used to look at how ecological processes have changed over different periods of time and across different areas, allowing researchers to analyze how sustainable ecosystems are. Both natural and human disturbances (like fire, tropical cyclones, insect outbreaks, pathogens, logging, and earthquakes) and ecological processes that may affect the composition, structure, and changes in plant life of a forest community are often recorded in the growth rings of trees. Understanding the effects of disturbances and how ecological processes operated in the past can help scientists to predict how forests will change and how sustainable their future ecosystems will be. This insight may be particularly important in an era of climate change.

Limitations of Dendrochronology

Tree rings are valuable as archives of environmental events and indicators of sustainability, but there are limits to what they can tell us. Ice cores (samples of ice from glaciers), ocean cores (samples from the ocean floor), speleothems (cave features, such as stalactites, that form after the cave itself has formed), and lake sediments all can provide longer-term records of past environments than tree rings can. On the other hand, trees produce more detailed information than these other indicators. Scientists face a trade-off, therefore, and must sacrifice detail as the period of time being analyzed gets longer.

Recently, dendrochronologists and scientists in other fields have been assessing whether tree rings can be used as valid indicators of climatic variability. A key issue to be resolved first, however, is that of divergence. Since the mid-twentieth century global temperatures have continued to rise while tree growth has appeared to decline, especially in higher-latitude locations. This pattern diverges from the usual one, since higher temperatures historically have resulted in wider tree rings. Dendrochronologists therefore must make sure that previous ideas about the climate–tree growth relationship are reliable before attempting to use growth-ring data as a climate variable.

The Future of Dendrochronology

As researchers discover new ways in which tree rings can be used to test sustainability theories, new fields of dendrochronology are emerging. The tropics are geographic frontiers, where annual growth rings are being discovered in tree species previously thought to be of little use to dendrochronological applications. Moreover, dendrochronologists continue to learn new ways in which the oxygen, carbon, and hydrogen embedded within tree rings can provide information on the links between processes taking place in the atmosphere, on land, and in the sea. New methods of extracting naturally occurring and human-made chemical compounds fixed within tree rings are constantly being developed as well. These new technologies are helping researchers look for changes in the levels of these elements and chemicals—changes that may be caused by pollution, which can be harmful to the sustainability of natural resources. Finally, as the number of tree-ring studies increase around the world, so does our ability to construct networks of tree-ring data. These networks of data can be used to answer questions about the sustainability of natural resources that affect everyone on Earth.

Grant L. HARLEY and Henri D. GRISSINO-MAYER
The University of Tennessee

See also Air Pollution Indicators and Monitoring; Biological Indicators (*several articles*); Challenges to Measuring Sustainability; Ecosystem Health Indicators; Global Strategy for Plant Conservation; Land-Use and Land-Cover Change; Long-Term Ecological Research (LTER); Reducing Emissions from Deforestation and Forest Degradation (REDD); Remote Sensing

FURTHER READING

Cook, Edward R., & Kairiukstis, Leonardas A. (Eds.). (1990). *Methods of dendrochronology: Applications in the environmental sciences.* Dordrecht, The Netherlands: Kluwer Academic Publishers.

Fritts, Harold C. (1971). Dendroclimatology and dendroecology. *Quaternary Research, 1,* 419–449.

Fritts, Harold C. (1976). *Tree rings and climate.* London: Academic Press.

Fritts, Harold C., & Swetnam, Thomas W. (1989). Dendroecology: A tool for evaluating variations in past and present forest environments. *Advances in Ecological Research, 19,* 111–188.

Mann, Michael E.; Bradley, Raymond S.; & Hughes, Malcolm K. (1999). Northern Hemisphere temperatures during the past millennium: Inferences, uncertainties, and limitations. *Geophysical Research Letters, 26,* 759–762.

Rice, Jennifer L.; Woodhouse, Connie A.; & Lukas, Jeffrey J. (2009). Science and decision making: Water management and tree-ring data in the western United States. *Journal of the American Water Resources Association, 45,* 1248–1259.

Schweingruber, Fritz H. (1987). *Tree rings: Basics and applications of dendrochronology.* Dordrecht, The Netherlands: Kluwer Academic Publishers.

Speer, James H. (2010). *Fundamentals of tree-ring research.* Tucson: University of Arizona Press.

Stoffel, Markus; Bollschweiler, Michelle; Butler, David R.; & Luckman, Brian H. (Eds.). (2010). *Tree rings and natural hazards: A state-of-the-art.* Berlin: Springer.

Stokes, Marvin A., & Smiley, Terah L. (1968). *An introduction to tree ring dating.* Chicago: University of Chicago Press.

Swetnam, Thomas W.; Allen, Craig D.; & Betancourt, Julio L. (1999). Applied historical ecology: Using the past to manage for the future. *Ecological Applications, 9,* 1189–1206.

Triple Bottom Line

The triple bottom line (TBL) is a conceptual and analytical framework for accounting and reporting on corporate performance not only in terms of economic achievement but also with regard to environmental and social impacts. Other organizations and even governments can also produce TBL reports. The challenge of measuring, accounting, and reporting on an organization's performance continues to invite debate over techniques and feasibility.

The triple bottom line (TBL or 3BL) is a conceptual and analytical framework for sustainable development in which environmental and social accounting are included to form three bottom lines, rather than the traditional single (financial) bottom line. Although the framework has primarily been applied to the performance of a business, and in this regard emphasizing organizational change for sustainability, the TBL performance of the world, a country, a location, or a nonbusiness organization can also be analyzed (see, for example, Henriques and Richardson 2004; Foran, Lenzen, and Dey 2005).

The TBL framework emerged as a challenge to the orthodoxy of conventional corporate governance in the 1990s through the idea of adding two additional bottom lines to the standard financial bottom line in business. This later developed into both a general way of thinking about an organization's broader responsibilities to sustainable development and a specific framework of accounting and reporting on organizational performance. The idea has been applied to at least four related areas: sustainable development, sustainability accounting, sustainability reporting, and corporate social responsibility (CSR). The framework has largely been advocated by consultants or through anecdotal accounts. There has been relatively little academic research on the topic (Norman and MacDonald 2004; Pava 2007).

The British corporate responsibility pioneer John Elkington (1997; 2004) provided one of the first definitions of TBL in terms of businesses and organizations achieving the three goals of social equity, environmental protection, and economic prosperity. An alternative and more popular definition uses the catchphrase *people, planet, and profit*. This convenient phrase is helpful in conveying the broad intent of TBL, but it is of little value in making the concept operational in terms of measurement at the organizational level. Elkington made the case that the only way a company could find out about its TBL performance was to carry out a sustainability audit guided by impact assessment, auditing, and life cycle assessment.

Interest in TBL was triggered by the *Exxon Valdez* oil spill in Prince William Sound, Alaska, in 1989. This disaster led to the creation of the Coalition for Environmentally Responsible Economies (Ceres) and the subsequent development of a ten-point code of corporate environmental conduct to be endorsed by companies either as an environmental mission statement or as a corporate ethic (Ceres 2012). The code of conduct included a periodic requirement to report on environmental management. The absence of any consistent metrics for reporting on performance subsequently led Ceres to launch the Global Reporting Initiative (GRI) in 1997.

Since then, the GRI has become an international program that provides guidelines for ostensibly transparent TBL reporting of economic, environmental, and social impacts of organizational performance. In addition to providing better reporting, the objectives of the reporting encourage effective stakeholder relations with communities, employees, customers, suppliers, and nongovernment organizations, as well as better investment decisions (GRI 2012). The GRI is on ongoing experiment in performance reporting on sustainability. Attempts for more comprehensive TBL reporting led to the proliferation of indicators to be reported on over time, recently reduced in number, as well as to the development of industry sector reports as a means to connect the producers of reports to their intended audience. Examples of environmental indicators include measurements of energy use, greenhouse gas emissions, other pollutants, and the total amount of waste by type and destination. The composition of social indicators includes performance measures on labor practices and decent work, human rights, society, and product responsibility. A focus on process at the expense of results—that is, actual measurement of performance—has led to criticism about companies selectively reporting good rather than bad news (if avoidable) and ignoring issues such as process and product responsibility. Self-promotion is not excluded in the TBL framework.

Discussions of TBL also occur in the context of CSR, and many companies have produced CSR reports using the TBL framework. The success of TBL in influencing major companies, most of the big accounting firms, the investment industry, governments, and not-for-profit organizations has been noted (Norman and MacDonald 2004). In this view, however, TBL is rhetorical jargon that cannot provide a meaningful measure of a social or environmental bottom line. The absence of a numeric metric to calculate social and environmental bottom lines means that TBL is nothing more than the old-fashioned financial bottom line plus vague commitments to social and environmental concerns.

A rather different account is provided by the business ethicist, Moses Pava:

One of the major limitations of the business ethics movement, to date, has been the inability to measure and track social and environmental performance in a meaningful, consistent, and comparable way. But blaming the advocates of triple bottom line reporting for this failure is to blame the only group that has noticed this problem and is trying to remedy it. Rather than criticizing triple bottom line reports for their failure to provide a magical number that aggregates ethical performance, academics should understand the real import of 3BL reporting and try to improve it. (Pava 2007, 108)

Whereas the measurement aspects of TBL represent a formidable and ongoing challenge, the professors Li-Chin Jennifer Ho and Martin Taylor reported on the more straightforward issue of which companies produce TBL reports. They investigated twenty TBL disclosure items in fifty of the largest US and Japanese companies and found that "the extent of reporting is significantly higher for firms with a large size, lower profitability, lower liquidity, and for firms with membership in the manufacturing industry" (Ho and Taylor 2007, 123). Their analysis shows that total TBL disclosure is primarily driven by noneconomic disclosures. So even though there are important measurement issues in TBL reporting, companies that do produce TBL reports at least are disclosing information related to their environmental and social performance that was not usually previously reported.

Although business interest in TBL continues, the concept is undertheorized. Central to Elkington's interest was its application within a capitalist system. In tackling the question "Is capitalism sustainable?" Elkington (1997) stated that we are a long way from sustainability because the changes required involve a complete economic-social-ecological system and cannot be defined for a single corporation. Building on the US environmentalist Paul Hawken's (1993) view about the *ecology of commerce*, capitalism could be sustainable if its innovative qualities led to more ecologically sustainable and restorative systems of commerce and production. This aspect of TBL has not been explored in any depth; rather, the focus has been on metrics development for guideline documents published by the GRI. The addition of *governance performance* to GRI's reporting requirements also shifts the framework to four bottom lines, which makes TBL sound more like a metaphor than a practice. In this regard, the 2004 critique by the ethicists Wayne Norman and Chris MacDonald raises many pressing, albeit not surprising, issues given the scope of the challenge. TBL continues to require a more robust and analytical discourse on how to make it effective as a measurement tool. Meanwhile dialogue continues on the theoretical proposition that the characteristics of a sustainable economic system differ enough from the current form of capitalism that the latter is unlikely to be sustainable (Gray and Milne 2004).

Robert GALE
University of New South Wales

See also Business Reporting Methods; Ecological Footprint Accounting; Environmental Justice Indicators; Framework for Strategic Sustainable Development (FSSD); Global Reporting Initiative (GRI); Human Development Index (HDI); International Organization for Standardization (ISO); National Environmental Accounting; Regulatory Compliance; Supply Chain Analysis; Taxation Indicators, Green; University Indicators

FURTHER READING

Ceres. (2012). History and impact. Retrieved January 21, 2012, from http://www.ceres.org/about-us/our-history

Elkington, John. (1997). *Cannibals with forks: The triple bottom line of 21st century business.* Oxford, UK: Capstone Publishing Limited.

Elkington, John. (2004). Enter the triple bottom line. In Adrian Henriques & Julie Richardson (Eds.), *The triple bottom line, does it all add up? Assessing the sustainability of business and CSR* (pp. 1–16). London: Earthscan.

Foran, Barney; Lenzen, Manfred; & Dey, Christopher. (2005). *Balancing act: A triple-bottom-line analysis of the Australian economy* (CSIRO Technical Report). Canberra, Australia: Commonwealth Scientific and Industrial Research Organisation (CSIRO).

Global Reporting Initiative (GRI). (2012). What is GRI? Retrieved January 21, 2012, from https://www.globalreporting.org/information/about-gri/what-is-GRI/Pages/default.aspx

Gray, Rob, & Milne, Markus. (2004). Towards reporting on the triple bottom line: Mirage, methods and myths. In Adrian Henriques & Julie Richardson (Eds.), *The triple bottom line, does it all add up? Assessing the sustainability of business and CSR* (pp. 70–80). London: Earthscan.

Hawken, Paul. (1993). *The ecology of commerce: A declaration of sustainability.* New York: HarperCollins.

Henriques, Adrian, & Richardson, Julie. (Eds.). (2004). *The triple bottom line, does it all add up? Assessing the sustainability of business and CSR.* London: Earthscan.

Ho, Li-Chin Jennifer, & Taylor, Martin. (2007) An empirical analysis of triple bottom-line reporting and its determinants: Evidence from the United States and Japan. *Journal of International Financial Management and Accounting, 18*(2), 123–150.

Norman, Wayne, & MacDonald, Chris. (2004). Getting to the bottom of "triple bottom line." *Business Ethics Quarterly, 14*(2), 243–262.

Pava, Moses. (2007). A response to "Getting to the bottom of 'triple bottom line.'" *Business Ethics Quarterly, 17*(1), 105–110.

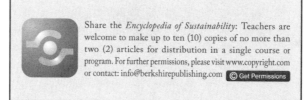

University Indicators

Universities differ from other organizations, given their distinctive power structure and their educational mission. Several groups are developing quality assessment tools for colleges and universities that can be used to evaluate whether they are acting environmentally responsibly. If the assessments employ useful and consistent indicators and are tied to the campus's strategy, they will influence campus stakeholders to create a more environmentally sustainable organization.

Universities are unique environments with a dual power structure shared between faculty and administration, students involved in parts of the functioning of a university's operations through clubs and research, a diversified curriculum, and decentralized decision making. This uniqueness calls for assessments different from other types of organizations. Environmental sustainability is no exception.

Sustainability as a concern for campus functioning, curriculum, and research is relatively new. Some attention has been paid to the overall measurement of environmental activities on campus, especially as related to campus operations; however, much of the focus has been on cutting energy costs or, for purposes of comparison, trying to determine which university is the "greenest" or most environmentally responsible.

Agreements and Organizations

Universities have tried to organize uniform agreements around commitments to sustainability. For example, the first such attempt, the Talloires Declaration (TD), is a ten-point action plan for incorporating sustainability and environmental literacy into teaching, research,

operations, and outreach at colleges and universities. It was initiated in 1990 at an international conference in Talloires, France, and has been signed by over 350 university presidents and chancellors in over forty countries.

Second Nature, a nonprofit organization established in 1993 in Boston, Massachusetts, works with higher education leaders to incorporate sustainability in the curriculum and in student and faculty practices within colleges and universities. It is the primary supporter for the American College and University Presidents' Climate Commitment (ACUPCC). The ACUPCC provides a framework and support for US colleges and universities to implement comprehensive plans in pursuit of climate neutrality. The organization was officially unveiled in June 2007 and currently numbers 683 signatories to its commitment statement. Its main function is to create a public forum in which universities declare their commitments to reduce carbon output.

A partner with Second Nature, the Association for the Advancement of Sustainability in Higher Education (AASHE) was established in 2006 as the first professional higher-education association for the campus sustainability community. AASHE works with all sectors of a campus integrating sustainability in campus governance, education, and research.

Other attempts to aid universities in their mission to become environmentally sustainable are the World Resources Institute's project for greening business colleges, Business-Environment Learning and Leadership, referred to as BELL; the Consortium for Environmental Education in Medicine; and the Association for University Leaders for a Sustainable Future. These are primarily attempting to make universities' physical plants more environmentally friendly.

Sustainability Measurement Systems

Despite these attempts, sustainability programs are still in their infancy at most universities. For example, many of the important university commitments originated only in the first decade of the twenty-first century, as did the organizations listed above. Therefore, methodologies that measure sustainability have not been fully developed.

The discussions below show several methodologies that illustrate the variety of approaches to measuring the extent to which universities are engaging in sustainable behavior and creating more environmentally friendly and socially responsible organizations. Major motivations behind collecting such data include using these measurements to help universities decide where to invest resources to achieve these goals, and benchmarking their organizations against best-in-class competitors. Interest in sustainability on campuses is increasing (Elder 2011), thus the need for effective measures is also increasing.

Sustainability Tracking, Assessment & Rating System (STARS)

STARS is an approach relatively widely used in the United States. It is supported by the Association for the Advancement of Sustainability in Higher Education (AASHE). STARS is a self-reporting tool that requires a university to collect information on a standard form that is submitted to AASHE, which then assigns the university a quality rating. STARS is currently in use at over 250 colleges and universities (AASHE 2011).

STARS has four analysis categories: education and research; operations; planning, administration, and engagement; and innovation. The ratings result in a designation of highest to lowest (Platinum, Gold, Silver, and Bronze), with an additional category of STARS Reporter for those who want to disclose information but not pursue a rating. These ratings are modeled after the Leadership in Energy and Environmental Design (LEED) categories for buildings, which is a standard environmentally sensitive methodology for rating building construction and renovation.

One of the benefits of STARS is that it allows universities to compare themselves to other universities and colleges and, by the nature of this comparison, to discover best practices among the STARS members' accomplishments. Among the program's drawbacks, however, are its self-report format and its lack of significant adaptation to a particular organizational mission. For example, the methodology is the same for large and small universities, which may put a smaller organization at a distinct disadvantage as it does not have the breadth or depth of activities that a larger organization might have. At the same time, the environmental footprint of a smaller school may be more environmentally favorable than that of a larger university, a fact not captured by STARS.

State of the Campus Environment Report

In 2008, the National Wildlife Federation (NWF) issued a report based on the results of surveys sent to nearly every college and university in the United States. The stated goal of the report was to "track trends and advance knowledge about environmental stewardship, sustainability activities and related curricular offerings in higher education" (NWF 2008, 1).

The survey contained assessments in the three broad, overarching categories of management, academics, and operations, which were then subdivided into subcategories. The report provided enough information so that universities could compare their responses to those of other institutions and determine best practices for themselves for becoming sustainable. Therefore, while this report was not individualized, it did provide some suggestions for how schools might improve.

The College Sustainability Report Card

The College Sustainability Report Card describes itself as the only independent evaluation of campus and endowment sustainability activities at colleges and universities in the United States and Canada. In contrast to the academic focus on sustainability in research and teaching, the Report Card examines colleges and universities, as institutions, through the lens of sustainability. The GreenReportCard.org website and the College Sustainability Report Card are both initiatives of the Sustainable Endowments Institute, a nonprofit organization engaged in research and education to advance sustainability in campus operations and endowment practices.

Sustainability Assessment Questionnaire (SAQ)

The Sustainability Assessment Questionnaire (SAQ) is supported by the University Leaders for a Sustainable Future (ULSF). Much like STARS, SAQ uses a self-assessment process that allows universities to evaluate themselves. The goal of SAQ is twofold: first, it assesses a university's sustainability at a given point in time; and secondly, SAQ seeks to encourage discussion at the university about sustainability and further steps that may be taken to improve the institution's overall sustainability.

SAQ divides its questionnaire into seven categories: curriculum; research and scholarship; operations; faculty and staff development and rewards; outreach and service;

student opportunities; and institutional mission, structure, and planning. SAQ is not a quantitative approach to sustainability assessment; it does not offer universities guidance on what improvements they can make, but rather it focuses on fostering discussion in the university community.

HEFCE's Environmental Report and Workbook

In 1998, the Higher Education Funding Council for England (HEFCE), a government agency, surveyed six universities in England. The report was particularly useful for providing benchmarks for universities against existing best practices, and the report was also careful to lay out the benefits that universities will receive should they choose to implement certain sustainability actions. This approach was particularly beneficial for guiding decision making for the individual universities.

On the other hand, there were some important issues that the assessment tool did not address. For example, while several universities were discussed, there was no obvious method for others to assess themselves. Additionally, the process provided little guidance on future steps that should be taken by universities.

Environmental Management System Self-Assessment

The Global Environmental Management Initiative (GEMI) developed its Environmental Management System Self-Assessment tool to cover a wide variety of organizations, including those in industry. The assessment tool was intended to meet draft international standards for environmental management systems put out by the International Organization for Standardization (ISO). ISO is the world's largest developer and publisher of international standards. It is a network of the national-standards institutes of 162 countries, one member standards organization per country, with a Central Secretariat in Geneva, Switzerland, that coordinates the system. ISO is a nongovernmental

organization that forms a bridge between the public and private sectors. On the one hand, many of its member institutes are part of the governmental structure of their countries or are mandated by their government. On the other hand, other members have their roots uniquely in the private sector, having been set up by national partnerships of industry associations.

The EMS assessment requires that the organization score itself on a scale from 0 to 2 in each subcategory, and the tool clearly lays out how points are awarded. It is broken into five categories, corresponding to parts of the ISO: commitment and policy, planning, implementation and operation, checking and corrective action, and management review. The tool also provides some suggestions for meeting certain criteria that are helpful but quite general. While this assessment tool is worthwhile and takes a global view, it does not look specifically at universities, so it fails to take into account important factors such as coursework and research focused on sustainability.

Effective Assessments

All of these programs and approaches have attempted to elevate the conversation about sustainability and to provide insights into campuses and their environmental sustainability. The methodologies still, however, need considerable research before the measurements they provide can be considered valid and reliable. For example, different assessment tools use different indicators, and some do not seem to practice what they preach; that is, they are not transparent in their methodology development and use (Sadowski 2011).

Certain characteristics of an effective measurement system can increase the usefulness of the methodologies and their levels of sophistication. For example, the information collected should cover topics and indicators that reflect the organization's significant economic, social, and environmental outcomes and that substantively assess organizational practices from various perspectives. A useful quality assessment thus identifies the organization's stakeholders (constituents important to it) and explains in the report how the organization has responded to their reasonable expectations and interests. These assessments need to be complete enough to create a valid representation of the organization's state of sustainability.

Quality reports cannot be divorced from the organization's overall strategy and its boundaries of operation. Global ratings suffer from their lack of sensitivity to a university's mission. For example, some community colleges do not engage in research, yet ratings such as STARS require them to rate this item on the assessment tool. This component, relating to the organization's strategy, is where most current assessment tools fail. Clarity, timeliness, balance (positive and negative commentary), and reliability are other important factors in quality assessments (GRI n.d.; Shriberg 2002, 256–257).

In sum, each of these methodologies needs much more rigorous analysis and development before it can be relied upon to accurately measure a campus's environmental sustainability. Also, most of the current assessment tools are insensitive to a college or university strategic direction.

Best-in-Class Universities

Certain universities' environmental sustainability programs and practices are especially instructive to other universities as they develop their environmental sustainability approaches and measurements. Arizona State University (ASU) has done extensive work on its physical plant, research agenda, and curriculum. ASU's Global Institute of Sustainability is the hub of the university's sustainability initiatives; it advances research, education, and business practices for an urbanizing world. Its School of Sustainability, the first of its kind in the United States, offers transdisciplinary degree programs focused on finding practical solutions to environmental, economic, and social challenges. The University of British Columbia (UBC) has also made exemplary progress in this area. Its university administration states "Sustainability defines UBC as a university. Through our collective efforts in education, research, partnerships and operations, we advance sustainability on our campus and beyond" (UBC n.d.). Stockholm University's Resilience Centre is an international center that advances transdisciplinary research for governance of social-ecological systems, with a special emphasis on resilience—the ability to deal with change and to continue to develop. The center is a joint initiative between Stockholm University, the Stockholm Environmental Institute, and the Beijer International Institute of Ecological Economics at the Royal Swedish Academy of Sciences. The Centre for Transdisciplinary Environmental Research (CTM) at Stockholm University and the Baltic Nest Institute are also part of the Stockholm Resilience Centre. The interconnectedness of these organizations promotes in-depth and extensive measurement of the university's activities, and the outcome is a university with a fully functional core focus on sustainability.

Educators and Role Models

Universities are organizations that wield special power for influencing the sustainability of our world. As educators, they can influence our future leaders and workforce and generate new knowledge, and as influential and respected organizations they can be models and facilitators for the communities in which they reside. They have the potential to act responsibly and to influence the behavior of other organizations, and, as sustainability assessments improve, to be models for other types of organizations.

Daniel S. FOGEL

Schools of Business and Center for Energy, Environment and Sustainability, Wake Forest University

Emily Yandle ROTTMANN

McGuireWoods, LLP

See also Challenges to Measuring Sustainability; Citizen Science; Focus Groups; International Organization for Standardization (ISO); Quantitative vs. Qualitative Studies; Transdisciplinary Research

FURTHER READING

Aspen Institute Business and Society Program. (2003). Where will they lead? 2003 MBA student attitudes about business and society. Retrieved December 15, 2011, from http://www.aspeninstitute.org/publications/where-will-they-lead-mba-student-attitudes-about-business-society-2003

Association for the Advancement of Sustainability in Higher Education (AASHE). (2010). Sustainability Tracking & Rating System (STARS). Retrieved March 20, 2011, from https://stars.aashe.org/

Association for the Advancement of Sustainability in Higher Education (AASHE). (2011). STARS Sustainability Tracking Assessment & Rating System: Version 1.1 technical manual. Retrieved March 20, 2011, from http://www.aashe.org/files/documents/STARS/stars_1.1_technical_manual_final.pdf

Devuyst, Dimitri. (2001). Introduction to sustainability assessment at the local level. In Dimitri Devuyst (Ed.), *How green is the city? Sustainability assessment and the management of urban environments.* New York: Columbia University Press.

Elder, James L. (2011). Higher education. In Chris Laszlo, Karen Christensen, Daniel S. Fogel, Gernot Wagner & Peter Whitehouse (Eds.), *Encyclopedia of sustainability: Volume 2. The business of sustainability* (pp. 137–140). Great Barrington, MA: Berkshire Publishers.

Fogel, Daniel S. (2012). *Baseline assessment of environmental sustainability.* Winston-Salem, NC: Wake Forest University.

Global Environmental Management Initiative (GEMI). (2000). ISO 14001 environmental management system self-assessment checklist. Retrieved March 21, 2011, from http://www.gemi.org/resources/ISO_111.pdf

Global Reporting Initiative (GRI). (n.d.). Homepage. Retrieved February 17, 2012, from https://www.globalreporting.org/Pages/default.aspx

Higher Education Funding Council for England (HEFCE). (1998). Report 98/61: Environmental report. Retrieved March 21, 2011, from http://www.hefce.ac.uk/pubs/hefce/1998/98_61.htm

Johnston, Paul; Everard, Mark; Santillo, David; & Robèrt, Karl-Henrik. (2007). Reclaiming the definition of sustainability. *Environmental Science Pollution Resources International, 14*(1), 60–66.

National Wildlife Federation (NWF). (2008). Campus environment 2008: A national report card on sustainability in higher education. *Campus Ecology.* Retrieved March 20, 2011, from http://www.nwf.org/campusEcology/docs/CampusReportFinal.pdf

New Jersey Higher Education Partnership for Sustainability (NJHEPS). (n.d.). Campus sustainability snapshot. Retrieved March 21, 2011, from http://www.njheps.org/assessment.htm

Net Impact. (2011). Homepage. Retrieved December 12, 2011, from http://netimpact.org/

Sadowski, Michael (2011). *Rate the rates: Phase four.* Washington, DC: SustainAbility.

Shriberg, Michael. (2002). Institutional assessment tools for sustainability in higher education: Strengths, weakness, and implications for practice and theory. *International Journal of Sustainability in Higher Education, 3*(3), 254–270.

University Leaders for a Sustainable Future (ULSF). (2008). Sustainability assessment questionnaire. Retrieved March 20, 2011, from http://www.ulsf.org/programs_saq.html

University of British Columbia (UBC). (n.d.). Our story. Retrieved February 18, 2012, from http://cirs.ubc.ca/about/our-story

Berkshire's authors and editors welcome questions, comments, and corrections. Send your emails about the *Berkshire Encyclopedia of Sustainability* in general or this volume in particular to: sustainability.updates@berkshirepublishing.com

Weak vs. Strong Sustainability Debate

Sustainability as a concept can be defined—and debated—in many different ways, but it generally falls into two categories: weak versus strong. Weak sustainability maintains that economic and social issues must be integrated in sustainability discussions and allows one form of capital (human, natural, social, constructed, cultural) to substitute for another. Strong sustainability theory, on the other hand, asserts that replacements do not exist for natural capital stocks.

Scholars in various disciplines approach the concept of sustainability in very different ways. The stakes can be high, as different approaches may lead to conflicting policy implications for how we regulate our economy, prioritize the allocation of public finances, and manage environmental impacts and resource stocks. These different conceptual approaches can be placed into two broad categories that serve as the foundation for an intellectual debate over what we mean by sustainability.

One of these categories focuses on the ecological imperatives of carrying capacity, biodiversity, and resilience as they relate to the natural capital stocks necessary for sustaining human society and life on Earth. This category is called *strong sustainability*. A key characteristic of strong sustainability theory is that natural capital stocks lack substitutes. Mitigation measures such as fish hatcheries or constructed wetlands that are built to offset declining natural capital are not consistent with strong sustainability. Strong sustainability performance indicators transform human activities and impacts into aggregated physical "footprint" measures of consumption or resource drawdown that can be compared to available flows of biophysical resources from the Earth's stock of natural capital.

The other category of sustainability theory focuses more broadly on the aggregate value of natural, human,

constructed, social, and cultural capital stocks, and thus allows for one form of capital to substitute for another. The idea here is that sustainability cannot ignore the economic and social problems of meeting basic human needs. This latter category is called *weak sustainability*. From this perspective one can argue that efforts to sustain natural capital must be integrated with addressing economic and social imperatives. Residents of failed states who are suffering from violent conflict, extreme poverty, and corruption, for example, are unlikely to sustain natural capital stocks for future generations until their pressing economic, social, and political problems are resolved. In contrast with strong sustainability, weak sustainability accommodates mitigation measures such as hatcheries and constructed wetlands, as well as policies that draw from resource stocks for economic and social development. Weak sustainability performance indicators usually convert the flows of services from these capital stocks, as well as any harmful or beneficial human impacts on these stocks, into aggregated monetary values.

While weak and strong sustainability theory each draws its own loyal advocates, perhaps it is more useful to think of them as complementary rather than as competing either–or theories. As these theories have developed, both have been heavily influenced by economic concepts and thus share elements of an economic worldview. Weak sustainability draws from the mainstream of economic thought, while strong sustainability derives from the emerging transdisciplinary field of ecological economics. Strong sustainability tells us that we must preserve the life support and ecosystem service functions that are essential for life. What are these essential elements of natural capital that lack any practical substitutes, and what steps are necessary to preserve them? Weak sustainability theory tells us that we must address the economic and social needs of people in addition to preserving natural capital. What are these essential economic and social needs, and how are they properly balanced with the need to preserve the functional integrity of natural capital?

Weak Sustainability

The weak sustainability concept originates from work in the early 1970s by Nobel laureate economist Robert Solow of the Massachusetts Institute of Technology and his colleagues. They were interested in understanding the conditions required for continued economic growth in a world with limited natural resources. From this anthropocentric perspective he argued that a sustainable path for the national economy is one that allows every future generation the opportunity to be as well off as its predecessors.

The development economist Sir Partha Dasgupta of Cambridge University articulates a view of weak sustainability that is built around the concept of *wealth,* which can be thought of as the value of productive capital stocks (human, constructed, natural, and so on). The total stock of wealth would thus represent the sum of the value of all forms of productive capital stocks. The basic idea is that weak sustainability occurs when total per capita wealth does not decrease over time. Development activity that expands one form of capital (e.g., constructed capital) through investment but depletes another (e.g., natural capital) only satisfies weak sustainability if total wealth is not reduced. A central element of weak sustainability theory therefore is the assumption that constructed capital can effectively substitute for natural capital and the services provided by ecological systems.

The economist John Hartwick of Queens University developed a simple weak sustainability rule that links depletion of natural capital stocks to investment in human or constructed capital. Under the *Hartwick rule,* in order to sustain constant levels of consumption over time, the gains that society today enjoys from depleting an exhaustible natural resource must be reinvested in human, constructed, or other forms of capital. Such a substitution of human or constructed capital for exhausted natural capital is justified so long as the value of the increase in human or constructed capital at least offsets the value of the loss of natural capital. As a result, a nondeclining aggregate consumption of goods and services flowing from all capital stocks can be maintained over time.

Strong Sustainability

From an ecological standpoint, running down the stocks of natural capital and replacing these stocks with constructed substitutes is not consistent with the requirements of sustainability. One concern is that the easier it is to substitute constructed capital for depleted natural capital, the less concern people have for the underlying carrying capacity of the environment to sustain development. Strong sustainability theory has developed from ecological science. It emphasizes the ecological imperatives of sustaining carrying capacity, biodiversity, and resilience. At a global scale, the regenerative life support system of the Earth's biosphere is the ultimate form of natural capital, and it clearly has no substitutes. Attempts to construct working replicas on a smaller scale (such as the $200 million for building Biosphere 2) have proven difficult and very costly. Strong sustainability is therefore concerned with limiting the cumulative adverse effects of natural capital depletion from human activity.

In the early 1990s the environmental economist David Pearce of University College London and his colleagues noted that arguments supporting strong sustainability theory, or undermining weak sustainability theory, include uncertainty, irreversibility, and discontinuities. The uncertainty argument is that the consequences of depleting natural capital in terms of the functional integrity and productivity of complex ecological systems are uncertain, as is the value of natural capital to future generations. Because of this uncertainty, it is not possible to know how much of an increase in human or constructed capital is necessary to compensate for declines in natural capital, as required by weak sustainability. The second argument is that certain forms of natural capital depletion, such as species extinction or global climate change, are irreversible and cannot be undone, adding greater significance to the problem associated with uncertainty. The third argument is that weak sustainability models usually assume smooth and continuous cause-and-effect relationships and trade-offs, while natural systems often feature discontinuities and threshold effects. Rising temperatures crossing the freezing point can trigger damaging flooding and inundation, for example, and wildlife population declines can reach a threshold beyond which the population crashes to extinction. The implication is that today's policy choices based on weak sustainability cannot be implemented with exact knowledge that they will avoid unintended consequences.

To summarize, strong sustainability theory is focused on the critical and irreplaceable life-support systems associated with natural capital, while weak sustainability theory is focused on the aggregate stocks of all forms of valuable capital. Strong sustainability is distinguished by the view that natural capital, and the resources and services that flow from natural capital, cannot be replaced by constructed alternatives. In contrast, weak sustainability allows for one form of capital to substitute for another. Another distinction is that weak sustainability theory is built on economic conceptions of smooth and continuous cause-and-effect relationships, while strong sustainability theory is premised upon an ecological systems approach that features discontinuities, discreteness, and thresholds in cause-and-effect relationships. Strong sustainability provides arguments for preserving natural capital stocks, while weak sustainability underlies processes such as mitigation, benefit/cost analysis, and sustainable development.

Applications and Future Directions

Environmental laws such as California's Environmental Quality Act require environmental studies (e.g., environmental impact reports) to identify significant environmental impacts from proposed projects, and to specify mitigations when impacts exceed thresholds of significance. While weak sustainability requires full mitigation, in practice these mitigations may fully or partially offset impacts. Examples already noted include constructed wetlands and fish hatcheries. Other examples include parks, creek restoration, or environmental education programs. At a broader scale, concerns about the inadequacy of per capita gross domestic product (GDP) as a measure of well-being have led to efforts to develop weak sustainability indicators. A number of measures have been developed that attempt to quantify and value constructed, human, natural, and social capital and reduce them to a single aggregated indicator of well-being. Examples include green GDP, genuine savings, and the genuine progress indicator, as well as the quantification of benefits and costs in policy analysis. Growing demands from policy makers and stakeholders for better information is driving researchers in the new field of ecological economics to refine methods for valuing natural capital and integrating those values with conventional economic measures. As a result, policies based on weak sustainability principles will grow in sophistication and influence.

Policies consistent with strong sustainability theory call for the application of a *safe minimum standard,* such as the US Endangered Species Act, that seeks to ensure sufficient populations of threatened or endangered plant and animal species to prevent extinction. The related concept of the *precautionary principle* calls for investment in natural capital (e.g., reducing greenhouse gas emissions) to be viewed as an "insurance premium" associated with preventing irreversible and potentially catastrophic harms. The ecological footprint is perhaps the best-known strong sustainability indicator. It is approximated by the area of ecologically productive land and water per capita that is necessary to support existing human consumption and to absorb many human-generated wastes. The ecological footprint is a useful tool for assessing

carrying capacity appropriated by human society. More recently, emerging concepts such as the carbon footprint and the water footprint have extended strong sustainability footprint indicators to new areas of critical concern. The trend is toward more collaboration between scientists and ecological economists, which will result in increasingly refined strong sustainability indicators as educational tools, advocacy tools, and guides for policy makers.

Steven C. HACKETT
Humboldt State University

See also Challenges to Measuring Sustainability; Development Indicators; Gross National Happiness; Intellectual Property Rights; *The Limits to Growth;* New Ecological Paradigm (NEP) Scale; Sustainability Science; Sustainable Livelihood Analysis (SLA); Systems Thinking

FURTHER READING

Brundtland, Gro. (Ed.). (1987). *Our common future: The World Commission on Environment and Development.* Oxford, UK: Oxford University Press.

Daly, Herman, & Farley, Joshua. (2004). *Ecological economics: Principles and applications.* Washington, DC: Island Press.

Dasgupta, Partha. (2010). Nature's role in sustaining economic development. *Philosophical Transactions of the Royal Society, 365*(1537), 5–11.

Gutes, Maite. (1996). Commentary: The concept of weak sustainability. *Ecological Economics, 17*(3), 147–156.

Hackett, Steven. (2011). *Environmental and natural resources economics: Theory, policy, and the sustainable society* (4th ed.). New York: M. E. Sharpe.

Hartwick, John. (1977). Intergenerational equity and the investing of rents from exhaustible resources. *American Economic Review, 67*(5), 972–974.

Hoekstra, Arjen. (2009). Human appropriation of natural capital: A comparison of ecological footprint and water footprint analysis. *Ecological Economics, 68*(7), 1963–1974.

Pearce, David, & Atkinson, Giles. (1993). Capital theory and the measurement of sustainable development: An indicator of weak sustainability. *Ecological Economics, 8*(2), 103–108.

Pearce, David; Markandya, Anil; & Barbier, Edward. (1989). *Blueprint for a green economy.* London: Earthscan.

Pearce, David, & Warford, Jeremy. (1993). *World without end: Economics, environment, and sustainable development.* Oxford, UK: Oxford University Press.

Rees, William, & Wackernagel, Mathis. (1996). Ecological footprints and appropriated carrying capacity: Measuring the natural capital requirements of the human economy. In Ann Marie Jansson, Carl Folke, Monica Hammer & Robert Costanza (Eds.), *Investing in natural capital: The ecological economics approach to sustainability* (pp. 362–390). Washington, DC: Island Press.

Solow, Robert. (1974). Intergenerational equity and exhaustible resources. *Review of Economic Studies, 41* (Symposium on the Economics of Exhaustible Resources), 29–45.

Wackernagel, Mathis; White, Sahm; & Moran, Dan. (2004). Using ecological footprint accounts: From analysis to applications. *International Journal of Environment and Sustainable Development, 3*(3), 293–315.

Index

A

AcountAbility 1000 (AA 1000), 38
Advertising, 2–5
    consumer culture, (consumerism), 2, 4–5
    culture jamming, 4–5
    green advertising, 2, 3–4
    social marketing, 2–3
Aerial Perspectives program, 278
Agenda 21, 6–10
Air Pollution Indicators and Monitoring, 11–16
allele, 20, 21
    See also DNA
Arizona State University (ASU) School of
    Sustainability, 355
assemblage assessment of fisheries, 134

B

Baltic Sea. *See* Helsinki Commission (HELCOM)
Barcode of Life Datasystem (BOLD), 327
barcoding, species. *See* **Species Barcoding**
biodiversity
    Biodiversity Indicators Partnership (BIP), 22
    conservation of, 168, 172
    Convention on Biological Diversity (CBD), 100, 168
    ecosystem diversity, 21
    ecosystem impact and, 99, 100
    genetic diversity, 20, 21–22, 24
    Shannon index, 139
    See also **Intergovernmental Science-Policy Platform
    on Biodiversity and Ecosystem Services
    (IPBES)**; species diversity; species richness
Biological Indicators—Ecosystems, 18–19, 138,
    139, 239
Biological Indicators—Genetic, 20–25

Biological Indicators—Species, 26–31
bottom-up approach (community development), 59
Building Research Establishment Environmental
    Assessment Method (BREEAM). *See* **Building
    Rating System, Green**
Brundtland report. See *Our Common Future*
Building Rating Systems, Green, 32–36
    Building Research Establishment Environmental
    Assessment Method (BREEAM) in UK, 32, 33,
    35, 74
    Leadership in Energy and Environmental Design
    (LEED) rating program, 32, 34, 35, 327
Busan Outcome, 207–208
Business Reporting Methods, 37–40
Bhutan. *See* **Gross National Happiness (GNH)**

C

Cameron County, Texas, USA (pesticide testing), 277–278
carbon credits, 292
carbon dioxide (CO_2)
    atmospheric, 47, 96, 264
    emission rates, 194–195
    equivalent quantities of carbon dioxide (CO_2e), 42
    uptake (sinks), 19, 95, 264, 265, 267, 268
Carbon Footprint 42–45
carrying capacity, 91
    See also T. Robert Malthus
Centre for Bhutan Studies, 183–184
Challenges to Measuring Sustainability, 46–52
China
    carbon emissions in, 44
    energy consumption in, 111
    green GDP of, 178, 258
    choice experiments (CE), 127

Bold entries and page numbers denote encyclopedia articles.